Complex Problem Solving:
Principles and Mechanisms

Complex Problem Solving: Principles and Mechanisms

Edited by
Robert J. Sternberg
Yale University
Peter A. Frensch
University of Missouri

LEA LAWRENCE ERLBAUM ASSOCIATES, PUBLISHERS
1991   Hillsdale, New Jersey   Hove and London

Lawrence Erlbaum Associates, Inc., Publishers
365 Broadway
Hillsdale, New Jersey 07642

Library of Congress Cataloging-in-Publication Data
Complex problem solving : principles and mechanisms / edited by Robert
  J. Sternberg, Peter A. Frensch.
     p.   cm.
  Includes bibliographical references and indexes.
  ISBN 0-8058-0650-4. — ISBN 0-8058-0651-2 (pbk.)
  1. Problem solving—Psychological aspects. 2. Thought and
thinking. 3. Cognitive styles. I. Sternberg, Robert J.
II. Frensch, Peter A.
BF449.C66 1991
153.4'3—dc20
                                                                91–7225
                                                                  CIP

Printed in the United States of America
10 9 8 7 6 5 4 3 2 1

This book is dedicated to *Herbert A. Simon,* whose pioneering work on complex problem solving has created and shaped the field as we know it today.

Contents

PART IV: GAMES

PART V: CONCLUSIONS

Preface

Although complex problem solving has emerged as a field of psychology in its own right, it is a field that usually occupies a single chapter in textbooks on thinking, a part of a chapter in textbooks on cognitive psychology, and a part of a part of a chapter in textbooks on introductory psychology. The literature on complex problem solving is far-flung, and is sometimes so technical that it is difficult for nonexperts to plow through. Moreover, many existing references represent a single point of view rather than a general overview of the field, which currently embraces diverse points of view.

Our goal in this book is to present in a single source a comprehensive, in-depth introduction to the field of complex problem solving. The chapters in this book cover much, although certainly not all, of the field. They are organized by areas of the field, and topics within each area. We have asked contributing authors to be comprehensive and catholic with respect to the points of view that have emerged in each area.

The book is divided into four main parts and a concluding part. The four main parts represent different areas of the field of complex problem solving. Consider each in turn.

Part I, Reading, Writing, and Arithmetic, contains three chapters, one on each of the topics within this area. In Chapter 1, *Reading as Constrained Reasoning,* Keith E. Stanovich and Anne E. Cunningham review the literature on reading from the standpoint of reading as a problem-solving activity, and conclude that reading cannot be well understood in terms of simple information-processing models. Rather, it requires for its understanding a more constructive conceptualization based on the notion of reading as a problem-solving process. In Chapter 2, *Going Beyond the Problem Given: Problem Solving in Expert and Novice*

Writers, Mary Bryson, Carl Bereiter, Marlene Scardamalia, and Elana Joram characterize writing as a problem-solving task. They note that it is more difficult than many other problem-solving tasks because often no explicit problem is given, and the author must not only solve problems, but construct them as well. In Chapter 3, *Cognitive Mechanisms in Calculation,* Scott M. Sokol and Michael McCloskey suggest that what seems like a simple and elementary task, arithmetic calculation, is actually a complex cognitive function requiring the interplay of diverse information-processing components. They suggest that the complexity of the processing involved has led some investigators to concentrate on specific types of calculations rather than to provide a general framework within which to understand calculation as a whole. The authors attempt to supply such a general framework.

Part II of this book deals with complex problem solving in the social sciences. The first chapter in this part, Chapter 4, is by James F. Voss, Christopher R. Wolfe, Jeanette A. Lawrence, and Randi A. Engle, and deals with political science. The chapter, *From Representation to Decision: An Analysis of Problem Solving in International Relations,* focuses on the information processing both experts and novices do when they try to solve problems in the field of international relations. Through their own work and that of others, the authors have found that experts and novices represent complex international problems in rather different ways, potentially leading to different kinds of solutions to these problems.

In Chapter 5, *Managerial Problem Solving,* Richard K. Wagner reviews the literature on management as complex problem solving. He notes that there are two schools of thought within management—one that views managers as rational technicians whose role it is to apply with brute force the knowledge and principles of management science, and the other that views managers as craftsmen who practice an art that cannot be reduced to a simple set of scientific principles. Wagner reviews these approaches, and provides a synthesis of approaches that suggests that management can be studied scientifically, but must be viewed in part as an art as well as a science. In Chapter 6, *Solving Complex Problems: Exploration and Control in Complex Social Systems,* Joachim Funke reviews the literature, much of it European, on solving very complex social-systems problems, such as those that would be faced by the mayor of a town or the ruler of an agrarian state. Funke reviews both computer simulations and human simulations, in which subjects are asked to imagine that they, for example, are in charge of a town and have to perform the duties that a mayor from that town would perform. In Chapter 7, *Do Lawyers Reason Differently from Psychologists? A Comparative Design for Studying Expertise,* Eric Amsel, Rosanne Langer, and Lynn Loutzenhiser compare legal reasoning to the reasoning of psychologists. The authors conclude that legal reasoning is distinct in certain respects from psychological (and hence scientific) reasoning, and they characterize some of the differences.

In Part III, Chapter 8, *Knowledge and Processes in Mechanical Problem Solving,* Mary Hegarty deals with how people solve mechanical problems, such as how hard a golfer should hit a golf ball, or how a car mechanic might diagnose what is wrong with a faulty brake system. She considers both domain-general and domain-specific principles of problem solving to formulate a fairly general model of how people solve problems in mechanics. In Chapter 9, *Complex Problem Solving in Electronics,* Alan Lesgold and Susanne Lajoie review the burgeoning literature on electronic troubleshooting. They combine both experimental and anecdotal data in their analysis of the cognitive processes brought to bear on electronics problems. In Chapter 10, *Computer Interaction: Debugging the Problems,* Dana S. Kay deals with problems such as the nature of the knowledge acquired when someone learns to use a computer, the transfer of computer programming skills to other domains, and the types of instruction that best lead to the acquisition of computer programming skills.

In Part IV, on game playing, a single chapter by Peter A. Frensch and Robert J. Sternberg, *Skill-Related Differences in Game Playing,* reviews the literature on the information processing involved when people strategically plan their moves in competitive and noncompetitive games.

And finally, in Part V, Chapter 12, *Some Comments on the Study of Complexity,* Earl Hunt summarizes and integrates the various chapters that constitute the book.

READING, WRITING, AND ARITHMETIC

1 Reading as Constrained Reasoning

Keith E. Stanovich
Ontario Institute for Studies in Education

Anne E. Cunningham
University of California, Berkeley

In two classic papers published over 50 years apart, both E. L. Thorndike (1917) and R. L. Thorndike (1973–1974) urged that, for the most part, reading was best thought of as reasoning. This assertion—that we view reading as essentially synonymous with reasoning—has always been at the heart of theoretical debates about reading. In this chapter we explore the validity of the theoretical assertion that reading can be conflated with reasoning.

In our introductory review of the classic global models of reading, we see that early bottom-up and top-down models of the reading process differed greatly in the assumptions made about how extensively reasoning processes infused the act of reading. We then briefly review the more contemporary models of Just and Carpenter (1980, 1987) and of Rayner and Pollatsek (1989). Although these more recent models relax some of the overly strong assumptions of the older top-down and bottom-up conceptualizations, both preserve a demarcation between processes taking place prior to and during lexical access (the process by which a word activates its meaning in memory) and those processes subsequent to lexical access. We then discuss the ideas of theorist Jerry Fodor (1983), whose concept of modularity most strongly demarcates prelexical word recognition processes from postlexical processing. We argue that the processing demarcations highlighted by the concept of modularity provide a convenient framework for addressing the question of whether reading is best conceptualized as a type of reasoning.

Our chapter then takes up the issue of individual differences; specifically, the issue of what components in the processing system are the source of individual differences in reading. Again, the distinction between prelexical word recognition processes and postlexical word recognition processes will loom large. In two sections we review the evidence on the cognitive differences between the skilled reader and the dyslexic reader defined by large aptitude/achievement discrepancies and the skilled reader and the poor reader without aptitude/achievement discrepancy.

After these discussions of how the distinction between pre- and postlexical processes bifurcates reading theory, we return to the issue of whether reading should reasonably be viewed as reasoning. One important consideration is the fact that even the postlexical components of reading that do involve processes more akin to reasoning are limited by the inputs delivered by modular systems. Because the operation of postlexical processes are limited by the hierarchical arrangement of the processing system, reading is best conceived as a particular form of constrained reasoning.

THE "CLASSIC" MODELS OF READING

During the late 1960s and early 1970s, cognitive psychologists began to apply their information processing perspective to the task of reading. There was a strong tendency for these cognitive theorists to depict information processing as a series of discrete stages, each performing a specific transformation on its input and passing on a new recoded representation as an input to a subsequent stage that did not initiate until the earlier stage was completed (LaBerge & Samuels, 1974; Massaro, 1978; Sperling, 1967). Because the sequence of processing operations proceeded from the incoming data (words on the page) to higher level encodings (comprehension), such conceptualizations were termed *bottom-up* models.

Although several bottom-up models were introduced into the literature, one of the most influential was presented by Gough (1972) in his seminal paper "One Second of Reading." The model is illustrated in Fig. 1.1. Although we need not be concerned with its details here, we do need to see how it embodies the serial, sequential-stage assumptions of bottom-up models. Visual information from an eye fixation is stored in iconic memory and then the letters of the word are scanned from left to right and stored in a character register. The letters are then transformed into systematic phonemes by a decoder that consults stored grapheme-to-phoneme correspondences. The resulting phonemic representation is used to access the word in the lexicon, and information concerning the word is entered into primary memory. A set of processes (dubbed "Merlin") then utilizes syntactic and semantic rules to construct a representation of the text and place it in the storage system called TPWSGWTAU ("The place where sentences go when they are understood").

Of course, the terms "Merlin" and "TPWSGWTAU" are joking references to the fact that, at the time Gough wrote, very little was known about these comprehension processes. Nevertheless, they do reflect the theoretical biases of the

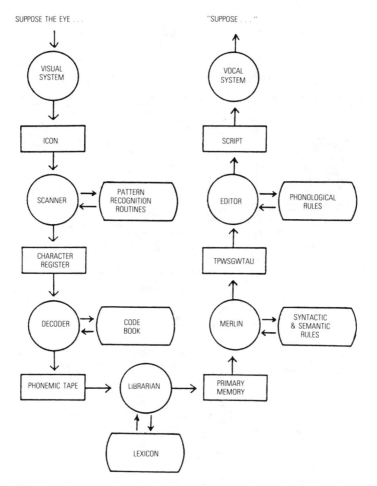

FIG. 1.1.   An example of a bottom-up model of reading (taken from Gough, 1972).

bottom-up perspective. For example, if we ask whether reading seems much like reasoning when viewed from within this perspective, the answer is clearly no. None of the processes that are emphasized seem very much like reasoning processes. The storage of visual information in iconic memory, the scanning of that information, the transfer of letters to the character register, the transformation to a phonemic representation, the access of the lexicon, and the placement of information into primary memory—all seem like processes that could be carried out in the absence of executive control and without draining much cognitive capacity. Certainly, problem-solving and reasoning-like processes might characterize "Merlin" or "TPWSGWTAU," but these do not receive any extended discussion or emphasis. The joke labels "Merlin" and "TPWSGWTAU" simply

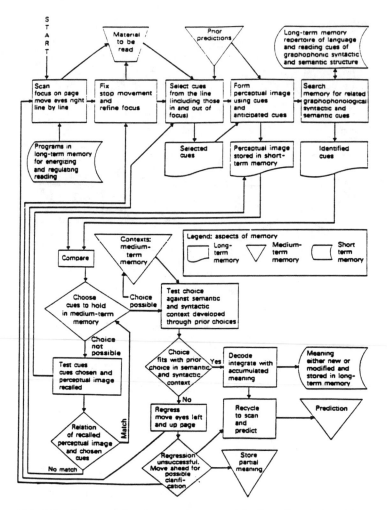

FIG. 1.2. An example of a top-down model of reading (taken from Goodman, 1972).

exist as commentaries on our lack of knowledge about such processes. Reading just does not look much like reasoning from the classic bottom-up perspectives (see also LaBerge & Samuels, 1974).

This stands in complete contrast to the top-down frameworks that were introduced into reading theory during roughly the same time period (Goodman, 1967, 1972; Hochberg, 1970; Kolers, 1972; Smith, 1971, 1973). The theorists who developed these reading models were heavily influenced by the New Look perspective in experimental psychology, which emphasized that perceptual processing was saturated with the organism's prior expectations (see Smith, 1971). They also drew on early models of recognition (see Neisser, 1967) emphasizing analysis-by-synthesis approaches whereby partially constructed stimulus representations were used to direct subsequent perceptual processing. A flow diagram depicting one of the early top-down reading models is displayed in Fig. 1.2. You will no doubt be pleased to learn that we do not bother to explicate its features in detail. The most important feature is the obvious one: in total contrast to the bottom-up model in Fig. 1.1, in Fig. 1.2 virtually everything interacts with everything else.

Top-down models posit that higher-level processes interact with, and direct the flow of information through, lower-level processes. Such models conceive of fluent readers as being engaged in hypothesis-testing as they proceed through text, only sampling information to confirm previously derived hypotheses. The reading process is thus driven by higher-level conceptual processes rather than by stimulus analysis, as in Fig. 1.1. The entire reading process is saturated with expectancies in top-down models. This can be most clearly seen at the top of Fig. 1.2, where the triangle labeled "prior expectations" is directly affecting the early perceptual processes of selecting visual cues and forming a "perceptual image." Thus, in top-down models, the entire reading process shares similarities with problem solving. Not only comprehension, but also the extraction of visual features in the stimulus array is driven by expectancies, the use of prior knowledge, and hypothesis-testing. Reading is manifestly reasoning under such a view.

RECENT MODELS: DEMARCATING LEXICAL ACCESS

More recent models of the reading process diverge from the earlier "classic" models in several ways. First, the newer conceptualizations are more data-based than earlier frameworks. The latter were naturally more apt to be influenced by philosophical preferences because they were developed in an era when there were many fewer empirical constraints on possible models. Second, these more recent models have relaxed some of the more objectionably strong assumptions of the early top-down and bottom-up models. For example, most current models more severely restrict where in the processing hierarchy expectancy-based processing can occur. Current models do not allow expectancy-based processing to influence feature extraction, as in the model portrayed in Fig. 1.2. Indeed, most current models largely restrict expectancy-based processing and hypothesis-testing mechanisms to the postlexical level (Henderson, 1982; Rayner & Pollatsek, 1989; Seidenberg, 1985; Stanovich, 1986b; Stanovich & West, 1983).

Additionally, however, several longstanding assumptions contained in bottom-up views have been modified. The idea of strict sequentiality of stages—the assumption that a later stage could not begin to execute until earlier stages had run to completion—has been abandoned. Most models now assume a cascade-like (see McClelland, 1979) processing structure where, even in a serial-stage model, later stages may begin their computations before earlier stages have completed processing. Also, the notion of serial left-to-right scanning of letters (e.g., Gough, 1972) has been abandoned (Gough, 1985).

Two examples of recent models—Just and Carpenter's (1980, 1987) production system model, READER, and Rayner and Pollatsek's (1989) model based on their recent research synthesis—are both notable for relying heavily on the empirical constraints derived from recent research on information processing during reading, particularly empirical results deriving from the precise study of eye-movement patterns during reading.

The general architecture of the Just and Carpenter model is illustrated in Fig. 1.3, although it has considerably more processing complications than can be captured in a schematic flow diagram (see Just & Carpenter, 1987). The heart of the model is a production system, which is a set of condition-act rules that operate on the contents of working memory. A particular production rule fires when it recognizes critical elements present in working memory. The production then carries out its particular operations, which could involve aspects of building a text structure or inserting new elements into working memory. Productions are executed in recognize-act cycles. During one such cycle the contents of working memory are simultaneously assessed by all the productions and those productions having their conditions satisfied then simultaneously execute their functions. Executing productions alter the contents of various memory systems, thus readying the system for the next recognize-act cycle.

Although it is clear that the Just and Carpenter model incorporates substantial

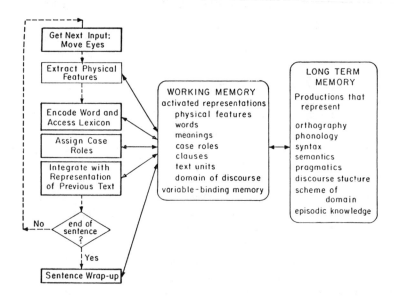

FIG. 1.3.   The Just and Carpenter (1987) model of reading.

parallel processing and that the strict seriality of earlier bottom-up models is violated, the architecture in Fig. 1.3 does share certain features of the bottom-up framework. Specifically, a stage of lexical access (the extraction of word meaning from the visual features) is demarcated, and later stages of case role assignment and text integration are dependent on the output from the lexical access stage. This allows the productions concerned with lexical processing to look in content (see Just & Carpenter, 1987) more like the bottom-up stimulus analysis mechanisms of the Gough (1972) model and the productions that utilize pragmatics and schema to instantiate a text representation to look at least somewhat like reasoning processes (see Just & Carpenter, 1987). Thus, the lexical level demarcates those processes that are "reasoning-like" from those that are not in the Just and Carpenter (1980, 1987) model.

A similar demarcation occurs in the model that Rayner and Pollatsek (1989) built, based on their extensive data using eye-movement contingent display technologies, where a computer can manipulate the text based on where the subject happens to be fixated. Unlike Just and Carpenter's model, which is a running computer simulation, Rayner and Pollatsek's model is summarized in a standard flow diagram (reproduced in Fig. 1.4). To understand exactly how the model works, one must consult the extensive list of specific findings—most deriving from studies of what text variables control the movement of the eyes and how they do so—that are scattered throughout Rayner and Pollatsek's excellent book. Nevertheless, the general framework is apparent from Fig. 1.4. Clearly this model bears more similarities to the earlier bottom-up models than to the top-down frameworks. It does, however, allow more alternative processing routes than did earlier bottom-up models. Nevertheless, while postlexical processes can trigger the eyes to refixate a word, expectations derived from the text representation and/or the thematic processor cannot direct the processes of feature extraction and visual encoding as in Fig. 1.2. To the point of lexical access, this model shares many features with early bottom-up models, although the potential routes to lexical access are more varied and complicated than those of the Gough (1972) model depicted in Fig. 1.1.

Again, we are not too far from a simplifying view whereby we conceptualize postlexical text integration processes as being "reasoning-like," in the manner of Thorndike (1973–74), but conceptualize prelexical mechanisms as being a much different type of stimulus-constrained, noncontrolled processing. Thus, there is a strong tendency in current reading theory to characterize prelexical and postlexical processing with very different explanatory mechanisms. That is, although processes of word recognition interface—and probably temporally overlap—with postlexical comprehension processes, the theoretical conceptualization of these different levels of processing is strongly divergent.

This distinction between levels of processing will take us quite far in understanding which processes and knowledge structures are unique to reading and which processes and knowledge structures reading shares with other tasks. It has

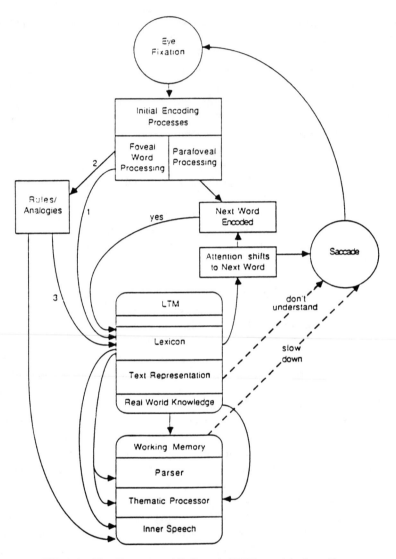

FIG. 1.4.   The Rayner and Pollatsek (1989) model of reading.

the additional advantage of tying disputes in reading theory directly to current debates within cognitive science. The reason for this is that the properties of the word recognition system, as outlined in the models of Gough (1972) and Rayner and Pollatsek (1989), as well as in the writings of other theorists (Forster, 1979; Henderson, 1982; Seidenberg, 1985; Stanovich & West, 1983) bear many similarities to the properties of modular processes in something approaching Fodor's

(1983) sense. Indeed, Fodor's distinction between central and modular processes provides a framework for the remainder of our review of the ways in which reading is both like and unlike reasoning.

MODULAR PROCESSES: THE PART OF READING NOT LIKE REASONING

Even more than the theorists we have already considered, Fodor (1983) is a theorist who strongly demarcated levels of processing. His differentiation between modular and central processes is useful in thinking about reading, because the distinction nicely demarcates the pre- and postlexical processing operations of reading. Fodor's concept of modularity, like the related concept of automaticity, is a complex construct that conjoins a number of separate properties (Forster, 1979; Humphreys, 1985; Logan, 1985; Stanovich, 1990). Nevertheless, the key property distinguishing modular processes from central ones is exactly the property that has loomed so large in disputes over global models of reading: whether a particular process is directed by expectancies based on prior knowledge structures stored in long-term memory.

We saw that in top-down models such as that illustrated in Fig. 1.2, knowledge-based expectancies are implicated in the very earliest processes prior to lexical access (selection of visual cues and perceptual "image" formation); whereas in Gough's model, and in Rayner and Pollatsek's, no such expectancies were implicated prior to lexical access. This latter situation—where previously-stored world knowledge does not influence the process in question—Fodor has termed "information encapsulation." It is the defining feature of modular process, according to his view. In Fodor's conceptualization, other properties—such as fast execution, domain specificity, and obligatory execution—tend to co-occur with information encapsulation. Central processes, according to Fodor (1983), have the converse set of properties. They are slow-acting, domain general, under strategic control, and, most importantly, they are informationally unencapsulated.

The reader should be warned that in recent theoretical writings in cognitive science the property of information encapsulation has traveled under a variety of different names. Humphreys (1985) mentioned some of these in his discussion of encapsulation:

> If word processing does proceed involuntarily on at least some occasions, there are some interesting implications concerning the control of such operations. For instance, one possibility is that control operates locally so that once a set of word processing procedures is activated, it runs to completion and cannot be amended by other higher order processes (i.e., it is "cognitively impenetrable;" see Pylyshyn, 1981). Such processes may be termed functionally autonomous (Forster, 1979). An

implication of this is that word processing cannot be benefited by other ongoing processes (e.g., see Fodor, 1983). This is a different prediction from that which holds that the effects of word processing cannot be prevented (cf. the argument that processing is involuntary), since it is feasible that subjects are unable to prevent a particular process but they may still supplement it when required. (pp. 292–293)

Thus, informational encapsulation (or the synonymous terms functional autonomy and cognitive impenetrability) means that the operation of a processing module is not controlled by higher level operations or supplemented by information from knowledge structures not contained in the module itself:

> The claim that input systems are informationally encapsulated is equivalent to the claim that the data that can bear on the confirmation of perceptual hypotheses includes . . . considerably less than the organism may know. That is, the confirmation function for input systems does not have access to all of the information that the organism internally represents; there are restrictions upon the allocation of internally represented information to input processes. (Fodor, 1983, p. 69)

Fodor (1983) viewed processes such as basic speech perception and face perception as candidates for modular input systems and in his book cited numerous instances of where, in these domains, "at least *some* of the background information at the subject's disposal is inaccessible to at least some of his perceptual mechanisms" (p. 66). Although Fodor rejected the idea of acquired modularity and equivocates in applying the modularity concept to reading, many other cognitive scientists have viewed the idea of acquired modularity as theoretically coherent (Forster, 1979; Humphreys, 1985; Logan, 1985; McLeod, McLaughlin, & Nimmo-Smith, 1985; Perfetti & McCutchen, 1987; Seidenberg, 1985; Sternberg, 1985). Others have applied the modularity concept to the process of word recognition and its development (Forster, 1979; Perfetti, in press; Perfetti & McCutchen, 1987; Seidenberg, 1985; Stanovich, 1986b, in press; Stanovich, Nathan, West, & Vala-Rossi, 1985; Stanovich & West, 1983). Interestingly, perhaps more actual empirical work has been done in the acquired domain of visual word recognition than in some of the other hypothesized modular domains that Fodor (1983) originally championed. In addition, it should also be noted that the theoretical claims in the area of visual word recognition have been more restricted to questions of the nature of information encapsulation (Seidenberg, 1985; Stanovich & West, 1983) and have not generally included the more far-reaching and tenuous claims that Fodor makes in his conceptualization of modularity (e.g., innateness, hard-wiring, specific ontogenic sequencing).

The important idea that information encapsulation could be acquired meshed perfectly with trends in the literature on context effects in the development of word recognition skills. During the early 1980s a longstanding puzzle in the literature on individual differences in reading skill was beginning to be resolved. It had consistently been found that children who were poor comprehenders invariably had poor word recognition skills. Additionally, and unexpectedly, however, they tended to show large linguistic context effects in many tasks. It had traditionally been assumed in reading theory that poor readers would display markedly attenuated contextual sensitivity (e.g., Smith, 1971). This seeming paradox was resolved by demonstrating that the greater contextual facilitation shown by poorer readers was confined to word recognition tasks and did not extend to reading tasks involving comprehension (Stanovich, 1980).

One particular model used to resolve the paradox proposed that the contextual facilitation of word recognition could result from either of two cognitive mechanisms that displayed very different properties (Neely, 1977; Posner & Snyder, 1975; Stanovich & West, 1979, 1983). Automatic spreading activation was a modular mechanism that produced contextual facilitation with no costs to other aspects of performance. In contrast, if conscious expectancy mechanisms (central processes) were employed, they would likewise facilitate word recognition performance, but at the cost of depleting the central cognitive resources available to other simultaneously operating comprehension processes. The puzzling data in the individual differences literature was explained by positing that the severely deficient word recognition processes of less-skilled readers caused them to rely on the conscious expectancy process because of the additional facilitation that it provided—but at the cost of further depleting the cognitive capacity available to higher-level comprehension processes. Fluent readers, in contrast, had word recognition mechanisms that were so efficient that they did not necessitate the use of the central expectancy mechanism and thus did not incur the costs of its use. The net result was that the poorer reader devoted more resources to the local level of word recognition, relied more on contextual mechanisms, but simultaneously further stressed an already inefficient comprehension system.

Consistent with these ideas, research has consistently indicated that the effects of background knowledge and contextual information attenuate as the efficiency of word recognition processes increases (Briggs, Austin, & Underwood, 1984; Perfetti, 1985; Perfetti & Roth, 1981; Pring & Snowling, 1986; Schwantes, 1985; Stanovich, 1980, 1986b; Stanovich et. al., 1985; Stanovich & West, 1983; Stanovich, West, & Feeman, 1981). This research evidence has led most developmental reading theorists to view word recognition as becoming increasingly encapsulated (informationally) as processing efficiency develops. Thus, even before the appearance of Fodor's monograph, reading theorists had featured the concept of information encapsulation more prominently in their theories. Fodor's terminology was simply adopted by a field already focused on issues of process encapsulation.

Why Modularity?

It is one thing to identify empirical evidence consistent with the idea of acquired modularity in the fluent reader, but it is another to have a principled explanation for why its incorporation into reading models makes theoretical sense. We may ask: Why is reading the type of task that benefits from having at least some of its processing components organized in a modular fashion? or: Why is information encapsulation a benefit to a processing system engaged in a task like reading? In short, is there a parsimonious way in which information encapsulation accounts for increased reading efficiency with increased experience and practice?

There are, in fact, many principled ways in which the encapsulation idea fits in with what is known about reading comprehension and the act of reading. The outline of the argument in reading theory is paralleled by several arguments in Fodor's (1983) monograph. Discussing the computer analogy to human information processing that is popular in some domains of cognitive science, Fodor argued that researchers have inappropriately de-emphasized the importance of making contact with the environment and have overly focused on Turing machines that are closed computational systems: "the sole determinants of their computations are the current machine state, the tape configuration, and the program, the rest of the world being quite irrelevant to the character of their performance; whereas, of course, organisms are forever exchanging information with their environments" (p. 39). What follows, according to Fodor, is that "what perception must do is to so represent the world so as to make it available to thought" (p. 40). In short, higher-level processing operations and inference-making processes will work more efficiently when perceptual processes deliver to them accurate representations of the world. The types of perceptual processes that do this best are modular ones—input systems that execute without accessing all of the organism's background information and beliefs. Modular cognitive processes are like reflexes in that "they go off largely without regard to the beliefs and utilities of the behaving organism" (Fodor, 1985, p. 2).

Modular processes are thus isolated from background knowledge, belief, and set. This confers two great advantages. One is the veridicality that results from the organism's ability to code—at least at some level—the features of the environment without distortion. As Fodor, in his inimitable style, pointed out: "The ecological good sense of this arrangement is surely self-evident. Prejudiced and wishful seeing makes for dead animals" (1985, p. 2). The second advantage—that of speed—follows along these same lines:

> Automatic processes are, in a certain sense, deeply unintelligent; of the whole range of computational . . . options available to the organism, only a stereotyped subset is brought into play. But what you save by this sort of stupidity is *not having to make up your mind,* and making your mind up takes time. (1983, p. 64)

Referring to Ogden Nash's "If you're called by a panther/don't anther," Fodor argued that what the organism needs is a panther identification mechanism that is fast and that errs only on the side of false positives. Thus, "we do not want to have to access panther-identification information from the (presumably very large) central storage . . . on the assumption that large memories are searched slowly" (1983, p. 70). In fact, even if such access were fast, it would not be efficacious because

> the property of being 'about panthers' is not one that can be surefootedly relied upon. Given enough context, practically everything I know can be construed as panther related; and I do not want to have to consider everything I know in the course of perceptual panther identification . . . The primary point is to so restrict the number of confirmation relations that need to be estimated as to make perceptual identifications fast. (1983, p. 71)

> Feedback is effective only to the extent that, *prior* to the analysis of the stimulus, the perceiver knows quite a lot about what the stimulus is going to be like. Whereas, the point of perception is surely that it lets us find out how the world is even when the world is some way that we don't expect it to be. (p. 67)

In short, an advantage accrues to encapsulation *when the specificity and efficiency of stimulus analyzing mechanisms is great relative to the diagnosticity of the background information that might potentially be recruited to aid recognition.* This is a point that has fundamental importance for understanding the role of modular input systems in reading.

The debate in the cognitive science literature regarding the benefits of encapsulation finds immediate correspondence with issues in the reading literature. One of Fodor's (1983, 1985) recurring themes was that "poverty of the stimulus" arguments inherited from the "New Look" period of perceptual research had led cognitive psychology astray. An analogous argument has influenced reading theory during the last decade.

Models of reading acquisition and individual differences in reading ability were dominated for a considerable time by top-down conceptualizations that borrowed heavily from the New Look in perception (e.g., Smith, 1971). These models strongly emphasized the contribution of expectancies and contextual information in the process of word recognition. Using the current terminology, top-down models posited that developmental changes in reading skill were characterized by word recognition processes that were more heavily penetrated by background knowledge and higher-level cognitive expectancies. As previously discussed, when the appropriate developmental and individual differences data were collected, they demonstrated exactly the opposite: reading skill increases as word recognition processes become increasingly encapsulated (Perfetti, 1985, in press; Perfetti & Roth, 1981; Stanovich, 1980, 1986b).

It appears that reading theory—at least regarding word recognition—went wrong by overgeneralizing "poverty of the stimulus" arguments. Reading theorists were considerably influenced by analysis-by-synthesis models of speech perception, and interactive models of recognition that derived from artificial intelligence work in speech perception (Rumelhart, 1977). The problem here is that the analogy to written language is not apt. The ambiguity in decontextualized speech is well known. For example, excised words from normal conversation are often not recognized out of context. This does not hold for written language, obviously. A fluent reader can identify written words with near perfect accuracy out of context. In short, the physical stimulus alone completely specifies the lexical representation in writing, whereas this is not always true in speech. The greater diagnosticity of the external stimulus in reading, as opposed to listening, puts a greater premium on an input system that can deliver a full representation of the stimulus to higher-level cognitive systems.

Another problem concerns the assumptions that have been made about the properties of contextual information. Laboratory demonstrations of contextual priming effects have often led to an overestimation of the magnitude of facilitation to be expected from contextual information, because these studies—often for sound theoretical reasons—employed stimulus materials that had strong semantic associations and that were vastly more predictable on a word-by-word basis than is natural text (Gough, 1983). Also, the writings of many reading theorists—ignoring evidence on text redundancy—often give the impression that predicting upcoming words in sentences is relatively easy and highly accurate. Actually, many different empirical studies have indicated that naturalistic text is not all that predictable. Alford (1980) found that for a set of SAT-type passages, subjects needed an average of more than four guesses to correctly anticipate upcoming words in the passage (the method of scoring actually makes this a considerable underestimate). Across a variety of subject populations and texts, a reader's probability of predicting the next word in a passage is usually between .20 and .35 (Aborn, Rubenstein, & Sterling, 1959; Gough, 1983; Miller & Coleman, 1967; Perfetti, Goldman, & Hogaboam, 1979; Rubenstein & Aborn, 1958). Indeed, as Gough has shown, this figure is highest for function words, and is often quite low for the very words in the passage that carry the most information content.

Thus, we have in reading precisely the situation where an enormous advantage accrues to encapsulation: the potential specificity of stimulus analyzing mechanisms is great relative to the diagnosticity of the background information that might be recruited to aid recognition. Of course, there is an analogy here to Fodor's "panther detector." The organism is much better off with a correct rendition of the stimulus as opposed to a sloppy stimulus representation and a geometric explosion of "panther-related" general information. Similarly, the reader is almost always better off having the proper lexical entry rapidly activated.

In summary, lexical access in the fluent adult reader is the part of reading that is *not* like reasoning or problem solving. It does not recruit information from general knowledge bases and is not directed by central processes of expectation and control. But lexical access is not all of reading, of course. A more appropriate realm for metaphors suggesting the view that "reading is reasoning" lies in the domain of postlexical comprehension processes, to which we now turn.

CENTRAL PROCESSES: THE PART OF READING THAT
IS LIKE REASONING

There is no question that beyond lexical access and basic sentence parsing processes, there are operating processes more akin to what would be commonly termed "reasoning" or "problem solving." Regardless of the extent to which such postlexical processes contribute to creating individual differences in reading—a matter in serious dispute (Perfetti, 1985; Perfetti & McCutchen, 1987)—they are certainly implicated in the act of general comprehension.

Understanding the part of reading that *is* more akin to "reasoning" has, for reading theorists, largely meant attempting to address two questions: How is prior knowledge used to elaborate the words in text via inferences? and: How do readers use metacognitive strategies to monitor and facilitate on-line comprehension? These questions correspond to what Perfetti and McCutchen (1987) term the "knowledge approach" and the "strategy approach" to understanding reading. Both of these approaches emphasize central, nonmodular processes because many of the strategies and knowledge bases can be applied across a number of domains outside of reading.

Knowledge and Comprehension

One principle that has become firmly established in reading theory is that readers must make extensive use of background knowledge in the postlexical phases of sentence processing. For example, disambiguation (distinguishing between different word-senses) and reference-finding (ascertaining the objects to which noun phrases, including pronouns, refer) are typically viewed as component processes in constructing propositions from text. Unlike lexical access and sentence parsing, however, these processes involve significant amounts of world knowledge, in addition to propositional information derived from previous text processing. Consider the following text fragment: "Mrs. Smith saw that SmithCorp stock was up 12. Her husband was having breakfast. Knowing he would want another cup, she stirred the arsenic into the coffee." A considerable amount of elaborative inferencing clearly occurs during the comprehension of this fragment. We infer that Mrs. Smith's husband owns SmithCorp stock and we make an inference of marital discord. We make use of a mutual base of knowledge and comprehension procedures that the writer takes advantage of to induce understanding in the reader without having to spell out every fact. This use of background knowledge in this manner is what has been the focus of recent research.

In the 1970s there was a revival of interest among reading researchers in Bartlett's (1932) observation that prior knowledge affects our ability to comprehend. This renewed interest spawned a flurry of studies demonstrating the extensive effects that prior knowledge can have on the comprehension and interpretation of passages. For example, variations in topic knowledge can extensively modify both the quantity and quality of the information recalled from text (Chiesi, Spilich, & Voss, 1979; Lipson, 1983; Pearson, Hansen, & Gordon, 1979; Spilich, Vesonder, Chiesi, & Voss, 1979; Steffensen, Joag-Dev, & Anderson, 1979; Taylor, 1985; Voss, 1984).

Beyond the demonstration of such effects, theorists became concerned with more refined questions. The issue of the nature of the organization of the knowledge used in the comprehension process, and the issue of which particular inferences are made during reading and what stored knowledge is employed to enable the inferences, became of great interest. The treatment of these issues of knowledge use within the domain of reading was considerably influenced by developments in other areas of cognitive science, particularly computational models of understanding. Many such theorists proposed variants of the idea that people possess a rich hierarchy of categories of complex, structured events (Charniak, 1973; Minsky, 1975; Schank & Abelson, 1977). For example, Minsky's proposed *frames* were intended to generalize the notion of category to cover event classes, and Schank and Abelson proposed *scripts* as specific structures describing event sequences. Reading researchers were even more strongly influenced by explications of the idea of content schemata by investigators such as Rumelhart and Anderson (Anderson, 1977; Anderson & Pearson, 1984; Anderson, Pichert, & Shirey, 1983; Anderson, Reynolds, Schallert, & Goetz, 1977; Rumelhart, 1975, 1980; Rumelhart & Ortony, 1977). There was a strong realization that many texts relied on the expectations and elaborations made possible by stored knowledge.

However we conceptualize the knowledge structures involved in reading, researchers must address the issue of what particular inferences are actually made during the reading process, because there are many classes of inference made possible by various kinds of prior knowledge (Gerrig, 1988; Graesser, Haberlandt, & Koizumi, 1987; Singer, 1988), and some investigators have proposed that all possible inferences are made. However, work in computer simulation has indicated that, even with very impoverished knowledge bases, programs adopting such a strategy were soon overwhelmed by the number of additional facts produced (Rieger, 1975; Schank & Abelson, 1977). Similarly, Schank and Abelson originally proposed that all of the slots of a script were instantiated with default values during processing, and this suggestion was eagerly adopted by many researchers in the psychology of reading. However, the goal of Schank and his colleagues was to build programs that could answer as many questions as possible about a piece of text contrived for the purposes of the demonstration. The text itself was constructed so that the small number of mechanisms in the program could succeed in deriving the small number of implications in the stories. Little attempt was made to mirror psychological data in this early work in cognitive science. It is possible that some of the stronger conclusions from this early work in computer simulation—conclusions not grounded in human data—were overgeneralized when applied in the field of reading.

Early applications of the schema concept in reading research assumed a model in which all slots of the activated schema were instantiated, whether or not the information was present in the text. This prevailing view was captured by Anderson, Reynolds, Schallert, and Goetz (1977): "The slots in the schemata from which an individual is trying to build an interpretation of a message 'beg' to be filled. They must be filled, even when the message contains no direct information, otherwise comprehension will fail" (p. 370). Thus, inferences are always made by the reader within this model, similar to other early conceptions of the operation of schema. In recall experiments it was found that readers could not easily distinguish between information present in the text and unstated information that was part of a hypothesized activated schema (Anderson & Pichert, 1978; Johnson, Bransford & Solomon, 1973; Paris & Lindauer, 1976). It was subsequently inferred from this evidence that extensive elaboration occurs during comprehension (Anderson et al., 1976; Johnson et al., 1973; Paris & Lindauer, 1976).

Recent research has questioned this standard interpretation. For example, it has been pointed out that as long as an explicit representation of the text is lost, schema-oriented recall could be due to inferences made at retrieval time (Alba & Hasher, 1983; Potts, Keenan, & Golding, 1988; Whitney, 1987). In fact, Corbett and Dosher (1978) found that information that could be inferred from an activated schema provided a good recall cue for text sentences even when the information in the text directly contradicted the schema inference. For example, 'shovel' is a *better* recall cue than 'pitchfork' for the sentence "The grocer dug a hole with a pitchfork." Similarly, Singer (1979, 1980) has presented evidence indicating that even highly likely case fillers may not be routinely inferred during processing of text.

Garnham (1982) provided an excellent theoretical analysis and experimental test of three basic theories concerning inference, or schema instantiation. He first distinguished between essential inferences, those that are needed to establish the correct structure for the propositions in the text, and elaborative inferences that simply enrich the representation of the subject matter. The former class of inferences are, according to Garnham, clearly made during the reading process. It is the latter class that are problematic, as the contradictory studies cited earlier indicate. The "immediate inference" theory explains recall of highly probable case fillers using immediate schema instantiation, whereas the "deferred inference" theory assumes reconstruction of these case fillers using prior knowledge at testing time. Garnham's formal analysis indicated that the immediate and deferred theories give identical predictions for the case in which an improbable case filler is actually present in the text. Garnham also showed that the predictions of the immediate inference theory are in all cases identical with those of an "omission theory" in which highly probable case fillers are always omitted from the memory trace whether or not they are explicitly present in the text, because they can always be reconstructed on demand. Garnham demonstrated that for recall experiments, all three apparently different models are in fact formally equivalent. He suggested, however, that only the omission theory appears to be consistent with evidence from other experiments, such as Singer's (1979, 1980) sentence verification tasks.

Other researchers have employed different techniques to derive some interesting conclusions regarding the details of inference in comprehension. McKoon and Ratcliff (McKoon & Ratcliff, 1980a; 1980b; 1981; Ratcliff & McKoon, 1981) designed a priming technique to test a simple model of resolving anaphoric references. Their experiments supported a model of anaphoric reference in which when an inference is necessary to render the text coherent, it is made by reactivating the referent and associated propositions in order to integrate the new information.

Whitney (1986; Whitney & Kellas, 1984) has used a Stroop priming methodology to distinguish between simple activation of concepts and actual generation of inferences. In a Stroop task, subjects are asked to name the color of a patch that also contains a written word. Depending on the prior level of activation of the concept represented by the written word, the naming of colors can be unaffected, slowed (Stroop interference) or speeded up (Stroop facilitation). Naming "bird" before testing "robin" causes interference, whereas naming "robin" before testing "robin" causes facilitation. Whitney first primed his subjects with a sentence containing a category word in a focus position (e.g., as the subject), such that there was a bias toward typical exemplars of the category: e.g., "the bird was in the tree." He found that facilitation occurred. In contrast, the prime "The bird was in the oven" did not result in facilitation, whether "robin" or "chicken" was tested for. Whitney suggested that this supports the view that instantiation of general terms does occur in limited contexts such as when the term is the subject and the context biases the interpretation towards typical exemplars.

Although a variety of experiments have confirmed the general importance of prior knowledge in comprehension, they have also demonstrated that the particular theory of knowledge structure that is needed to explain the effects still remains undetermined. For example, whether anything more specific than a generalized activation theory is required is still a matter of dispute. In more recent work, Schank (1982) has argued for a model in which schemata, rather than being predefined bodies of facts, are dynamically assembled from smaller units (see also Sharkey & Mitchell, 1985). Whitney (1987) simply viewed the knowledge base as "an associative network of hierarchically and thematically connected concepts" (p. 307). Kintsch's (1988) construction-integration model made similar assumptions. What is confirmed, however, is that previously stored world knowledge interacts with the construction of text representations, and that the reading shares the recruitment of such knowledge with listening, general understanding, and problem solving.

Cognitive and Metacognitive Strategies for Comprehension

The other class of nonmodular, central processes that loom large in cognitive theories of reading might generally be termed "comprehension strategies." Research interest here has grown out of the more general reconceptualization of the learner as an active information processor that has occurred in the last two decades (Rohwer, 1973; Rohwer & Ammon, 1971; Wittrock, 1974, 1978). Such an emphasis in our characterization of the reading process is, of course, not completely new. Huey (1908), Thorndike (1917), and Dewey (1910) all viewed cognitive monitoring as a central activity of reading.

The work of Flavell, (1971, 1978) and Brown (1975) on children's self-regulatory or metacognitive abilities also had a seminal influence on reading theory. Subsequent to their seminal work, many researchers interested in reading comprehension began framing their questions within the context of metacognitive skills. Most of the metacognitive strategies to be considered are mechanisms for facilitating understanding that have some generality and that are not unique to reading. Most recruit information from a variety of cognitive knowledge bases. Therefore, they may be considered to be nonmodular, central processes within Fodor's framework.

Although traditionally it was believed that young children did not possess the ability to reflect upon their own thought processes in an abstract manner, both Flavell (1978, 1981) and Brown (1975) demonstrated that relatively young children were able to establish their own internal criteria for learning and to monitor their progress towards that goal. Brown and her associates (Baker & Brown, 1984; Brown, Armbruster, & Baker, 1986; Brown, Bransford, Ferrara, & Campione, 1983; Brown, Campione, & Day, 1981) have highlighted the importance of differentiating a number of metacognitive abilities. For example, in reading, the child must have knowledge of their own cognitive resources and the relative match between these resources and the text at hand. This knowledge entails awareness of necessary strategies for enhancing comprehension of text, such as skimming or paraphrasing, that assist in the understanding and remembering of information.

Children must also have knowledge of the task itself, such as the purpose for reading a particular passage, and the associated task requirements, such as writing a report or summarizing of the passage. Knowledge of how textual features such as its structure, clarity, and difficulty influence subsequent memory and comprehension is another component of metacognitive ability. Additionally, knowledge of one's own "learner characteristics" such as level of motivation for the task and familiarity with the topic, is important. Paris and his colleagues

(Paris, Lipson, & Wixson, 1983; Cross & Paris, 1988) have argued that meta-cognition is a complex array of knowledge and skills that include the type of knowledge Brown has described and more. Paris argued that metacognition is defined as declarative knowledge (knowing that paraphrasing is a strategy), procedural knowledge (knowing how to paraphrase), and conditional knowledge (knowing when to paraphrase and why).

Simply being knowledgeable of the influence of these components is not sufficient, however. Metacognition also involves the "orchestration" of these variables via self-regulation (Brown, 1987). This aspect of metacognition has been characterized as control or management of strategies (Brown et al., 1986; Wagner & Sternberg, 1987). Thus, knowledge of the interactions of the metacognitive variables and how they affect learning outcomes is an important aspect of control.

There is a wealth of correlational evidence linking strategies and megacognitive ability to reading comprehension skill. Typically, strategic processing has been examined in light of the performance of expert versus novice readers. Myers and Paris (1978), for example, observed that older children were more aware of the value and utility of strategies for reading comprehension than younger children. In another study, Paris and Myers (1981) found that good and poor readers differed in their knowledge of reading strategies and their use of them. Expert readers monitored and repaired comprehension difficulties, whereas novice readers were passive comprehenders. Garner and Reis (1981) observed that expert comprehenders recognized comprehension errors and applied a "look back" or rereading strategy more readily than poorer comprehenders. Forrest and Waller (1979) observed that younger and less-skilled readers had less knowledge of fix-up strategies and were less successful at evaluating their own comprehension than older and more skilled readers. This lack of knowledge of the use of strategies, inability to choose appropriate strategies, and ineffective monitoring of strategies has been characterized as a strategic deficiency that tends to be more commonly found in novice readers (Forrest-Pressley & Gillies, 1983; Scardamalia & Bereiter, 1983).

One important aspect of metacognition related to reading comprehension is understanding the purpose of reading text. Current research has focused on the establishment of reader purpose as one of the first steps in monitoring text comprehension (e.g., Paris & Winograd, 1988). Markman (1981) in particular, assigned a large role to the establishment of purpose for reading. She argued that decisions regarding the comprehensibility of a passage will depend, in part, on the type of material being read, but that comprehension will vary as a function of one's purpose or goal for reading. Thus, individual differences can be observed among skilled and less-skilled readers along this dimension. Younger and less-skilled readers are found to be less aware of the purpose of reading than older and more skilled readers (Johns & Ellis, 1976; Myers & Paris, 1978). Furthermore, expert readers have been show to adjust their reading behaviors according to the purpose of reading more readily than novice readers (Forrest & Waller, 1979). Smith (1967) asked novice and expert adults to either read for details or read to obtain the gist of the story. He observed that expert readers were able to adjust their reading to accommodate this instruction, whereas novice readers used the same behaviors for both purposes.

Baker and Brown (1984) showed that novice readers are not always sensitive to levels of text difficulty. Novice readers' ratings of structural importance differs from expert readers. When asked to differentiate the important, less important, and least important features of a text, younger and less-skilled readers were less likely to reliably rate the structural importance of ideas in a story. Novice readers were also not able to distinguish between the three levels of importance in a study by Brown and Smiley (1977). Novice readers tend to focus more on lexical items rather than intersentence logical consistency (Baker & Anderson, 1982; Glenberg, Wilkinson, & Epstein, 1982). Thus, it appears that younger and less-skilled readers often take a "piecemeal" approach to comprehension and, as a result, integration of information is minimal (Garner, 1987; Markman, 1981).

What an individual knows about their own characteristics as learners, including capacity limitations, background knowledge, and motivational level also appears to be important for monitoring one's current state of learning. Research in metamemory has shown developmental trends in children's knowledge of whether they will/can remember something. Older children, for example, are more aware of their limitations in remembering a list of words than younger children (Cavanaugh & Perlmutter, 1982). Younger children display inordinately poor knowledge of effective study skills and the amount of time needed to study for a test (Brown, Campione, & Barclay, 1979). Expert readers are more aware that they have a limited capacity for remembering large chunks of text and therefore apply strategies such as summarizing to facilitate comprehension (Brown et al., 1986). Expert readers also make more attempts to personalize text by fitting it into their own experiences (Bransford, Stein, Shelton, & Owings, 1981).

The process of "cognitive orchestration," as previously mentioned, have also received some research attention. For example, Wagner and Sternberg (1987) examined the importance of control processes in adult reading comprehension and observed that expert readers monitored their performance and revised their comprehension strategies more often than novice readers. Expert readers monitor their comprehension and retention and evaluate their progress more often than novice readers (Baker & Brown, 1984). Novice readers are much less aware of the need to check, evaluate, and monitor their comprehension (Baker & Brown, 1984). Interestingly, Brown (1980, 1981) argued that the expert reader engages in comprehension monitoring but it is typically an automatic process (see also Perfetti & McCutchen, 1987). The expert reader's "bottom up and top down skills (Rumelhart, 1980) are so fluent that she operates on automatic pilot until a triggering event alerts her to a comprehension failure" (Baker & Brown, 1984, p.

356). This triggering event causes the reader to slow down and allocate time and attention to repairing the comprehension failure.

Strategy Instruction in Reading Comprehension

The linkage between metacognitive strategies and reading comprehension has been indirectly confirmed by the results of several instructional interventions that are predicted on such a connection. Much recent instructional research has indicated that increasing a reader's knowledge of strategies and their associated use does facilitate comprehension (Haller, Child, & Walberg, 1988; Hansen, 1981; Palinscar, 1986a; Paris, Wasik, & Van der Westhuizen, 1988; Raphael & McKinney, 1983; Raphael & Pearson, 1982, 1985; Raphael & Wonnacott, 1985), although it remains difficult to exercise the proper amount of methodological control in such studies (see Carver, 1987; Paris, Wasik, & Van der Westhuizen, 1988; Pressley, Forrest-Pressley, & Elliott-Faust, 1988). Such training appears to be particularly effective with less-skilled readers (Hansen & Pearson, 1983). It does not, however, appear to be helpful or sufficient solely to provide readers with instruction of strategies at the control or self-management level (Short & Ryan, 1984). Control processes can be taught (Brown & Campione, 1978; Brown, Campione, & Day, 1981), but they only appear to be generalized when they are combined with a task analysis of the reading act itself (Brown & Day, 1983; Day, 1980; Kurtz & Borkowski, 1985).

One notable program of cognitive strategy training in reading that is representative of the work done in this area is the Informed Strategies for Learning approach (Paris, Cross, & Lipson, 1984; Paris, Saarnio, & Cross, 1986). This approach instructs children in three broad comprehension processes: (a) constructing text meaning through elaboration, priming background knowledge and summarizing; (b) monitoring comprehension through questioning and look-back strategies; and (c) identifying meaning by summarizing the main idea and inferencing. Children are taught to regulate their own cognitive processes using instructional techniques based on a cognitive coaching approach (Paris, 1985, 1986). The experimental studies examining this approach have demonstrated that children who receive metacognitive instruction are significantly more aware of comprehension strategies and their functions (Paris & Jacobs, 1984). Moreover, they display greater control or self-regulation processes as evidenced by their propensity to utilize strategies to facilitate text comprehension (Paris, Cross, & Lipson, 1984 Paris; & Oka, 1986).

In the cognitive strategy instruction technique known as reciprocal teaching (Palinscar & Brown, 1984, 1987; Palinscar, 1986b; Palinscar, Brown, & Martin, 1987), training occurs via an interplay between student and teacher. The goal of this process is for teacher and student to jointly arrive at an understanding of the text via turn-taking and questioning. Palinscar and Brown's (1984) version of reciprocal teaching utilizes four activities: a) summarizing segments of the text;

b) forming questions about the text; c) clarifying aspects of the text; and d) making predictions about future content. These activities encourage children to monitor comprehension, make inferences, activate background knowledge, concentrate on the main idea, and maintain attention to the purpose of reading. The reciprocal teaching approach, as well as other strategy training programs, have been found to have facilitative effects on reading comprehension. Across these studies, however, the size of the effect often varies depending upon the expertise of the reader. Novice readers, for example, tend to benefit from manipulations of this type significantly more than do expert readers (Hansen & Pearson, 1983; Yuill & Oakhill, 1988).

WHERE ARE THE DIFFERENCES BETWEEN SKILLED AND LESS-SKILLED READERS?

The demarcation between prelexical and postlexical processes in reading provides a framework for understanding individual differences in reading subskills. In this section, we briefly review research aimed at identifying the cognitive subskills that differentiate skilled from less-skilled readers among groups of children and adults who have been selected without regard to aptitude. In the next section we consider the cognitive subskills that differentiate skilled readers from children who are unskilled relative to their aptitude—the so-called "dyslexic," or specifically disabled poor reader.

At the prelexical level, processes of visual perception are sharply differentiated for phonological processing skills as correlates of individual differences in reading. The relationship between visual processing abilities and reading skill appears to be either weak or nonexistent in the general population. While a few studies have demonstrated a relationship between reading ability and visual processing efficiency (e.g., Gross & Rothenberg, 1979), a large number of well-controlled studies have failed to uncover a relationship (Arnett & DiLollo, 1979; Ellis, 1981; Fisher & Frankfurter, 1977; Gupta, Ceci, & Slater, 1978; Hulme, 1981; Liberman & Shankweiler, 1979; Mason, 1975; Morrison, Giordani, & Nagy, 1977; Stanley, 1976; Stanovich, 1981; Swanson, 1978, 1983; Vellutino, 1979).

Although the bulk of the evidence supports a minimal or nonexistent relationship between basic visual processing operations and reading ability, the issue should not be decided by merely adding up the number of studies on either side. Instead, we should invoke Calfee's (1977) concept of a "clean" psychological test, the idea being that before a deficit in a specific processing operation is hypothesized, investigators should ensure that the tasks employed isolate (as much as is feasible) that particular process without heavily involving other cognitive processes that could contaminate the inference of a specific processing deficit (see Stanovich, 1978; Torgesen, 1975, 1979; Vellutino, 1979). When this point is emphasized, the research literature appears to support Vellutino's conclusion: The more an experiment specifically isolates a visual process, the smaller the difference between good and poor readers. As a result of applying the clean test criterion, the general conclusions of several recent reviews of the research in this area all have converged on the conclusion that visual processing abilities are, at best, weakly related to reading acquisition (Aman & Singh, 1983; Carr, 1981; Mitchell, 1982; Rutter, 1978; Vellutino, 1979).

The results of training studies in this area agree with the findings from correlational studies in questioning a strong linkage between visual processing deficits and poor reading. It is generally accepted that visual perception training programs have been ineffective in promoting reading acquisition (Bateman, 1979; Coles, 1978; Hammill & Larsen, 1974, 1978; Kavale & Mattson, 1983; Larsen & Hammill, 1975; Larsen, Parker, & Hammill, 1982; Mann, 1970; Seaton, 1977; Vellutino, 1979). The literature on perceptual training thus is consistent with the correlational research in casting doubt on a large causal role for visual perception in reading disabilities. Of course, the existing empirical evidence does not rule out the possibility that basic visual processes do account for some proportion of reading variance, or that a small group of poor readers may be characterized by visual deficits. However, the literature suggests that the numerical upper bounds on these two possibilities must be very low.

The conclusion that basic visual processes do not account for a large proportion of reading variance should not be interpreted as indicating the cognitive processes operating at the word and subword level in reading are not implicated in reading acquisition; quite the contrary. It is well established that the speed and accuracy of word recognition is related to reading comprehension ability (Cunningham, Stanovich, & Wilson, in press; Perfetti, 1985; Stanovich, 1980, 1986b). However, it appears to be phonological processes, rather than visual processes, that determine the wide variation in the speed with which children acquire word recognition skills.

From the very earliest stages of skill acquisition, phonological processes are strongly linked to reading ability (see Maclean, Bryant, & Bradley, 1987). Children must, at some point, acquire skill at breaking the spelling-to-sound code (Gough & Hillinger, 1980; Liberman, 1982). This is necessary if the child is to gain the reading independence that eventually leads to the levels of practice that are a prerequisite to fluent reading (see LaBerge & Samuels, 1974; Stanovich, 1986b).

However, several prerequisite and facilitating subskills are critical to success at spelling-to-sound code-breaking. One, clearly, is the ability to discriminate letters, the visual segments of words. This, as discussed, appears not to be a source of difficulty for problem readers. Letters, however, must be mapped onto phonemic segments, and here appears a critical point of difficulty for the poor reader. There is now voluminous evidence indicating that phonological segmentation skills that are based on linguistic awareness at the phoneme level are strongly linked to the speed of initial reading acquisition (Blachman, 1989; Bradley & Bryant, 1978, 1983; Fox & Routh, 1976, 1980, 1983; Goldstein, 1976; Liberman, 1982; Liberman & Shankweiler, 1979; Mann, 1986; Perfetti, Beck, Bell, & Hughes, 1987; Stanovich, 1986b, 1987; Stanovich, Cunningham, & Cramer, 1984; Stanovich, Cunningham, & Feeman, 1984; Vellutino & Scanlon, 1987; Wagner, 1988; Wagner & Torgesen, 1987; Williams, 1980, 1984; Yopp, 1988). Although the linkage is probably one characterized by reciprocal causation (Ehri, 1979, 1985; Morais, Alegria, & Content, 1987; Perfetti et al., 1987), there is mounting evidence that phonological sensitivity is causally related to later reading and spelling skill (Bradley, 1987; Bradley & Bryant, 1983, 1985; Fox & Routh, 1976; Lundberg, Frost & Peterson, 1988; Maclean et al., 1987; Mann, 1986; Perfetti et al., 1987; Torneus, 1984; Treiman & Baron, 1983).

Early difficulty in becoming aware of phonemes as the segments of spoken words quite naturally leads to a delay in developing the spelling-to-sound linkages that are necessary for word decoding. It should not be surprising, therefore, that the ability to accurately and rapidly access the lexicon via phonological coding is strongly related to reading skill (Barron, 1981; Hogaboam & Perfetti, 1978; Jorm & Share, 1983; Perfetti & Hogaboam, 1975). The linkage has been demonstrated in a wide variety of tasks that tap facility of grapheme-to-phoneme conversion. For example, in the large literature on individual differences in reading ability, one of the tasks that most clearly differentiates good and poor readers is the speed and accuracy with which they name pseudowords (Cunningham et al., in press; Jorm & Share, 1983).

Skill at grapheme-phoneme conversion might confer another processing advantage in addition to providing a more efficient mode of word recognition. During reading, sequences of words must be held in short-term memory, while comprehension processes operate on the words to integrate them into a meaningful conceptual structure that can be stored in long-term memory. There is evidence (e.g., Baddeley, 1966; Conrad, 1964) that, for this purpose, the most stable short-term memory code is a phonetic code. Thus, it has been suggested that the ability to rapidly form a stable phonological code in short-term memory may be related to reading comprehension ability (see Perfetti & McCutchen, 1982, for an important discussion of this issue). This conjecture has received considerable support from research indicating that the inferior performance of less-skilled readers on many memory tasks may be due to inefficient phonological coding of stimuli and/or an inability to maintain a phonological code in working memory (Brady, Shankweiler, & Mann, 1983; Byrne, 1981; Byrne & Shea, 1979; Mann, Liberman, & Shankweiler, 1980; Olson, Davidson, Kliegl, & Davies, 1984; Perfetti & Lesgold, 1977, 1979; Perfetti & McCutchen, 1982; Shankweiler, Liberman, Mark, Fowler, & Fischer, 1979; but see Hall, Wilson, Humphreys, Tinzmann, & Bowyer, 1983). The conclusion also is supported by the results of several studies that show that poor readers display memory deficits on tasks where the stimuli are easily labeled, but that the same poor readers do not show performance deficits when the stimuli are not verbally codable (Hulme, 1981; Katz, Shankweiler, & Liberman, 1981; Mann, 1984; Swanson, 1978, 1983).

In fact, there is considerable evidence indicating that performance on a wide variety of short-term memory tasks is related to reading ability (Bauer, 1982; Cohen, 1982; Daneman & Carpenter, 1980; Goldman, Hogaboam, Bell, & Perfetti, 1980; Manis & Morrison, 1982; Masson & Miller, 1983; Newman & Hagen, 1981; Payne & Holzman, 1983; Torgesen, 1977a, 1977b, 1978–1979; Torgesen & Goldman, 1977; Wong, Wong, & Foth, 1977). Of course, the finding that poor readers display short-term memory deficits has the status of correlational evidence. However, because comprehension processes depend on the ability of short-term memory to hold recently accessed information, short-term memory deficits could directly impair the ability to comprehend text. Thus, there is some reason to assume a causal connection between short-term memory deficits and reading ability.

Two general explanations have been advanced to account for the memory deficits displayed by poor readers. One, the hypothesis of a deficit in the formation and maintenance of phonological codes in short-term memory, was previously discussed. The other explanation hypothesizes that poor readers are less prone to employ the active, planful, memorization strategies (e.g., verbal rehearsal, imagery, and elaboration) that have been shown to facilitate memory performance. Untangling the proportion of variance that is associated with each of these hypotheses may be difficult (e.g., strategies such as verbal rehearsal may be difficult to separate from phonological coding processes) because they are not mutually exclusive (see Cohen, 1982; Torgesen, 1978–1979; Torgesen & Houck, 1980). Indeed, the research evidence suggests that poor readers may display inferior short-term memory performance due to deficits in both phonological processing and strategic planning.

Research has shown that poor readers are less likely to employ a variety of cognitive strategies that facilitate memory performance (Bauer, 1982; Newman & Hagen, 1981; Torgesen, 1977a, 1977b, 1978–1979, 1980; Torgesen & Goldman, 1977; Wong et al., 1977). For example, findings such as depressed primacy effects in the serial-position curves of poor readers indicate that they are less likely to use a verbal rehearsal strategy. However, Torgesen (1977a) and Torgesen and Goldman (1977) have shown that instruction in the use of memory strategies can attenuate the performance deficits displayed by poor readers (see also Newman & Hagen, 1981). Thus, poor readers appear less prone actually to employ cognitive strategies even when the strategies are within their capabilities, a conclusion supported by other research (see following). Also implicating strategy usage in the memory problems of the poor reader is the finding that performance deficits are somewhat reduced (although usually not entirely eliminated; see Cohen, 1982; Torgesen & Houck, 1980) in tasks that are designed to preclude the use of strategies (Cermak, Goldberg, Cermak, & Drake, 1980). Poor readers display particularly marked performance deficits on memory tasks that require several different strategies and control processes for successful completion (e.g., Foster & Gavelek, 1983).

Clearly, the research on short-term memory functioning in less skilled readers has extended the theoretical locus of the processing deficits beyond merely the "holding" operations of memory into more general areas of cognitive planning and study strategies. Thus, the nature of the differences that have been hypothesized to explain depressed performance on short-term memory tasks are such that they could encompass more complex text-level processing operations. The empirical evidence currently available indeed indicates such a linkage.

The question of whether deficits in more general comprehension strategies are associated with reading skill interfaces with a closely related issue in the reading research literature—whether processes beyond decoding are responsible for individual differences in reading skill. This question is usually answered in the affirmative. Although there is no question that a considerable amount of reading variance is explained by individual differences in decoding skill (Cunningham et al., in press; Stanovich, Cunningham, & Feeman, 1984), it has been demonstrated that processes independent of decoding ability are also linked to reading ability (Oakhill, 1982; Wilkinson, 1980). This is particularly true at the more advanced levels in reading acquisition (Stanovich, Cunningham, & Feeman, 1984). For example, almost all studies of subjects beyond the early elementary grades report significant correlations between listening-comprehension ability and reading skill. The relationship is particularly strong in adults (Cunningham et al., in press; Daneman & Carpenter, 1980; Jackson, 1980; Jackson & McClelland, 1979; Palmer, MacLeod, Hunt, & Davidson, 1985; Sticht & James, 1984), moderately strong in the middle grades, and weak, but still significant, in the early elementary grades (Berger, 1978; Chall, 1983; Curtis, 1980; Duker, 1965; Stanovich, Cunningham, & Feeman, 1984). These findings are consistent with the data indicating that, as the absolute reading level of the sample under study increases, the proportion of reading variance accounted for by listening comprehension ability also increases (Carver & Hoffman, 1981; Chall, 1983; Curtis, 1980; Fletcher, Satz, & Scholes, 1981; Kintsch, 1979; Stanovich, Cunningham, & Feeman, 1984; Sticht & James, 1984).

Berger (1978) studied a group of fifth grade children and found that the listening comprehension of the less-skilled readers was just as depressed as their reading performance. Similarly, Smiley, Oakley, Worthen, Campione, and Brown (1977) observed strikingly inferior listening comprehension in a group of seventh grade poor readers. These comprehension problems are probably implicated in the well-known fact that poor readers display inferior performance on close tasks (Bickley, Ellington, & Bickley, 1970; Perfetti et al., 1979; Perfetti & Roth, 1981; Ruddell, 1965; Siegel & Ryan, 1984). The pervasive comprehension deficits that research has uncovered could result from a very generalized lack of linguistic and metacognitive awareness that is characteristic of poor readers and that was detailed in several studies reviewed in the previous section.

WHERE ARE THE DIFFERENCES
BETWEEN THE SPECIFICALLY DISABLED READER
AND THE NONDISABLED READER?

The research reviewed in the foregoing indicates that explanations of the performance differences between skilled and less-skilled readers implicated processes at both the pre- and postlexical levels. Processes subserving both word decoding and text integration have been linked to reading skill differences. The situation promises to be different when we search for the performance deficits displayed by the specifically disabled reader (or dyslexic; the terms are used interchangeably here). This is because the disabled reader is defined by reference to an aptitude/achievement discrepancy, rather than with reference to the absolute level of reading ability.

For example, the World Federation of Neurology characterized developmental dyslexia as "A disorder manifested by difficulty in learning to read despite conventional instruction, adequate intelligence, and socio-cultural opportunity. It is dependent upon fundamental cognitive abilities which are frequently of constitutional origin" (Critchley, 1970, p. 11). This particular definition highlighted the well-known "exclusionary criteria" that subsequently caused much dispute in discussions of dyslexia (e.g., Applebee, 1971; Ceci, 1986; Doehring, 1978; Rutter, 1978). In particular, this definition excluded from the dyslexia classification children of low intelligence, those who suffered from inadequate environments, and those who underachieved due to lack of educational opportunity.

The exclusionary criteria were carried over into the definition of learning disability employed in the landmark Education for All Handicapped Children Act (PL 94–142) passed in 1975.

> Specific learning disability means a disorder in one or more of the basic psychological processes involved in understanding or in using language spoken or written, which may manifest itself in an imperfect ability to listen, think, speak, read, write, spell, or to do mathematical calculations. The term includes such conditions as perceptual handicaps, brain injury, minimal brain dysfunction, dyslexia, and developmental aphasia. The term does not include children who have learning problems which are primarily the result of visual, hearing, or motor handicaps, of mental retardation, of emotional disturbance, or of environmental, cultural, or economic disadvantage.

The essential features of these older definitions have been carried over into the more recent definitions of The National Joint Committee for Learning Disabilities (Hammill, Leigh, McNutt, & Larsen, 1981) and the Interagency Committee on Learning Disabilities established by the U.S. Health Research Extension Act of 1985 (Kavanagh & Truss, 1988).

All of these professional and legal definitions are vague regarding the specific behavioral criteria that should be used to classify children on an individual basis (Reynolds, 1984–85). In dealing with learning disabilities in the domain of reading, state and local educational authorities have most often operationalized these verbal definitions in terms of quantitative discrepancies between individually administered reading comprehension tests and intelligence tests (Frankenberger & Harper, 1987; Kavale, 1987; Kavale & Nye, 1981; Reynolds, 1985; Shepard, 1980).

Thus, all of the professional, legal, and research definitions of dyslexia rest, either explicitly or implicitly, on what has been termed *the assumption of specificity in learning disabilities* (see Hall & Humphreys, 1982; Stanovich, 1986a, 1986b). This is the idea that a child with this type of learning disability has a brain/cognitive deficit that is reasonably specific to the reading task. That is, the concept of dyslexia requires that the deficits displayed by such children not extend too far into other domains of cognitive functioning. If they did, this would depress the constellation of abilities we call intelligence and thus reduce the reading/intelligence discrepancy that is central to all the definitions of dyslexia.

The assumption of specificity puts severe restrictions on the type of processing deficit that one can propose as the explanation of the reading problem of the dyslexic child. Any hypothesis that attempts to explain dyslexia while at the same time undermining the assumption of specificity (that the disability is localized in only a thin slice of the cognitive domain, rather than in more global aspects of intellectual functioning) will lead to a crisis in the application of the concept of dyslexia (see Stanovich, 1986a, 1988b). Thus, it is unlikely that the cognitive deficits of the dyslexic reader will be located in all of the domains— both pre- and postlexical—that have characterized comparisons between the general skilled and less-skilled readers that we reviewed previously. The reason is that postlexical processes like general linguistic awareness, strategic functioning, active/inactive learning, and metacognition are too global in nature. The problem with all of these is that they are central processes (Fodor, 1983), too critically intertwined with other aspects of intellectual functioning (Sternberg, 1985). Deficits in such processes would lower the child's general intellectual functioning, thereby reducing the intelligence/achievement discrepancy that is the defining feature of specific reading disability. In short, children with such deficits are almost logically precluded from being classified as dyslexic.

The best candidates for key processing mechanisms underlying reading disability will be those that are somewhat modular (Fodor, 1983). The important point is that modular processes are not strongly interactive with central processes; they may provide data for central processing procedures but they do not direct those central procedures, nor are they directed by them. This means that a modular system may fail without disrupting the operations of central processes that do not depend on its output—the defining cognitive pattern for the concept of dyslexia. For these, and other reasons, there is a wide research consensus that the key to the dyslexic performance pattern resides at the word recognition level (e.g., Aaron, 1989; Gough & Tunmer, 1986; Morrison, 1984, 1987; Perfetti, 1985; Siegel, 1985, 1988; Siegel & Faux, 1989; Stanovich, 1986b, 1988b; Vellutino, 1979).

Thus, much recent research has been directed at isolating the locus of the flaw in the word recognition module of the dyslexic reader. Several "classic" hypotheses that placed the cognitive locus of difficulty in the visual domain have proven to be incorrect. The sequencing and reversal errors (b/d, was/saw) that loomed so large in the early study of dyslexia have proven to be a dead end (and indeed, a useful lesson in how case study evidence can be misleading; see Stanovich, 1982). Much recent evidence has indicated that such errors do not have the unique diagnosticity that has been attributed to them and that verbal/linguistic factors rather than visual factors are implicated in their occurrence (Calfee, 1977; Cohn & Stricker, 1979; Fischer, Liberman, & Shankweiler, 1978; Harman, 1982; Holmes & Peper, 1977; Park, 1978–1979; Shankweiler & Liberman, 1972, 1978; Valtin, 1978–1979; Vellutino, 1979). Systematic studies of the distribution of error types across reading ability have indicated that poor readers make more errors of all types, but that their number of reversal errors as a proportion of the total number of errors is no higher than that displayed by good readers.

Of course, many other studies have been conducted in order to investigate whether basic processes of visual perception were implicated in dyslexia. Several different kinds of visual tasks (e.g., masking tasks, fusion paradigms, detection tasks, partial-report paradigms, and reaction-time tasks) have been used to study various aspects of visual perception (e.g., feature extraction, visual segmentation, encoding, and visual persistence). Whereas some studies have demonstrated a relationship between reading ability and visual processing efficiency (e.g., Babcock & Lovegrove, 1981; Slaghuis & Lovegrove, 1985, 1987), most reviews of this large literature question whether visual processing differences are implicated in dyslexia (Aman & Singh, 1983; Liberman & Shankweiler, 1979; Mitchell, 1982; Rutter, 1978; Stanovich, 1986a; Vellutino, 1979).

Finally, there is the longstanding hypothesis that deficient eye movements cause reading problems. Actually, there is very little evidence supporting this hypothesis, either in the older literature (Aman & Singh, 1983; Lahey, Kupfer, Beggs, & Landon, 1982; Rayner, 1978; Taylor, 1965; Tinker, 1958) or in more recent studies (Brown, Haegerstrom-Portnoy, Adams, Yingling, Galin, Herron, & Marcus, 1983; Olson, Kliegl, & Davidson, 1983; Stanley, Smith, & Howell, 1983). The consensus of researchers in the field remains that erratic eye movement patterns are the result, not the cause, of poor reading.

In contrast to the largely negative results in the area of visual processing differences, research in the last ten years has firmly established that dyslexic children display deficits in various aspects of phonological processing. They have difficulty making explicit reports about sound segments at the phoneme level, they display naming difficulties, their utilization of phonological codes in short-term memory is inefficient, their categorical perception of certain phonemes may be other than normal, and they may have speech production problems (Bradley & Bryant, 1978, 1985; Cossu, Shankweiler, Liberman, Katz, & Tola, 1988; Kamhi & Catts, 1989; Liberman & Shankweiler, 1985; Liberman, Meskill, Chatillon, & Schupack, 1985; Mann, 1986; Pennington, 1986; Pratt & Brady, 1988; Snowling, 1987; Stanovich, 1988b; Taylor, Lean, & Schwartz, 1989; Vellutino & Scanlon, 1987; Wagner & Torgesen, 1987; Werker & Tees, 1987; Wolf & Goodglass, 1986). Presumably, lack of phonological sensitivity makes the learning of grapheme-to-phoneme correspondences very difficult.

For example, Snowling (1980) compared the performance of a group of children who had been diagnosed as dyslexic with that of a younger group of nondyslexic children who were matched on reading ability. Despite some performance similarities on some of the tasks administered, the two groups responded differently on a nonsense word, visual-auditory matching task that mimicked the grapheme-phoneme conversion process in reading. The dyslexic subjects were markedly inferior in this condition. Furthermore, within the dyslexic group of children, there was no correlation between reading level and performance on the visual-auditory matching task, unlike the case in the nondyslexic sample where a significant correlation was obtained. Snowling has suggested that normal development in reading is characterized by an increase in grapheme-phoneme decoding ability and in the size of sight vocabulary, whereas the development of reading skill in dyslexic subjects is due primarily to increases in sight vocabulary because the development of grapheme-phoneme decoding skills in this group is severely delayed. Results consistent with Snowling's have been produced in a wide variety of different experimental laboratories (Olson et al., 1985; Pennington, 1986; Stanovich, 1986b).

Thus, research has been successful in locating a critical flaw in the word processing module of dyslexic readers. In short, there is now voluminous evidence indicating that phonological deficits are the basis of the dyslexic performance pattern. However, the possibility of core deficits in the realm of orthographic processing does still remain, and there is growing evidence for the utility of distinguishing a group of dyslexics who have severe problems in accessing the lexicon on a visual/orthographic basis (Stanovich & West, 1989). Suggestive evidence comes from the work on acquired reading disability that has revealed the existence of surface dyslexia (Patterson, Marshall, & Coltheart, 1985) and from multivariate investigations indicating that efficient phonological processing is a necessary but not sufficient condition for attaining advanced levels of word recognition skill (Juel, Griffith, & Gough, 1986; Tunmer & Nesdale, 1985).

But as regards orthographic processing deficits, two crucial caveats are in order. First, there is a very large body of evidence indicating that this group of children must be numerically quite smaller than the group with phonological difficulties (Aaron, 1989; Freebody & Byrne, 1988; Gough & Hillinger, 1980; Liberman & Shankweiler, 1985; Pennington, 1986; Perfetti, 1985; Vellutino, 1979). Secondly, the problem encountered by these children is not similar to the "visual perception" problems popular in the early history of the study of dyslexia, but now widely recognized to have been overstated (Aman & Singh, 1983; Morrison, Giordani, & Nagy, 1977; Stanovich, 1986a; Vellutino, 1979). The actual problems in orthographic processing must be much more subtle and localized than these older views suggested. However, the performance patterns of any smaller group of dyslexics with orthographic deficits would mirror the group with phonological deficits group in all other aspects.

These critical processing differences have been characterized within the phonological-core variable-difference model of individual differences in reading (Stanovich, 1988a, 1988b). The term *variable differences* refers to the key performance contrasts between the dyslexic and the poor reader without aptitude/achievement discrepancy. Gough and Tunmer (1986) have termed the latter group of children "garden-variety" poor readers. Recent research has indicated that the cognitive status of the garden-variety poor reader is well described by a developmental lag model (Stanovich, Nathan, & Zolman, 1988). Cognitively, they are remarkably similar to younger children reading at the same level. A logical corollary of this pattern is that the garden-variety poor reader will have a wide variety of cognitive deficits when compared to CA controls who are reading at normal levels. Support for this hypothesis was presented in the previous section's review of the cognitive factors differentiating generally skilled from unskilled readers. Less-skilled readers of the garden variety were characterized by numerous cognitive deficiencies, some extending into the broad domain of comprehension processes.

However, it is important to understand that the garden-variety poor reader does share the phonological problems of the dyslexic reader, and these deficits appear also to be a causal factor in their poor reading (Perfetti, 1985; Stanovich, 1986b). But for the garden-variety reader, the deficits—relative to CA controls—extend into a variety of domains (see Ellis & Large, 1987) and some of these (e.g., vocabulary, language comprehension) may also be causally linked to reading comprehension. Such a pattern does not characterize the dyslexic, who has a deficit localized in the phonological core.

The phonological-core variable-difference model assumes multidimensional continuity for reading ability in general and for all its related cognitive subskills. That is, it conceives of all of the relevant distributions of reading-related cognitive skills as being continuously arrayed in a multidimensional space and not distributed in clusters. There is considerable evidence from a variety of different sources supporting such a continuity assumption (Ellis, 1985; Jorm, 1983; Olson et al., 1985; Scarborough, 1984; Seidenberg, Bruck, Fornarolo, & Backman, 1985; Share, McGee, McKenzie, Williams, & Silva, 1987; Silva, McGee, & Williams, 1985). However, the fact that the distribution is a graded continuum does not render the concept of dyslexia scientifically useless, as many critics would like to argue. Ellis (1985) has drawn the analogy with obesity. No one doubts that it is a very real health problem, despite the fact that it is operationally defined in a somewhat arbitrary way by choosing a criterion in a continuous distribution.

The framework of the phonological-core variable-difference model meshes nicely with the multidimensional continuum notion. Consider the following characterization: As we move in the multidimensional space—from the dyslexic to the garden-variety poor reader—we will move from a processing deficit localized in the phonological core to the global deficits of the developmentally lagging garden-variety poor reader. Thus, the actual cognitive differences that are displayed will be variable depending upon the type of poor reader who is the focus of the investigation. The differences on one end of the continuum will consist of deficits located only in the phonological core (the dyslexic) and will increase in number as we run through the intermediate cases that are less and less likely to pass strict psychometric criteria for dyslexia. Eventually we will reach the part of the multidimensional space containing relatively "pure" garden-variety poor readers who clearly will not qualify for the label dyslexic (by either regression or exclusionary criteria), will have a host of cognitive deficits, and will have the cognitively immature profile of a developmentally lagging individual.

This framework provides an explanation for why almost all processing investigations of reading disability have uncovered phonological deficits, but also why some investigations have found deficits in *other* areas as well (see Stanovich, 1988b). This outcome is predictable from the fact that the phonological-core variable-difference model posits that virtually all poor readers have a phonological deficit, but that other processing deficits emerge as one drifts in the multidimensional space from "pure" dyslexics toward garden-variety poor readers.

In summary, a consideration of the cognitive differences between various types of poor readers reinforces the importance of the distinction between modular decoding processes and nonmodular comprehension processes. The different performance patterns characterizing poor readers of the garden variety from that of dyslexics fit nicely within our framework for addressing the question of whether to view "reading as reasoning." The dyslexic—by definition of high aptitude—should not have deficits in broad processing areas that would be candidates for the term "reasoning." The localization and restriction of their deficits to the phonological domain are consistent with this idea. In contrast, studies of garden-variety poor readers—who are not psychometrically constrained to display deficits only in domain-specific areas—could well uncover deficits in nonmodular processes of general language comprehension, and indeed much recent research described above has indicated this pattern.

READING AS CONSTRAINED REASONING?

Current reading theory is thus quite interestingly bifurcated. The idea that background knowledge should saturate central processes of text inferencing, comprehension monitoring, and global interpretation is now widely accepted (Anderson, 1984; Anderson & Pearson, 1984; Fincher-Kiefer, Post, Greene, & Voss, 1988; Paris, 1987; Paris, Lipson, & Wixson, 1983; Spiro, Bruce, & Brewer, 1980; Wixson & Peters, 1987), while at the same time the advantage of modularly organized lexical processes is acknowledged. Indeed, the dangers of cognitive penetrability that is too pervasive have become apparent in discussions of nonaccommodating reading styles (Kimmel & MacGinitie, 1984; Maria & MacGinitie, 1982). As Evans and Carr (1985) point out:

> If print-specific encoding mechanisms send incomplete or erroneous data to the language comprehension processes, what could result but an incomplete or erroneous understanding of the text? In addition, the more powerful the language skills that are applied to the erroneous data, the greater the chance that a seemingly acceptable interpretation can be constructed. (p. 342)

This bifurcation of reading theory might lead us to endorse a restricted version of Thorndike's (1973–1974) suggestion that we view "reading as reasoning." We might say that subsequent to input processing, reading begins to look much more like reasoning. But it is reasoning of a special type, because of the sequential arrangement of pre- and postlexical processes. That is, the modular input processes deliver the data that central processes of text-model construction must work with. The lexical entries activated by the input processes put severe constraints on the nature of the text model that can be constructed. Thus, if we conceive of processes such as text-model construction based on knowledge integration as "reasoning" processes, then they are subject to prior constraints that are unusually strong compared to the type of central processes that we might identify as involved in reasoning or problem solving. Thus, the proper metaphor might be to conceive of reading as "constrained reasoning."

Indeed, recent theories of reading comprehension have emphasized the constraints imposed by input processes and deemphasized the degrees of freedom available to postlexical comprehension ("reasoning") processes. For example, in the development of his construction-integration model of reading comprehension, Kintsch (1988) is at pains to reject early AI assumptions (e.g., Schank, 1978) of context-driven and knowledge-saturated perceptual processing. In the construction phase of his model, a network of text-based propositions is formed and linked to knowledge structures in a purely bottom-up manner. In the integration phase, activation spreads through the network and stabilizes in a connectionist manner to determine a coherent interpretation. In the construction-integration model, text information contacts and shares activation with knowledge structures, but comprehension is not "driven" by knowledge-based expectations in the traditional top-down fashion. Thus, models of reading like Kintsch's have migrated away from expectancy and "strong" schema theories toward theories stressing autonomous processing, undifferentiated networks, and/or connectionist architectures (see Rumelhart & McClelland, 1986; Schneider, 1987; Sejnowski & Rosenberg, 1986; Tanenhaus, Dell, & Carlson, 1987; Tanenhaus & Lucas, 1987).

Like Kintsch (1988), Perfetti's most recent theorizing (1985, in press; Perfetti & Curtis, 1986; Perfetti & McCutchen, 1987) has emphasized the constraints on processing imposed by cognitive impenetrable processes like lexical access and sentence parsing and has deemphasized the nonmodular processes, particularly as sources of individual differences: "Ability in reading depends on linguistically based processes that support word identification, parsing, and proposition encoding. It depends less on abilities to apply special knowledge, draw inferences, make elaborations. . . . We see no reason yet to identify reading with problem solving or thinking" (Perfetti & McCutchen, 1987, p. 122).

Perfetti's strong position followed from a principled distinction that is made between achieving a meaning for a text and achieving an interpretation of a text, and Perfetti and McCutchen (1987) argued that "Identifying comprehension only with interpretation leads to the claim that comprehension depends on knowledge. Identifying comprehension with meaning leads to a different perspective: Comprehension depends on meaning, a symbol-based process, whereas interpretation depends on meaning plus knowledge" (p. 113). But the crux of their argument is that the words that determine the meaning of a sentence strongly constrain the possible interpretations in most instances, thus severely limiting the effects of nonmodular processes of knowledge elaboration.

Perfetti and McCutchen (1987) questioned the conclusions typically drawn from the studies that have demonstrated various effects of prior knowledge on comprehension. They pointed out that such classic studies as that of Bransford and Johnson (1973) and Anderson et al. (1976)

have used very odd texts. Even a cursory examination of the Bransford and Johnson texts . . . show their vagueness of reference. . . . Readers either fail to construct an interpretation or construct one based on individual experiences. It is far from clear that ordinary texts, written to communicate rather than obfuscate, would show such a strong effect of knowledge. . . . In ordinary texts, interpretation and meaning are usually highly overlapping. In these experimental texts, they are not. (p. 115)

Indeed, Sadoski (1981) has called these passages "the verbal counterpart of the optical illusions used to demonstrate figure-ground perception in early Gestalt psychology experiments" (p. 601).

Similarly, Perfetti and McCutchen (1987) used two sentences from a study by Anderson and Ortony (1975) in order to demonstrate how their own theory diverges from the typical contextual approach:

1. The accountant pounded the stake.
2. The accountant pounded the desk.

Taking no issue with the finding that "hammer" is a better recall cue for (1) and "fist" a better recall cue for (2), Perfetti and McCutchen insisted only that "The words strongly constrain the representation to elaborations consistent with the basic semantics of the word" and cited:

3. The accountant pounded the stake with his fist;

to demonstrate that mentioning an instrument

> fills in the variables allowed by the verb frame and, no matter how pragmatically unconventional, forces an interpretation of (3) that is, at the action level, more similar to (2) than (1). What is not possible, in general, is to use 'The accountant pounded the stake' to mean the accountant pounded the desk. Nor can it mean that the accountant pulled up the stake or that the bartender pounded the desk. The fact is that mental representations are constrained by *meanings*. One cannot use any sentence to carry any interpretation. (p. 114)

Perfetti and Kintsch are not the only theorists who have called into question the strong assumptions about knowledge and strategy use that have been present in the schema-based and strategy approaches to modeling reading. These approaches have often been criticized for utilizing formalisms that are too powerful, given the minimal constraints in our current data base (Iran-Nejad, 1987; Whitney, 1987). As mentioned in the previous review of the knowledge approach, many of the empirical findings in this area can be accounted for by much simpler, nonactive network models. Also, it appears that much of the elaborative inferencing indicated by earlier experiments was taking place at the time of recall rather than on-line during the comprehension process itself (Dosher & Corbett, 1982; Kardash, Royer, & Greene, 1988; Potts, Keenan, & Golding, 1988; Whitney, 1987).

But what about the demonstrated linkage between strategic ability and reading skill observed in several of the studies we have reviewed? Perfetti and McCutchen (1987) pointed out that such strategies are most often efficacious for the poor comprehender:

The interesting thing about all strategies . . . is that the good reader can get by without them. The skilled reader may be doing the *functional equivalent* of summarizing or self-questioning when he or she derives a higher-order representation of text sentence . . . Such knowledge activation and inference making may be more appropriately thought of as tied to basic text processes than as detachable strategies. They are, in ordinary circumstances, triggered by comprehended text elements. (p. 110)

They viewed the demonstrated lack of strategy use on the part of poorer readers as an epiphenomenon of inefficiencies in their basic language processing skills.

The problem of separating "strategy use" from "decoding epiphenomenon" explanations of the deficiencies in higher-level processing displayed by less-skilled readers is a perennial problem in reading research (Stanovich, 1984, 1986b). The reason for this is the hierarchically organized modular logic of reading subprocesses. Higher-level postlexical processes always depend upon the quality of the data provided by modular input processes. If processes of lexical access ("decoding") are deficient, the inadequate data that they provide to higher level text processes may degrade the performance of the latter (Markman, 1985). Inferring a separate deficiency in the higher-level processing strategies of poorer readers requires proof that the integrity of the input to these processes is not compromised. In strategy studies in reading, this means demonstrating that their decoding is accurate and, importantly, fluent (rapid). This requirement is rarely met in strategy studies in the text comprehension literature (Perfetti, 1985; Perfetti & McCutchen, 1987; Stanovich, 1986b), although some studies have achieved close matches on decoding accuracy (e.g., Yuill & Oakhill, 1988).

It should be noted, however, that viewing the correlational linkage of strategy use and reading as epiphenomenal is not to deny that the teaching of such strategies as a *compensatory* mechanism (see Perfetti, 1988) might not be efficacious. To the contrary, we have reviewed the ample evidence indicating that strategy and metacognitive awareness training does seem to be effective in giving poor readers access to discriminative cognitive judgments that allow better coordination of processing during reading. The point to be emphasized here is simply that this does not mean that the cognitive scaffolding that is used during such training should become a model of the on-line processing taking place during fluent reading.

Other evidence that cautions against overgeneralizing the "strategy approach" into a generic model of reading comes from research on comprehension monitoring and comprehension calibration in adults. In an extensive series of experiments, Glenberg and Epstein (Glenberg, Wilkinson, & Epstein, 1982; Epstein, Glenberg, & Bradley, 1984) observed that readers often reported understanding text passages that they had not really comprehended. They labelled this phenomenon the "illusion of knowing" and operationally defined it as a reader's belief that contradictory material was understood. The finding was ubiquitous in adult college readers who would presumably be relative experts in the metacognitive skill of "comprehension monitoring," at least compared to the general population.

In a series of later studies, Glenberg and associates (Glenberg & Epstein, 1985, 1987; Glenberg, Sanocki, Epstein, & Morris, 1987) developed a measure of the calibration of comprehension. Subjects were asked to read texts, to rate their confidence in their ability to verify an inference made from a principle central to the text, and then to identify such an inference as true or false according to the text. The salient finding from the extensive series of experiments converged with the results of the "illusion of knowing" experiments: Subjects were extremely poorly calibrated.

Glenberg and Epstein (1987) found that even the comprehension of experts within their field of expertise was poorly calibrated, although across domains there was a correlation between confidence and performance. This finding indicates that experts were more likely to rate their abilities to verify correct inferences not on their comprehension of particular texts, but on their familiarity with the domain or subject matter. When there are gross differences in domains between the two passages, experts are able to correctly calibrate; but when reading two passages within a domain, experts are just as likely as novices to poorly calibrate. Thus, Glenberg and Epstein conclude that domain familiarity rather than actual comprehension monitoring is the major determinant of confidence in comprehension. Assessing domain familiarity is easier than assessing the knowledge one may or may not have gained from a particular text.

Although comprehension monitoring and calibration is not always so poor in experiments employing other paradigms (e.g., Maki & Swett, 1987; Zabrucky & Ratner, 1986), Pressley and Ghatala (1988) have confirmed the findings of the Glenberg group by demonstrating that performance calibration on multiple choice reading comprehension tests was significantly worse than performance calibration for verbal analogies and word opposites problems. In the case of reading comprehension, but not the other two tasks, the adult subjects were almost as confident of incorrect responses as of correct responses. The results of Glenberg and Epstein (Glenberg & Epstein, 1985, 1987; Glenberg, Sanocki, Epstein, & Morris, 1987) indicate that the monitoring of ongoing comprehension is no trivial thing, even for the fluent adult reader, who is insensitive to on-line processing in many cases. Some people perform the act of comprehension considerably better than others, and some considerably worse. But their awareness of their relative performance seems to be only tenuously related to their actual comprehension.

CONCLUSION

It is widely known that reading theory has been evolving in a fairly unidirectional manner in the past 15–20 years. Theorists have been slowly abandoning the positivist-inspired early information processing models and moving toward more constructivist conceptualizations. The earlier models put the key information in the text and were concerned with its veridical transformation through information processing stages into an understanding completely constrained by the text itself. Schema theory, strategy approaches, and other constructivist accounts have gradually altered the mainstream conceptualization (the "modal model") in the direction of emphasizing that comprehension is in part determined by the reader's prior expectations, use of world knowledge to supplement the text, and the general preexisting schemata for classifying text elements (Oransanu & Penny, 1986).

It appears, though, that a backlash against the more extreme elements of the constructivist conceptualization is beginning to set in, as it is increasingly recognized that strong constructivist assumptions are not squaring with what is becoming known about how the autonomous, encapsulated input processes that act on the external stimulus actually work (Rayner & Pollatsek, 1989). Theory is drifting back and being tempered by a consideration of how the external stimulus constrains belief fixation (Fodor, 1985; Perfetti & McCutchen, 1987; Rayner & Pollatsek, 1989).

Also, it is beginning to be recognized that the applicability of these various conceptualizations is bound to vary with the type of text being read and the purposes of reading—in short, with the particular reading situation. For example, the concept that "readers . . . rather than reading texts merely for information, may be participating in an interpretive activity having little to do with the author's intentions—however these may be reconstructed and understood by readers" (Beers, 1987, p. 374) may be quite fine in the domain of imaginative fiction. But it is not a good model (theoretically or instructionally) with which to conceptualize the reading of: "In case of fire, pull the red handle and close all doors," or "Send the package to Toledo, Ohio by Federal Express," or "Do not take aspirin while using this drug." Only a small proportion of the actual reading taking place among the general populace is of imaginative fiction (Sharon, 1973–1974; Venezky, 1982). Most reading is of mundane expository material; and even the most modern of literary theorists will at least now admit that "Interpreting a poem *is* in an important sense freer than interpreting a London underground notice" (Eagleton, 1983, p. 88).

Misreading, or using a nonaccommodating text strategy (e.g., Maria & MacGinitie, 1982), has many real negative consequences when reading in the natural ecology of print, which is highly meaning constrained (Perfetti & McCutchen, 1987). For example, when our physicians consult a medical volume in the course of our treatment, most of us are hoping that his/her processing will not be characterized by an unrestrained constructivism whereby meanings are imposed on the information in the text. We wish the same thing when obtaining advice about legal documents, or when our auto mechanic orders a part for us. Such situations are more representative of reading in the real world. In such situations, the more constrained Perfetti and McCutchen (1987) conception seems the better choice for a model of optimal performance: meaning and interpretation almost entirely overlapping—but not entirely, so that relevant knowledge structures and expectations can play a small part in "fine-tuning" the interpretation arrived at.

Interestingly, this is what constructivist theorists themselves seem to want when others read their works. In disputes, it is not uncommon for such theorists to complain that their critics did not read their writings correctly—that the critic has come to the wrong interpretation (e.g., "There are so many misrepresentations of my position" [Goodman, 1976–1977a, p. 578]; "And try, next time, someplace in your meanderings to deal directly with my work" [Goodman, 1976–1977b, p. 604]; "This leads him to misrepresent my model" [Goodman, 1981, p. 477]). But why not apply their own dictums to their own theory? Why is the critic's interpretation—saturated as it is with the critic's own prior theory and expectations—not acknowledged as just as "real" and "valid" an interpretation, equal in status to the constructivist's own interpretation? Of course, it is not acknowledged as such. Instead, the constructivist is at pains to lead the critic to the "right" interpretation, which—we can infer from the constructivist's protestations—is clearly not one saturated with the critic's prior schemata and expectations. Indeed, the existence of the passionate advocate of constructivism convincingly demonstrates that "one can never completely escape objectivism: it is, among other things, a necessary condition of polemic" (Goodheart, 1983, p. 217). Constructivist theorists, when dealing with reader responses to their own texts, adopt a model of constrained processing. Our point is, of course, a version of a common rejoinder to constructivist and skeptical positions in literary theory and the philosophy of science (Booth, 1983; Gellner, 1975; Newton-Smith, 1982; Phillips, 1983; Putnam, 1981, 1983; Siegel, 1980, 1987; Toulmin, 1970).

It will be an interesting test of whether reading theory is responsive to empirical evidence if indeed the current philosophical predilection is reversed because of experimental results. Theoretical preferences in reading theory have often marched in tandem with conceptual developments in philosophy of science and literary theory (Beers, 1987; Golden, 1983). The latter two fields have shared philosophical disputes and trends during the last thirty years (Bernstein, 1983; Booth, 1974; Goodheart, 1983). Both have marched away from positivist assumptions that data strongly constrained theory (in the first case) and that the text strongly constrained interpretation (in the latter case) toward more constructivist conceptualizations emphasizing that data collection is theory laden (Brown, 1977; Kuhn, 1970; Lakatos & Musgrave, 1970; McMullin, 1988) and that literary interpretation is in some part reader determined and not solely constrained by the text (Eagleton, 1983; Fish, 1980; Golden, 1983). Thus, reading theory shares the postpositivist unidirectional march toward constructivism with these other two fields. The only way we will know whether reading theory is more empirical behavioral science than hermeneutical discipline is for the perfect correlation among paradigmatic historical trends in the three fields to be broken. In the next few years we may well witness something like an existence proof that will decide this issue.

ACKNOWLEDGEMENTS

The authors would like to thank Stewart Russell for extensive consultation on sections of early drafts of the manuscript. Co-editors Robert Sternberg and Peter Frensch are thanked for their comments on an early version of the manuscript.

REFERENCES

Aaron, P. G. (1989). *Dyslexia and hyperlexia*. Dordrecht, The Netherlands: Kluwer Academic.

Aborn, M., Rubenstein, H., & Sterling, T. D. (1959). Sources of contextual constraint upon words in sentences. *Journal of Experimental Psychology, 57*, 171–180.

Alba, J. W., & Hasher, L. (1983). Is memory schematic? *Psychological Bulletin, 93*, 203–231.

Alford, J. (1980, May). *Predicting predictability: Identification of sources of contextual constraint on words in text*. Paper presented at the meeting of the Midwestern Psychological Association, St. Louis, MO.

Aman, M., & Singh, N. (1983). Specific reading disorders: Concepts of etiology reconsidered. In K. Gadow & I. Bialer (Eds.), *Advances in learning and behavioral disabilities* (Vol. 2, pp. 1–47). Greenwich, CT: JAI Press.

Anderson, R. C. (1977). The notion of schemata and the educational enterprise: General discussion of the conference. In R. Anderson, R. Spiro, & W. Montague (Eds.), *Schooling and the acquisition of knowledge* (pp. 415–431). Hillsdale, NJ: Lawrence Erlbaum Associates.

Anderson, R. C. (1984). Some reflections on the acquisition of knowledge. *Educational Researcher, 13*(9), 5–10.

Anderson, R. C., & Ortony, A. (1975). On putting apples into bottles—A problem of polysemy. *Cognitive Psychology, 1*, 167–180.

Anderson, R. C., Pichert, J., Goetz, E., Schallert, D., Stevens, K., & Trollip, S. (1976). Instantiation of general terms. *Journal of Verbal Learning and Verbal Behavior, 15*, 667–679.

Anderson, R. C., & Pearson, P. D. (1984). A schema-theoretic view of basic processes in reading comprehension. In P. D. Pearson (Ed.), *Handbook of reading research* (pp. 255–291). New York: Longman.

Anderson, R. C., & Pichert, J. W. (1978). Recall of previously unrecallable information following a shift in perspective. *Journal of Verbal Learning and Verbal Behavior, 17*, 1–12.

Anderson, R. C., Pichert, J. W., & Shirey, L. L. (1983). Effects of the reader's schema at different points in time. *Journal of Educational Psychology, 75*, 271–279.

Anderson, R. C., Reynolds, R. E., Schallert, D. L., & Goetz, E. T. (1977). Frameworks for comprehending discourse. *American Educational Research Journal, 14*, 367–382.

Applebee, A. N. (1971). Research in reading retardation: Two critical problems. *Journal of Child Psychology & Psychiatry, 12*, 91–113.

Arnett, M., & DiLollo, V. (1979). Visual information processing in relation to age and to reading ability. *Journal of Experimental Child Psychology, 27*, 143–152.

Babcock, D., & Lovegrove, W. (1981). The effects of contrast, stimulus duration, and spatial frequency on visible persistence in normal and specifically disabled readers. *Journal of Experimental Psychology: Human Perception and Performance, 7*, 495–505.

Baddeley, A. (1966). Short-term memory for word sequences as a function of acoustic, semantic, and formal similarity. *Quarterly Journal of Experimental Psychology, 18*, 362–365.

Baker, L., & Anderson, R. C. (1982). Effects of inconsistent information on text processing: Evidence for comprehension monitoring. *Reading Research Quarterly, 17*, 281–294.

Baker, L., & Brown, A. L. (1984). Metacognitive skills and reading. In P. D. Pearson (Ed.), *Handbook of reading research* (pp. 353–394). New York: Longman.

Barron, R. (1981). Reading skill and reading strategies. In A. Lesgold & C. Perfetti (Eds.), *Interactive processes in reading* (pp. 299–327). Hillsdale, NJ: Lawrence Erlbaum Associates.

Bartlett, F. (1932). *Remembering*. Cambridge: Cambridge University Press.

Bateman, B. (1979). Teaching reading to learning disabled and other hard-to-teach children. In L. Resnick & P. Weaver (Eds.), *Theory and Practice of Early Reading. Vol. 1* (pp. 227–259). Hillsdale, NJ: Lawrence Erlbaum Associates.

Bauer, R. (1982). Information processing as a way of understanding and diagnosing learning disabilities. *Topics in Learning & Learning Disabilities*, *2*, 33–45.

Beers, T. (1987). Schema-theoretic models of reading: Humanizing the machine. *Reading Research Quarterly*, *22*, 369–377.

Berger, N. (1978). Why can't John read? Perhaps he's not a good listener. *Journal of Learning Disabilities*, *11*, 633–638.

Bernstein, R. J. (1983). *Beyond objectivism and relativism: Science, hermeneutics, and praxis.* Philadelphia: University of Pennsylvania Press.

Bickley, A., Ellington, B., & Bickley, R. (1970). The cloze procedure: A conspectus. *Journal of Reading Behavior*, *2*, 232–249.

Blachman, B. A. (1989). Phonological awareness and word recognition: Assessment and intervention. In A. G. Kamhi & H. W. Catts (Eds.), *Reading disabilities* (pp. 133–158). Boston: MA: College-Hill Press.

Booth, W. C. (1974). *Modern dogma and the rhetoric of assent.* Chicago: The University of Chicago Press.

Booth, W. C. (1983). A new strategy for establishing a truly democratic criticism. In S. Graubard (Ed.), *Reading in the 1980s* (pp. 193–214). New York: R. R. Bowker.

Bradley, L. (1987, December). *Categorising sounds, early intervention and learning to read: A follow-up study.* Paper presented at the meeting of the British Psychological Society, London.

Bradley, L., & Bryant, P. E. (1978). Difficulties in auditory organization as a possible cause of reading backwardness. *Nature*, *271*, 746–747.

Bradley, L., & Bryant, P. E. (1983). Categorizing sounds and learning to read: A causal connection. *Nature*, *301*, 419–421.

Bradley, L., & Bryant, P. E. (1985). *Rhyme and reason in reading and spelling.* Ann Arbor: University of Michigan Press.

Brady, S., Shankweiler, D., & Mann, V. (1983). Speech perception and memory coding in relation to reading ability. *Journal of Experimental Child Psychology*, *35*, 345–367.

Bransford, J. D., & Johnson, M. K. (1973). Considerations of some problems of comprehension. In W. G. Chase (Ed.), *Visual information processing* (pp. 383–438). New York: Academic Press.

Bransford, J. D., Stein, B. S., Shelton, T. S., & Owings, R. A. (1981). Cognition and adaptation: The importance of learning to learn. In J. Harvey (Ed.), *Cognition, social behavior and the environment*. Hillsdale, NJ: Lawrence Erlbaum Associates.

Briggs, P., Austin, S., & Underwood, G. (1984). The effects of sentence context in good and poor readers: A test of Stanovich's interactive-compensatory model. *Reading Research Quarterly*, *20*, 54–61.

Brown, A. L. (1975). The development of memory: Knowing, knowing about knowing, and knowing how to know. In H. W. Reese (Ed.), *Advances in child development* (Vol. 10, pp. 103–152). New York: Academic Press.

Brown, A. L. (1980). Metacognitive development and reading. In R. J. Spiro, B. C. Bruce, & W. F. Brewer (Eds.), *Theoretical issues in reading comprehension* (pp. 453–481). Hillsdale, NJ: Lawrence Erlbaum Associates.

Brown, A. L. (1981). Metacognition: The development of selective attention strategies for learning from texts. In M. Kamil (Ed.), *Thirtieth Yearbook of the National Reading Conference* (pp. 21–43). Clemson, SC: National Reading Conference.

Brown, A. L. (1987). Metacognition, executive control, self-regulation, and other more mysterious mechanisms. In F. E. Weinert, & R. N. Kluwe (Eds.), *Metacognition, motivation, and understanding*. Hillsdale, NJ: Lawrence Erlbaum Associates.

Brown, A. L., Armbruster, B. B., & Baker, L. (1986). The role of metacognition in reading and studying. In J. Orasanu (Ed.), *Reading comprehension: From research to practice* (pp. 49–75). Hillsdale, NJ: Lawrence Erlbaum Associates.

Brown, A. L., Bransford, J. D., Ferrara, R. A., & Campione, J. C. (1983). Learning, remembering and understanding. In J. H. Flavell & E. M. Markman (Eds.), *Handbook of child psychology* (Vol. 3, pp. 77–166). New York: Wiley.

Brown, A. L., & Campione, J. C. (1978). Permissible inferences from cognitive training studies in developmental research. *Quarterly Newsletter of the Institute for Comparative Human Behavior, 2*, 46–53.

Brown, A. L., Campione, J. C., & Barclay, C. R. (1979). Training self-checking routines for estimating test readiness: Generalization from list learning to prose recall. *Child Development, 50*, 501–512.

Brown, A. L., Campione, J. C., & Day, J. D. (1981). Learning to learn: On training students to learn from text. *Educational Researcher, 10*, 14–21.

Brown, A. L., & Day, J. D. (1983). Macrorules for summarizing texts: The development of expertise. *Journal of Verbal Learning and Verbal Behavior, 22*, 1–14.

Brown, A. L., & Smiley, S. S. (1977). Rating the importance of structural units of prose passages: A problem of metacognitive development. *Child Development, 48*, 1–8.

Brown, B., Haegerstrom-Portnoy, G., Adams, A., Yingling, C., Galin, D., Herron, J., & Marcus, M. (1983). Predictive eye movements do not discriminate between dyslexic and control children. *Neuropsychologia, 21*, 121–128.

Brown, H. I. (1977). *Perception, theory and commitment: The new philosophy of science*. Chicago: The University of Chicago Press.

Byrne, B. (1981). Deficient syntactic control in poor readers: Is a weak phonetic memory code responsible? *Applied Psycholinguistics, 2*, 201–212.

Byrne, B., & Shea, P. (1979). Semantic and phonetic memory codes in beginning readers. *Memory & Cognition, 7*, 333–338.

Calfee, R. (1977). Assessment of independent reading skills: Basic research and practical applications. In A. S. Reber & D. L. Scarborough (Eds.), *Toward a psychology of reading* (pp. 289–323). Hillsdale, NJ: Lawrence Erlbaum Associates.

Carr, T. (1981). Building theories of reading ability: On the relation between individual differences in cognitive skills and reading comprehension. *Cognition, 9*, 73–113.

Carver, R. P., & Hoffman, J. (1981). The effect of practice through repeated reading on gain in reading ability using a computer-based instructional system. *Reading Research Quarterly, 16*, 374–390.

Cavanaugh, J. C., & Perlmutter, M. (1982). Metamemory: A critical examination. *Child Development, 53*, 11–28.

Ceci, S. J. (1986). *Handbook of cognitive, social, and neuropsychological aspects of learning disabilities* (Vol. 1). Hillsdale, NJ: Lawrence Erlbaum Associates.

Cermak, L., Goldberg, J., Cermak, S., & Drake, C. (1980). The short-term memory ability of children with learning disabilities. *Journal of Learning Disabilities, 13*, 25–29.

Chall, S. (1983). *Stages of reading development*. New York: McGraw-Hill.

Charniak, E. (1973). *Toward a model of children's story comprehension* (Tech. Rep. No. 266). Cambridge, MA: MIT Artificial Intelligence Laboratory.

Chiesi, H. L., Spillich, G. J., Voss, J. F. (1979). Acquisition of domain related information in relation to high and low domain knowledge. *Journal of Verbal Learning and Verbal Behavior, 18*, 257–274.

Cohen, R. (1982). Individual differences in short-term memory. In N. Ellis (Ed.), *International Review of Research in Mental Retardation* (Vol. 11, pp. 43–77). New York: Academic Press.

Cohn, M., & Stricker, G. (1979). Reversal errors in strong, average, and weak letter namers. *Journal of Learning Disabilities, 12*, 533–537.

Coles, G. (1978). The learning disabilities test battery: Empirical and social issues. *Harvard Educational Review, 48*, 313–340.

Conrad, R. (1964). Acoustic confusions in immediate memory. *British Journal of Psychology, 55*, 75–84.

Corbett, A. T., & Dosher, B. A. (1978). Instrumental inferences in sentence encoding. *Journal of Verbal Learning and Verbal Behavior, 17*, 479–491.

Cossu, G., Shankweiler, D., Liberman, I. Y., Katz, L., & Tola, G. (1988). Awareness of phonological segments and reading ability in Italian children. *Applied Psycholinguistics, 9*, 1–16.

Critchley, M. (1970). *The dyslexic child*. London: William Heinemann Medical Books.

Cross, D. R., & Paris, S. G. (1988). Developmental and instructional analyses of children's metacognition and reading comprehension. *Journal of Educational Psychology, 80*, 131–142.

Cunningham, A. E., Stanovich, K. E., & Wilson, M. R. (in press). Cognitive variation in adult students differing in reading ability. In T. Carr & B. A. Levy (Eds.), *Reading and its development: Component skills approaches*. San Diego: Academic Press.

Curtis, M. (1980). Development of components of reading skill. *Journal of Educational Psychology, 72*, 656–669.

Daneman, M., & Carpenter, P. (1980). Individual differences in working memory and reading. *Journal of Verbal Learning and Verbal Behavior, 19*, 450–466.

Day, J. D. (1980). *Training summarization skills: A comparison of teaching methods*. Unpublished doctoral thesis, University of Illinois.

Dewey, J. (1910). *Educational essays*. London: Blackie & Son.

Doehring, D. G. (1978). The tangled web of behavioral research on developmental dyslexia. In A. L. Benton & D. Pearl (Eds.), *Dyslexia* (pp. 123–135). New York: Oxford University Press.

Dosher, B., & Corbett, A. (1982). Instrument inferences and verb schemata. *Memory & Cognition, 10*, 531–539.

Eagleton, T. (1983). *Literacy theory: An introduction*. Minneapolis: University of Minnesota Press.

Ehri, L. (1979). Linguistic insight: Threshold of reading acquisition. In T. Walker & G. Mackinnon (Eds.), *Reading research: Advances in research and theory* (Vol. 1, pp. 63–114). New York: Academic Press.

Ehri, L. C. (1985). Effects of printed language acquisition on speech. In D. Olson, N. Torrance, & A. Hildyard (Eds.), *Literacy, language, and learning* (pp. 333–367). Cambridge: Cambridge University Press.

Ellis, N. (1981). Visual and name coding in dyslexic children. *Psychological Research, 43*, 201–218.

Ellis, N., & Large, B. (1987). The development of reading: As you seek so shall you find. *British Journal of Psychology, 78*, 1–28.

Epstein, W., Glenberg, A. M., & Bradley, M. M. (1984). Coactivation and comprehension: Contribution of text variables to the illusion of knowing. *Memory & Cognition, 12*, 355–360.

Evans, M. A., & Carr, T. H. (1985). Cognitive abilities, conditions of learning, and the early development of reading skill. *Reading Research Quarterly, 20*, 327–350.

Fincher-Kiefer, R., Post, T. A., Greene, T. R., & Voss, J. F. (1988). On the role of prior knowledge and task demands in the processing of text. *Journal of Memory and Language, 27*, 416–428.

Fischer, F., Liberman, I., & Shankweiler, D. (1978). Reading reversals and developmental dyslexia: A further study. *Cortex, 14,* 496–510.

Fish, S. (1980). *Is there a text in this class?* Cambridge, MA: Harvard University Press.

Fisher, D., & Frankfurter, A. (1977). Normal and disabled readers can locate and identify letters: Where's the perceptual deficit? *Journal of Reading Behavior, 9,* 31–43.

Flavell, J. H. (1971). Stage-related properties of cognitive development. *Cognitive Psychology, 2,* 421–453.

Flavell, J. H. (1978). Metacognitive development. In J. M. Scandura & C. J. Brainerd (Eds.), *Structural/process models of complex human behavior* (pp. 213–224). The Netherlands: Sijthoff & Noordoff.

Flavell, J. H. (1981). Cognitive monitoring. In W. P. Dickson (Ed.), *Children's oral communication skills* (pp. 35–60). New York: Academic Press.

Fletcher, J., Satz, P., & Scholes, R. (1981). Developmental changes in the linguistic performance correlates of reading achievement. *Brain and Language, 13,* 78–90.

Fodor, J. A. (1983). *Modularity of mind.* Cambridge: MIT Press.

Fodor, J. A. (1985). Precis of *The Modularity of Mind. Behavioral and Brain Sciences, 8,* 1–42.

Forrest, D. L., & Waller, T. G. (1979, March). *Cognitive and metacognitive aspects of reading.* Paper presented at the meeting of the Society for Research in Child Development, San Francisco.

Forrest-Pressley, D. L., & Gillies, L. A. (1983). Children's flexible use of strategies during reading. In M. Pressley & J. R. Levin (Eds.), *Cognitive strategy research: Educational applications* (pp. 133–156). New York: Springer-Verlag.

Forster, K. I. (1979). Levels of processing and the structure of the language processor. In W. E. Cooper & E. Walker (Eds.), *Sentence processing: Psycholinguistic studies presented to Merrill Garrett* (pp. 27–85). Hillsdale, NJ: Lawrence Erlbaum Associates.

Foster, R., & Gavelek, J. (1983). Development of intentional forgetting in normal and reading-delayed children. *Journal of Educational Psychology, 75,* 431–440.

Fox, B., & Routh, D. (1976). Phonemic analysis and synthesis as word attack skills. *Journal of Educational Psychology, 68,* 70–74.

Fox, B., & Routh, D. (1980). Phonemic analysis and severe reading disability. *Journal of Psycholinguistic Research, 9,* 115–119.

Fox, B., & Routh, D. (1983). Reading disability, phonemic analysis, and dysphonic spelling: A follow-up study. *Journal of Clinical Child Psychology, 12,* 28–32.

Frankenberger, W., & Harper, J. (1987). States' criteria and procedures for identifying learning disabled children: A comparison of 1981/82 and 1985/86 guidelines. *Journal of Learning Disabilities, 20,* 118–121.

Freebody, P., & Byrne, B. (1988). Word-reading strategies in elementary school children: Relations to comprehension, reading time, and phonemic awareness. *Reading Research Quarterly, 23,* 441–453.

Garner, R. (1987). Strategies for reading and studying expository texts. *Educational Psychologist, 22,* 299–312.

Garner, R., & Reis, R. (1981). Monitoring and resolving comprehension obstacles: An investigation of spontaneous text lookbacks among upper-grade good and poor comprehenders. *Reading Research Quarterly, 16,* 569–582.

Garnham, A. (1982). Testing psychological theories about inference making. *Memory & Cognition, 10,* 341–349.

Gellner, E. (1975). Beyond truth and falsehood. *British Journal of Philosophy of Science, 26,* 331–342.

Gerrig, R. J. (1988). Text comprehension. In R. J. Sternberg & E. E. Smith (Eds.), *The psychology of human thought* (pp. 242–266). Cambridge: Cambridge University Press.

Glenberg, A. M., & Epstein, W. (1985). Calibration of comprehension. *Journal of Experimental Psychology: Learning, Memory, and Cognition, 11*, 702–718.

Glenberg, A. M., & Epstein, W. (1987). Inexpert calibration of comprehension. *Memory & Cognition, 15*, 84–93.

Glenberg, A. M., Sanocki, T., Epstein, W., & Morris, C. (1987). Enhancing calibration of comprehension. *Journal of Experimental Psychology: General, 116*, 119–136.

Glenberg, A. M., Wilkinson, A. C., & Epstein, W. (1982). The illusion of knowing: Failure in the self-assessment of comprehension. *Memory & Cognition, 10*, 597–602.

Golden, J. M. (1983). If a text exists without a reader, is there meaning? Insights from literary theory for reader-text interaction. In B. A. Hutson (Ed.), *Advances in reading/language research* (Vol. 2, pp. 139–163). Greenwich, CT: JAI Press.

Goldman, S., Hogaboam, T., Bell, L., & Perfetti, C. (1980). Short-term retention of discourse during reading. *Journal of Educational Psychology, 72*, 647–655.

Goldstein, D. (1976). Cognitive-linguistic functioning and learning to read in preschoolers. *Journal of Educational Psychology, 63*, 680–688.

Goodheart, E. (1983). The text and the interpretive community. In S. Graubard (Ed.), *Reading in the 1980s* (pp. 215–231). New York: R. R. Bowker.

Goodman, K. S. (1967). Reading: A psycholinguistic guessing game. *Journal of the Reading Specialist, 6*, 126–135.

Goodman, K. S. (1972). The reading process: Theory and practice. In R. Hodges & E. Rudorf (Eds.), *Language and learning to read*. Boston: Houghton-Mifflin.

Goodman, K. S. (1976–77a). From the strawman to the tin woodman: A response to Mosenthal. *Reading Research Quarterly, 12*, 575–585.

Goodman, K. S. (1976–77b). And a principled view from the bridge. *Reading Research Quarterly, 12*, 604.

Goodman, K. S. (1981). [Letter to the editors.] *Reading Research Quarterly, 16*, 477–478.

Gough, P. B. (1972). One second of reading. In J. Kavanagh & I. Mattingly (Eds.), *Language by ear and eye* (pp. 331–358). Cambridge, MA: MIT Press.

Gough, P. B. (1983). Context, form, and interaction. In K. Rayner (Ed.), *Eye movements in reading* (pp. 203–211). New York: Academic Press.

Gough, P. B. (1985). One second of reading: Postscript. In H. Singer & R. Ruddell (Eds.), *Theoretical models and processes of reading* (3rd ed., pp. 687–688). Newark, DE: International Reading Association.

Gough, P., & Hillinger, M. (1980). Learning to read: An unnatural act. *Bulletin of the Orton Society, 30*, 171–196.

Gough, P. B., & Tunmer, W. E. (1986). Decoding, reading, and reading disability. *Remedial and Special Education, 7*, 6–10.

Graesser, A. C., Haberlandt, K., & Koizumi, D. (1987). How is reading time influenced by knowledge-based inferences and world knowledge? In B. K. Britton & S. M. Glynn (Eds.), *Executive control processes in reading* (pp. 217–251). Hillsdale, NJ: Lawrence Erlbaum Associates.

Gross, K., & Rothenberg, S. (1979). An examination of methods used to test the visual perceptual deficit hypothesis of dyslexia. *Journal of Learning Disabilities, 12*, 670–677.

Gupta, R., Ceci, S., & Slater, A. (1978). Visual discrimination in good and poor readers. *Journal of Special Education, 12*, 409–416.

Hall, J., & Humphreys, M. (1982). Research on specific learning disabilities: Deficits and remediation. *Topics in Learning and Learning Disabilities, 2*, 68–78.

Hall, J., Wilson, K., Humphreys, M., Tinzmann, M., & Bowyer, P. (1983). Phonemic-similarity effects in good vs. poor readers. *Memory & Cognition, 11*, 520–527.

Haller, E. P., Child, D. A., & Walberg, H. J. (1988). Can comprehension be taught? *Educational Researcher, 17*, 5–8.

Hammill, D., & Larsen, S. (1974). The effectiveness of psycholinguistic training. *Exceptional Children, 41*, 5–15.

Hammill, D., & Larsen, S. (1978). The effectiveness of psycholinguistic training: A reaffirmation of position. *Exceptional Children, 44*, 402–417.

Hammill, D., Leigh, J., McNutt, G., & Larsen, S. (1981). A new definition of learning disabilities. *Learning Disability Quarterly, 4*, 336–342.

Hansen, J. (1981). The effects of inference training and practice on young children's comprehension. *Reading Research Quarterly, 16*, 391–417.

Hansen, J., & Pearson, P. D. (1983). An instructional study: Improving the inferential comprehension of good and poor fourth-grade readers. *Journal of Educational Psychology, 75*, 821–829.

Kardash, C., Royer, J. M., & Greene, B. (1988). Effects of schemata on both encoding and retrieval of information from prose. *Journal of Educational Psychology, 80*, 324–329.

Harman, S. (1982). Are reversals a symptom of dyslexia? *The Reading Teacher, 35*, 424–428.

Henderson, L. (1982). *Orthography and word recognition in reading*. London: Academic Press.

Hogaboam, T., & Perfetti, C. (1978). Reading skill and the role of verbal experience in decoding. *Journal of Educational Psychology, 70*, 717–729.

Hochberg, J. (1970). Components of literacy: Speculation and exploratory research. In H. Levin & J. Williams (Eds.), *Basic studies in reading* (pp. 80–123). New York: Basic Books.

Holmes, D., & Peper, R. (1977). An evaluation of the use of spelling error analysis in the diagnosis of reading disabilities. *Child Development, 48*, 1708–1711.

Huey, E. B. (1968). *The psychology and pedagogy of reading*. Cambridge: MIT Press. (Original work published 1908).

Hulme, C. (1981). The effects of manual training on memory in normal and retarded readers: Some implications for multi-sensory teaching. *Psychological Research, 43*, 179–191.

Humphreys, G. W. (1985). Attention, automaticity, and autonomy in visual word processing. In D. Besner, T. Waller, & G. MacKinnon (Eds.), *Reading research: Advances in theory and practice* (Vol. 5, pp. 253–309). New York: Academic Press.

Iran-Nejad, A. (1987). The schema: A long-term memory structure or a transient structural phenomena. In R. J. Tierney, P. L. Anders, & J. N. Mitchell (Eds.), *Understanding readers' understanding* (pp. 109–127). Hillsdale, NJ: Lawrence Erlbaum Associates.

Jackson, M. (1980). Further evidence for a relationship between memory access and reading ability. *Journal of Verbal Learning and Verbal Behavior, 19*, 683–694.

Jackson, M., & McClelland, J. (1979). Processing determinants of reading speed. *Journal of Experimental Psychology: General, 108*, 151–181.

Johns, J., & Ellis, D. (1976). Reading: Children tell it like it is. *Reading World, 16*, 115–128.

Johnson, M. K., Bransford, J. D., & Solomon, S. K. (1973). Memory for tacit implications of sentences. *Journal of Experimental Psychology, 98*, 203–205.

Jorm, A. (1983). Specific reading retardation and working memory. A review. *British Journal of Psychology, 74*, 311–342.

Jorm, A., & Share, D. (1983). Phonological recoding and reading acquisition. *Applied Psycholinguistics, 4*, 103–147.

Juel, C., Griffith, P. L., & Gough, P. B. (1986). Acquisition of literacy: A longitudinal study of children in first and second grade. *Journal of Educational Psychology, 78*, 243–255.

Just, M. A., & Carpenter, P. A. (1980). A theory of reading: From eye fixations to comprehension. *Psychological Review, 4*, 329–354.

Just, M., & Carpenter, P. (1987). *The psychology of reading and language comprehension*. Boston: Allyn & Bacon.

Kardash, C., Royer, J. M., & Greene, B. (1988). Effects of schemata on both encoding and retrieval of information from prose. *Journal of Educational Psychology, 80*, 324–329.

Kamhi, A., & Catts, H. (1989). *Reading disabilities: A developmental language perspective*. Boston: College-Hill Press.

Katz, R., Shankweiler, D., & Liberman, I. (1981). Memory for item order and phonetic recoding in the beginning reader. *Journal of Experimental Child Psychology*, *32*, 474–484.

Kavale, K. A. (1987). Theoretical issues surrounding severe discrepancy. *Learning Disabilities Research*, *3*, 12–20.

Kavale, K. A., & Nye, C. (1981). Identification criteria for learning disabilities: A survey of the research literature. *Learning Disability Quarterly*, *4*, 363–388.

Kavanagh, J. F., & Truss, T. J. (Eds.). (1988). *Learning disabilities: Proceedings of the national conference*. Parkston, MD: York Press.

Kimmel, S., & MacGinitie, W. H. (1984). Identifying children who use a perseverative text processing strategy. *Reading Research Quarterly*, *19*, 162–172.

Kintsch, W. (1979). Concerning the marriage of research and practice in beginning reading instruction. In L. B. Resnick & P. Weaver (Eds.), *Theory and practice of early reading* (pp. 319–330). Hillsdale, NJ: Lawrence Erlbaum Associates.

Kintsch, W. (1988). The role of knowledge in discourse comprehension: A construction-integration model. *Psychological Review*, *95*, 163–182.

Kolers, P. A. (1972). Experiments in reading. *Scientific American*, *227*, 84–91.

Kuhn, T. S. (1970). *The structure of scientific revolutions* (2nd ed.). Chicago: University of Chicago Press.

Kurtz, B. E., & Borkowski, J. G. (1985). Children's metacognition: Exploring relations among knowledge, process, and motivational variables. *Journal of Experimental Child Psychology*, *37*, 335–354.

LaBerge, D., & Samuels, S. (1974). Toward a theory of automatic information processing in reading. *Cognitive Psychology*, *6*, 293–323.

Lahey, B., Kupfer, D., Beggs, V., & Landon, D. (1982). Do learning-disabled children exhibit deficits in selective attention? *Journal of Abnormal Child Psychology*, *10*, 1–10.

Lakatos, I., & Musgrave, A. (1970). *Criticism and the growth of knowledge*. Cambridge: Cambridge University Press.

Larsen, S., & Hammill, D. (1975). Relationship of selected visual perception abilities to school learning. *Journal of Special Education*, *9*, 281–291.

Larsen, S., Parker, R., & Hammill, D. (1982). Effectiveness of psycholinguistic training: A response to Kavale. *Exceptional Children*, *49*, 60–67.

Liberman, I. (1982). A language-oriented view of reading and its disabilities. In H. Myklebust (Ed.), *Progress in learning disabilities* (Vol. 5, pp. 81–101). New York: Grune & Stratton.

Liberman, I., & Shankweiler, D. (1979). Speech, the alphabet, and teaching to read. In L. Resnick & P. Weaver (Eds.), *Theory and practice of early reading* (Vol. 2, pp. 109–132). Hillsdale, NJ: Lawrence Erlbaum Associates.

Liberman, I., & Shankweiler, D. (1985). Phonology and the problems of learning to read and write. *Remedial and Special Education*, *6*, 8–17.

Lieberman, P., Meskill, R. H., Chatillon, M., & Schupack, H. (1985). Phonetic speech perception deficits in dyslexia. *Journal of Speech and Hearing Research*, *28*, 480–486.

Lipson, M. Y. (1983). The influence of religious affiliation on children's memory for text information. *Reading Research Quarterly*, *18*, 448–457.

Logan, G. D. (1985). Skill and automaticity: Relations, implications, and future directions. *Canadian Journal of Psychology*, *39*, 367–386.

Lundberg, I., Frost, J., & Peterson, O. (1988). Effects of an extensive program for stimulating phonological awareness in preschool children. *Reading Research Quarterly*, *23*, 263–284.

Maclean, M., Bryant, P., & Bradley, L. (1987). Rhymes, nursery rhymes, and reading in early childhood. *Merrill-Palmer Quarterly*, *33*, 255–281.

Maki, R. H., & Swett, S. (1987). Metamemory for narrative text. *Memory & Cognition*, *15*, 72–83.

Manis, F., & Morrison, F. (1982). Processing of identity and position information in normal and disabled readers. *Journal of Experimental Child Psychology*, *33*, 74–86.

Mann, L. (1970). Perceptual training: Misdirections and redirections. *American Journal of Orthopsychiatry, 40,* 30–38.

Mann, V. (1984). Reading skill and language skill. *Developmental Review, 4,* 1–15.

Mann, V. (1986). Why some children encounter reading problems. In J. Torgesen & B. Wong (Eds.), *Psychological and educational perspectives on learning disabilities* (pp. 133–159). New York: Academic Press.

Mann, V., Liberman, I., & Shankweiler, D. (1980). Children's memory for sentences and word strings in relation to reading ability. *Memory & Cognition, 8,* 329–335.

Maria, K., & MacGinitie, W. H. (1982). Reading comprehension disabilities: Knowledge structures and non-accommodating text processing strategies. *Annals of Dyslexia, 32,* 33–59.

Markman, E. M. (1981). Comprehension monitoring. In W. P. Dickson (Ed.), *Children's oral communication skills* (pp. 61–84). New York: Academic Press.

Markman, E. M. (1985). Comprehension monitoring: Developmental and educational issues. In S. F. Chipman & J. W. Segal (Eds.), *Thinking and learning skills* (Vol. 2, pp. 275–291). Hillsdale, NJ: Lawrence Erlbaum Associates.

Massaro, D. W. (1978). A stage model of reading and listening. *Visible Language, 12,* 3–26.

Mason, M. (1975). Reading ability and letter search time: Effects of orthographic structure defined by single-letter positional frequency. *Journal of Experimental Psychology: General, 104,* 146–166.

Masson, M., & Miller, J. (1983). Working memory and individual differences in comprehension and memory of text. *Journal of Educational Psychology, 75,* 314–318.

McClelland, J. L. (1979). On the time relations of mental processes: An examination of systems of processes in cascade. *Psychological Review, 86,* 287–330.

McKoon, G., & Ratcliff, R. (1980a). The comprehension processes and memory structures involved in anaphoric reference. *Journal of Verbal Learning and Verbal Behavior, 19,* 668–682.

McKoon, G., & Ratcliff, R. (1980b). Priming in item recognition: The organization of propositions in memory for text. *Journal of Verbal Learning and Verbal Behavior, 19,* 369–386.

McKoon, G., & Ratcliff, R. (1981). The comprehension processes and memory structures involved in instrumental inferences. *Journal of Verbal Learning and Verbal Behavior, 20,* 671–682.

McLeod, P., McLaughlin, C., & Nimmo-Smith, I. (1985). Information encapsulation and automaticity: Evidence from the visual control of finely timed actions. In M. Posner & O. Marin (Eds.), *Attention and performance* (Vol. 11, pp. 391–406). Hillsdale, NJ: Lawrence Erlbaum Associates.

McMullin, E. (1988). The shaping of scientific rationality: Construction and constraint. In E. McMullin (Ed.), *Construction and constraint* (pp. 1–47). Notre Dame, IN: University of Notre Dame Press.

Miller, G. R., & Coleman, E. B. (1967). A set of thirty-six prose passages calibrated for complexity. *Journal of Verbal Learning and Verbal Behavior, 6,* 851–854.

Minsky, M. A. (1975). A framework for representing knowledge. In P. H. Winston, (Ed.), *The psychology of computer vision* (pp. 211–277). New York: McGraw-Hill.

Mitchell, D. (1982). *The process of reading: A cognitive analysis of fluent reading and learning to read.* New York: John Wiley.

Morais, J., Alegria, J., & Content, A. (1987). The relationships between segmental analysis and alphabetic literacy: An interactive view. *Cahiers de Psychologie Cognitive, 7,* 415–438.

Morrison, F. (1984). Word decoding and rule-learning in normal and disabled readers. *Remedial and Special Education, 5,* 20–27.

Morrison, F. J. (1987). The nature of reading disability: Toward an integrative framework. In S. Ceci (Ed.), *Handbook of cognitive, social, and neuropsychological aspects of learning disabilities* (pp. 33–62). Hillsdale, NJ: Lawrence Erlbaum Associates.

Morrison, F., Giordani, B., & Nagy, K. (1977). Reading disability: An information-processing analysis. *Science, 196,* 77–79.

Myers, M., & Paris, S. G. (1978). Children's metacognitive knowledge about reading. *Journal of Educational Psychology, 70,* 680–690.

Neely, J. H. (1977). Semantic priming and retrieval from lexical memory: Roles of inhibitionless spreading activation and limited-capacity attention. *Journal of Experimental Psychology: General, 106*, 226–254.

Neisser, U. (1967). *Cognitive psychology*. New York: Appleton-Century-Crofts.

Newman, D., & Hagen, J. (1981). Memory strategies in children with learning disabilities. *Journal of Applied Developmental Psychology, 1*, 297–312.

Newton-Smith, W. (1982). Relativism and the possibility of interpretation. In M. Hollis & S. Lukes (Eds.), *Rationality and relativism* (pp. 106–122). Cambridge, MA: MIT Press.

Oakhill, J. (1982). Constructive processes in skilled and less skilled comprehenders' memory for sentences. *British Journal of Psychology, 73*, 13–20.

Olson, R., Davidson, B., Kliegl, R., & Davies, S. (1984). Development of phonetic memory in disabled and normal readers. *Journal of Experimental Child Psychology, 37*, 187–206.

Olson, R., Kliegl, R., & Davidson, B. (1983). Dyslexia and normal readers' eye movements. *Journal of Experimental Psychology: Human Perception and Performance, 9*, 816–825.

Olson, R., Kliegl, R., Davidson, B., & Foltz, G. (1985). Individual and developmental differences in reading disability. In G. E. MacKinnon & T. Waller (Eds.), *Reading research: Advances in theory and practice* (Vol. 4, pp. 1–64). London: Academic Press.

Orasanu, J., & Penney, M. (1986). Introduction: Comprehension theory and how it grew. In J. Orasanu (Ed.), *Reading comprehension: From research to practice* (pp. 1–9). Hillsdale, NJ: Lawrence Erlbaum Associates.

Palincsar, A. S. (1986a). Metacognitive strategy instruction. *Exceptional Children, 53*, 118–124.

Palincsar, A. S. (1986b). The role of dialogue in providing scaffolded instruction. *Educational Psychologist, 21*, 73–98.

Palincsar, A. S., & Brown, A. L. (1984). Reciprocal teaching of comprehension-fostering and comprehension-monitoring activities. *Cognition and Instruction, 1*, 117–175.

Palincsar, A. S., & Brown, D. A. (1987). Enhancing instructional time through attention to metacognition. *Journal of Learning Disabilities, 20*, 66–75.

Palincsar, A. S., Brown, A. L., Martin, S. M. (1987). Peer interaction in reading comprehension instruction. *Educational Psychologist, 22*, 231–253.

Palmer, J., MacLeod, C. M., Hunt, E., & Davidson, J. E. (1985). Information processing correlates of reading. *Journal of Memory and Language, 24*, 59–88.

Paris, S. G. (1985). Using classroom dialogues and guided practice to teach comprehension strategies. In T. L. Harris & E. J. Cooper (Eds.), *Reading, thinking, and concept development* (pp. 133–144). New York: College Entrance Examination Board.

Paris, S. G. (1986). Teaching children to guide their reading and learning. In T. Raphael (Ed.), *The contexts of school-based literacy* (pp. 115–130). New York: Random House.

Paris, S. G. (1987). Introduction to current issues in reading comprehension. *Educational Psychologist, 22*, 209–212.

Paris, S. G., Cross, D. R., & Lipson, M. Y. (1984). Informed strategies for learning: A program to improve children's reading awareness and comprehension. *Journal of Educational Psychology, 76*, 1239–1252.

Paris, S. G., & Jacobs, J. E. (1984). The benefits of informed instruction for children's reading awareness and comprehension skills. *Child Development, 55*, 2083–2093.

Paris, S. G., & Lindauer, B. K. (1976). The role of inference in children's comprehension and memory for stories. *Cognitive Psychology, 8*, 217–227.

Paris, S. G., Lipson, M. Y., & Wixson, K. K. (1983). Becoming a strategic reader. *Contemporary Educational Psychology, 8*, 293–316.

Paris, S. G., & Myers, M. (1981). Comprehension monitoring, memory, and study strategies of good and poor readers. *Journal of Reading Behavior, 13*, 5–22.

Paris, S. G., & Oka, E. R. (1986). Children's reading strategies, metacognition, and motivation. *Developmental Review, 6*, 25–56.

Paris, S. G., Saarnio, D. A., & Cross, D. R. (1986). A metacognitive curriculum to promote children's reading and learning. *American Journal of Psychology, 38*, 107–123.

Paris, S. G., Wasik, B. A., & Van der Westhuizen, G. (1988). Meta-metacognition: A review of research on metacognition and reading. In J. E. Readence & R. S. Baldwin (Eds.), *Dialogues in literacy research: Thirty-seventh yearbook of the National Reading Conference* (pp. 143–166). Chicago, IL: National Reading Conference.

Paris, S. G., & Winograd, P. (1988). Metacognition in academic learning and instruction. In B. F. Jones & L. Idol (Eds.), *Dimensions of thinking and cognitive instruction*. Hillsdale, NJ: Lawrence Erlbaum Associates.

Park, R. (1978–1979). Performance on geometric figure-copying tests as predictors of types of errors in decoding. *Reading Research Quarterly, 14*, 100–118.

Patterson, K., Marshall, J., & Coltheart, M. (1985). *Surface dyslexia*. London: Lawrence Erlbaum Associates.

Payne, M., & Holzman, T. (1983). Auditory short-term memory and digit span; Normal versus poor readers. *Journal of Educational Psychology, 75*, 424–430.

Pearson, P. D., Hansen, J., & Gordon, C. (1979). The effect of background knowledge on young children's comprehension of explicit and implicit information. *Journal of Reading Behavior, 11*, 201–209.

Pennington, B. F. (1986). Issues in the diagnosis and phenotype analysis of dyslexia: Implications for family studies. In S. D. Smith (Ed.), *Genetics and learning disabilities* (pp. 69–96). San Diego: College-Hill Press.

Perfetti, C. A. (1985). *Reading ability*. New York: Oxford University Press.

Perfetti, C. (1988). Verbal efficiency in reading ability. In M. Daneman, G. E. MacKinnon, & T. G. Waller (Eds.), *Reading research: Advances in theory and practice* (Vol. 6, pp. 109–143). San Diego: Academic Press.

Perfetti, C. A. (in press). The representation problem in reading acquisition. In P. Gough (Ed.), *Reading acquisition*. Hillsdale, NJ: Lawrence Erlbaum Associates.

Perfetti, C. A., Beck, I., Bell, L., & Hughes, C. (1987). Phonemic knowledge and learning to read are reciprocal: A longitudinal study of first grade children. *Merrill-Palmer Quarterly, 33*, 283–319.

Perfetti, C. A., & Curtis, M. E. (1986). Reading. In R. F. Dillon & R. J. Sternberg (Eds.), *Cognition and instruction* (pp. 13–57). New York: Academic Press.

Perfetti, C. A., Goldman, S., & Hogaboam, T. (1979). Reading skill and the identification of words in discourse context. *Memory & Cognition, 7*, 273–282.

Perfetti, C., & Hogaboam, T. (1975). Relationship between single word decoding and reading comprehension skill. *Journal of Educational Psychology, 56*, 461–469.

Perfetti, C., & Lesgold, A. (1977). Discourse comprehension and sources of individual differences. In M. Just & P. Carpenter (Eds.), *Cognitive processes in comprehension* (pp. 141–183). Hillsdale, NJ: Lawrence Erlbaum Associates.

Perfetti, C., & Lesgold, A. (1979). Coding and comprehension in skilled reading and implications for reading instruction. In L. B. Resnick & P. Weaver (Eds.), *Theory and practice of early reading* (pp. 57–84). Hillsdale, NJ: Lawrence Erlbaum Associates.

Perfetti, C., & McCutchen, D. (1982). Speech processes in reading. In N. Lass (Ed.), *Speech and language: Advances in Basic Research and Practice* Vol. 7 (pp. 237–269). New York: Academic Press.

Perfetti, C. A., & McCutchen, D. (1987). Schooled language competence: Linguistic abilities in reading and writing. In S. Rosenberg (Ed.), *Advances in applied psycholinguistics* (Vol. 2, pp. 105–141). Cambridge: Cambridge University Press.

Perfetti, C. A., & Roth, S. (1981). Some of the interactive processes in reading and their role in reading skill. In A. Lesgold & C. Perfetti (Eds.), *Interactive processes in reading* (pp. 269–297). Hillsdale, NJ: Lawrence Erlbaum Associates.

Phillips, D. C. (1983). After the wake: Postpositivist educational thought. *Educational Researcher, 12*(5), 4–12.

Posner, M. I., & Snyder, C. R. R. (1975). Facilitation and inhibition in the processing of signals. In P. Rabbitt & S. Dornic (Eds.), *Attention and performance* (Vol. 5, pp. 669–682). London: Academic Press.

Potts, G., Keenan, J., & Golding, J. (1988). Assessing the occurrence of elaborative inferences: Lexical decision versus naming. *Journal of Memory and Language, 27*, 399–415.

Pratt, A. C., & Brady, S. (1988). Relation of phonological awareness to reading disability in children and adults. *Journal of Educational Psychology, 80*, 319–323.

Pressley, M., Forrest-Pressley, D., & Elliott-Faust, D. J. (1988). What is strategy instructional enrichment and how to study it: Illustrations from research on children's prose memory and comprehension. In F. E. Weinert & M. Perlmutter (Eds.), *Memory development: Universal changes and individual differences* (pp. 101–130). Hillsdale, NJ: Lawrence Erlbaum Associates.

Pressley, M., & Ghatala, E. S. (1988). Delusions about performance on multiple-choice comprehension tests. *Reading Research Quarterly, 23*, 454–464.

Pring, L., & Snowling, M. (1986). Developmental changes in word recognition: An information-processing account. *Quarterly Journal of Experimental Psychology, 38A*, 395–418.

Putnam, H. (1981). Philosophers and human understanding. In A. F. Heath (Ed.), *Scientific explanation* (pp. 99–120). Oxford: Clarendon Press.

Putnam, H. (1983). *Realism and reason: Philosophical papers* (Vol. 3). Cambridge: Cambridge University Press.

Pylyshyn, Z. W. (1981). The imagery debate: Analogue media versus tacit knowledge. *Psychological Review, 88*, 16–45.

Raphael, T. E., & McKinney, J. (1983). An examination of fifth and eighth grade students' question answering behavior: An instructional study in metacognition. *Journal of Reading Behavior, 15*, 67–86.

Raphael, T. E., & Pearson, P. D. (1982). *The effect of metacognitive training on children's question-answering behavior* (Tech. Rep. No. 238). Urbana: University of Illinois, Center for the Study of Reading.

Raphael, T. E., & Pearson, P. D. (1985). Increasing students' awareness of sources of information for answering questions. *American Educational Research Journal, 22*, 217–236.

Raphael, T. E., & Wonnacott, C. A. (1985). Heightening fourth-grade students' sensitivity to sources of information for answering comprehension questions. *Reading Research Quarterly, 20*, 282–296.

Ratcliff, R., & McKoon, G. (1981). Automatic and strategic priming in recognition. *Journal of Verbal Learning and Verbal Behavior, 20*, 204–215.

Rayner, K. (1978). Eye movements in reading and information processing. *Psychological Bulletin, 85*, 618–660.

Rayner, K., & Pollatsek, A. (1989). *The psychology of reading*. Englewood Cliffs, NJ: Prentice Hall.

Reynolds, C. R. (1984–1985). Critical measurement issues in learning disabilities. *The Journal of Special Education, 18*, 451–475.

Reynolds, C. R. (1985). Measuring the aptitude-achievement discrepancy in learning disability diagnosis. *Remedial and Special Education, 6*, 37–55.

Rieger, C. (1975). Conceptual memory and inference. In R. C. Schank (Ed.), *Conceptual information processing* (pp. 157–288). Amsterdam: North-Holland.

Rohwer, W. D., Jr. (1973). Elaboration and learning in childhood and adolescence. In H. W. Reese (Ed.), *Advances in child development and behavior*, Vol. 8. New York: Academic Press.

Rohwer, W. D., Jr., & Ammon, M. S. (1971). Elaboration training and learning efficiency in children. *Journal of Educational Psychology, 62*, 376–383.

Rubenstein, H., & Aborn, M. (1958). Learning, prediction, and readability. *Journal of Applied Psychology, 42*, 28–32.

Ruddell, R. (1965). The effect of similarity of oral and written patterns of language structure on reading comprehension. *Elementary English, 42*, 403–410.

Rumelhart, D. E. (1975). Notes on a schema for stories. In D. G. Bobrow & A. M. Collins (Eds.), *Representation and understanding: Studies in cognitive science* (pp. 211–236). New York: Academic Press.

Rumelhart, D. E. (1977). Toward an interactive model of reading. In S. Dornic (Ed.), *Attention and performance* (Vol. 6, pp. 573–603). New York: Academic Press.

Rumelhart, D. E. (1980). Schemata: The building blocks of cognition. In R. J. Spiro, B. C. Bruce, & W. F. Brewer (Eds.), *Theoretical issues in reading comprehension* (pp. 245–278). Hillsdale, NJ: Lawrence Erlbaum Associates.

Rumelhart, D. E., & McClelland, J. L. (1986). *Parallel distributed processing: Explorations in the microstructure of cognition* (Vol. 1). Cambridge: MIT Press.

Rumelhart, D. E., & Ortony, A. (1977). The representation of knowledge in memory. In R. C. Anderson, R. J. Spiro, & W. E. Montague (Eds.), *Schooling and the acquisition of knowledge* (pp. 99–136). Hillsdale, NJ: Lawrence Erlbaum Associates.

Rutter, M. (1978). Prevalence and types of dyslexia. In A. Benton & D. Pearl (Eds.), *Dyslexia: An appraisal of current knowledge* (pp. 5–28). New York: Oxford University Press.

Sadoski, M. (1981). Right forest, wrong tree? *Reading Research Quarterly, 16*, 600–603.

Scarborough, H. S. (1984). Continuity between childhood dyslexia and adult reading. *British Journal of Psychology, 75*, 329–348.

Scardamalia, M., & Bereiter, C. (1983). Child as coinvestigator: Helping children gain insight into their own mental processes. In S. G. Paris, G. M. Olson, & H. W. Stevenson (Eds.), *Learning and motivation in the classroom* (pp. 61–82). Hillsdale, NJ: Lawrence Erlbaum Associates.

Schank, R. (1978). Predictive understanding. In R. Campbell & P. Smith (Eds.), *Recent advances in the psychology of language—Formal and experimental approaches* (pp. 91–101). New York: Plenum.

Schank, R. (1982). *Dynamic memory: A theory of learning in computers and people*. Cambridge: Cambridge University Press.

Schank, R. C., & Abelson, R. (1977). *Scripts, plans, goals, and understanding*. Hillsdale, NJ: Lawrence Erlbaum Associates.

Schneider, W. (1987). Connectionism: Is it a paradigm shift for psychology? *Behavior Research Methods, Instruments, & Computers, 19*, 73–83.

Schwantes, F. M. (1985). Expectancy, integration, and interactional processes: Age differences in the nature of words affected by sentence context. *Journal of Experimental Child Psychology, 39*, 212–229.

Seaton, H. (1977). The effects of a visual perception training program on reading achievement. *Journal of Reading Behavior, 9*, 188–192.

Seidenberg, M. (1985). The time course of information activation and utilization in visual word recognition. In D. Besner, T. Waller, & G. MacKinnon (Eds.), *Reading research: Advances in theory and practice* (Vol. 5, pp. 199–252). New York: Academic Press.

Seidenberg, M. S., Bruck, M., Fornarolo, G., & Backman, J. (1985). Word recognition processes of poor and disabled readers? Do they necessarily differ? *Applied Psycholinguists, 6*, 161–180.

Sejnowski, T. J., & Rosenberg, C. R. (1986). *NETtalk: A parallel network that learns to read aloud*. (Tech. Rep. No. JHU/EECS-86/01). Baltimore: Johns Hopkins University, Department of Electrical Engineering and Computer Science.

Shankweiler, D., & Liberman, I. (1972). Misreading: A search for causes. In J. Kavanagh & I. Mattingly (Eds.), *Language by ear and eye*. (pp. 293–317). Cambridge: MIT Press.

Shankweiler, D., & Liberman, I. (1978). Reading behavior in dyslexia: Is there a distinctive pattern? *Bulletin of the Orton Society, 28*, 114–123.

Shankweiler, D., Liberman, I., Mark, L., Fowler, C., & Fischer, F. (1979). The speech code and learning to read. *Journal of Experimental Psychology: Human Learning and Memory, 5*, 531–545.

Share, D. L., McGee, R., McKenzie, D., Williams, S., & Silva, P. A. (1987). Further evidence relating to the distinction between specific reading retardation and general reading backwardness. *British Journal of Developmental Psychology*, *5*, 35–44.

Sharkey, N. E., & Mitchell, D. C. (1985). Word recognition in a functional context: The use of scripts in reading. *Journal of Memory and Language*, *24*, 253–270.

Sharon, A. T. (1973–1974). What do adults read? *Reading Research Quarterly*, *9*, 148–169.

Shepard, L. (1980). An evaluation of the regression discrepancy method for identifying children with learning disabilities. *The Journal of Special Education*, *14*, 79–91.

Short, E. J., & Ryan, E. B. (1984). Metacognitive differences between skilled and less skilled readers: Remediating deficits through story grammar and attribution training. *Journal of Educational Psychology*, *76*, 225–235.

Siegel, H. (1987). *Relativism refuted: A critique of contemporary epistemological relativism.* Dordrecht, The Netherlands: D. Reidel.

Siegel, L. S. (1985). Psycholinguistic aspects of reading disabilities. In L. Siegel & F. Morrison (Eds.), *Cognitive development in atypical children* (pp. 45–65). New York: Springer-Verlag.

Siegel, L. S. (1988). Evidence that IQ scores are irrelevant to the definition and analysis of reading disability. *Canadian Journal of Psychology*, *42*, 201–215.

Siegel, L. S., & Faux, D. (1989). Acquisition of certain grapheme-phoneme correspondences in normally achieving and disabled readers. *Reading and Writing: An Interdisciplinary Journal*, *1*, 37–52.

Siegel, L.S., & Ryan, E. (1984). Reading disability as a language disorder. *Remedial and Special Education*, *5*, 28–33.

Silva, P. A., McGee, R., & Williams, S. (1985). Some characteristics of 9-year-old boys with general reading backwardness or specific reading retardation. *Journal of Child Psychology and Psychiatry*, *26*, 407–421.

Singer, M. (1979). Processes of inference during sentence encoding. *Memory & Cognition*, *7*, 192–200.

Singer, M. (1980). The role of case-filling inferences in the coherence of brief passages. *Discourse Processes*, *3*, 185–201.

Singer, M. (1988). Inferences in reading comprehension. In M. Daneman, G. E. MacKinnon, & T. G. Waller (Eds.), *Reading research: Advances in theory and practice* (Vol. 6, pp. 177–219). San Diego: Academic Press.

Slaghuis, W. L., & Lovegrove, W. S. (1985). Spatial-frequency dependent visible persistence and specific reading disability. *Brain & Language*, *4*, 219–240.

Slaghuis, W. L., & Lovegrove, W. S. (1987). The effect of field size and luminance on spatial-frequency dependent visible persistence and specific reading disability. *Bulletin of the Psychonomic Society*, *25*, 38–40.

Smiley, S., Oakley, D., Worthen, D., Campione, J., & Brown, A. (1977). Recall of thematically relevant material by adolescent good and poor readers as a function of written versus oral presentation. *Journal of Educational Psychology*, *69*, 381–387.

Smith, F. (1971). *Understanding reading.* New York: Holt, Rinehart & Winston.

Smith, F. (1973). *Psycholinguistics and reading.* New York: Holt, Rinehart & Winston.

Smith, H. K. (1967). The responses of good and poor readers when asked to read for different purposes. *Reading Research Quarterly*, *3*, 53–84.

Snowling, M. (1980). The development of grapheme-phoneme correspondence in normal and dyslexia readers. *Journal of Experimental Child Psychology*, *29*, 294–305.

Snowling, M. (1987). *Dyslexia.* Oxford: Basil Blackwell.

Sperling, G. (1967). Successive approximations to a model for short-term memory. *Acta Psychologica*, *27*, 285–292.

Spillich, G. J., Vesonder, G. T., Chiesi, H. L., & Voss, J. F. (1979). Text processing of domain-related information for individuals with high and low domain knowledge. *Journal of Verbal Learning and Verbal Behavior, 18*, 275–290.

Spiro, R. J., Bruce, B. C., & Brewer, W. F. (Eds.). (1980). *Theoretical issues in reading comprehension*. Hillsdale, NJ: Lawrence Erlbaum Associates.

Stanley, G. (1976). The processing of digits by children with specific reading disability. *British Journal of Educational Psychology, 46*, 81–84.

Stanley, G., Smith, G., & Howell, E. (1983). Eye movements and sequential tracking in dyslexic and control children. *British Journal of Psychology, 74*, 181–187.

Stanovich, K. E. (1978). Information processing in mentally retarded individuals. In N. R. Ellis (Ed.), *International review of research in mental retardation* (Vol. 9, pp. 29–60). New York: Academic Press.

Stanovich, K. E. (1980). Toward an interactive-compensatory model of individual differences in the development of reading fluency. *Reading Research Quarterly, 16*, 32–71.

Stanovich, K. E. (1981). Relationships between word-decoding speed, general name-retrieval ability, and reading progress in first-grade children. *Journal of Educational Psychology, 73*, 809–815.

Stanovich, K. E. (1982). Individual differences in the cognitive processes of reading I: Word decoding. *Journal of Learning Disabilities, 15*, 485–493.

Stanovich, K. E. (1984). The interactive-compensatory model of reading: A confluence of developmental, experimental, and educational psychology. *Remedial and Special Education, 5*, 11–19.

Stanovich, K. E. (1986a). Cognitive processes and the reading problems of learning disabled children: Evaluating the assumption of specificity. In J. Torgesen & B. Wong (Eds.), *Psychological and educational perspectives on learning disabilities* (pp. 87–131). New York: Academic Press.

Stanovich, K. E. (1986b). Matthew effects in reading: Some consequences of individual differences in the acquisition of literacy. *Reading Research Quarterly, 21*, 360–407.

Stanovich, K. E. (1987). Perspectives on segmental analysis and alphabetic literacy. *Cahiers Psychologie Cognitive, 7*, 514–519.

Stanovich, K. E. (1988a). Explaining the differences between the dyslexic and the garden-variety poor reader: The phonological-core variable-difference model. *Journal of Learning Disabilities, 21*, 590–612.

Stanovich, K. E. (1988b). The right and wrong places to look for the cognitive locus of reading disability. *Annals of Dyslexia, 38*, 154–177.

Stanovich, K. E. (1990). Concepts in Developmental Theories of Reading Skill: Cognitive Resources, Automaticity, and Modularity. *Developmental Review, 10*, 72–100.

Stanovich, K. E., Cunningham, A. E., & Cramer, B. (1984). Assessing phonological awareness in kindergarten children: Issues of task comparability. *Journal of Experimental Child Psychology, 38*, 175–190.

Stanovich, K., Cunningham, A., & Feeman, D. (1984). Intelligence, cognitive skills, and early reading progress. *Reading Research Quarterly, 19*, 278–303.

Stanovich, K. E., Nathan, R. G., West, R. F., & Vala-Rossi, M. (1985). Children's word recognition in context: Spreading activation, expectancy, and modularity. *Child Development, 56*, 1418–1429.

Stanovich, K. E., Nathan, R. G., & Zolman, J. E. (1988). The developmental lag hypothesis in reading: Longitudinal and matched reading-level comparisons. *Child Development, 59*, 71–86.

Stanovich, K. E., & West, R. F. (1979). Mechanisms of sentence context effects in reading: Automatic activation and conscious attention. *Memory & Cognition, 7*, 77–85.

Stanovich, K. E., & West, R. F. (1983). On priming by a sentence context. *Journal of Experimental Psychology: General, 112*, 1–36.

Stanovich, K. E., West, R. F., & Feeman, D. J. (1981). A longitudinal study of sentence context effects in second-grade children: Tests of an interactive-compensatory model. *Journal of Experimental Child Psychology, 32*, 185–199.

Stanovich, K. E., & West, R. F. (1989). Exposure to print and orthographic processing. *Reading Research Quarterly*, *24*, 402–433.

Steffensen, M. S., Joag-Dev, C., & Anderson, R. C. (1979). A cross-cultural perspective on reading comprehension. *Reading Research Quarterly*, *15*, 10–29.

Sternberg, R. J. (1985). Controlled versus automatic processing. *Behavioral and Brain Sciences*, *8*, 32–33.

Sticht, T. G., & James, J. H. (1984). Listening and reading. In P. D. Pearson (Ed.), *Handbook of reading research* (pp. 293–317). New York: Longman.

Swanson, L. (1978). Verbal encoding effects on the visual short-term memory of learning-disabled and normal readers. *Journal of Educational Psychology*, *70*, 539–544.

Swanson, L. (1983). A study of nonstrategic linguistic coding on visual recall of learning-disabled readers. *Journal of Learning Disabilities*, *16*, 209–216.

Tanenhaus, M. K., Dell, G. S., & Carlson, G. (1987). Context effects in lexical processing: A connectionist approach to modularity. In J. Garfield (Ed.), *Modularity in knowledge representation and natural language understanding*. Cambridge, MA: MIT Press.

Tanenhaus, M. K., & Lucas, M. M. (1987). Context effects in lexical processing. *Cognition*, *25*, 213–234.

Taylor, B. M. (1985). Good and poor readers' recall of familiar and unfamiliar text. In H. Singer & R. Ruddell (Eds.), *Theoretical models and processes of reading* (3rd ed.) (pp. 494–500). Newark, DE: International Reading Association.

Taylor, H. G., Lean, D., & Schwartz, S. (1989). Pseudoword repetition ability in learning-disabled children. *Applied Psycholinguistics*, *10*, 203–219.

Taylor, S. (1965). Eye movements while reading: Facts and fallacies. *American Educational Research Journal*, *2*, 187–202.

Thorndike, E. L. (1917). Reading as reasoning: A study of mistakes in paragraph reading. *Journal of Educational Psychology*, *8*, 323–332.

Thorndike, R. L. (1973–1974). Reading as reasoning. *Reading Research Quarterly*, *2*, 135–147.

Tinker, M. (1958). Recent studies of eye movements in reading. *Psychological Bulletin*, *55*, 215–231.

Torgesen, J. (1975). Problems and prospects in the study of learning disabilities. In M. Hetherington & J. Hagen (Eds.), *Review of child development research*. (Vol. 5, pp. 1–25). New York: Russell Sage Foundation.

Torgesen, J. (1977a). Memorization processes in reading-disabled children. *Journal of Educational Psychology*, *69*, 571–578.

Torgesen, J. (1977b). The role of nonspecific factors in the task performance of learning disabled children: A theoretical assessment. *Journal of Learning Disabilities*, *10*, 27–34.

Torgesen, J. (1978–1979). Performance of reading disabled children on serial memory tasks. *Reading Research Quarterly*, *14*, 57–87.

Torgesen, J. (1979). What shall we do with psychological processes? *Journal of Learning Disabilities*, *12*, 514–521.

Torgesen, J. (1980). Conceptual and educational implications of the use of efficient task strategies by learning-disabled children. *Journal of Learning Disabilities*, *13*, 364–371.

Torgesen, J., & Goldman, T. (1977). Verbal rehearsal and short-term memory in reading disabled children. *Child Development*, *48*, 56–60.

Torgesen, J., & Houck, D. (1980). Processing deficiencies of learning-disabled children who perform poorly on the digit span test. *Journal of Educational Psychology*, *72*, 141–160.

Torneus, M. (1984). Phonological awareness and reading: A chicken and egg problem? *Journal of Educational Psychology*, *70*, 1346–1358.

Toulmin, S. (1970). Does the distinction between normal and revolutionary science hold water? In I.

Lakatos & A. Musgrave (Eds.), *Criticism and the growth of knowledge* (pp. 39–47). Cambridge: Cambridge University Press.

Treiman, R., & Baron, J. (1983). Phonemic-analysis training helps children benefit from spelling-sound rules. *Memory & Cognition, 11*, 382–389.

Tunmer, W. E., & Nesdale, A. R. (1985). Phonemic segmentation skill and beginning reading. *Journal of Educational Psychology, 77*, 417–427.

Valtin, R. (1978–1979). Dyslexia: Deficit in reading or deficit in research? *Reading Research Quarterly, 14*, 201–221.

Venezky, R. L. (1982). The origins of the present-day chasm between adult literacy needs and school literacy instruction. *Visible Language, 16*, 113–126.

Vellutino, F. (1979). *Dyslexia: Theory and research*. Cambridge, MA: MIT Press.

Vellutino, F., & Scanlon, D. (1987). Phonological coding, phonological awareness, and reading ability: Evidence from a longitudinal and experimental study. *Merrill-Palmer quarterly, 33*, 321–363.

Venezky, R. L. (1982). The origins of the present-day chasm between adult literacy needs and school literacy instruction. *Visible Language, 16*, 113–126.

Voss, J. F. (1984). On learning and learning from text. In H. Mandl, N. L. Stein, & T. Trabasso (Eds.), *Learning and comprehension of text* (pp. 193–212). Hillsdale, NJ: Lawrence Erlbaum Associates.

Wagner, R. K. (1988). Causal relations between the development of phonological processing abilities and the acquisition of reading skills: A meta-analysis. *Merrill-Palmer Quarterly, 34*, 261–279.

Wagner, R. K., & Sternberg, R. J. (1987). Executive control in reading comprehension. In B. K. Britton & S. M. Glynn (Eds.), *Executive control processes in reading* (pp. 1–21). Hillsdale, NJ: Lawrence Erlbaum Associates.

Wagner, R. K., & Torgesen, J. K. (1987). The nature of phonological processing and its causal role in the acquisition of reading skills. *Psychological Bulletin, 101*, 192–212.

Werker, J. F., & Tees, R. C. (1987). Speech perception in severely disabled and average reading children. *Canadian Journal of Psychology, 41*, 48–61.

Whitney, P. (1986). Processing category terms in context: Instantiations as inferences. *Memory & Cognition, 14*, 39–48.

Whitney, P. (1987). Psychological theories of elaborative inferences: Implications for schema-theoretic views of comprehension. *Reading Research Quarterly, 22*, 299–310.

Whitney, P., & Kellas, G. (1984). Processing category terms in context: Instantiation and the structure of semantic categories. *Journal of Experimental Psychology: Learning, Memory, & Cognition, 10*, 95–103.

Wilkinson, A. (1980). Children's understanding in reading and listening. *Journal of Educational Psychology, 72*, 561–574.

Williams, J. (1980). Teaching decoding with an emphasis on phoneme analysis and phoneme blending. *Journal of Educational Psychology, 72*, 1–15.

Williams, J. (1984). Phonemic analysis and how it relates to reading. *Journal of Learning Disabilities, 17*, 240–245.

Wittrock, M. C. (1974). Learning as a generative process. *Educational Psychologist, 11*, 87–95.

Wittrock, M. C. (1978). The cognitive movement in instruction. *Educational Psychologist, 13*, 15–29.

Wixson, K. K., & Peters, C. W. (1987). Comprehension assessment: Implementing an interactive view of reading. *Educational Psychologist, 22*, 333–356.

Wolf, M., & Goodglass, H. (1986). Dyslexia, dysnomia, and lexical retrieval: A longitudinal investigation. *Brain and Language, 28*, 154–168.

Wong, B., Wong, R., & Foth, D. (1977). Recall and clustering of verbal materials among normal and poor readers. *Bulletin of Psychonomic Society, 10,* 375–378.

Yopp, H. K. (1988). The validity and reliability of phonemic awareness tests. *Reading Research Quarterly, 23,* 159–177.

Yuill, N., & Oakhill, J. (1988). Effects of inference awareness training on poor reading comprehension. *Applied Cognitive Psychology, 2,* 33–45.

Zabrucky, K., & Ratner, H. H. (1986). Children's comprehension monitoring and recall of inconsistent stories. *Child Development, 57,* 1401–1418.

2

Going Beyond the Problem as Given: Problem Solving in Expert and Novice Writers

Mary Bryson
University of British Columbia

Carl Bereiter
Marlene Scardamalia
Elana Joram
Ontario Institute for Studies in Education

Paris Review Interviewer: "Are there any tricks or devices that seem to help?"

Elizabeth Hardwick (Author): "For me, writing has not become easier after all these years. It is harder—perhaps because of the standards you set for your work. I suppose you have, by effort, a greater command than you imagine. The fact that writing remains so difficult is what puzzles." (Writers at Work, Vol. 7, p. 131)

Common sense wisdom suggests that for novices and experts alike, written composition is a difficult and complex task. The argument (e.g., Ferreiro, 1984) that the acquisition of literacy skills represents a cognitively sophisticated developmental achievement for young learners (or for society; e.g., Havelock, 1986) is not particularly counterintuitive. However, it is not so intrinsically obvious to explain why writing tasks might remain problematic despite (or in spite of) the acquisition of expert levels of domain-relevant competence. Nor is it necessarily the case that the same set of factors makes writing tasks difficult for both novices and experts. Perhaps writing is so demanding because it is a complex task that is best tackled as a problem solving endeavor (i.e., with a well-regulated application of strategies, monitoring, automated subprocedures, and appropriate content knowledge), but is, in essence, a task in which no problem is given. The theme, story line, or argument must be constructed by the author through cycles of deliberative thinking directed toward constructing a problem representation that includes multiple constraints (e.g., originality, coherence, and interestingness).

In this chapter, we review literature on the composing processes of both novice and expert writers and discuss research pertaining to the question of how expert-like problem solving in written composition is fostered by instruction. We review two models of competence in written composition, which are differentiated according to level of expertise in the domain. We start by exploring domain-general aspects of expertise as well as the unique demands of written composition. This approach may help us to see the relationship between the exigencies of literacy and the radically different ways in which experts and novices cope with written composition tasks.

In this chapter, *written composition* refers to academic-type writing tasks, the object of which is both to inquire into a particular topic and also to inform or persuade one or more readers of the fruits of an investigation. Such tasks might include opinion-type assignments such as: "Should children be able to choose the subjects they study in school?" (from Bereiter, Burtis, & Scardamalia, 1988), or informative-type assignments such as: "Write about your job for the readers of *Seventeen* magazine, 13–14-year-old girls" (from Flower & Hayes, 1980). Excluded by this definition are other kinds of writing tasks, such as storying, writing a shopping list, or composing a set of directions. In characterizing problem solving in written composition, we restrict our discussion to the kinds of knowledge that appear to play a central role in the inquiry processes which culminate in the production of both new knowledge and texts; namely, content knowledge, discourse knowledge, and higher-order, or metacognitive knowledge (that is, epistemological knowledge and regulatory skills). We do not consider at length the role played by, or the acquisition of, handwriting, spelling, linguistic, or grammatical knowledge.

COMPLEX PROBLEM SOLVING

Expertise and Problem Solving

In virtually every area where problem solving expertise has been studied, a consistent pattern of change has been observed as expertise increases (for integrative reviews, see Larkin, McDermott, Simon, & Simon, 1980, or Lesgold, 1984). Beginners must construct solution paths by laborious means-ends analysis, often working backward from the goal to identify subgoals that will advance them toward a solution. Experts, by contrast, are able to move from their starting place to the goal by a more efficient forward-acting process. This is made possible by their having accumulated a large repertoire of problem schemata. They can recognize the immediate situation as an instance of some problem type and then apply previously learned procedures appropriate to the problem type. For example, Lesgold, Feltovich, Glaser, and Wang (1981) reported that in the domain of radiology, expert physicians make use of organized and elaborated anatomical knowledge retrieved in the form of schemata in order to diagnose pathologies from patterns seen in x-ray plates. Likewise, in the domain of chess, Chase and Simon (1973) found that chess masters could quickly and efficiently recognize and retrieve appropriate moves in response to 10,000–100,000 meaningful board patterns. Thus, in certain domains, experts appear to solve complex—though familiar—problems by making strategic use of extensive and well-structured domain knowledge, rather than relying on effortful problem solving procedures (Larkin, 1981; Simon & Simon, 1978).

Writing as Problem Solving

Although no comparable research has been done on expert writers, it seems likely that they must also acquire a vast number of schemata applicable to writing problems. Yet, testimonies of professional writers, like that of Elizabeth Hardwick at the beginning of the chapter, indicate that for many of them, writing never becomes easy. Writers' notebooks, such as those of Dostoyevsky (1860/1971), display agonizing amounts of means-ends analysis, not to mention false starts, clutching at straws, expressions of discouragement and dismay—all the behaviors of people not in command of their craft. Thinking-aloud protocols analyzed in research on the composing processes of expert writers (e.g., Berkenkotter, 1983; Flower & Hayes, 1980) reveal a tremendous investment of mental effort in the elaboration, the coordination, and the execution of complex goals and subgoals, such as how to shape content for a particular audience, how to express conceptual intentions in the language of prose, or how to construct a catchy title. To add to the paradox, there are indications that for many novices— ordinary school children—writing is handled in a manner normally characteristic of experts. Given a writing assignment, they set to work and proceed directly toward their goal in a forward-acting manner. Their thinking-aloud protocols reveal hardly any means-ends analysis; false starts and uncertainties as to how to proceed are rare (see Bereiter & Scardamalia, 1987).

Another significant characteristic of writing is that it involves solving problems at a number of different levels, with considerable interaction among levels (Beaugrande, 1984; McCutchen, 1986). Interaction here means that solutions achieved at one level influence those at another. A choice of text organization, for instance, may affect the kinds of arguments that may be advanced, or a choice of type of appeal to make to readers may constrain the choice of vocabulary. Differences in writing expertise may appear both in the levels of problems addressed (inexpert writers may simply fail to address certain high-level problems) and in the extent of interaction among levels (inexpert writers may solve problems of syntax, organization, and content in relative isolation, whereas experts solve them in an integrative way).

Beaugrande (1984) proposed a "multilevel parallel-stage interaction model" of composing processes (see Fig. 2.1), which focuses on the kinds of symbolic

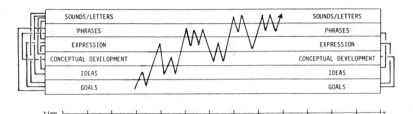

FIG. 2.1.   A parallel-stage interaction model. From "Text production: Toward a science of composition" by R. de Beaugrande, 1984: Ablex Publishing.

structures manipulated during text production and on the interactions between component processes. A critical feature of this model is that the organization of component processes is based on notions of parallel interactive processing (e.g., Hinton & Anderson, 1981; Rumelhart & McClelland, 1982), such that activity at any single level can influence (and be influenced by) activity at any other level/levels of the model. As the model depicted in Fig. 2.1 suggests, the various levels are organized so as to represent "processing depth," with the shallowest level at the top (Sounds/Letters) and the deepest at the bottom (Goals). The jagged line moving from left to right suggests that, with time, composing-related thinking gradually shifts from primarily deep to primarily shallow levels of processing, albeit with considerable allowances for departures from a simple linear trend. Beaugrande suggests that it is critical for student-writers to automatize text production factors, such as mechanics, due to the heavy processing load created by the coordination of writing processes.

Flower and Hayes (1980, 1981) emphasized both the goal-directed and the recursive nature of problem solving during writing, and suggested that much mental effort during composing is directed toward the elaboration and coordination of plans designed to reduce cognitive strain. These authors noted that: "As a dynamic process, writing is the act of dealing with an excessive number of simultaneous demands or constraints. Viewed this way, a writer in the act is a thinker on a full-time cognitive overload" (p. 33).

To view writing as problem solving, therefore, is to view it in a somewhat paradoxical light. The paradox can be largely removed by adopting the premise that expert and nonexpert are solving different problems. This premise is reasonable because of the ill-structured nature of writing problems. In particular, the goal state in writing tasks is usually defined in only general terms, leaving the specification up to the writer. Consequently, it is possible for writers who are ostensibly engaged in carrying out the same assignment to be pursuing radically different goals. Even allowing for differences in goals, however, there remain some serious questions about problem solving in novice and expert writers. These questions have to do with the cognitive load imposed by the sheer multiplicity of problems that must be addressed or circumvented in some way in order for written composition to proceed. Although the overload conception of writing difficulty seems plausible and has been endorsed by many commentators, it immediately raises two questions:

1. Why, if the cognitive load is so high, does it not prove crippling to novice writers, for whom few of the subcomponents of writing have been automated? Why does the process not break down altogether for them? That it does not is evident to anyone walking into a well-conducted elementary school writing session, with children peacefully absorbed in what appears to be for them a pleasant and rewarding process. Biemiller, Gang, and Regan (1986) found that elementary children typically compose at close to their maximum handwriting speed, which argues strongly against the notion that they are being overwhelmed by the additional cognitive demands of the task.

2. Why are written composition problems not perceptibly easier for experts than for novices? Or, to put it differently, why, given that goals are under the command of the writer, do expert writers keep redefining writing problems so as to maintain a high level of difficulty? Clearly, certain writing subskills, such as transcription and spelling, become perceptibly easier and less resource-demanding as efficacy and automaticity increase. Nonetheless, expert writers' systematic escalation of problem complexity ensures that writing remains a difficult task despite the acquisition of sophisticated domain-specific expertise.

We believe that the answers to both of these questions depend on the different models of the composing process that characterize novice and expert writers. One is a model that avoids many of the problems of writing and that, even for relatively young writers, makes efficient use of highly practiced skills. The other is a model that contains within it a dynamic that tends to escalate the complexity of writing problems. Before describing these models and the answers that they suggest to these questions, however, we need to look at empirical evidence bearing on how experts and novices deal with the major varieties of problems involved in writing and the knowledge resources that they have available for doing so.

PROBLEMS IN WRITTEN COMPOSITION

Goal Formulation and Planning

In complex problem solving tasks, planning serves to bridge the gap between an initial state and a final goal state by providing a manageable set of signposts for negotiating uncharted territory. Thus, a good plan reduces a large and unmanageable problem into a series of reasonable subproblems (Miller, Galanter, & Pribram, 1960). Expert writers are trying to deal with multiple goals simultaneously during composing, such as goals pertaining to truth and novelty of the content as well as clarity and interestingness of the final text (Hayes & Flower, 1986; Scardamalia & Paris, 1985). Breuleux (1987) used Frederiksen's (1975, 1987) propositional analysis system in order to conduct detailed analyses of the thinking-aloud protocols of expert writers. He reported that writers plan extensively throughout composing, and that their plans are typically shallow so as to "allow contextual refinements or inexpensive reorganizations at lower levels according to local properties of the problem-state" (p. 1). This view of planning is consistent with data gathered from expert and nonexpert writers' thinking-aloud protocols reported by Flower and Hayes (1980), who suggested that: "Good plans are rich enough to work from and argue about, but cheap enough to throw away" (p. 43).

As Flower and Hayes suggested, the expert writer is dealing with an entirely different range of problems during composing from those faced by the novice. For the expert writer, the writing problem is not given by the topic statement, but emerges in multiple attempts made by the writer to: (a) interpret the significance of the topic on a different, generally more abstract level; and (b) transform the topic so that it can be placed within a personally meaningful epistemological perspective. Studies which have compared expert and novice writers reveal that, indeed, skilled writers' thinking-aloud protocols exhibit a high density of goal-directed epistemological search operations in the construction and solution of problems throughout composing (Bereiter, Burtis, & Scardamalia, 1988; Berkenhotter, 1983; Breuleux, 1987; Flower & Hayes, 1980; Paris, 1986; Scardamalia & Paris, 1985). The expert writer's goals for a given text are described as "emergent"; that is, whereas the writer represents various general or superordinate goals at the beginning of a writing session, subgoals are constructed on-line during composing, which may modify, in significant ways, the nature of the initial goal structure.

Novice writers' thinking-aloud protocols typically reveal little or no planning activity (Burtis, Bereiter, Scardamalia, & Tetroe, 1983; Hayes & Flower, 1986; Perl, 1979). Amount of planning appears largely to be a function of level of expertise in writing, and not primarily an age-related, developmental phenomenon. The college-age novice writers in Perl's study started writing a few minutes after getting the topic, initiated a string of free association searches to particular words in the topic sentence as their primary content planning strategy, and interrupted content-related thinking frequently with surface-feature concerns about spelling or punctuation. At the earliest stages of written language development, planning seems to consist of activities such as drawing pictures or making telegraphic notes that are designed to delimit a chunk of content that will reappear unchanged in the final text. In an ethnographic study of a first grade student's composing behaviors, Himley (1988) suggested that for emergent writers, the task of writing is conflated with surface features of the final product, and there appears to be little or no awareness of the communicative or intentional dimensions of writing. For school-age writers, planning appears to consist of the elaboration of content rather than the representation of goals and subgoals for achieving specific rhetorical or ideational effects. Scardamalia and Paris (1985) reported that when school-age writers were asked to state their main goal after writing, they tended to provide a summary of their main idea, or to rephrase the topic. Likewise, when asked to recall details of text, such as how often they had used a certain word, novice writers relied almost exclusively on their memory of surface features of their texts whereas expert writers made reference to goal statements as a means to reconstruct textual features.

Content Generation

Beaugrande suggests that this level of processing includes: "all activities that create an IDEA: a configuration of conceptual content that acts as a control center for building the text-world model (the total configuration of knowledge activated for processing the text" (p. 109). This implies a good deal more than "thinking of what to say." It is a problem at one level higher in abstraction than generating particular items of content. It is the level at which main ideas or main points are determined. Bereiter, Burtis, and Scardamalia (1988) reported that expert writers spent significantly longer than novices in the development of main points during composing. The expert writers' main points were rated as representing a substantial transformation of the topic assignment, which indicates that mental effort was invested in "going beyond the problem as given." These authors also presented evidence from path analyses that suggests that the effect of age on the rated quality of text-based statements of main point was almost entirely mediated by amount of problem solving during composing. Novice writers arrived at their main points in half a minute or less and devoted the rest of their composing time to generating specific content.

The extent to which writers exhibit on-line construction of ideas, themes, or main points during text composition is mediated by the problem representation (Flower & Hayes, 1980). Flower and Hayes reported a study in which thinking-aloud protocols were collected from both expert and novice writers in response to the topic: "Write about your job for the readers of Seventeen magazine, 13–14-year-old girls." Analyses of the expert writers' thinking-aloud protocols in this study indicated that a great deal of thinking was directed toward the elaboration of what the authors refer to as a "rhetorical problem," which consists of "information about the rhetorical situation and information about the writer's own purpose and goals" (p. 25). The authors reported that the expert writers generated most of their ideas (67%) by setting goals related to the rhetorical problem. Novice writers, by contrast, generated the majority of their ideas (83%) in response to the assigned topic.

The contribution of domain knowledge to content generation processes in written composition has received very little substantive attention by researchers working in this area. Folk wisdom about writing has it that we write best about what we know best. No evidence has yet been reported that would permit a definitive judgment about the truth-value of this widely accepted notion. In other related domains, such as socio-political argumentation (Voss, Greene, Post, & Penner, 1983), expert-novice studies have revealed that domain knowledge substantively influences problem solving processes. Scardamalia, Bereiter, and Woodruff (1980) report a study in which elementary school children wrote two compositions, one on a high-familiarity topic and one on a low-familiarity topic. Text-based analyses showed no effect of topic familiarity on any dependent measures. McCutchen (1986) investigated the role of domain knowledge (football) on texts written by children from Grades 4, 6, and 8. Analyses of texts included measures of local coherence, hierarchical conceptual structure, and level of detail of content. Results indicate that high-knowledge students, irrespective of age, wrote texts about football which were more coherent and included more elaborative detail than did low-knowledge students. Neither of these studies sheds any light on how domain knowledge might influence a writer's thinking processes during text composition.

Written Language Production

In addition to attending to the development of an ideational structure, writers also have to devote cognitive resources to a multiplicity of text production processes, such as handwriting, spelling, punctuation, word choice, and style. Beaugrande (1984) used the term *linearization* to describe the process of mapping ideational content (nonlinearly structured) onto language expressions (linearly structured). Collins and Gentner (1980) suggested that idea production and text production are two different categories of processes which are best dealt with in successive, separate stages. They argued that "one of the most damaging habits for a novice writer to have is that of confusing idea manipulation with text manipulation . . . the effort to perfect text may cause the writer to lose track of the desired content" (p. 53). The extent to which linearization processes compete with cognitive resources required by higher-order processes in novice and expert writers suggests a nonlinear, U-shaped relationship between competence and attention devoted to text production factors.

Primary grade children frequently subvocalize words and letters during transcription (Simon, 1973), suggesting a lack of automaticity with transcription. King and Rentel (1981) found that the dictated stories of first and second graders were more fully developed than their handwritten texts, suggesting adverse cognitive effects resulting from a lack of fluency in transcription processes. Scardamalia, Bereiter, and Goelman (1982) reported that by Grade 4, however, the mechanics of writing are automatized, and no longer compete for cognitive resources. Zbrodoff (1984) found that fifth graders required about 3 seconds of start-up time after being assigned a topic before launching directly into text production, suggesting that linearization poses few problems for novice writers once transcription has been automatized. McCutchen (1988) argued that one of the critical facets of expert writers' thinking consists of the development of strategic control over text production processes. She included a segment from an experienced writer's protocol (generated in preparing an editorial column for a newspaper) that indicates continuous interaction between levels (as in Beaugrande, 1984) as follows:

> I'm in a delicate situation as far as commenting on unions in that I'm management here and I'm also a member of a union; I'm a member of AFTRA. So I'm going to point that out immediately in my answer to this letter because if I don't, I would think it would have some effect on my credibility.
>
> I'm trying to think of how to phrase this labor and management relationship. (pause) I'll contrast my two stands.
>
> I don't want to confuse the issue any more than I have to so I'm going to change an "incarnation" to a "hat." (p. 309)

Evidence in support of McCutchen's argument that expert writers devote attention to written language production problems was reported by Kaufer, Hayes, and Flower (1986), who found that: (a) the subprocesses involved in the construction of written sentences are available to conscious control at the level of plans and intentions; and (b) text production processes can, likewise, exert reciprocal control over higher level concerns.

Reprocessing

Data from studies of writers' revision activities reveal conclusively that experts, in sharp contrast to novices, (a) think of revision as a process of rethinking that can be applied to mental entities, like main points, goals, and plans, as well as to textual entities, such as words and sentences (Flower, Hayes, Carey, Schriver, & Stratman, 1986; Murray, 1978); (b) engage in significantly more revision than novices (Sommers, 1980); and (c) make substantive changes to texts that are correlated with higher ratings of text quality (Bridwell, 1980).

Summary

Clearly, expert writers are wrestling with problems during composing which bear little resemblance to those faced by novices. Yet novices manage to generate texts and novice writing can produce relatively sophisticated compositions (Hairston, 1984). Therefore, at this point, we deal with the exigencies of written language and discuss the cognitive requirements of composition tasks which might induce typical novice composing strategies.

ALTERNATIVE ORGANIZATIONS
OF THE COMPOSING PROCESS

In Plato's Phaedrus, Socrates has a great deal to say about written composition that is relevant to our consideration of the problematic nature of written composition. Socrates argued that because written texts are composed without the input and "benevolent disputation" provided in the social context afforded by dialogue, writers will be tempted to compose unreflectively, thereby committing unworthy ideas to a text form whose permanence provides the illusion of substantive content. Socrates contrasts the goals of a philologist, or lover of discourses, with those of a philomathist, or lover of learning. He notes that in order to compose texts, the lover of discourses relies on formulaic discourse knowledge provided by rhetorical devices that are superficially used as a "form of flattery . . . a routine and a knack". For the lover of learning, content knowledge, discourse forms, and rhetorical devices are subordinated during the composing process to a superordinate goal characterized by an unending search for the truth. Socrates argues that this search is optimally carried out in a dynamic social context.

In a similar vein, Plato (1925/1987) suggested that:

> The study of virtue and vice must be accompanied by an inquiry into what is false and what is true of existence in general and must be carried on by constant practice throughout a long period. . . . After practicing detailed comparisons of names and definitions and visual and other sense perceptions, after scrutinizing them in benevolent disputation by the use of question and answer without jealousy, at last in a flash of understanding of each blazes up, and the mind as it exerts all its powers to the limit of human capacity, is flooded with light. (p. 344b)

Socrates distinguished between two kinds of discourse, one of which has relatively little engagement with the higher levels of mental life and the other of which is seen as vital to them. The first can be carried out by the solitary writer but the second requires disputation. Since Socrates' day, however, writing has evolved into forms that are capable of supporting deeply reflective thought without the direct involvement of disputants. What Olson (1977) calls *essayist technique* utilizes the internal constraints of written text itself to achieve logical consistency, explanatory adequacy, and the like. Thus, writing, is this highly literate form, may be seen as a cultural invention over and above the inventions of written language itself. Plato's dialogues, which preserve the forms and substance of oral disputation, refined into written text, may be seen as a transitional form in the development of an epistemically powerful form of writing.

Analysts of literacy (Goody, 1968; Havelock, 1986; Olson, 1977; Ong, 1982) have generally sought to explain its epistemic effects on the basis of characteristics of written language and text and the conditions under which it is produced and read. These considerations fail, however, to provide answers to the questions raised by expert-novice differences. They do not explain why literate people in modern societies may fail to master essayist technique and instead produce the kind of unreflective prose that Socrates warned against. They suggest why writing may be difficult, but they do not explain the twin questions of why it is not overwhelmingly difficult for novices and why it does not eventually get easier for many experts. For the beginnings of answers to these questions, it seems necessary to look into the cognitive processes involved in essayist technique, in comparison to those involved in more casual or superficial writing.

The Dialectic Between Rhetorical and Content Problems

There are numerous testimonials from writers indicating that writing itself plays an important role in the development of their understanding (Murray, 1978). Henry Miller suggested that: "Writing, like life itself, is a voyage of discovery." In a recent interview, Sam Shepard (Sessums, 1988) said that:

> The great thing about writing is that in the course of going after it, it teaches you something. You start out thinking you know something about it, but then you discover you hardly know anything. And the more you do it, the more things begin to inform you about where you're going. (p. 78)

Likewise, Robert Frost reported that: "I have never started a poem whose end I knew. Writing a poem is discovering."

In pursuing the question of what it is in the writing process that can have such surprise-inducing effects on the writer's own understanding, Scardamalia and Bereiter (1985) considered and rejected the hypothesis that composing involves an internal dialogue between disputants à la Socrates. Thinking-aloud protocol data offered no signs of a more subtle kind of conversational process. Writing involves solving two general kinds of problems—content problems, which are problems of the writer's own knowledge and beliefs, and rhetorical problems, which are problems having to do with achieving the goals of the composition. Socrates' concern was that the writer dealt only with rhetorical problems, leaving content problems—the problems of truth—unexamined. Scardamalia and Bereiter proposed that not only does the expert writer deal with both kinds of problems, but the two kinds of problems interact. Problems arising in the "rhetorical space" are often translated into problems requiring solution in the "content space." New decisions arrived at in the content space create new problems in the rhetorical space, and so on in a dialectical fashion. The result will often be that by the end of the composing process, both the writer's ideas and the nature of the written product have evolved in unexpected ways. Hence the experience of writing as discovery.

The dialectical interaction of rhetorical and belief-related problems is illustrated in the following segment from an expert writer's thinking-aloud protocol (from a study conducted by Paris, 1986).

Segment from a Thinking-Aloud Protocol
(content statements underlined)

- So, I'm looking for examples of programs that could be argued . . . that could be argued were good influences on children.
- Now I know I already don't believe this, but *Sesame Street comes to mind as a possible good influence,*
- And I find myself trying to work it out.
- So I'm going to say . . .
- I'm making up two columns here . . . and just trying to respond to my own thought processes.
- *Sesame Street jumped to mind as a good influence.*
- So I guess what I need is three columns here . . . I need a column just for the specific and the example. And I can work back and forth between columns.
- *Sesame Street is good because it could be argued that it educates.*
- *And educates in a specific way . . . giving children basic information, A.B.C.'s etcetera.*
- But immediately when I say it's a good influence, I have reservations about it.
- Now I'm just trying to clarify for myself the reservations about it . . .

This dialectical process is the distinctive characteristic of what Bereiter and Scardamalia (1987) have elaborated as the knowledge-transforming model of composition (see Fig. 2.2). In this model, knowledge growth may or may not be a goal of the writer, but the interactive working out of rhetorical and content problems can lead to knowledge transformation as an effect in either case. Of more immediate relevance to the present discussion, however, is that this dialectical process provides a mechanism by which the complexity of writing problems escalates. A more liner approach to writing (such as is often recommended in composition textbooks) would settle all the content issues first, after which the composition would be planned and carried out in a straightforward manner (reminiscent of the forward-acting problem-solving strategies exhibited by experts in other domains). But, as we have noted, expert composing processes are

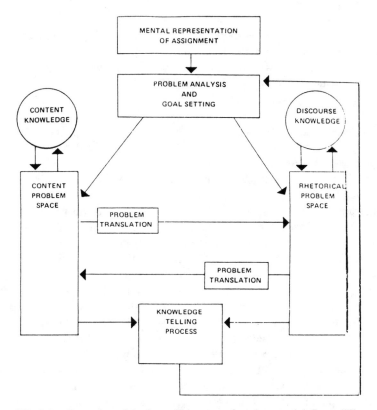

FIG. 2.2.   Structure of the knowledge-transforming model. From "The psychology of written composition" by C. Bereiter and M. Scardamalia, 1987: Lawrence Erlbaum Associates.

characterized by recursion, so that planning keeps being reactivated throughout. By responding to the content implications of rhetorical decisions and vice versa, the knowledge-transforming writer engages in a process that can, in principle, exponentiate the problems of composition without limit, therefore truly courting mental overload.

Knowledge-Telling as a Problem-Reducing Strategy

Although the interactive solving of rhetorical and content-related problems can overload the most skillful writer, just coping with the rhetorical problems—the problems of producing a successful written product—would seem sufficient to overload the novice. Sometimes they do. Studies of writing block among university students indicate that often it amounts to collapse under an excess of constraints, often unwisely applied (Rose, 1985; Selfe, 1985). Something similar may occur with young school children who, after writing 50 words or so, protest that they can think of nothing more to write, even though very simple supports will enable them to write a great deal more. Still, the most remarkable thing about young or inexpert writers is how easily they cope with the writing task as they construe it.

If inexpert writing were just stream-of-consciousness or babble, it would need no explaining. What needs explaining is how novice writers, whose thinking-aloud protocols show little or no evidence of planning, or concern about main ideas or about form, who start writing almost instantly and proceed about as rapidly as they can move the pencil, manage nevertheless to produce coherent prose that fits some appropriate literary form and that is sometimes imaginative, colorful, and well-conceived.

According to the knowledge-telling model (Bereiter & Scardamalia, 1987), novice writers follow a procedure that enables them to reduce the problems of writing to a routine procedure for "telling what one knows about the topic" (Scardamalia & Bereiter, 1986, p. 792). According to this model (see Fig. 2.3), knowledge-tellers, once provided with a writing assignment (e.g., *Is television a good influence on children?*) begin automatically to retrieve knowledge using two kinds of cues. Topic identifiers (e.g., "television shows," "good aspects," and "children") serve as cues that prime associated concepts through a process of spreading activation (Anderson, 1983). Discourse knowledge provides a second type of cue. For instance, a writer whose opinion essay schema consisted of: Say what you believe about the question and give reasons; would use Say what you believe and reasons as retrieval cues, which in combination with topic identifiers, would retrieve ideas relevant to defending an opinion about children and television. Information typically is transcribed as it is called up from long-term memory, or in short circuit "think-say" cycles, rather than being transformed by rhetorical and more broadly based content goals.

The following segment of a Grade 6 student's thinking-aloud protocol (from a study conducted by Paris, 1986) illustrates the forward-moving and additive flow of knowledge-telling in response to general topic and discourse structure cues.

Segment from a Thinking-Aloud Protocol
(content statements underlined)

- *I think it is good and bad for children to watch television because I like the cartoons and some sad movies.*
- *But I like good movies that come on TV because they are good to watch.*
- *But usually it is good to watch comedy shows because they are very funny.*
- *They keep you laughing almost every time you watch them.*
- *It is good to watch interesting movies.*

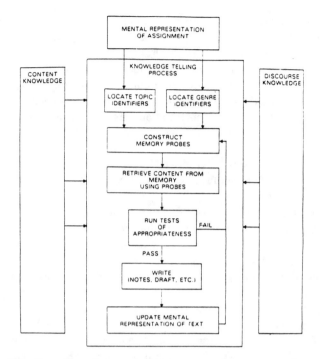

FIG. 2.3. Structure of the knowledge-telling model. From "The psychology of written composition" by C. Bereiter and M. Scardamalia, 1987: Lawrence Erlbaum Associates.

- *Interesting shows like Young and the Restless, All My Children, and General Hospital . . . because it's sometimes exciting.*
- *But pay TV has some very good movies like Splash, Police Academy, Romancing the Stone.*
- *But sometimes I watch sports.*
- *My favorite sport is baseball.*
- *I like football, but not that much.*
- *I hate golf and tennis and all the other stuff except soccer.*
- *But I usually watch wrestling at my friend's house because it's kind of exciting and I like the way they fight.*

The overall picture of the composing process exhibited by this Grade 6 writer during thinking-aloud is characteristic of the kinds of content-based thinking typically manifested by novice writers as predicted by the knowledge-telling model. The predominant activity is generating topic- and genre-appropriate content. The knowledge-teller does not represent the task of composing as a goal-directed one in which epistemological and rhetorical problems must be jointly resolved (Scardamalia & Paris, 1985). Rather, the novice writer's greatest difficulty seems to be that of accessing a sufficient quantity of relevant knowledge in order to satisfy length and genre requirements. Problem-solving episodes are infrequent in knowledge-tellers' thinking-aloud protocols because the task routine manages to bypass most content-related as well as rhetorical problems.

THE SHIFT FROM KNOWLEDGE-TELLING
TO KNOWLEDGE-TRANSFORMING

The proposal that there are two quite different composing processes that result in radically different sorts of problem situations for different writers raises questions about how the two models are related. What determines which one a writer will acquire, and what would be involved in shifting from one to the other? The assumption is that knowledge-telling is developed at an early age as a way in which novice writers can deal with the complexity of the writing task. The knowledge-transforming process only develops through efforts to cope with significant problems of content on one hand: What do I really believe? Is this belief really tenable? What are my true feelings?; and significant problems of communication on the other. Knowledge telling is not abandoned. It remains an efficient way to deal with routine tasks. But knowledge transforming develops as a way of doing "serious" writing.

Many people grew up seldom or ever doing serious writing, however, and so it is not surprising that many people never develop a knowledge-transforming approach. The blame is often placed on schools for treating writing as an exercise and never engaging students with its epistemic aspects (Applebee, 1981; Emig, 1971; Graves, 1983). That may be a justifiable charge, but it cannot be the full explanation. Expert writers have emerged from unpromising school backgrounds. And school educators have reported to us that even with a very enlightened writing program, in which writing activities are designed to engage students' interests and concerns as fully as possible, many children who start out as serious and thoughtful writers begin, by the middle years of school, to lapse into mindless routines and to avoid writing that really challenges their abilities. It seems reasonable, therefore, to suppose there are also cognitive barriers to developing the knowledge-transforming process.

A way to investigate cognitive barriers to problem solving in writing is through instruction aimed at supporting a shift from knowledge telling to knowledge transforming. Instructional studies in this domain could be divided into two primary categories, as follows. The first type of intervention we discuss aims at encouraging expert writing indirectly, by liberating novice writers from the necessity to attend simultaneously to low- and high-level concerns. The second type aims directly at fostering expert-like problem solving during composing through the provision of learning environments which feature explicit cognitively-based instruction in modeling of, and support for, knowledge-transforming-type writing strategies.

Reducing Cognitive Load during Composing

Several instructional interventions for improving writing arise from the assumption that problem solvers have a finite set of mental resources that can be devoted to a task, and that all writers have higher-level strategies available, but that they are suppressed as a result of attending to lower-level concerns. One such intervention for teaching writing is "free writing" (Elbow, 1973; Stover, 1988; Tomkins & Camp, 1988), in which writers are instructed to ignore low-level problems like spelling during first draft composing in order to free their mental capacity for higher-level concerns such as planning.

In order to test the idea that reduction in writers' attention to production factors would enhance written composition, Scardamalia, Bereiter, and Goelman (1982) compared children's handwritten and dictated texts. They found that students produced longer texts when freed from mechanical concerns, but that the quality of dictated texts was not superior to those that were handwritten.

In a study by Joram, Lindsay, Bryson, and Woodruff (1986), average and above average Grade 8 students were instructed not to attend to errors during first draft composing, and to postpone correcting their texts to a subsequent writing session. Students wrote with either paper and pencil or with word processors throughout and were directed to think aloud during all writing sessions. Although word processors are often thought of as tools that liberate writers from mechanical concerns, writing with word processors required a considerable amount of attention to mechanics for these students because despite their two years of computer experience, text editing and typing were not automatic skills.

Ratings of final drafts indicated that instruction to postpone editing was only of benefit when students wrote with word processors, while when writing with paper and pencil, they performed best when permitted to edit as usual. Students' final drafts were rated as more creative in this condition, but not as being holistically superior. Analyses of thinking-aloud protocols indicated that when writing with word processors, students made more general evaluative statements when they were permitted to edit their texts. Under these circumstances, students appeared to be quite concerned with the mechanical errors incurred from using computers, and thus instructions not to worry about making errors was an effective intervention. The fact that instructions not to edit was of no benefit in the paper and pencil condition suggests that even above average Grade 8 writers did not engage in high-level problem solving when their attentional capacity was freed up. Typical of adolescent writers (Burtis, Bereiter, Scardamalia, & Tetroe, 1983), there was little evidence in their thinking-aloud protocols of high-level planning or metacognitive statements.

Accordingly, these results provide no evidence that novice writers have at-hand a repertoire of high-level problem solving strategies that are ready to emerge when low-level attentional demands are reduced. Instructions to imma-ture writers to ignore low-level concerns do not free them to focus on high-level problem solving because they are not engaged in solving high-level problems.

Cognitively-Based Instructional Environments which Foster Expert-Like Problem Solving

An instructional study was conducted by Bryson (1989) that investigated the role of reflective problem solving during argument construction. The study's two main goals were (a) to determine the role, if any, played by reflective problem solving in normally achieving and reading disabled adolescent students' argu-ment construction processes; and (b) to investigate the extent to which reflec-tivity in argument construction could be enhanced through the provision of a specially designed computer-supported instructional environment called M.U.S.E.[1] (for a complete description of this environment, see Bryson & Scar-damalia, 1988). Research on reading disabled students' cognitions during aca-demic tasks indicates that these students exhibit a particularly low frequency of problem solving strategies and a high frequency of passive, dysfunctional, or "learned helplessness" responses to in-process difficulties (Butkowski & Willows, 1984).

The term reflectivity was used to refer to problem solving which takes knowl-edge and experience as objects of thought (as in Brown, 1987; Locke, 1690/1924; Pylyshyn, 1978). Deliberative, goal-directed, and autocritical (Bin-et, 1909) thought has been reported to be characteristic of experts' problem solving during argument construction (Paris, 1986; Voss, Tyler, & Yengo, 1983). Research reported by Scardamalia and Paris (1985) suggested that it is not fruitful to attempt to improve reflection in the composition of arguments by teaching students discourse knowledge, or the structural components of a good argument (as in the textbook for courses on reasoning by Toulmin, Rieke, & Janik, 1979). Scardamalia and Paris reported a study where this kind of interven-tion did not increase any knowledge-transforming behaviors during writing. Rather, novice writers seem to lack "heuristics for reflection"; that is, both knowledge of and the ability to make use of executive strategies for making use of what they already know in order to extend current knowledge.

Thinking-aloud protocol data and argument-type expository texts were col-lected from 31 Grade 10 students before and after exposure to instruction. Stu-

---

[1]*Monitoring Understanding + Strategic Execution*

dents in the experimental group were taught specific procedures for reflecting on the adequacy of knowledge accessed in the generation of arguments. Experimental students received direct instruction in a set of reflective operations, as well as in the general processes of dialectical inquiry. The operations included: Plan, Identify New Learning, Identify Confusions, Build an Argument, Challenge its Assumptions, Elaborate Statements, Search for Additional Ideas, and Put it Together. Students in the control group were provided with instruction in the structural elements of persuasive arguments (as per Toulmin, 1958). Control group students got the same exposure to modeling argument construction via thinking-aloud by the instructor and the students, as in the Experimental group. Rather than being provided with thinking prompts, control group students were provided with definitions of each of the elements in a discourse knowledge model of a persuasive argument. These elements included: (a) beliefs on both sides; (b) reasons on both sides; (c) facts, descriptions, and examples; and (d) conclusions.

Pretest results indicate that the normally achieving students' texts received higher quality and complexity ratings than did those written by reading disabled students. However, both normally achieving and reading disabled students tended for the most part to construct arguments which were one-sided, and engaged in little or no in-process problem solving during composing. The protocols generated by the reading disabled students contained clusters of task-irrelevant and self-denigrating statements in response to perceived failure. These statements led them to dead ends. In contrast, negative self-statements by the more confident and capable students were frequently followed by shifts in the kind of activity they were engaged in and consequent revision or refinement of ideas. Thus, for the higher-performing students, signals of difficulty were somehow translated into a more productive course of action.

Posttest results indicated a significant increase in problem solving during argument construction for both normally achieving and reading disabled experimental students. Path analyses of the results indicated that level of rated main point in students' texts was mediated by the amount of in-process problem solving activity. Experimental reading disabled students' protocols contained significantly fewer negative, self-denigrating attributional-type statements at posttesting. Texts written by the normally achieving students continued to receive higher text ratings than did those written by reading disabled students. However, experimental reading disabled students' texts were rated more highly at posttesting than at pretesting.

Achievements at different levels of sophistication were linked to the ability to represent persuasive-essay tasks at increasingly complex levels, and, in turn, to the availability of strategies for coping with increasingly problematic composing episodes. Analyses suggest that internal models of argument develop from conceptions grounded in fighting, to those of back-and-forth verbal exchanges, to those of reconciling opposing arguments by shifting to a more comprehensive level of analysis. The strategies that underlie these different levels of task representation correspondingly reflect those that young writers bring to bear when they are, respectively, fighting, engaging in verbal exchanges, or reflecting on different points of view. The highest level of task representation, that requiring reflection on different points of view, was lacking in much of the data collected. The posttest results suggest that it is, nonetheless, possible to foster reflective problem solving during writing by providing students with on-line "thinking tools" embedded in an environment that enables novice writers to sustain reflective inquiry independently; that is, without the external source of feedback provided by a teacher.

CONCLUSIONS

We have argued that for expert writers, problem solving consists of a dialectical interaction between content goals and rhetorical goals. Expert writers construct problem representations that: (a) are more complex than those of novice writers; and (b) include goals for constructing new knowledge, as compared with novice writers' goals, which are restricted to the retrieval and transcription of topic- and genre-related knowledge. Thus, written composition seems to involve complex problem solving to the extent that the writer elaborates a problem representation that (a) is emergent; that is, which evolves recursively during text production; (b) demands effortful cognitive operations in order to bridge the gap between the initial state and the final goal state that are not available as a single automatized procedure; and (c) necessitates dealing simultaneously with multiple (and possibly competing) goals.

The expert writers' deliberate construction of a complex problem representation is probably comparable to expert artists' "problem-finding" behaviors reported by Getzels and Csikszentmihalyi (1976) in a longitudinal expert-novice study. In this experiment, 33 second and third year male art college students artists were assessed on a variety of tasks both at the college, and six years after graduation. At the college, students were provided with a collection of materials and objects for a drawing task. Time spent exploring and manipulating the materials proved to be a significant predictor of later real world success as an artist. Likewise, during the drawing phase, amount of revision and time devoted to successive problem reformulations were significantly longer for successful, as compared with unsuccessful, artists. Similar differences between expert and novice artists were reported by Eindhoven and Vinacke (1952). The task in this study was to produce a painting to illustrate a poem. Expert artists (compared with novices) spent twice as long reading the poem during the first session, sketched more, and spent longer elaborating particular details in a single sketch. Likewise, Lesgold (1988) reported that expert radiologists spent proportionately more problem solving time generating a problem representation than did novices.

These findings seem to indicate that across domains, the tendency to effortfully construct complex problem representations constitutes a hallmark of expert task performance. Also, evidence suggests that the to-be-solved problems represented by experts are qualitatively distinct from those represented by novices. In open-ended tasks like written composition, where there is no ceiling on the possible complexity of problem representation, expertise is associated with the strategic coordination of "learning goals" (which serve the purpose of increasing competence, Dweck & Leggett, 1988; Elliott & Dweck, 1988) and task goals. Perhaps it makes sense to conclude that novices in this most exacting craft need to learn to think like writers, for whom it seems that composing is, and will always remain, a particularly difficult and demanding intellectual pursuit. As Ernest Hemingway suggested: "We are all apprentices in a craft where no one ever becomes a master."

REFERENCES

Anderson, J. R. (1983). *The architecture of cognition.* Cambridge, MA: Harvard University Press.

Applebee, A. N. (1981). *Writing in the secondary school: English and the content areas.* Urbana, IL: National Council of Teachers of English.

Beaugrande, R. de. (1984). *Text production: Toward a science of composition.* Norwood, NJ: Ablex.

Bereiter, C., Burtis, P. J., Scardamalia, M. (1988). Cognitive operations in constructing main points in written composition. *Journal of Memory and Language, 27,* 261–278.

Bereiter, C., & Scardamalia, M. (1987). *The psychology of written composition.* Hillsdale, NJ: Lawrence Erlbaum Associates.

Berkenhotter, C. (1983). Decisions and revisions: The planning strategies of a publishing writer. *College Composition and Communication, 34,* 156–169.

Bridwell, L. (1980). Revising strategies in twelfth grade students' transactional writing. *Research in the Teaching of English, 14,* 197–122.

Biemiller, A., Gang, D., & Regan, E. (1986). *Handwriting fluency, oral story production, and written story production.* Paper presented at a meeting of the Canadian Psychological Association (CPA). Toronto.

Binet, A. (1909). *Lesidees Modernes sur les Enfants.* Paris: Errest Flamcrion.

Breuleux, A. (1987). *Expert writers' planning.* Paper presented at a meeting of the American Educational Research Association (AERA), Washington D.C.

Brown, A. (1987). Metacognition, executive control, self-regulation and other more mysterious mechanisms. In F. Weinert & R. Kluwe (Eds.), *Metacognition, motivation, and understanding* (pp. 65–116). Hillsdale, NJ: Lawrence Erlbaum Associates.

Bryson, M. (1989). *Computer-supported composition: Fostering reflectivity in the products and the processes of normally achieving and reading disabled student-writers.* Unpublished doctoral dissertation, University of Toronto, Toronto.

Bryson, M., & Scardamalia, M. (1988). M.U.S.E.: A computer-based learning environment for novice and supernovice student-writers. *Proceedings of the Intelligent Tutoring Systems Conference* (pp. 357–364) Montreal.

Burtis, P., Bereiter, C., Scardamalia, M., & Tetroe, J. (1983). The development of planning in writing. In G. Wells & B. Kroll (Eds.), *Explorations in the development of writing* (pp. 153–174). Chicester, England: John Wiley.

Butkowski, I., & Willows, D. M. (1984). Cognitive-motivational characteristics of children vary-ing in reading ability: Evidence for learned helplessness in poor readers. *Journal of Educational Psychology*, *72*, 408–422.

Chase, W. G., & Simon, H. A. (1973). Perception in chess. *Cognitive Psychology*, *4*, 55–81.

Collins, A., & Gentner, D. (1980). A framework for a cognitive theory of writing. In L. Gregg & E. Steinberg (Eds.), *Cognitive processes in writing*. Hillsdale, NJ: Lawrence Erlbaum Associates.

Dostoyevsky, F. (1971). *The unpublished Dostoyevsky notebooks and journals, 1860–1861*. Liter-atwnoye Nasledstvo, Vol. LXXXIII, Moscow.

Dweck, C., & Leggett, E. (1988). A social-cognitive approach to motivation and personality. *Psychological Review*, *95*, 256–273.

Eindhoven, J. E., & Vinacke, W. E. (1952). Creative processes in painting. *The Journal of General Psychology*, *47*, 139–164.

Elbow, P. (1973). *Writing without teachers*. New York: Oxford University Press.

Elliott, E. S., & Dweck, C. (1988). Goals: An approach to motivation and achievement. *Journal of Personality and Social Psychology*, *54*, 5–12.

Emig, J. (1971). *The composing processes of twelfth graders* (Research Report No. 13). Cham-paign, IL: National Council of Teachers of English.

Ferreiro, E. (1984). What is written in a sentence? A developmental answer. *Journal of Education*, *160*, 25–39.

Flower, L., & Hayes, J. R. (1980). The cognition of discovery: Defining a historical problem. *College Composition and Communication*, *31*, 21–32.

Flower, L., & Hayes, J. R. (1981). A cognitive process theory of writing. *College Composition and Communication*, *32*, 365–387.

Flower, L., Hayes, J. R., Carey, L., Schriver, K., & Stratman, J. (1986). Detection, diagnosis, and the strategies of revision. *College Composition and Communication*, *37*, 16–55.

Frederiksen, C. H. (1975). Representing logical and semantic structure of knowledge acquired from discourse. *Cognitive Psychology*, *7*, 371–458.

Frederiksen, C. H. (1987). Cognitive models of discourse analysis. In C. R. Cooper & S. Green-baum (Eds.), *Written Communication Annual, Volume 1: Linguistic approaches to the study of written discourse*. Beverly Hills, CA: Sage Press.

Getzels, J. W., & Csikszentmihalyi, M. (1976). *The creative vision: A longitudinal study of prob-lem-finding in art*. Toronto: John Wiley & Sons.

Goody, J. (1968). *Literacy in traditional societies*. Cambridge: Cambridge University Press.

Graves, D. (1983). *Writing: Teachers and children at work*. Exeter, NH: Heinemann Educational Books.

Hairston, M. (1984). Working with advanced writers. *College Composition and Communication*, *35*, 196–208.

Havelock, E. A. (1986). *The muse learns to write*. New Haven: Yale University Press.

Hayes, J. R., & Flower, L. (1986). Writing research and the writer. *American Psychologist*, *41*, 1106–1113.

Himley, M. (1988). Becoming a writer. *Written Communication*, *5*, 82–107.

Hinton, G. E., & Anderson, J. A. (1981). *Parallel models of associative memory*. Hillsdale, NJ: Lawrence Erlbaum Associates.

Joram, E., Lindsay, P., Bryson, M., & Woodruff, E. (1986). *The effects of editing on the planning phase of the writing process*. Paper presented at the Conference on Computers and Writing, LRDC, Pittsburgh, Pennsylvania.

Kaufer, D., Hayes, J. R., & Flower, L. (1986). Composing written sentences. *Research in the Teaching of English*, *20*, 120–140.

King, M., & Rentel, V. M. (1981). Research update: Conveying meaning in written texts. *Lan-guage Arts*, *58*, 721–728.

Larkin, J. H. (1981). Enriching formal knowledge: A model for learning to solve textbook physics problems. In J. Anderson (Ed.), *Cognitive skills and their acquisition* (pp. 311–334). Hillsdale, NJ: Lawrence Erlbaum Associates.

Larkin, J. H., McDermott, J., Simon, D. P., & Simon, H. (1980). Expert and novice performance in solving physics problems. *Science, 208,* 1335–1342.

Lesgold, A. M. (1984). Acquiring expertise. In J. R. Anderson & S. Kosslyn (Eds.), *Tutorials in learning and memory: Essays in honor of Gordon Bower* (pp. 31–60). San Francisco, CA: W. H. Freeman.

Lesgold, A. M. (1988). Problem solving. In R. J. Sternberg & E. E. Smith (Eds.), *The psychology of human thought* (pp. 188–209). New York: Cambridge University Press.

Lesgold, A. M. Feltovich, P., Glaser, R., & Wang, Y. (1981). *The acquisition of perceptual diagnostic skill in radiology* (Tech. Rep. No. PDS-1). University of Pittsburgh, LRDC.

Locke, J. (1690/1924). *An essay concerning human understanding* (A. L. Pringle-Pattison, Ed.). Oxford: Clarendon Press.

McCutchen, D. (1986). Domain knowledge and linguistic knowledge in the development of writing ability. *Journal of Memory and Language, 25,* 431–444.

McCutchen, D. (1988). "Functional automaticity" in children's writing. *Written Communication, 5,* 306–324.

Miller, G. A., Galanter, E., & Pribram, K. H. (1960). *Plans and the structure of behavior.* New York: Holt, Rinehart & Winston.

Murray, D. M. (1978). Internal revision: A process of discovery. In C. R. Cooper & L. Odell (Eds.), *Research on composing* (pp. 85–103). Urbana, IL: National Council of Teachers of English.

Olson, D. (1977). From utterance to text: The bias of language in speech and writing. *Harvard Educational Review, 47,* 257–281.

Ong, W. J. (1982). *Orality and literacy.* London: Methuen.

Paris, P. (1986). *Goals and problem solving in written composition.* Unpublished doctoral dissertation, York University, Downsview, Canada.

Perl, S. (1979). The composing processes of unskilled college writers. *Research in the Teaching of English, 13,* 317–336.

Plato (1925/1987). Seventh letter (L.A. Post, Trans.). In E. Hamilton & H. Cairns (Eds.), *The collected dialogues of Plato.* Princeton: Princeton University Press.

Plato (1952). *Phaedrus* (R. Hackforth, Trans.). New York: Cambridge University Press.

Pylyshyn, Z. (1978). Computational models and empirical constraints. *The Behavioral and Brain Sciences, 1,* 93–99.

Rose, M. (Ed.). (1985). *When a writer can't write.* New York: The Guilford Press.

Rumelhart, D. E., & McClelland, J. L. (1982). An interactive activation model of context effects in letter perception: Part 2. The contextual enhancement effect and some tests and extensions of the model. *Psychological Review, 89,* 60–94.

Scardamalia, M., & Bereiter, C. (1985). The development of dialectical processes in writing. In D. Olson, N. Torrance, & A. Hildyard (Eds.), *Literacy, language and learning: The nature and consequences of reading and writing.* Cambridge: Cambridge University Press.

Scardamalia, M., & Bereiter, C. (1986). Research on written composition. In M. C. Wittrock (Ed.), *Handbook of research on teaching* (pp. 778–803). New York: Macmillan.

Scardamalia, M., & Paris, P. (1985). The function of explicit discourse knowledge in the development of text representations and composing strategies. *Cognition and Instruction, 2,* 1–39.

Scardamalia, M., Bereiter, C., & Goelman, H. (1982). The role of production factors in writing ability. In M. Nystrand (Ed.), *What writers know: The language, process, and structure of written discourse* (pp. 173–210). New York: Academic Press.

Scardamalia, M., Bereiter, C., & Woodruff, E. (1980). *The effects of content knowledge on writing.* Paper presented at the meeting of the American Educational Research Association, Boston.

Selfe, C. (1985). An apprehensive writer composes. In M. Rose (Ed.), *When a writer can't write*. New York: The Guilford Press.

Sessums, K. (1988, September). Sam Shepard: Geography of a horse dreamer. *Interview*, pp. 72–80.

Simon, D. P., & Simon, H. A. (1978). Individual differences in solving physics problems. In R. S. Siegler (Ed.), *Children's thinking: What develops?* (pp. 325–348). Hillsdale, NJ: Lawrence Erlbaum Associates.

Simon, J. (1973). *La langue ecrite de l'enfant. Children's Written Language*. Paris: Presses Universitaires de France.

Sommers, N. (1980). Revision strategies of student writers and experienced adult writers. *College Composition and Communication, 31*, 378–388.

Stover, K. (1988). In defense of freewriting. *English Journal, 77*, 61–62.

Tompkins, G., & Camp, D. (1988). Rx for writer's block. *Childhood Education, 64*, 209–214.

Toulmin, S. E. (1958). *The uses of argument*. Cambridge: Cambridge University Press.

Toulmin, S. E., Rieke, R., & Janik, A. (1979). *An introduction to reasoning*. New York: Macmillan.

Voss, J. F., Greene, T. R., Post, T., & Penner, B. (1983). Problem solving skill in the social sciences. In G. Bower (Ed.), *The psychology of learning and motivation: Advances in research theory* (Vol. 17, pp. 165–213). New York: Academic.

Voss, J. F., Tyler, S., & Yengo, L. (1983). Individual differences in the solving of social science problems. In R. F. Dillon & R. R. Schmech (Eds.), *Individual differences in cognition* (Vol. 1, pp. 205–232). New York: Academic Press.

Zbrodoff, N. J. (1984). *Writing stories under time and length constraints*. Unpublished doctoral dissertation, University of Toronto, Toronto.

3 Cognitive Mechanisms in Calculation

Scott M. Sokol
Massachusetts General Hospital and Harvard Medical School

Michael McCloskey
Johns Hopkins University

Arithmetic calculation is a complex cognitive function requiring the interplay of a number of distinct processing components. Perhaps due to this complexity, most previous studies of calculation have focused on describing one or another aspect of the system (e.g., retrieval of "table facts," procedural knowledge, general number concepts), typically without reference to a general framework within which to understand the individual contributions of component processes, or their interactions. A major goal of this chapter is therefore to provide such a framework. In so doing, we rely heavily upon a somewhat unusual source of data: patterns of impaired performance in brain-damaged patients with number-processing and calculation deficits, a class of disorders collectively termed "dyscalculia." (For clinical neuropsychological reviews of dyscalculia, see Boller & Grafman, 1983, and Levin & Spiers, 1985).

The use of performance data from brain-damaged subjects as a basis for drawing inferences about normal cognition is fast becoming an established methodology in several research areas, including reading (e.g., Beauvois & Derouesne, 1979; Patterson, 1982), sentence processing (e.g., Hildebrandt, Caplan, & Evans, 1987; Miceli, Mazzuchi, Menn, & Goodglass, 1983), spelling (e.g., Ellis, 1982; Goodman & Caramazza, 1986), number processing (e.g., McCloskey, Sokol, & Goodman, 1986; McCloskey, Sokol, Goodman-Schulman, & Caramazza, 1990; Sokol & McCloskey, 1988), and calculation itself (e.g., Caramazza & McCloskey, 1987; McCloskey, Caramazza & Basili, 1985; Sokol, McCloskey & Cohen, 1989; Warrington, 1982). Two assumptions motivate this "cognitive neuropsychological" approach. The first is that one may consider performance in the domain under study to be mediated by an information processing system which comprises a number of functionally distinct components. Second, one assumes that brain damage may selectively disrupt this information processing system without bringing about a qualitatively different organization of function *de novo* (see Caramazza, 1986; Caramazza & McCloskey, 1988; McCloskey & Caramazza, 1988, for further discussion on the assumptions of cognitive neuropsychological research). Given these assumptions, one may approach data from brain-damaged subjects by asking the question: What must the normal system be like in order that, subsequent to selective damage, performance breaks down in just the ways observed? In this way, data may be used both to delineate the general functional architecture of a cognitive system (i.e., the major components and the flow of information among them), and to articulate the internal structure and functioning of the various components.

In this chapter we first present a general model of the cognitive calculation system, and describe patterns of impaired calculation performance that support the model's principal assumptions. We then examine in greater detail the major processing mechanisms specified by the model, surveying relevant research involving normal children and adults, and also presenting some additional findings from our studies of brain-damaged patients.

THE FUNCTIONAL ARCHITECTURE OF THE CALCULATION SYSTEM

McCloskey et al. (1985; see also Caramazza & McCloskey, 1987) have proposed a general model of the cognitive mechanisms underlying number comprehension, number production, and calculation. On the most general level, the model distinguishes between the number-processing system and the calculation system. The number-processing system comprises the mechanisms for comprehending and producing numbers in various forms (e.g., Arabic numbers, such as 345, and verbal numbers, such as *three hundred forty-five*). The calculation system consists of processing components required specifically for carrying out calculations. The relationships among number processing and calculation components are depicted in Fig. 3.1.

Within the calculation system (see Fig. 3.2) the McCloskey et al. (1985) model distinguishes among cognitive mechanisms for (a) comprehension of operation symbols or words (e.g., × or times); (b) execution of calculation procedures; and (c) retrieval of arithmetic facts (e.g., 6 × 9 = 54).

Consider the following multiplication problem

$$\begin{array}{r} 26 \\ \times\ 37 \\ \hline \end{array}$$

For this problem, processing of the operation sign (×) would serve to identify multiplication as the to-be-performed operation. Accordingly, the multiplication procedure would be activated. This procedure, which provides an ordered plan

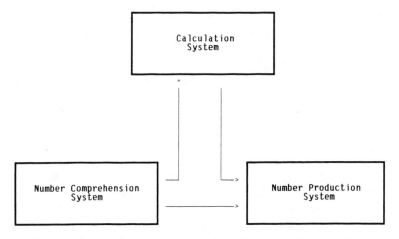

FIG. 3.1.   Schematic representation of number-procesing and calculation systems.

for the solution of multiplication problems, might call first for encoding the
rightmost digit in the bottom number (i.e., 7). Arabic number comprehension
processes would thus be recruited to translate this digit into a mental representation for use in the computation. This representation is assumed to be a modality-
independent semantic representation (McCloskey, et al., 1986; Sokol & Mc-
Closkey, 1988). The multiplication procedure might then call for encoding of the
rightmost digit in the top number (i.e., 6), which would again be accomplished
by Arabic number comprehension mechanisms.

   The next step specified in the multiplication procedure would presumably be
that of retrieving the product of the two encoded numbers from an arithmetic fact
store. Thus, the semantic representations of the operands along with a representation of the arithmetic operation would serve as input to the fact retrieval
component, which would return a semantic representation of the product (i.e.,
42). The multiplication procedure might then call for the ones portion of the
product to be written in Arabic form beneath the rightmost column of the prob-

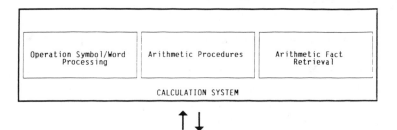

FIG. 3.2.   Schematic representation of calculation mechanisms.

lem. To accomplish this, Arabic number production mechanisms would be recruited to translate the semantic representation into a representation specific to the digit 2. This digit representation would then be processed by motor mechanisms to generate the written output.

Processing would continue in this fashion until all partial products had been computed. At this point the addition procedure would be called upon, and the partial products would be summed and written under control of this procedure.

Conceptual Knowledge

In addition to arithmetic facts and calculation procedures, at least one other aspect of arithmetic knowledge may be of some importance to calculation, namely conceptual knowledge (e.g., understanding of arithmetic operations and laws pertaining to these operations). For example, one may know that multiplication can be understood in terms of taking successive sums. Likewise, one may understand that $(a \times b) \times c = a \times (b \times c)$—the law of associativity—, or that $a \times b = b \times a$—the law of commutativity. That people typically acquire at least some understanding of the principles underlying arithmetic seems apparent. Nevertheless, the role of conceptual knowledge in calculation performance is not entirely clear.

RELEVANT EVIDENCE

The distinctions drawn among the number processing and calculation components have been informed and supported by patterns of performance observed in dyscalculic subjects. In this section, we outline a few illustrative examples of these patterns within the calculation system. (Dissociations of number-processing performance fall outside the scope of this chapter; for discussions of such dissociations see McCloskey & Caramazza, 1987; McCloskey et al., 1986; McCloskey et al., 1990; Sokol & McCloskey, 1988).

Selective Disruption of Operation Symbol/Word Comprehension

The ability to process operation symbols or words can be disrupted selectively by brain damage. For example, Ferro and Botelho (1980; see also Grewel, 1952) describe a patient who was unable to comprehend the operation symbols (e.g., +, ×), but was otherwise intact in arithmetic performance. When presented with a written arithmetic problem (e.g., 3 + 5), she often performed the wrong operation (e.g., 3 × 5 = 8; 35 + 24 = 840). However, when problems were presented aurally (e.g., speaking the problem as "three times five"), the patient showed excellent performance. The normal performance on spoken problems, and the fact that on written problems the wrong operations were performed correctly, imply that the patient was unimpaired in comprehending numbers as well as in retrieving arithmetic facts and using arithmetic procedures. Further, the patient's ability to identify the appropriate operation for aurally-presented problems indicates intact comprehension of spoken operation words. Her sole impairment seems to be in the processing of written operation symbols.

Dissociations of Arithmetic Facts and Procedures

The distinction drawn between arithmetic facts and arithmetic procedures has been supported by several reports that collectively provide a double dissociation. That is, in certain brain-damaged patients fact retrieval is impaired while the ability to use calculation procedures is spared, whereas in other patients fact retrieval remains intact in the face of impaired execution of arithmetic procedures.

Selective Disruption of Arithmetic Facts

A clear case of selective disruption of arithmetic fact retrieval is provided by patient P.S., reported in Sokol et al. (1989). This brain-damaged patient, who holds a bachelor's degree in finance, showed largely intact number comprehension and number production, but was substantially impaired in the retrieval of arithmetic facts, especially in multiplication.

Single-digit Multiplication.   In each of 23 blocks of trials, P.S. was presented with the 100 single-digit multiplication problems (i.e., 0×0 through 9×9). She responded incorrectly to 451 of the 2300 problems (19.6%). Table 3.1

TABLE 3.1
Percentage of Errors for Patient P.S. on Individual Problems

First Operand	Second Operand									
	0	1	2	3	4	5	6	7	8	9
0	0	48	44	48	39	39	48	39	39	35
1	39	13	0	4	0	0	0	4	0	0
2	39	0	0	0	0	0	9	4	0	4
3	39	0	0	30	4	0	4	0	13	9
4	39	0	0	4	52	4	9	4	17	74
5	44	4	0	0	0	4	9	17	26	30
6	48	0	0	4	4	26	0	30	13	9
7	39	4	0	0	13	9	52	78	52	83
8	39	0	0	9	17	22	9	26	61	0
9	44	0	0	17	83	22	26	91	0	100

presents P.S.'s error rate for each of the individual problems. The rows in the table represent the first operand in a problem, and the columns represent the second operand. For example, the entry in row 4 column 9 indicates that P.S.'s error rate was 74% for the problem 4 × 9. It is apparent from the table that impairment was not uniform over problems. Rather, the error rate was very high for some problems, and very low for others. In general, problems with large operands (e.g., 9 × 7) showed greater impairment than those with small operands (e.g., 2 × 3), but there were several clear exceptions (e.g., 9 × 8, 4 × 4). It is also notable that P.S. had substantial difficulty with 0's problems. We discuss her performance on multiplication by 0, and the implications of this performance, in a later section.

For problems not involving 0's, P.S.'s errors fell predominantly into two categories: (a) omission errors, in which she failed to give an answer to a problem; and (b) operand errors, in which she produced a number that was correct for a problem sharing an operand with the stimulus problem (e.g., 7 × 8 = 63, in which the erroneous answer is correct for 7 × 9).

The nonuniformity of impairment across problems suggests that arithmetic fact retrieval need not break down in an all-or-none fashion; rather, retrieval of some individual fact representations may be disrupted while the ability to access the representations of other facts remains intact. Further, the error pattern suggests that, at least in P.S., the fact retrieval impairment manifested itself in two ways: (a) as an inability to retrieve facts (leading to omission errors); and (b) as a tendency to retrieve stored answers to problems other than the stimulus problem, especially answers to problems sharing an operand with the stimulus problem (leading to operand errors).

Multi-digit Multiplication.   Over the same period of time in which P.S. was tested on single-digit multiplication, she was also presented with 145 multi-digit multiplication problems. She responded incorrectly to 66 of these problems (46%). Examination of the errors revealed that virtually all were attributable to her fact retrieval impairment. In the example presented in Fig. 3.3A, P.S. retrieved 32 as the answer to 4 × 9, and 72 as the answer to 9 × 9. In the example in Fig. 3.3B she retrieved 54 as the answer to 7 × 9.

Although P.S. showed impaired fact retrieval on the multi-digit problems, her execution of calculation procedures was virtually flawless. She consistently carried out the appropriate fact retrievals in the correct order (although not always successfully). For example, in the problem in Fig. 3.3B, she first multiplied 7 × 3, then 7 × 9, then 7 × 1, and next multiplied 1 by 3, 9, and 1. Further, P.S. dealt appropriately with the retrieved products (e.g., writing the ones digit and carrying the tens digit, aligning written answers correctly), and executed the addition procedure correctly when adding the partial products. Thus, P.S. presents with a clear dissociation between retrieval of arithmetic facts (impaired) and execution of calculation procedures (intact). McCloskey et al. (1985) describe a similar dis-

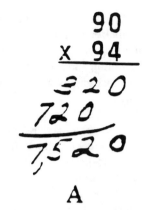

A

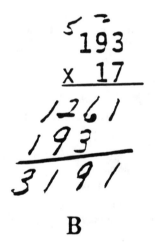

B

FIG. 3.3.   Performance of Patient P.S. on two multidigit multiplication problems, illustrating fact retrieval errors.

sociation in another patient (M.W.). These dissociations support the assumption that arithmetic facts and calculation procedures are functionally distinct.

Selective Disruption of Calculation Procedures

In contrast to patterns in which facts are impaired and procedures are intact, certain patients present with the complementary pattern: intact fact retrieval and impaired execution of calculation procedures. One fairly common procedural deficit involves the failure to separate intermediate sums or products into ones and tens digits, in order that the tens digit can be carried. Instead, the patient writes down the complete intermediate sums or products. Fig. 3.4 shows examples of this type of deficit in addition and multiplication, as noted by McCloskey et al. (1985). (Note that in these examples, as well as in the other examples we present in this section, the individual fact retrievals are correct.) Head (1926) and Grewel (1969) have also described deficits of this sort.

A particularly interesting type of procedural deficit involves the apparent confusion of component steps for one operation with the steps of another operation. As shown in Fig. 3.5, McCloskey et al.'s (1985) patient W.W. apparently used components of the multiplication procedure in an addition problem: the patient added 45 and 8 by first adding 8 and 5, and then 8 and 4. Note that the patient also wrote down the complete intermediate sum, rather than carrying the tens digit.

Finally, the arithmetic procedures may be more drastically disrupted, as illustrated in Fig. 3.6. In the example on the left, the patient obtained the answer 28 for the problem 68 + 59, saying while he worked the problem, "8 + 9 is 17, 6 + 5 is 11, 17 + 11 is 28." In the example on the right, the patient is grossly impaired in organizing the steps of the multiplication procedure, and in arranging the intermediate products (McCloskey et al., 1985).

ARITHMETIC FACTS, PROCEDURES, AND CONCEPTS

In this section we examine in greater detail the major components of the cognitive calculation system: arithmetic facts, calculation procedures, and conceptual knowledge of arithmetic. We briefly discuss relevant research with normal children and adults, and also present some recent findings from our laboratory. Our aim is not to provide an exhaustive review, but simply to highlight some issues of current interest.

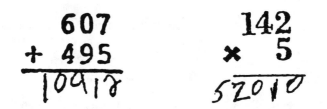

FIG. 3.4. Examples of procedural errors involving failure to separate ones and tens digits of retrieved sums or products.

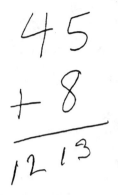

FIG. 3.5. Example of a procedural error involving apparent confusion of the steps of one procedure with those of another.

ARITHMETIC FACTS

Developmental Studies

Prior to learning arithmetic facts, children seem to solve basic arithmetic problems (specifically addition and subtraction) by counting. Gelman and Gallistel (1978; see also Fuson, 1982; Steffe, Thompson & Richards, 1982) have shown that preschool children are not merely able to count by rote, but possess sophisti-

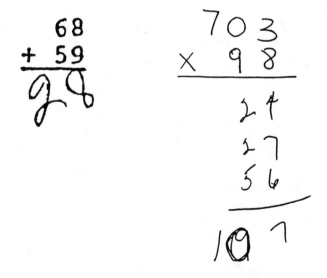

FIG. 3.6. Examples of procedural errors involving drastic disruption of procedures.

cated counting algorithms that they can use selectively in different situations. For example, children can select forward counting to solve addition problems and backward counting to solve subtraction problems, thus demonstrating an understanding of the relationship of counting to these basic arithmetic operations (Starkey & Gelman, 1982).

Several researchers (e.g., Ashcraft, 1982; Ashcraft & Fierman, 1982; Groen & Parkman, 1972; Parkman & Groen, 1971) have suggested that counting strategies persist in early school years. Groen and Parkman, for example, claim that in solving simple addition problems first-graders typically use a *min* strategy that involves "counting-on" from the larger of the numbers to be added (e.g., given 6 + 3, count up from 6 three units to arrive at 9). However, as children memorize the arithmetic facts, problem-solving by direct fact retrieval comes to predominate (e.g., Ashcraft, 1982; Ashcraft & Fierman, 1982). For example, the study by Ashcraft and Fierman found that whereas third-graders used both counting and fact retrieval strategies in solving single-digit addition problems, fourth- and sixth-graders relied primarily on retrieval of memorized facts. Thus, the acquisition of arithmetic fact knowledge seems to involve a gradual shift from counting to fact retrieval. Development beyond the initial memorization of the facts may involve simply a quantitative improvement in the speed and reliability of the fact retrieval process, although it has also been suggested that some form of automaticity may develop (e.g., Ashcraft & Fierman, 1982; Zbrodoff & Logan, 1986).

Models of Arithmetic Fact Retrieval

As just noted, children come to memorize arithmetic facts in their elementary school years. How these facts are organized and retrieved once "memorized" is a question that has stimulated considerable research. In studies of normal arithmetic fact retrieval, children or adults are typically asked to make speeded true/false decisions to single-digit problems presented with correct or incorrect answers (e.g., $8 \times 7 = 56$, $5 + 4 = 10$). Data thus take the form of reaction time (RT) measures, and inferences are drawn from the mean RTs computed over groups of subjects (e.g., Ashcraft & Battaglia, 1978; Ashcraft & Stazyk, 1981; Geary, Widaman, & Little, 1986; Groen & Parkman, 1972; Miller, Perlmutter, & Keating, 1984; Parkman, 1972; Parkman & Groen, 1971; Stazyk, Ashcraft, & Hamann, 1982; Winkelman & Schmidt, 1974). The principal finding to emerge from these studies is the so-called "problem-size effect," the tendency for RT to be longer for problems with large operands (e.g., 7 + 8) than for problems with smaller operands (e.g., 4 + 3).

Table-search Models.   Largely on the basis of the problem-size effect, several researchers have proposed that arithmetic fact retrieval involves a search through a table-like representation. Table-search models have been proposed to account for fact retrieval performance in addition (e.g., Ashcraft & Battaglia,

1978; Ashcraft & Stazyk, 1981; Widaman, Geary, Cormier, & Little, 1989), and in multiplication (e.g., Geary et al., 1986; Miller et al., 1984; Parkman, 1972; Stazyk et al., 1982). For both addition and multiplication, arithmetic fact representations are assumed to be organized into a two-dimensional table with rows and columns corresponding to problem operands. In a typical model the rows and columns are headed by "entry" or "parent" nodes representing the values 0 through 9. The answer to a problem is assumed to be stored at the intersection of the appropriate row and column. In a multiplication table, for example, the answer 63 would be stored at the intersection of the row with entry node 7 and the column with entry node 9.

When a problem is presented, the corresponding row and column entry nodes are activated (e.g., the row for 4 and the column for 8 given the problem 4×8), and activation spreads along the row and down the column until an intersection occurs at the location where the correct answer is stored. Latency to respond is assumed to reflect the time needed for the search process to reach the appropriate location in the table. In general, as the size of a problem's operands increase, so will the distance that must be traversed within the table in order to retrieve the answer. For example, activation must spread a greater distance down a column and across a row in the case of 8×7 than in the case of 3×2. In this way the table-search models interpret the problem-size effect.

Proponents of table-search models, although agreeing on the basic assumption of a table-like organization for arithmetic facts, have debated the details of the representations and the retrieval process. In particular, questions about how the table is entered and searched have been the point of departure for much research over the last 15 years. These questions have been addressed primarily through regression analyses in which competing "structural variables" are compared in an effort to determine which best predicts the RT data obtained in studies of fact retrieval. The "winning" variable is then incorporated into some theoretical account. Some of the more popular structural variables hypothesized to date are the sum of the operands (e.g., Stazyk et al., 1982), the sum-squared (e.g., Ashcraft & Battaglia, 1978), and the product (e.g., Miller et al., 1984).

A number of questions can be raised about the fruitfulness of the research program just described. For one thing, the search for the single structural variable that best accounts for the data is unlikely to yield any clear result. This is due to the fact that most of the variables considered in the analyses are highly intercorrelated (e.g., sum and sum-squared) and thus often difficult to differentiate empirically.

A more fundamental issue concerns the viability of the basic assumption of a table-like organization for arithmetic facts. As noted above, this assumption is motivated primarily by the empirical finding of a problem-size effect. However, as several researchers have recently pointed out, the empirical result does not in fact take the form required by the table-search models.

Table-search models predict that RT will increase monotonically with (some measure of) problem size. Yet, whereas numerous studies have found that larger problems tend to show longer RT than smaller ones, systematic departures from monotonicity have been documented. Certain subsets of facts have been found to yield faster response times than their size parameters would suggest. For example, it has been reported by many researchers that the so-called "tie problems" (i.e., problems with two identical operands such as 7 + 7) all show approximately equal RT, and are typically quicker than non-tie problems overall. Thus, verification RT for 7 + 7 = 14 is about the same as for 3 + 3 = 6, and both are quicker than 4 + 7 = 11. This tie effect has been an especially robust finding in addition (e.g., Groen & Parkman, 1972; Ashcraft & Battaglia, 1978), although some differences between tie and non-tie problems have been reported in multiplication as well (e.g., Miller et al., 1984).

Other departures from the pattern of monotonically increasing RT with problem size have also been reported. For example, problems where one of the operands is 5 (e.g., 5 × 6) tend to show relatively fast RTs (Campbell & Graham, 1985). In fact, based on reanalyses of Miller et al.'s (1984) data, Campbell and Graham conclude that " . . . only the 4, 8, and 9 times problems occupied the rank order RT position predicted by structural variables [i.e., measures of problem size]" p. 432).

More generally, idiosyncrasies appear to be widespread in arithmetic fact retrieval (e.g., Miller et al., 1984). That is, individuals differ in the relative ease with which particular facts are accessed. Such differences are generally reflected in slower reaction times and/or higher error rates to certain problems than to others. When averaging performance over groups of subjects, these differences are often masked, and therefore what appear as general trends on an individual basis (i.e., larger problems tend to take longer to respond to than smaller ones) may be interpreted as steadfast processing rules (cf. Siegler, 1987). In the light of the above considerations, it seems that the primary empirical motivation for table-search models (i.e., the problem-size effect) may be more apparent than actual.

These problems have not gone unrecognized by researchers hypothesizing table-search models. Miller et al. (1984), in fact, note many of the points we have discussed:

> In addition to the practical difficulties facing attempts to differentiate between similar models of the structure of the representation underlying arithmetic, it may well be the case that a general table-like representation of arithmetic information is only a first approximation of the cognitive structure underlying adults' performance of arithmetic. Such a network may be complicated by the persistence into adulthood of widespread idiosyncrasies in individual subjects' representation and performance of arithmetic. (p. 57)

Unfortunately, no adequate solutions for these problems have been proposed within the table-search framework.

Another shortcoming of the table-search models is that these models have little or nothing to say about errors. In producing or verifying arithmetic facts, normal adults who know the facts well nevertheless err occasionally, and their errors are highly systematic (e.g., Campbell, 1987a, 1987b; Campbell & Graham, 1985; Miller et al., 1984). However, table-search theorists have failed to specify how errors might come about in the course of searching a table-like representation, and it is not clear that the models could be extended in any straightforward way to account for errors.

Finally, table-search models offer no insights into the patterns of fact-retrieval impairment observed in brain-damaged patients. For example, why does Patient P.S. have difficulty with certain problems but not with others? The finding that impairment was, in general, greater for problems with large operands than for problems with small operands might appear consistent with the assumption of a table-like representation. However, as with the problem-size effect in RT data from normal subjects, there are clear exceptions to the generalization of greater impairment for large than for small problems (see Table 3.1). Further, how do the errors come about in the first place? Although ad hoc accounts for observed patterns of impairment might possibly be developed within the table-search framework, conceptualizing the deficits in terms of a disrupted table-search process seems unlikely to prove fruitful.

Direct Association Models.   Recently, a somewhat different type of arithmetic fact retrieval model has been proposed by Siegler and his colleagues (e.g., Siegler, 1988; Siegler & Shrager, 1984), and Campbell and his colleagues (e.g., Campbell, 1987a, 1987b; Campbell & Graham, 1985). Although the Siegler and Campbell models differ in some respects, their assumptions are fundamentally similar. In the following discussion we consider the two models together, presenting a generic version that reflects the essential features of both without corresponding precisely to either. We refer to this generic model as a *direct-association model.*

The direct-association model assumes that problems are associated directly with candidate answers. For example, the problem 6×7 may be associated in memory with the correct answer 42, but also with some incorrect answers such as 48, 36, or 43. The associations vary in strength, such that at least in the normal adult system a problem is usually associated most strongly with the correct answer.

When a problem is presented, associated answers become activated in proportion to their strengths of association to the problem. Given that the correct answer has the strongest association, this answer is usually selected by the retrieval process, and produced as the response. Occasionally, however, an incorrect answer associated with the problem may be retrieved instead (due, for example, to activation of that answer during the processing of an earlier problem; see Campbell, 1987b).

Direct association models interpret the problem-size effect as reflecting differences between large and small problems in amount of practice (e.g., Campbell & Graham, 1985; Siegler, 1988). That is, small problems may be encountered more often than large problems, leading to stronger associations between problems and correct answers for the former. This interpretation has the advantage of not requiring RT to increase monotonically with problem size. Exceptions to the general trend of more practice for smaller problems (e.g., extensive practice on large tie problems) would be expected to yield departures from strict monotonicity. (See also Campbell & Graham, 1985, for discussion of another factor that may contribute to the problem-size effect.)

Direct association models also hold promise for interpreting errors. As discussed above, errors are assumed to occur when an incorrect answer associated with a problem is retrieved instead of the correct answer. Finally, this type of model may prove useful for understanding the patterns of impairment observed in brain-damaged patients. If brain damage is conceived of as weakening associations between problems and answers, or as adding noise to the process of activating candidate responses, we might expect to observe impairment that varies in severity across problems (depending upon the initial strength of association between problems and correct or incorrect answers). Further, we might expect brain-damaged patients, although erring more often than normal individuals, to make the same sorts of errors as those observed in studies of normal subjects. (And, indeed, this is what we have typically found.)

Although the direct association models proposed by Siegler and Campbell appear promising, some aspects of these models are in need of further development. For example, both Siegler and Campbell have made some attempt to specify the types of incorrect answers that become associated with a problem, and the sources of these associations (see especially Siegler, 1988). However, more explicit assumptions, and further efforts to derive testable consequences of these assumptions, will be required before the models can be considered adequately constrained. In the absence of specific, testable claims, any observed pattern of errors could be interpreted simply by postulating associations between problems and the observed incorrect answers.

Arithmetic Facts and Arithmetic Rules:
The Facts About Zero

Both table search and direct association models assume that the answers to most basic arithmetic problems are stored as individual fact representations (e.g., $6 \times 7 = 42$ for the problem 6×7, and $6 \times 8 = 48$ for the problem 6×8). Some arithmetic facts, however, may be stored in the form of general rules. For example, several researchers (e.g., Ashcraft, 1983; Ashcraft, Fierman, & Bartolotta, 1984; Baroody, 1983, 1984; Campbell & Graham, 1985; Miller et al., 1984; Parkman, 1972; Stazyk et al., 1982) have suggested that the answers to 0's multiplication problems may be stored not as individual facts (e.g., $0 \times 1 = 0, 0 \times 2 = 0$, etc.), but rather as a rule that applies to all 0s problems (e.g., any number times 0 is 0). Although this suggestion appears reasonable, little if any relevant evidence has emerged from studies of normal calculation. However, results from several brain-damaged patients tested in our laboratory provide clear support for the 0-rule hypothesis.

Patient P.S.   In all 23 blocks of single-digit multiplication problems, P.S. responded correctly to the problem 0×0. However, for problems of the form $0 \times n$ or $n \times 0$ (where n is a non-zero number, as in 6×0 or 0×4), she presented with a pattern of severe impairment followed by sudden and dramatic improvement. In the first 9 blocks of trials, P.S. erred on 98% of the $0 \times n$ and $n \times 0$ problems, in all instances giving the number n as her response (e.g., $6 \times 0 = 6, 0 \times 4 = 4$). In Blocks 10–23, however, P.S. was 95% *correct* on $0 \times n$ and $n \times 0$ problems.

A striking feature of the $0 \times n/n \times 0$ results is that each individual problem showed the same performance pattern. Table 3.2 presents results for the individual problems in Blocks 1–9, and Blocks 10–23. It is apparent from the table that all of the problems were initially impaired to the same extent, and all improved to the same extent. Further, the sudden improvement in performance occurred at the

TABLE 3.2
Performance of Patient P.S. on $0 \times N$ and $N \times 0$
Problems in Blocks 1–9 and 10–23

	Number of Correct Responses	
Problem	Blocks 1–9	Blocks 10–23
0×1	0	13
0×2	1	12
0×3	0	12
0×4	1	13
0×5	0	14
0×6	0	12
0×7	0	14
0×8	0	14
0×9	1	14
1×0	0	14
2×0	0	14
3×0	0	14
4×0	0	14
5×0	0	13
6×0	0	12
7×0	0	14
8×0	0	14
9×0	1	12

same point in testing for each of the problems. P.S. was incorrect on all of the $0 \times$ n/n $\times$ 0 problems in Block 9, but correct on all of these problems in Block 10. Finally, the nature of the errors (i.e., responding n to $0 \times$ n or n $\times$ 0) was the same for all problems.

P.S.'s performance on $0 \times$ n/n $\times$ 0 problems stands in contrast to her performance on problems with two non-zero operands (which we will refer to as m $\times$ n problems). As discussed in an earlier section (see Table 3.1), impairment was not uniform over the set of m $\times$ n problems. Even within individual rows and columns of the table, the degree of impairment varied across problems. For example, examination of the 8s row reveals that the error rate was very low for $8 \times 1, 8 \times 2, 8 \times 3, 8 \times 6$, and 8×9, somewhat higher for $8 \times 4, 8 \times 5$, and 8×7, and higher still for 8×8.

Further, although P.S.'s performance on m $\times$ n problems improved over the course of testing, the improvement differed from that observed for the $0 \times$ n and n $\times$ 0 problems in two respects. First, improvement on m $\times$ n problems for the most part took the form of a gradual decrease in the likelihood of an error, rather than a sudden transition from floor to ceiling performance. Second, improvement for the m $\times$ n problems was not uniform across problems. Rather, the extent and timing of improvement varied across problems, even within the individual rows and columns of the m $\times$ n table.

To summarize the relevant data, P.S.'s performance in single-digit multiplication by zero was strikingly uniform across problems. All 18 $0 \times$ n/n $\times$ 0 problems were initially impaired, and all were impaired to the same extent. Further, all of the problems showed recovery, and all recovered to the same extent and at the same time. In contrast, P.S.'s performance was not uniform across the m $\times$ n problems. Her error rate, the amount of improvement she exhibited over the testing period, and the timing of the improvement varied across problems. These results strongly suggest that whereas responses to m $\times$ n problems (with the possible exception of the 1s problems) are generated by retrieving stored representations of individual facts (e.g., $9 \times 4 = 36; 9 \times 5 = 45$), 0's problems are solved by reference to a general rule that applies to all of these problems.

The postulation of a multiplication-by-0 rule permits a straightforward explanation for P.S.'s performance on 0's problems: All 0's problems showed the same pattern of performance because all are solved by reference to a single rule representation. More specifically, we may assume that in the first 9 blocks of trials P.S. was unable to access the 0 rule, and consequently showed impairment on all 0's problems. However, beginning with Block 10, P.S. regained access to the rule, with the result that all problems showed improvement. (The reasons for P.S.'s recovery of the rule are beyond the scope of the present discussion; see Sokol, McCloskey, Cohen, & Aliminosa, 1991.)

If we do not posit a 0 rule, but instead assume that performance on 0's problems is mediated by retrieval of individual fact representations (e.g., 6×0

= 0 for the problem 6 × 0, 7 × 0 = 0 for the problem 7 × 0), then P.S.'s performance pattern is difficult to explain. We would have to assume that although m × n fact representations were disrupted nonuniformly, disruption of 0's fact representations was for some reason entirely uniform. Further, we would have to assume that whereas access to m × n representations improved nonuniformly, access to all 0's fact representations improved at the same time and to the same extent. These assumptions are at best unmotivated.

Converging Evidence for the 0-Rule Hypothesis: Patient G.E.   A second patient we have studied, G.E., presented with a performance pattern similar in many respects to that of P.S. Like P.S., G.E. showed largely intact number comprehension and production, but was impaired in arithmetic fact retrieval. (Over 22 blocks of 100 single-digit multiplication problems, G.E.'s error rate was approximately 25%).

Table 3.3 presents G.E.'s error rates for each of the individual problems. It is apparent from the table that his performance differed dramatically depending on whether or not a problem involved multiplication by zero. For m × n problems (i.e., those with two non-zero operands) G.E.'s error rate was only 9%, and the level of impairment was nonuniform across problems. For 0 × n/n × 0 problems, however, G.E. was uniformly and drastically impaired: He responded incorrectly to all of these problems (amounting to almost 400 errors). Like P.S., G.E. always gave the non-zero operand as his response (e.g., 3 × 0 = 3). This pattern of uniform impairment across the 0 × n/n × 0 problems clearly supports the hypothesis that all of the problems are solved by reference to a single rule.

Patient A.T.   Additional support for the 0-rule hypothesis comes from a remediation study we conducted with another brain-damaged patient, A.T. In

TABLE 3.3
Percentage of Errors for Patient G.E. on Individual Problems

First Operand	Second Operand									
	0	*1*	*2*	*3*	*4*	*5*	*6*	*7*	*8*	*9*
0	0	100	100	100	100	100	100	100	100	100
1	100	27	18	18	14	23	9	14	0	0
2	100	14	0	0	0	0	9	0	5	0
3	100	23	5	5	10	9	5	5	5	45
4	100	9	0	9	14	0	9	14	0	0
5	100	14	0	5	0	9	0	23	9	32
6	100	5	0	5	10	0	19	5	14	14
7	100	9	5	9	5	10	9	36	14	23
8	100	0	5	5	0	9	14	10	0	5
9	100	9	0	14	0	0	14	25	5	9

initial testing this patient presented with a severe impairment in arithmetic fact retrieval, including an inability to solve correctly any single-digit problems involving zero.

Once this pattern was documented, A.T. was selectively retrained on several multiplication facts, including two involving zero ($0 \times 6 = 0$, and $3 \times 0 = 0$). After remediation, A.T. responded correctly to all $0 \times n/n \times 0$ problems, suggesting that training on the two individual 0's problems led to recovery (or creation) of a rule applying to all of the 0's problems. Recovery of nonstudied facts was observed only for the 0's facts; no recovery was observed for any nonstudied $m \times n$ fact. For example, before training, A.T. was 0% correct for the problem 3×4. She remained completely impaired on this fact after training even though a number of different facts involving the operands 3 and 4 were trained.

CALCULATION PROCEDURES

Developmental Studies

The solution of single-digit arithmetic problems requires only the retrieval of basic arithmetic facts. In contrast, solving multidigit problems requires both fact retrieval and the execution of calculation procedures. Although the majority of research in calculation has concentrated on fact retrieval, several recent studies have addressed the development of calculation procedures. One theme emerging from such research is that children's procedural errors are systematic, and result from the application of "buggy" algorithms (e.g., Brown & Burton, 1978; Brown & VanLehn, 1980, 1982; Resnick, 1982; Young & O'Shea, 1981). For example, a child with an incomplete understanding of the subtraction algorithm may systematically subtract the smaller number from the larger, regardless of which number happens to be on top:

$$
\begin{array}{r}
83 \\
-67 \\
\hline
24
\end{array}
$$

Bugs may arise either from misunderstanding of instructional material, or from children's attempts to "repair" incomplete algorithms (i.e., attempts to determine the appropriate action in situations to which an incomplete algorithm does not apply; see Brown & VanLehn, 1980, 1982). For example, the subtract-smaller-from-larger bug may arise when a child whose subtraction algorithm does not include a borrowing routine encounters problems that require borrowing. These notions of bugs and repairs may prove important for understanding not only the development of calculation procedures, but also the procedural impairments observed in brain-damaged patients.

Consideration of the characteristics of bugs has led certain researchers to question the relationship between procedural knowledge and conceptual knowledge. For example, Resnick (1982) asks whether explicit conceptual knowledge about the base ten nature of our number system could prevent the development of certain bugs among children learning subtraction.

Special-Case Procedures in Calculation

Researchers studying bugs in children's calculation procedures have typically assumed that the endpoint of the learning process is a set of general-purpose algorithms for carrying out multi-digit computations. Results from our studies of patients P.S. and G.E. suggest, however, that procedural knowledge may also encompass "special-case" procedures that bypass the general algorithm under certain conditions, and thereby increase the speed or efficiency of problem-solving.

As we noted in an earlier section, P.S. made fact retrieval errors in solving both single- and multidigit multiplication problems. Indeed, her fact retrieval performance was virtually identical for single- and multidigit problems. When the multidigit problems were scored for performance on individual $m \times n$ facts (i.e., those involving two non-zero operands), it was found that P.S.'s error rate was almost exactly the same as for single-digit problems. Furthermore, she made the same types of errors, and tended to err on the same problems. For example, a comparison of error rates for individual facts across single- and multidigit problems revealed a correlation of .92.

However, one clear exception to the correspondence between single- and multidigit problems was observed: P.S. demonstrated quite different performance with the $0 \times n/n \times 0$ problems across single- and multidigit problems. During the period in which she was only 2% correct on single-digit $0 \times n/n \times 0$ problems, she was 100% correct on 0's facts occurring in the context of multidigit problems. Fig. 3.7 presents two examples of her performance on multidigit problems involving 0s. Both of these problems were solved during a session in which P.S. responded incorrectly to every $0 \times n$ and $n \times 0$ item in a block of single-digit problems.

Interpretations for the Dissociation.   At least two possible interpretations may be suggested for the dissociation between the single- and multidigit 0's problems. One possibility is that for some unspecified reason, P.S. was able to access the 0's multiplication rule in the context of multidigit multiplication problems, but not in the context of single-digit problems. This interpretation seems somewhat implausible given that performance on the $m \times n$ facts was virtually identical in the single- and multidigit problem contexts. However, it might be argued that whereas $m \times n$ facts are regularly retrieved in both single-digit and multidigit contexts, single-digit 0s problems are rarely encountered.

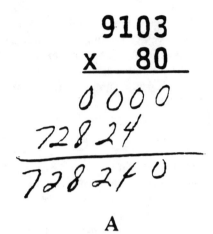

A

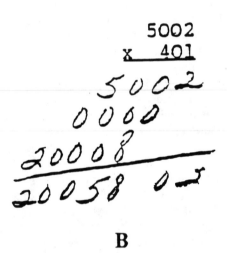

B

FIG. 3.7. Examples of P.S.'s performance on multidigit multiplications problems involving 0s during the period in which she was virtually always incorrect on single-digit 0s problems.

That is, multiplication by 0 is required almost exclusively in the context of multidigit problems. As a consequence, the 0 rule may conceivably be more difficult to access in the context of single-digit problems than in the context of multidigit problems. If this were the case, then disruption of arithmetic fact retrieval might well result in impaired access to the 0 rule in single- but not multidigit multiplication.

An alternative account of the 0's dissociation postulates special-case procedures for processing 0s in multidigit multiplication problems. On this account, certain context-sensitive procedures circumvent the application of the general-purpose multiplication algorithm to 0's in multidigit problems, generating appropriate responses by other means. For example, one special-case 0's procedure might specify something like the following: "If the current top row operand is a 0, bring down the carry from the preceding fact retrieval or, if there is no carry, write 0." Applied to the problem in Fig. 3.7A, this procedure would generate the 2 next to the 4 in the second row of partial products simply by bringing down the carry digit from the multiplication of 3 by 8. In contrast, application of the general-purpose multiplication algorithm would involve retrieval of the product of 8 and 0 (which would require accessing the 0 rule), and then the adding of the carry digit to the retrieved product. The special-case procedures account would explain the 0's dissociation by assuming that whereas the 0 rule was initially inaccessible in both single- and multidigit multiplication contexts, the special-case procedures for processing 0s in multidigit problems were intact.

P.S.'s performance pattern offers no clear basis for choosing between these two accounts. However, results from Patient G.E. provide strong evidence in favor of the special-case procedures interpretation.

Evidence from Patient G.E.   In addition to 22 blocks of single-digit multiplication problems, G.E. was given 109 multidigit multiplication problems. He erred on 35 of the problems (32%). For the most part, G.E.'s incorrect responses resulted from fact retrieval errors of the same sorts he made on single-digit problems. This similarity between single- and multidigit problems noted, separate inspection of the 56 multidigit problems which contained zeros within their operands revealed a striking dissociation. Whereas G.E. was 0% correct on single-digit 0s problems, he was virtually 100% correct on 0's portions of multidigit problems. Most importantly, on the multidigit problems he never made an error interpretable in terms of impaired retrieval of a 0's fact (or rule). Thus, in multiplication by 0, G.E. presented with a pattern of performance very similar to that of P.S.

Although P.S.'s performance dissociation between single- and multidigit 0's problems was somewhat equivocal with respect to the two explanations offered above, G.E.'s performance allows us to choose between them. We asked G.E. to provide verbal reports of the steps he took in solving multidigit multiplication problems, while we visually observed his solution strategy. Fig. 3.8 presents four multidigit multiplication problems he was asked to solve. Below each is the verbal report he gave as well as relevant observations of the experimenter.

The problem in Fig. 3.8A illustrates the procedure of writing a 0 as a place holder when it appears in the right-most position in the bottom column (in G.E.'s terms "zero stands for the top line" or alternately "bring down the zero"). In the problem in Fig. 3.8B, G.E. writes down three 0 place holders (saying each as he writes), takes the product of 2 and 7, holds the carry digit in his head, takes the product of 2 and 8, and finally adds the carry.

A)

$$
\begin{array}{r}
618 \\
\times\ \ 90 \\
\hline
55620
\end{array}
$$

"This zero stands for all of the top line so that [referring to the zero] goes down there [writing the right-most zero]."

B)

$$
\begin{array}{r}
87 \\
\times\ 2000 \\
\hline
174000
\end{array}
$$

"Zero, zero, zero [writing down three zeroes right to left], uh two times seven is fourteen, two times eight is sixteen is seventeen."

C)

$$
\begin{array}{r}
904 \\
\times\ 307 \\
\hline
6328 \\
27120 \\
\hline
277528
\end{array}
$$

"Twenty-eight, put it down because zero is there on this seven so nine times seven is sixty-three. Alright, so zero covers everything up here. Two carry the one, so that's twelve automatically, and nine times three is twenty-seven."

D)

$$
\begin{array}{r}
3006 \\
\times\ \ \ 28 \\
\hline
24048 \\
6012 \\
\hline
84168
\end{array}
$$

"Forty-eight, because this zero being placed there [points to the right-most zero], this 6 x 8 is automatically forty-eight. Bring down the zero. Eight times three is twenty-four..."

FIG. 3.8. Examples of G.E.'s performance on multidigit multiplications problems involving 0's, illustrating his use of special-case procedures.

The problem in Fig. 3.8C is more complicated in that it contains zeros in the middle of the operands. G.E. demonstrates a number of procedures in solving this problem. First, he knows that he may write the entire product 28 "because zero is there." In fact, he writes '28' from left-to-right rather than the typical right-to-left. Next, he takes the product of 7 and 9. He then writes down a 0 on the next line saying that "zero covers everything up here." In taking the product of 3 and 4 he elaborates his report to include the carry step over the 0 but still writes the "12" product left-to-right saying, "two carry the one so that's twelve automatically." He then completes the problem by taking the final product and summing.

In the problem in Fig. 3.8D, G.E. correctly solves a problem containing two internal 0s in succession. In so doing, he applies two different procedures to the respective zeros. First, he writes the product "48" left-to-right saying, "Forty-eight, because this zero being placed there, this six times eight is automatically forty-eight." He then "brings down the [next] zero" as a place holder, and then completes the rest of the problem in normal fashion.

It is clear from these verbal reports that G.E. does not solve 0's portions of problems with the general multiplication algorithm (which would treat a 0 like any other digit, and hence would require fact retrievals for the 0's portions of problems). Rather, G.E. applies special-case procedures. Contrast for example, what he says when solving 0's portions of the problem in Fig. 3.8C, versus those not involving zero. For 0's portions his reports include statements such as " . . . zero covers everything up here"; for non-zero portions his statements are of the order " . . . nine times three is twenty-seven." Note that G.E. never says of zero portions, a statement such as "zero times three is zero." (Indeed, if he were to do so, he might be expected to err.)

Even in the absence of G.E.'s verbal reports, it could be concluded that he used special-case 0's procedures. If G.E. had applied the general-purpose multiplication algorithm, and therefore had retrieved a fact for each product involving zero, he would presumably have written each zero down just as required with non-zero products. For example, in the problem in Fig. 3.8A, he should have written three 0s on the first solution line to correspond to each product, rather than the place holder zero.

CONCEPTUAL KNOWLEDGE

Developmental Studies

Although a substantial body of research addresses issues concerning the development of number concepts (e.g., Gelman & Gallistel, 1978), less effort has been devoted to the acquisition of concepts related specifically to arithmetic. Piaget (1951), in his seminal work *The Child's Conception of Number,* stressed the importance not only of conservation, but also of inversion and compensation (for a description and critique of some of this work, see Starkey & Gelman, 1982). Inversion refers to a relation such as that expressed in the following equation: $a + b - b = a - b + b = a$. That is, adding a particular quantity to a number can be negated by subtracting the same quantity from the number. This relationship is obviously at the crux of an understanding of the complementary nature of addition and subtraction. Compensation refers to a relation such as that expressed by the logical equation: if $a = b$, then $a + c = b + c$ (or if $a > b$, then $a + c > b + c$). That is, if a particular relation between two numbers holds (e.g., equal to, greater than), then the addition of a third number to the first can be compensated for by addition of the third number to the second. A number of experiments have been conducted to examine children's understanding of inversion and compensation (e.g., Cooper, Starkey, Blevins, Goth & Leitner, 1978; Gelman, 1972; Smedslund, 1966). The development of other conceptual properties such as commutativity and associativity has not, however, received as much attention.

In general, though, it is becoming increasingly clear that an understanding of children's early concepts involving numbers and arithmetic operations is extremely important both to basic calculation research and to applied research on improving mathematics education (Davydov, 1982). Further, it is also important to consider the degree to which development of arithmetic concepts may be supported by prior or parallel development of more general conceptual knowledge (Case, 1982).

Relationship of Arithmetic Facts and Conceptual Knowledge

Is knowledge of arithmetic facts and calculation procedures inextricably bound up with knowledge of the conceptual underpinnings of these facts and procedures? Or is the knowledge of facts and procedures distinct from the conceptual knowledge? Recent studies involving brain-damaged patients with arithmetic fact retrieval impairments shed some light on this issue. For example, Warrington (1982) has described a patient, D.R.C., who presented with difficulties in accessing arithmetic facts as indicated by errors (e.g., $5 + 7 = 13$), and abnormally slow response times. This patient was able, however, to give reasonable definitions of the four arithmetic operations. For example, he defined subtraction as " . . . the reduction of the magnitude of a particular number by the magnitude of another number . . ." (p. 34).

Based on this and other related findings, Warrington concluded that in D.R.C.'s case, "it was his knowledge of arithmetical *facts* and not his knowledge of arithmetical *operations* which was impaired" (emphasis in original; p. 45). Warrington's result suggests that in some brain-damaged patients, access to certain arithmetic concepts may remain intact in the face of impaired knowledge of arithmetic facts.

McCloskey et al. (1985) noted a related impairment in their patient M.W. Like Warrington's patient, M.W. presented with a selective impairment in retrieval of arithmetic facts; his knowledge of arithmetic operations, however, appeared intact. Furthermore, M.W. was able on occasion to solve multiplication problems in spite of an inability to retrieve particular facts, by relying instead upon conceptual understanding of arithmetic operations. For example, when unable to remember the answer to 7×7, he calculated the product correctly as $70 (7 \times 10) - 21 (7 \times 3)$. Spiers (1987) reported a similar ability in a "Wernicke's aphasic," who had pronounced difficulty accessing multiplication facts. To compensate for this impairment, this patient resorted to a strategy of using successive addition to solve multiplication problems.

Perhaps the clearest evidence that conceptual knowledge of arithmetic is functionally distinct from knowledge of arithmetic facts comes from a study conducted in our laboratory with patient I.E. (Sokol et al., 1989). I.E. is a 56-year-old right-handed woman who underwent surgery for removal of a benign brain tumor. She is a high school graduate, and was employed prior to her surgery as the secretary to the president of an insurance company, with duties including claim adjustment and bookkeeping.

I.E. was substantially impaired in retrieval of multiplication facts, and also evidenced difficulty in accessing some addition facts, specifically those in which the sum was greater than 10. I.E. was well aware of her problems in retrieving arithmetic facts. However, she claimed that if permitted to "work out" answers, she would be able to do so accurately.

This claim turned out to be well-founded. For addition problems, I.E. relied heavily on knowledge about the operand combinations that add to ten, using this knowledge to arrive at correct solutions for facts she was unable to access directly. Two verbal reports of the steps she takes in solving such addition problems follow:

9 + 2: "Nine plus two. That's easy because I add one to nine to get my ten
        and then I have only one left, so it's eleven."
8 + 5: "Eight plus five. Let's see, I have to take two off [of five] to get [from
        eight] to ten which gives me three more, so it's thirteen."

I.E.'s ability to figure out addition problems for which the stored fact is inaccessible reflects substantial conceptual knowledge about arithmetic. For example, she clearly understands the law of associativity for addition which enables her (in the first example above) to recast the problem [9 + 2] as [9 + (1 + 1)] and then as [(9 + 1) + 1].

I.E.'s ability to calculate multiplication problems for which the stored fact was inaccessible provides further evidence of her ability to use conceptual level knowledge in arithmetic problem solving. During three separate testing sessions, I.E. was asked to solve the 100 single-digit multiplication problems. For each problem I.E. was instructed first to attempt to retrieve the answer from memory. If she was unable to retrieve an answer, or if she simply wanted to check her answer for accuracy, she was permitted to do so after an initial response (or "don't know" response) was given.

Although her initial responses were as impaired as in earlier testing, I.E. was virtually always correct when permitted to work the problems out. Fig. 3.9 shows two examples in which I.E. solved problems with a conceptually based strategy.

A)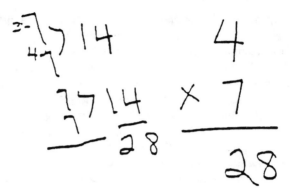

B)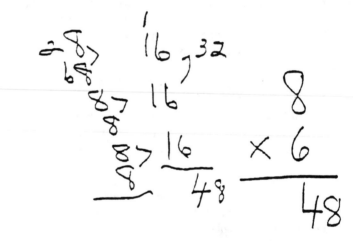

FIG. 3.9. Examples of I.E.'s strategy for working out multiplication facts she is unable to solve through fact retrieval.

I.E. clearly understands on a conceptual level that the process of multiplication is equivalent to successive additions. For example, in the first problem (4 × 7), she adds 7 four times. In employing the successive addition strategy, I.E. always chooses to add the large operand a number of times corresponding to the smaller operand. This choice on her part is not only highly efficient (i.e., it minimizes the number of computations needed for correct solution), but also demonstrates knowledge of the law of multiplicative commutativity. I.E.'s knowledge of commutativity was also revealed more explicitly on a number of occasions when she was unable to retrieve the response for an ordered operand combination, but knew its complement. For example, on one occasion when I.E. was unable to access the answer to the problem 8×7, she said, "I don't know, but it's the same as 7×8 so it must be 56."

I.E.'s ability to keep track of the various steps needed in her multiplication problem solving is particularly striking when considered in light of her difficulty with addition. In the example shown in Fig. 3.9B, I.E. first decides to work out the product of 8 and 6 by taking six successive additions of 8, but then, not knowing what $8 + 8$ equals, must compute this initial sum by determining that 8 is two less than 10, that taking 2 from (the other) 8 leaves 6, and that adding the 6 and the 10 yields 16. Next, she adds the three 16s (again using her addition strategy), finally arriving at the answer 48.

The performance of I.E. and the other patients discussed earlier suggests that arithmetic fact retrieval may be disrupted while conceptual knowledge of arithmetic remains intact, and hence that conceptual and fact knowledge are functionally distinct. This finding is perhaps not surprising in that arithmetic facts may often be learned essentially by rote, with no necessary connection to conceptual knowledge of arithmetic operations. The results also demonstrate that conceptual knowledge may be used to compensate for impaired fact retrieval. Of course, this finding does not necessarily imply that conceptual knowledge plays a functional role in basic arithmetic for individuals with intact calculation systems.

CONCLUDING REMARKS

The Importance of Specialized Knowledge in Problem-Solving

Calculation provides a very clear if obvious illustration of the general principle that development of problem-solving expertise in a domain often involves acquisition of facts and procedures dedicated specifically to solving problems in that domain. As we have seen, problem-solving in basic arithmetic makes use of a variety of specialized facts, rules, and procedures (e.g., $9 \times 5 = 45$, $0 \times n/n \times 0 = 0$, the general multidigit multiplication algorithm, special-case procedures for processing 0s). In principle, however, arithmetic problems could be solved without these facts and procedures. General reasoning processes, coupled with conceptual knowledge of numbers and arithmetic operations, would probably suffice. For example, the single-digit multiplication problem 7×6 might be solved by recognizing that multiplication can be conceived of as successive addition, so that the problem could be restated as $7 + 7 + 7 + 7 + 7 + 7$. Pairs of 7s might then be added by counting, and the resulting 14s might be dealt with in a similar fashion, leading ultimately to the answer 42. Alternatively, one might recognize that the product of 7 and 6 corresponds to the area of a rectangle 7 units long and 6 units wide. Thus, one might draw such a rectangle, marking off the units, and counting the resulting squares. These approaches could also be applied to multidigit problems.

Although problems could in principle be solved in these ways, the solution process would obviously be extremely slow (and probably also error-prone), especially in the case of multidigit problems. From this perspective, the calculation mechanisms we have described in this chapter may be seen as a set of specialized facts and procedures well-designed for rapid and accurate problem-solving. For example, in the realm of multiplication, memorization of the single-digit products ensures that these products will be available quickly when needed, and will not have to be laboriously worked out. The advantage gained thereby may be appreciated by examining the attempt of patient I.E. to solve a simple multidigit problem in the absence of an ability to retrieve the necessary single-digit facts. As shown in Fig. 3.10, when presented with the problem 39 × 24, I.E. had to work out each individual fact. Although she arrived at the correct answer, the time and effort required were considerable.

Similarly, the multidigit multiplication procedure provides a straightforward method for decomposing large problems into small (i.e., single-digit) problems, the answers to which have been memorized, and then combining the answers to the small problems to obtain the answer to the problem as a whole.

Special-case procedures for processing 0s in multidigit multiplication offer an especially clear example of the role of specialized knowledge in promoting

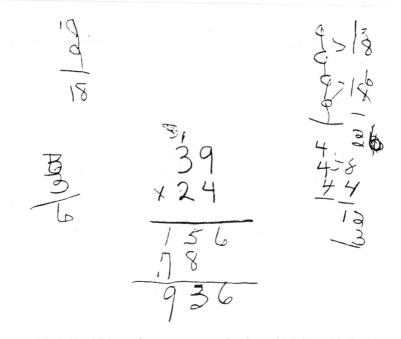

FIG. 3.10.   I.E.'s performance on a simple multidigit multiplication problem.

efficient problem-solving. The special-case procedures are not necessary for solving multidigit multiplication problems that include 0s; the general-purpose multiplication algorithm applies to 0s as well as to non-zero digits in the operands of a multidigit problem. For example, the problem in Fig. 3.8A could be solved without special-case procedures, by multiplying 0×8, then 0×1, and then 0×6, writing a 0 after each of these operations. Thus, the special-case procedures apparently function simply to increase the speed and/or accuracy of the problem-solving process.

Finally, the development of skill levels beyond those normally encountered may involve the acquisition of additional facts and procedures specialized for use in problem-solving within the calculation domain. For example, one "lightning calculator" we have tested uses special-case procedures for computing squares, and also claims to have memorized all products from 0×0 through 99×99.

Cognitive Research with Brain-Damaged Subjects

In this chapter we have presented analyses of patterns of impaired performance exhibited by several brain-damaged subjects with acquired dyscalculia. Our aim was to motivate claims about normal cognitive mechanisms underlying calculation, and not to elucidate the functions of specific brain areas or the nature of cognitive deficits underlying a particular clinical syndrome. As in traditional cognitive research with normal subjects, we drew conclusions from the subjects' performance on cognitive tasks, and not from neurophysiological or neuroanatomical data (e.g., lesion localization).

Our choice of a brain-damaged subject population was not an arbitrary one. In recent years, there has been a growing realization that the performance of subjects with acquired cognitive deficits represents a rich and oftentimes unique source of information about normal cognitive processes. The advantages attached to cognitive research with brain-damaged subjects stem from the fact that brain damage may selectively impair particular components of a cognitive system in ways that are rarely observed and often impossible even to simulate in normal subjects (cf. McCloskey et al., 1990). Detailed analyses of the resulting patterns of impaired performance may reveal in a clear (and sometimes even dramatic) fashion the componential structure of the damaged cognitive system, as well as the inner workings of the various components. The convergence of findings from several patients with various forms of impairment to a cognitive function may therefore lead to rapid progress in the development of a well-articulated model of that function.

ACKNOWLEDGMENTS

This research was supported by NIH grant NS21047. We thank Donna Aliminosa for assistance in testing patients and analyzing data, and Valentina Ruzecki for helpful comments on an earlier draft.

REFERENCES

Ashcraft, M. H. (1982). The development of mental arithmetic: A chronometric approach. *Developmental Review*, *2*, 213–236.

Ashcraft, M. H. (1983). Procedural knowledge versus fact retrieval in mental arithmetic: A reply to Baroody. *Developmental Review*, *3*, 231–235.

Ashcraft, M. H., & Battaglia, J. (1978). Cognitive arithmetic: Evidence for retrieval and decision processes in mental addition. *Journal of Experimental Psychology: Human Learning and Memory*, *4*, 527–538.

Ashcraft, M. H., & Fierman, B. A. (1982). Mental addition in third, fourth, and sixth graders. *Journal of Experimental Child Psychology*, *33*, 216–234.

Ashcraft, M. H., Fierman, B. A., & Bartolotta, R. (1984). The production and verification tasks in mental addition: An empirical comparison. *Developmental Review*, *4*, 157–170.

Ashcraft, M. H., & Stazyk, E. H. (1981). Mental addition: A test of three verification models. *Memory and Cognition*, *9*, 185–196.

Baroody, A. J. (1983). The development of procedural knowledge: An alternative explanation for chronometric trends of mental arithmetic. *Developmental Review*, *3*, 225–230.

Baroody, A. J. (1984). A reexamination of mental arithmetic models and data: A reply to Ashcraft. *Developmental Review*, *4*, 148–156.

Beauvois, M. F., & Derouesne, J. (1979). Phonological alexia: Three dissociations. *Journal of Neurology, Neurosurgery, & Psychiatry*, *42*, 1115–1124.

Boller, F., & Grafman, J. (1983). Acalculia: Historical development and current significance. *Brain and Cognition*, *2*, 205–223.

Brown, J. S., & Burton, R. R. (1978). Diagnostic models for procedural bugs in basic mathematical skills. *Cognitive Science*, *2*, 155–192.

Brown, J. S., & VanLehn, K. (1980). Repair theory: A generative theory of bugs in procedural skills. *Cognitive Science*, *4*, 379–426.

Brown, J. S., & VanLehn, K. (1982). Towards a generative theory of "bugs." In T. P. Carpenter, J. M. Moser, & T. A. Romberg (Eds.), *Addition and subtraction: A cognitive perspective* (pp. 117–135). Hillsdale, NJ: Lawrence Erlbaum Associates.

Campbell, J. I. D. (1987a). Network interference and mental multiplication. *Journal of Experimental Psychology: Learning, Memory, & Cognition*, *13*, 109–123.

Campbell, J. I. D. (1987b). Production, verification, and priming of multiplication facts. *Memory & Cognition*, *15*, 349–364.

Campbell, J. I. D., & Graham, D. J. (1985). Mental multiplication skill: Structure, process, and acquisition. *Canadian Journal of Psychology*, *39*, 338–366.

Caramazza, A. (1986). On drawing inferences about the structure of normal cognitive systems from the analysis of patterns of impaired performance: The case for single-patient studies. *Brain and Cognition*, *5*, 41–66.

Caramazza, A., & McCloskey, M. (1987). Dissociations of calculation processes. In G. Deloche & X. Seron (Eds.), *Mathematical disabilities: A cognitive neuropsychological perspective.* (pp. 221–234). Hillsdale, NJ: Lawrence Erlbaum Associates.

Caramazza, A., & McCloskey, M. (1988). The case for single-patient studies. *Cognitive Neuropsychology*, *5*, 517–528.

Case, R. (1982). General developmental influences on the acquisition of elementary concepts and algorithms in arithmetic. In T. P. Carpenter, J. M. Moser, & T. A. Romberg (Eds.), *Addition and subtraction: A cognitive perspective* (pp. 157–170). Hillsdale, NJ: Lawrence Erlbaum Associates.

Cooper, R. G., Starkey, P., Blevins, B., Goth, P., & Leitner, E. (1978, May). *Number development: Addition and subtraction.* Paper presented at the meeting of the Jean Piaget Society, Philadelphia.

Davydov, V. V. (1982). The psychological characteristics of the formation of elementary mathematical operations in children. In T. P. Carpenter, J. M. Moser, & T. A. Romberg (Eds.), *Addition and subtraction: A cognitive perspective* (pp. 224–238). Hillsdale, NJ: Lawrence Erlbaum Associates.

Ellis, A. W. (1982). Spelling and writing (and reading and speaking). In A. W. Ellis (Ed.), *Normality and pathology in cognitive functions* (pp. 113–146). London: Academic Press.

Ferro, J. M., & Botelho, M. A. S. (1980). Alexia for arithmetical signs: A cause of disturbed calculation. *Cortex, 16*, 175–180.

Fuson, K. (1982). An analysis of the counting-on solution procedure in addition. In T. P. Carpenter, J. M. Moser, & T. A. Romberg (Eds.), *Addition and subtraction: A cognitive perspective* (pp. 67–81). Hillsdale, NJ: Lawrence Erlbaum Associates.

Geary, D. C., Widaman, K. F., & Little, T. D. (1986). Cognitive addition and multiplication: Evidence for a single memory network. *Memory & Cognition, 14*, 478–487.

Gelman, R. (1972). Logical capacity of very young children: Number invariance rules. *Child Development, 43*, 75–90.

Gelman, R., & Gallistel, C. R. (1978). *The child's understanding of number.* Cambridge, MA: Harvard University Press.

Goodman, R. A., & Caramazza, A. (1986). Aspects of the spelling process: Evidence from a case of acquired dysgraphia. *Language and Cognitive Processes, 1*, 263–296.

Grewel, F. (1952). Acalculia. *Brain, 75*, 397–407.

Grewel, F. (1969). The acalculias. In P. J. Vinken & G. W. Bruyn (Eds.), *Handbook of clinical neurology: Vol 4* (pp. 181–194). New York: Wiley.

Groen, G. J., & Parkman, J. M. (1972). A chronometric analysis of simple addition. *Psychological Review, 79*, 329–343.

Head, H. (1926). *Aphasia and kindred disorders of speech.* London: Cambridge University Press.

Hildebrandt, N., Caplan, D., & Evans, K. (1987). The man$_i$ left t$_i$ without a trace: A case study of aphasic processing of empty categories. *Cognitive Neuropsychology, 4*, 257–302.

Levin, H. S., & Spiers, P. A. (1985). Acalculia. In K. M. Heilman & Valenstein (Eds.), *Clinical neuropsychology* (pp. 97–114). New York: Oxford University Press.

McCloskey, M., & Caramazza, A. (1987). Cognitive mechanisms in normal and impaired number processing. In G. Deloche & X. Seron (Eds.), *Mathematical disabilities: A cognitive neuropsychological perspective* (pp. 201–219). Hillsdale, NJ: Lawrence Erlbaum Associates.

McCloskey, M., & Caramazza, A. (1988). Theory and methodology in cognitive neuropsychology: A response to our critics. *Cognitive Neuropsychology, 5*, 583–623.

McCloskey, M., Caramazza, A., & Basili, A. (1985). Cognitive mechanisms in number-processing and calculation: Evidence from dyscalculia. *Brain and Cognition, 4*, 171–196.

McCloskey, M., Sokol, S. M., & Goodman, R. A. (1986). Cognitive processes in verbal number production: Inferences from the performance of brain-damaged subjects. *Journal of Experimental Psychology: General, 115*, 307–330.

McCloskey, M., Sokol, S., Goodman-Schulman, R., & Caramazza, A. (1990). Cognitive representations and processes in number production: Evidence from cases of dyscalculia. In A. Caramazza (Ed.), *Advances in cognitive neuropsychology and neurolinguistics.* (pp. 1–32). Hillsdale, NJ: Lawrence Erlbaum Associates.

Miceli, G., Mazzuchi, A., Menn, L., & Goodglass, H. (1983). Contrasting cases of Italian agrammatic aphasia without comprehension disorder. *Brain and Language, 19*, 65–97.

Miller, K., Perlmutter, M., & Keating, D. (1984). Cognitive arithmetic: Comparison of operations. *Journal of Experimental Psychology: Learning, Memory, & Cognition, 10*, 46–60.

Parkman, J. M. (1972). Temporal aspects of simple multiplication and comparison. *Journal of Experimental Psychology, 95*, 437–444.

Parkman, J. M., & Groen, G. (1971). Temporal aspects of simple addition and comparison. *Journal of Experimental Psychology, 89*, 335–342.

Patterson, K. E. (1982). The relation between reading and phonological coding: Further neuropsychological observations. In A. W. Ellis (Ed.), *Normality and pathology in cognitive functions* (pp. 77–111). London: Academic Press.

Piaget, J. (1951). *The child's conception of number* (C. Gattegno & F. M. Hodgson, Trans.). London: Routledge & Kegan Paul. (Original work published 1941).

Resnick, L. B. (1982). Syntax and semantics in learning to subtract. In T. P. Carpenter, J. M. Moser, & T. A. Romberg (Eds.), *Addition and subtraction: A cognitive perspective* (pp. 136–155). Hillsdale, NJ: Lawrence Erlbaum Associates.

Siegler, R. S. (1987). The perils of averaging data over strategies: An example from children's addition. *Journal of Experimental Psychology: General, 116*, 250–264.

Siegler, R. S. (1988). Strategy choice procedures and the development of multiplication skill. *Journal of Experimental Psychology: General, 117*, 258–275.

Siegler, R. S., & Shrager, J. (1984). A model of strategy choice. In C. Sophian (Ed.), *Origins of cognitive skills* (pp. 229–293). Hillsdale, NJ: Lawrence Erlbaum Associates.

Smedslund, J. (1966). Microanalysis of concrete reasoning, I. The difficult of some combinations of addition and subtraction of one unit. *Scandinavian Journal of Psychology, 7*, 145–156.

Sokol, S., & McCloskey, M. (1988). Levels of representation in verbal number production. *Applied Psycholinguistics, 9*, 267–281.

Sokol, S. M., McCloskey, M., & Cohen, N. J. (1989). Cognitive representations of arithmetic knowledge: Evidence from acquired dyscalculia. In A. F. Bennett and K. M. McConkie (Eds.), *Cognition in individual and social contexts* (pp. 577–591). Amsterdam: Elsevier.

Sokol, S. M., McCloskey, M., Cohen, N. J., & Aliminosa, D. (1991). Cognitive representations and processes in arithmetic: Inferences from the performance of brain-damaged patients. *Journal of Experimental Psychology: Learning, Memory, & Cognition, 17*, 355–376.

Spiers, P. A. (1987). Acalculia revisited: Current issues. In G. Deloche & X. Seron (Eds.), *Mathematical disabilities: A cognitive neuropsychological perspective.* (pp. 1–25). Hillsdale, NJ: Lawrence Erlbaum Associates.

Starkey, P., & Gelman, R. (1982). The development of addition and subtraction abilities prior to formal schooling in arithmetic. In T. P. Carpenter, J. M. Moser, & T. A. Romberg (Eds.), *Addition and subtraction: A cognitive perspective* (pp. 99–116). Hillsdale, NJ: Lawrence Erlbaum Associates.

Stazyk, E. H., Ashcraft, M. H., & Hamann, M. S. (1982). A network approach to mental multiplication. *Journal of Experimental Psychology: Learning, Memory, & Cognition, 8*, 320–335.

Steffe, L. P., Thompson, P. W., & Richards, J. (1982). Children's counting in arithmetical problem solving. In T. P. Carpenter, J. M. Moser, & T. A. Romberg (Eds.), *Addition and subtraction: A cognitive perspective* (pp. 83–97). Hillsdale, NJ: Lawrence Erlbaum Associates.

Warrington, E. K. (1982). The fractionation of arithmetical skills: A single case study. *Quarterly Journal of Experimental Psychology, 34A*, 31–51.

Widaman, K. F., Geary, D. C., Cormier, P., & Little, T. D. (1989). A componential model for mental addition. *Journal of Experimental Psychology: Learning, Memory, and Cognition, 15*, 898–919.

Winkelman, J. H., & Schmidt, J. (1974). Associative confusions in mental arithmetic. *Journal of Experimental Psychology, 102*, 734–736.

Young, R. M., & O'Shea, T. (1981). Errors in children's subtraction. *Cognitive Science, 5*, 153–177.

Zbrodoff, N. J., & Logan, G. D. (1986). On the autonomy of mental processes: A case study of arithmetic. *Journal of Experimental Psychology: General, 115*, 118–130.

II SOCIAL SCIENCES

4

From Representation to Decision: An Analysis of Problem Solving in International Relations

James F. Voss
Christopher R. Wolfe
University of Pittsburgh

Jeanette A. Lawrence
University of Melbourne

Randi A. Engle
Dartmouth College

The focus of this chapter is upon the complexities of problem solving that are found in the field of international relations, the discipline that involves the analysis of conflict and cooperation between countries.

International problems arise when the leaders of one country develop political, economic, and/or cultural policies that produce antagonistic interactions with other countries. Such problems of course vary in their importance, scope, and complexity. A crisis may occur between two superpowers, a trade agreement may require negotiation, a border dispute may require mediation, or a cultural exchange program may be implemented. Many of the problems, such as those confronted by desk officers of the United States Department of State, are solved by routine procedures (cf. Pruitt, 1965), whereas other problems require considerable study and analysis at various levels of government.

Perhaps due to the fact that this discipline is relatively new or perhaps due to the nature of the contents of the discipline, the field of international relations does not have a single paradigm or orientation that is employed in the analysis of international problems. Indeed, there are differences of opinion concerning the theoretical assumptions of the discipline, such differences largely focused upon the unit of analysis.

The traditional theoretical orientation analysis is termed the *realist* position (cf. Carr, 1946; Morgenthau & Thompson, 1978). According to this view, the unit of analysis is the state, and the basic assumptions are that the primary motive of each state is power and that the interaction among states is a function of the distribution of power. Furthermore, at least to some authors, the interaction of states may be viewed in terms of the interaction of systems, systems that obey laws (cf. Kaplan, 1967; Morgenthau & Thompson, 1978; Singer, 1961). This position, moreover, generally holds that the international system is essentially independent of the individual; that is, regardless of what individual or group has the leadership role of a state, the state's position in the international system will not change appreciably.

In contrast there are a number of investigators who are not satisfied with the realist view, pointing out that the view cannot explain a number of observations such as why states fail to use their superior power when they would be able to do so. Among the investigators who feel that the realist position is lacking are those who have adopted a more cognitive approach to the study of international relations, an approach that places substantial emphasis upon foreign policy decision making. The argument is essentially that international relations involves making decisions and that decision making is done by people, not states. Therefore, understanding how foreign policy decisions are made becomes an integral part of the field of international relations. Furthermore, this view holds that the study of the decision making process requires taking into account not only the cognitive factors, but it must also address issues such as affect and the role of the bureaucracy in decision making (e.g., de Rivera, 1968; Falkowski, 1979; Holsti, 1976; Snyder, Bruck, & Sapin, 1954, 1962).

Cognition and International Relations

Literature involving the interface of cognition and international relations has focused upon two general topics, perception and decision making. (A third possible issue is negotiation; see Mandel, 1986). The most widely cited work dealing with perception is a book by Jervis (1977) entitled *Perception and Misperception.* Jervis cites a number of historical incidents, including some of considerable magnitude such as the December 7, 1941 attack of the Japanese on Pearl Harbor, that were influenced by misperception. Of greater concern to the present chapter, however, is the interface involving international relations and decision making; to place the work described in this chapter in the appropriate perspective, some background concerning problem solving in the international context is considered.

One of the most important aspects of solving problems in a field such as international relations compared to the solving of problems in a number of other domains is that the problems in international relations usually are quite ill-structured. When a problem is defined, the "givens" may include the statement of a well-defined goal as well as the noting of other constraints. In addition, the solver may have a good idea of the steps that are necessary. When a problem is defined, the "givens" may include the statement of a well-defined goal, the inclusion of constraints and the steps that are required to solve the problem may be reasonably apparent. Furthermore, the solution to the problem may be established; that is, there is agreement among people knowledgeable in the particular domain regarding the established solution. This description is that of a well-structured problem. On the other hand, one or more of the components listed above may be missing or only vaguely stated; that is, the goal may be vaguely defined, no constraints may be stated, and little may be known about how to solve the problem. Furthermore, there may not be consensual agreement regarding what a good solution would be. This latter description is that of an ill-structured problem (Reitman, 1965; Voss & Post, 1988). The problems of international relations are, by-and-large, ill-structured; the exceptions being problems that are fairly well-established and that are solved by standard operating procedures.

In addition to the fact that the problems are ill-structured, the foreign policy decision maker works in a political context that has at least three other characteristics. One of the characteristics is that the information available to the decision maker is usually incomplete and sometimes inaccurate and/or ambiguous. Speeches or writings of foreign leaders, for example, require analysis, and it is not always clear for whom a leader's speech is intended; is it for foreign consumption or for strengthening one's domestic position? Even actions of countries usually require considerable interpretation, and explanations for actions need to be looked upon critically. For example, the Soviet invasion of Afghanistan was interpreted in terms of a Soviet predisposition toward aggression, as a desire to move toward obtaining a warm water port, and as a move to prevent Moslems from taking power. Which explanation(s) is correct? Recently the Soviets withdrew from Afghanistan. How should this move be interpreted? What effect should it have upon American policy? An American analyst with a Cold War orientation may suggest that it was American pressure brought about by support of the rebels that produced withdrawal. Another analyst may suggest that the costs the Soviets had to absorb in Afghanistan became greater than the benefits, and that American presence had a minimal effect.

A second characteristic involved in foreign policy decision making is that the amount of information that must be processed by the decision maker is quite substantial. This means that there are processing load problems that lead to the need to select information and the need to simplify. One way to deal with this problem is via use of a hierarchical bureaucratic organization that allows for filtering of the information, but this can produce biased selection. Indeed, presidents may be told only what they want to hear. Alexander George (1980) has written on how such a situation may be avoided.

The need to process a large amount of information also leads to simplification; that is, the individual may employ images or stereotypes of particular countries (Cottam, 1977; Herrmann, 1984), and such images may influence the problem solving process. For example, an expert was given a problem on US-Soviet relations, and initially he responded by saying that what is important is whether you view the Soviet Union as aggressive or as reactive. This individual then indicated his view was the latter, and he proceeded to justify it at length before even addressing the given problem (Voss, Greene, Post, & Penner, 1983). The solution posed was then consistent with a reactive view but would probably not have been adapted by a person holding a strong Cold War view. Thus, the beliefs of the solver may and usually do play a critical role in the process of interpretation. Moreover, the role of belief would be of special importance when the amount of available information is large and/or ambiguous. Also, the beliefs are often not verbalized in the course of the decision process, per se.

A third characteristic involved in the solving of international relations problems is that the number of goals that must be taken into account in the problem solving process is often quite large. For example, in the Cuban Missile Crisis, goals which President Kennedy was aware of were avoiding a nuclear war, getting the missiles out of Cuba, avoiding domestic criticism, and taking an action that would not antagonize allies. Such a variety of goals, when considered in relation to Kennedy's beliefs about Khrushchev as a person, the Soviet Union in general, Castro, and others, portrays just how complex the factors are that feed into the decision making process. Moreover, to this complexity Etheredge (1985) has added another dimension. He claims that leaders get caught up in a drama-like world in which they are both the writers of history and the actors, and they become concerned about their impact. Etheredge also argues that this drama-world leads to overconfidence and loss of touch with the "real world."

Even if a person is not in a high level position, but provides input to the decision process, there also are complex factors operating. Individuals in government often assume they need to take a position that maximizes the role of their own departments, a bureaucratic view of decision making. The saying is "Where you stand depends upon where you sit." Furthermore, people in government, as elsewhere, are often highly concerned with their own careers and advancement. They also may be intimidated by a more experienced and previously successful individual or by status.

As suggested by the preceding paragraphs, problem solving in an international political context is a complex process. In the present chapter we focus upon the relation of the information processing model of problem solving, especially as applied to the solving of ill-structured problems, to an aspect of classical decision theory. More specifically, the paper addresses the issue of the extent to which alternatives are generated in solving ill-structured problems and how the alternatives generated are related to the decision that is made. In order to develop this issue in more detail, the relation of problem representation development to decision making is now considered.

Problem Representation and Decision Making

The information-processing model of problem solving (Newell & Simon, 1972) places substantial emphasis upon problem representation as the primary factor in the solution process, the argument being that the nature of the representation in large part dictates or at least leads to the solution or decision that is made. For example, in work involving the problem of Soviet agricultural productivity, protocols were collected from Soviet experts regarding how they would solve that problem, as well as regarding how they would deal with problems of Soviet-American relations (Voss, Greene, Post, & Penner, 1983; Voss, Tyler, & Yengo, 1983). The solution process typically involved the development of a representation of the problem, followed by the statement of a solution. Moreover, in developing the representation, the solver usually analyzed the problem with respect to its primary causal factors. This analysis was usually supported by argument in which the role of a causal factor was justified. For example, one expert traced the history of the Soviet agriculture problem, describing the early solutions and why they did not work, concluding that the primary cause of the problem was a lack of modernization in the agricultural industry.

The lack of modernization led to a solution involving provision for greater technological development in agriculture, although the expert realized that such a solution, to be effective, would need to take into account a number of problems. These problems included how to convince the economic planning agency to place greater emphasis upon agriculture, how to educate the peasants to use more modern methods, and how to develop an infrastructure which included transportation, storage, and plastics. In addition, the expert provided support for his solution by indicating how modernization would improve the current state of affairs. This brief account suggests that if the representation of the problem includes isolation of the causes of the problem, then a solution to the problem may be proposed by alleviating or eliminating these causes. Furthermore, the solution that is proposed must be evaluated with respect to its potential positive and negative effects.

Of note in this account is that nothing was said about the generation of alternative solutions during the solving process. The experts did not say that to solve the Soviet agriculture problem one needs to generate a large number of alternatives, evaluate each alternative, and then decide which course to follow. A possible reason for this lack of alternative generation is that with the representation that was developed, the solution was apparent and the need to consider alternatives did not exist. If this is true, then a reasonable hypothesis is that individuals, when presented with a problem, try to develop a representation that will point to a unique solution. However, when the representation does not permit this, alternative solutions need to be generated as a way of developing the representation and arriving at a solution. Viewed from this perspective, alternative generation is a step in the development of a problem representation that occurs when a representation does not yield a unique solution.

The question of how an individual selects one from a number of alternatives has of course been the focus of classical decision theory. This model starts not with a problem representation but with a decision tree that assumes the existence of a number of alternatives in a particular choice situation. The alternatives are presumed to be evaluated in terms of the probability of particular outcomes for each alternative as well as the desirability or utility of each outcome. The choice of alternative is then made via the application of a decision rule (cf. Hogarth, 1980).

Classical decision theory has received substantial criticism. Simon (1959), for example, has argued that individuals examine alternatives only until one is found that is acceptable, a process termed *satisfycing*. Simon further argued that the reason satisfycing occurs is that the human information processing system is of limited capacity, and simultaneous consideration of all alternatives usually constitutes too much of a processing load. The criticism most cogent to the present paper is that decision theory typically does not indicate the origin of the alternatives that are generated (Simon, 1980). There have been attempts, however, to develop procedures for generating alternatives (cf. Pitz, Sachs, & Heerboth, 1980).

The position suggested here is that the particular alternatives generated are a function of the characteristics of the problem representation. It is assumed that the goals of the solver as well as the solver's perception of other constraints are the primary factors of the representation that determine the alternatives that are generated. The alternatives thus constitute an extension of the representation, with the evaluated possible outcomes constituting additional constraints. In information processing terms, one's problem space is being expanded. This view of the solving process is of course a version of constraint satisfaction (cf. Newell, 1980).

FOUR CASE STUDIES

In the present chapter four studies are presented. Two pertain to the Cuban Missile Crisis and the American intervention in Korea. These two issues have received considerable attention in the international relations literature, in large part because accounts of the respective decision making processes have become available. The two other studies pertain to the nuclear threat and the hypothetical reunification of Germany, with each of these involving the collection and analysis of individual protocols.

While the analysis of problem solving developed in the present chapter focuses upon the relation of the problem representation to alternative generation and selection, the specific cases studied provide for the investigation of other issues. Specifically, the nuclear problem involves comparison of the representations established by Australian and American activists and as such provides for the cross-cultural comparison of the problem solutions generated by the activists of the two problems. In addition, the German reunification problem involves comparison of representational differences in reference to novices, postnovices, and experts. The other two issues, those of Korean and Cuban crises, involve comparison of possible representational differences of individuals who were members of a high government level decision making body.

The Nuclear Problem as Viewed by American and Australian Activists

This study was concerned with the problem of how to reduce the threat of nuclear war. Four Australians and four Americans who, with one exception, were informed activists served as subjects, that is, informed regarding nuclear issues. The one exception was US3 who was an arms control expert.

Each person was given the "Nuclear Armament/Disarmament Problem," and was asked to generate his or her solution, thinking aloud while doing so, that is, saying whatever came to mind. The problem statement was: "One of the major issues of current international concern is the problem of nuclear armament and disarmament. What do you understand that problem to be, and what solution to the problem would you propose?" The protocols were analyzed in terms of their respective problem representations and the related solutions. In addition, the role of cultural perspective in the solution process was studied by analyzing the referential use of plural pronouns such as "we," "us," "them," and "the people."

Problem Representations and Solutions.   AUS1 decomposed the problem into two subproblems, one consisting of the possibility of disaster occurring by design or by accident and the second involving the pressure placed upon non-nuclear countries by countries with nuclear capability. While AUS1 suggested the former was not being solved by arms control negotiations, AUS1's solution to both subproblems was to change peoples' attitudes, overcoming hatred and discrimination. AUS1 did not indicate how to implement this solution.

AUS2 defined the problem in terms of the need to halt nuclear proliferation and the need to reduce the arms of the major powers. No rationale or support for this representation was presented. AUS2 presented a relatively lengthy solution, advocating that public awareness had to be raised and pressure had to be placed upon political leaders "to stop the madness." But then he raised a problem related to proliferation, namely, that we live in an age of militarism that when combined with nationalism, forces military solutions to world problems.

AUS2's solution was to form a world government which presumably could get rid of the "tribal attitude" (nationalism). To do this, he appealed to the need to increase public awareness, primarily via education. AUS2 cited Australia's appointment of an Ambassador for Disarmament as a step in this direction, and he also indicated that a peace movement, as found in Australia, is needed around the world. Thus, AUS2's solution rested primarily in the hands of citizens and their awareness, with such awareness needed to have a world government.

AUS3 defined the problem as the threat of genocide and also as a political issue, primarily that the United States has the myth of excessive Soviet aggression. He argued that Soviet actions have included presenting peace-oriented resolutions in the United Nations, which the United States rejected. AUS3 also noted that Australia usually voted with the United States on such matters.

AUS3 presented a relatively extensive solution advocating that the world needs a change of heart and must realize that survival of the human race is at stake. For the more specific political problem, AUS3 advocated that the United States must make pledges like the Soviet Union has made and must freeze production and stockpiling of nuclear weapons, a move which Australia's President Hayden has supported. AUS3 also noted that the United States needed to get rid of weapons placed in other countries. But, he also noted that Australia seemed happy to have the American nuclear weapons, a fact that AUS3 tended to blame in part on the American military-industrial complex. AUS3's solution, like that of AUS1 and AUS2, thus involved a change in basic attitude, a "change of heart." But for the more specific political problem, AUS3 essentially indicated that the United States needed to behave more like the Soviet Union. This solution was thus related closely to the problem as defined.

AUS4 defined the problem as a failure of arms control negotiations and a lack of trust between the nuclear powers, blaming vested interests within both the United States and the Soviet Union for making arms development desirable. She also argued that each superpower exaggerated the aggressiveness of the other side, therefore further justifying the need for arms. AUS4's solution was that you need to "chip away" at the nuclear establishment at every opportunity. She cited as an example that if there were a nuclear accident on a ship in the Indian Ocean, Australia would be more likely to rule against nuclear ships entering any western Australian ports. AUS4 also argued that the United States was more responsible for the arms race than the Soviet Union because the United States usually was technologically ahead, which forces the Soviet Union to catch up. AUS4 also stated that one must be careful because you did not want to be anti-American. Her solution was thus related to United States' responsibility, but only suggested one should "chip away," whatever that may mean.

Turning to the American protocols, US1 decomposed the problem into two subproblems, one technical and the other political. The technical problem consisted of nuclear proliferation, a technical problem because countries could develop a nuclear potential by "peaceful" use of nuclear energy. The political problem is that the two superpowers are in an economic conflict, a statement supported by the need of the United States and the Soviet Union to exploit the Third World. In addition, US1 discussed a history of the nuclear policy, pointing out how the United States has felt the need to stay ahead of the Soviet Union. Finally, he indicated difficulties in knowing the reliability of missiles if they were used.

US1 offered two solutions. First, US1 stressed the need to increase human awareness and emphasized that individuals need to learn more about the problem so that they would be able to refute the positions of their leaders. As a specific case, he indicated that the nuclear freeze movement should be expanded, with more groups being developed that emphasize social responsibility. Secondly, US1 advocated greater dialogue of American and Soviet leaders. A solution to the proliferation problem per se was not articulated. The solution to the US-USSR economic competition problem was to increase US-USSR dialogue, a rather vague objective.

US2 decomposed the problem into three subproblems. One was that of managing the forces we already have; that is, that the development of nuclear weapons has in itself become a force and the systems developed to control this force are open to question. He also pointed out the irreversibility of the situation. The second subproblem was that of managing bureaucracies that foster arms development. The third subproblem was the political rivalry between the United States and the Soviet Union. In support, US2 argued that the issue does not revolve around nuclear parity and calculation of capability because when the United States and Soviet Union were the closest to war during the Cuban Missile Crisis, the United States had a nuclear advantage. Thus, US2 argued that the problem is political in nature and does not involve nuclear issues per se.

With respect to solutions, US2 advocated better control of existing systems, and felt there has been some progress in this regard. He did not provide a solution for a more effective system control, however. US2 also advocated that political action groups need to be active in order to reduce the control exerted by the bureaucracies. With respect to American-Soviet relations, US2 indicated that a new administration in the United States is needed. In support he provided a brief analysis of the Reagan and the Carter administrations, showing them as insufficient. Then, US2 indicated the need to appeal to group action to deal with bureaucracies.

US3, the arms control expert, considered the problem as one of the possibility of destabilization. He considered two related subproblems. One is that rather than considering American-Soviet relations, he discussed what is engendered when a country declares itself to be a nuclear power and the destabilization that results from this position, noting how countries like Israel may be responded to if it declared itself a nuclear power. The other subproblem is that disarmament can also produce destabilization because one side may perceive the other as weaker. The solution provided was that arms control, not disarmament, or a freeze, is needed, because it is the most likely way to have stabilization. He also noted that while the effects of future technological development cannot be foreseen, technological advancement will produce an increase in strike precision, which in turn will reduce the amount of total striking power that is needed.

US4 stated the problem to be that we currently have weaponry that could destroy everything, thus making war obsolete. At the same time we have outgrown national sovereignty, since a nation is no longer able to provide security. Furthermore, US4 noted governments erroneously feel that they can enhance security by building more and better weapons. This procedure, he indicated, is analogous to primitive religions, which appeased gods by sacrificing virgins. When the process did not work, more virgins were sacrificed. Similarly, US4 argued that building more weapons does not enhance security.

US4's solution was to abolish war. This solution, while he defended it, lacked a statement of how to accomplish this global objective. He did cite the example of Gandhi in bringing about peaceful change. He also argued that the position is not naive and idealistic, but realistic. He furthermore argued that arms control does not work and that while historically governments use aggression and power, people within a country can resist this. US4 also suggested that global institutions be established rather than being preoccupied with maintaining national institutions. He suggested that issues such as food distribution and the control of the ocean's resources have shown that international cooperation is possible. US4's idea of developing international institutions does follow from the problem defined as inadequacy of national security.

Before considering the protocols as a whole, data are presented which suggest that Americans and Australians identified rather strongly with their respective countries and that the identification yielded somewhat different cultural perspectives. Identification was addressed by assessing the use of plural personal pronouns.

Each use of a plural pronoun, including "we," "us," "you," "they," "them," "their," and cognates, was coded in reference to one of five uses: (a) an individual country or region, referring to Australia, the United States, or the Soviet Union; (b) global, international, generic human references, with no nation or regional connotations; (c) an individual nation or small region other than Australia, the United States, or the Soviet Union; (d) rhetorical use within the subject's conversation, with no specific reference (e) individuals not identified with particular nations, for example, "scientists." Interjudge agreement for 553 instances was 85%.

The results indicated that American use of plural personal pronouns referred significantly more to the United States, the Soviet Union, and Australia than did

TABLE 4.1
Distribution of Plural Pronouns for the American
and Australian Subjects

Referent	US	AUS	df	X^2
(1) AUS, US, or USSR	46.3%	25.0%	1	17.98***
(2) Global, generic human	19.7%	54.6%	1	58.72***
(3) Region other than 1	6.3%	3.8%	1	
(4) Rhetorical	21.6%	9.9%	1	8.36**
(5) Not relevant	6.2%	6.8%	1	

** = significant at .01 level
*** = significant at .001 level

TABLE 4.2
Examples of Local and Global Pronoun Usage

Localized	
(1) "The US . . . and we do this under the rubric of national defense"	US4
(2) "We (US) could knock them (SU) out"	US1
(3) "Our relations with the SU"	US2
(4) "The most serious danger occurred not when we (US) had the least nuclear advantage." (re: Cuban crisis)	US2
(5) "Major powers such as the SU and us"	US3
(6) "On our side . . . and the other side"	US3
(7) "The Russians might tell us . . . and we could tell them"	US4
(8) "Our obligations under the ANZUS Treaty"	AUS4
(9) (Re: Tomahawk in teh Pacific area) . . . "in Japan, people were very, very disturbed, . . . and we, of course, should be very, very disturbed about it as well"	AUS4
Global	
(10) "We've lived in a state where the world could be obliterated"	AUS1
(11) "While there's one nuclear weapon, we have problems"	AUS1
(12) "We have so many nuclear weapons in the world"	AUS2
(13) "How can we reduce the level of risk, how can we prevent further nuclear proliferation"	AUS3
(14) "It is not possible for them (US) to say that we (generic) can't trust the SU"	AUS4
(15) "We are the human race, and either all the human race survives, or we all go under"	AUS4

the Australian usage, 46.3% to 25.0%, respectively, while Australian usage of pronouns such as "we" referred more frequently to individuals in a more global and/or humanistic sense, 54.6% to 19.7%. This analysis thus suggests that Australians had a more global sense of "we" than did Americans. Specific examples of statements by Americans include "We (the United States) could knock them (the Soviet Union) out;" "Our relations with the Soviet Union;" "Major powers such as the Soviet Union and us." Australian statements include "We have so many nuclear weapons in the world;" "It is not possible for them (the United States) to say that we can't trust the Soviet Union;" "We are the human race, and either all the human race survives or all the race goes under."

One other analysis was performed to identify concerns, events, and entities mentioned by both groups that reflected a local orientation. Americans made specific references to the American defense program at Los Alamos (US1), the Cuban crisis (US2), the administration (US3), local politicians (US1, US4), and cities, personalities, and institutions such as Amtrak (US2, US4). Australians referred to their country's export of uranium, United States defense treaties and the related Australian alignment (AUS2, AUS3), the Pacific region's problems

(AUS4), and national political identities (AUS3, AUS4). These findings indicate that the examples used tended to come from within one's national perspective.

Considering now the representation-solution contingency across all protocols, the problem as presented in the problem statement was generally converted into another problem that could be more readily addressed than the problem as stated. This conversion produced the problem representation. The representations developed varied substantially in specificity. Probably the most specific representation was that of US3, the arms control expert, who rejected the problem phrased in terms of disarmament, rephrasing it in terms of arms control with the goal of stability. His solution was then oriented in relation to stability maintenance.

The most common representation was that of the conflict of the Soviet Union and the United States and the failure of these governments to take appropriate steps to reduce the nuclear threat. The solutions for this representation varied, ranging from increased USSR-US dialogue to the need for a new U.S. administration and the need for U.S. pledges. Another representation that occurred with relatively high frequency was that there is a nuclear threat that has the potential to destroy life as we know it, and not enough is being done to reduce this threat. After all, human survival is at stake. This representation depicts a type of frustration, and solutions tended to be offered in relation to it. Three of the solutions were global in nature, referring to "change the hearts" or attitudes of people and bring pressure to bear on government leaders so that they take appropriate action. Or, form a world government and/or outlaw war, a solution that suggests existing government structures cannot deal with the problem. Another solution involved "chipping away" at the problem, helping in the nuclear freeze movement, or taking whatever action one can at an individual level to do something.

Taking the protocols as a whole, the degree of generality or specificity of the solution was related to the respective generality or specificity of the problem representation. However, the protocols also indicated that individuals did not generate a number of possible solutions and subsequently evaluate them. Instead, individuals provided solutions that were generally appropriate to the respective representation, and, if more than one solution was presented, it was not an alternative but an additional way to try to solve the problem.

The cultural differences obtained between Australians and Americans are of two general types. Perspective differences were demonstrated by the pronoun analyses, which reflect the differences of perception of US-Soviet relations. In addition, the Australians felt relatively separated from the superpowers whereas the Americans had more of an US/THEM mentality. Secondly, while one's cultural perspective was related to representational differences in US-Soviet relations, general representations of the nuclear threat were shared. Representations led to solutions involving the need for awareness and a change of attitude of people and the need to place pressure upon governments.

The Reunification of Germany

Specialists in the field of international relations sometimes develop hypothetical scenarios as an exercise in reasoning about the affairs of nations. The work reported in this section involves problem representation and solution processes as found in "think aloud" protocols given in response to a problem involving German reunification. The subjects were two professors specializing in the Soviet Union, four advanced graduate students, and two undergraduates enrolled in their first course in international relations.

Subjects were given a scenario concerning hypothetical events in the Federal Republic of Germany (Appendix 4.A). The subjects were asked, "What options do you think the Soviet Union has in responding to the events described above? Indicate which option they are most likely to pursue, and provide your rationale for selection this option." The task was designed to encourage the generation of a number of possible solutions.

Protocols of the Experts.   A rather striking difference occurred between the two experts. Expert E1 maintained that the Soviet reaction to German reunification would be essentially negative: "I think from a Soviet point of view, this (reunification) is absolutely not something they would envision with any positive reactions at all." E2 saw the orientation of the Soviet union as essentially positive: "Historically speaking, the Soviet side has always been interested and, at various times, has supported the idea of negotiations towards a unified, neutral German state."

Despite this difference, there is a basic similarity in the protocols of the two experts. E1 began with a review of the history of the situation, noting that the Soviets persuaded General Secretary Honecker to cancel a trip to West Germany in 1984. E1, noting the task instructions, then said, "If the idea is to sketch out as many options as possible, and then indicate which one they are most likely to pursue, let me do that without regard at first to the likelihood or attractiveness, but just sort of sketch options." He then outlined three options starting with an "extremely favorable reaction" including the withdrawal of troops. He also included a "neutral position" of stating that "this is an affair of the German people," while at the same time the Soviets would offer no strong position in private. Finally, E1 suggested the possibility of "high pressure opposition" including "whipping up hysteria," making overtures to the French, and bringing strong pressure on East Germany, just short of involving troops.

After stating these options, E1 provided an assessment of the situation as a whole, stating, "I think the attractiveness to the Soviet Union of a neutralized West Germany, that they would gain from such a thing, a neutralized Germany, would be overcome by their fear, by number one a loss of East Germany, and a fear of where this country could go." Thus, he saw the Soviet Union's goal as one of maintaining the status quo. He then noted some constraints on the Soviets, including the reaction of the United States and public opinion in East Germany and elsewhere.

Having laid out the goal and some constraints, E1 proceeded with a more detailed description of the Soviets' most likely response:

> I think their reaction would be at first firm, negative, moving very quickly to a more strident negative, and they would, in that situation, employ all of the options which they have available: public pressure coordinated among the allies, Warsaw Pact meetings, meetings of first secretaries of the parties, (etc.)

E1 then engaged in a process of evaluation. First he noted that the reason the Soviets have so many troops in East Germany is to ensure that no decisions would be taken concerning the future of Germany without Soviet influence. Finally E1 stated, "I'm trying to think if there's a domestic component on the Soviet side, that is, any domestic factors, differences, factions that might produce a different reaction in the Soviet Union, and I don't think there are."

E2 also started with an historical analysis of the situation, noting that in 1952 the Soviets supported efforts towards reunification, although the idea had not surfaced recently. He then dismissed the idea that the Soviets would immediately withdraw 300,000 troops.

> They'd say, I think, that we would like to see the negotiations go forward, and if the possibility of a central, unified neutral state not allied to Warsaw or to NATO, after certain progress has been made there, then we will entertain the possibility of a 300,000 troop withdrawal.

He then supported this assertion by claiming that withdrawing troops would be giving up too much too early in the process.

E2 next raised a constraint, that the Soviet military would never accept this withdrawal as long as there were NATO forces in the Federal Republic. Thus the Soviet response would involve two sets of negotiations, one focusing on the reunification of Germany as a peaceful, neutral state, and the other on the eventual withdrawal of troops from East Germany. According to E2, the goal of the Soviet Union in this case would be the demilitarization of central Europe.

> Almost 40 years ago they entertained the possibility of selling the G.D.R. out in order to create a sort of free zone in the center of Europe, and if, I think, the shape of Germany is right, that is, if it is genuinely, permanently not a member of NATO and severely demilitarized, then I think that's something they would entertain again.

To support his position, E2 noted that a neutral state served two important goals. First, it addressed security concerns because it would create a situation where the two major alliances are not directly confronting each other. Second, "It opens up possibilities of a totally different sort of Western Europe than the one you have now," in which the Soviet Union may exert a greater degree of influence.

Although the two experts viewed the situation differently, there were many similarities between their protocols. Both start with a discussion of the historical context of the problem. Each gives a fairly clear description of the goals of the Soviet Union, the experts agreeing for the most part with respect to the possible goals. Other constraints were also considered, and each presents a course of action that follows from these goals. Finally, each expert critically evaluates the course of action prescribed relative to the stated goals.

The differences between the experts can be understood in terms of their representation of the goals of the Soviet Union. E1 believed that the Soviets fear losing East Germany more than they desire seeing a demilitarized, unified Germany. E2, on the other hand, felt that the security needs of the Soviet Union would be well served by a "free zone" in central Europe, and that such an arrangement would open the way for new possibilities for the Soviet Union in Europe. Thus, the experts were led to different conclusions because of the differences in their perceptions of Soviet goals.

An interesting characteristic of the protocols produced by both experts is the way they generated alternatives. Rather than producing a wide range of alternatives and evaluating them systematically, they produced relatively few alternatives, and often did little more than state them as possibilities. For example, E1 generated options, partially in response to the specific task instructions. However, after laying out the possibilities, he essentially disregarded all but his preferred option. E2 produced few alternatives, and at no time did he explicitly raise and consider them. It appears that these experts were able to develop a solution within their respective perceptions of the Soviet goals and constraints, thus making generating a list of alternatives unnecessary.

Protocols of the Undergraduate Novices.   In contrast to the experts, the undergraduate novices showed little in the way of an explicit representation of the problem. Instead, these subjects primarily focused on the options themselves. Consider the first sentences uttered by each of the novices. One undergraduate (U1) said, "Well, obviously I think they're not going to support unification to begin with." U2 started with, "Well, the first option would be to withdraw the 300,000 troops in a show of good faith, which I doubt that they would do." U1 went on to say that it's in neither superpower's best interest, and that both would work together in the U.N. Security Council to keep reunification from happening. U1 went on to say that "their clearest option would just be to really kind of take charge of East Germany in terms of the pressure they can put on those people." The subject then stated that "clamping down" would be a more direct approach than working with other nations diplomatically. U2 went a little farther in stating the Soviet's goals: "They would definitely want to get their relations with West Germany, considering that they're going to a socialist government." Thus, U2 stated that the Soviets would try to "aid them and sway them to turn away from the NATO alliance . . . and start up stronger relations with the Soviet Union." This subject also qualified this position, saying, "I can't imagine that they would be too forceful in going in there, because there would be such a tenuous situation that they would probably have to be very careful about the channels that they used while they were trying to influence them." This is all that either undergraduate offered as a constraint. Each of the undergraduates revealed little in terms of evaluation, specifying goals, or posting constraints. In generating four or five alternatives, they seemed to be concerned with concrete actions more than with abstractions (cf. Voss, Greene, Post, & Penner, 1983).

Protocols of the Graduate Student Postnovices.   The graduate student protocols constituted a position somewhere between the professors and the undergraduates. Like the experts, one graduate student, G1, started with an historical discussion,

> The Soviet stance on reunification has shifted over the years, so that eventual reunification is something particularly under the Gorbachev regime that is never spoken about publicly but is implied, so that academic writings and commentary have used other cases to perhaps illustrate that reunification is something that's good.

G1 also cited a number of constraints including the situation in Poland, the state of Gorbachev's reforms, and the state of arms control talks.

By way of contrast, another graduate student (G2) started by generating a list of options in the manner of the undergraduates. First this subject dismissed the option of withdrawing one third of the troops. Then G2 stated, "Another option would be to make it clear to Mr. Honecker that this is not something that they're enamored of, and that he ought to cease and desist with his courting of reunification." The subject then stated that this is the most likely scenario. When prompted as to whether there are any other actions the Soviets might take, G2 simply responded, "Other than indicating to Mr. Honecker that they don't agree with his steps, no. I don't think there is much else they would need to do outside of that."

Summary.   The German reunification scenario produced a variety of options ranging from "clamping down" on the East Germans to actively supporting talks leading to the reunification of Germany. The scenario also highlighted differences in the reasoning of experts and novices; the experts spending more effort constructing a representation of the situation, in historical terms as well as in the defining of goals and constraints, findings in agreement with Voss, Greene, Post, and Penner (1983). The experts also explicitly laid out the Soviets goals, defined constraints, and developed solutions that matched these goals and constraints. Finally, the experts engaged in a critical evaluation of their interpretation of the situation, and the prescribed course of action.

The novices were relatively concrete in their thinking. They first rejected the course of action suggested by the West Germans (removing troops), and then offered alternatives of their own without describing the Soviets goals or external constraints. The novices demonstrated little in the way of a critical evaluation of these options. Graduate student protocols depicted a transition phase in which they would use a historical analysis to try to define contemporary goals and constraints.

Of particular interest is the finding that despite the instructions to generate alternatives, the generation and evaluation of alternatives was not an integral part of the solution process. Subjects seemed to be generating alternatives because they were instructed to do so. Especially in the case of the experts and even with the graduate students, alternative solutions were not seriously considered.

Comparison of the protocols obtained in the nuclear and German unification cases suggests the following points. First, performance was not characterized by the generation and evaluation of alternatives; instead, subjects proposed solutions that were appropriate to the particular representation that had been developed. This finding supports the idea that the generation of alternative solutions is not an intrinsic component of the solving process; indeed, even when instructed to generate alternatives, subjects either did so because of the instructions or did so without serious consideration of most alternatives.

Secondly, although the solutions provided were generally quite consistent with the nature of the representation, generally speaking, the solution was not readily predicted from the representation. However, greater specificity of the representation was associated with greater specificity of the solution, as well as greater likely predictability of the solution. The two experts providing solutions for the German reunification problem as well as US3 in the nuclear problem provided the most detailed representations and solutions and these are also the most predictable. This result raises the possibility that for other individuals their protocols did not reflect their representations or, perhaps what is more likely given that the other individuals lacked expertise, their lack of knowledge prohibited the development of representations that would lead to more specific solutions. Virtually all of the other nuclear protocols involved general goals such as human awareness, world government, etc., and these goals were stated as the solutions, solutions that of course were vague because little was usually stated with respect to how to reach such goals. Even viewing the nuclear problem in terms of the need for better US-Soviet relations, the issue of how to reach the goal was stated in vague terms, such as "increasing the dialogue between the two superpowers." Negotiation possibilities, for example, were not mentioned. In contrast, the experts analyzed the reunification problem in relation to their perception of Soviet goals and constraints, and these solutions were relatively specific.

Thirdly, the protocols support the findings of Voss, Greene, Post, and Penner (1983) in that factors such as cultural perspective, knowledge, and attitude were shown to affect the nature of the representation that is developed. In particular, cultural perspective was shown generally to provide a different global perspective for the Australians and Americans; perceptions that led to differences in some concrete actions that could or should be taken, as well as differences in the perception of the role of the superpowers. At the same time, a number of solutions were shared, general solutions as increasing awareness. This commonality likely reflects a common concern that governments have not made a strong enough commitment to deal with the nuclear issue. Also, had the subjects provided ways to implement such goals, then differences attributable to cultural perspective would quite possibly have been obtained.

Fourthly, the more sophisticated problem solving included an evaluation component whereas less-sophisticated solvers usually did not include a solution evaluation process. Evaluation, as previously noted, refers to considering how the proposed solution will solve the problem and also considering any difficulties the solutions may pose and what should be done about them. It may of course be that the German reunification problem lended itself to evaluation more readily than the nuclear threat problem, but in any event, evaluation was essentially absent from the protocols of all but the two experts.

UNITED STATES INTERVENTION
IN THE KOREAN WAR

An Account of Events

Whereas in an ideal world decision makers would have all of the necessary information before making a decision, in reality, decisions are made with inadequate and sometimes faulty data. In the case of the intervention in Korea, it was necessary to re-represent the problem as new information was obtained, an action which led to a sequence of decisions. In effect, the changes in representation were necessary because the outcome of a prior decision was different than expected.

Most of the important decisions concerning U.S. involvement in the Korean war were made by the President and fourteen of his advisors during the week after the North Korean invasion of South Korea. The decisions were made in a series of five meetings, the initial meeting held at Blair House in the capital. Our discussion consists of an examination of the major decisions made in these meetings. A chronology of events pertaining to the Korean war intervention is presented in Appendix 4.B.

On Sunday, June 25, 1950, President Truman asked Secretary of State Dean Acheson to arrange a dinner meeting with the President's top advisors. This group (see Appendix 4.C) remained essentially intact throughout the week. The President called upon Secretary of State Acheson to give a detailed account of the situation. Acheson noted that a full-scale invasion of South Korea was in progress. He described the actions taken in the United Nations Security Council, which had passed a U.S. sponsored resolution demanding a cessation of hostilities. He then stated a number of suggestions for group consideration:

1) That General MacArthur be authorized to furnish the South Koreans with military equipment over and above that already authorized under the Mutual Defense Assistance Program; 2) that American planes be employed to cover the evacuation of American women and children from Inchon; 3) that the Air Force be authorized to destroy North Korean tanks and airplanes interfering with the evacuation; 4) that consideration be given to what further assistance might be given to Korea pursuant to the Security Council resolution; and 5) that the Seventh Fleet be ordered to prevent a Chinese Communist invasion of Formosa as well as to prevent operations by the Chinese Nationalists against the mainland. (Paige, 1968, p. 127)

Following the Secretary of State's presentation, the President asked each member of the group to comment on Acheson's proposals and to add any suggestions of his own. No other suggestions were advanced by other members of the group. Secretary of Defense Johnson announced that his department had come to no specific conclusions as of yet. General Bradley, Chairman of the Joint Chiefs of Staff, pointed out that Korea was of no strategic importance to the United States in the event of a global war with the Soviet Union. The military consensus was that although the situation appeared serious, the South Koreans could probably contain the attack. At the conclusion, the President asked for a second meeting on the following day, and ordered a complete reappraisal of Soviet strength around the world.

The second Blair House conference was held on Monday, June 26, 1950. President Truman asked General Bradley to open the conference by presenting an overview of the military situation. The General said that the South Korean resistance had not been effective, and that the South Korean government had been forced to retreat from Seoul because the capital was about to be taken. He noted that "South Korean casualties as an index to fighting have not shown adequate resistance capabilities or the will to fight and our estimate is that a complete collapse is imminent" (Paige, 1968, p. 162).

In the face of the new situation, the President once again called on Secretary of State Acheson for suggestions. Apparently in view of the lack of effectiveness of the previously proposed actions, the Secretary of State proposed:

1) That the Navy and Air Force be instructed to give the fullest possible support to the South Korean forces and that such support should be limited to the area south of the 38th parallel; 2) that orders be issued to the Seventh Fleet to prevent an attack upon Formosa, that the Chinese Nationalist government be told desist from operations against the mainland, and that the Fleet be ordered to secure the compliance of the latter; 3) that American forces in the Philippines be strengthened and that increased military assistance be rendered to the Philippine Government; 4) that military assistance to Indochina be accelerated and that a military mission be sent there; and 5) that Ambassador Austin be instructed to report any action taken under the above recommendations to the United Nations. (Paige, 1968, p. 164)

Following Acheson's proposals, the President asked each of the members present for additional opinions. Once again no further suggestions were proposed. Secretary of Defense Johnson later explained,

Neither I nor any member of the Military Establishment in my presence recommended we go into Korea. The recommendation came from the Secretary of State, but I want to repeat that it was not opposed by the Defense Department all the members of which had severally pointed out the trouble, the trials, tribulations, and the difficulties. (Paige, 1968, p. 164)

The military leaders agreed that South Korea was strategically a poor place to fight. They further agreed, however, that with American air and sea power, the South Korean Army should have little trouble repulsing the attack.

The Blair House group also discussed the possibility of direct Soviet or Chinese involvement, and concluded that the chance of either occurring was remote. They also agreed that the United States should do only what was necessary to repel the attack, and that all actions should be taken within the framework of the United Nations. There was no opposition to Acheson's proposal to use the Seventh Fleet off the coast of Formosa. In the final analysis, the consensus of the Blair House group was that the "aggression must be resisted," and all of the Secretary of State's proposals were adopted.

On Thursday, June 29th, Secretary of Defense Johnson called the President and requested another meeting of the group. The Korean situation had deteriorated considerably. Seoul had fallen, and a report was received which estimated South Korean casualties at 50 percent and warned that the Korean army might not be able to hold the Han River line.

The meeting centered around factors hindering the military operations in Korea. Johnson stated that the major obstacles to effective military performance were restrictions of the Air Force and Navy from operating north of the 38th parallel, poor air to ground communications with the South Korean Army, and inadequate means of transporting American munitions to the front. Johnson presented a number of proposals made by General MacArthur and approved by the Joint Chiefs of Staff. The proposals were to permit MacArthur to extend air and naval operations to North Korea, "to employ Army service forces in South Korea such as transportation or signal units and to commit a limited number of combat infantrymen to protect a port-airfield beachhead in the vicinity of the southeastern coastal city of Pusan" (Paige, 1968, p. 245).

The decision to use combat troops was made to protect the evacuation of United States citizens. A group of advisors, including Secretary of the Army Frank Pace, Jr., expressed concern over a possible escalation of the conflict into a war with the Soviet Union. However, most of this discussion concerned the wording of the orders to General MacArthur. The consensus of the group was that the bombing of North Korea should be restricted to essential military targets. The final orders to General MacArthur were that "You are authorized to extend your operations in Northern Korea against air bases, depots, tanks, farms, troop columns, and other purely military targets, if and when this becomes essential for the performance of your mission" (Paige, 1970, p. 150). President Truman said that he wanted "to take every step necessary to push the North Koreans back to the 38th parallel. But I wanted to be sure that we would not become so deeply committed in Korea that we could not take care of other situations as they might develop" (Paige, 1968, p. 246). At the conclusion of the meeting the proposal was adopted, and a new set of orders were sent to General MacArthur.

At 4:57 a.m. on Friday, June 30th, President Truman received a phone call from Secretary Pace. Pace had received a communication from General Mac-Arthur stating that the South Korean army was in a state of disarray, and that the only hope of defending the Han River line was an immediate commitment of "a United States regimental combat team to the combat area in Korea as a nucleus of a possible buildup of two divisions from Japan" (Paige, 1968, p. 254). In fact, by the time the President received the message, the Han River line had already been broken. The President immediately authorized the use of one regimental combat team, and told Pace that a decision on the buildup of two divisions would be postponed until he met with his advisors.

At 9:30 President Truman met with his advisors in the White House. The President briefed the group on the situation and asked whether other divisions should be included. He also asked for opinions concerning a Nationalist Chinese offer to commit 33,000 troops to the Korean conflict. Finally he asked the group to consider possible responses by the Soviets and the Communist Chinese. There was no opposition to the proposal to commit ground forces. The consensus was that the two divisions would be able to stop the North Korean advance. The advisors contended that the possibility of Soviet or Communist Chinese involvement remained small. However, the advisors disagreed with the President on the issue of Nationalist Chinese involvement. This was thought to increase the probability of Communist Chinese involvement, and increase the chances of an invasion of Formosa. When the meeting was concluded the President agreed to decline the Nationalist Chinese offer. He also decided to give MacArthur the authority to use all of the forces under his command.

The final decision was that of sending United Nations troops across the 38th parallel, which of course occurred later in the conflict. Unfortunately little is known about the process that led to this decision. The official United Nations resolution was passed on October 7, 1950. The U.S. First Cavalry crossed the parallel on the same day. However President Truman's decision was made nearly a month earlier on September 11th. At that time the United States was considering the high-risk Inchon landing. Over two months of fighting had resulted in unexpectedly high levels of casualties, but if the Inchon landing was successful, it would mean that the North Korean's supply lines would be cut and they would be forced to fight the war on two fronts. It was in this context that the President decided that if the landing was successful, efforts should be made to unify the country. The Inchon landing took place on September 15th, and that day a directive was sent to General MacArthur authorizing him to send U.N. forces into North Korea pending the approval of the United Nations, and provided that there was no change of Soviet or Communist Chinese involvement.

MacArthur's orders specifically stated that the United States did not want to "become engaged in a general war with Communist China" (Spanier, 1959, p. 95). Yet there were numerous warnings that the Chinese Communists would become involved if United Nations forces entered North Korea. Intelligence sources reported an increase in Chinese forces in Manchuria from "180,000 to at least 320,000 troops" (Whiting, 1960, p. 111). Moreover, the leaders of the People's Republic of China had repeatedly stated their intention to enter the war if the "imperialists" crossed the 38th parallel. For example, on October 1, Chou En-lai announced that although the Chinese people want peace, "They will not tolerate foreign aggression and will not stand aside should the imperialists wantonly invade the territory of their neighbor" (Spanier, 1959, p. 86). The warnings were interpreted as a bluff. In fact, of course, the United States did become involved in a war with the Communist Chinese. The fighting continued until the Armistice of July 19, 1953. The cease fire line, today the North-South border, roughly approximates the 38th parallel.

The Forming of the Blair House Group

The Blair House group was formed by Secretary of State Acheson as an ad hoc committee of advisors to the President. Although President Truman had an especially close working relationship with Acheson, the Secretary of State and Secretary of Defense Johnson "obviously disliked and distrusted each other personally" (de Rivera, 1968, p. 215). Because the participant membership was in part determined by government position, it was not possible for Acheson to exclude Johnson. However, it was possible to include some members whose position did not necessitate their participation. The Assistant Secretary of State for U.N. affairs, John Hickerson, and the Ambassador at Large, Philip Jessup, could have easily been excluded from the group. Their presence can be interpreted in terms of the Secretary of State's desire to see the American response to the Korean invasion conducted in the framework of the United Nations. Both Hickerson and Jessup were strong supporters of the United Nations and by including them in the group. Acheson thus gained two allies in the event of a confrontation with Johnson.

Conversely, it would have been reasonable to include State Department Counselor George Kennan. He was considered to be an expert on Soviet intentions, and the North Korean invasion was thought to have been directed by the Soviet Union. In fact, Kennan was on the Secretary of State's original list of participants, but he was not invited to any of the Blair House meetings. Part of the reason for this apparently stems from Kennan's belief that the United Nations would restrict American flexibility. Kennan was apparently the only high-ranking member of the State Department to hold this position. After an early State Department meeting, Kennan volunteered to brief American allies on the Korean situation. The Counselor presented the decision as justified by America's role as the leader of the free world, rather than as a defense of the United Nations charter. The State Department responded by "preventing him from giving any more briefings" (de Rivera, 1968, p. 210). After a few months Kennan resigned, frustrated that he had been excluded from the foreign policy decision-making process.

The decision of who participates in group decision making is of course critical. Clearly, if one person is responsible for participant membership, then the individual may use what degrees of freedom are available for group membership. The membership thus is critical in the development of the representation of the problem and in the making of decisions.

The Dynamics of the Group

It is evident that President Truman employed a highly directive style of leadership while at the same time concentrating upon the building of consensus. The President opened each meeting by defining the issues at hand, and concluded by announcing his decisions. The purpose of the meetings was to help the President make up his mind about the issues. The opinions of others were taken into consideration but "the buck" stopped with the President. Furthermore, in presenting his proposals as Secretary of State, Acheson was the most powerful member of the group next to the President. In the early meetings Truman called on Acheson to present his proposals and most of the discussion revolved around them. In the end they were accepted by the group.

Although each person was asked to comment on the proposals, two aspects of this procedure should be noted. One is that the problem was essentially "defined" via the briefings provided by Acheson. Perhaps if there had been general discussion before Acheson stated his proposals, the results would have been different. The other aspect is that it is not clear how each person perceived the problem. Members of the group later expressed favorable attitudes about the group and the decisions. One participant, for example, described the atmosphere as "the finest spirit of harmony I have ever known" (Paige, 1968, p. 179). This feeling of harmony likely stems in part from the President's desire to achieve consensus on each major decision. Indeed, Ambassador Jessup recalled feeling "proud of the President." Secretary Johnson felt that the President had made the "right decisions." These comments suggest that participating individuals had similar representations, although this conclusion cannot really be verified.

An interesting characteristic of the deliberations is the limited number of alternatives seriously considered by the group. In the first two meetings Acheson's proposals were the only options given serious consideration. In the third and fourth meetings discussion centered around Secretary Johnson's presentations. However, in each of the latter meetings, Secretary Johnson failed to propose any specific suggestions. Whether he was, in a sense, deferring to Acheson, or whether he did not want to be the person advocating the use of American troops, as was suggested, is not clear.

The Groupthink Hypothesis

One of the problems with consensus formation in group decision making has been referred to by Irving Janis as *groupthink*. The expression refers to "a deterioration of mental efficiency, reality testing, and moral judgment that results from in-group pressures" (Janis, 1982, p. 9). The heart of the groupthink phenomenon lies in the need for group cohesiveness. Groupthink occurs when the pressures for uniformity and adherence to group norms are unduly high.

Janis describes seven major defects in decisions resulting from groupthink. First, "the group decisions are limited to a few alternative courses of action without a survey of the full range of alternatives" (p. 10). Second, the group does not adequately survey its objectives. Third, "the group fails to reexamine the course of action immediately preferred by the majority" (p. 10). Fourth, members fail to reconsider alternatives that were initially rejected. Fifth, members seldom attempt to obtain information from outside experts. Sixth, members spend little effort considering facts or opinions that don't support their initial preferences. Finally, members spend little time deliberating about how their decisions might be hindered. Janis hypothesizes that groupthink is responsible for a number of American foreign policy fiascoes including the Bay of Pigs invasion, the escalation of the Vietnam war, and the decision to cross the 38th parallel in the Korean war. Janis notes that "the President set the tone at all the meetings with his advisors, strongly shaping the group consensus" (p. 68). This high level of cohesion coupled with a highly directive leader seeking consensus indicates that the conditions for groupthink were ripe.

The factors in the Korean intervention supporting the groupthink hypothesis included the small number of alternatives considered and the group spending little effort exploring their objectives or considering contrary evidence. By dismissing the Chinese warnings as "bluffing," the Blair House group also failed to consider evidence that was contrary to the group's position. There is, however, also evidence against the groupthink hypothesis. After the September 11th meeting, the President sought the opinions of General MacArthur and others outside the group. They agreed that is was unlikely that the Communist Chinese would become involved. Similarly, in the early meetings, the group used information from outside experts that consistently underestimated the strength of the North Koreans. In addition, there were instances where the Blair House group participants disagreed with the President and each other. For example, the decision to decline the Nationalist Chinese offer of military support runs contrary to the groupthink hypothesis.

Problem Representation and Decision

With respect to the representation process, the first phase consisted of interpreting the North Korean invasion. The United States had previously indicated that South Korea was not of strategic military importance, a position that should call for an evaluation of whether South Korea should be defended. However, at that time, in the midst of the Cold War period, the invasion was believed to have been produced by the Soviet Union, possibly as the first of a number of worldwide actions. As noted, President Truman asked for an appraisal of strength around the world. Furthermore, the repeated proposal to position the Seventh Fleet to prevent a Chinese Communist invasion of Formosa indicates that China was also regarded as part of the potential communist worldwide attack. Thus, despite the fact that the United States had previously made statements about the strategic insignificance of South Korea, the United States viewed the North Korean invasion as a case of communist aggression, and, as such, it needed to be stopped. Indeed, President Truman is supposed to have stated with respect to the invasion that he did not want another Munich.

Given the representation of the North Korean invasion as Soviet-inspired and as one possible action of many in the Cold War, the decision that the invasion had to be resisted was virtually a given. The goal of the decision process was thus established. To consider means, it was clear that particular constraints needed to be taken into consideration. One was to minimize American involvement with respect to commitment of forces and another was to frame the resistance as a United Nations action rather than an exclusive United States action. Indeed, one wonders whether the initial judgments suggesting that the South Korean army would be able to repel the invasion was not a misperception motivated by the desire for minimal United States involvement rather than by an appraisal of the South Korean military strength and strength of will (cf. Jervis, 1977).

Although the overall goal of resistance to communism was maintained, the goals of implementation required greater and greater commitment of American resources. Thus, while the local implementation of the goal was modified, the goal itself remained constant, at least until the new goal of Korean unification was articulated. Each decision served as a precursor to the subsequent one, and the costs correspondingly increased. The decisions made by the Blair House group were largely "logical" extensions of earlier decisions. As Secretary Pace noted, "the decision to employ Army units 'logically followed' the decisions taken earlier in the week and had been 'practically made for us' by subsequent events" (Paige, 1968, p. 261).

Two further points may be noted with respect to the decision-making process. One is that the establishment of the general goal of resistance to Soviet aggression was such a strong constraint that it virtually forced the decision sequence. "The decision-making process in the Korean case was not characterized by the consideration of multiple alternatives at each stage. Rather a single proposed course of action emerged from the definition of the situation" (Snyder & Paige, 1962, p. 245–246). A second aspect of the decision process is that there was little evaluation of preceding decisions. This is understandable, however, because, given the goal of stopping the aggression, what was apparent is that at each step there was a need to use more resources. Postmortem discussion would not solve the need to use greater resources. Furthermore, the solution process did not involve reevaluating basic assumptions, that is, resistance to Soviet aggression. Instead, it involved reevaluation to a more immediate goal, that of providing enough strength to stop the invasion.

What is less clear is how the decision to include the goal of Korean unification was developed. Perhaps the perceived military necessity was instrumental in producing this goal. What also is not clear is why there was not a more realistic appraisal of Chinese involvement.

In summary, the perception of the North Korean invasion as part of a global movement of communist aggression made the decision to resist almost inevitable. In addition, there was the interesting political decision to define the resistance in terms of a U.N. action and not a unilateral action of the United States. The initial failures in resisting the invasion led to a relaxation of the constraint of U.S. minimal involvement. Earlier decisions were not reevaluated and they acted as constraints on subsequent decisions. Alternatives were evidently not seriously considered, except for such matters as use of Nationalist Chinese troops. Furthermore, there apparently was little analysis regarding why the North Korean invasion took place, except to note it as communist aggression.

THE CUBAN MISSILE CRISIS

The Cuban Missile Crisis took place over a 13 day period, October 16 to October 28, 1962, although a more extensive analysis of the causes of the crisis as well as of the closing negotiations and aftereffects, of course, involves a much larger time period (cf. Garthoff, 1987). On October 16, President Kennedy was given photographs of Cuba, taken via a U-2 reconnaissance plane, indicating that Soviet-designed missile launching pads had been placed in Cuba, launching pads that could be used for offensive missiles. From October 16 to October 22, meetings of President Kennedy and what was later termed the *ExCom Committee* (Executive Committee of the National Security Council) took place in which reaction to the missile placement was considered. (Appendix 4.D lists the members of this committee.) From October 22 to October 28, the Soviet-American confrontation occurred via the quarantine of Soviet ships. The matter was resolved on October 28 when Premier Khrushchev agreed to withdraw the missiles from Cuba and President Kennedy pledged not to invade Cuba. Much has been written about the decision process of the ExCom committee, and, early in 1989, meetings were held in Moscow in which Soviet, American, and Cuban officials discussed the crisis. In the present account, the possible Soviet representation of the issue is considered followed by consideration of the American representation.

The Soviet Perspective

In March of 1960, President Eisenhower approved the development by the CIA of a plan to overthrow Castro, a plan developed over the next months and inherited by John Kennedy upon his election in November, 1960. The plan was presented, modified, and ultimately put into action with the Bay of Pigs "invasion" of Cuba on April 15, 1961, an action that failed. The planning of the Bay of Pigs operation has been discussed and its goals and problems are not considered here. (See, e.g., Etheredge, 1985).

Following this failure, the Kennedy administration, still viewing Castro as a serious threat, initiated a policy called Mongoose. This policy was aimed at destabilizing the Castro regime via covert operations including economic harassment and sabotage (Etheredge, 1985). A number of attempts to assassinate Castro were included. However, an invasion of Cuba by the United States was not planned.

Although a number of ideas have been advanced about why the Soviets placed missiles in Cuba, two seem most plausible. One is that, based upon the aggressive posture of the United States toward Cuba, Castro and the Soviets were expecting the United States to invade Cuba. Given this threat, the Soviets regarded sending Soviet troops as undesirable and impractical, and yet the Soviets wanted to support Castro against what likely would be an overwhelming force. The missiles were then placed, with the serious intent of possibly using them, or at least using them as a bargaining chip. Later, even though the missiles were removed, Khrushchev regarded the outcome as a triumph, feeling that it was better to have communism in Cuba with no missiles than not to have communism there at all. This rationale thus indicates that the Soviet-Cuban representation was a reaction to the American threat, and with the Soviets quite limited in their available alternatives, they sent the missiles.

A second factor in the Soviet placement of missiles involved the relative missile strengths of the United States and the Soviet Union at that time. The 1989 Soviet-American-Cuban conference yielded the information that, at that time, the Soviet Union had relatively few ICBMs, compared to the United States. However, by placing their intermediate-range missiles in Cuba, the Soviet Union would reduce the strike differential of Soviet and American forces. The decision to plant the missiles in Cuba thus provided a way to work toward the goal of Soviet equalization of strike force.

The American Perspective

The development of the American representation of the crisis serves as an excellent example of the difficulties of complex problem solving when the stakes are quite high. In some respects, the representation of the Cuban Missile Crisis problem was quickly determined. Once it was established that there were in fact offensive missiles in Cuba, 90 miles from the United States, the missiles were perceived as a threat, and as such, a strong action had to take place to remove them. However, this position was not held initially by all ExCom members. Interestingly, Defense Secretary McNamara, in making the comment that "A missile is a missile," essentially was asking what is so special about these missiles. After all, the Soviets have missile-carrying submarines which can easily get within 90 miles of the American coastline. But clearly there was something special about these missiles. Why were these missiles so special?

The military regarded the missile placements as special because they cut considerably into the warning time of a possible Soviet attack. The missiles thus placed the American military at a disadvantage with respect to time to prepare for an attack. A second way in which these missiles were special was that they were being placed in a Western hemisphere country, an event not acceptable by long-standing tradition that began with the Monroe doctrine. A third reason that the missiles were special lies in the timing of the placement. This was a Cold War period and there were strong anticommunism feelings in the United States. Other international problems such as Berlin and Laos were also on the table. This was therefore not a time to show any sign of weakness to the Soviets. Moreover, because of the public feelings about communism, President Kennedy suggested that if action was not taken, he would be impeached. So, the representation involved not only the military threat but the strength of the United States as it may be perceived by Americans, by allies, and by the communist world. What should be done about the problem, however, was not clear.

From a problem-solving perspective, we see that the representation did not beget a solution in the manner of the Korean intervention. Indeed, the positions described in the immediately preceding paragraph indicate that the representation varied somewhat with committee members. In this case, therefore, the position advocated in this chapter is that it was necessary to generate alternatives. Initially, discussion included the question of whether to do nothing or to take diplomatic action. Brady strongly argued for a diplomatic approach, possibly confronting Gromyko or Khrushchev about the missiles, indicating that withdrawal was necessary. He argued that a diplomatic approach be taken first rather than taking action without the opportunity for negotiation (Allison, 1971, p. 196). Doing nothing was unacceptable to President Kennedy and, similarly, diplomatic action was not strong enough. One solution that, according to Sorenson (1966), seemed to have an early consensus was that of a "surgical" air strike which would be aimed at destroying only the missile bases. An air strike was favored by Acheson, Dillon, and McCone. However, the military was not convinced that such an air strike could be effective. Instead, the military argued that is also was necessary to attack fuel depots, airfields, and other targets (Allison, 1971). Moreover, when an air strike was considered, McNamara and Robert Kennedy were opposed to it, with Robert Kennedy reported to have written a note to his brother suggesting how he did not want his brother to be another Tojo. Robert Kennedy also made a statement regarding how the struggle with the Soviet Union was not only a struggle of physical power but a struggle of ideals, and by its actions the United States should not give up its ideals (Allison, 1971, p. 197). This is an extremely interesting comment from a problem-solving perspective, because with it, Bobby Kennedy moved away from the crisis per se and pointed out that rather abstract American traditions and ideals were also involved. As Allison notes, after the crisis President Kennedy indicated his lack of respect for military judgment, and that it was a positive thing that McNamara was the Secretary of Defense (p. 198). Another alternative considered was an invasion, which was favored by the military, and yet another was the one eventually adopted, that of a blockade. The blockade of course was a more moderate action than an invasion or air strike, although a blockade is regarded as an act of war.

Allison (1971) reports that the alternatives were narrowed within a few meetings to an air strike or a blockade, or "quarantine." In evaluating these alternatives, President Kennedy asked two questions about the surgical air strike possibility. One was whether it was possible, with the military feeling a more inclusive strike was necessary. Some of the ExCom members apparently sought private advice on the feasibility of an air strike, receiving the judgment that it would be possible. But that information was likely available to President Kennedy only after his decision for a blockade was made.

The second question repeatedly asked by Kennedy was what the Soviets would do in the event of an air strike of Cuba. He did not receive an answer that was satisfactory. To the answer of "nothing" he pointed out that the Soviets would need to do something just as the Americans needed to do something about the missiles. The more conservative blockade action was then adopted, apparently because the threat of a nuclear war seemed less than would be the case with an air strike.

With respect to the issue of alternative generation, Anderson (1987) studied the issue of the number of alternatives generated in the ExCom meetings, using a sampling procedure. Although Anderson does not present data regarding the nature of the alternatives, he reported that whereas alternatives were generated, most were not pursued in the course of discussion. Anderson also pointed out that statements of alternatives were characteristically made in conjunction with statements of goals, as perhaps one would expect. Finally, Anderson also provided evidence supporting the notion that the alternatives generated tended to be in the domain of the expertise of the individual. Thus, a military man would produce a military solution. Secretary of Defense McNamara, interestingly, was opposed to any bombing or invasion of Cuba.

In one sense, the Cuban Missile Crisis is of particular interest because most of the members of the ExCom Committee apparently had similar interpretations of the missile threat per se, but they varied considerably in what action should be taken. The question, then, is how the representations differed. The most important dimension of difference probably was one's perception of the Soviet Union as an enemy and how that perception was related to how a particular action would be related to a risk of nuclear war. In other words, one person may view the Soviet Union as a quite serious threat to the United States, to the extent that one should be willing to risk a nuclear war in order to "contain Soviet aggression." This view could also be accompanied by the idea that the Soviet Union would likely back down anyway if the United States adopted a strong posture. On the other hand, a person may feel the Soviet Union is a threat, but not such a serious threat that a risk of nuclear war should be entertained. The representation thus was not only a function of the situation but of the individual's value system and how that value system interacted with the situation. Indeed, McNamara was initially opposed to the blockade but later was in favor of it because it was better than an air strike with respect to the possibility of war. On the other hand, the Secretary of the Navy, Anderson, indicated after the crisis that he felt that the United States had "been had" (Garthoff, 1987, p. 58).

Comparison of the Korean Intervention and Cuban Missile Crisis

With respect to the question of relation of the problem representation, alternative generation, and alternative evaluation, the Korean intervention and the Cuban Missile Crisis provide interesting similarities and differences. Each situation was precipitated by a communist action. There was a greater sense of urgency in the Korean case, although time was also not plentiful in the Cuban case because of the need to preempt the missiles being placed into launch position. Nevertheless, the accounts differ in that whereas Acheson's proposals were made and accepted without much discussion, the Cuban situation produced considerable discussion. It could be argued that the decision making process in the Cuban Missile Crisis occurred as it did because the need to generate alternative plans of action stemmed from the variety of representations that existed among the ExCom members. Interestingly, whereas individuals did not spend time on reviewing their respective attitudes and feelings about the Soviet Union, as well as their attitudes toward the importance of avoiding a nuclear war, discussion of particular alternatives gave evidence of such differences. As noted, whether such a discussion in the Korean meetings would have evoked such variety is open to question, but the odds are that it would not have, the reason being that the representations would have been more homogeneous than found in the Cuban situation.

With respect to the possible operation of groupthink, Janis (1982) uses the Cuban Missile Crisis as a case in which groupthink did not operate, due to the consideration of alternatives, the use of outside sources, and other factors.

That beliefs and also values are of extreme importance in providing solutions to international problems is demonstrated within the context of the present four studies. Subjects educated with respect to the nuclear threat did not, in fact, present well-developed solutions, but they maintained their position based upon the belief that nuclear war was a threat to all life. This is a value judgment. The Korean intervention was based upon a belief system embracing communism as an international threat. The Cuban Missile Crisis evoked representations that were based upon beliefs of Soviet retaliation intention, with those advocating the strongest actions against Cuba apparently the most convinced of the invincibility of the United States, and willing to risk a nuclear action. Beliefs and values were at the core of the decision process. One may wonder how history would have changed had the United States either bombed or invaded Cuba. Indeed, today no doubt there are individuals who would say that the more aggressive action is what should have been done.

SOME TENTATIVE CONCLUSIONS

The Representation-Solution Relationship

A major focus of this chapter has been upon the relation that exists between the problem representation and the proposed solution, including the role of the generation and selection of alternatives. Two questions are of particular importance, namely, how closely are the representation and solution related, and what is the role of alternative generation and evaluation.

The four cases of the present chapter suggest that the relationship between the representation that is established and the solution that is stated is a function of the specificity of the representation. In the nuclear problem, most protocols yielded representations which contained quite general goals, and, because of this, the solutions were also general. Indeed, what much of the data suggest is frustration. Individuals want to do something to reduce the nuclear threat but in most cases the solutions indicate little regarding how the goal should be accomplished.

Subjects were not able to state the constraints that would provide a more specific solution. On the other hand, experts in the German reunification case tended to define the problem in such a way that their decision involving Soviet involvement was specific. The same type of result is found for US3, the arms control expert in the nuclear study.

Major differences were obtained between the Korean and Cuban decision processes, even though they both involved a President meeting with advisors. Probably foremost of these differences was that the Korean case gives evidence of the committee members having a similar representation, whereas the representation of the committee members in the Cuban Missile Crisis was quite diverse, especially with respect to the perception of the Soviet Union and the willingness to risk nuclear war. As previously noted, there may have been substantial differences in the individual representations in the Korean case, but if there were, the decision making process did not bring them out in the open. The differences were probably not great, given the period of time and the strong feeling of the need to resist communist aggression.

The differences in the representations of different individuals in the Cuban case, we would argue, led to the need to generate and evaluate alternative courses of action. The process of considering alternatives and evaluating their outcomes may readily be seen as a process of determining how particular actions and how the anticipated outcomes of those actions would impact upon one's representation and provide further constraints for the solving process. Moreover, prioritizing the goals also must then play a large role in the evaluation of alternatives. Furthermore, in the Cuban crisis, the data suggest that the number of alternatives quickly narrowed to two, not because some alternatives were evaluated and dismissed, but because President Kennedy rejected particular alternatives because of his own position.

Comparison of the two individual problem solving studies to the Korean and Cuban situations suggests two further points of interest. First, one would expect that a group decision process would be more penetrating in that proposed representations and solutions set forth by one person may be viewed critically by other group members (cf. Snyder & Diesing, 1977). But, as noted, this is not necessarily so, for although it appeared to be true in the Cuban study it did not appear to be true in the Korean study. Indeed, looking at the individual studies, experts in the German unification case submitted their own ideas for evaluation while other individuals did not. A decision to evaluate thus does not seem to be intrinsic to the group case.

A second issue involving comparison of the individual and group cases is that the former were of low stakes. They were "thought" experiments involving, at most, planning. On the other hand, the Korean and Cuban situations were "real" and quite important. This difference seemed to lead to a more specific plan of action being developed in the latter, which of course is not surprising.

A third and important component is that the group case can evoke the goals of each group member, and each member may have personal vested interests as well as perceptions and related goals that differ from others of the group. Such a situation can then lead to debate and argument, as it did in the Cuban case. Yet, in principle, the process of decision making in the Cuban case was not fundamentally different than what one finds in the individual case. Basically, in the Cuban case, what was needed was a representation of the problem that would provide for the best "avoid nuclear war/stand firm" strategy. No doubt some individuals thought an air strike or even an invasion of Cuba would be the best strategy in effecting this goal combination, but it was those who weighed the avoidance of war more heavily, as they interpreted the risk, who dominated in the decision process.

Interestingly, although some of the actors in the Cuban situation changed positions (Allison, 1971), the decision process was not one of basic argument and persuasion. The process seemed to be more one of classification and of evaluating outcomes based upon one's goal structure. This observation supports the findings of Axelrod (1977) in that the solutions to problems posed at a high level of government are not to be characterized by a classical debate model of persuasion.

The Evaluation Process

The evaluation of the solution of a problem of international relations is difficult. It seems appropriate, however, to make a distinction of "on-line" and "a posteriori" evaluation. The former refers to the evaluation of a decision or a solution at the time it is made; the latter refers to an evaluation which occurs some time after the decision is made, as the outcomes of the decision become known. A question of importance then is what criteria can be used to evaluate a solution in each of these cases.

For on-line evaluation, two criteria seem to be the most important. One is whether the proposed solution or decision takes into account the goals and objectives that the decision is supposed to accomplish as well as whether the solution can be implemented. To what extent will the decision or solution yield results that are commensurate with one's goals and priority of goals? A second criterion is whether all possible information is taken into account in arriving at the decision or solution. This includes the possibility of alternative solutions and the possibility of alternative outcomes, as well as the existence of other events, ideas, or information that is germane to the representation. Nevertheless, even though one may have on-line criteria, there is the need to say "Let's see what happens" as the decision is implemented, and only when the effects are known can one say it was a "good" decision. Unfortunately, such a criterion is of no use to the decision makers at the time of making the decision.

This mode of on-line problem solving is traceable to basic rhetoric (Corbett, 1971). What the solver is doing is building a case for the offered solution, arguing what the effects of the solution will be. Thus, whereas the Cuban Missile Crisis decision-making did not portray a debate format, the implicit goal of the process was how to achieve our goals, in terms of what action will yield the outcomes most consistent with the goals, taking into account possible undesirable outcomes.

With respect to a posteriori evaluation, probably the question is whether the decision worked out as well as or better than you expected it to. Indeed, even if it does not, one may maintain that it was the right decision but "I did not know X would react the way he did" or "It must have been a problem of implementation." Rationalization of decisions that do not work out as desired is of course a major political skill. Indeed, Holsti and Rosenau (1977) have demonstrated that the "lessons" learned from Vietnam varied substantially with one's position regarding United States involvement in that conflict.

Comparison of Expert and Novice Performance

Although the present studies were not primarily concerned with the issue of expert and novice performance, two points may nevertheless be made regarding this topic. First, compared to individuals in numerous studies who would be termed *experts,* it seems clear that virtually anyone who participated in meetings involving the Korean or Cuban situations could be legitimately called an expert. Yet, it also is clear that the experts, at least in the Cuban case, varied considerably with respect to their goals and preferred solutions. When dealing with well-structured problems, there is little doubt that the solutions of experts would be in substantial agreement. However, in international relations, most problems provide for varied representations, this largely being a function of the goals and perceptions of the different experts. Thus, in international relations, it is not uncommon to have disagreement among highly knowledgeable experts; the disagreement largely based upon interpretation differences, perception, beliefs, and values.

Secondly, the expert performance in the German reunification case was quite similar to that previously reported by Voss, Greene, Post, and Penner (1983). Moreover, the performance of the two experts provided further evidence for differences among experts, in this case attributed to different perceptions of Soviet goals and how they would be accomplished.

Cross-Cultural Factors

One of the studies presented in this chapter involved similarities and differences of cross-cultural performance. This work showed that cultural background can be influential in various components of problem representation development as well as in providing support for one's representation. But the study also indicated that, with respect to the nuclear problem, a common thread or lifeline running across the Pacific is a sense that individual people need to take action. They must try to put pressure on their governments to reduce the likelihood of nuclear war, or, there must be a higher system of government because the current notion of state sovereignty is not working. Yet, the solutions in most cases ended at this point. Mechanisms for implementation were missing, and perhaps this reflects a difference of those who are active in setting forth goals and those who need to work out arms control and/or reduction via negotiations.

Perhaps the cross-cultural data are best viewed as providing support for concern of issues related to one's values and concern for the general welfare of individuals, even though how that concern can manifest itself in realistic solutions was not clear.

ACKNOWLEDGMENT

Preparation of this chapter was supported by the Office of Educational Research and Improvement via support of the Center for the Study of Learning of the Learning Research and Development Center of the University of Pittsburgh. Additional support was provided by the Mershon Center of Ohio State University. The opinions expressed in this chapter do not necessarily reflect those of any of these organizations.

REFERENCES

Allison, G. T. (1971). *Essence of decision: Explaining the Cuban Missile Crisis.* Boston: Little, Brown.

Anderson, P. A. (1987). What do decision makers do when they make a foreign policy decision? The implications for the comparative study of foreign policy. In C. F. Hermann, C. W. Kegley, Jr., & J. N. Rosenau (Eds.), *New Directions in the study of foreign policy* (pp. 285–308). Boston: MA: Allen & Unwin.

Axelrod, R. (1977). Argumentation in foreign policy settings. *Journal of Conflict Resolution, 21,* 727–744.

Carr, E. H. (1946). *The twenty years' crisis, 1919–1939.* London: Macmillan. New York: Harper Torchbooks.

Corbett, E. P. J. (1971). *Classical rhetoric for the modern student* (2nd ed.). New York: Oxford University Press.

Cottam, R. W. (1977). *Foreign policy motivation: A general theory and a case study.* Pittsburgh, PA: University of Pittsburgh Press.

de Rivera, J. (1968). *The psychological dimensions of foreign policy.* Columbus, OH: Charles E. Merrill Publishing.

Etheredge, L. S. (1985). *Can governments learn? American foreign policy and Central American revolutions.* Elmsford, NY: Pergamon Press.

Falkowski, L. S. (1979). Predicting flexibility with memory profiles. In L. S. Falkowski (Ed.), *Psychological models of international politics* (pp. 49–69). Boulder, CO: Westview Press.

Garthoff, R. L. (1987). *Reflections on the Cuban Missile Crisis*. Washington, DC: The Brookings Institute.

George, A. (1980). *Presidential decisionmaking in foreign policy: The effective use of information and advice*. Boulder, CO: Westview Press.

Herrmann, R. K. (1984). Perceptions and foreign policy analysis. In D. A. Sylvan & S. Chan (Eds.), *Foreign policy decision making* (pp. 25–52). New York: Praeger.

Hogarth, R. M. (1980). *Judgment and choice: The psychology of decision*. Chichester, England: Wiley.

Holsti, O. R. (1976). Foreign policy decisions viewed cognitively. In R. Axelrod (Ed.), *The structure of decision* (pp. 18–54). Princeton, NJ: Princeton University Press.

Holsti, O. R., & Rosenau, J. N. (1977). The meaning of Vietnam: Belief systems of American leaders. *International Journal, 32*, 452–474.

Janis, I. L. (1982). *Groupthink*. Boston: Houghton Mifflin.

Jervis, R. (1977). Minimizing misperception. In G. M. Bonham & M. J. Shapiro (Eds.), *Thought and action in foreign policy* (pp. 154–189). Basel and Stuttgart: Birkhauser Verlag.

Kaplan, M. (1967). *System and process in international politics*. New York: John Wiley.

Mandel, R. (1986). Psychological approaches to international relations. In M. G. Hermann (Ed.), *Political psychology* (pp. 251–278). San Francisco: Jossey-Bass.

Morgenthau, H. J., & Thompson, K. W. (1978). *Politics among nations: The struggle for power and peace* (6th ed.). New York: Alfred A. Knopf.

Newell, A. (1980). One final word. In D. T. Tuma & F. Reif (Eds.), *Problem solving and education: Issues in teaching and research* (pp. 175–189). Hillsdale, NJ: Lawrence Erlbaum Associates.

Newell, A., & Simon, H. A. (1972). *Human problem solving*. Englewood Cliffs, NJ: Prentice-Hall.

Paige, G. D. (1968). *The Korean decision*. New York: Free Press.

Paige, G. D. (1970). *1950: Truman's decision*. New York: Chelsea House.

Pitz, G. F., Sachs, N. J., & Heerboth, J. (1980). Procedures for eliciting choices in the analysis of individual decisions. *Organizational Behavior and Human Performance, 26*, 396–408.

Pruitt, D. G. (1965). Definition of the situation as a determinant of interactional action. In H. C. Kelman (Ed.), *International behavior: A social-psychological analysis* (pp. 393–432). New York: Holt, Rinehart, & Winston.

Reitman, W. (1965). *Cognition and thought*. New York: John Wiley.

Simon, H. (1959). Theories of decision making in economics and behavioral science. *American Economic Review, 49*, 253–283.

Simon, H. A. (1980). Problem solving and education. In D. T. Tuma & F. Reif (Eds.), *Problem solving and education: Issues in teaching and research*. Hillsdale, NJ: Lawrence Erlbaum Associates.

Singer, J. D. (1961). The level-of-analysis problem in international relations. In K. Knorr & S. Verba (Eds.), *The international system: Theoretical essays* (pp. 77–92). Princeton, NJ: Princeton University Press.

Snyder, G., & Diesing, P. (1977). *Conflict among nations*. Princeton, NJ: Princeton University Press.

Snyder, R. C., Bruck, H. W., & Sapin, B. (1954). Decision-making as an approach to the study of international politics. *Foreign policy analysis project series*, No. 3, Princeton, NJ.

Snyder, R. C., Bruck, H. W., & Sapin, B. (1962). *Foreign policy decision-making: An approach to the study of international politics*. New York: Free Press.

Snyder, R. C., & Paige, G. D. (1962). *The United States decision to resist aggression in Korea*. In R. C. Snyder, H. W. Bruck, & B. Sapin (Eds.), *Foreign policy decision making*. New York: Free Press.

Sorensen, T. C. (1966). *Kennedy*. New York: Bantam.

Spanier, J. W. (1959). *The Truman-MacArthur controversy and the Korean war*. Cambridge, MA: Belknap Press.

Voss, J. F., Greene, T. R., Post, T. A., & Penner, B. C. (1983). Problem solving skill in the social sciences. In G. H. Bower (Ed.), *The psychology of learning and motivation: Advances in research theory* (Vol. 17, pp. 165–213). New York, NY: Academic Press.

Voss, J. F., & Post, T. A. (1988). On the solving of ill-structured problems. In M. T. H. Chi, R. Glaser, & M. J. Farr (Eds.), *The nature of expertise* (pp. 261–285). Hillsdale, NJ: Lawrence Erlbaum Associates.

Voss, J. F., Tyler, S. W., & Yengo, L. A. (1983). Individual differences in the solving of social science problems. In R. F. Dillon & R. R. Schmeck (Eds.), *Individual differences in cognition* (pp. 205–232). New York: Academic Press.

Whiting, A. S. (1960). *China crosses the Yalu*. Stanford, CA: Stanford Press.

APPENDIX 4.A

The Reunification of Germany Scenario

Suppose that an accident occurred in a nuclear power plant near Kassel, West Germany in the spring of 1990. The accident cost the lives of one hundred thirty-eight people and contaminated an area of nearly sixty square kilometers, including twenty square kilometers in East Germany. In the wake of the accident, confidence in the regime of the Christian Democracies is shattered and new elections are held in West Germany. The result of this election is a new coalition government formed by the Social Democrats and the rapidly growing Green Party. This new government is headed by the left-leaning Oskar Lafontaine.

One of the first acts of the new government was to schedule a series of high-level meetings between representatives of the governments of East and West Germany. The purpose of these meetings is to "coordinate clean-up operations and facilitate communication in times of crisis." Following a face to face meeting between President Oskar Lafontaine and East German General Secretary Honecker, the conservative West German daily the *Frankfurter Allgeheimne Zeitung* published a startling report. Citing inside sources, the newspaper produced an account of the meeting which claimed that the leaders discussed "the eventual reunification of Germany to its rightful position as a single unified nation."

The discussion of reunification was strongly condemned in a front page editorial in the *Allgeheimne Zeitung*. However, the public reaction of the West German people is unexpectedly strong and favorable. In the following weeks, reunification has become the dominant topic of conversation in West Germany. Public opinion polls indicate that seventy-nine percent of the public approves of the notion in principle, and sixty-two percent approve of Oskar Lafontaine's conduct in the East-West meetings. The notion of a unified German nation is thought to be even more popular in East Germany.

Recently there have been proposals made by segments of the Green Party for a complete withdrawal of U.S. and Soviet forces from Germany as a first step towards eventual reunification. Recognizing the concern of NATO allies, most members of parliament have focused their attention on the presence of Soviet forces in the east. In an open letter to Mikhail Gorbachev, a majority of the members of the West German parliament have asked for the unilateral withdrawal of a third of the 300,000 Soviet troops in East Germany. The letter states that the withdrawal would be seen as an act of good faith, reducing the need for outside assistance in matters of security.

What options do you think the Soviet Union has in responding to the events described above? Indicate which option they are most likely to pursue, and provide your rationale for selecting this option.

APPENDIX 4.B

Chronology of Events

June 24, 1950	North Korean invasion
June 25, 1950	U.N. Security Council meets
June 25, 1950	1st Blair House conference
June 26, 1950	2nd Blair House conference
June 27, 1950	North Korea captures Seoul
July 1, 1950	U.S. Battalion arrives in Korea
August 11, 1950	First major U.N. victory
Sept. 11, 1950	President approves crossing 38th parallel
Sept. 15, 1950	Inchon landing
Sept. 15, 1950	Directive to MacArthur to cross 38th parallel
Sept. 19, 1950	U.N. refuses PRC entry
Oct. 1, 1950	ROK troops cross 38th parallel
Oct. 7, 1950	U.N. resolution to unite Korea
Oct. 7, 1950	U.S. 1st Calvary crosses the 38th parallel
Oct. 15, 1950	Truman–MacArthur conference
Oct. 16, 1950	Chinese secretly enter North Korea
Nov. 24, 1950	MacArthur launches drive towards China
Nov. 28, 1950	Chinese attack U.S. forces
April 10, 1951	Truman fires MacArthur
July 19, 1953	Armistice

(Sources: de Rivera, 1968; Paige, 1968, 1970; Spanier, 1959; Whiting, 1960.)

APPENDIX 4.C

The Decision Makers

Secretary of State	Dean G. Acheson
Chairman, Joint Chiefs of Staff	Omar N. Bradley
Chief of Staff, U.S. Army	J. Lawton Collins
Secretary of the Air Force	Thomas K. Finletter
Asst. Secretary for U.N.	John D. Hickerson
Ambassador at Large	Philip C. Jessup
Secretary of Defense	Louis A. Johnson
Secretary of the Navy	Francis P. Matthews*
Deputy Under Sec. of State	H. Freeman Matthews**
Secretary of the Army	Francis Pace, Jr.
Asst. Secretary of State	Dean Rusk
Chief of Naval Operations	Forrest P. Sherman
President of the United States	Harry S. Truman
Chief of Staff U.S. Air Force	Hoyt S. Vandenberg
Under Secretary of State	James E. Webb*

*Attended first Blair House conference only
**Attended second Blair House conference only

(Source: Paige, 1968, 1970)

APPENDIX 4.D

The Members of the ExCom Committee in addition to President Kennedy

McGeorge Bundy	National Security Advisor
Dean Rusk	Secretary of State
Robert McNamara	Secretary of Defense
Robert Kennedy	Attorney General
Maxwell Taylor	Chair of the Joint Chiefs of Staff
John McCone	Director of CIA
Douglas Dillon	Secretary of Treasury
Theodor Sorenson	Special Council

George Ball	Undersecretary of State
U. Alexis Johnson	Deputy Undersecretary of State
Edwin Martin	Assistant Secretary of State
Llewellyn Thompson	Soviet Expert
Roswell Gilpatric	Deputy Secretary of Defense
Paul Nitze	Assistant Secretary of Defense
Dean Acheson	Former Secretary of State
Robert Lovett	Former Secretary of Defense

5 Managerial Problem Solving

Richard K. Wagner
Florida State University

MANAGERIAL PROBLEM SOLVING

The field of management is split in two. The split is between those who view managers as rational technicians whose role it is to apply the knowledge and principles of management science, and those who view managers as craftsmen who practice an art that is not reducible into a set of scientific principles (Schon, 1983). The view of managers as craftsmen is the longer standing of the two; the split began early in the present century when Taylor (1947) popularized the view that management could be explained in terms of a set of scientific principles, just as one might attempt to explain mechanical and natural phenomena. This split has divided managerial theory, practice, and training.

I begin this chapter by reviewing rational approaches to managerial problem solving. These approaches exemplify the managerial science perspective on problem solving. Next I consider some limitations of rational approaches to managerial problem solving, and describe a number of recent attempts to understand more about the art of managerial problem solving. Finally, I draw some conclusions.

THE RATIONAL APPROACH TO MANAGERIAL PROBLEM SOLVING

Management science has spawned a number of approaches to managerial problem solving that collectively are referred to as *rational* approaches to problem solving (Isenberg, 1984). The hallmark of rational approaches to managerial problem solving is a set of problem-solving principles with nearly universal applicability. Consider two examples of rational approaches.

The Rational Manager

Kepner and Tregoe (1965) proposed a system for solving managerial problems in what has become a classic text on rational management. I describe the problem-solving principles that comprise the system, and then apply them to a managerial problem.

1. *Problems are identified by comparing actual performance to an expected standard of performance.* Effective managers engage in an ongoing comparison between what should be happening and what is happening. A significant discrepancy between what is happening and what should be happening identifies the existence of a problem.

2. *Problems are defined as deviations from expected standards of performance.* Problem definition is a trivial step in Kepner and Tregoe's system. The problem is defined by the discrepancy between actual and expected performance that alerted a manager to the existence of a problem in the first place. For example, assume that the normal percentage of defective automobiles produced in a Marysville, Illinois, plant is 2%. If the percentage of defective automobiles increases to 4%, a problem is identified. The problem is defined as "the percentage of defective automobiles produced at the Marysville plant has doubled."

3. *Prerequisite to identifying the cause of a problem is generating a precise and complete description of the problem.* Describing a problem precisely and completely consists of describing exactly: (a) *what* is happening; (b) *where* it is happening; (c) *when* it is happening; and (d) *to what extent* it is happening. Part of the descriptive process is to identify the boundaries of the problem by describing what is not happening (i.e., what is not problematical), where it is not happening, when it does not happen, to what extent it does not happen.

4. *The cause of the problem will be found by comparing situations in which the problem is found to similar situations in which the problem is not found.* Problems rarely affect everything. For example, a quality control problem may affect one plant and not another, one work shift and not another, or one product and not another. Determining what differentiates the situation in which the problem is found from similar situations in which the problem is not found is the key to determining the cause of the problem. For example, if the quality control problem is confined to one shift of workers, the manager would search for the cause of the problem by examining differences across shifts in workers, their supervision, and the nature of their task.

5. *Problems are the result of some change that has caused an unwanted deviation from expectations.* Assuming the problem is of recent origin, some-

thing must have changed to produce it. Further, the change will be related to one of the characteristics that distinguishes the problem situation from other, similar situations in which the problem is not found. For example, the quality control problem might have begun when a new employee was hired on the suspect shift. Perhaps the new employee has been poorly trained or is careless.

I illustrate this approach to managerial problem solving by applying it to a problem involving rancid butterfat (adapted from Kepner & Tregoe, 1965).

The vice-president of a butterfat manufacturer received a call from a customer of her midwestern plant. Some recent bags of butterfat that the customer received have turned rancid during the manufacture of various food products. The discrepancy between the actual level of performance—some of the butterfat was turning bad—and the expected standard of performance, was the vice-president's indication that a problem existed. She defined the problem in terms of a deviation from the expected standard, thus defining the problem as "some bags of butterfat produced in the midwestern plant turn rancid before they should."

Being a rational manager, the vice-president resisted her first impulse—which was to fly to the midwestern plant to inspect things first hand—and instead began to think through the situation. Having defined the problem, the vice-president began to describe the problem as precisely and completely as possible. By making a number of phone calls, she learned the following facts: (a) the problem appeared to be limited to bags of butterfat that were produced at the company's midwestern plant; (b) none of the midwestern plant's other customers experienced the problem; (c) the problem was confined to approximately 20% of the bags that the customer used; and (d) the problem began about a week ago.

The vice-president resisted her first thought, namely, that because none of the midwestern plant's other customers experienced the problem, the customer must be doing something wrong, and continued her problem-solving analyses. Having described the problem as precisely as possible, she next searched for anything that distinguished when the problem occurred from when it did not. An afternoon on the phone turned up potentially interesting additional facts. First, the customer was by far the midwestern plant's largest customer, a consequence of which was that the customer's bags were handled differently from those of other customers. Specifically, bags for the large customer were stacked in cubes on pallets before being frozen for shipment. However, this did not really explain the problem because the customer's bags had been handled this way for several years, yet the problem appeared only a week ago. Second, the midwestern plant's quality control inspector was a new employee who began a week ago. However, even if the quality control inspector was not doing his job, that would only explain why it was a customer rather than plant personnel who discovered the problem, and not why a plant that typically turns out good butterfat began turning out bad butterfat. Third, a new freezer was brought on line a week ago in the midwestern plant that is used to freeze the bags of butterfat before shipping. If the new machine were not working as effectively as the old one, it is possible that some of the bags of butterfat were not completely frozen, and thus could turn rancid. However, why would only the one customer be affected?

None of the these facts when considered individually provided an adequate explanation of the problem, but perhaps a combination of factors was at work. One combination that might explain the problem involved the new freezer and stacking the bags of butterfat in cubes for the customer. Suppose the new freezer was not as effective as the old one. Bags of butterfat near the outside of the cube might freeze completely, but perhaps bags near the center of the cube would not. This explanation could account for what was known about the problem. Only one customer was affected because it was only the large-order customer whose bags were stacked in cubes. Only some cubes were affected because the bags near the outside of the cube would freeze whereas those near the center of the cube might not. The problem began only a week ago because that is when the new freezer was first used.

Having come to an explanation that apparently accounted for what was known about the problem, the next step was to test the proposed explanation. The vice-president asked the plant manager to insert temperature probes into one of the cubes, some near the center of the cube and some near the outside, and then use the new freezer to freeze the cube. The results of this test indicated that the bags near the outside froze very quickly, but the bags near the center cooled little, if at all. Apparently, the frozen bags on the outside of the cube insulated the inner bags from the cold of the freezer.

Having found the source of the problem, the vice-president decided to stick with the new freezer because it was so much more cost-effective, but to change the way the bags were handled for the customer. Instead of building the bags into a solid cube, the bag handlers were instructed to leave at least one inch of space between the columns. A subsequent test using temperature probes showed that the space between columns resulted in all bags being frozen completely. The vice-president finished by calling the customer to explain the problem and how it was corrected.

The Proactive Manager

A more recent example of a rational approach to managerial problem solving is provided by Plunkett and Hale (1982). Their system of managerial problem solving is based on principles similar to those outlined by Kepner and Tregoe (1965), and consists of the following seven steps:

1. *State the problem.* The first step in problem solving is to state the problem and the desired resolution. Plunkett and Hale offer little guidance for completing this step; as was true for Kepner and Tregoe, problem identification and formulation are assumed to be perfunctory parts of the problem-solving process.

2. *Describe the problem.* The second step is to describe the problem carefully in terms of: (a) what object, unit, or person appears to be affected by the problem; (b) what exactly is wrong; (c) where the problem is found; (d) when the problem began; and (e) how many of the total number of objects, units, or persons that could be affected by the problem actually are affected.

3. *Identify differences between affected and unaffected objects, units, or persons.* Differences between affected and unaffected objects, units, or persons provide clues about the underlying cause of the problem.

4. *Identify changes that are associated with the problem.* When something is operating at the expected level of performance, it is assumed that this level of performance will continue indefinitely unless something changes. Thus, when a problem develops, one searches for a change that might have caused it.

5. *Generate likely causes.* Once changes that are associated with the problem have been identified, the problem solver attempts to determine how a particular change, either alone or in combination with other changes or factors, might have caused the problem.

6. *Consider most likely cause.* Here the problem solver determines whether the most likely cause provides an adequate explanation for the problem, focusing on whether the cause can explain why the problem appears in some situations and not in others.

7. *Verify most likely cause.* The goal here is to find some independent means to verify that one has uncovered the actual cause of the problem rather than a potential cause.

Evaluation of Rational Approaches to Managerial Problem Solving

Rational approaches to managerial problem solving such as those proposed by Kepner and Tregoe (1965) and Plunkett and Hale (1982) have a number of obvious strengths. First, the approaches are *explicit.* One easily may communicate the steps used in problem solving to others who might be involved in the process, and training managers how to use approaches such as these is a straightforward endeavor. Second, the approaches are *general,* across both problems and problem solvers. The same principles apply regardless of the nature of the specific problem or of the characteristics of the manager who is responsible for solving the problem. The generality of rational approaches to managerial problem solving has served as a rationale for creating a class of general managers who can move from position to position and yet be effective problem solvers. By adopting rational approaches to managerial problem solving, problems are interchangeable as are problem solvers. Thus, organizations gain enormous flexibility in staffing managerial positions. Third, the approaches are *based on sound principles of logic and scientific reasoning.* Managers attempt to minimize bias and avoid jumping to conclusions prematurely. They generate alternative potential explanations of a problem, and they search for independent confirmation of the explanation they settle on.

Given these obvious strengths, one might imagine that the science of management would have displaced the art of management in no time at all. In fact, proponents of rational management are at best holding their own ground with little likelihood of making further inroads in management theory or practice. For example, rational approaches receive little consideration in recent handbooks of managerial problem solving (e.g., Albert, 1980; Virga, 1987). What has limited the influence of rational approaches to managerial problem solving?

Mintzberg's (1973) influential studies of what managers actually do, as opposed to what they are supposed to do or what they say they do, provided unwelcome news to proponents of rational approaches to managerial problem solving. Mintzberg found that even successful managers rarely if ever employed rational approaches. Rather than following a step-by-step sequence from problem definition to problem solution, managers typically groped along with only vague impressions about the nature of the problems they were dealing with, and with little idea of what the ultimate solution would be until they had found it (Mintzberg, Raisinghani, & Theoret, 1976). Isenberg (1984) reached a similar conclusion in his analysis of how senior managers solve problems. The senior managers he studied did not follow the rational model of first defining problems, next assessing possible causes, and only then taking action to solve the problem. Instead they worked from general overriding concerns, and they worked simultaneously at a number of problems. Note that it is not just that senior managers appeared to be applying a rational approach to a number of problems in parallel, as opposed to seeing one problem through to completion before tackling the next. Rather, they violated the principles of rational management. For example, the senior managers often took action throughout the problem-solving process. In fact, evaluating the outcomes of their preliminary actions appeared to be one of their more useful tools for problem formulation.

A second problem for rational approaches to managerial problem solving is growing skepticism about the power of general principles of problem solving in the absence of content knowledge of the problem-solving domain (McCall & Kaplan, 1985). Proponents of rational approaches have argued that one of their major strengths is that managers can apply them without having prior knowledge of, or experience with, the problems they confront. For example, Kepner and Tregoe (1965) find it notable that a particular manager was able to solve a problem with ". . . no special know-how or detailed technical information about this problem. He relied instead on a thorough knowledge of the process of problem analysis" (p. 130). That some problems may be intractable in the face of rational approaches was recognized even by the consummate rational problem solver, Sherlock Holmes, who near the end of a baffling case was observed to remark to Watson:

> What is the meaning of it, Watson? What object is served by this circle of misery and violence and fear? It must tend to some end, or else our universe is ruled by chance, which is unthinkable. But what end? There is the great standing problem to which human reason is as far from an answer as ever. (cited in Eames, 1978)

A third problem for rational approaches to managerial problem solving is a growing awareness of the biases and other limitations that characterize the rational thinking of individuals including managers (see, e.g., Hogarth, 1987; Kahneman, Slovic, & Tversky, 1982; Nisbett & Ross, 1980; Tversky & Kahneman, 1983, 1986). Hogarth (1987) provided a catalog of common biases that affect the acquisition of information, the processing of information, and response selection, which I have summarized in the context of managerial problem solving.

Acquisition Biases.   Managers must acquire a tremendous amount of information as they attempt to understand the problems they confront and to identify potential solutions. Biases that affect the acquisition of information include the following:

1. *Managers overestimate the frequency of occurrence of highly salient or publicized events and underestimate the frequency of occurrence of less salient or publicized events (i.e., the availability heuristic).* Consequently, their view of events associated with the problem to be solved may be distorted.

2. *Information acquired early in the problem-solving process receives too much weight; information acquired late in the problem-solving process receives too little weight.* Managers conceptualize their problems (i.e., develop a problem-solving "set") on the basis of the initial information that is available to them. Subsequent information is interpreted in terms of the conceptualization that emerged from analysis of the initial information, and thus subsequent information may not receive the weight it should receive.

3. *Managers have difficulty conceptualizing problems in ways that transcend their own prior knowledge and experience.* Consequently, every problem a marketing manager is given is seen as a marketing problem, every problem that a personnel manager is given is seen as a personnel problem, and so on.

4. *Managers discover what they expect to discover.* What managers anticipate influences what they perceive. In addition, managers seek out information that is consistent with their views, and disregard or suppress information that is inconsistent with their views.

5. *When making comparisons, managers give greater weight to the total number of successes rather than to a ratio of the number of successes to the number of success and failures.* When, for example, managers must decide whom to promote, they tend to evaluate candidates on the basis of the absolute number of previous "hits" (i.e., times when the candidate really came through on an assignment), forgetting to consider a candidate's "misses." Thus, a newer candidate who has had more hits per assignment will lose out to a candidate with a longer, yet poorer, track record.

6. *Concrete information (e.g., personal experience) is given more weight than abstract information (e.g., evaluative reports), even when the abstract information is likely to be much more valid.* Managers pay more attention to things they observe firsthand, even when what they can observe firsthand presents a less-representative picture than that obtainable from other sources.

Processing Biases.   Once relevant information has been acquired, it must be processed. Due to limitations in managers' ability to process information, a number of biases influence their performance:

1. *Managers apply evaluative criteria inconsistently when they must evaluate a number of courses of action.* Because evaluative criteria shift, comparable courses of action are unlikely to be valued equally.

2. *Once an opinion has been formed, it is not likely to be changed even in the face of new information.* Managers quickly become invested in their opinions. New information that suggests the need to revise prior opinions tends to be discounted.

3. *Managers are not able to estimate the products of nonlinear relations.* For example, a cost that increases exponentially will be underestimated.

4. *Managers are likely to continue using an alternative that has worked before even when it no longer is appropriate.* Personnel managers rely on selection tests as predictors of managerial performance. The predictive power of such tests is modest, at best, yet managers will rely on test scores when making decisions about individuals for whom criterion information is available.

5. *Managers overestimate the stability of data based on small samples.* When managers go beyond qualitative opinion and collect data relevant to solving a particular problem, they are likely to overestimate the stability of the data they have collected.

6. *Managers make predictions by adjusting expectations relative to an anchor without questioning the continued validity of the anchor.* For example, sales managers may set a goal of increasing sales by 10 percent over last quarter, without considering any special circumstances that might have affected last quarter's sales figures.

Response Biases.   Managers are prone to two biases affecting their selection of responses to problems:

1. *Managers are prone to engage in wishful thinking.* As a consequence, they judge the probability of outcomes they favor to be greater than the data warrant, and the probability of outcomes they fear to be less than the data warrant.

2. *Managers succumb to the illusion of control.* The illusion of control refers

to an overestimation of the potency of one's actions. By planning for the future, managers may come to believe that they have more control over future outcomes than they in fact have, and to underestimate the importance of factors such as luck and economic conditions, over which they have no control.

With a growing awareness of the limitation of rational approaches to managerial problem solving, researchers recently have become more interested in the art of managerial problem solving as it is practiced by effective managers. In the next section, I review the early results of some recent approaches to understanding the art of managerial problem solving.

THE ART OF MANAGERIAL PROBLEM SOLVING

How might the art of managerial problem solving be conceptualized and examined? I consider five approaches to answering this question. The first approach to be considered, that of Isenberg (1986), suggests that managers deviate from the rational model especially in terms of their propensity to act before the facts are in.

Thinking While Doing

Isenberg has used a variety of methods for studying how experienced managers solve problems. In a recent study (1986), he compared the thinking-aloud protocols of 12 general managers and 3 college students who planned to pursue business careers, as they solved a short business case. (The small number of subjects is typical for verbal protocol research, but does suggest the need for cross-validation on other samples.) The case involved the Dashman company (Harvard Business School Case Services, 1947):

> Mr. Post was recently appointed vice-president of purchasing. The Dashman company has 20 plants, and in an effort to avoid shortfalls in essential raw materials required by the plants, Mr. Post decided to centralize part of the purchasing process the plants must follow. Mr. Post's experienced assistant objected to the change, but Mr. Post proceeded with the new procedures anyway. He sent a letter describing the new purchasing process to plant managers responsible for purchasing, and received supportive letters from the managers of all 20 plants. However, none of the managers complied with the new purchasing process.

The case was presented in parts on seven cards. Participants were free to rearrange the cards, and to work on the case in any manner they chose. The participants' task was to identify Mr. Post's problems and determine what he should do about them. Their verbal protocols were transcribed and coded into 17 categories that covered encoding information (e.g., ponders specific information, clarifies meaning, evaluates information), reasoning (e.g., causal reasoning, conditional reasoning, analogical reasoning), and planning action (makes reference to goals when planning, puts self in place of another when deciding what to do, establishes contingencies). In addition to coding the verbal protocols, the effectiveness of the participants' solutions to Mr. Post's problems was rated by several professors at the Harvard Business School who had used the Dashman case in their teaching over the years.

A number of differences were found between the managers' and students' performance on the task. Compared to students, the experienced managers: (a) began planning action sooner; (b) asked for less additional information; (c) made more inferences from the data; and (d) were less reflective about what they were doing and why. In many cases, managers began suggesting problem solutions after reading only half of the cards containing the case, even though they were not under time pressure and additional information was available merely by turning over the remaining cards! The best predictor of rated effectiveness of proposed problem solutions was the degree to which the managers reasoned analogically from their personal experience (e.g., "I had a similar problem last year with a new payroll procedure I tried").

To summarize the results from the verbal protocol study, experienced managers behaved differently than a rational model of managerial problem solving would suggest. They were action-oriented very soon into the problem-solving process. Their analyses were cursory, rather than exhaustive, and were based on their personal experience with analogous problems rather than on more formal principles of problem solving. Consistent with Mintzberg (1973), these results suggest that managers are people of action rather than of analysis. Peters and Waterman (1982) noted that effective organizations capitalize on managers' penchant for action by promoting a "bias for action."

Isenberg (1984) has documented other ways that managers depart from traditional conceptions of managerial problem solving. The traditional view is that managers carefully choose a strategy, formulate well-specified goals, establish clear and quantifiable objectives, and determine the most effective way to reach them. Whereas the traditional view might present an accurate picture of how junior managers approach problems, senior managers do their jobs differently. Using detailed interviews and observation, Isenberg learned that senior managers work from one or a small number of very general concerns or preoccupations. These preoccupations apparently guide their actions on a day-to-day basis. However, the preoccupations are not explicitly incorporated in detailed objectives, strategies, or action plans. For example, one senior manager saw his task as establishing discipline in a division that had become too loose, lacking enough order and predictability. This overriding concern guided his actions in discouraging a "fire-fighting" mentality among his managers and encouraging problem prevention through routine procedures that anticipated problems or at least caught them before they became full-blown. The concern for establishing discipline also resulted in a sharply critical evaluation of managers' poor preparation for corporate reviews. Senior managers also deviated from traditional conceptions of managerial problem solving by: (a) relying on intuition; (b) managing a large number of problems in various stages of completion; and (c) accepting considerable ambiguity, misinformation, and a lack of information.

Perhaps the major finding of Isenberg's work is the degree to which managers take action very early in the problem-solving process. The next approach I describe suggests that managers indeed may act on very little information, but that bringing a solution to fruition involves much more than one act on the part of a manager.

Nonlinear Problem Solving

Solving managerial problems by proceeding linearly through the stages of problem recognition, analysis, and solution is the exception rather than the rule; managerial problem solving typically is a recursive phenomenon that involves numerous delays, interruptions, revisions, and restarts (Mintzberg et al., 1976). Consider several examples.

No problem of consequence arrives on the desk of a manager correctly formulated (Mintzberg et al., 1976). There are occasions when a superior presents a problem that not only has been formulated properly but also comes with a solution (e.g., "We don't have enough help to handle this job. Hire someone!"), but this amounts to carrying out a task—doing what the superior has said to do— rather than problem solving. Most problems can be formulated in ways that make reaching a solution nearly impossible. Whether a formulation is the optimal one is rarely apparent until attempts have been made at finding and implementing solutions. Thus, solving managerial problems can involve recursive cycles of problem reformulation and solution seeking. Finding a solution tends to be a recursive phenomenon as well. Managers may search for ready-made solutions that can be applied directly or modified slightly. Usually, custom-made solutions are required. Custom-made solutions are put together, bit by bit, by managers who are guided only by a vague notion of some ideal solution, and who often do not know what the ultimate solution will look like until it has been completely crafted together. Implementing solutions also tends to be a recursive phenomenon. Solutions cannot be implemented without authorization, and for important problems, managers usually must seek authorization from others. The authorization process can be recursive, cycling back and forth among several levels of the organization and the manager. To make matters worse, interruptions and delays are common to all phases of managerial problem solving.

Extensive interviews with managers on the job by McCall and Kaplan (1985) confirm Mintzberg's observations about the nonlinear character of managerial problem solving, especially when the problems are important ones. McCall and Kaplan describe the process of solving important problems as one involving *convoluted action.* Convoluted action takes a long time to complete, typically months or even years as opposed to days or weeks. There are many people involved, with different interest groups competing for their stake in the outcome. Exhaustive searches are carried out to find solutions to problems, each of which is scrutinized before implementation is considered.

An advantage of convoluted action is that it appears to meet organizational needs. Problems often are caused by and affect a web of interrelated groups and individuals in an organization. Solutions to such problems must involve the cooperative efforts of many parties if they are to succeed. Convoluted action provides the opportunity for all interested parties to attempt to influence the process. Opportunities arise for persuading those who can be persuaded and neutralizing those who cannot. Because political considerations are a part of the process of finding solutions, there is less likelihood of political considerations causing a solution to derail in the implementation phase. A disadvantage of convoluted action is that the problem-solving process can be taken over by power politics, with competing interests in an organization being more interested in using the opportunity to get the best of their competitors than in solving the problem. By far the biggest liability of convoluted action is the frequency with which the process breaks down before a solution is identified and implemented. Because so many individuals are involved, and because each has the opportunity to derail or at least delay the process, it is not an unusual outcome for a solution to be put on the shelf rather than be implemented, if the process even makes it to the point of solution implementation. Problems are much more likely to be solved through convoluted action if they have a "champion" who refuses to let the problem-solving process derail until it has been completed (Peters & Waterman, 1982). An important role of a problem's champion is to manage the inevitable conflict that surrounds efforts to attack significant problems. Managers who deal effectively with such conflict tend to rely on several strategies (McCall & Kaplan, 1985). First, they engage the various parties in bilateral discussion, and do what is possible to avoid much interaction among other parties that could result in a coalition against them. Second, they put people ahead of issues. They take advantage of relationships they have cultivated and make their interactions personal rather than abstract. Third, they engage in "horse-trading" by getting the support of a given individual in return for something the individual would find useful. They make sure that all interested parties believe that they have won something. Fourth, they are very good at seeing things from another's point of view, and thus are able to prepare in advance for many of the objections they will face.

Not all problem solving in organizations involves convoluted action. Some problems simply cannot wait for convoluted action to run its course. These problems require *quick action,* the characteristics of which are, as you might expect, just the opposite of those of convoluted action (McCall & Kaplan, 1985). The goal of the manager is to implement a solution to the problem as quickly as possible. The manager takes sole responsibility for deciding on a solution and makes the decision unilaterally, although others may be consulted for advice if they are available. The search for information and alternative solutions is necessarily cursory. There simply is not time to get all of the information that might be helpful, so the manager must focus on a few key facts and must rely heavily on past experience.

An advantage of quick action is that action is not thwarted on problems that are not clearly understood, and more may be learned about the nature of some problems by studying the reaction to a quick action than by analysis without action. A political advantage of quick action is that it informs others in the organization that the problem is being dealt with. The obvious disadvantages of quick action include the fact that the chances of choosing an ineffective or even a deleterious solution are nontrivial, and that the manager who takes quick action is likely to bear complete responsibility for a failure.

McCall and Kaplan (1985) have identified several characteristics of managers who seem to be able to make quick action work. First, they have ready access to the one or two individuals who can provide trustworthy information about the problem. Second, they tend to drop everything and attend to the problem directly rather than delegating parts of the problem-solving process. Third, and perhaps most importantly, they avoid taking quick action unnecessarily. When presented with an emergency, their first response is to question why this must be handled today, as opposed to tomorrow or next week. Usually, only one aspect of the problem is really urgent, and that aspect can be dealt with by some limited response that will buy some time for addressing the complete problem.

In summary, managerial problem solving often is not characterized by a linear progression through the stages of problem formulation, solution search, and solution implementation, but may be characterized by either a recursive and interrupted cycling through the various stages (i.e., convoluted action), or a compressed response that truncates part of the problem-solving process (i.e., quick action).

The results of the approaches that have been discussed so far suggest that managers do not follow a rational model of first reflecting and then acting. The next approach to be considered has yielded results that support this conclusion, but it also suggests that there is an important role for reflection in managerial problem solving. Effective managers do reflect, but during, rather than prior to, action.

Reflection-in-Action

Schon (1983) assumes that managers are confronted not with simple, isolated problems, but with dynamic situations involving many complex, interwoven problems, each of which must be restructured to make it soluble. Because problems are complex and interconnected and environments are turbulent, rational analytic methods will not suffice. What is required is a manager who can imagine a more desirable future, and invent ways of reaching it.

Much of managerial competence appears as action that is nearly spontaneous, and based more on intuition than on rationality (Schon, 1983). When asked to explain their behavior, managers either are at a loss for words, or will make up an explanation that may be fictitious, perhaps not intentionally, but only in the spirit of trying to satisfy the questioner. To use Schon's own words, "Our knowing is ordinarily tacit, implicit in our patterns of action and in our feel for the stuff with which we are dealing. It seems right to say that our knowing is *in* our action" (p. 49).

A number of attempts have been made to characterize the idea that managers are able to know more than they can say. Barnard (1938/1968) believed such knowledge to come from nonlogical processes that cannot be expressed in words but that are demonstrated in judgment and action. For example, people are able to make quite accurate judgments of things such as the distance to the pin in golf and the trajectory to throw a ball so that it reaches its intended target, yet they are not able to describe how they make their judgments.

Although managers are not able accurately to describe how they are able to do what they do, many do occasionally attempt to reflect on their actions as they perform them. These *reflections-in-action* are on-the-spot examination and test-ing of a manager's intuitive understanding of a situation, often in the form of a reflective conversation with the situation (Schon, 1983). For example, a manager might ask herself why she feels uneasy about a decision she is about to make, or whether she might come up with a new way of framing an intractable problem. Although the practice of reflection-in-action is widespread among managers, managers rarely if ever reflect on their reflection-in-action. Consequently, they rarely discuss it with others, nor do they teach others how to do it.

Marketing provides a good example of the need for and use of reflection-in-action. The success of a business depends upon its ability to identify, create, and adapt to markets. The study of market phenomena is a highly specialized one; the field of marketing research has generated quantitative models of market phe-nomena and methods for predicting the response of a particular market to a particular product. However, the vast majority of the work managers do during the course of product development and marketing requires them to transcend the techniques and knowledge of market research. One reason for the limited effec-tiveness of market research on product development is a mismatch in timing. To be of much use in development, knowledge about a product's potential markets needs to be available early in product development, before considerable re-sources have been invested in a particular design. Yet market researchers cannot make accurate predictions until the product has been fully developed and can be test marketed. Market researchers can ask individuals how interested they would be in a yet to be developed product that will do x, y, and z, but the individuals' responses are poor predictors of their subsequent behavior, should the product subsequently appear in a store. Market researchers can give prototypes of the product to carefully selected consumer panels, but the reactions of consumer panels to product prototypes are not very predictive of real consumers' interest when the actual product reaches the marketplace.

Schon (1983) describes the marketing of a new type of tape by the 3M Corporation shortly after World War II as an example of reflection-in-action.

> The 3M Corporation had developed a clear cellulose acetate tape that was coated on one side with an adhesive. The intended use of the tape was for mending books that might otherwise be thrown away, hence the name Scotch Tape. The initial marketing plan, which reflected the intended use of mending books, was a complete flop. Very few consumers were interested in mending their books. However, some Scotch Tape was being bought by consumers who used it for a variety of other purposes such as wrapping packages, fastening labels, and curling hair. Subsequently, the marketing managers dumped the original marketing plan and the company brought out different types of Scotch Tape, each designed optimally for a particular use such as wrapping packages or curling hair. (p. 245)

What made the product the success it has become was not the ability of the market managers to foresee the market—they were dead wrong. What they did well was to take some action (i.e., the initial marketing plan), and to adaptively reflect on the outcome of their action. They might have viewed the initial marketing plan as a failure, and tried another approach to get consumers to use the tape for mending books. They might have ignored the information they turned up about the surprising uses consumers were finding for Scotch Tape. What they did was to capitalize on what they learned from the initial marketing plan by adapting the product to previously overlooked consumer needs.

The next approach to be described shares with that of Schon (1983) the assumption that much of a manager's problem-solving knowledge is tacit. The results to be described suggest that managerial tacit knowledge can be measured and studied, and that tacit knowledge is consequential to managerial effectiveness.

Tacit Knowledge

If much of managers' problem-solving knowledge is tacit, then the result of simply asking managers to describe what they know and do will be an incomplete, and perhaps erroneous, picture of managerial problem solving. The approach to be described represents an attempt to study managerial tacit knowledge by studying managers as they solve simulated problems that have been constructed to elicit tacit knowledge (Wagner, 1987; Wagner & Sternberg, 1985).

Tacit Knowledge is defined as practical know-how that usually is not openly expressed or stated (Oxford English Dictionary, 1933). It typically is acquired through informal learning, either from one's own experience or from that of a mentor or colleague. Managerial tacit knowledge can be classified according to its content, its context, and its orientation (Wagner, 1987).

The Content of Tacit Knowledge.   Three contents of managerial tacit knowledge have been studied. Tacit knowledge about *managing oneself* refers to practical know-how about self-organizational and self-motivational aspects of managerial performance. An example of tacit knowledge about managing oneself is knowing how to overcome the problem of procrastination. Tacit knowledge about *managing others* refers to practical know-how about managing one's subordinates, and one's relationships with peers and superiors. An example of tacit knowledge about managing others is knowing how to provide criticism that provokes a constructive rather than defensive response. Tacit knowledge about *managing tasks* refers to practical know-how about how to perform specific tasks well. An example of tacit knowledge about managing tasks is knowing how to give an effective oral presentation.

The Context of Tacit Knowledge.   Tacit knowledge with a *local* context refers to practical know-how concerning the short-term accomplishment of a task at hand. The focus is confined to the immediate task or problem, ignoring for the moment the larger context in which the problem exists. An example of tacit knowledge with a local context is knowing what steps to take so as to be able to finish a report that is due tomorrow. Tacit knowledge with a *global* context refers to practical know-how concerning long-term accomplishment. The focus is on how the present task or problem fits into the larger context. An example of tacit knowledge with a global context is knowing that there is a long-term payoff (i.e., developing more able subordinates) to the near-term inefficient strategy of assigning tasks to employees who have little experience with that particular task, in the hope of promoting the development of new skills.

The Orientation of Tacit Knowledge.   Problem solutions differ in their ideal quality and practicality. Tacit knowledge with an *idealistic* orientation refers to practical know-how concerning the ideal quality of an idea without regard to its practicality. Tacit knowledge with a *pragmatic* orientation refers to practical know-how concerning how workable an idea is, without regard to its ideal quality. It usually is a mistake to be concerned exclusively with only one of the two.

Combining Content, Context, and Orientation.   By crossing the three contents, two contexts, and two orientations of tacit knowledge, the framework depicted in Fig. 5.1 emerges. Consider examples of the kinds of knowledge that are represented by each block of the cube. For handling the problem of procrastination, forcing yourself to spend five minutes on a task in the hope that you

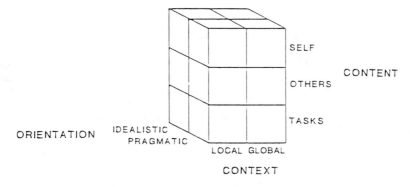

FIG. 5.1.   The tacit-knowledge framework.

will continue working once you have begun, is an example of tacit knowledge about managing self, with a local context. If it so happens that the task is an important report to your superior, reminding yourself of the long-term consequences to your career of not completing the assignment also may help to avoid procrastination. This is an example of tacit knowledge about managing self, with a global orientation. Regarding making oral presentations, knowing that it helps to inform your audience in advance about what you intend to say is an example of tacit knowledge about managing tasks, with a local context. Recognizing the importance of doing well in an upcoming oral presentation to superiors in the organization whom you have not yet met is an example of tacit knowledge about managing tasks, with a global context. Regarding the unpleasant task of firing an employee, knowing how to fire the employee in a manner that is not unnecessarily punishing is an example of tacit knowledge about managing others, with a local context. Realizing that you may need to get feedback on your personnel practices because you have fired more employees than your peers is an example of tacit knowledge about managing others, with a global context. Finally, for each of the judgments and decisions just mentioned, one might weigh separately how good each is ideally as well as practically.

Measuring Tacit Knowledge.   Having described a framework for describing tacit knowledge, how might it be measured? The approach I describe involves presenting managers with scenarios. The scenarios describe managerial problems that require tacit knowledge to solve effectively. The managers' task is to read the scenarios and then rate the quality of possible responses to them. A scenario and a sampling of its associated response alternatives is presented in Table 5.1. This particular scenario was constructed to measure tacit knowledge about managing others with a global context. Responses can be scored using several methods, the more common of which is to compare item ratings to a prototype derived from the responses of an expert group.

TABLE 5.1
A Scenario Used to Measure Managerial Tacit Knowledge

You have just been promoted to head of an important department in your organization. The previous head has been transferred to an equivalent position in a less important department. Your understanding of the reason for the move is that the performance of the department as a whole was mediocre. There were not any glaring deficiencies, just a perception of the department as so-so rather than as very good. Your charge is to shape up the department. Results are expected quickly. Rate the quality of the following strategies for succeeding in your new position.

___ a. Meet with your superiors to describe your strategy for improving the performance of the department.
___ b. Resist the pressure to turn things around in a hurry because quick improvements may come at the expense of long-term negative consequences.

. . .

___ g. Buy some time from your superiors by taking quick, but limited action, then consider what needs to be done in the long run.

Representative Findings.   A number of recent studies of managerial tacit knowledge (Wagner, 1987; Wagner & Sternberg, 1985, in press) have yielded the following findings:

1. *Performance on measures of managerial tacit knowledge differentiates experts and novices.* Wagner and Sternberg (1985) gave a measure of managerial tacit knowledge to three groups of subjects, totaling 127 subjects in all, whose members differed in amount of managerial experience. A professional manager group consisted of 54 managers; a business graduate student group consisted of 51 graduate students in business schools; and a novice group consisted of 21 undergraduates with no managerial experience. Participants in the study read scenarios depicting managerial problems and then rated the quality of various responses to the problems. Item ratings were correlated with a "dummy" variable that indicated whether an individual was a member of the professional manager, business graduate student, or novice group. With a total of 166 items, 8 reliable correlations between item ratings and the dummy variable would be expected by chance. In fact, significant correlations were found for 39 of 166 item ratings. A binomial test of the probability of obtaining this many significant correlations due to chance alone yielded $p < .001$.

Wagner (1987) gave a different measure of managerial tacit knowledge to 64 professional managers, 25 business graduate students, and 60 novices with no managerial experience. Responses were scored by deviating them from a prototype constructed from the responses of an expert group of highly successful and experienced managers. When performance is scored in this manner, lower scores (i.e., smaller deviations from the expert prototype) indicate better performance.

Average total scores were 254.2, 296.8, and 363.6 for the professional managers, business graduate students, and novices, respectively. A test for a linear trend was significant, $F(1, 132) = 31.9, p < .001$, and a Newman-Keuls follow-up indicated that all differences between pairs of means were significant at $p < .01$.

2. *Performance on measures of tacit knowledge predicts criterion measures of managerial performance.* Wagner and Sternberg (1985) examined correlations between performance on a measure of managerial tacit knowledge and a variety of criterion measures of managerial performance. For a group of professional managers, reliable correlations were found between tacit knowledge and the managerial criterion measures of salary (.46) and whether or not one's organization was at the top of the Fortune 500 list (.34). For a group of bank managers for whom more detailed performance data were available, reliable correlations were found between tacit knowledge and the criterion measures of percentage of salary increase (based on merit) (.48) and a rating of the managers' success at generating new business for the bank (.56). Recently, Wagner and Sternberg (in press) reported a significant correlation between amount of tacit knowledge and rated performance in a managerial problem-solving situation of .61 for a group of managers who participated in a Leadership Development Program at the Center for Creative Leadership.

3. *Individual differences in tacit knowledge are not closely related to individual differences in IQ.* Correlations between IQ and performance on measures of managerial tacit knowledge consistently are not reliably different from zero. For example, Wagner and Sternberg (1985) reported a correlation between IQ and managerial tacit knowledge of .16 (n.s.). Wagner (1987) reported a correlation between IQ and managerial tacit knowledge of $-.12$ (n.s.), and Wagner and Sternberg (in press) reported a correlation between IQ and managerial tacit knowledge of $-.14$ (n.s.).

Other results reported by Wagner and Sternberg (in press) provide further support for viewing tacit knowledge as a predictor of managerial problem solving that is independent of both IQ and personality factors as measured by common self-report measures. They carried out a series of hierarchical regression analyses to determine whether tacit knowledge would predict performance in a managerial problem-solving simulation after partialling out the effects of IQ and personality variables from scales such as the California Personality Inventory, the Myers-Briggs, the Fundamental Interpersonal Relations Orientation-Behavior (FIRO-B), the Hidden Figures Test, and other measures. In every case, tacit knowledge accounted for a reliable and large proportion of the variance in performance on the managerial problem-solving simulation regardless of the other variables that were partialled out.

4. *At least some tacit knowledge appears to be quite general.* Factor analyses of measures of tacit knowledge suggest that individual differences are largely a function of a general factor. For example, Wagner (1987) factor-analyzed a

managerial tacit knowledge measure and found that the first principal component accounted for 44% of the total variance in the correlation matrix, and 76% of the total variance when the correlations were disattenuated for unreliability. The residual matrix after extracting the first principal component was nonsignificant in both cases. The results of a confirmatory factor analysis were comparable. A model with a general factor and no group factors provided an excellent fit to the data.

Using a complementary approach to assess the generality of tacit knowledge, Wagner (1987) gave a measure of managerial tacit knowledge and a measure of tacit knowledge that was constructed for the field of academic psychology to the same group of individuals. The reliable correlation between performance on the two measures of .58 ($p < .001$) provides further evidence of the generality of tacit knowledge.

In summary, experienced managers differ from novices with little or no managerial experience in having acquired tacit knowledge about managerial problem solving. Differences in the amount of tacit knowledge acquired have been related to a wide variety of criterion measures of managerial success, but such differences are not closely related to differences in IQ. Finally, a substantial part of tacit knowledge appears to be broadly applicable as opposed to highly situation specific.

Each of the reviewed approaches to studying aspects of the art of managerial problem solving assume that much is lost when problem solving is reduced to a set of general principles. This assumption would appear to have consequences for the way students are trained to become managers. An example of a training approach that attempts to go beyond the teaching of general problem-solving principles is considered next.

The Case Approach

Illustrative cases have played a central role in medical and legal education from before the turn of the century. The origin of a case approach to teaching management is usually traced to the Harvard Business School (McNair, 1954). In 1909 the dean of the business school requested that student discussion be used to supplement the traditional practice of lecturing. For the next 10 years, executives were invited to classes to present problems they faced on the job. Students were asked to analyze the problems and make recommendations. In 1921, the first written collection of cases was produced, and a new dean, Wallace B. Donham, who happened to be a lawyer trained in law by the case method, pressed to have the case method adopted by the entire business school (Leenders & Erskine, 1973). Today, the case method has many adherents who are motivated by the belief that important aspects of managerial problem solving cannot be conveyed directly as decontextualized principles or methods. Thus, the students read descriptions of specific business situations and participate in class discussions that are designed to illuminate problem solving as it occurs in the context of the specific situation under discussion (Schoen & Sprague, 1954). The intent is that students learn to solve a variety of managerial problems by working through a large number of varied cases. The cases vary in length and complexity. The following is an example of an unusually short case:

> Mr. Thomsen accepted the position of plant manager at the Carmen Canning Company in Jamaica. He spent his first few months familiarizing himself with the various operations and management practices. Although he had extensive experience in the fruit canning industry in Hawaii, the Jamaican situation was substantially different.
>
> Mr. Thomsen faced all of the problems of a new manager stepping into an ongoing operation, and he was anxious to do his job well without appearing over eager to upset standard practice. One matter of particular concern to him dealt with a general lack of responsibility shown by the employees. Among other things, this was manifested by what seemed to Mr. Thomsen to be a high absentee rate. Workers often were late, or did not show up for work and sent notice after the shift had started. General employee attitude to foremen showed little respect also. In an effort to get to the heart of the situation, Mr. Thomsen gathered the following information: company background information; payroll records and time sheets for lateness; warning slips issued, including names and records; and labor records, including numbers of employees, their seniority, and the jobs they perform. (Leenders & Erskine, 1973, p. 127)

Many of the recent business situations that are used in the case method are much more involved, and are presented as a series of cases. For example, a case about NIKE, Inc. actually consists of 15 cases that report company operations at all levels of management as the company evolves from an entrepreneurial firm to a billion-dollar organization (Christensen, 1987).

It is difficult to describe the case method in much detail because there are no formal procedures or guidelines to govern case analysis or evaluation of problem solutions. Most who use the case method rely on their prior teaching experience with the cases to determine how to guide class discussion. However, Christensen (1987) has enumerated characteristics of the case method as practiced at the Harvard Business School:

1. *The case method emphasizes situational analysis.* By making the student deal with a problem in a particular situation, the student cannot simply deal with abstractions in hypothetical situations, but must confront the reality of the particular situation at hand. Necessary information may be missing, available information may be in conflict, a deadline may be approaching, and competing political forces may be causing interference. Yet the manager must do something (even if it is to decide to do nothing). Thus, solving problems presented in the context of

a specific situation with its various shortcomings and pressures prepares students for the kind of problem solving they will face later as managers.

2. *The case method relates analysis and action.* Academic researchers in business schools are rewarded for acquiring, analyzing, and disseminating knowledge. Managers, however, must act. The case method can be a vehicle for relating analysis and action. By forcing students to recommend actions that will begin to solve problems, they must derive recommended actions from their analyses. This fact has implications for the kind of analyses that pay off. For example, it may be more practical to restrict one's analyses to those that are relevant to planning a first step for handling a problem, rather than attempting to come up with a complete solution.

3. *The case method forces active intellectual involvement.* Advocates of the case method argue that just as one cannot learn to play tennis merely by listening to a lecture on the subject, one cannot learn to solve managerial problems merely by taking notes in a lecture hall. The playing out of the case is viewed as a simulation of real business problems. Case discussion provides students practice in skills such as analysis of information while listening and convincing others of the value of one's solution.

Even instructors who are considered masters of the case method are able to say little about what it is they actually do. However, contrasting the case method used in business schools with that common to law schools may help to understand the role of underlying principles in the case method. In law schools, the Socratic method is often used to get students to distill the case into its essence (referred to as "stating the case"), and then to derive general legal principles from the specific case. In contrast, students in business schools are questioned about the adequacy of their analysis and the appropriateness of their action plan, for the purpose of coming up with a solution to the problem faced by the organization as described. Little or no attention is paid to deriving general principles. The emphasis is on: (a) understanding the unique aspects of the context in which the problem is found; (b) defining the scope of the problem, including the organizational forces that are at work; (c) appreciating the interconnectedness of problems, and of the organization's various structures and functions; and (d) taking action that improves the organization's position relative to the problems presented in the case (Christensen, 1987).

SUMMARY AND CONCLUSIONS

The emphasis of rational approaches to managerial problem solving is on basic principles that apply regardless of the specific nature of the problem to be solved. Advantages of rational approaches include: (a) a reliance on sound principles of logic and scientific reasoning that are intended to result in objective problem analysis and to minimize the effects of bias; (b) their generality—the set of methods applies to any managerial problem; and (c) their explicitness, a consequence of which is that the approaches can be described and taught to others directly. Although the bulk of this chapter has been concerned with limitations of, and alternatives to, rational approaches to managerial problem solving, it would be a mistake to regard them merely as "straw men." When confronted with a novel problem for which a manager has little or no relevant prior knowledge to draw upon, it is hard to imagine a more effective approach to problem solving. What is at issue is the extent to which effective managers actually use rational approaches in problem solving, and the validity of the assertion by advocates of rational approaches that knowledge of how to employ the approach is *sufficient* for effective problem solving (Kepner & Tregoe, 1965).

What evidence exists does not support the view that managers rely heavily on rational approaches in their on-the-job problem solving (Mintzberg, 1973; Isenberg, 1984). Rational approaches may be difficult for managers to employ because of the biases that are inherent in information acquisition, processing, and response selection (Hogarth, 1987). The most consistently documented deviation of managerial practice from that prescribed by rational approaches is a bias for acting rather than merely reflecting, especially in the initial stages of problem solving (Isenberg, 1984, 1986; Mintzberg, 1973). When managers do reflect, it is likely to be while taking action rather than as a precursor to action. One possible explanation for the reliance on early action is that a substantial portion of managers' problem-solving knowledge ordinarily is tacit, and becomes available only indirectly in the context of action (Schon, 1983). The results of a series of studies of managerial tacit knowledge indicate that: (a) having acquired tacit knowledge differentiates expert and novice managers; (b) individual differences in tacit knowledge are related to criterion measures of managerial performance; (c) individual differences in IQ are not closely associated with individual differences in tacit knowledge; and (d) some portion of managerial tacit knowledge is relatively general (Wagner, 1987; Wagner & Sternberg, 1985, in press).

Problem solving in real organizations is much more complicated than typical textbook treatments of the topic would suggest. An unbroken progression from identifying a problem, coming up with a solution, and implementing the solution is the exception rather than the rule. Problem solving is a recursive process that commonly is delayed as a consequence of numerous interruptions (Mintzberg et al., 1976). Although it is possible for action to be initiated abruptly when a problem is identified, action carried out to solve problems often is the product of a drawn out convoluted process that involves a number of individuals and parts of an organization (McCall & Kaplan, 1985).

One response by business schools to the discrepancy between problem solving as it is described in textbooks and as it occurs in the context of real organizations has been the adoption of the case method to managerial training. The case method emphasizes understanding the situational context of a problem. By requiring students to recommend action in response to the case problem, analysis is constrained much as it is in actual business situations (Christensen, 1987).

Although the work that has been reviewed gives clear indication that progress is being made to understand complexities associated with the art of managerial problem solving, much remains to be done. A substantial portion of the data have been generated by interview and observational procedures that necessarily are less rigorous than is optimal. Much of the work is sketchy, largely because it is based on approaches to the study of managerial problem solving that are of very recent origin. The case method is a notable exception in that it has been in use for close to 70 years, but the method has received little empirical scrutiny.

The approaches to the study of the art of managerial problem solving are similar to rational approaches in that both kinds of approaches represent analytic attempts to describe problem solving in terms of some set of generalizations. Without generalizations, one must give up hope of ever understanding how managers solve problems. If the early results from these approaches are any indication, forthcoming generalizations about the art of problem solving will differ from the principles of rational problem solving in terms of: (a) an emphasis on the situational context in which the problem is embedded; (b) an appreciation of the complexity of the problem-solving process as it is carried out by managers in organizations; and (c) an acknowledgement that a substantial proportion of the knowledge and skills that managers bring to the problem-solving process is tacit, and thus is knowable only indirectly through careful study of what managers do when they solve problems as opposed to what they say they do.

Managers are noted for thinking in terms of the bottom line. The bottom line on managerial problem solving is that it is clear that rational approaches represent only a small part of the total picture of managerial problem solving. Recent work on understanding some of the neglected complexities of managerial problem solving is promising, but to date, it has provided only a rough outline of some of the missing parts to the picture.

ACKNOWLEDGMENTS

Preparation of this chapter was supported by contract MDA90385K0305 from the Army Research Institute. Appreciation is expressed to Carol Rashotte who provided helpful comments.

REFERENCES

Albert, K. J. (Ed.). (1980). *Handbook of business problem solving*. New York: McGraw-Hill.
Barnard, C. (1938/1968). *The functions of the executive*. Cambridge, MA: Harvard University Press.

Christensen, C. R. (1987). *Teaching and the case method.* Boston: Harvard Business School.

Eames, H. (1978). *Sleuths, Inc.: Studies of problem solvers Doyle, Simeon, Hammett, Ambler, Chandler.* Philadelphia: Lippincott.

Hogarth, R. M. (1987). *Judgment and choice.* New York: John Wiley & Sons.

Isenberg, D. J. (1984). How senior managers think. *Harvard Business Review, 62,* 81–90.

Isenberg, D. J. (1986). Thinking and managing: A verbal protocol analysis of managerial problem solving. *Academy of Management Journal, 4,* 775–788.

Kahneman, D., Slovic, P., & Tversky, A. (Eds.). (1982). *Judgment under uncertainty: Heuristics and biases.* New York: Cambridge University Press.

Kepner, C. H., & Tregoe, B. B. (1965). *The rational manager: A systematic approach to problem solving and decision making.* New York: McGraw-Hill.

Leenders, M. R., & Erskine, J. A. (1973). *Case research.* London, Ontario: University of Western Ontario.

McCall, M. W., & Kaplan, R. E. (1985). *Whatever it takes: Decision makers at work.* Englewood Cliffs, NJ: Prentice-Hall.

McNair, M. P. (Ed.). (1954). *The case method at the Harvard Business School.* New York: McGraw-Hill.

Mintzberg, H. (1973). *The nature of managerial work.* New York: Harper & Row.

Mintzberg, H., Raisinghani, D., & Theoret, A. (1976). The structure of "unstructured" decision processes. *Administrative Science Quarterly, 21,* 246–275.

Nisbett, R. E., & Ross, L. (1980). *Human inference: Strategies and shortcomings of social judgment.* Englewood Cliffs, NJ: Prentice-Hall.

Oxford English Dictionary. (1933). Oxford: Clarendon Press.

Peters, T. J., & Waterman, R. H. (1982). *In search of excellence.* New York: Harper & Row.

Plunkett, L. C., & Hale, G. A. (1982). *The proactive manager.* New York: John Wiley & Sons.

Schoen, D. R., & Sprague, P. A. (1954). The case method as seen by recent graduates. In McNair, M. P. (Ed.), *The case method at the Harvard Business School* (p. 76). New York: McGraw-Hill.

Schon, D. A. (1983). *The reflective practitioner.* New York: Basic Books.

Taylor, F. W. (1947). *Scientific Management.* New York: Harper & Brothers.

Tversky, A., & Kahneman, D. (1983). Extensional versus intuitive reasoning: The conjunction fallacy in probability judgment. *Psychological Review, 90,* 293–315.

Tversky, A., & Kahneman, D. (1986). Rational choice and the framing of decisions. *Journal of Business, 59,* 251–278.

Virga, P. H. (Ed.). (1987). *The National Management Association handbook for managers.* Englewood Cliffs, NJ: Prentice Hall.

Wagner, R. K. (1987). Tacit knowledge in everyday intelligent behavior. *Journal of Personality and Social Psychology, 52,* 1236–1247.

Wagner, R. K., & Sternberg, R. J. (1985). Practical intelligence in real-world pursuits: The role of tacit knowledge. *Journal of Personality and Social Psychology, 48,* 436–458.

Wagner, R. K., & Sternberg, R. J. (in press). Street smarts. In K. Clark & M. Clark (Eds.), *Measures of leadership.* Greensboro, NC: Center for Creative Leadership.

6 Solving Complex Problems: Exploration and Control of Complex Systems

Joachim Funke
University of Bonn/FRG

SOLVING COMPLEX PROBLEMS: EXPLORATION AND CONTROL OF COMPLEX SYSTEMS

Studying complex problem solving by means of computer-simulated scenarios has become one of the favorite themes of modern theorists in German-speaking countries who are concerned with the psychology of thinking. Following the pioneering work of Dietrich Dörner (University of Bamberg, FRG) in the mid-70s, many new scenarios have been developed and applied in correlational as well as in experimental studies (for a review see Funke, 1988). Instead of studying problem-solving behavior in restricted situations (like the "Tower of Hanoi" or "Cannibals and Missionaries"; cf. Greeno, 1974; Jeffries, Polson, & Razran, 1977), the new approach focuses on semantically rich domains that provide a touch of reality that was not inherent in the older research (see also Bhaskar & Simon, 1977). In the computer-administered scenario "LOHHAUSEN," for instance, subjects have to take over the regentship of a little town (Dörner, Kreuzig, Reither, & Stäudel, 1983). In other work, subjects take over the roles of a manager of a little shop (Putz-Osterloh, 1981), of an engineer in a developmental country (Reither, 1981), or of a pilot flying to the moon (Thalmaier, 1979). In general, the new approach deals with the *exploration and control of complex and dynamic systems by human individuals.*

This chapter is divided into four main parts. First, I give a working definition of what I mean by "complex problem solving" and suggest how complex tasks can be profitably analyzed and compared to each other across domains. Second, I summarize recent research on complex problem solving, analyze the main streams of current research, and discuss the underlying principles and mechanisms uncovered so far. Also, I consider how people learn to solve complex problems and discuss expert-novice differences in complex problem solving. Third, I describe my own approach to studying complex problem solving in which it is conceptualized as a dynamic process of knowledge acquisition and of knowledge application. I briefly describe the so-called DYNAMIS project and the DYNAMIS shell for scenarios, and report the results of some studies within this framework. Finally, I give perspectives for future research.

DEFINITION OF COMPLEX PROBLEM SOLVING

I argue that complex problem solving can be understood by contrasting it with "simple," noncomplex problem solving in terms of the following, non-orthogonal criteria:

1. Availability of information about the problem, that is, transparency of the problem situation.
2. Precision of goal definition, that is, whether a goal is defined, and whether there are multiple goals, some of which may be contradictory.
3. "Complexity" of the problem as defined by the number of variables, the degree of connectivity among the variables, and the type of functional relationship (linear vs. nonlinear).
4. Stability properties of the problem, that is, time dependencies in the course of the problem-solving process ("Eigendynamik").
5. "Richness" of the problem's semantic embedding. Rich semantic embeddings often reduce the uncertainty to a large degree.

A complex problem-solving situation is one that can be characterized by the following features (with respect to the previously mentioned criteria):

1. "Intransparency": In complex problem-solving situations, only some variables lend themselves to direct observation. Often, only knowledge about "symptoms" is available, from which one has to infer the underlying state. This is a case of intransparency. Other cases of intransparency arise if variables can be assessed in principle, but their huge number requires selection of a few relevant ones.

2. "Polytely" (from the Greek words *poly telos* = many goals): Frequently, complex problem-solving situations are characterized by the presence of not one, but multiple goals. Problems can arise when some of the goals are contradictory (e.g., the manager who wants to make a lot of money, but has to pay high wages in order to find good workers), and a reasonable trade-off is required.

3. "Complexity of the situation": This feature concerns the number of identification and regulation processes involved. A complex problem-solving situation

is not only characterized by a large number of variables that have to be considered, but also by their complex connectivity pattern, by the possibilities to control the system, and by the dynamic aspects of the system. The growing complexity of situational demands may conflict with the limited capacity of the problem solver.

4. "Connectivity of variables": A high degree of connectivity describes a situation in which changes in one variable affect the status of many other, related variables. Complex problems often contain a high degree of connectivity, that is, it is very difficult to anticipate all possible consequences of a given situation.

5. "Dynamic developments": Complex problem-solving situations often change decrementally and worsen, forcing a problem solver to act immediately, under considerable time pressure. Also, spontaneous changes in the other direction are possible, causing less stress but making the situation less predictable.

6. "Time-delayed effects": Not every action shows immediate consequences. In complex problem-solving situations, effects often occur with time delay. This makes it necessary for the actor to wait patiently, in sharp contrast to the aforementioned situation, in which immediate action is required.

The features outlined differ not only from those traditionally emphasized in research on problem solving and thinking, but also from those employed in conventional intelligence tests. They do, however, allow for a more precise characterization of complex problem situations than do more traditional classifications, like the classification into well-defined and ill-defined situations. For example, Duncker's (1935) "radiation problem," although useful in studying analogical transfer (e.g., Gick & Holyoak, 1983), might not be classified as a complex problem according to the present classification scheme, because it lacks the feature of dynamic development as well as that of complexity.

Complex problem solving has also been a topic in recent man-machine research. With increasingly more automation and computerization, the operator of a complex technical system becomes a complex problem solver, rather than merely a controller (cf. Bainbridge, 1987). Process control tasks are used in the laboratory or observed in the field to address questions of systems design and of optimal training procedures of system-relevant knowledge. Because this research comes more from the applied, engineering point of view, however, it will not be reported in detail in this paper (see, e.g., Rasmussen, Duncan, & Leplat, 1987).

RECENT RESEARCH ON COMPLEX PROBLEM SOLVING

In the following, I consider some of the research on complex problem solving that has been conducted over the past 15 years. Following this review, I summarize: (a) the domain-specific and domain-general principles and mechanisms underlying complex problem solving; (b) the acquisition of complex problem solving; and (c) expert-novice differences in complex problem solving.

Review of Studies on Complex Problem Solving

Because the research themes diverge and the domains that have been chosen are very heterogeneous, it is not easy to arrange the various studies in a systematic way. Even the simulation systems can only be compared superficially. For reasons of simplicity, the systems are, in the following, grouped according to their number of variables, a criterion which is sometimes seen as an essential indicator of complexity. Because no objective general measure of complexity exists, the number-of-variables criterion is just an expedient for orienting purposes. In this section, I give a short description of the major systems used in empirical research (for a more elaborated review see Funke, 1988).

Systems With up to 10 Variables.   Systems with up to 10 variables are the most commonly used ones. Despite the fact that only a small number of variables is utilized, the complexity of these systems should not be underestimated. Table 6.1 gives an overview of the major systems in this category.

A major advantage of small systems is that all information relevant to the problem-solving situation can be displayed on a single computer screen, thus allowing the subject directly to interact with the system. For the small systems, the equations are given if known to the author. Systems are discussed in alphabetical order.

BLACK BOX.   In Mackinnon and Wearing's (1985) BLACK BOX, subjects are asked to control an abstract, first-order feedback system for 75 trials. The behavior of the system can be described by a complicated formula (cf. Mackinnon & Wearing, 1985, p. 165). The subject's task is to maintain the goal value of a single system variable by controlling a single input variable. No information about system characteristics is given. BLACK BOX is a transparent system (no hidden variables) that has a single goal variable. The connectivity function is complex. There is no time pressure. The system develops dynamically. Effects of time-delayed feedback can be manipulated experimentally.

In an experimental study using BLACK BOX, Mackinnon and Wearing manipulated two factors: the value of the boundary function which amplified or attenuated the input value, and the intensity of feedback, operationalized via a short versus long "memory" of past inputs. For the data of 32 subjects, Mackinnon and Wearing found no significant effect of the amplification factor: Subjects were able to quickly adapt their inputs to different boundary parameters. In contrast, intensity of feedback did have a significant effect on subjects' problem-solving behavior. Results showed significantly better system control for the longer memory of past inputs. The authors concluded that a systems-analytical

TABLE 6.1
Overview of Simulation Systems: Systems With up to 10 Variables

Name	# of Variables	Reference
BLACK BOX	2	Mackinnon & Wearing (1985)
COLD-STORAGE DEPOT	6	Reichert & Dörner (1988)
ECONOMIC SYSTEM	4	Broadbent, FitzGerald, & Broadbent (1986)
ECOSYSTEM	6	Funke (1985)
GAS-ABSORBER	6	Hübner (1987)
HAMURABI	8	Gediga, Schöttke, & Tücke (1983)
INVENTORY PROBLEM	3	Kleiter (1970)
MINI-LAKE	6	Opwis & Spada (1985)
MOONLANDING	3	Thalmaier (1979)
PORAEU	8	Preussler (1985)
SIM002	10	Kluwe & Reimann (1983)
SINUS	6	Funke & Müller (1988)
SUGAR FACTORY	4	Berry & Broadbent (1987)
TRANSPORTATION	4	Broadbent (1977)
WORLD	4	Eyferth et al. (1982)

approach might be helpful in identifying the demands a problem-solving task makes upon the problem solver and might also make the comparison of different tasks and the ordered exploration of the range of possible tasks easier.

COLD-STORAGE DEPOT. In Reichert and Dörner's (1988) system, COLD-STORAGE DEPOT, subjects have to control a cold-storage depot by means of a steering wheel (u) with which the temperature of the depot (r) can be changed according to the following formula which is unknown to the subjects (s = outside temperature and v = delay factor; see Reichert, 1986):

$$r(t) = r(t - 1) + (s(t) - r(t - 1))*0.1 - q(t - 1),$$
$$q(t) = (r(t - v) - u(t))*0.3.$$

This simulation system is transparent, has a single goal, dynamic development, time pressure, and, most importantly, time-delayed effects which require a careful control strategy.

In one of the studies using the COLD-STORAGE DEPOT, 54 student subjects had the opportunity to perform 100 interventions. Subjects were told that the automatic steering was defective and human control was necessary in order to prevent the food from being spoiled. The results of the study showed that only one-fifth of the subjects were able to run the depot successfully. The main difficulty for subjects was the time-delay of the nonlinear function relating subjects' interventions and the system's responses; some subjects recognized this delay and planned their actions adequately, that is, ahead of time, whereas other students changed their interventions immediately after receiving feedback. Interestingly, some of the "good" problem solvers were not able to verbalize the rules they were using so effectively. Reichert and Dörner developed what they called a "simulation of the simulation," that is, a psychological model that simulated the simulation game, which was able to produce a synthetic behavior almost indistinguishable from the behavior of real subjects.

ECONOMIC SYSTEM. Broadbent, FitzGerald, and Broadbent's (1986) ECONOMIC SYSTEM modeled an imaginary country, in which subjects can raise or lower the levels of taxation (R) and of government expenditure (G) in order to control the rates of unemployment (U) and of inflation (I) according to the following formulas (cf. Broadbent et al., 1986, p. 41):

$$U(t + 1) = 12.8 - ((1 - R)*(G + 7650)/730),$$
$$I(t + 1) = I(t)*(1.45 - 0.15*U(t)).$$

Broadbent et al. argued that their findings demonstrate a dissociation between verbal reports and actions. I return to this topic later when related work of the Broadbent group (SUGAR FACTORY, TRANSPORTATION) will be presented.

ECOSYSTEM. In ECOSYSTEM (Funke, 1985), subjects are asked to control the amounts of insects (Y1), leaves (Y2), and water pollution (Y3) in an ecosystem through the manipulation of poison (X1), vermin eaters (X2), and fertilizer (X3), according to the following system structure:

$$Y1(t + 1) = 0.9*Y1(t) + 1.0*X2(t),$$
$$Y2(t + 1) = 1.0*Y2(t) + 10.0*X3(t),$$
$$Y3(t + 1) = 1.0*Y1(t) - 0.1*X1(t).$$

ECOSYSTEM is a transparent, polytelic, complex, and dynamic system, in which time delay and connectivity can be manipulated as experimental variables.

The system simulates a total of five trials, each consisting of seven cycles. In the first four trials, subjects are encouraged to familiarize themselves with the system by actively exploring the system ("knowledge-acquisition phase"). In the last trial ("knowledge-application phase"), in contrast, subjects are asked to actively steer the system toward achieving a given goal state. Funke found that two critical system attributes, namely, the "connectivity of the variables" and the "degree of time delay," had a large effect on subjects' quality of the knowledge representation (a subject's diagnosed "mental model" of the system) as well as on the degree to which the goal was achieved, although the effects of time delay appeared to be weaker than the effects of connectivity. In a similar study, Fritz and Funke (1988) demonstrated differences between pupils with minimal cerebral dysfunction and matched controls with respect to discriminatory and integrational abilities in the process of hypothesis development and hypothesis testing.

GAS-ABSORBER. Hübner (1987) simulates a GAS-ABSORBER with one input variable (u) and three states (x):

$$x(t + 1) = \begin{bmatrix} 0.365 & 0.219 & 0.066 \\ 0.186 & 0.421 & 0.219 \\ 0.048 & 0.186 & 0.365 \end{bmatrix} x(t) + \begin{bmatrix} 0.019 \\ 0.100 \\ 0.389 \end{bmatrix} u(t)$$

The GAS-ABSORBER is a transparent, dynamic, complexly interconnected system with dynamic and time-delayed effects. The system's structure is, at a formal level, precisely defined and analyzed (see also Hübner, 1989).

In a study by Hübner (1987), two different learning conditions produced no differences with respect to the quality of control (measured as distance from a given objective point). However, distance to the goal at the beginning of the intervention phase proved to be very important: If the goal could be achieved in two steps, less input error was made than if the goal could be achieved in three steps. These results are consistent with those obtained in manual tracking studies (see Bösser, 1983).

HAMURABI.   HAMURABI is the name of the absolute ruler of the agrarian state of "Summaria." In Gediga, Schöttke, and Tücke's (1983) system, subjects have the task of keeping alive as much of the population of Summaria as possible by using four manipulations: purchasing and selling arable acreage, deciding the area to be sown with corn, and determining the quantity of food required by each member of the community. Subjects run through two trials, each simulating a time period of 30 years. The system partly depends on randomly varying variables. Gediga et al. claim to have demonstrated that, on the one hand, problem situations with an exponential change over time were mastered by only a few subjects; on the other hand, the hypotheses of many subjects were in accordance with the complex problem situation and led to better performance.

HAMURABI is an intransparent, polytelic, complex system with dynamic components. Because of the random effects, it is not easy to determine the pure effects of subject interventions.

INVENTORY PROBLEM.   Kleiter (1970) uses a situation in which a retailer stocks a product which spoils if it is not sold by the end of a certain period of time. For every unit sold, the amount won increases; the units not sold decrease the amount won. The formula combining the input supply (A) with the output of the demand (Z) and a random component (e) under an "optimism condition" is as follows:

$$Z(t + 1) = 0.25*(A(t) - Z(t)) + Z(t) + e.$$

Under the "pessimism condition," a weight of -0.25 instead of 0.25 is used. The system is transparent, has a single goal, is low on complexity and connectivity, but shows dynamic developments. A random component makes subjects' performances more difficult to interpret.

For the "optimism condition," Kleiter found that the demand for the product increased when a higher amount than the last one was stocked; for the "pessimism condition," it was the other way around. The results of 40 subjects working with this system for a maximum of 50 trials demonstrated that only 2 subjects in each condition were able to accumulate a win whereas 6 subjects in the optimism and 12 in the pessimism condition did not even reach the minimum win.

MINI LAKE. The ecosystem MINI LAKE (Opwis & Spada, 1985) is a biological population model (with isolated as well as integrated parts) that is transparent, complex, and interconnected, has multiple goals, dynamic development, and no time-delayed effects. Subjects managing the system are asked to infer the conditions of change that operate in the system to make predictions about future states. Subjects are given precisely designated objectives and are asked to take adequate action. They can change the amount of phosphate fertilizer (u1) and fish biomass (u2) to control for two kinds of phytoplankton (x1, x2) and zooplankton (x3, x4), according to the following matrices:

$$\dot{x}(t) = \begin{bmatrix} 0 & 0 & -0.244 & -0.122 \\ 0 & 0 & -0.110 & -0.220 \\ 0.036 & 0.018 & 0 & 0 \\ 0.016 & 0.032 & 0 & 0 \end{bmatrix} x(t) + \begin{bmatrix} 0.507 & 0 \\ 0.418 & 0 \\ 0 & -0.246 \\ 0 & -0.200 \end{bmatrix} u(t)$$

Opwis and Spada argue that the nature of reliable and valid problem-solving indicators is problematic in most systems: with unrestricted access to the system, unknown solubility of the task, and ignorance of subjects' internal mental representations of the system, the experimental examination of thought processes is virtually impossible. Opwis and Spada, therefore, use a research plan that allows control of these stated variables. A model based on subjects' individual knowledge data was able accurately to predict approximately 80% of subjects' answers to questions about the system.

MOONLANDING. Thalmaier (1979) uses the dynamic system MOON-LANDING in which subjects have to control the landing maneuver of a space craft on the lunar surface. Thalmaier argues that the mathematical description of the problem type (e.g., the simulated system) and an understanding of the system's properties is a necessary prerequisite for understanding the behavior of experimental subjects. In his studies, Thalmaier found that 20 mathematics students who served as subjects were, indeed, able during a total of 20 practice landings, to recognize the dynamic aspects of the problem as well as its nonlinear development. Thalmaier concludes that subjects are not overtaxed from the beginning by nonlinear extrapolations. However, relative to an optimal steering strategy, subjects' difficulties in exploring and understanding the system were paramount. The successive recognition of the structure of the system through an input-output analysis had to occur first.

Empirical findings concerning this paradigm also come from a study by Funke and Hussy (1984), who presented the MOONLANDING task in two different domains, in its original domain and as a similarly structured COOKING problem. Funke and Hussy predicted that experience with the two different reality domains would affect problem-solving performance. Twenty-four male and female subjects (assumed to be experts in the domains of MOONLANDING or COOKING because of sex-specific socialization) were used. The results, however, did not confirm the hypotheses. The main effects of the experimental conditions "domain" and "previous experience" on the dependent variable "quality of problem solving" were weak, and the expected interaction did not materialize. Statistical arguments did not allow an expanded interpretation of this finding.

In a similar study with the modified target-approach paradigm, Hussy and Granzow (1987; Hussy, 1989) showed that problem-solving quality (measured as distance to a target state) decreased as a function of the increasing number of variables as well as of nonlinear interweaving functions, and of lower problem transparency. Hussy and Granzow found a significant correlation between test intelligence and problem-solving quality—but only under transparent conditions with few variables, which seems to support earlier findings reported by Putz-Osterloh (1981).

MOONLANDING is low on complexity but contains dynamic components. Experimental manipulation of domain effects, of complexity, and of transparency effects demonstrate the usefulness of this scenario in analyzing different influences on problem-solving behavior.

PORAEU. PORAEU (Preussler, 1985) is a small nonlinear predator-prey model in which subjects have to anticipate the number of robbers and swags in a simulated ecosystem at each of the 35 discrete time points.

In a prediction experiment, Preussler crossed three semantic conditions (helpful: the growth of the robbers was bad for humans; hindering: growth of robbers was good for humans; or neutral: an abstract version of the system without semantic labels), two prognosis conditions (only robber values had to be predicted vs. the prediction of robber and swag values was requested), and two presentation forms (number of robbers and swags with or without graphical displays). Subjects did not receive any information about system variables and the connectivity structure. Because the author used more than 20 dependent variables in this experiment and tested more than 30 different hypotheses, it is difficult to summarize the results of this work in a few words. The main effects of the three factors on the predictive behavior were all nonsignificant; individual interactions, however, showed more distinct effects. Based upon an additional examination of response effects, the author concluded that individuals are not able to make predictions concerning exponential development trends. Interestingly, under conditions of graphical feedback, subjects approximated nonlinear developments by linear functions. Introducing graphical feedback by showing the growth functions improved the quality of predictions, especially at later points in simulation time.

PORAEU is not a very complex system, but realizes a nonlinear dynamic development that is difficult for subjects to handle despite its transparency and the fact that only a single goal has to be controlled.

SIM002. Stimulated by a critical review of the studies on complex problem solving, Kluwe and Reimann (1983) derived an abstract system called SIM002. Kluwe and Reimann were less interested in pursuing the aim of simulating reality, rather, they wanted to develop systems that could be fit to many experimental inquiries. A more detailed description is given in the next section for the similar system, SIM00X.

SINUS. Funke and Müller (1988) were concerned with the effects of different demands of activity on the handling of an unknown dynamic system called SINUS. The system consists of living creatures from a distant planet called SINUS. The dependent variables are given the nonsense names, "Gaseln" (Y1), "Schmorken" (Y2), and "Sisen" (Y3); the independent variables are called "Olschen" (X1), "Mukern" (X2), and "Raskeln" (X3). The system has the following structure:

$$Y1(t + 1) = 10.0*X1(t) + 1.0*Y1(t),$$
$$Y2(t + 1) = 3.0*X3(t) + 1.0*Y2(t) + 0.2*Y3(t),$$
$$Y3(t + 1) = 2.0*X2(t) + 0.5*X3(t) + 0.9*Y3(t).$$

The task of the subjects is to explore the system and to control the dependent variables with respect to given goal states.

In their study, Funke and Müller manipulated (a) the possibility to actively or passively explore the system; and (b) whether the next system state had to be predicted or not. The amount of system knowledge subjects had acquired and the quality of problem solving served as dependent variables. Funke and Müller expected (a) the "interveners" to be superior to the pure "observers" with regard to amount of knowledge as well as to efficient operations; and (b) the "predictors" to accumulate more knowledge than the "nonpredictors." Subjects were 32 college students. Path-analytical evaluation of the data supported the expectations only partially: "interveners" were, indeed, better in dealing with the system, but seemed to know less than "observers" (cf. the similar dissociations reported by Broadbent et al., 1986; Putz-Osterloh, 1987). "Predictors" were more knowledgeable than "nonpredictors," but only in a special mode. Knowledge about the system was generally a good predictor of operating performance. Interestingly, there was a negative relation between the duration of the experiment and the quality of performance. Detailed analyses of so-called "experimental twins"—pairs of subjects who dealt with the same system situations—indicated high interindividual variability, thus showing the relevance of person-specific ways of data-evaluation.

SINUS is a transparent, complex, interconnected, dynamic system with multiple goals and no time delays. It is an ideal instrument for experimental manipulation of system attributes.

SUGAR FACTORY.   In Berry and Broadbent's SUGAR FACTORY (1984), subjects are asked to manage a small sugar-production factory in order to reach and maintain a given target production level. The size of the work force (W) can be varied in 12 discrete steps, yielding a level of production (P) according to the formula:

$$P(t + 1) = 2*W(t) - P(t).$$

A second, mathematically equivalent task called PERSONAL INTERACTION used the same structure, but now the subject could choose between 12 styles of behavior (very rude, rude, very cool, cool, . . . , loving) in order to produce and maintain a target behavior in a fictitious person called Clegg. After two sets of 30 trials, results of a posttask questionnaire were correlated with control performance, yielding nonsignificant coefficients of about -0.50 (Exp. 1).

In a later study, the SUGAR FACTORY simulation was combined with the PERSONAL INTERACTION task (Berry & Broadbent, 1987; Marescaux, Luc, & Karnas, 1989) to make relationships more or less salient. The input variables were now the number of employed workers (W; 1–12) and the behavior toward the union chief (B; 1–10); the variables to be controlled were the level of sugar output (P; 1–21) and the behavior of the union chief (G; 1–10), according to the formulas:

$$P(t + 1) = 1.8*W(t) - 0.45*B(t),$$
$$G(t + 1) = 0.8*B(t) + 0.45*W(t).$$

Results with this system illustrated the role of salience of relationships: No explicit knowledge about nonsalient relationships was acquired even when the system was handled very well.

TRANSPORTATION.   In this system, first used by Broadbent (1977), subjects have to control the bus load (L) and vacant parking spaces (VS) in a fictitious city parking lot by manipulating the time intervals between bus arrivals (T) and the amount charged for use of the lot (F). The formulas are:

$$L(t + 1) = 200*T(t) + 80*F(t),$$
$$VS(t + 1) = 4.5*F(t) - 2*T(t).$$

As in earlier mentioned studies, Broadbent (1977) reported a dissociation between the verbal statements of the subjects and their actual ability to control the system. I discuss this phenomenon later in the context of development of knowledge.

SUGAR FACTORY, PERSONAL INTERACTION TASK, and TRANSPORTATION are all systems at the lower end of the complexity scale. They have no time delays, no intransparencies, no dynamic developments, and represent a situation with a single respectively a double goal. One might ask, therefore, if these systems would really represent complex problems.

WORLD.   Eyferth, Hoffmann-Plato, Muchowski, Otremba, Rossbach, Spiess, & Widowski (1982) examine the coping possibilities—the "genesis of handling competence"—in a novel situation. WORLD exists as a series of pictures on a screen, upon which a few objects can carry out computer-controlled maneuvers and can move or interact with each other according to a set of fixed rules. The observer can use the keyboard to interrupt maneuvers and to become actively involved. The task is to understand the system rules and to manipulate the objects toward achieving a certain purpose. Four numbered squares move on the screen in various ways, changing after collisions. The observer can (a) vary the speed with which the squares move over the screen; (b) change the squares' directions of movement; and (c) stop the system. WORLD is a single-rule system, with dynamic development, no time delays, and a single goal.

The results of an exploratory study (Eyferth et al., 1982) indicated that subjects gradually construct a system representation and connect it to existing schemata.

Systems With up to 100 Variables.   Table 6.2 shows the systems that belong to this category.

DAGU.   DAGU (Reither, 1981) simulates the climatic, ecological, and ethnic situation of a fictional African developing area. Subjects' goals are to create better living conditions for the people of DAGU and to increase the population, but to prevent overpopulation. Seven operational areas (i.e., with the possibility for interventions) are used: food, animal fodder, birth control, medical supply, preventive actions against tse-tse flies, set-up of irrigation projects, and sale of produce. The results of Reither's research on DAGU are reported later in the section on expert-novice differences.

DAGU as well as the following DORI and EPIDEMIC systems can be classified as a highly interconnected, complex, dynamic, and intransparent system with multiple goals. The DORI and EPIDEMIC system are offsprings of the DAGU program and their features are very similar to DAGU's.

DORI.   DORI simulates the living conditions of a nomad tribe in the Sahel region, whose livelihood depends on cattle rearing. Hesse (1982) compares a semantic version of DORI to a structurally identical, nonsemantic version in

TABLE 6.2
Overview of Simulation Systems: Systems With up to 100 Variables

Name	# of Variables	Reference
DAGU	12	Reither (1981)
DORI	12	Hesse (1982)
EPIDEMIC	13	Hesse, Spies, & Lüer (1983)
FACTORY	>20	Zimolong (1987)
FIRE FIGHTING	>10	Brehmer (1987)
MEDICAL DECISION	>10	Kleinmuntz & Kleinmuntz (1981)
MORO	49	Strohschneider (1986)
SIM00X	15	Kluwe, Misiak, Ringelband, & Haider (1986)
TAILORSHOP	24	Putz-Osterloh (1981)
TANALAND	54	Dörner & Reither (1978)
TANK SYSTEM	14	Moray, Lootsteen, & Pajak (1986)

which the variables were designated by Latin letters. In addition, Hesse crossed the semantic factor with a factor transparency, whose two levels were the presence or absence of a graphical display of the connections between the variables. Hesse found that notes were more heavily consulted in the abstract, nonsemantic conditions, but that subjects in the semantic group asked more pointed questions and organized their actions better. In general, the observed differences between good and poor problem solvers suggested a difference in strategy that was related to the content area. In the abstract condition, there was a positive relation between intelligence test scores and problem-solving quality. This result is in line with previously observed correlations between transparency and IQ in a study by Putz-Osterloh (1981).

EPIDEMIC. EPIDEMIC is a system that is very similar to DORI. EPIDEMIC, however, uses a different content area and also new individual connections. Subjects are asked to take charge of the health authority of a small town in the aftermath of an epidemic disaster (Hesse, Spies, & Lüer, 1983; the system variables and equations as well as the similarities to the DORI system are fully described in Spies & Hesse, 1987). Their decisions are aimed at reducing the number of illnesses. Subjects have a choice among seven possible interventions. EPIDEMIC's main concern is the effect of personal distress, which is realized by simulating two kinds of epidemics, each of which is presented to different subject groups. Whereas a reduced level of distress is supposedly induced by a simulated influenza epidemic, a higher level of distress is induced by a dangerous smallpox epidemic. In both cases, the same structural equations are used, only the semantic labels of the variables are changed. The findings of the experiment point out the effectiveness of the variable semantic content upon problem-solving quality:

the highly distressed students obtained higher quality values, worked harder, took more effective actions, and recognized effective measures more readily.

FACTORY. Zimolong's (1987) FACTORY is a real-time, interactive, computer-simulation program that simulates a manufacturing system containing up to seven machine stations. The spatial design of the machine places, the pathway of the material handling system through the production unit, and the launching point of the parts are arbitrarily adjustable. The characteristics of the individual machine stations can be changed in different ways. The screen image (showing the machines and their actual state) is updated every second; the subjects can check and maintain the state of the machinery in order to prevent breakdown of the factory. FACTORY is a highly dynamic and real-time environment, with many variables, time delay effects, and partial intransparency.

Empirical work by Zimolong (1987) showed that, after one hour of practice with the simulation system, risk-taking behavior (measured as time to expected tool wear failure) under conditions of complete human control was less developed than under conditions of limited control. Zimolong concluded from these results that the job design in a flexible manufacturing system should care for an active operator instead of automated conditions.

FIRE FIGHTING. Brehmer (1987) is interested in the mental models problem solvers develop on the basis of direct, interactive experience with a system. Brehmer describes a "dynamic decision problem" as one in which (a) a series of interdependent decisions is required to reach the goal; (b) the environment changes over time; and (c) the decisions change the state of the world, thus creating new decision problems. Based on a general computer program for simulating dynamic decision problems called DESSY (Dynamic Environmental Simulation System), the FIRE FIGHTING scenario simulates "the decision problems facing a fire chief who obtains information about forest fires from a reconnaissance plane" (p. 115). The information is displayed on a VDU, and the subject has command over eight fire-fighting units. The goal is to prevent the fire from reaching the base as well as minimizing the area that is burned down. FIRE FIGHTING is a complex, dynamic system with multiple goals and with time delayed effects.

Brehmer's studies (see also Brehmer & Allard, 1991) demonstrated that complexity (measured in number and efficiency of fire fighting units) had "little or no effect on performance, so long as the total efficiency of the units as a whole is kept constant" (p. 118). In contrast, delay of even minimal feedback had disastrous effects. Brehmer concluded that subjects do not manage to form any truly predictive model of the system, but, instead, base their reactions only on direct feedback.

MEDICAL DECISION TASK. Kleinmuntz and Kleinmuntz (1981) use a simulated medical decision task environment that is based on probabilistic relations between symptoms, diseases, and treatments. Within this scenario, a person (the doctor) is confronted with an ill patient complaining of three symptoms and suffering from one out of five possible diseases. The doctor can, at each point in time, request a test for any of 30 symptoms; in addition, she can choose among 12 different treatments. The task is dynamic insofar as the disease generally causes the patient to get progressively closer to death from trial to trial (linear trend), because each test for a symptom has a detrimental effect, and because the same treatments can have vastly different effectivenesses depending upon the disease of the patient. Comparing the strategies of (a) expected utility, (b) heuristic decision, and (c) generate-and-test, Kleinmuntz and Kleinmuntz found strategy (a) to be best, (b) slightly worse, and (c) less good. Data from human subjects were not reported.

MEDICAL DECISION TASK has conflicting goals and dynamic components, but is not very complex and interconnected.

MORO. Strohschneider (1986), Putz-Osterloh (1987), Putz-Osterloh & Lemme (1987), and Stäudel (1987) use the scenario MORO, which simulates the situation of a small nomad tribe in the southern Sahara. MORO is a polytelic, intransparent system with highly interconnected and dynamic variables, which partly show time-delayed effects.

In one of the studies using MORO, Strohschneider (1986) deals with the question of just how far this research instrument can be used to gather stable data and what evidence for the external validity of these data can be found. Concerning test-retest stability, Strohschneider concluded that behavioral indices (e.g., the number of questions posed) show a higher reliability than measures of the system's condition (e.g., the number of starving people). From an exhaustive debriefing of the subjects, Strohschneider concluded that subjects perceive the demands on their problem-solving ability as valid in the simulated scenario as in everyday complex problem solving.

SIM00X. SIM00X is a descendant of SIM002, which therefore will be described first. The system SIM002 consists of 10 system variables, whose relations are fixed in a first-order parameter matrix. The system states are displayed in the form of a histogram on the monitor of a personal computer, and the subjects can change as many of the variables as they want to at any given time. The goal of the problem solver is to reach a nominal value displayed on the screen; the difference between achieved state and goal determines the quality measure.

A more recent version of the system SIM002 is the system SIM00X, in which the number of variables have been increased to 15 and the system variables have been arranged into groups. Unrestricted access to the system is followed by a step-by-step confining of the status display. At uneven intervals, subjects have to reproduce the previous system states or to anticipate the next ones.

The SIM00X systems are complex, interrelated, dynamic systems with partial intransparency and multiple goals. System characteristics can easily be changed for experimental purposes.

A central assumption of the work using SIM002 and SIM00X concerns the postulate of various states of construction of mental models, which are identified in individual studies of longer duration. The authors see the elapsing complex learning processes under the perspective of "chunk" construction. Because an ideal intervention into the system with respect to the stated aim can be designated at any time (because of the system construction), the process of learning can be described accurately. An increase in proficiency is coupled with a gain in time, which (as with chunk building) is open to large individual differences. At the end of a long steering period (200 simulation tacts per subject), the subjects have a verbalizable system knowledge with respect to the connections of the variables as well as to the specific qualities of individual variables.

TAILORSHOP.   TAILORSHOP (Putz-Osterloh, 1981; see also Putz-Osterloh & Lüer, 1981; the systems equations are fully published in Funke, 1983) is a miniature system in which subjects take over the management of a tailor shop: By purchasing raw materials and modifying the production capacity in terms of workers and machines used, shirts are to be produced and to be sold at a profit. The goal is to describe and examine the sine qua nons of complex problem solving and of intelligence test tasks, and which problem-solving processes can be used to surmount these requirements. In addition, complex problems should be more strongly equated with everyday problem situations than intelligence tests presently are. In a complex problem, as opposed to an IQ-test item, the construction and derivation of problem-solving objectives requires a choice of actions leading to the achievement of the goals and the active search for information about relevant system variables. TAILORSHOP is an intransparent, complex, dynamic, interconnected system with imprecise goals and time-delayed effects.

A study by Putz-Osterloh and Lüer (1981) tested the hypothesis that test-intelligence and problem-solving performance are related through a comparison of a transparent with a nontransparent condition (N = 70 student subjects). The two experimental conditions were the presence or absence of an illustration, which presented the connections between the system variables. Only under the transparent condition did the authors find a statistically significant correlation between problem-solving performance and IQ. They interpreted this result as a criticism of common intelligence tests in which transparency is generally high. They argued that "real" problems are rather intransparent and highly complicated and therefore demand behavior that cannot be measured by intelligence tests.

TANALAND.   The TANALAND system (Dörner & Reither, 1978) was one of the earliest simulation studies published. The ecosystem of an African landscape with various flora and fauna as well as human groups, the "Tupis" and "Moros," who live by cattle and sheep farming, is simulated. The 50 or more system variables are connected through a complicated process of "positive and negative feedback." Subjects are to assume the role of a technical agronomy advisor to improve the living conditions of the native population. The system is very difficult to handle. As Dörner and Reither have shown, almost no subject is able to succeed in this task. The observed failures mirror deficits of a more general nature. It appeared that the subjects did not possess enough cognitive ability to be able to cope with complex systems. The failure of "linear thinking" was proposed. In the realized systems, which were described in terms of such features as dynamics, complexity, connectivity, and opaqueness, thinking in the form of causal networks should be considered.

TANK SYSTEM.   Interested in the acquisition of process control skills, Moray, Lootsteen, and Pajak (1986) use a tank system consisting of four subsystems. Each subsystem consists of one tank with input and output valves and a heater. Temperature and level of each tank are shown on a VDU in analog and digital form. The task is to control either one or all of the tanks with respect to given required set points for level, temperature, and flow rate; the required points should be reached as rapidly as possible. Each of the 12 trials is run until these goal points are reached. TANK SYSTEM is an interconnected, transparent, complex system with multiple goals and dynamic development.

Discussing the problems of data analysis, the authors concluded that it would make no sense to average individual data. Rather, the data should be analyzed separately for each operator. Looking at the graphs of the system variables as a function of time, they concluded further that operators develop good "mental models" of the system. "One aspect of the more complex skill is, therefore, the discovery of causal relations and their use to develop control tactics" (p. 498). Starting with closed-loop control, good operators later developed almost perfect open-loop control. Switching from the control of one tank to the control of four tanks simultaneously, learning slowed down and interference effects occurred. Despite the enormous variety in sequences used to achieve the required goal, strategies emerged that were related to the development of the mental model "which represents the dynamics and causality of the system and leads to more efficient control" (p. 504).

Systems with more than 100 variables.   Only two systems (see Table 6.3) that have more than 100 variables and were used in scientific research are known to this author. One of them—LOHHAUSEN—is the most prominent example of the new way of studying problem-solving processes. (For a short description of LOHHAUSEN in English language see Dörner, 1987.)

TABLE 6.3
Overview of Simulation Systems: Systems With
More Than 100 Variables

Name	# of Variables	Reference
ENERGY SUPPLY	>2000	Vent (1985)
LOHHAUSEN	>2000	Dörner, Kreuzig, Reither, & Stäudel (1983)

ENERGY SUPPLY.   The "Energieversorgung" (ENERGY SUPPLY) of private households in the Federal Republic of Germany was simulated in a large-scale system in which individual energy choice preferences were projected over time and space (Vent, 1985). The author was concerned with the effect of various presentation and feedback forms that stimulate certain ways of thinking (for instance, analytical or holistic thinking). In one condition, he presented the system's data numerically and in the other, graphically. The results supported the superiority of a visual-holistic way of thought over an analytic style of thought as measured by the quality of decisions. There have been no follow-up studies with this system.

LOHHAUSEN.   If TANALAND was the first scenario to study complex problem solving, then LOHHAUSEN was its expansion. The simulated reality domain (a small city called LOHHAUSEN) contains more than 2000 variables. Dörner, Kreuzig, Reither, and Stäudel's (1983) comprehensive monograph introduced the five years of work on this unique study with the following sentences:

> The following report states the results of a relatively long-term psychological experiment. We tried to find out something about the conditions and forms of actions in ambiguous and complex situations. For this we systematically observed 48 subjects over a relatively long period and processed the manifold results of these observations. (p. 13)

LOHHAUSEN, originally the name of the simulated town, has since become the name of a research program: a deepening of cognitive psychology through new paradigms of problem-solving research; paradigms that, in contrast to the traditional types of problems such as mind games or mental exercises, contain the characteristics of complexity and uncertainty. Subjects, who took over the role of mayor of LOHHAUSEN, were instructed to "take care of the future prosperity of the town over the short and long term," that is, over a simulated 10-year period. Testing was done in eight two-hour sittings. Approximately 100,000 data points per subject resulted, from which the authors hoped to successfully separate the important from the trivial, and accidental from meaningful information.

The analysis of the findings—with a few exceptions, such as case studies of selected experimental subjects—was based upon aggregated data. The authors first agglomerated the objective and subjective measures of problem-solving quality to a single "General Quality Criterion," which made it possible to split the total sample into two extreme groups (N = 12) of good and poor problem solvers. Results comparing the two groups showed that different variables in the LOHHAUSEN system (such as earnings of the industry, funds of the town, stocks of the bank, production and trade data, number of inhabitants, and rate of employment) developed more detrimentally when worked on by the poor problem solvers than by the good problem solvers. Even the "good problem solvers" were not what their designation suggested, however: System experts (the experimenters) achieved even higher values on some of the variables.

The behavioral effects were less interesting than the connected thought, planning, and decision processes: Besides formal characteristics (e.g., the frequency and consistency of decisions) and content biases (e.g., "financial situation of the watch factory") of the experimenters' "gross protocol," there were interesting references in the "think-aloud protocols" that the subjects were encouraged to produce. Subjects' problem-solving quality and their test intelligence were found not to be correlated. Neither Raven's Advanced Progressive Matrices (APM) nor Cattell's Culture Fair Intelligence Test (CFT) correlated substantially with the solution quality. Rather, what correlated significantly with problem-solving performance was the experimenters' spontaneous judgment that a "subject makes an intelligent impression."

Although the authors were right in pointing out the shortcomings of classical IQ-tests (e.g., not taking information search into account), they themselves did not take a possible shortcoming of their own findings into account: the possible lack of reliability of their problem-solving measures. It is known that intelligence tests, when used repeatedly, produce homogeneous results. Also, the sample limitations (students with a restricted range of IQ scores) should not have been ignored when the results were interpreted.

Further findings of the LOHHAUSEN study were concerned with personality characteristics and their relation to solution quality. The construct of "self-confidence" has to be given a special mention in this context; it had a strong positive relation to complex problem solving and was introduced to set off "the total failure of intelligence tests." Also, prior knowledge was not a significant predictor of success.

The condensed theory of this comprehensive study contains a list of elementary information processing methods for dealing with complex problems such as, for example, component and dependence analysis as well as sub- and superordination processes. The construction and pursuit of partial objectives by a subject is subsumed under an intention management model. Based upon the emotional embedding of cognitive processes (Dörner, Reither, & Stäudel, 1983), the intellectual emergency reaction—a quick and general reaction of the cognitive system to unspecified danger situations—can be brought into connection with the actual competence of the actor. Self-confidence can be used as an indicator for heuristic competence, which refers to the ability "to be able to create adequate ways of dealing even with unknown situations" (Dörner, Reither, & Stäudel, 1983, p. 436; cf. Stäudel, 1987). Central to the theory is the concept of control: Control competence guarantees action in uncertainty, and loss of control leads to the negative emotional consequences, which override problem-solving thought.

LOHHAUSEN not only stands for a new field of research in cognitive psychology; it is also an appeal against the prevalent "analytical procedure" in scientific endeavor. The examination of the highly complicated cognitive system of "mankind"—following Dörner—cannot be pursued using strictly experimental means because the isolation of a few chosen variables in a laboratory says little about the "normal" interplay of processes that are interactively embedded within other variables (see also Dörner, 1989). The demand for an intensified "collecting of beetles and butterflies," that is, the exact description of the observed phenomena, goes hand in hand with the search for an overlapping conceptual framework concerning the complete workings of the psychic system. (A first impression of this framework can be found in Dörner, Schaub, Stäudel, & Strohschneider, 1988).

At the end of this section, the question has to be raised as to what sense it makes to permanently create new systems. It is surprising, for instance, that no replication of the famous LOHHAUSEN study exists; in fact, many of the previously mentioned systems lack this basic scientific requirement. From this author's point of view, if new systems are, indeed, needed, existing systems should be modified, rather than new systems created, in order to fulfill certain experimental requirements. If different systems are used in different studies, results can neither be compared nor heterogeneous conclusions clearly attributed to certain system attributes. What is missing, then, is a descriptive schema of systems that allows us directly to compare different systems with respect to such attributes as complexity, connectivity, transparency, etc. The following section offers a taxonomy of influence factors that might help to organize the different studies.

Main Streams of Current Research

Main streams of current research as revealed in the material reviewed center around the following three topics, which might serve as a taxonomy of possible influential determinants: (a) personal factors (poor vs. good problem solvers), (b) situational determinants of complex problem solving, and (c) system characteristics.

The *role of personal factors* can be differentiated in three ways: (a) cognitive abilities, (b) emotional and motivational factors, (c) personality characteristics in a broader sense. Concerning the *cognitive abilities,* one would probably expect intelligence to play an important role in handling complex situations. "Whatever *intelligence* may be, *reasoning* and *problem solving* have traditionally been viewed as important subjects of it. Almost without regard to how *intelligence* has been defined, *reasoning* and *problem solving* have been part of the definition" (Sternberg, 1982, p. 225). The empirical support for the effect of intelligence on the quality of complex problem solving is rather poor, however: most empirical studies report either low or even zero correlations. Correlations tend to increase, however, when the problem-solving situation is made more similar to the intelligence-test situation; that is, when the problem situation is made more transparent. Also, a more differentiated diagnosis of intelligence reveals higher correlations on subtest-level rather than on a global one (see Thomas, Hörmann, & Jäger, 1989; Hussy, 1989).

Concerning *emotional and motivational factors,* one has to acknowledge that in the course of action, many situations develop that might evoke emotional reactions; for example, critical events that demonstrate a person's inability to cope with the given situation. There are presumably many feedback loops between "pure" cognitive processes and these evaluation processes; in case of luck, or of good interventions, they could be stabilizing; otherwise, one might expect a lot of disturbances stemming from the noncognitive area. Dörner, Kreuzig, Reither, and Stäudel (1983) reported an "intellectual emergency reaction" for some of their subjects, a quick and general reaction of the cognitive system to unspecified danger situations. The effects of this reaction were (a) a general increase in activation, (b) an externalization of behavior control (reduction of situation analysis and growing use of dogmatic principles), and (c) the activation of unspecific, precautionary behavior.

Personality characteristics in a broader sense seem to have a great influence primarily in the beginning stages and especially under conditions of intransparency. In these cases, cognitive abilities and knowledge are less required than, for example, a stable personality that shows no overload due to the huge amount of uncertainty. One can imagine that people with high anxiety and/or low self-confidence will tend to retreat from these situations. It is, thus, evident that a lot of nonintellectual abilities are necessary to cope with uncertain situations. These abilities are *not* problem-solving qualities themselves, but, rather, reflect the importance of individual differences due to different state and trait personality characteristics.

The *role of situational determinants* is related to (a) the transparency of the situation, and (b) the concrete task demands with which a subject has to cope.

As previously mentioned, the *transparency of a situation* depends on the degree to which a subject has direct access to system information. This factor can be manipulated easily by the experimenter. Putz-Osterloh (1981), for example, used a diagram that displayed the relations among the system variables: under a transparent condition, subjects could see this diagram; under intransparency, they could not. Degree of (in)transparency of system connections is not the only way of manipulating this variable, however. Another frequently used method consists of varying how subjects get the information they want: under transparent conditions, subjects are shown all interesting variables on a VDU; the subject thus has direct access to the system. Under intransparency, the experimenter is the mediator between system and subject; every time a subject wants some information (i.e., about the actual values of a certain variable), he or she has to ask the experimenter who will give an answer if possible.

Additional situational determinants are the *concrete task demands* subjects have to fulfill. Sometimes they have to control an (unknown) system right from the start, sometimes they are allowed to explore the system in a previous phase. Demands vary also with respect to goals: sometimes no goals are given at all (the finding of an adequate goal is part of the task), sometimes a few selected variables, and sometimes all variables, have to be controlled.

Brehmer (1989) conceptualizes the tasks of process control as "dynamic decision tasks"—in contrast to static or sequential decision tasks—with the following four characteristics: "(a) a series of decisions are required; (b) these decisions are interdependent; (c) the decision problem changes, both autonomously and as a consequence of the decision maker's action; and (d) the decisions are made in real time" (p. 144). Based on the assumption that the human decision-maker does not want to resolve discrete choice dilemmas, but, rather, attempts to achieve control, Brehmer (see also Brehmer & Allard, 1991) characterizes dynamic decision tasks more precisely, differentiating between (a) complexity (in relation to control); (b) feedback quality (the problem of indicators); (c) feedback delay (which implies feedforward instead of feedback control); (d) possibilities for decentralization (i.e., give control to local decision makers); (e) rate of change (controlling the economy of a country vs. flying a jet); and (f) the relation between the control process and the to-be-controlled process.

Understanding the *role of system characteristics* requires a differentiation between (a) formal aspects and (b) aspects with regard to the contents.

The *formal aspects* are related to the number of variables, their connectivity, the resulting stability of the system, the degree of time delays, and so on. Also, the distinction between time-continuous and time-discrete systems is useful as is that of linear versus nonlinear systems. The question of deterministic versus stochastic modeling of the domain has to be answered, too.

The *aspects with regard to content* are not so easy to specify. Primarily, one is concerned with the semantic embedding of the system in question, but also with the relation between the actually implemented structure and the structure which is assumed by the subject because of previous knowledge.

Principles and Mechanisms Underlying Complex Problem Solving

It is not easy to list the principles and mechanisms that govern complex problem-solving activity by a human operator. One may ask, in fact, if there are any special mechanisms and principles that are applied to complex problem-solving tasks, or if it is simply sufficient to look for the mechanisms applicable to the solving of simple problems. As Tversky and Kahneman (1974) have claimed:

"People rely on a limited number of heuristic principles which reduce complex tasks to simpler judgmental operations." (p. 1124) The reason to look for special principles comes from the new demands that the complex control tasks require. As mentioned in the introduction, complex problems have unique features that they do not share with simple problems. Therefore, one has good reason to assume that special mechanisms are needed to deal with these features.

On the other hand, there are also reasons to assume that a general model could be applied to this situation. Knaeuper and Rouse (1983), for example, suggest the application of the production-system formalism. They specify four tasks that an operator has to perform: (a) transition tasks (bringing the system into a certain state), (b) steady-state tuning, (c) detection and diagnosis of failures, and (d) compensation for failures. Therefore, they postulate, the operator needs knowledge about (a) how the system would evolve if left alone; (b) what effects the control actions would have; and (c) which of the four abovementioned tasks is the appropriate one.

For purposes of clarity, I first give a brief sketch of how—under ideal conditions—structural knowledge about an unknown system can be acquired and used; then the development and use of strategic knowledge is described. The separate presentations should not be taken as suggesting that the two aspects can be seen as unconnected parts, however.

The Development of Structural Knowledge. In the following, a normative stage model of structural knowledge acquisition is outlined for which empirical data have still to be delivered. Yet, despite the missing empirical base, the model might serve as a useful frame of reference for discussing the principles and mechanisms of solving complex problems in terms of knowledge acquisition and knowledge application processes.

Complex problem solving requires the development of structural knowledge, which describes the functional or causal relationships between variables. This explicit knowledge is the condensed result of a hypothesis-formation and hypothesis-evaluation process. It can be assumed that this knowledge starts from simple observation of contingencies between subsequent system states. At its first stage, such knowledge is restricted to the pure identification of a relation between at least two variables (relational knowledge). At the second stage, such observations lead to a more differentiated view that allows a statement about the sign of the relation (sign knowledge). At the third stage, finally, the precise influence factor can be specified (numerical knowledge).

The three kinds of knowledge are expected to be in a declarative format. The basic unit looks like the following quadruple:

$$H_t: = \langle V_1, V_2, C, B \rangle,$$

that is, a hypothesis at time t (H_t) consists of four components: specifications of (a) a variable 1 (V_1), (b) a variable 2 (V_2), (c) a connectivity form (C), and (d) a degree of belief (B) in the hypothesis. For example, for a hypothesis on the causal influence of "advertise" (V_1) on "demand" (V_2), the connectivity form (C) of a hypothesis could be "positive linear," the degree of belief (B) "high."

One could argue that this conceptualization of a hypothesis is similar to a schema with four slots. If one knows the semantics of V_1 and V_2, for example, connectivity (C) and degree of belief (B) may be default values due to prior experience.

In addition to the explicit knowledge, implicit knowledge also emerges. In a series of studies, Berry and Broadbent (1984, 1987; cf. Broadbent & Aston, 1978; Broadbent et al., 1986) found evidence that, despite low explicit task knowledge (as measured by a questionnaire), subjects were able to control small systems with good performance. These results are not without problems: Haider (1989), on the basis of a simulation study, argued that, for the control of these systems, complete explicit knowledge is not necessary. However, one has to accept the possibility that subjects acquire a lot of information above the degree that is usually assessed by diagnostic procedures. The results of a recent series of studies by Sanderson (1989) point to the same conclusion. Using the TRANS-PORTATION system originally introduced by Broadbent et al. (1986), Sanderson demonstrated association as well as dissociation effects between task performance and verbalizable knowledge depending on amount of practice, kind of display, and cover story. Interestingly, Sanderson's results contradict the common thesis that, with growing practice, verbal task knowledge decreases (e.g., Anderson, 1983).

The Development of Strategic Knowledge.   It is by far more complicated to describe how strategic knowledge develops in the course of action. In most cases, this is essentially a problem of application, and not of developing, the concepts. Like structural knowledge, the strategic procedures used by, and known to, a subject depend primarily on previous experience. Unlike structural knowledge, however, it is not as easy to construct experimental conditions under which the influence of previous strategic knowledge is minimized. Some kind of "naive experimentation," the use of concepts like "isolated (or systematic) variation of conditions," "Eigendynamik," "side effects," etc., are part of this strategic inventory which a subject possesses.

Learning to Solve Complex Problems

Learning to solve complex problems has two aspects. The first aspect concerns the improvement in handling a system over the course of repeated experiences (domain-specific learning). The second aspect concerns the potential transfer from one complex problem to another (domain-general learning). Generally, one is interested in improving complex problem-solving performance by some kind of training.

One example of this approach is a training study by Streufert, Nogami,

Swezey, Pogash, and Piasecki (1988). They used a design in which 56 subjects first had to work with one of two complex scenarios (either as coordinator of a disaster control center or as governor of a developing country) for six hours. Then, a first group (17 of the participants) received extensive training on domain-general rules (especially on structural management styles) and on their concrete operationalization. A second group (7 persons) received only the specific training, and a third, control group (31 persons) received no training at all. After that, all subjects had to work with the second system in order to assess training effects. As was expected, condition (a) yielded significant improvements in 8 out of 13 performance measures compared with only 4 improvements and 1 impairment under condition (b) and 5 impairments without any improvement under the no-training condition.

Many training methods for improving learning abilities exist (for a review see Derry & Murphy, 1986), including microcomponent training as well as metastrategy approaches. But one has to consider that training an executive control mechanism that would automatically assess and combine learning skills whenever needed can only gradually be developed and requires time. Derry and Murphy, therefore, concluded that, "The choice of which taxonomy to use and which learning skills to train is a matter of selecting what is appropriate for the student population, the training time allowed, and the type of learning material involved" (p. 32). With respect to complex problem solving, one might expect that a lot of time is needed for improving behavior. Hays and Singer (1989) give a good overview of problems and possible solutions in designing and evaluating training systems.

Differences between Experts and Novices

Differences between novices and experts in "normal" problem solving were summarized by Mayer (1988), who stated "that experts and novices differ with respect to their tendency by using chunking in free recall, to use comprehensive plans in solving problems, and to classify problems based on their underlying solution requirements" (p. 572).

For complex problem solving, too, the observed differences between novices and experts are a relevant source for theorizing.

Reither (1981), using the DAGU simulation system, compared the results of 12 development-aid workers with 6 to 8 years of practical experience in third world countries with those of 12 subjects who were about to begin their first mission in developmental aid. Subjects working in groups of three had to create better living conditions for the people of Dagu and to increase their population smoothly. The results showed differences between novices and experts insofar as novices thought more in causal chains than in causal webs (i.e., thinking mainly in terms of "straight-on" main effects instead of taking possible side effects into their deliberations), showed more thematic jumps, and made more "metastatements." The hallmark of expertise was experts' blind coping, that is, the fact that experts arrived at conclusions under all circumstances, thereby demonstrating a continuity of action under every condition. Interestingly, even the experts were not able to stabilize the critical variable "population size," however.

Putz-Osterloh (1987; see also Putz-Osterloh & Lemme, 1987) conducted a study in which she analyzed complex problem solving by experts (7 professors in economy, aged between 40 and 49) and novices (30 randomly selected students, aged between 19 and 27) who had to control the previously described business system TAILORSHOP for 15 months first and then the developmental scenario MORO for 20 months. Data analysis was concerned with the first six simulated months of each system, evaluating (a) the quality of interventions (analysis of subjects' behavior according to a complicated rating scale); (b) the frequency of use of domain-general strategies (according to a classification of verbal statements during thinking aloud); and (c) system knowledge (also derived from thinking-aloud protocols). Results indicated that professors of economy were better with respect to all three kinds of criteria in the TAILORSHOP situation. In the MORO situation, experts were better only with respect to strategies and knowledge, but not with respect to the quality of intervention. Putz-Osterloh concluded that experts differ from novices not because of different amounts of available data, but because of differences in processing these data: experts generate more correct hypotheses, more frequently and correctly analyze the relations between variables, and verbalize more often the expected effects of their planned interventions.

Critical remarks concern the operationalization of expertise, which is markedly confounded with age and therefore with life experience. Also, the dependent variables are primarily of a verbal nature, a kind of data that, in the opinion of this author, should not be the only source relied upon to characterize expert-novices differences.

SOLVING COMPLEX PROBLEMS AS KNOWLEDGE ACQUISITION AND KNOWLEDGE APPLICATION

In this section, I briefly describe my own work on complex problem solving. First, I describe the experimental setting, the scenario, that I used in various studies, and second, I summarize the theoretical framework underlying the studies.

Description of Research Within the DYNAMIS-Project

From the beginning, research about solving complex problems had to cope with a number of difficulties (see the critical aspects mentioned by Funke, 1984). One central difficulty was the measurement of problem-solving quality. Because there was no "best" intervention (due to the partially nonlinear relationships between the variables for which no optimal solution could be found), one could never be quite sure if a subject's solution to a problem was really better or worse than any others. Therefore, problem-solving quality often was rated by "experts."

The line of research done in our laboratory adheres to the following principles (Funke, 1986):

1. It should always be possible to define the quality of a given problem solution by comparing it with an optimal solution strategy.

2. The problem-solving situations should take into account the aforementioned features of complex problem solving insofar as possible.

3. A differentiated diagnostic procedure should reveal the subject's development of hypotheses about the system. This implies repeated measurements and/or the use of thinking-aloud techniques under certain conditions.

4. There should be a clear distinction between a phase of knowledge acquisition (mainly realized by letting the subjects experiment with the system) and a phase of knowledge application, in which given states of the problem space should be reached by the subjects as quickly as possible.

The DYNAMIS Shell for Scenarios

Control of complex systems with dynamic behavior requires knowledge from the operator that has previously been acquired. To study the acquisition as well as the application of knowledge, we confront our subjects with computer-simulated scenarios. A universal tool for constructing these scenarios is the computer program DYNAMIS. It works like a shell, in that the user can implement in a simple way different types of simulation systems that follow one general frame of reference. This general frame of reference is a *linear equation system* (see, e.g., Steyer, 1984), which consists of an arbitrary number of exogenous ($=x$) and endogenous ($=y$) variables according to the following equation:

$Y(t + 1) = A*Y(t) + B*X(t)$,
where $Y(t + 1)$ and $Y(t)$ are vectors representing the state of the y-variables at times $t + 1$ and t,
$X(t)$: a vector representing the values chosen by the subject for the x-variables,
A, B: weight matrices.

The construction of the equation system follows theoretical considerations about the influence of certain system attributes on task complexity (e.g., the effect of self-dynamic, side effects or effects due to interdependencies). It is not intended to simulate a domain of reality adequately because this kind of simulation demands too many constraints on the attributes of the system. Consequently, most of the simulation systems used in our research group are artificial ones. Regarding a distinction made by Hays and Singer (1989), one can say we do not want physical fidelity of our simulation systems but do want functional fidelity (for a taxonomy of simulation fidelity considerations see also Alessi, 1988).

Experimental Procedure

In our experiments, subjects pass through at least two phases. In the first phase, the *knowledge acquisition* phase, the subject is allowed to explore the system and its behavior (see also Moray et al., 1986). Subjects can take actions (i.e., make an intervention on one or more of the exogenous variables) and observe the resulting effects on the endogenous variables. From time to time, we measure the acquired knowledge by asking the subject for a graphical representation of his or her structural knowledge. In the second phase, called *knowledge application,* the subject has to reach a defined system state and try to keep the variables on the defined values. In this phase, we measure the quality of the operator's control by assessing the distance between the reached and the defined values for all endogenous variables. Some remarks on measuring structural knowledge and system performance seem necessary at this point because of their central role in each study. Empirical studies based on this procedure have been done by Fritz and Funke (1988, "ECOSYSTEM"), Funke (1985, "ECOSYSTEM"), and by Funke and Müller (1988, "SINUS").

Measuring Structural Knowledge and System Performance

Measuring knowledge and performance seems only on the first view to be an easy problem (for an overview, see Kluwe, 1988; Spada & Reimann, 1988). At a closer view, there are a lot of difficulties, some of which are mentioned and possible solutions presented. A good review of problems in diagnosing "mental models" is given by Rouse and Morris (1986).

Starting with *system performance quality,* the goal is to determine how well a given goal state is approximated by the operator's interventions. The classical approach requires the measurement of the deviation from the target system state by means of the root-mean-squares criterion (RMS). This indicator reflects the mean deviation, independent of sign, and weighs the individual deviations more heavily the further away they are from the target state. A good discussion of the frequently used RMS criterion can be found in Bösser (1983).

There is an aspect that reflects an ugly property of this kind of system performance evaluation, however. Assume that an operator has knowledge about the system. Reaching the goal is of little or no difficulty for him and the resulting RMS will be low and near zero. But what about the operator with little or missing knowledge? The resulting distance to the goal state as measured by RMS varies with his (random) interventions. According to certain system characteristics, this would result in a large variety of measured distances. Therefore, different values of the RMS do not, in this case, reflect different degrees of quality of system performance. The argument here is one of different reliabilities of the RMS criterion for different states of an operator's knowledge, which is best in the case of correct knowledge (RMS indicating reliable values near zero) and worst in the case of pure random intervention (RMS indicating a huge range of values due to decreasing reliability).

One potential solution for this problem is a logarithmic transformation of the RMS. This transformation leads to an evaluation of distances which is more efficient: larger distances are now not weighed as more important but, rather, as less important. It does not matter if someone failed the goal by 10,000 or 100,000 points, as this is of the same importance as the difference between a deviation of 1 and 10. The transformation, thus, reduces the error variance that increases with the operator's distance to the goal state.

Measuring the *structural knowledge* an operator has acquired about a system requires also some kind of distance or similarity measurement, in this case between the assumed and the real existing structural relations. For this purpose, the operator marks on a sheet (or, in some versions, directly on the screen) the assumed causal relationships at certain points in time. The problems with this kind of measurement are:

1. Subjects differ with respect to their response tendency. Therefore, one has to count not only the hits (i.e., correspondence between assumed and existing relation), but also the false alarms.

2. Subjects differ with respect to the quality of knowledge they can talk about: Sometimes any relationship between two variables is assumed (relational knowledge), sometimes the sign of the relation is known (sign knowledge), sometimes even the numerical weights are known (numerical knowledge).

3. A false model can be useful for system control, at least within a restricted area of values. The functionality of a model is somewhat independent of its correctness.

4. Subjects take certain assumptions as givens but do not talk about them. For example, if a variable does not change over the time, the weight for that relation is assumed to be equal to one. The subject often does not find worth mentioning this kind of knowledge.

5. It is not clear if a subject follows only one single model or if there exist some models concurrently.

For problems (3) to (5), no solution can be given at present. Problems (1) and (2), however, can be solved by using a quantification of the following kind: For each specification of a subject, one first counts whether it belongs to one of the three classes of knowledge (relational, sign, numerical) and whether it is right or wrong with respect to the implemented system. Then, for each level one can determine the "quality of system identification" (QI) as the difference between "hits" (HI) and "false alarms" (FA), weighted by some kind of "guessing" probability (P) according to the following scheme, which closely resembles the discrimination index Pr from the two-high threshold model for recognition memory (see Snodgrass & Corwin, 1988; the proposed "correction for guessing" goes back to Woodworth, 1938):

$$QI = (1 - p)*HI/max(HI) - p*FA/max(FA),$$
$$-P \leq QI \leq (1 - P).$$

The guessing probability for numerical parameters in a dynamic system could, for instance, be set equal to zero, so all hits count relative to the maximal number of hits. If one sets the guessing probability to 0.5 in the case of sign knowledge, then errors lead to a reduction in the QI index for that stage.

Note that it is not required that the operator have a complete and correct model of the system in question, because good control is possible with models that are partly incorrect (but see Conant & Ashby, 1970). The reason for this stems from the functionality a false structure can have: With respect to a restricted range of values, different models can be functionally equivalent (to the degree of control they allow). This might be one reason for the fact that in everyday life we often use wrong models that are nevertheless functional (see, for example, Kempton, 1986, who could show that up to 50% of Americans do not have a correct theory of home-heating control).

Relation to Research on Scientific Reasoning

Klahr and Dunbar (1988; see also Klahr, Dunbar, & Fay, in press) have recently developed an integrated model of scientific reasoning that seems to be applicable to our scenarios. At the core of their model is the Generalized Rule Inducer (GRI) (Simon & Lea, 1974), augmented by (a) a mechanism for the identification of relevant attributes (because in scientific situations these attributes are not given as in concept-learning tasks) and (b) a more complex "instance generator." Klahr and Dunbar argue "that scientific reasoning can be conceptualized as a search through two problem spaces: an hypothesis space and an experiment space" (1988, p. 7). These spaces result from the task a scientist has, may he be a skilled one or a naive one:

> The successful scientist, like the successful explorer, must master two related skills: knowing where to look and understanding what is seen. The first skill— experimental design—involves the design of experimental and observational procedures. The second skill—hypothesis formation—involves the formation and evaluation of theory. (p. 2)

Working with the toy "BigTrak"—a computer-controlled robot tank that can be programmed (see also Shrager & Klahr, 1986)—Klahr and Dunbar asked their subjects to explore the functions of the device, especially the function of the RPT-key. A fine analysis of verbal protocols of their subjects (Experiment 1) showed that the hypothesis space was very small: Only eight different "common" hypotheses concerned with four attributes were found. A frame representation of the concept of the RPT key was important insofar as once a subject had constructed a particular frame, the task became one of filling in or verifying the contents of the slots in this frame.

With respect to the experiment space, Klahr and Dunbar showed that there are six different "regions" (combinations of values for two critical parameters) with different conclusions to be drawn. Incidentally, the experiment space is not the representation a subject has, but one that allows classifying subjects' experimental procedures.

Data from their Experiment 1 demonstrated that there were at least two groups of subjects: so-called "Experimenters" and "Theorists." The difference between the two groups stems from the strategy according to which they shifted their frames: If subjects switched their frame as a consequence of a certain experimental outcome, they were called "Experimenters"; if subjects searched in their hypothesis space and came to a shift, they were labeled as "Theorists."

This theoretical framework seems applicable to the research topic of this chapter insofar as the experimental situation Klahr and Dunbar were concerned with—exploration of a hitherto unknown object—is basically identical to the situation of handling an unknown system. Furthermore, Klahr and Dunbar conceptualize the process of knowledge acquisition in terms of hypotheses that are more or less deductively or inductively developed.

Aside from the similarities in the experimental procedures and in the theoretical frames of reference, however, there are some differences. The main difference can be seen in the way subjects' knowledge is measured. Klahr and Dunbar use primarily verbal data (see Bainbridge, 1979, for a comment on verbal data in this context), whereas in our procedure different approaches are taken to diagnose the structural knowledge a subject acquires. This difference is partly due to our "object" of exploration: subjects explicitly have to anticipate the next states of the system, they have to write down their hypotheses about structural relationships, and they have to control the system as well as possible.

PERSPECTIVES FOR FUTURE RESEARCH

Three tasks for future research are outlined briefly: (a) a differentiation between factors influencing complex problem solving resulting from the individual as well as from the situational and the system attributes; (b) reliability and validity research on complex problem-solving scenarios; and (c) adequate measurement of the actual "mental model" and of the potential heuristics that complex problem solvers use, also over time.

Concerning the first task, separation of person, situation, and system influences on performance measures, the approach taken by Streufert et al. (1988) seems to point in the right direction: instead of using "free" simulations in which decisions can change a system's state quite drastically, they use a "quasi-experimental simulation technology," in which the system reacts in part independently from subjects' interventions such that each subject receives comparable informations and events. Despite this fact, subjects still believe that they have direct or delayed impact on the system. This technique should be extended further in order to standardize the conditions under which subjects' performance quality is measured independent from system attributes.

Concerning Task 2, reliability and validity aspects, there is a lot of work to do: up to now, mainly face validity exists. Jäger (1986) speaks of "uncovered checks" that have to be cashed in subsequent research (p. 274). It is simply not enough to show that there are no correlations to standard intelligence tests, because many reasons can account for that result. Rather, one has to show positive connections to other psychometric instruments as well as to external criteria. One possible line of research could be the use of the learning test concept (e.g., Guthke, 1982), according to which intelligence is not a static variable but, rather, is to be interpreted as "learning potential." It seems plausible that there exists a relation between learning potential and the ability to solve complex problems.

With respect to reliability, work also has to be done. One promising way of evaluating reliability of complex problem-solving indicators was recently proposed by Müller (1989). Following the concepts of consistency and stability developed by Steyer (1987), Müller applied this design to studies of complex problem solving. His procedure is as follows: at two times of measurement (TM_1 and TM_2), two parallel forms of a system (PF_1 and PF_2) are given to the same subjects, yielding the four observed variables y_{11}, y_{21}, y_{12}, and y_{22} (first index for the system parallel form, second index for time of measurement; see Fig. 6.1).

In this design (and when certain assumptions about uncorrelated residuals, etc., are met), it is possible, based on covariances, to determine the degree of measurement accuracy (=consistency) as well as the stability of the measured construct (the problem-solving "competence").

Concerning Task 3, the adequate measurement of the operator's mental model and his heuristics, one has to develop instruments that sensitively assess those relevant parts of human memory that are required for exploration and control. Whereas in the area of assessing structural (or declarative) knowledge some useful techniques exist, there are clear deficits in diagnosing the heuristic knowledge on which human problem solvers operate. Also, more attention should be given to developing measurement techniques that reveal the implicit knowledge of an operator.

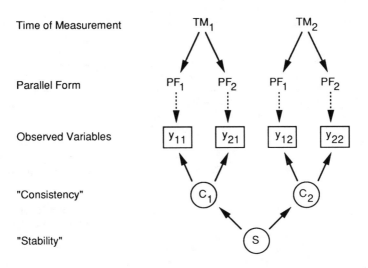

Time of Measurement

Parallel Form

Observed Variables

"Consistency"

"Stability"

FIG. 6.1. Design of a study for assessing consistency and stability data (from Müller, 1989).

Concerning the general research strategy, it seems more useful to manipulate critical variables in systems that already exist than to create new systems. Only the strategy of analyzing the effects of small variations—the experimental method—can offer new insights into the principles and mechanisms that govern complex human problem solving.

ACKNOWLEDGMENTS

Preparation of this chapter was supported in part by a grant from the "Deutsche Forschungsgemeinschaft (DFG)" to the author (Az. Fu 173/1). Thanks to Edgar Erdfelder, Horst Müller, and Uwe Kleinemas for valuable comments on a draft version of this chapter. Special thanks to Peter Frensch who corrected my German English and provided many comments that made the chapter more precise and understandable.

REFERENCES

Alessi, S. M. (1988). Fidelity in the design of instructional simulation. *Journal of Computer-Based Instruction, 15,* 40–47.

Anderson, J. R. (1983). *The architecture of cognition.* Cambridge: Harvard University Press.

Bainbridge, L. (1979). Verbal reports as evidence of the process operator's knowledge. *International Journal of Man-Machine Studies, 11,* 411–436.

Bainbridge, L. (1987). Ironies of automation. In J. Rasmussen, K. Duncan, & J. Leplat (Eds.), *New technology and human error* (pp. 271–283). Chichester, England: Wiley.

Berry, D. C., & Broadbent, D. E. (1984). On the relationship between task performance and associated verbalizable knowledge. *Quarterly Journal of Experimental Psychology, 36,* 209–231.

Berry, D. C., & Broadbent, D. E. (1987). The combination of explicit and implicit learning processes in task control. *Psychological Research, 49,* 7–15.

Bhaskar, R., & Simon, H. A. (1977). Problem solving in semantically rich domains: an example from engineering thermodynamics. *Cognitive Science, 1,* 193–215.

Bösser, T. (1983). Eine nichtlineare Regelstrategie bei der manuellen Regelung [A nonlinear control strategy at manual control]. *Zeitschrift für Experimentelle und Angewandte Psychologie, 30,* 529–565.

Brehmer, B. (1987). Development of mental models for decision in technological systems. In J. Rasmussen, K. Duncan & J. Leplat (Eds.), *New technology and human error* (pp. 111–120). Chichester, England: Wiley.

Brehmer, B. (1989). Dynamic decision making. In A. P. Sage (Ed.), *Concise encyclopedia of information processing in systems and organizations* (pp. 144–149). New York: Pergamon Press.

Brehmer, B., & Allard, R. (1991). Dynamic decision making: The effects of task complexity and feedback delay. In J. Rasmussen, B. Brehmer, & J. Leplat (Eds.), *Distributed decision making: Towards a basis for modeling* (pp. 319–334). Chichester, England: Wiley.

Broadbent, D. E. (1977). Levels, hierarchies, and the locus of control. *Quarterly Journal of Experimental Psychology, 29,* 181–201.

Broadbent, D. E., & Aston, B. (1978). Human control of a simulated economic system. *Ergonomics, 21,* 1035–1043.

Broadbent, D. E., FitzGerald, P., & Broadbent, M. H. P. (1986). Implicit and explicit knowledge in the control of complex systems. *British Journal of Psychology, 77,* 33–50.

Conant, R. C., & Ashby, W. R. (1970). Every good regulator of a system must be a model of that system. *International Journal of System Science, 1,* 89–97.

Derry, S. J., & Murphy, D. A. (1986). Designing systems that train learning ability: From theory to practice. *Review of Educational Research, 56,* 1–39.

Dörner, D. (1987). On the difficulties people have in dealing with complexity. In J. Rasmussen, K. Duncan & J. Leplat (Eds.), *New technology and human error* (pp. 97–109). Chichester, England: Wiley.

Dörner, D. (1989). Die kleinen grünen Schildkröten und die Methoden der experimentellen Psychologie [The little green turtles and the methods of experimental psychology]. *Sprache & Kognition, 8,* 86–97.

Dörner, D., Kreuzig, H. W., Reither, F., & Stäudel, T. (1983). *Lohhausen. Vom Umgang mit Unbestimmtheit und Komplexität* [Lohhausen. On dealing with uncertainty and complexity]. Bern: Huber.

Dörner, D., & Reither, F. (1978). Über das Problemlösen in sehr komplexen Realitätsbereichen [On problem solving in very complex domains of reality]. *Zeitschrift für Experimentelle und Angewandte Psychologie, 25,* 527–551.

Dörner, D., Reither, F., & Stäudel, T. (1983). Emotion und problemlösendes Denken [Emotion and problem solving thinking]. In H. Mandl & G. L. Huber (Eds.), *Emotion und Kognition* (pp. 61–84). München: Urban & Schwarzenberg.

Dörner, D., Schaub, H., Stäudel, T., & Strohschneider, S. (1988). Ein System zur Handlungsregulation oder—Die Interaktion von Emotion, Kognition und Motivation [A system for action regulation or—The interaction of emotion, cognition, and motivation]. *Sprache & Kognition, 7,* 217–232.

Duncker, K. (1935). *Zur Psychologie des produktiven Denkens* [The psychology of productive thinking]. Berlin: Julius Springer.

Eyferth, K., Hoffmann-Plato, I., Muchowski, L., Otremba, H., Rossbach, H., Spiess, M., &

Widowski, D. (1982). *Studienprojekt Handlungsorganisation* [Project: Organization of action]. Berlin: Institut für Psychologie der TU Berlin (Forschungsbericht Nr. 82–4, korrigierter Nachdruck).

Fritz, A., & Funke, J. (1988). Komplexes Problemlösen bei Jugendlichen mit Hirnfunktionsstörungen [Complex problem solving with pupils who have minimal cerebral dysfunctions]. *Zeitschrift für Psychologie, 196,* 171–187.

Funke, J. (1983). Einige Bemerkungen zu Problemen der Problemlöseforschung oder: Ist Testintelligenz doch ein Prädiktor [Some comments to problems of problem solving research, or: An intelligence test is a predictor, isn't it?] *Diagnostica, 29,* 283–302.

Funke, J. (1984). Diagnose der westdeutschen Problemlöseforschung in Form einiger Thesen [Diagnosis of problem solving research in the FRG in form of some theses]. *Sprache & Kognition, 3,* 159–171.

Funke, J. (1985). Steuerung dynamischer Systeme durch Aufbau und Anwendung subjektiver Kausalmodelle [Control of dynamic systems through development and application of subjective causal models]. *Zeitschrift für Psychologie, 193,* 443–465.

Funke, J. (1986). *Komplexes Problemlösen. Bestandsaufnahme und Perspektiven* [Complex problem solving. State of the art and perspectives]. Heidelberg: Springer.

Funke, J. (1988). Using simulation to study complex problem solving. A review of studies in the FRG. *Simulation & Games, 19,* 277–303.

Funke, J., & Hussy, W. (1984). Komplexes Problemlösen: Beiträge zu seiner Erfassung sowie zur Frage der Bereichs- und Erfahrungsabhängigkeit [Complex problem solving: contributions to its measurement and to the question of the effects of context and prior experience]. *Zeitschrift für Experimentelle und Angewandte Psychologie, 31,* 19–38.

Funke, J., & Müller, H. (1988). Eingreifen und Prognostizieren als Determinanten von Systemidentifikation und Systemsteuerung [Intervention and prediction as determinants of systems identification and system control]. *Sprache & Kognition, 7,* 176–186.

Gediga, G., Schöttke, H., & Tücke, M. (1983). Problemlösen in einer komplexen Situation [Problem solving in a complex situation]. *Archiv für Psychologie, 135,* 325–339.

Gick, M. L., & Holyoak, K. J. (1983). Schema induction and analogical transfer. *Cognitive Psychology, 15,* 1–38.

Greeno, J. G. (1974). Hobbits and orcs: Acquisition of a sequential concept. *Cognitive Psychology, 4,* 270–292.

Guthke, J. (1982). The learning test concept—An alternative to the traditional static intelligence test. *German Journal of Psychology, 6,* 306–324.

Haider, H. (1989, March). *Die Bedeutung impliziten Lernens beim Problemlösen* [The importance of implicit learning in problem solving]. Paper presented at the "31. Tagung experimentell arbeitender Psychologen," Bamberg, FRG.

Hays, R. T., & Singer, M. J. (1989). *Simulation fidelity in training system design. Bridging the gap between reality and training.* New York: Springer.

Hesse, F. W. (1982). Effekte des semantischen Kontexts auf die Bearbeitung komplexer Probleme [Effects of semantic context on the processing of complex problems]. *Zeitschrift für Experimentelle und Angewandte Psychologie, 29,* 62–91.

Hesse, F. W., Spies, K., & Lüer, G. (1983). Einfluß motivationaler Faktoren auf das Problemlöseverhalten im Umgang mit komplexen Problemen [On the effect of motivational variables at solving complex problems]. *Zeitschrift für Experimentelle und Angewandte Psychologie, 30,* 400–424.

Hübner, R. (1987). Eine naheliegende Fehleinschätzung des Zielabstandes bei der zeitoptimalen Regelung dynamischer Systeme [An obvious fallacy on the distance to the criterion in time optimal control of dynamic systems]. *Zeitschrift für Experimentelle und Angewandte Psychologie, 34,* 38–53.

Hübner, R. (1989). Methoden zur Analyse und Konstruktion von Aufgaben zur kognitiven Steuerung dynamischer Systems [Methods for analysis and construction of tasks for cognitive control of dynamic systems]. *Zeitschrift für Experimentelle und Angewandte Psychologie, 36*, 271–238.

Hussy, W. (1989). Intelligenz und komplexes Problemlösen [Intelligence and complex problem solving]. *Diagnostica, 35*, 1–16.

Hussy, W., & Granzow, S. (1987). Komplexes Problemlösen, Gedächtnis und Verarbeitungsstil [Complex problem solving, memory, and kind of processing]. *Zeitschrift für Experimentelle und Angewandte Psychologie, 34*, 212–227.

Jäger, A. O. (1986). Validität von Intelligenztests [Validity of intelligence tests]. *Diagnostica, 32*, 272–289.

Jeffries, R., Polson, P. G., & Razran, L. (1977). A process model for missionaries-cannibals and other river crossing problems. *Cognitive Psychology, 9*, 412–440.

Kempton, W. (1986). Two theories of home heat control. *Cognitive Science, 11*, 75–90.

Klahr, D., & Dunbar, K. (1988). Dual space search during scientific reasoning. *Cognitive Science, 12*, 1–48.

Klahr, D., Dunbar, K., & Fay, A. L. (in press). Designing good experiments to test bad hypotheses. In J. Shrager & P. Langley (Eds.), *Computational models of discovery and theory formation*. Hillsdale, NJ: Lawrence Erlbaum Associates.

Kleinmuntz, D. N., & Kleinmuntz, B. (1981). Decision strategies in simulated environments. *Behavioral Science, 26*, 294–305.

Kleiter, G. D. (1970). Trend control in a dynamic decision making task. *Acta Psychologica, 34*, 387–397.

Kluwe, R. H. (1988). Methoden der Psychologie zur Gewinnung von Daten über menschliches Wissen [Psychological methods for data acquisition about human knowledge]. In H. Mandl & H. Spada (Eds.), *Wissenpsychologie* (pp. 359–385). München: Psychologie Verlags Union.

Kluwe, R. H., & Reimann, H. (1983). *Problemlösen bei vernetzten, komplexen Problemen: Effekte des Verbalisierens auf die Problemlöseleistung* [Problem solving with complex problems: Effects of verbalizing on problem solving quality]. Hamburg: Bericht aus dem Fachbereich Pädagogik der Hochschule der Bundeswehr.

Kluwe, R. H., Misiak, C., Ringelband, O., & Haider, H. (1986). Lernen durch Tun: Eine Methode zur Konstruktion von simulierten Systemen mit spezifischen Eigenschaften und Ergebnisse einer Einzelfallstudie [Learning by doing: A method for construction of simulated systems with specific traits and results of a single case study]. In M. Amelang (Ed.), *Bericht über den 35. Kongress der DGfPs in Heidelberg 1986* (p. 208). Göttingen: Hogrefe.

Knaeuper, A., & Rouse, W. B. (1983). A model of human problem solving in dynamic environments. In A. T. Pope & L. D. Haugh (Eds.), *Proceedings of the Human Factors Society* (Vol. 2, pp. 695–699). Santa Monica, CA: Human Factors Society.

Mackinnon, A. J., & Wearing, A. J. (1985). Systems analysis and dynamic decision making. *Acta Psychologica, 58*, 159–172.

Marescaux, P. J., Luc, F., & Karnas, G. (1989). Modes d'apprentissage sélectif et non-sélectif et connaissances acquises au contrôle d'un processus: évaluation d'un modèle simulé [Selective vs. unselective learning and knowledge acquisition about process control: Evaluation of a simulation model]. *Cahier de Psychologie Cognitive, 9*, 239–264.

Mayer, R. E. (1988). From novice to expert. In M. Helander (Ed.), *Handbook of human-computer interaction* (pp. 569–580). Amsterdam: Elsevier Science Publishers.

Moray, N., Lootsteen, P., & Pajak, J. (1986). Acquisition of process control skills. *IEEE Transactions on Systems, Man, & Cybernetics, 16*, 497–504.

Müller, H. (1989, March). *Zur Reliabilität verschiedener Indikatoren beim Bearbeiten komplexer dynamischer Systeme* [On the reliability of different indicators of dealing with complex dynamic systems]. Paper presented at the "31. Tagung experimentell arbeitender Psychologen," Bamberg, FRG.

Opwis, K., & Spada, H. (1985). Erwerb und Anwendung von Wissen über ökologische Systeme [Acquisition and application of knowledge about ecological systems]. In D. Albert (Ed.), *Bericht über den 34. Kongress der DGfPs in Wien 1984* (pp. 258–260). Göttingen, FRG: Hogrefe.

Preussler, W. (1985). *Über die Bedingungen der Prognose eines bivariaten ökologischen Systems* [On the determinants of forecasting a bivariate ecological system]. Bamberg: Memo No. 31 at the chair Psychology II at the University of Bamberg.

Putz-Osterloh, W. (1981). Über die Beziehung zwischen Testintelligenz und Problemlöseerfolg [On the relationship between test intelligence and success in problem solving]. *Zeitschrift für Psychologie, 189,* 79–100.

Putz-Osterloh, W. (1987). Gibt es Experten für komplexe Probleme [Are there experts for complex problems?] *Zeitschrift für Psychologie, 195,* 63–84.

Putz-Osterloh, W., & Lemme, M. (1987). Knowledge and its intelligent application to problem solving. *German Journal of Psychology, 11,* 286–303.

Putz-Osterloh, W., & Lüer, G. (1981). Über die Vorhersagbarkeit komplexer Problemlöseleistungen durch Ergebnisse in einem Intelligenztest [On the predictability of complex problem solving through intelligence test scores]. *Zeitschrift für Experimentelle und Angewandte Psychologie, 28,* 309–334.

Rasmussen, J., Duncan, K., & Leplat, J. (Eds.). (1987). *New technology and human error.* Chichester, England: Wiley.

Reichert, U. (1986). *Die Steuerung eines nichtlinearen Regelkreises durch Versuchspersonen* [The control of a nonlinear system by subjects]. Bamberg: Memo No. 42 at the chair Psychology II at the University of Bamberg.

Reichert, U., & Dörner, D. (1988). Heurismen beim Umgang mit einem "einfachen" dynamischen System [Heuristics in the control of a "simple" dynamic system]. *Sprache & Kognition, 7,* 12–24.

Reither, F. (1981). About thinking and acting of experts in complex situations. *Simulation & Games, 12,* 125–140.

Rouse, W. B., & Morris, N. M. (1986). On looking into the black box: Prospects and limits in the search for mental models. *Psychological Bulletin, 100,* 349–363.

Sanderson, P. M. (1989). Verbalizable knowledge and skilled task performance: Association, dissociation and mental models. *Journal of Experimental Psychology: Learning, Memory, and Cognition, 15,* 729–747.

Shrager, J., & Klahr, D. (1986). Instructionless learning about a complex device. *International Journal of Man-Machine Learning, 25,* 153–189.

Simon, H. A., & Lea, G. (1974). Problem solving and rule induction: A unified view. In L. W. Gregg (Ed.), *Knowledge and cognition* (pp. 105–127). Hillsdale, NJ: Lawrence Erlbaum Associates.

Snodgrass, J. G., & Corwin, J. (1988). Pragmatics of measuring recognition memory: Applications to dementia and amnesia. *Journal of Experimental Psychology: General, 117,* 34–50.

Spada, H., & Reimann, P. (1988). Wissensdiagnostik auf kognitionswissenschaftlicher Basis [Diagnosis of knowledge from a cognitive science point of view]. *Zeitschrift für Differentielle und Diagnostische Psychologie, 9,* 183–192.

Spies, K., & Hesse, F. W. (1987). Problemlösen [Problem solving]. In G. Lüer (Ed.), *Allgemeine Experimentelle Psychologie* (pp. 371–430). Stuttgart: Gustav Fischer.

Stäudel, T. (1987). *Problemlösen, Emotionen und Kompetenz. Die Überprüfung eines integrativen Konstrukts* [Problem solving, emotions and competence. The evaluation of an integrative construct]. Regensburg, FRG: Roderer.

Sternberg, R. J. (1982). Reasoning, problem solving, and intelligence. In R. J. Sternberg (Ed.), *Handbook of human intelligence* (pp. 225–307). Cambridge: Cambridge University Press.

Steyer, R. (1984). Causal linear stochastic dependencies: An introduction. In J. R. Nesselroade &

A. von Eye (Eds.), *Individual development and social change: Explanatory analysis* (pp. 95–124). New York: Academic Press.

Steyer, R. (1987). Konsistenz und Spezifität: Definition zweier zentraler Begriffe der Differentiellen Psychologie und ein einfaches Modell zu ihrer Identifikation [Consistency and specificity: Definition of two central concepts of differential psychology and a single model for their identification]. *Zeitschrift für Differentielle und Diagnostische Psychologie, 8,* 245–258.

Streufert, S., Nogami, G. Y., Swezey, R. W., Pogash, R. M., & Piasecki, M. T. (1988). Computer assisted training of complex managerial performance. *Computers in Human Behavior, 4,* 77–88.

Strohschneider, S. (1986). Zur Stabilität und Validität von Handeln in komplexen Realitätsbereichen [On the stability and validity of action in complex domains of reality]. *Sprache & Kognition, 5,* 42–48.

Thalmaier, A. (1979). Zur kognitiven Bewältigung der optimalen Steuerung eines dynamischen Systems [On the cognitive mastering of the optimal control of a dynamic system]. *Zeitschrift für Experimentelle und Angewandte Psychologie, 26,* 388–421.

Thomas, M., Hörmann, H. J., & Jäger, A. O. (1988). Systemwissen als Indikator der Bewältigung von Komplexität [System knowledge as indicator for coping with complexity]. In W. Schönpflug (Ed.), *Bericht über den 36. Kongress der Deutschen Gesellschaft für Psychologie in Berlin 1988* (pp. 301–302). Göttingen, FRG: Hogrefe.

Tversky, A., & Kahneman, D. (1974). Judgment under uncertainty: Heuristics and biases. *Science, 185,* 1124–1131.

Vent, U. (1985). *Der Einfluß einer ganzheitlichen Denkstrategie auf die Lösung von komplexen Problemen* [The effect of a holistic strategy of thinking on the solution of complex problems]. Kiel: Institut for Pedagogic of Natural Science at the University of Kiel (= IPN working paper No. 61).

Woodworth, R. S. (1938). *Experimental psychology.* New York: Holt.

Zimolong, B. (1987). Decision aids and risk taking in flexible manufacturing systems. A simulation study. In G. Salvendy (Ed.), *Cognitive engineering in the design of human-computer interaction and expert systems* (pp. 265–272). Amsterdam: Elsevier Science Publishers.

7

Do Lawyers Reason Differently From Psychologists? A Comparative Design for Studying Expertise

Eric Amsel*
Rosanna Langer**
and Lynn Loutzenhiser***
University of Saskatchewan

Legal reasoning has a logic of its own.

—E. H. Levi (1949)

Lawyers are experts in solving complex problems in their domain of expertise. For example, how a case ought to be presented, a contract drawn up, and when and when not to go to court are types of problems best left to lawyers who are trained to deal with them. Generally speaking, people appreciate the value of legal expertise. Very few people hire a psychologist to solve their legal problems or a lawyer to solve their psychological problems, although, as any good episode of "L.A. Law" suggests, people sometimes confuse their psychological problems with their legal ones. Such confusions of problem-states notwithstanding, people see both lawyers and psychologists as equipped to solve different problems by virtue of their training and experience.

This basic insight is not challenged, or even addressed, in this chapter. We address a different question: Does the training and experience of lawyers equip them to solve the same problem differently than experts in other professions? This may not be the theoretical focus that the reader expected. However, we believe that this question better addresses the central issue of this book: How are complex problems solved, and what are the underlying principles and mechanisms of such problem-solving skills? By examining whether lawyers and other groups of novices and experts solve the same problems differently, we can begin

*Now at the Department of Psychology, Vassar College.
**Faculty of Law, University of Saskatchewan.
***Now at the Department of Psychology, University of Guelph.

to say something about the existence of a uniquely legal style of reasoning and problem solving. A unique legal style of reasoning has been written about (Golding, 1984; Levi, 1949) and presented in popular culture in such films as *The Paper Chase,* but does it really exist? In this chapter, we compare and contrast problem-solving processes among lawyers, psychologists, and professionally novice adults. In particular, we examine theoretically and empirically the processes of causal reasoning among members of these groups. We start by outlining a comparative design for studying expertise and reviewing relevant research. Then, we review the theoretical literative on goals, structures, and processes of causal reasoning in legal and psychological contexts, and in everyday contexts. On the basis of the review, we present two studies evaluating the claim that lawyers' organization of causal inference rules is different than psychologists' and novice adults'.

Central to our position is the claim that the traditional manner of studying expertise cannot answer the question of the existence of a uniquely legal style of reasoning. In the traditional design, the cognitive processes used to solve problems unique to the expert's domain are isolated, categorized, and compared to the processes of novices (cf. Chi, Glaser, & Rees, 1982, on physics problem solving). The same traditional research design has been used on legal practitioners, focusing on novices' and experts' reasoning on tasks unique to the job descriptions of members of the legal profession; for example, sentencing (Lawrence, 1988), reading case law (Lundeberg, 1987), and legal argumentation (Hofer, 1987). Such an analysis tells us how to solve those problems uniquely faced by legal practitioners, but it tells us less about "legal reasoning" and more about "reasoning on legal tasks" than we prefer.

A Comparative Design for Studying Legal Reasoning

We believe that the best approach for studying the existence of a legal style of reasoning is to examine whether such a style is distinguishable from other styles of reasoning. For example, lawyers can be compared with psychologists, who are trained in a "social-scientific" style of reasoning. We call this a "comparative design for studying expertise" because the traditional comparison between the task performance of an expert and a novice group is augmented by comparisons between the different expert groups. These comparisons address the question of the specific influence of the experts' training and experience on their task performance, permitting a distinction between the expert groups. For example, a finding that the expert groups perform differently from each other on a task, and that each performs differently still from the novice group, suggests that task performance is influenced uniquely by the training and experience of each expert group. This, in turn, suggests that the training and experience led to different styles of reasoning. In summary, the choice of the comparative or traditional design for studying expertise ought to be based on whether one's interest is in isolating characteristics of a style of reasoning (e.g., legal reasoning), or in isolating expert strategies for solving a type of problem (e.g., legal problems).

A comparative design like that described was used in a study by Lehman, Lempert, and Nisbett (1988). They examined the effects of graduate training in law, psychology, medicine, and chemistry on such inference skills as statistical, conditional, and causal reasoning about everyday events. In both cross-sectional and longitudinal analyses, they found that graduate training in psychology and medicine enhances performance on all the reasoning tasks; training in law enhances performance only on the conditional reasoning task; and training in chemistry enhances performance on none of the tasks.

The findings were taken by Lehman et al. to support the claim that there are domain-general "pragmatic" reasoning schemas (Cheng & Holyoak, 1985). Domain-general reasoning schemas are defined by inference rules that are applied to various content domains (Cheng & Holyoak, 1985). Pragmatic reasoning schemas refer to how such rules are mentally represented and activated. The rules are not thought to be represented as a logical structure or activated by conditions that are independent of the subjects' goals; rather, pragmatic reasoning schemas "capture regularities among problem goals and among event relationships that people encounter in their everyday life" (Lehman et al., 1988, p. 432). The pattern of performance is explained by students' differential practice in the use of pragmatic reasoning schemas (contractual schemas, causal schemas, and statistical rules) as a function of professional or graduate school. The use of all these rules is practiced in the course of training in the probabilistic sciences of medicine and psychology; practice in the use of contractual schemas occurs during training in the nonscience of law; and no practice in the use of pragmatic inference rules takes place during training in the deterministic science of chemistry.

Alternative Interpretations

The Lehman et al. findings appear to cast doubt on the existence of a uniquely legal style of reasoning. They argue that professionals improve upon and generalize to everyday problems those pragmatic reasoning schemas that will help them in solving problems specific to their profession: Lawyers and psychologists reason no differently than would otherwise be expected because of the kind of tasks that they reason about. Our problem with the "inferential practice" explanation of the different patterns of improvement among the students centers on the finding of differential improvements of law and psychology students in causal reasoning. Only psychology and medical students' causal reasoning scores improved over the course of graduate education, presumably because they, and not law and chemistry students, exercise causal inference schemas in the course of graduate education.

This explanation conflicts with our understanding of the professional duties of lawyers, which include engaging in causal inquiry. Causal inquiry refers to the processes for establishing the existence of causal connections. In their classic book on causation in the law, Hart and Honore (1985) argue that for legal liability in civil trials, "causal connection is often a necessary element in responsibility and sometimes sufficient" (p. xxxv). The amount of legal scholarship devoted to the topic of causation rivals that of social-scientific scholarship. For example, just as a recent volume of *Child Development* is devoted to the topic of causation (Volume 58,1, 1987, which is devoted to causal modeling), so is one recent edition of the *Chicago-Kent Law Review* (Volume 63,3, 1987, which is devoted to causation in the law of torts). Moreover, the topic of causation is almost as inevitable a topic in first year law courses (particularly in torts) as it is in first year graduate courses in methodology and statistics. We shall wait until later to go into further detail about the similarities and differences in the process of causal inquiry in law and psychology. For now, we want to impress upon the reader that the issue of causation is as central a topic in law (Hart & Honore, 1985) and legal education as it is in psychology (Cook & Campbell, 1979, 1986) and in graduate education in the social sciences. Yet, in contrast to the theoretical and pedagogical importance of causation in law and psychology, Lehman et al.'s "differential practice" explanation suggests that only graduate education in psychology or medicine provides sufficient practice to improve students' causal reasoning performance.

Our problem with Lehman et al.'s explanation lies with the insensitivity of their causal reasoning task. Perhaps if the causal reasoning task were improved, psychology and law students would show a pattern of improvement over graduate training consonant with our argument of the theoretical and pedagogical centrality of the topic of causation in law and psychology. Like Lehman et al., we believe that there are empirical and theoretical reasons for believing that causal reasoning is a good candidate for being the quintessential domain-general reasoning process. Empirically, systematic causal inference strategies have been demonstrated among infants (Leslie, 1987), preschoolers (Bullock, Gelman, & Baillargeon, 1982; Shultz, 1982), and adults (Kelley, 1967). Theoretically, the existence of domain-general causal inference strategies is acknowledged even by theorists who otherwise seek to explain all of cognitive development in terms of changes in domain-specific cognitive processes (Carey, 1985a, 1985b).

In the Lehman et al. task, subjects read stories that presented a causal relation between events, and were instructed to criticize the existence of the causal relation based on the presence of confounded variables. For example, the task assessed subjects' ability to apply control group concepts and the principle of self-selection. Thus, the task actually measures subjects' ability to inhibit making causal inferences, given certain conditions, rather than measuring the process by which such inferences are made. There is evidence that children become better at inhibiting causal inferences in the presence of confounding variables, although even adults are not particularly adept at it (Kuhn, Amsel, & O'Loughlin, 1988). Moreover, practice in solving "confounded causation" problems has been shown to be helpful, but not for all subjects (Kuhn & Phelps, 1982; Schauble, 1990). These findings suggest that the skills for inhibiting invalid causal inferences are not particularly central in children's or novice adults' causal reasoning. It would seem that the Lehman et al. causal reasoning task assesses only a subset of inference rules used by children and novice adults in reasoning about causation. This leaves open the question of how children and novice adults engage in causal inquiries, and how professional training alters this process.

THE NATURE OF LEGAL, PSYCHOLOGICAL AND "EVERYDAY" CAUSAL INQUIRIES

The differences between lawyers', psychologists', and novice adults' causal inquiries are examined by comparing and contrasting theoretical discussions of and empirical research on the process of legal, psychological, and everyday causal inquiry. For example, there may be differences between lawyers, psychologists, and novices in what causal information is acquired, how the information is acquired, and when the inquiry is initiated. To examine such differences we distinguish three psychologically relevant aspects of a causal inquiry: its goals, its structures, and its processes. By the goals of a causal inquiry we are referring to the use of the causal knowledge that is enabled by the inquiry. The structure of a causal inquiry refers to its procedural characteristics as they are constrained by the inquirer or the task. The process of a causal inquiry refers to the inferential and information-gathering procedures available for conducting the inquiry. Unless otherwise stated, the comparison we make is between scientific and legal causal inquiries. However, to limit the discussion at particular points, we examine causal inquiry in the "softer" side of psychology, particularly social psychology, and in civil law or Torts, particularly harm-causing.

Goals

The knowledge gathered by everyday causal inquiries can serve a variety of purposes. Weiner (1985) found that adults spontaneously engage in causal inquiries when they are confronted with unexpected results or when they don't attain desired goals. Besides explaining the unexplained or unexpected, everyday causal inquiries serve as one basis for assessing blame and responsibility by adults and children (Fincham & Jaspers, 1980; Shaver, 1985; Shultz & Schleifer, 1983; Shultz, Wright, & Schleifer, 1986; Wollert & Rowley, 1987).

The dual goals of explanation and the attribution of blame and responsibility are central not only in everyday causal inquiries but also in the distinction between psychological and legal causal inquiries. According to a number of legal scholars, the goals of explanation and the attribution of blame or responsibility require different types of causal inquiry. Hart and Honore (1985) distinguish between causal inquiries in which explanation is the goal and those in which the attribution of blame or responsibility is the goal. They claim that

> after it is clearly understood how some harm happened, the courts have, because of the form of legal rules, to determine whether such harm can be attributed to the defendant's action as its consequence, or whether he can properly be said to have caused it. (p. 24)

According to this traditional legal view, the explanation of the occurrence of a harm is only one step in the process; the second step involves assessing the defendant's role in causing the harm on the basis of legal policy. Hart and Honore label the two steps as *explanatory* and *attributive contexts*. Discussing these two kinds of causal inquiries in law, Strachan (1970) writes:

> There are, of course, two distinct causal problems. The first is concerned with whether there is a causal relationship between the defendant's conduct and the plaintiff's injury. . . . If the first of these questions is answered affirmatively the second inquiry arises as to whether the injury incurred was sufficiently proximate to the defendant's negligent action for liability to be imposed. The first question therefore is basically one which is divorced from matters of legal policy and turns on a question of 'pure' causation, while the second is intimately concerned with policy considerations of where and to what extent liability should lie. The distinction broadly corresponds to what Hart and Honore have called the 'explanatory' context, . . . and the 'attributive' inquiry . . . American legal terminology expresses this 'bifurcation of causal questions' as a distinction between causation-in-fact and causation-in-law. (p. 286)

The separation between causation-in-fact and causation-in-law amounts to a separation between fact-based causal inquiry and a policy-based inquiry. Weinrib (1975) clarifies the rationale for the distinction:

> Inherent in the division of cause into factual causation and proximate causation is the belief that the ascertainment of facts should be distinguished from elucidation of values. The former task requires the adducing of evidence, whereas the latter involves decisions of policy, usually expressed in terms of reasonable forseeability, as to whether certain interests have been or should be placed within the law's protective sphere. (p. 529)

The separation of fact from value in a two-staged legal inquiry is not universally accepted by legal scholars, some of whom argue that no separation is necessary (e.g., Epstein, 1973; Calabresi, 1975; although see Borgo, 1979) and others who argue for a third stage (e.g., Wright, 1985a). But, even if we ignore the issues of proximate causation (causation-in-law) and limit the discussion to explanatory causal inquiries (causation-in-fact), legal and scientific causal inquiries nonetheless continue to have different goals. Specifically, Williams (1961) notes that causal generalizations are a central concern in scientific but not factual legal causal inquiries:

> For the scientist, the notion of causation involves the idea that the same effect can be repeated by reproducing the cause. In other words, the scientist is concerned with causal generalizations. But in historical and legal statements this notion of generalization and reproducibility hardly figures at all. (p. 66)

Williams' argument is that the goal of legal and historical causal inquiries is the generation of singular causal statements (e.g., "c causes e"; where c and e refer to unique events or states). However, in scientific causal inquiries the goal is to generate general causal statements (e.g., "C's cause E's"; where C and E refer to classes of events or states) required for causal prediction and control.

A slightly different view of the role of generalizations in legal causal inquiries is presented by Hart and Honore (1985). They claim that causal generalizations do constitute a part of the background of causal statements in attributive contexts to the extent that a reliance on general knowledge is exhibited. That is, the general causal statement is implicit in singular causal statements. However, they claim that this implicit relation is not true of all types of singular causal statements. The two main types of causal statements are distinguished according to whether a causal statement refers to: a) an event caused by a physical event, human action or a complex set of conditions; or b) a certain human relationship or interpersonal transaction. The central notion of this second type of statement is that the first person's words or actions constitute the reason or part of the reason why the second acted as he did. They argue that no appeal to generalizations is required for the defense of this latter statement, and that generalizations are no part of the implicit meaning of such a statement.

Yet a third position on the role of causal generalizations in legal contexts is presented by Mackie (1980), who contends, "No specific generalization needs be known in advance to support the interpretation of an observed sequence as causal; all that is required is the assumption that what happened is an instance of some regularity" (p. 79). His claim is that causal generalizations play some role in all legal contexts, "if only to aid in the exclusion of irrelevancies" (p. 122). Jensen (1957), like Mackie, argues that causal generalizations are part of causal inquiries in law. He suggests that relevant causal factors are derived from causal laws or probability rules, but that this derivation is overlooked because causal inquiry in law is not concerned with making predictions as to future occurrences:

> The law is not concerned, in negligence cases, with predicting and controlling accidents: it is concerned with the question whether a particular occurrence was the cause of a certain accident. The relevant causal factors are probably derived from common-sense causal generalizations or probability rules, e.g., if a driver turns around to chat with those at the back of his car he will have an accident. Not being

concerned with prediction and control, lawyers do not bear in mind the causal laws from which their relevant causal factors have been derived. (p. 84)

Regardless of the precise role of generalizations in causal inquiries in law (if any), the consensus among theorists indicates that legal and scientific (e.g., psychological) causal inquiries have a different focus. Causal inquiries in law focus on the unique and specific content of a particular case, whereas a particular instance or case is only relevant in causal inquiries in science to the extent that it confirms the general causal law. Hart and Honore (1985) best characterized the difference in goals of explanatory causal inquiries in law and science. They wrote:

> The lawyer and the historian are both primarily concerned about *particulars,* to establish that on some particular occasion some particular occurrence was the effect or consequence of some other particular occurrence. . . . This characteristic concern with causation is . . . to *apply* generalizations which are already known or accepted as true and even platitudinous to particular concrete cases. . . . By contrast, in the experimental sciences . . . the focus of attention is the discovery of generalizations and the construction of theories. (Italics in the original, pp. 9–10)

The differences in goals between everyday, legal, and scientific causal inquiries appear to be a matter of emphasis: Everyday goals of explanation and attribution of responsibility become further differentiated and highly specialized in legal and scientific causal inquiries. Nonetheless, the goals of explanation and attribution of responsibility are so much part of everyday causal inquiries that children and adults have been characterized as intuitive scientists (Amsel, 1989; Ross, 1977) and intuitive lawyers (Fincham & Jaspers, 1980; Hamilton, 1980). That is, there remains a continuity between the goals of the intuitive psychologist/lawyer and the professional psychologist and lawyer.

Structure

Besides differences in goals, the structure of lawyers', psychologists', and novice adults' causal inquiries are different. The structure of an inquiry refers to constraints on its procedure due to characteristics of the inquirer or task. For example, one way in which the structure of legal and psychological inquiries differentially constrains lawyers and psychologists is that lawyers take a perspective on whether the defendant's action is or is not causal and find evidence in support of it; whereas psychologists, like other scientists, are ideally supposed to be objective, if not to seek evidence falsifying their causal hypotheses (Popper, 1965). That is, lawyers and psychologists are constrained by different sets of methodological prescriptions.

There are other differences between legal and scientific causal inquiries that are more pertinent to the present discussion because they focus on constraints due to characteristics of the causal inquiry performed by lawyers and psychologists. For example, a factual causal inquiry in law is retrospective, being initiated to determine whether a particular event or act was the cause of an effect (damage or harm-doing) that has already occurred. Wright (1985a) notes that the characteristic specificity of a causal inquiry in law is made possible by the retrospective causal inquiry:

> The actual causation requirement invokes . . . a backward-looking, individualized and factual inquiry, which asks, ex-post, after the tortious conduct of the defendant has already occurred, whether the tortious (negligent, intentional, ultrahazardous) aspect of the defendant's conduct in fact contributed to a legally redressible injury to the plaintiff. (p. 437)

A causal inquiry in law is retrospective in two senses; not only has the event sequence already occurred (i.e., the inquiry is historically-oriented), but also the inquiry focuses on the cause of a given effect (i.e., the inference is from effect to cause or diagnostic). Hart and Honore (1985) note the diagnostic nature of legal inquiries, which they capture with the term *inquest:*

> It is, however, vital to see that logically the demands of the situation in which we ask for the cause of what has happened, and that in which we are concerned to predict are very different. In the first case it is an inquest that we are conducting. The 'effect' has happened: it is a particular puzzling or unusual occurrence, or divergence from the standard state or performance of something with whose ordinary states or modes of functioning we are familiar; and when we look for the cause of this, we are looking for something, usually earlier in time, which is abnormal or an interference. (p. 46)

Hart and Honore's characterization of a cause in legal inquiries as a particular puzzling or unusual occurrence suggests that the diagnostic nature of causal inquiries in law constrains the kinds of events that will be identified as causal. Moreover, the diagnostic nature of the inquiry permits an indefinitely long sequence to be evaluated, unless some criteria, legal or otherwise, are present for limiting the relevance to a particular case. This infinite sequence leading to an effect has been called "Adam-and-Eve-causation" (Williams, 1961). Cooper-Stephenson and Saunders (1981) note that the selection of the cause in retrospective legal inquiries is not completely arbitrary, or factual, but informed by legal policy.

In contrast to the retrospective nature of causal inquiry in law, causal inquiry in psychology is prospective. There are two senses to the prospective nature of the psychologist's causal inquiry. A psychological causal inquiry not only begins with predictions about the outcome of a future experiment (i.e., the inquiry is future-oriented), but it involves the manipulation of an independent variable—a cause—in order to produce variation in a dependent variable—an effect (i.e., the inference is from cause to effect, or prognostic). The prognostic nature of causal inferences in psychology is due to the experimental and quasi-experimental requirement of manipulating the independent (treatment) variable. Philosophers such as Collingwood (1972) and von Wright (1971) claim that the locus of influence of human activity is central for understanding causation, a point that is extended by Cook and Campbell (1979, 1986) to include causal inquiries in psychology. They claim that underlying causal inferences in psychological research is the pragmatic notion that causation can be inferred when, by manipulating one factor, another factor is also manipulated. As evidence of their belief in the centrality of manipulation in causal inquiries in psychology, Cook and Campbell (1979, 1986) characterize the meaningfulness of a cause as related to its potential for manipulation:

> The paradigmatic assertion in causal relationships is that the manipulation of a cause will result in the manipulation of an effect. . . For many valid causal laws we may not in practice be able to manipulate the putative cause at will, if at all. This has grave consequences for our ability to test the law, but this does not negate its truthfulness. However, it does decrease the immediate practical importance of the law, for it suggests that the causal powers implicit in the law cannot be easily used to make desirable changes in persons or environments. . . . If we define the meaningfulness of causes in terms of their ability to create testable, dependable, and planned changes, then the most meaningful causes are those which can be deliberately manipulated. Such a concept of cause mirrors the unique feature of experimentation—the manipulation of putative causes. (p. 36)

Just as the diagnostic nature of legal causal inquiries constrains the kinds of events that lawyers entertain as causes, so it is in psychological causal inquiries: The prognostic nature of experimental inquiries constrains the kinds of events psychologists find as meaningful causes. Thus, the prospective/retrospective difference in legal and psychological causal inquiries is not trivial but rather reflects a significant constraint on the nature of the inquiry and the characteristics of the "cause" identified. Everyday causal inquiries have structural characteristics in common with both prospective psychological causal inquiry and retrospective legal causal inquiry. Some everyday inquiries are historically-oriented and diagnostic (e.g., determining who was the cause of the broken radio), and others are future-oriented and prognostic (e.g., determining if the placement of the radio will improve the quality of reception).

A more significant constraint on the process of everyday inquiries than their prospective or retrospective nature is the constraint due to children's and adults' cognitive systems. Lay adults' causal inquiries fail to measure up to models of how causal inquiries ought to proceed (c.f., Nisbett & Ross, 1980; Schustack, 1988; Kahneman, Slovic, & Tversky, 1982). For example, lay adults engage in limited searches of evidence (Shaklee & Fishoff, 1982), make inappropriate causal inferences regarding evidence (Kuhn et al., 1988; Kahneman et al., 1982), and inadequately revise their prior causal beliefs on the basis of the evidence (Kuhn et al., 1988; Nisbett & Ross, 1980). Such findings have been interpreted as the consequence of a limited cognitive system; that is, people are generally thought to be "bounded" in their rationality (Fishoff, 1976; Simon, 1981). More recently, researchers have interpreted examples of cognitive "limitations" as the consequence of a pragmatically driven inference system. For example, Holland, Holyoak, Nisbett, and Thagrad (1987) have characterized people's rules of induction as being geared to the generation of accurate predictions of the aspect of the world that happens to be focused upon at the time. There is no spontaneous search for coherence other than a local one.

These findings portray the cognitive system of the inquirer as the major source of difference between the causal inquiries of legal and scientific professionals and nonprofessionals (although see Faust, 1984, for examples of limits on the cognitive system of scientists constraining their causal inquiries). However, there also appear to be sources of continuity between professional and nonprofessional causal inquiries. For example, rules of causal inference, such as covariation detection, counterfactual reasoning, sensitivity to and use of mechanism information, spatial-temporal contiguity, and similarity, appear to be available to and used by lay adults, lawyers, and psychologists (Cook & Campbell, 1979, 1986; Einhorn & Hogarth, 1986; Hart & Honore, 1985; Shultz, Fischer, Pratt, & Rulf, 1986; Wells, Taylor, & Turtle, 1987). The nature and use of these rules will be discussed more fully in the following section.

Processes

Given the differences between the goals and structures in lay adults', psychologists', and lawyers' causal inquiries, it is not surprising to find differences in the processes of such inquiries as well. By processes of causal inquiry we mean the inferential and data-gathering rules used to make causal judgments. We outline three kinds of inference rules, then discuss how the rules might be used and organized by novice adults, psychologists, and lawyers. The three rules are mechanism-based, covariation-based, and context-based.

Mechanism-based.   One manner of making causal judgments is to assess whether a cause produces an effect through a mechanism. Use of such a rule has been demonstrated in children and adults (Bullock, 1985; Bullock et al., 1982; Koslowski & Okagaki, 1986; Shultz, 1982; Shultz & Kestenbaum, 1985; Shultz, Fischer, Pratt, & Rulf, 1986). For example, Shultz (1982, Experiment 1) presented preschoolers and adults with a candle that is blown out by one of two blowers that are directed at the candle. One blower is on and is producing a wind whereas the other is off and is producing no wind. Preschool children and adults overwhelmingly judged that the "on" blower was the cause of the candle going out, demonstrating that even young children make causal judgments on the basis of mechanism information. Shultz (1979, 1983; Bindra, Clarke, & Shultz, 1983) has argued that causal judgments made on the basis of mechanism are irreducible to a logical form (e.g., logical necessity or sufficiency) or to probability calculus. Therefore, Mary's belief that her drinking coffee this morning caused her mental alertness because of the stimulant drug caffeine in the coffee may be consistent with, but can not be reduced to, the claim that drinking coffee is a logical condition of mental alertness or that drinking coffee is associated statistically with mental alertness.

Covariation-based.   Another manner of making causal judgments is to assess whether a cause and an effect are associated statistically. This type of causal inference rule is available to children and adults in the form of covariation and other statistical rules (Einhorn & Hogarth, 1986; Kuhn et al., 1988; Shaklee & Tucker, 1980). Related to the use of covariation and statistical rules is classical attribution theory (Kelley, 1967). The central characteristic of the covariation-based causal inference rule is the use of prior association between the cause and effect as the basis for and justification of causal inferences. For example, Susan's belief that her drinking coffee this morning caused her mental alertness is justified by the association in the past between drinking coffee and mental alertness. Put schematically, "the belief that 'C causes E' is justified by the past association between C-type events and E-type events."

Context-based.   A third manner of making causal judgments is to assess information from the causal context itself. Contextual information includes information about temporal contiguity, spatial contiguity, or similarity between events. Causal inference rules based on spatial and temporal contiguity and similarity between cause and effect events have been shown to be used by children and adults in making causal judgments (Sedlack & Kurtz, 1981; Shultz & Kestenbaum, 1985).

More recently, another kind of contextual rule, the counterfactual rule, has been demonstrated in adults (Tversky & Kahneman, 1982; Wells & Gavanski, 1989; Wells, Taylor, & Turtle, 1987). Counterfactual reasoning involves comparing an actual sequence of events leading to an effect to a hypothetical sequence undoing the effect. An actual event in the sequence leading to the effect is judged as causal if an imagined hypothetical sequence that does not include the target event "undoes" the effect. For example, Mary may give as evidence for her belief that her drinking coffee this morning caused her mental alertness the argument that she would not be so alert, had she not had the coffee. Although Mary may or may not know that coffee contains the stimulant drug caffeine and that there is a statistical association between coffee and mental alertness, her counterfactual argument does not directly mention or imply such knowledge.

This lack of a direct appeal to knowledge beyond the causal context makes counterfactual reasoning a context-based causal inference rule.

It has been shown that all three kinds of causal inference rules are used by adults. Some researchers have argued that the rules serve as "cues" to causality and so causal judgments are made by a weighting of information derived from use of multiple rules (Einhorn & Hogarth, 1986). Other researchers have argued that despite arguments to the contrary, all rules are variants of the same underlying statistical principle (Cheng & Novick, 1989). A third view is that each of the rules is psychologically unique and that there are organizing principles for selecting among rules (Shultz, Fischer, Pratt, & Rulf, 1986; Shultz & Kestenbaum, 1985). At present, this third approach seems to be the most promising because: a) it is the most consistent with the view of the cognitive system that is multi-ruled, pragmatically-driven, and capacity-limited (Holland et al., 1987); and b) the approach has been successfully applied in other content domains (Siegler & Shrager, 1984).

The primary organizing principle for selecting a causal inference strategy identified by Shultz is *fundamentality,* which is defined as the adaptational success of the rule in predicting true causes. According to Shultz, the mechanism-based rule is the most fundamental, meaning that mechanism is the primary source of information used to make causal inferences. If mechanism is unavailable, other rules are selected on the basis of the following four secondary principles: *salience* (the degree to which the relevant evidence for rule deployment is perceptible); *facility* (the relative ease with which the relevant information for rule deployment can be processed); *plausibility* (whether the deployed rule will generate a causal attribution that is consistent with imagined or hypothesized causal mechanisms); and *discriminability* (whether the rule selected will serve the goal of discriminating between the potential causes of interest).

Shultz's principles were derived from research on novice adults and children. It is our claim that, in contrast to novice adults, psychologists and lawyers would have a different hierarchy of causal inference rules. For example, among psychologists, covariation-based causal inference rules would seem as important as mechanism-based rules. Cook and Campbell (1979, 1986) described causal inference in psychology as requiring a combination of the covariation rule to reason about statistical evidence, and the mechanism rule to reason about various influences on the internal and external validity of an experiment.

Similarly, our argument is that, compared to novice adults and children, lawyers' causal inquiries seem to require an increased likelihood of use of context-based rules, particularly the counterfactual rule. In legal contexts, the "but-for" test is a counterfactually structured argument in which the necessity of the causal sequence is tested by "undoing" the outcome in a hypothetical sequence. The "but-for" factual causation test for the claim that "x caused y" amounts to acknowledging the truth of the proposition that "but for x, y would not have occurred." For example, a homeowner would be held as the cause-in-fact for the visitor's injuries if, in the context, it can be reasonably concluded that "but for the homeowner's improper care for the staircase, the visitor would not have been injured."

However, there is disagreement regarding whether the "but-for" test can be used as the basis of both causal inclusion and exclusion. Weinrib (1975) contended that, although the overall cause-in-fact inquiry can be used to exclude potential defendants, the "but-for" test is one of inclusion only. The author first argued that the cause-in-fact inquiry functions to exclude defendants without having to decide if their conduct was culpable, but then went on to note that the "but-for" test is unable to exclude irrelevant causes; it operates only to include causal factors:

> If a function of cause-in-fact is to exclude whatever conduct is irrelevant to the plaintiff's inquiry, it is a function which the 'but-for' test is inherently incapable of performing. This test can operate as a criterion only of inclusion, not of exclusion; it can tell us whether the factor in question is a cause but it cannot determine that it is not a cause. (pp. 521–522)

Cooper-Stephenson and Saunders (1981), among other legal scholars, observed that the use of the counterfactual "but-for" as a test of exclusion can be problematic when applied in cases of concurrent or successive multiple causes (where each of two events, with other normal conditions, is sufficient for the effect). The problem in these and similar cases of causal overdetermination is that the "but-for" test cannot distinguish among sufficient causes. Thus it can be argued that each sufficient cause can elude the label of a "but-for" cause by conceding it to another event in the "but-for" test. (See Cooper-Stephenson & Saunders, 1981, pp. 653–654; Hart and Honore, 1985, pp. 122–128; Malone, 1956, pp. 88–90; Thompson, 1987, p. 482; Williams, 1961, p. 75; Wright, 1985b, pp. 1775–1777).

Attempts to remedy this situation have led to the addition of new legal tests of cause-in-fact or alterations of the "but-for" test. Nonetheless, it is clear from this discussion that the "fundamental" causal inference rule for the lawyer may well not be the mechanism rule, as Shultz claimed it is for professionally novice adults.

In summary, the process of causal inquiry for lawyers, psychologists, and novices would be different if they organize causal inference rules differently. To make this argument more concrete, imagine that David kicked a TV set and its picture became clear. Was David's kick a (factual) cause of the clear TV picture? One could justify the sequence of events leading from the kick to the clear picture as causal on the basis of a covariation argument (other times David kicked the TV its picture became clear), a counterfactual argument (if David had not kicked the TV, there would not have been a clear picture), or a mechanism argument

(David's kick rearranged loose wires to produce a clear picture). It is argued that these justification strategies are differentially adequate or convincing for lawyers, psychologists, and untrained adults. Untrained adults would be most convinced by mechanism, psychologists by mechanism and covariation, and lawyers by counterfactual as well as other arguments. This conceptualization of the difference between psychologists, lawyers, and novice adults in the organization of causal inference rules was tested in two experiments.

EXPERIMENTS

We carried out two studies based on the aforementioned discussion of differences in the goals, structures, and processes of psychologists', lawyers', and novice adults' causal inquiries. The studies examined whether the acquisition of expertise in law and psychology involves a characteristically different organization of novices' causal inference rules. Causal inference rules were assessed by subjects' preferred manner for justifying that an event is causally and not coincidentally related to an effect. The task parallels the kinds of situations argued in courts, discussed in journals, and overheard in college dormitories—a protagonist trying to convince an antagonist that a sequence of events is causally rather than coincidentally related.

Hypotheses

The hypothesis of a change with acquisition of expertise in the organization of causal inference rules was tested in four ways. First, causal inference rules were assessed in a comparative design, using a group of undergraduate "novices" and groups of experts in law and psychology. If there is a reorganization of causal rules, then there should be differences not only between undergraduates and lawyers and between undergraduates and psychologists in their organization of causal inference rules, but there should also be differences between lawyers and psychologists.

Second, a control group of professionals (police officers) was included. If there are differences in causal reasoning among novices, lawyers, and psychologists due to their professional training, then a control group of professionals who are not trained in law or the social sciences should reason like novices. Police officers served as a control group, because like social scientists, police officers evaluate evidence, and like lawyers they must have some understanding of the law. However, because police officers are not trained specifically in legal or social scientific reasoning, we predicted that their organization of causal inference rules would be similar to that of undergraduates.

Third, causal reasoning was assessed within and outside the lawyers' and psychologists' domains of expertise. Preferred causal justifications were examined in three content domains: a legal domain, a psychological domain, and an everyday domain. If there is a reorganization of lawyers' and psychologists' causal inference rules, and if the rules are general, then their manner of testing for causal relations should generalize to domains outside their domain of expertise.

Fourth, it is proposed that differences in the justification of sequences as causal and not merely coincidental reflect differences in the organization of causal inference rules. As such, professional differences in preferences for justifications should relate to differences in the processing of evidence and not merely to differences in the manner of expressing that a sequence of events is causal.

Study 1

In the first study, subjects read nine scenarios, each depicting a different causal relation. The scenario consisted of an initial sentence introducing a protagonist and describing an event sequence believed by the protagonist to be causal, followed by four *evidence sentences* about the event sequence in question. These four evidence sentences presented information about the situation prior to the presence of the cause, noting that the effect was also absent (contextual evidence), prior association of the cause and effect (past association evidence), other consequences of a plausible mechanism that links the putative cause and effect (mechanism evidence), and irrelevant evidence. The order of these four pieces of evidence was randomized across stories.

At the end of each causal scenario, we introduced an antagonist who believed that the event sequence, believed by the protagonist to be causal, is merely coincidental. Subjects then were presented with three *causal justification statements* that provided arguments against the protagonist's claim. The causal justification statements were designed on the basis of the three causal inference rules: counterfactual, covariation, and mechanism. The counterfactual causal justification statement was the claim that, had the cause been absent, then the effect would not have occurred (If C had not occurred, then E would not have occurred). The covariation causal justification statement was the claim that the cause and the effect covaried regularly (C is associated with E in the past), and the mechanism causal justification statement was the claim about how the cause produced the effect (C causes E through mechanism M). Subjects rated each causal justification statement as to how "convincing" it was (on a scale from one to five) as an argument against the antagonist's claim and in support of the protagonist's claim, selected the "most convincing" causal justification statement, and then rated each evidence sentence as to how relevant it was to their judgment of the most convincing statement. The nine scenarios presented causal relations in three domains—legal, scientific, and everyday—with three causal scenarios in each domain. Figure 7.1 presents an example of a causal inference item.

David, an avid sports fan, found a unique way of getting a clearer picture on his TV to watch the Grey Cup game. In telling a friend about this incident David points out that:

• He kicked the TV to get a clearer picture of the Curling and Hockey match.____

• The vertical and horizontal hold on the TV was stable after he kicked it.____

• David watches TV sports in the living room and sits on the couch.____

• He had a poor picture of the Grey Cup game until he kicked the TV.____

David thinks that the clearer picture of the Grey Cup game was caused by his kicking the TV. His friend thought that David's kicking his TV and the clearer picture of the Grey Cup game is just a coincidence.

Suppose you were asked to convince David's friend that a causal relation does indeed exist. Rate each of the following three statements, on a scale from 1-5, by how convincing it is of David's claim.

1	**2**	**3**	**4**	**5**
Not at all	**Somewhat**	**Moderately**	**Highly**	**Very Highly**
Convincing	**Convincing**	**Convincing**	**Convincing**	**Convincing**

A If David had not kicked the TV, there would not have been a clearer picture.____

B David tends to get a clearer picture whenever he kicks the TV.____

C By kicking the TV, loose wires got jolted and so the picture got clearer. ____

Now that you have rated the above statements, choose the one (A, B, or C) that you find to be the most convincing. _____

Finally, rate each piece of information in the story, on a scale from 1-5, by how relevant it was in making the judgment of the most convincing statement.

1	**2**	**3**	**4**	**5**
Not at all	**Somewhat**	**Moderately**	**Highly**	**Very Highly**
Relevant	**Relevant**	**Relevant**	**Relevant**	**Relevant**

FIG. 7.1. A causal reasoning task item (everyday domain).

There were four groups of subjects. The psychologist group was composed of psychology professors and Ph.D. students; the lawyer group of practicing lawyers and third-year law students; the police group of police officers; and the undergraduate group of students enrolled in first- and second-year psychology courses.

A pretest was conducted to determine whether the three causal justification statements given at the end of each scenario were equally supported by the evidence present in the scenario. This was to ensure that differences in the ratings of convincingness could be attributed to preferred ways of justifying a sequence of events as causal, and not to differences in the perceived support for the causal justification statements. Subjects in the pretest read 27 scenario/statement pairs (3 statements for each of the 9 scenarios) in random order and rated the statements for the degree to which they were supported by the evidence sentences in the scenario. Analysis revealed that there were no differences in the support for the three causal statements overall or across domains.

The major hypothesis of the study, that novice adults (undergraduates and police officers) would be most convinced by mechanism, psychologists by mechanism and covariation, and lawyers by counterfactual as well as other causal justification statements, was tested with a 3 (domain) by 4 (profession) by 3 (statements) mixed-model, repeated-measures ANOVA on the frequency with which a statement was selected as the "most convincing." Figure 7.2 presents the mean number of times (out of 9) that each causal justification statement was judged to be the most convincing for each profession. The results revealed that: (a) the lawyers chose the counterfactual causal justification statement to be the most convincing significantly more often than any other group; and (b) the psychologists chose the covariation causal justification statement to be the most convincing more often than the lawyers and the undergraduates, but not more often than police officers. Domain had no effect, nor did it interact with profession in any analysis. This finding suggests that lawyers and psychologists were convinced by justifications (counterfactual and covariation respectively) that were infrequently found to be convincing by novice adults.

More generally, the data in Fig. 7.2 suggest that the undergraduates and police had a three-tier hierarchy of preferences for the causal justification statements. Both novice groups most frequently used the mechanism justification to justify causation, followed by, in order, the covariation and the counterfactual justifica-

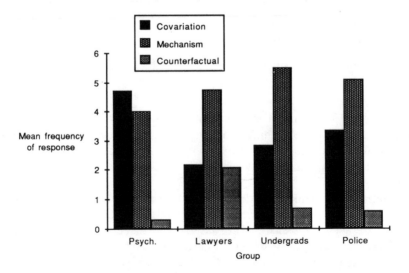

FIG. 7.2. Mean percent judgment across scenarios of the most convincing causal justification by group.

TABLE 7.1
Correlation coefficients between ratings of causal justifications and
evidence sentences (the evidence sentence that is
most highly correlated with a particular causal
justification statement is in boldface).

Evidence Sentences	Causal Justification Statements		
	Counter-factual	Covariation	Mechanism
Contextual	**.32**	.52	.34
	***p* < .01**[a]	*p* < .001	*p* = .004
Past Association	.30	**.68**	.28
	p = .01	***p* < .001**	*p* = .02
Mechanism	.23	.42	**.63**
	p = .057	*p* < .001	***p* < .001**
Irrelevant	.21	.08	.19
	p = .09	*p* = .51	*p* = .11

[a] 2-tailed tests.

tions. In contrast, the lawyers and psychologists had a two-tier hierarchy for justifying causal statements. The psychologists used the mechanism and the covariation causal justification statements equally frequently, followed by the counterfactual justification. The lawyers used the mechanism causal justification primarily, but secondarily used the covariation and the counterfactual justifications equally often. The interpretation of the data in terms of hierarchies of preferences for justifications confirmed the major hypothesis of the study that undergraduates and police professionals (adult novice groups) would have a similar organization of causal inference rules, but that their organization would be different from that of lawyers and psychologists, who in turn would differ in organization from each other.

To assess whether differences in ratings of justification statement convincingness reflected superficial linguistic or deeper information-processing differences, we examined Pearson product-moment correlations between convincingness ratings for the justification statements and relevance ratings for the evidence sentences (see Table 7.1). If differences in justification statement convincingness reflect linguistic preferences, then each causal justification statement should show the same pattern of correlation with the evidence sentences. Such a pattern of correlation would show that the variation in the convincingness ratings of each causal justification statement did not correspond to a unique pattern of ratings regarding the relevance of evidence sentences. On the other hand, if differences in justification statement convincingness reflect differences in how the evidence was processed, then each causal justification statement should show a unique pattern of correlation with the evidence sentences. Such a pattern of correlation would show that the variation in the convincingness ratings of each justification statement corresponds to a unique pattern of ratings regarding the relevance of evidence sentences. The pattern of correlation coefficients between ratings of evidence sentences and each causal statement revealed that of all the evidence sentences: (a) the contextual evidence sentence was most strongly correlated with the counterfactual statement; (b) the past association evidence sentence was most strongly correlated with the covariation statement; and (c) the mechanism evidence sentence was most strongly correlated with the mechanistic statement. None of the correlations between the convincingness ratings of causal justification statements and the relevance ratings of the irrelevant evidence sentence were significant. These data suggest that the best predictor of the variation in justification convincingness was the relevance rating for the corresponding evidence sentence. The data support the hypothesis that variation in ratings of statement convincingness reflect differences in how the evidence was processed.

Study 2: Replication

If the data in Fig. 7.2 are best described as different hierarchical patterns of preferences for justification statements, then subjects' preference judgments should be transitive. That is, if undergraduates employ the predicted three-tier preference hierarchy for justifying a sequence of events as causal, then they should prefer the mechanism justification over the covariation justification, the mechanism justification over the counterfactual justification, and the covariation justification over the counterfactual justification. We carried out a second study to test whether lawyers', psychologists', and undergraduates' preference hierarchies for causal justification statements would generate predicted transitive judgments. Eight second- and third-year law students, eight second- and third-year MA psychology students (mean age of 27 years for both groups), and eight first- and second-year undergraduates (mean age 19 years) served as subjects. The replication study paralleled the first study except that there were four scenarios in each domain (pretested as in Study 1 and found to be adequate) and the scenarios were presented on a microcomputer. Each scenario was presented and then three pairs of causal justification statements were presented in random order (e.g., mechanism vs. covariation, mechanism vs. counterfactual, covariation vs. counterfactual). The subjects' task was to choose the more convincing statement in each pair.

Represented below are the eight possible patterns that could be generated from a subject's response on each of the three comparisons to a scenario (the symbol "M > Co" means that the mechanism justification is judged to be more convincing that the covariation justification):

		Comparison		
	1	2	3	
	M ? C	M ? Cf	Co ? Cf	
Pattern #		Transitive		Label
1	M > Co	M > Cf	Co > Cf	M > Co > Cf
2	M > Co	M > Cf	Cf > Co	M > Cf > Co
3	Co > M	M > Cf	Co > Cf	Co > M > Cf
4	Co > M	Cf > M	Co > Cf	Co > Cf > M
5	M > Co	Cf > M	Cf > Co	Cf > M > Co
6	Co > M	Cf > M	Cf > Co	Cf > Co > M
		Intransitive		
7	Co > M	M > Cf	Cf > Co	Intrans
8	M > Co	Cf > M	Co > Cf	Intrans

Response patterns 7 and 8 are intransitive, meaning that each causal justification statement is judged once to be more convincing than another. For the purpose of analyses, patterns 7 and 8 were collapsed and treated as a single pattern. The six transitive response patterns (patterns 1–6) reflect different transitive judgments regarding the causal justification statements. In each of the six transitive patterns, one causal justification statement is selected twice as being "more convincing," another statement is selected once, and a third statement is not selected at all. The label given to transitive response patterns 1 through 6 has the symbol for the twice-selected justification presented first, followed by the symbol for the once-selected justification, and then the symbol for the justification not selected. Subjects were assigned a response pattern for each of the 12 scenarios.

Over 90% of subjects' response patterns were intransitive, suggesting that their preferences for causal justification statements were hierarchically organized. If subjects were randomly responding, then 75% ($\frac{6}{8}$) of their response patterns would be transitive. The rest of the analysis was performed on the percentage of transitive response patterns subjects generated. Fig. 7.3 presents mean percentage of transitive response patterns generated for subjects in each group.

The percentage with which each of the six response patterns were generated was not the same. A 3 (Groups) by 3 (Domains) by 6 (Response Patterns) ANOVA on the percentage of response patterns subjects generated revealed a main effect of response pattern. There was neither a group by response pattern nor a group by domain by response pattern interaction effect. An analysis of the simple main effects revealed that each group differentially generated response patterns at a level that was significant or approached significance (Psychologists: $p = .066$, Lawyers: $p = .049$, Undergraduates: $p < .001$).

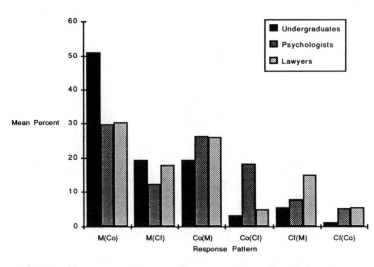

FIG. 7.3.   Mean percent generation across scenarios of the six transitive response patterns by group.

We analyzed whether specific response patterns generated by subjects were consistent with their predicted preference hierarchy for causal justification statements. It was predicted that undergraduates would generate a higher percentage of response pattern 1 than any other pattern. In response pattern 1, mechanism is preferred over covariation, covariation over counterfactual, and mechanism over counterfactual. As predicted, t-test[1] comparisons demonstrated that the percentage of response pattern 1 was significantly higher than each of the other five transitive response patterns (all p's < .01). This supports the interpretation that undergraduates have primarily a three-tier hierarchy of preferences for causal justifications, with the mechanism justification being preferred over covariation, and covariation over the counterfactual justification.

Psychology students' preference hierarchy for causal justifications was predicted to be two-tier with the covariation and the mechanism causal justification statements equally preferred and both preferred over the counterfactual justification statement. The psychology students generated a higher percentage of pattern 1 than patterns 5 and 6 (all p's < .05). However, unlike the undergraduates, the psychology students' percentage of pattern 1 was not different from their percentage of patterns 2, 3 and 4. Patterns 1 and 2 are those in which the mechanism

---

[1]We used t-tests because we wanted a sensitive measure of the difference between the frequency with which various response patterns were generated, despite the fact that the multiple comparisons increase Type II error. Our justification for this choice lies in the fact that only a subset of significant differences could be reasonably interpreted as consistent with the predicted hierarchical pattern of preferences. Thus, although not an a priori use of t-tests, there was a strong constraint in interpreting the results.

justification is the most convincing, whereas patterns 3 and 4 are the ones in which the covariation justification statement is the most convincing. Thus, as argued above, and by Cook and Campbell (1979, 1986), the psychologists judged covariation and mechanism as an effective justification of causation.

Law students' preference hierarchy was predicted to be two-tier, with the mechanism justification preferred over the counterfactual and covariation justification statements, which would be equally preferred. The law students' percentage of response pattern 1 was higher than patterns 4 and 6 (all p's < .05), suggesting that, unlike both the undergraduate and psychology students, the law students' frequency of generating pattern 1 was not different from their frequencies of generating patterns 2, 3, and 5. Thus, as predicted above, the mechanism justification (patterns 1 and 2) was used more often than the covariation (pattern 3) and counterfactual (pattern 5) justifications. This finding suggests that law students sometimes found each of the three causal justifications to be effective in justifying a sequence of events as causal.

SUMMARY AND CONCLUSIONS

The two studies presented were designed to examine a basic question regarding legal reasoning: whether lawyers have a unique style of problem solving. Rejecting the traditional expertise literature as unhelpful, and motivated by results from Lehman et al., who showed that psychologists but not lawyers demonstrate superior causal reasoning performance over the course of professional training, we examined whether psychologists and lawyers engage in causal inquiries differently. A review of the goals, structures, and process of legal, psychological, and everyday causal inquiry suggested one psychologically relevant source of variance between the three groups: their organizations of causal inference rules. To measure differences in lawyers', psychologists', and adults' organization of causal inference rules, we examined preferences for arguments justifying a sequence of events as causal.

The results of the two studies can be summarized by examining the four hypotheses previously presented. First, in Study 1, lawyers judged counterfactual justifications as the "most convincing" more often than any other group, and psychologists judged covariation justifications as "most convincing" more often than lawyers and undergraduates. This finding confirmed the hypothesis that there are differences between undergraduates and lawyers, undergraduates and psychologists, and lawyers and psychologists, in use of causal inference rules.

Study 1 also demonstrated that the best predictor of variation in ratings of each justification statement convincingness was the relevance ranking of the corresponding evidence sentence. This finding supported the claim that differences in the use of causal justifications reflect differences in the processing of evidence, and not merely differences in the manner of expressing that a sequence of events is causal. Moreover, there was no evidence in either study that the groups were differentially influenced by domain, suggesting that the causal hierarchies are domain-general.

Finally, the undergraduate and police groups (novice groups) had the same three-tier hierarchy of preferences for causal justifications, whereas the expert groups had different two-tier hierarchies, which was consistent with the claim that a control group of professionals, who are not trained in law or the social sciences, should reason like novices. The last finding was further confirmed by the subjects' preferences of response patterns in Study 2. The undergraduates preferred the response pattern in Study 2 that was the pattern identified in Study 1; they preferred (in order) the mechanism, covariation, and counterfactual justifications.

More generally, the results suggested that subjects' organization of causal inference rules was hierarchical in a manner consistent with Shultz (1982). Subjects' choices of convincing causal justifications could not be attributed to characteristics of the scenarios because pretesting insured that each causal justification was judged to be equally supported by the information in the scenarios. Thus, subjects' choices were preferences that we believe reflect the tendency to execute causal inference rules. However, the studies were not designed to test alternatives to Shultz's conceptualization (e.g., Cheng & Novick, 1989; Einhorn & Hogarth, 1986). Thus, we make no claim that the data support exclusively a hierarchical theory of the organization of causal inference rules. For one thing, the hierarchical organization may be adequate to explain the initial order of execution of causal inference rules. However, a complex causal problem may require the execution of multiple rules over time, and the search for consistency between inferences generated by different rules. Nonetheless, our data suggest that one principle of complex causal problem solving is that of the hierarchical organization of causal inference rules.

The results regarding the differences between the novice and expert groups' preferences for causal justifications are consistent with previous research on the novice-expert shift (cf., Chi et al., 1982). The hierarchies of lawyers and psychologists are more complex compared to that of undergraduate novices. Experts' hierarchies are more complex than novices' in that more kinds of causal justifications are seen as relevant by the experts and not by the novices, and the justifications are used in combination.

The results further suggest that lawyers' and psychologists' causal inference rules are organized differently. As discussed in the review of the goals, structures, and processes, the use of experiments as a basis of psychologists' goal of generating causal generalizations requires use of future-oriented and prognostic causal inference rules, which suggests a limited preference for context-based rules. Moreover, on the basis of Cook and Campbell's (1979, 1986) discussion of causal reasoning, it was predicted that the mechanism rule (to generate hypotheses and evaluate the internal and external validity of an experimental design) and the covariation rule (to evaluate statistical evidence) would be preferred. Such an organization of causal inference rules was demonstrated in Studies 1 and 2. In contrast, lawyers' goal of making causal inferences about particular event sequences required use of past-oriented and diagnostic causal inference rules, which suggests an increased preference for the counterfactual rule. However, on the basis of discussion of the limits of the "but-for" test of causation-in-fact, it was predicted that the other rules would be used as well. Lawyers generated multiple hierarchies of causal inference rules in Studies 1 and 2, thus lending support to this hypothesis.

The difference in the organization of causal inference rules among lawyers and psychologists is directly relevant to Lehman et al.'s (1988) argument that psychologists but not lawyers exercise causal reasoning schemas during graduate education. The findings of this study suggest that the processes of training in law and psychology induce professional differences in causal reasoning. Thus, Lehman et al. found a change in psychologists' and not lawyers' causal reasoning performance over graduate school because their task assessed a manner of causal reasoning trained exclusively in the social sciences. However, the data confirm a central point of Lehman et al., that professional education can induce general changes in reasoning. Our argument for the role of training in professional differences in causal reasoning is based on the similarity between the two novice groups (undergraduates and police professionals) in Study 1, and the difference between the novice groups and each expert group in Studies 1 and 2.

Undergraduates who go on to study law or psychology are trained not merely in the content of a discipline, but in a manner of reasoning characteristic of that discipline. Cross-sectional and longitudinal analyses of students in professional schools is necessary before inferences can be drawn about the precise role of professional education on the induction of causal inference rules. For example, research could examine whether the induction of a professionally-consistent manner of causal reasoning is a direct or indirect result of instruction. Nonetheless, the finding of differences between lawyers, psychologists, and professionally novice adults in causal reasoning is one step in a line of research that could demonstrate the uniqueness of legal logic. Causal reasoning is one of many domain-general inference rules that may vary across profession. Further research comparing lawyers with a variety of professionals on a multitude of inference rules may yet support Levi's (1948) epigrammatic comment about the uniqueness of legal logic.

ACKNOWLEDGMENTS

The research reported in this chapter was carried out by the third author, supervised by the first. Support by a SSHRCC postdoctoral fellowship, a University of Saskatchewan president's NSERC, and a NSERC operating grant to the first author is gratefully acknowledged. The authors would like to thank Judith Amsel, Jack Carroll, Michael Davidson, Peter Frensch, Leona Schauble, Bob Sternberg, and Ying Zhu for their help. Special appreciation is extended to Professor Lucinda Findley and the members of her Torts class (1986–1987) at the Yale Law School who allowed E.A. to audit.

REFERENCES

Amsel, E. (1989). *The development of scientific reasoning: Are children like scientists?* Unpublished manuscript, University of Saskatchewan.

Bindra, D., Clarke, K., & Shultz, T. R. (1980). Understanding predictive relations of necessity and sufficiency in formally equivalent "causal" and "logical" problems. *Journal of Experimental Psychology: General, 109,* 422–443.

Borgo, John. (1979). Causal paradigms in tort law. *Journal of Legal Studies, 8,* 419–455.

Bullock, M. (1985). Causal reasoning and developmental change over the preschool years. *Human Development, 29,* 169–191.

Bullock, M., Gelman, R., & Baillargeon, R. (1982). The development of causal reasoning. In W. Friedman (Ed.), *The developmental psychology of time* (pp. 209–254). New York: Academic Press.

Calabresi, G. (1975). Concerning cause and the law of torts: An essay for Harry Kalven, Jr. *University of Chicago Law Review, 43,* 69–101.

Carey, S. (1985a). *Conceptual change in childhood.* Cambridge, MA: MIT Press.

Carey, S. (1985b). Are children fundamentally different kinds of thinkers and reasoners than adults? In S. Chipman, J. Segal, & R. Glaser (Eds.), *Thinking and learning skills: Research and open questions* (Vol. 2, pp. 485–517). Hillsdale, NJ: Lawrence Erlbaum Associates.

Cheng, P., & Holyoak, K. (1985). Pragmatic reasoning schemes. *Cognitive Psychology, 17,* 391–416.

Cheng, P., & Novick, L. (1989). *Covariation and pragmatics: A qualitative contrast model of causal induction.* Unpublished manuscript, UCLA.

Chi, M., Glaser, R., & Rees, E. (1982). Expertise in problem solving. In R. J. Sternberg, (Ed.), *Advances in the psychology of human intelligence* (Vol. 1, pp. 7–75). Hillsdale, NJ: Lawrence Erlbaum Associates.

Collingwood, R. G. (1972). *Essay on metaphysics.* Chicago: Henry Regnery.

Cook, T., & Campbell, D. T. (1979). *Quasi-experimentation: Design and analysis issues for field settings.* Chicago: Rand McNally.

Cook, T., & Campbell, D. T. (1986). The causal assumptions of quasi-experimental practice. *Synthese, 68,* 141–180.

Cooper-Stephenson, K., & Saunders, D. (1981). *Personal injury damages in Canada.* Toronto: Carswell.

Einhorn, H. J., & Hogarth, R. M. (1986). Judging probable cause. *Psychological Bulletin, 99,* 3–19.

Epstein, R. (1973). A theory of strict liability. *Journal of Legal Studies, 2,* 151–204.

Faust, D. (1984). *The limits of scientific reasoning.* Minneapolis, MN: University of Minnesota Press.

Fincham, F. D., & Jaspers, J. M. (1980). Attribution of responsibility: From man the scientist to man the lawyer. In L. Berkowitz (Ed.), *Advances in experimental social psychology* (Vol. 13, pp. 81–138). New York: Academic Press.

Fishoff, B. (1976). Attribution theory and judgments under uncertainty. In J. H. Harvey, W. J.

Ickes, & R. F. Kidd (Eds.), *New directions in attribution research* (Vol. 1, pp. 421–452). Hillsdale, NJ: Lawrence Erlbaum Associates.

Golding, M. P. (1984). *Legal reasoning.* New York: Alfred Knopf.

Hamilton, V. L. (1980). Intuitive psychologist or intuitive lawyer? Alternative model of the attribution process. *Journal of Personality and Social Psychology, 39,* 767–772.

Hart, H. L. A., & Honore, T. (1985). *Causation in the law* (2nd ed.). Oxford: Oxford University Press.

Hofer, P. J. (1987). *Cognitive strategies for interpreting law.* Unpublished doctoral dissertation, Johns Hopkins University, Baltimore.

Holland, J., Holyoak, K., Nisbett, R., & Thagrad, P. (1987). *Induction: Processes of inference, learning, and discovery.* Cambridge, MA: MIT Press.

Jensen, O. C. (1957). *The nature of legal argument.* Oxford: Basil Blackwell.

Kahneman, D., Slovic, P., & Tversky, A. (1982). *Judgments under uncertainty: Heuristics and biases.* New York: Cambridge University Press.

Kahneman, D., & Tversky, A. (1982). The simulation heuristic. In D. Kahneman, P. Slovic, & A. Tversky (Eds.), *Judgments under uncertainty: Heuristics and biases* (pp. 201–210). New York: Cambridge University Press.

Kelley, H. H. (1967). Attribution theory in social psychology. In D. Levine (Ed.), *Nebraska symposium on motivation* (Vol. 15, pp. 192–238). Lincoln, NE: University of Nebraska Press.

Koslowski, B., & Okagaki, L. (1986). Non-Humian indices of causation in problem-solving situations: Causal mechanism, analogous effects, and the status of rival alternative accounts. *Child Development, 57,* 1100–1108.

Kuhn, D., Amsel, E., & O'Loughlin, M. (1988). *The development of scientific thinking skills.* Orlando, FL: Academic Press.

Kuhn, D., & Phelps, E. (1982). The development of problem-solving strategies. In H. Reese (Ed.), *Advances in child development and behavior* (Vol. 17, p. 5). New York: Academic Press.

Lawrence, J. A. (1988). Expertise on the bench: Modelling magistrates' judicial decision making. In M. T. Chi, R. Glaser, & M. J. Farr (Eds.), *The nature of expertise* (pp. 229–259). Hillsdale, NJ: Lawrence Erlbaum Associates.

Lehman, D., Lempert, R., & Nisbett, R. E. (1988). The effects of graduate training on reasoning: Formal discipline and thinking about everyday-life events. *American Psychologist, 43,* 431–442.

Leslie, A. M. (1987). Do six-month-old infants perceive causality? *Cognition, 25,* 265–288.

Levi, E. H. (1949). *An introduction to legal reasoning.* Chicago: University of Chicago Press.

Lundeberg, M. A. (1987). Metacognitive aspects of reading comprehension: Studying understanding in legal case analysis. *Reading Research Quarterly, 22,* 407–432.

Mackie, J. L. (1980). *The cement of the universe: A study of causation.* Oxford: Oxford University Press.

Malone, W. S. (1956). Ruminations on cause-in-fact. *Stanford Law Review, 9,* 60–99.

Nisbett, R., & Ross, L. (1980). *Human inference: Strategies and shortcomings of social judgment.* Englewood, NJ: Prentice-Hall.

Popper, K. (1965). *The logic of scientific discovery* (2nd ed.). New York: Harper & Row.

Ross, L. (1977). The intuitive scientist and his shortcomings: Distortions in the attribution process. In L. Berkowitz (Ed.), *Advances in experimental social psychology* (Vol. 10, pp. 173–220). New York: Academic Press.

Schauble, L. (1990). The role of prior knwoledge and strategies for generating evidence. *Journal of Experimental Child Psychology, 49,* 31–57.

Schustack, M. (1988). Thinking about causality. In R. J. Sternberg & E. E. Smith (Eds.), *The psychology of human thought.* New York: Cambridge University Press.

Sedlack, A., & Kurtz, S. (1981). A review of children's use of causal inference principles. *Child Development, 52,* 759–784.

Shaklee, H., & Tucker, D. (1980). A rule analysis of judgments of covariation between events. *Memory and Cognition, 8,* 459–467.

Shaklee, H., & Fishoff, B. (1982). Strategies of information search in causal analysis. *Memory and Cognition, 10,* 520–530.

Shaver, K. G. (1985). *The attribution of blame: Causality, responsibility, and blameworthiness.* New York: Springer-Verlag.

Shultz, T. R. (1979, July). *Causal and logical reasoning.* Paper presented at the International Congress of Psychology of the Child, Paris.

Shultz, T. R. (1982). Rules of causal attribution. *Monographs of the Society for Research in Child Development, 47,* (Serial No. 194).

Shultz, T. R. (1983, April). Causal and probablistic reasoning. In M. Bullock (Chair), *New directions in causal reasoning.* Symposium presented at the biennial meeting of the Society for Research in Child Development, Detroit.

Shultz, T. R., Fischer, G., Pratt, C., & Rulf, S. (1986). Selection of causal rules. *Child Development, 57,* 143–152.

Shultz, T. R., & Kestenbaum, M. (1985). Causal reasoning in children. In G. Whitehurst (Ed.), *Annals of child development* (Vol. 2, pp. 195–249). Greenwich, CT: JAI Press.

Shultz, T. R., & Schleifer, M. (1983). Towards a refinement of attribution concepts. In J. D. Jaspers, F. D. Fincham, & M. Hewstone (Eds.), *Attribution theory and research: Conceptual, developmental, and social dimensions* (pp. 37–62). London: Academic Press.

Shultz, T. R., Wright, K., & Schleifer, M. (1986). Assignment of moral responsibility and punishment. *Child Development, 57,* 177–184.

Siegler, R., & Shrager, J. (1984). Strategy choices in addition and subtraction: How do children know what to do? In C. Sophian (Ed.), *Origins of cognitive skills: The Eighteenth Annual Carnegie Symposium on Cognition* (pp. 229–293). Hillsdale, NJ: Lawrence Erlbaum Associates.

Simon, H. A. (1981). *The science of the artificial* (2nd ed). Cambridge, MA: MIT Press.

Strachan, D. M. A. (1970). The scope and application of the "but-for" causal test. *Modern Law Review, 33,* 386–395.

Thomson, J. J. (1987). Causality and rights. *Chicago-Kent Law Review, 63,* 471–496.

von Wright, G. H. (1971). *Explanation and understanding.* Ithaca, NY: Cornell University Press.

Weiner, B. (1985). "Spontaneous" causal thinking. *Psychological Bulletin, 97,* 74–84.

Weinrib, E. J. (1975). A step forward in factual causation. *Modern Law Review, 38,* 518–534.

Wells, G., & Gavanski, I. (1989). Mental simulation of causation. *Journal of Personality and Social Psychology, 56,* 161–169.

Wells, G., Taylor, B. R., & Turtle, J. W. (1987). The undoing of scenarios. *Journal of Personality and Social Psychology, 53,* 421–430.

Wollert, R., & Rowley, J. (1987). Concurrent and longitudinal patterns among sanctions, mood, and attributions. *Journal of Personality and Social Psychology, 53,* 608–613.

Williams, G. (1961). Causation in the law. *Cambridge Law Journal,* 62–85.

Wright, R. W. (1985a). Actual causation vs. probabilistic linkage: The bane of economic analysis. *Journal of Legal Studies, 14,* 435–456.

Wright, R. W. (1985b). Causation in tort law. *California Law Review, 73,* 1735–1828.

NATURAL SCIENCES

8 Knowledge and Processes in Mechanical Problem Solving

Mary Hegarty
University of California, Santa Barbara

When a golfer figures out how hard to hit a golf ball, when a car mechanic diagnoses what is wrong with a faulty brake system, and when a physicist formulates a theory of the motion of the planets, all are solving mechanical problems. All of these problems involve forces acting on objects, causing them to move. This is the subject matter of mechanics. This chapter provides both a general account of mechanical problem solving and a discussion of the different knowledge and processes used to solve diverse types of mechanical problems.

The chapter has three major themes. One theme is the knowledge required to solve mechanical problems. In examining this knowledge, we are particularly concerned with understanding which knowledge is *specific* to problem solving in the mechanics domain and which knowledge is more *general* to all types of problem solving. Not only can knowledge be specific to the mechanics domain, but it can also be specific to particular problems within mechanics. I make distinctions between different types of mechanical problems, and the knowledge that is required to solve these different types of problems.

A second theme of the chapter is the information-processing mechanisms that are involved in solving mechanics problems. One of the most important mechanisms that I examine is that of finding the knowledge relevant to solving a particular type of problem. I also examine the role of spatial information-processing mechanisms for solving mechanical problems. Because motion takes place over space and time, spatial information processes may be more central to solving mechanical problems than to other types of problems.

The third theme of the chapter is the development of problem-solving ability in mechanics. I consider mechanical problem-solving processes not as static processes, but as processes that change and develop as a person gains more experience with mechanical phenomena. I examine how a person's conceptual knowledge of mechanical principles and his or her problem-solving mechanisms develop with such experience. Finally, I review some recent research that draws on these developmental results to design more effective methods of instruction for students of mechanics.

BASIC PRINCIPLES

Principles of Problem Solving

Before examining problem solving in the *specific* domain of mechanics, it is worthwhile to review some *general* principles of problem solving that have been established in previous research, and that I take for granted in the remainder of the chapter.

General Principles of Problem Solving

A problem has three main components: a given state, a goal state, and a set of operators for transforming the given state into the goal state (Newell & Simon, 1972). So, for example, if the problem is to diagnose what is wrong with your car engine, the given state is the fact that your car will not start; the goal state is the identification of the faulty component; and the operators include actions such as looking under the hood of the car, reading the car manual, and relating the particular symptoms of the fault to your knowledge of different components of a car engine. In this theoretical framework, the process of solving a problem is essentially one of searching for a set of operators that allows you to get from the given state of the problem to the goal state.

Problem Solving in Semantically Rich Domains

In a *semantically rich* domain, such as mechanics, problem solving involves searching one's knowledge of the domain in addition to the problem statement, in order to find the operators necessary for solving the problem. Research on the use of knowledge in problem solving in several different domains, for example, in chess (Chase & Simon, 1973; de Groot, 1965), in mechanics (Chi, Feltovich, & Glaser, 1981; Larkin, McDermott, Simon, & Simon, 1980), in computer programming (Adelson, 1984; Jeffries, Turner, Polson, & Atwood, 1981) and in social studies (Voss, Greene, Post, & Penner, 1983) suggests that people use two types of domain-specific knowledge to solve problems: *conceptual* knowledge and *procedural* knowledge.

Conceptual knowledge is knowledge of the principles of the domain. This knowledge is used to elaborate the basic statement of a problem, so that the start state for a given problem may include not only the basic information given in the problem statement, but also the solver's interpretation of this information, which is elaborated by his or her knowledge of the domain. For example, in solving a textbook physics problem, an expert physics problem solver might recognize that a situation described in the problem involves the principle of conservation of energy. His or her representation of the problem would then be elaborated to include knowledge of this physics principle (Chi et al., 1981).

Procedural knowledge is knowledge of how to carry out operations, that is, mechanisms of problem solving. One example of a general problem solving procedure is means-end analysis, which involves assessing the difference between the current problem state and the goal state, and choosing an operator that will reduce that difference (Newell & Simon, 1972). In addition to such general problem solving procedures, people develop specialized procedures for solving problems in domains with which they are familiar. For example, a basic procedure for solving a physics problem might be to draw a force diagram, identifying all the forces operating in the mechanical system that is asked about in the problem (Heller & Reif, 1984).

Conceptual and procedural knowledge of a domain can be thought of as organized into problem schemata, which are general frameworks of knowledge that correspond to categories of problems. Problem solving in complex domains has been characterized as finding an appropriate problem schema in long-term memory, and filling in this schema with the specific parameters of the problem at hand (Chi et al., 1981; Chi, Glaser, & Rees, 1982; Hinsley, Hayes, & Simon, 1977). The problem schema that is retrieved in any particular case is a crucial determinant of how the problem is solved because it determines what conceptual knowledge is used to elaborate the problem statement, and what procedures are used to solve the problem.

The foregoing account of problem solving could apply to any semantically rich domain. But what is specific to solving mechanical problems? To answer this question, we must first examine the nature of mechanical principles and mechanical problems.

Principles of Mechanics

Motion is typically described at the level of mechanical systems. Mechanical systems are made up of *components,* each of which can be in a number of different *states.* Motion arises from the *interaction of components* in a mechanical system. That is, the states of each component are constrained by the states of the other components with which it comes in contact. These interactions can be described as *kinematic* relations, that is, the relations between the motions of connected components. They can also be described as *dynamic* or kinetic relations, that is, in terms of the forces that the different components exert on each other.

To illustrate these points, take, for example, a type of simple machine, a pulley system, as shown in Fig. 8.1. This pulley system is made up of two pulleys, a rope, and a weight. These components can be in different states. For example, the upper pulley can be either stationary, moving clockwise, or moving counterclockwise. The state of each component is constrained by the states of the other components with which it comes in contact. For example, pulling the rope causes the upper pulley to move in a clockwise direction as the rope moves over this pulley. Understanding how the pulley system works is largely a matter of understanding the relations among its components.

The dynamics of the system can be described as follows. If the system is in equilibrium, the sum of the upward forces at any point in the system is equal to the sum of the downward forces. If a person exerts a unit force on the pull rope, there will be a force equal to two units acting on the weight because there are two rope strands pulling up on the weight, one on either side of the movable pulley. Thus, a person could support a 20 lb weight by exerting a force of 10 lbs on the rope of this pulley system. The ratio of the weight to be lifted to the effort exerted to lift this weight is the mechanical advantage of the pulley system. This pulley system has a mechanical advantage of 2.

Examples of Mechanical Problems

Now consider the three different problems about pulley systems that are presented in Fig. 8.2.

The Bale of Hay problem is a practical problem in a real-world context. This problem has several distinctive characteristics that contrast it with the other mechanical problems in Fig. 8.2. First, the solution does not have to be exact. That is, it does not matter if the boy ends up pulling the rope with a force of 16 or 17 lbs, rather than 20, once the force needed is no more than 20 lbs. Second, in deciding what configuration of pulleys to use, the boy has to take into account the weight of the pulleys because, depending on the configuration he chooses, he may have to pull up some pulleys as well as the 60 lb bale. He might also have to consider whether the pulleys are rusty, or whether the rope is rough; both factors

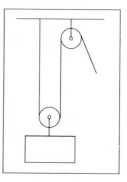

FIG. 8.1. A pulley system.

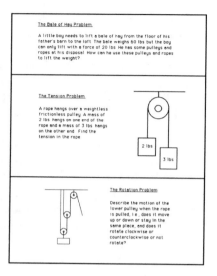

The Bale of Hay Problem

A little boy needs to lift a bale of hay from the floor of his father's barn to the loft. The bale weighs 60 lbs but the boy can only lift with a force of 20 lbs. He has some pulleys and ropes at his disposal. How can he use these pulleys and ropes to lift the weight?

The Tension Problem

A rope hangs over a weightless frictionless pulley. A mass of 2 lbs. hangs on one end of the rope and a mass of 3 lbs hangs on the other end. Find the tension in the rope

2 lbs

3 lbs

The Rotation Problem

Describe the motion of the lower pulley when the rope is pulled, i.e., does it move up or down or stay in the same place, and does it rotate clockwise or counterclockwise or not rotate?

FIG. 8.2. Examples of three different types of mechanical problems involving pulley systems.

that would add to friction in the system. Finally, there are several practical subproblems that the boy has to solve, such as how to attach the pulleys to the ceiling of the barn.

The Tension problem is a typical problem from an introductory physics text. The first thing we notice about this problem is that it is stated in terms of physics concepts such as mass and tension so that knowledge of these concepts is necessary to solve the problem. Second, unlike the Bale of Hay problem, this problem requires a precise, quantitative answer. Finally, this problem describes an ideal world in which such real-world factors as pulley weight and friction can be ignored.

The Rotation problem is different again in that the goal state of this problem is information about the kinematics of the pulley system rather than the system dynamics. This problem has one correct answer, but the answer is qualitative rather than quantitative. That is, it asks about a general direction of motion of the pulley rather than a precise speed of motion. The most striking feature of this problem is that it is very visual. When people solve this type of problem they often report having the experience of "mentally animating" a representation of the pulley system.

These examples demonstrate that there are many different types of mechanical problems. These problems can be classified as everyday mechanical problems that can be solved on the basis of common sense knowledge of how objects move in the physical world, and formal problems that require knowledge of the science of mechanics. The Bale of Hay problem and the Rotation problem are examples of everyday mechanics problems, whereas the Tension problem is a formal problem.

Earlier studies of mechanical problem solving focused on the solution of formal problems (Chi et al., 1981; Larkin, McDermott, Simon, & Simon, 1980; Simon & Simon, 1978). More recently, researchers have been interested in characterizing informal knowledge of mechanics and how this knowledge is used in problem solving (e.g., diSessa, 1983; McCloskey, Caramazza, & Green, 1980; White, 1983). This movement reflects both a general interest in understanding cognition in everyday, practical situations (Brown, Collins, & Duguid, 1989; Rogoff & Lave, 1984; Sternberg & Wagner, 1986) and the insight that expert problem solving is often based on informal knowledge in addition to the formal quantitative laws of mechanics (Bobrow, 1985; deKleer & Brown, 1984; Forbus, 1984; Roschelle & Greeno, 1987).

In the remainder of this chapter, I consider the knowledge of mechanical principles and the information-processing mechanisms that are used in solving these different types of problems, examining which knowledge and mechanisms are specific to particular problem types, and which are more general.

CONCEPTUAL KNOWLEDGE OF MECHANICS PRINCIPLES

The account of mechanical principles suggests that in order to understand a mechanical system, one has to know what its basic components are, the possible states of these components, and how these components are interrelated. Furthermore, the relations between components can be described purely in terms of their motions, or in terms of the forces that bring about these motions.

Knowledge of the relations between components of a mechanical system allow people to predict and mentally simulate the behavior of mechanical systems. Such knowledge can be characterized as empirical rules stating relations among the system configuration, kinematics, and dynamics. For example, a rule relating configuration and kinematics is the rule that if two gears are interlocking, and one of the gears is rotating, then the other gear must be rotating in the opposite direction. This type of knowledge is sometimes called a *mental model* of a mechanical system (Gentner & Stevens, 1983). Although the term mental model is not well defined in the literature (see Rips, 1986), it is an appropriate term to denote conceptual understanding of mechanical systems, because it emphasizes that this knowledge allows the problem solver to internally model the behavior of dynamic systems.

Mental models can encompass a variety of different levels of understanding. They can be specific to a particular type of machine, or more general, and they can represent mechanical systems quantitatively or qualitatively. For example, Newton's theory of mechanics might be thought of as a very general, quantitative mental model of mechanical phenomena. To solve problems such as the Bale of Hay problem, the Tension problem, and the Rotation problem in Fig. 8.2, one calls on different types of mental models of mechanical phenomena; I now discuss the nature and origins of these knowledge types.

Types of Conceptual Knowledge of Mechanics

People accumulate knowledge of mechanical principles from three sources. First, they learn about motion and mechanical phenomena just by observing the way objects move in our everyday environment. I use the term *intuitive knowledge* to refer to this type of knowledge of mechanical principles. A second type of knowledge stems from active interactions with machines, for example, activities such as operating and learning to diagnose faults in machines. I use the term *practical knowledge* to refer to this type of knowledge. Third, people accumulate knowledge of mechanical principles by taking physics courses that deal with theoretical principles of mechanics. I use the term *theoretical knowledge* to refer to this type of knowledge.

What are the differences between these types of knowledge? What are their origins? What types of problems can they be used to solve? In this section, I examine intuitive, practical, and theoretical knowledge with respect to these questions.

Intuitive Knowledge of Mechanical Principles

The earliest and most basic knowledge of mechanical principles is derived from an individual's observations of moving objects in his or her environment. These intuitions about motion are constructed as part of the individual's attempt to make sense of their environment. For example, one such mechanical principle might be the rule that a force applied to an object, such as a ball, usually causes the object to move in the direction of the force. The construction process is essentially one of inducing rules of mechanical reasoning from the specific examples of motion phenomena that are observed in the everyday world. Research on intuitive knowledge of mechanical principles has been concerned with its origins, accuracy, and consistency.

Origins of Mechanical Intuitions.

Intuitions about motion seem to originate as memories of prototypical mechanical events and later become more abstract causal rules (diSessa, 1983; Forbus & Gentner, 1986; Hardiman, Pollatsek, & Well, 1986; Kaiser, McCloskey, & Proffitt, 1986; Kaiser, Proffitt, & McCloskey, 1985). This developmental progression can be illustrated by some interesting data on the development of children's understanding of the trajectories of moving objects. Take, for example, the situation of the ball released from a curved tube shown in Fig. 8.3. Young children (preschool and kindergarten children) typically predict correctly that the ball will move in a straight line once released (61% correct responses), as

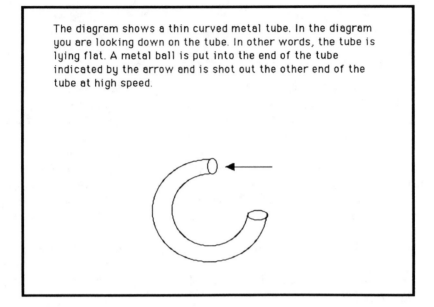

The diagram shows a thin curved metal tube. In the diagram you are looking down on the tube. In other words, the tube is lying flat. A metal ball is put into the end of the tube indicated by the arrow and is shot out the other end of the tube at high speed.

FIG. 8.3.   A problem used by McCloskey (1983a, 1983b; McCloskey et al., 1980) to assess subjects' naive intuitions about motion. Subjects are asked to predict the trajectory of the ball when it emerges from the tube.

do the majority of college students (65%). However, older children (grades one through six) typically predict that the ball will move in a curved line (Kaiser, McCloskey, & Profitt, 1986), so that this age group has a correct-response rate of only 25%.

Kaiser, McCloskey, and Profitt (1986) suggest that young children deal with the problem at a concrete level, perhaps thinking about other situations in which they observed a ball rolling. Older children have begun to formulate general rules of motion, for example, the rule that an object set in motion will continue to move in the same path for some time; however, they overgeneralize these rules. Later development of mechanical rules might involve understanding their conditions of applicability. Thus, the development of empirical rules of motion follows a u-shaped curve, similar to that which has been observed in the development of linguistic rules (cf. Brown, 1973).

Accuracy of Mechanical Intuitions

Because naive mechanical rules are abstracted from experience, they are affected by the limitations of the perceptual system. Objects in the physical world often move too fast to accurately observe their trajectories, or are judged against the wrong frame of reference. For example, an object dropped from a moving object (e.g., an airplane) is often erroneously judged to fall straight down, because its motion is compared to the frame of reference of the airplane rather than the environment (McCloskey, 1983a). These frame-of-reference errors also affect the development of conceptions of motion. Thus, slower developmental progressions have been observed in understanding the trajectories of objects dropping from moving objects than from stationary objects (Kaiser et al., 1985).

Possibly as a result of these perceptual limitations, intuitive theories of motion are best described as rules of thumb that provide an approximate account of many motion phenomena but do not predict the motions of objects consistently (Holland, Holyoak, Nisbett, & Thagard, 1986; White, 1983). The impetus model of motion (McCloskey, 1983a) is a good example of a naive mental model having these properties. This model accounts for the general observation that when a force is applied to an object, it tends to continue to move in the direction of the force for some time; an observation that can be derived from many different experiences, such as throwing a ball in the air, hitting a golf ball, or riding a bicycle. The impetus model of motion explains these phenomena in terms of a force or "impetus" that becomes internal to the moving object and that gradually dissipates. This model is common among people with no training in theoretical mechanics and was the dominant theory of motion in the Middle Ages.

The impetus model is clearly a good qualitative description of many motion phenomena. However, it leads to several erroneous predictions about motion. For example, it implies that if an object is moving in a certain direction, it must be subject to a force in that direction. People holding this theory say that in the situation shown in Fig. 8.4, there is an upward force acting on the ball while it is

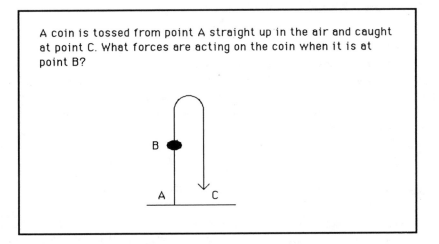

A coin is tossed from point A straight up in the air and caught at point C. What forces are acting on the coin when it is at point B?

FIG. 8.4.   A problem used by Clement (1983) to assess subjects' naive intuitions of motion.

rising (Clement, 1983), whereas in reality, the only force acting on the ball at this stage is gravity, which is a downward force.

Inconsistencies in Intuitive Mental Models

Intuitive mental models are often specific to situations with particular surface features, so that they lead people to make different predictions about situations which are physically similar. For example, when asked to predict the trajectory of an object emerging from a curved tube (see Fig. 8.3), many people predict a curved trajectory when the object is a ball, but predict a correct straight trajectory when the situation is described as water emerging from a curved hose (Kaiser, Jonides, & Alexander, 1986). Such inconsistencies suggest that intuitive mental models often retain some of the surface characteristics of the situations from which they are induced.

Mitchell and Pellegrino (in preparation) investigated the consistency of misconceptions of motion by analyzing subjects' error patterns over a variety of different problems, previously demonstrated to elicit incorrect models. They found that many individuals were inconsistent in the models that they appeared to apply to these problems. For example, among the 22 subjects who made most errors in their study, 16 could not be characterized as using a single incorrect model more than two-thirds of the time, and these subjects used 3.8 different mental models, on average, to generate their incorrect solutions. These data suggest that subjects' incorrect mental models are tied to surface features of problems, rather than reflecting a single incorrect mental model, such as the impetus model.

Practical Knowledge of Mechanics

A second source of knowledge of mechanical principles stems from people's interactions with machines. These interactions allow a person to understand mechanical principles on a more practical level. That is, they lead to an understanding of how mechanical principles can be applied to performing particular functions such as multiplying force, multiplying speed, or changing the direction of force. Whereas intuitive theories of mechanics are often characterized as "naive physics," this type of knowledge is more like "naive engineering." Practical mechanical problems include problems of operating, troubleshooting, and designing machinery. The Bale of Hay problem in Fig. 8.2 is a design problem—it requires the problem solver to design a configuration of pulleys and ropes that will allow the boy to perform a specific function: lifting the 60 lb bale of hay.

Practical mechanics problems have a long history of research in the psychometric tradition. However, the psychometric movement was concerned with developing tests that would predict performance in mechanical occupations such as machine assembly, and repair (Bennett, 1969; Ghiselli, 1955; Vernon & Parry, 1949), rather than characterizing the type of mechanical knowledge that is used to solve these practical problems. Recently, researchers have been more interested in understanding the nature of people's conceptual knowledge of machines and how they use this conceptual knowledge in mechanical reasoning and problem solving (deKleer & Brown, 1983; Forbus, 1984; Hegarty, Just, & Morrison, 1988; Mayer, 1989).

Causal Models of Mechanical Systems

It has been argued that knowledge of practical mechanical principles takes the form of *causal models* of specific machines or devices (deKleer & Brown, 1984; Forbus, 1984; Hegarty et al., 1988; Lancaster & Kolodner, 1987; Mayer, in press). These models contain rules stating causal relations among the components of the machine, which describe how these components work together to achieve the function of the machine. For example, a causal model of the cam-driven valve in Fig. 8.5 is described as follows:

When the cam shaft rotates, the high point—lobe—of the cam raises the valve to its open position. As the shaft continues to rotate, the high point of the cam is

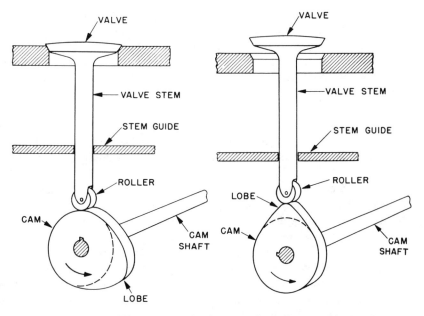

FIG. 8.5.   Two different states in the operation of a cam-driven valve (Bureau of Naval Personnel, 1971).

passed and the valve is lowered to its closed position. (Bureau of Naval Personnel, 1971, p. 36)

Causal models can differ in the *depth of understanding* that they characterize (Miyake, 1986). Understanding a mechanical system on one level often involves discovering a lower-level mechanism. In her studies of people's causal models of a sewing machine, Miyake found that people's understanding of a function of the machine at one level (e.g., making stitches) was explained in terms of a mechanism at a lower level (e.g., the looping of the upper thread around the lower thread). But this looping mechanism is itself a function that must be explained in terms of a lower-level mechanism. Forbus and Gentner (1986) have proposed that with experience, mental models progress from being purely descriptive to including understanding of the lower level mechanisms or processes that bring about the behavior of the system.

Effects of Causal Models on Problem-Solving Performance

Success in problem solving about mechanical systems is related to the quality of the problem solver's causal model of the system. In a series of studies involving problem solving about different types of machines, Mayer and his colleagues (see Mayer, 1989) have influenced the quality of subjects' causal models of machines by giving them different descriptions of how these machines work. For example, one group of subjects might be given labelled diagrams of a mechanical system, such as a bicycle pump, along with a description of the causal chain of events when the handle of the pump is pushed. Another group might be given only information about the components of the system. Giving subjects a description of the causal chain of events in the system enabled them to answer practical problems, such as how to make a pump more reliable, or more effective, or how to diagnose when a pump is not functioning properly. Similarly, in the domain of electronics, Kieras and Bovair (1984) have found that giving subjects a causal model of how an electronic device works enhances their ability to operate the device.

Why do such causal models enhance the solution of practical problems? One possibility is that these models encompass a deeper understanding of a mechanical system by specifying the underlying processes or mechanisms by which the machines achieve their function, rather than merely stating the input and output of the system (Forbus & Gentner, 1986; Miyake, 1986). A related possibility is that these models allow people to mentally image the motion of the components of the device as it operates (deKleer & Brown, 1983). I take up this suggestion later in the chapter when I discuss spatial information-processing mechanisms for solving mechanical problems.

Theoretical Knowledge of Mechanical Principles

Through formal instruction in physics, people are introduced to the concepts of motion phenomena that reflect the cumulative knowledge of the science of mechanics. In this context, they learn to analyze mechanical situations at a highly abstract, general, and precise level (Heller & Reif, 1984; Reif & Heller, 1982). The basic units of analysis in theoretical concepts of motion are particles and systems. Particles are objects sufficiently small or simple to be adequately described by geometric points, and systems are objects consisting of a number of interacting particles.

Through formal instruction, people also learn the meaning of precise concepts such as mass, tension, and acceleration. Finally, they learn a system of quantitative mechanical principles, such as Newton's laws, that specify how the motions of particles and systems change as a function of their interactions. These laws are general in that they can account for all motion in the universe, from the motion of planets and stars in space to the motions of atomic and subatomic particles.

Organization of Theoretical Knowledge

People with different levels of expertise in theoretical mechanics have been found to differ in the organization of their theoretical knowledge (Chi et al., 1981). Expert knowledge is organized into problem schemata that are based on specific physics principles (e.g., the principle of conservation of energy), and include procedures for solving problems that are based on these principles. In contrast, novices appear not to have problem schemata, or have schemata based on surface features of problems, such as whether a problem involves a pulley or an inclined plane. These conclusions are primarily based on how experts and novices categorize different types of problems. Later in the chapter, I examine how the organization of knowledge into problem schemata affects problem-solving efficiency.

Summary

In summary, everyday observations of motion, interactions with mechanical systems, and formal physics instruction lead to qualitatively different types of knowledge of mechanical phenomena. Mechanical intuitions, constructed from our everyday experiences, can be described as causal, qualitative, general rules. These rules are often situation specific, they are not always a completely accurate account of motion phenomena, and they can contradict each other. Practical knowledge of mechanics is best described as a set of causal models of specific mechanical systems, which specify how the components of these systems interact to achieve the function of the system. Theoretical knowledge is quantitative, applies to all motion phenomena, and is based on theoretical concepts. In the next section of the chapter, I discuss how people apply these different types of knowledge to solving mechanical problems.

MECHANISMS OF MECHANICAL PROBLEM SOLVING

Problem-solving mechanisms transform the given state of a problem into its goal state by operating on the information stated in the problem and the problem solver's conceptual knowledge of mechanics. In this review of problem-solving mechanisms, I focus on two types of processes that are particularly important to mechanical problem solving: processes for manipulating spatial information and processes for accessing the relevant conceptual and procedural knowledge to solve a problem.

Spatial Mechanisms in Mechanical Problem Solving

Given that mechanics concerns the movement of objects in space, one would expect problem solvers to make extensive use of spatial representations and spatial processes when solving mechanical problems. This may be the basis of a consistent finding in the psychometric literature, that spatial and mechanical ability are highly correlated (Bennett, 1969; Smith, 1964). In this section, I discuss how problem solvers operate on spatial representations to solve mechanical problems.

There are at least two ways in which spatial representations can be used in solving mechanical problems. First, a spatial representation can serve as an index of the information relevant to solving a problem. Second, a problem solver can operate on a static spatial representation of a mechanical system to infer the kinematics and dynamics of the system.

Spatial Representations as Indices to Information

One advantage of a spatial representation is that it can allow information to be grouped in a way that reduces search for relevant information in a problem. Larkin and Simon (1987) proposed that spatial representations have this property because they allow information to be indexed by location. Information that must be related in solving the problem is often present at the same location in the representation, whereas cues to the next logical step in a problem may be present in an adjacent location.

This property of spatial representations makes them particularly suitable for solving mechanical problems. In a mechanical system, the interactions between components depend on their configuration, that is, their relative locations in space. Components that affect each other's motions are typically connected. A particularly useful strategy in determining a property of a component in a mechanical system is to gather information about the states of the other system components with which it is connected.

Spatial representations can be used as indices to the information in any type of mechanical problem. Larkin and Simon (1987) used computer simulation to demonstrate that a spatial representation of the problem considerably reduced search in solving a textbook physics problem. It is easy to imagine that a process of tracing the interactions of contiguous components might also reduce search in a more practical problem such as troubleshooting. Furthermore, this property of spatial representations is not specific to mechanics problems. For example, spatial representations are useful indices of information in geometry (Larkin & Simon, 1987), and planning in computer programming (Reiser, Ranney, Lovett, & Kimberg, 1989).

Inferring the Behavior of Mechanical Systems

The process of inferring how a mechanical system operates is another type of problem-solving mechanism that can involve spatial information processing. This process uses knowledge of the spatial and mechanical constraints among the components of the system to infer how these components behave when the system is in operation, that is, infer a causal model of the system. The process of inferring the behavior of a system is central to many types of mechanical tasks, such as machine operation, fault diagnosis, and machine design. For example, a mechanic diagnosing a fault in a device has to envision the correct functioning of the different components of a machine in order to determine which component is not functioning correctly.

There have been several theoretical accounts of how individuals infer the kinematics and dynamics of mechanical systems from information about their structure (e.g., de Kleer & Brown, 1983, 1984; Nielsen, 1988; Stanfill, 1983). For example, in de Kleer and Brown's scheme, this ability involves two processes. One process, which they call *envisioning*, operates on a representation of the structure of the device to infer how each component of the device affects the other components with which it comes in contact. The resulting representation corresponds to a causal model of a mechanical system. A second process, *running*, uses these functional relations to mentally simulate the operation of the device.

Spatial Processes in Inferring System Behavior.   The accounts of several highly successful engineers suggest that they rely on spatial information processing in their problem solving. These engineers report that they design machines by imaging the configuration of components of the machine and mentally tracing the stages of the dynamic process (Ferguson, 1977; Shepard, 1978). For example, Oliver Evans, who invented the automatic flour mill, reported that he first put the system together in his head, mentally imaging the operation of the device (Ferguson, 1977). A particularly extreme account suggests that the inventor Tesla, before constructing a physical machine, would first run a mental model of the device for weeks in order to determine what parts were most subject to wear (O'Neill, 1944; Shepard, 1978). Accounts such as these led Sir Francis Galton to conclude that inventive mechanics "invent their machines as they walk, and see them in height, breadth, and depth as real objects, and they can also see them in action" (Galton, 1907, p. 78; Ferguson, 1977).

The spatial nature of mechanical problem-solving processes is also supported by research on how people construct mental models of mechanical systems by reading text accompanied by diagrams (Hegarty, 1988; Hegarty & Just, 1989). In these studies, subjects' eye fixations were monitored as they read a text and diagram describing the configuration and kinematics of simple mechanical systems like the pulley system shown in Fig. 8.1. The system behavior was described in the text accompanying the diagram. By observing subjects' diagram inspections as they constructed mental models of the mechanical systems, Hegarty and Just could infer the extent to which this construction process involved spatial information processing.

Subjects frequently interrupted their reading of the text to inspect the diagram, suggesting that inspection of the spatial representation in the diagram was an important process in their construction of an internal representation of the device. The majority of these diagram inspections (about 80%) were on the components of the mechanical system described in the most recent section of text read, suggesting that subjects inspected the diagram either to construct a spatial representation of the most recent section of text read, or to check this representation. Furthermore, subjects spent more time inspecting the diagram after reading clauses describing the kinematics of the system than after clauses describing the system configuration. Hegarty (1988) has proposed that this extra time was required to mentally animate the static representation of the pulley system to construct a representation of the kinematics of the system.

Knowledge in Inferring System Behavior.   A central question regarding how individuals infer the motions of components of mechanical systems is whether this process is purely one of spatial visualization, or whether it is dependent on specific knowledge of mechanics. On one hand, the ability to determine the relative directions of motion of interlocking gears in a gear chain (such as those shown in Fig. 8.6A) does not seem to depend on specific knowledge of gears. On the other hand, relatively simple kinematic events, such as the direction of rotation of a yoyo when the string is pulled, shown in Fig. 8.6B, are counterintuitive (Anzai & Yokoyama, 1984; diSessa, 1983), so that determining the correct direction of rotation is dependent on the analysis of forces in the situation.

Several sources of evidence suggest that the ability to infer the kinematics and dynamics of a mechanical system is influenced by knowledge. One source of

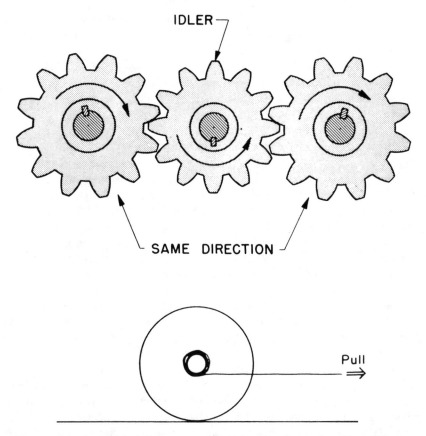

FIG. 8.6.   (a) Diagram of a gear chain, showing that successive gears rotate in opposite directions. (b) Diagram of a yoyo used by diSessa (1983) to study intuitive understanding of motion. Subjects are asked to predict which way the yoyo will roll on being pulled.

evidence comes from studies of how people construct representations of mechanical systems by reading text and diagrams. Another comes from studies of how people evaluate animated diagrams of mechanical systems.

The effects of knowledge on construction of the representation of a mechanical system is evident in situations in which the system is not described adequately in the text, so that individuals cannot depend on the text to direct their diagram processing. Subjects with low mechanical ability spend less time inspecting the diagram in these situations, suggesting that these subjects are unable to extract information from a diagram alone, that is, without direction from an accompanying text. In contrast, high-ability subjects appear to compensate for the omission of relevant information from the text (Hegarty & Just, 1989) and disorganization of the information in the text (Hegarty, 1988) by increasing the time they spend inspecting the diagram. Consequently, their comprehension is less impaired.

A recent study in my laboratory suggests that low-ability subjects have most difficulty extracting kinematic information from a diagram alone. In this study, subjects were given either a text alone, a diagram alone, or text and diagrams describing a mechanical system. They were later asked questions about the configuration and kinematics of these systems. Low-ability subjects who had studied only diagrams of the mechanical systems were severely limited in their ability to answer questions about the kinematics of the systems in this comprehension test. They answered only 18.7% of the comprehension questions correctly, compared to an average of 51% correct for low-ability subjects who had studied both the text and diagram. High-ability subjects showed a similar decrement in comprehension (from 80% correct to 49.5% correct) when the text was omitted, although their comprehension scores were higher in general.

Further evidence for the importance of knowledge in inferring kinematic information can be seen in studies of how individuals evaluate animated diagrams of mechanical systems. Fallside (1988) presented subjects with animated diagrams of a pulley system. In some of the displays, the motion of one of the components was inconsistent with the motions of the other components in the system. For example, a pulley might be rotating in the wrong direction or at the wrong speed. The subjects' task was to determine whether each pulley system was realistic or unrealistic (i.e., contained an inconsistent part).

Subjects' eye-fixations as they inspected the pulley system animations indicated that they evaluated the pulley system descriptions by sampling individual components for inspection until a possible inconsistency was detected. When an inconsistency was detected, it was evaluated by a more directed confirmation process in which the inconsistent component was compared to a reference component.

Subjects low in mechanical ability were both slower and less accurate in evaluating the realism of the pulley systems. Furthermore, their errors could be attributed to the absence of knowledge of particular kinematic relations between components of the pulley systems.

Summary and Implications.   In summary, the ability to infer the behavior of a mechanical system appears both to involve spatial information processing and to be influenced by general familiarity with mechanical systems, as measured by tests of mechanical ability. This is consistent with reports of famous engineers and scientists, as previously discussed, suggesting that they have unusually complex mental imagery in this domain.

It would be interesting to study how this ability develops as an individual gains more familiarity with mechanical systems. One possibility is that the basis for this ability is a general ability to manipulate spatial images, and that as people gain more experience with mechanical systems, they learn the kinematic relations between common subsystems of mechanical devices and learn to chunk components of mechanical systems into these subsystems (cf. Egan & Schwartz, 1979). Another possibility is that when people encounter a novel mechanical device, they initially visualize the mechanical interactions, and later abstract rules of mechanical reasoning from these visualizations. Such a developmental progression was observed by Metz (1985) in her studies of children's understanding of gear systems. When asked to predict the direction of motion of a gear in a gear chain, younger children imagined the motion of successive gears from the input of the system to the gear in question, whereas older children used the general rule that every other gear moves in the same direction.

Further research is also required to determine the limitations of the process of mentally animating a mechanical device. For example, this research could investigate how complex a machine people at a given level of ability can "mentally animate." It is also possible that certain types of motion or mechanical constraints are more difficult to represent than others. The existing research (Fallside, 1987) suggests that ability to mentally animate a device is limited to qualitative judgments. That is, people are able to identify inconsistencies in the *direction* of motion of a component, but not in the *speed* of that motion.

Mechanisms for Accessing Problem-Relevant Knowledge

Different types of mental models and problem schemata are appropriate for solving different types of problems. For example, imagine that a physics student was asked to solve the Bale of Hay problem in Fig. 8.2. She or he might express the possible input force to the pulley system (the boy's 20 lb pull) as a ratio of the output force needed (60 lbs) and decide that the boy needs a pulley system with a mechanical advantage of 3. This answer would be sufficient if we could assume that the weight of the pulleys and the friction in the system could be ignored, assumptions that are often made in textbook physics problems, but this is not the case in the real-world situation presented in this problem. Therefore the little boy in the problem has to construct a pulley system with a mechanical advantage of more than 3. The physics student's solution to the problem would be inadequate because it did not take account of the practicalities of the problem.

Similarly, suppose we gave the "tension" problem in Fig. 8.2 to a person who has had a lot of experience with rigging different types of pulley systems on a sailboat but who has never taken a physics course. This person would probably be immediately confused as to the precise meanings of the terms "mass" and "tension" so that she or he would be unable to solve the problem.

These examples demonstrate that problem solving is largely a matter of finding the appropriate knowledge to solve the problem at hand. This is true of problem solving in all semantically rich domains. However, it is perhaps more crucial to mechanical problem solving because of the variety of different types of mechanical problems and different types of mechanical knowledge.

Research presented herein suggests that people sometimes have multiple types of conceptual knowledge that can be brought to bear on solving a given problem. People may have multiple intuitions about motion, abstracted from different situations. They may have specific causal models of different machines. If they have taken a physics class, they may also have theoretical concepts of mechanics. How do they choose between these competing representations of mechanics when faced with a particular mechanical problem?

There are several possible ways in which a particular representation might be chosen. One possibility is that the different representations conflict in specifying how a problem should be solved, and the most salient features of the problem dictate which representation is chosen. Another possibility is that the different representations are organized into a higher level structure, specifying when it is appropriate to use each representation. A third possibility is that these two accounts characterize different groups of subjects. I examine this issue by first taking a specific example of a problem situation that involves selection among a number of different causal rules. I then consider the generality of the findings in this specific example by examining the problem-solving procedures of individuals with different abilities, individuals at different developmental levels, and individuals with different amounts of expertise.

Pulley Problems: An Example

Pulley problems of the type used in psychometric tests of mechanical ability (e.g., Bennett, 1969) provide a good domain in which to examine how people choose among competing mental models or mechanical rules in solving mechanical problems. In a typical pulley problem (see Fig. 8.7), the subject is asked to decide which of two pulley systems will require more force to lift a weight. The two pulley systems can differ in a number of attributes, such as the number of pulleys or ropes in the system, the configuration of the system, or the weight of the object to be lifted.

Hegarty, Just, and Morrison (1988) required subjects to solve a set of pulley problems that systematically varied the number and type of attributes that distinguished the two systems depicted in each problem. Their goals were both to provide a general account of how people solve these types of problems, and to account for individual differences in the solution processes. To this end, they assigned the subjects to groups of high-scoring and low-scoring subjects on the basis of accuracy in solving the problems.

The correct solution to these problems can be found by analyzing the balance of forces to determine the mechanical advantage of each system. However, our subjects rarely solved the pulley problems in this way. Instead, they compared the pulley systems on a number of visible attributes, such as the number of pulleys, the number of load-bearing ropes, or the size of the pulleys. To solve a

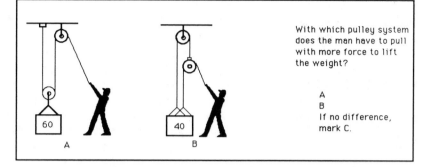

FIG. 8.7.   A typical pulley problem of the type studied by Hegarty et al., (1988).

problem, subjects first decided which of these attributes were relevant to reducing the effort required to lift the weight and then answered the question on the basis of rules of mechanical reasoning, relating these attributes to the amount of effort required to lift the weight. For example, a very common rule could be stated as "a pulley system with more pulleys requires less force to lift a weight." The attributes on which subjects based their answers were either relevant attributes, such as the number of pulleys or rope strands, that covary with mechanical advantage, or irrelevant attributes, such as the size of the pulleys and the height of the system, attributes that have no effect on the mechanical advantage of the system.

Subjects' protocols and responses to different problems revealed that they based their answers on several different rules of mechanical reasoning, rather than on a single rule. Because subjects used a number of different rules, they frequently encountered problems in which their rules predicted different answers to the problem. Take, for example, the problem presented in Fig. 8.5 and consider that it is being solved by a person who has the following rules of mechanical reasoning:

1. A system with fewer pulleys requires more effort.
2. A system with fewer ceiling attachments requires more effort.
3. A system with more weight requires more effort.

Each of these different rules predicts a different answer to the problem. Rule 1 predicts Answer C, Rule 2 predicts Answer B, and Rule 3 predicts Answer A.

Individual Differences in Selection of Mechanical Rules

Hegarty et al. (1988) found that high-scoring subjects used three different methods to resolve conflicts between different rules that were applicable in a situation. First, they demonstrated *preferences* among their rules, so that when a number of different rules were applicable in a situation, these subjects reliably preferred the answer based on one of the rules. Consequently, their responses across different problems were very consistent. In contrast, low-scoring subjects did not have such preferences, so that their responses were inconsistent across different problems.

Second, high-scoring subjects sometimes *combined* the information given by two rules, and these combinations could be either qualitative or quantitative. Subjects who made qualitative combinations tried to assess the size of the difference between the two pulley systems on the two attributes that were in conflict, for example, weight and ceiling attachments. On the basis of these estimates, they decided that either the difference in one outweighed the difference in the other, or that the two differences compensated for each other. Subjects quantitatively combined the information given by two rules by computing a ratio of the weight to some attribute of the system, for example, the amount of weight per pulley. In contrast, low-scoring subjects preferred to base their answers on a single attribute of the systems, usually the weight.

Third, high-scoring subjects appeared to augment their rules of mechanical reasoning with *conditions of applicability* of those rules. Their search for information in a problem was organized so that they used their most complex rules (quantitative rules) only in situations in which a simpler rule was insufficient. If the relative effort required in the two pulley systems could be determined by comparing a single attribute (rather than by quantitatively combining two attributes), then just that attribute was evaluated and compared. In contrast, for low-scoring subjects, the order of search for information was random.

In summary, the study by Hegarty et al. (1988) suggests that high-scoring subjects have developed preferences between their rules of mechanical reasoning, have combined rules, and have developed conditions of applicability for these rules. Thus, their mental models of pulley systems correspond to an organized system of rules, whereas the mental models of low-scoring subjects are better described as a set of isolated rules that compete in the solution of individual problems. I now consider how general these conclusions are to other subject populations and other mechanical rules.

Developmental Differences in the Selection of Knowledge

Similar differences in the organization of rules of mechanical reasoning have been observed in the developmental literature. In studies of children's solutions to balance beam problems, Siegler (1978, 1981) found that children demonstrated different preferences among their rules at different developmental stages, and that individuals at the highest developmental stages combined rules quantitatively.

In a typical problem, the child is shown a balance beam with a number of

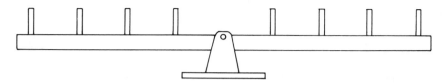

FIG. 8.8.   The balance beam apparatus used by Siegler (1978, 1981).

weights on either side, which are located on one of four pegs spaced at different distances from the fulcrum (see Fig. 8.8). The task is to predict which side of the balance will go down when a lever, which holds the scale motionless, is released.

Preferences among rules of mechanical reasoning are evident at Stages 1 and 2 of Siegler's account of the development of mechanical reasoning. At Stage 1, children base their answers on rules based on the amount of weight on each side of the balance scale, ignoring the distance dimension. At Stage 2, they take the distance into account, but they have a preference for the weight rule, so that if both weight and distance vary in a problem, they base their answer on the weight dimension.

The strategy of combining the information from two conflicting attributes was also observed in Siegler's studies. Subjects at Stage 4 in his account always consider both the weight and distance dimensions and know the appropriate quantitative rule for combining them (multiplying the weight by the distance). It should be noted that in both the developmental studies of the balance beam task, and the study of individual differences in the pulley task, combination of rules was associated with a shift from a qualitative to a quantitative mental model. This shift occurred only at the highest levels of ability and development and may have reflected formal instruction rather than development of purely intuitive mental models.

Expert-Novice Differences in the Selection of Knowledge

The development of conditions specifying when particular representations are applicable to solving a problem is a general phenomenon associated with the development of expertise in a domain. Because mental models or problem schemata are initially specific to the situations from which they were induced, the selection of a mental model or problem schema by a novice is largely determined by the surface features of the problem. With experience, mental models become indexed by the mechanics principles that they embody, rather than the surface features of problems, so that their conditions of applicability are more suited to the appropriate solution process (Chi et al., 1981).

These differences in the organization of formal knowledge lead to several differences between expert and novice problem solving. Experts' problem solving is faster and less effortful than that of novices, because once experts evoke a problem schema, they automatically access the procedures for solving the problem and these procedures can be carried out without further effort. Experts evoke equations, substitute values for the variables, and solve equations all in one step; whereas for novices, these are separate, effortful steps (Simon & Simon, 1978). Furthermore, the protocols of novices contain more metastatements expressing subgoals and uncertainties.

Differences in the organization of knowledge also lead to differences in the order of search for information to solve a problem. Experts work forward from the givens of the problem, deriving information from the problem statement, regardless of whether it is required to solve the problem (Larkin et al., 1980). This is essentially a process of instantiating a problem schema. In contrast, novices work backward from the goal of the problem, searching for equations that will allow them to derive the information that the problem asks about. Thus experts are more schema driven, whereas novices are more goal driven in solving problems.

This characterization of expert and novice performance is also true of other domains, such as programming. Rist (1989) has recently shown that working backward from the goal of a problem is a default strategy that both experts and novices use when there is no schema available for a given type of problem. Furthermore, he found that working backwards from the goal of a problem typically leads to the creation of a problem schema, which is subsequently used in solving similar problems. Thus, the essential difference between experts and novices then may be in the number of problem schemata that they have created as a result of their problem-solving experience.

Choosing between Formal and Intuitive Mental Models. Solving formal mechanical problems also includes choosing between using everyday, informal knowledge or more formal knowledge to solve the problem. Concrete, qualitative representations, characteristic of intuitive knowledge, can be useful in solving formal physics problems, because they allow problem situations to be compared with familiar cases that are well specified and well understood (Reif, 1987). These representations can also be useful for generating equations for solving formal problems, checking errors, and inferring information not stated explicitly in the problem. To be useful, however, these representations must be integrated with formal scientific knowledge; they must be testable against such formal knowledge; and they must incorporate discriminations needed to avoid confusions with incorrect naive conceptions (Reif, 1987). This can be problematic, especially because novice problem solvers often retain some of their naive misconceptions of mechanical systems (Champagne, Klopfer, & Anderson, 1980; Clement, 1982; White, 1983).

In solving formal problems, novices evoke either their theoretical knowledge or their intuitive knowledge of mechanics, but not both, and the knowledge that they evoke is largely determined by surface features of the problem. Anzai and Yokoyama (1984) found that when faced with an unfamiliar physics problem, novice students were likely to interpret the problem in terms of their naive intuitions rather than their correct theoretical knowledge. However, they could be induced to switch their problem representations to the correct theoretical representations when additional information in the diagram of the problem statement cued them to the relevant information in the problem. As well as demonstrating novices' dependence on surface features, this result shows that novices do not always invoke all the relevant knowledge that they have for solving a problem.

In contrast, studies of expert problem solving suggest that experts have integrated their formal knowledge with their everyday knowledge of mechanical phenomena. For example, Roschelle and Greeno (1987) reported that when solving mechanics problems, experts alternated between two different representations of the problem: a qualitative simulation of the motions of objects in the situation, and a theoretical model including the mechanical forces and constraints operating in the situation. Experts solved the problems by first qualitatively simulating the situation described in the problem, and then checking this simulation against the theoretical model, resolving inconsistencies between the two models, if necessary. Similarly, when asked questions testing their understanding of the concept of acceleration, experts answered using both formal definitional knowledge and less formal knowledge about specific cases (Reif, 1987). These examples demonstrate that experts often solve problems by working within two different but integrated representations, a formal and an informal representation.

Summary

In summary, the choice of a mental model or a problem schema to be applied to solving a problem appears to be governed by similar factors in solving practical and more theoretical problems. Problem solving at lower levels of skill, ability, or development seems to involve competition among different types of conceptual knowledge, and the type of knowledge that wins this competition is largely determined by the surface features of the problem. At higher levels of skill or development, the choice of conceptual knowledge appears to be more suited to the requirements of the problem at hand, suggesting that experts' representations are organized or integrated into a higher level structure, including conditions under which the different mental models are applicable to solving a problem. In the final section of the chapter, I consider the development of conceptual knowledge of mechanics in more detail, suggesting how instruction can aid this development.

DEVELOPMENT OF MECHANICAL KNOWLEDGE

I have examined the mechanical knowledge and problem solving of individuals with different abilities, individuals at different developmental levels, and individuals with different amounts of expertise. The dimensions underlying the differences in the three cases are similar. In each case, differences between individuals can be described in terms of a progression of conceptual knowledge of mechanical phenomena that involves three types of changes.

One dimension on which concepts change is in their *level of specificity* (diSessa, 1983; Forbus & Gentner, 1986; Holland et al., 1986; Kaiser, McCloskey, & Proffitt, 1986). Mechanical intuitions, causal models, and problem schemata are induced from problem solving and observation in specific situations such that they initially retain some of the specificity of these situations. With development, they become more general and indexed by the underlying mechanical principles operating in a situation, rather than the surface features of the situation (Chi et al., 1981).

Another way in which mechanical concepts change is from *qualitative* to *quantitative* (Forbus & Gentner, 1986; Hegarty et al., 1988; Siegler, 1981; White & Frederiksen, 1986). Intuitive knowledge of mechanical phenomena is generally qualitative. It is only at the highest levels of mechanical ability and development that people tend to use quantitative models. Furthermore, as previously noted, this latter development may not be a purely spontaneous development in intuitive knowledge and is usually influenced by formal schooling.

Finally, a third progression in conceptual knowledge concerns the *consistency* of its use. At lower levels of ability, development, or expertise, people appear to apply mechanical concepts inconsistently to solving problems (Hegarty et al., 1988; Kaiser, Jonides, & Alexander, 1986; Mitchell & Pellegrino, in preparation; White, 1983). This is because they have many situation-specific mechanical rules and no clear preferences among these rules. With experience, they develop preferences for their more correct rules of mechanical reasoning and augment their models with conditions stating when these rules are applicable. Thus, people's problem-solving methods become more consistent and more correct.

Future Research

These conclusions are based on limited evidence of the development of conceptual knowledge. More research is needed to study the progression of mental models systematically and in other domains. Furthermore, studies are needed which monitor the progression of people's understanding as they gain experience in a domain rather than inferring these progressions from studies of mental models at different stages of a developmental continuum.

In addition to documenting the stages of the developmental sequence, we must also consider the learning mechanisms underlying the sequence. A number of different learning mechanisms have been proposed. For example, changes in preferences between different rules of mechanical reasoning might be accounted for by a strengthening mechanism that increases the preference of successful rules and decreases the preference of unsuccessful rules (Hegarty et al., 1988; Holland et al., 1986). An analogy mechanism could account for the application of general rules to new unfamiliar situations (Forbus & Gentner, 1986; Gentner, 1983). Finally, Williams, Hollan, and Stevens (1983) have proposed a checking mechanism that checks that consistency of models abstracted from different situations.

Instruction: Fostering the Development of Mechanical Knowledge

Normally the development of mechanical knowledge occurs with difficulty. In particular, novices have many difficulties integrating the general, quantitative concepts of theoretical mechanics with their existing intuitive understanding of mechanics. There are several reasons for these difficulties. First, formal instruction in mechanics requires students to master new concepts, and this is particularly difficult because many mechanics concepts, such as mass and acceleration, have everyday meanings that do not correspond to their meanings in theoretical mechanics (Reif, 1987). A related reason is that students' intuitive mechanical knowledge often conflicts with theoretical laws (Clement, 1982; diSessa, 1982; White, 1983). Third, physics instruction requires students to master new quantitative skills for solving problems in a domain that they are used to thinking about qualitatively (Champagne et al., 1980). Fourth, the knowledge required to solve physics problems is largely procedural, and current physics instruction does not explicitly teach procedures for solving problems (Heller & Reif, 1984; Reif & Heller, 1982).

Recently, researchers have attempted to develop new approaches to teaching mechanical problem solving that take account of these difficulties. One approach is to structure students' experiences of mechanical phenomena to foster a smoother progression of mechanical understanding. This can be achieved with computer "microworlds" that simulate motion in the real world (diSessa, 1982; White, 1984; White, in press). Another approach is to teach students explicit procedures for solving physics problems (Heller & Reif, 1984; Reif & Heller, 1982). I consider each of these approaches in turn.

Microworlds for Teaching Formal Mechanics

The ThinkerTools curriculum, developed by White (in press) is a specific example of a computer microworld designed to teach theoretical mechanics. In this curriculum, students develop a set of increasingly complex concepts of motion by experimenting and problem solving within a set of microworlds that gradually increase in complexity. For example, the first microworld introduces motion in one dimension, the second introduces two dimensional motion, and the third introduces continuous forces. The microworlds allow students to construct increasingly complex concepts of motion in which the model at each level builds on the concepts understood at the previous level.

The microworlds allow students to link their real-world knowledge of motion with more theoretical knowledge by incorporating several different representations of motion. For example, the microworlds simultaneously show both the appearance of moving objects (real-world representation) and vectors showing the horizontal and vertical velocities of that motion (theoretical representation). This allows students to construct concepts which link the visible physical phenomena of motion to abstract theoretical representations of motion.

A central component of the activity of interacting with the microworld is the formulation and evaluation of general laws of motion (for example, the rule that whenever you give an object a push, it speeds up). This activity is useful both in developing students' concepts of the nature of scientific laws, and allowing them to confront and evaluate their own intuitive laws of motion. For example, a student who held the naive impetus model of motion (McCloskey, 1983a) could test it in the context of the microworld, and discover that motion is in fact inconsistent with this intuitive law.

Preliminary data suggest that the ThinkerTools curriculum is very successful in teaching Newtonian mechanics to relatively young children. Two classes of sixth graders exposed to the ThinkerTools curriculum performed better on a set of mechanics problems than either physics-naive sixth graders or high school students (White, in press). These data demonstrate the general effectiveness of the curriculum. Further research is required to assess the separate effects of each of the educational innovations embodied in the curriculum, that is, the progression of microworlds, the linked representations, and the focus on scientific laws.

Teaching Problem-Solving Procedures

Another approach to improving instruction in formal mechanics is to teach students explicit procedures for solving problems and for comparing their formal and informal knowledge, rather than leaving them to derive these procedures for themselves from declarative definitions of the concepts or from textbook examples.

In one study (Heller & Reif, 1984), students were given a list of instructions for generating a problem representation that included: (a) procedures for representing the motions of the relevant systems in the problem and the forces in these systems; and (b) procedures for checking that the motion and force representations were consistent. These instructions contrast with standard physics instruction that emphasizes the description of forces but not motion, does not specify *how* to enumerate forces, and does not include checking procedures. The explicit instructions produced large gains in problem-solving success, indicating that providing such procedural directions is one way to improve problem-solving performance, at least in the short term. Further research is required to assess the long-term effects of such instruction.

In another study, Labudde, Reif, and Quinn (1988) found that teaching students explicit procedures for determining the acceleration of a particle caused them to revise their highly deficient previous conceptions of acceleration and allowed them to interpret the concept almost flawlessly across a diverse set of problems. These studies demonstrate that people can be taught procedures for representing and solving physics concepts and problems, that they do not derive these procedures for themselves from existing instruction, and that these procedures improve their problem-solving performance.

CONCLUSION

In this chapter, I have examined the knowledge of mechanical phenomena and the information-processing mechanisms that are involved in solving mechanical problems. I have been particularly concerned with which knowledge and principles are specific to the mechanics domain and which are more general. Furthermore, I have viewed mechanical problem solving as an ability that is learned and developed as an individual gains more experience of mechanical phenomena.

Clearly, knowledge of mechanical systems and mechanical principles is specific to solving mechanical problems. In this review, we have seen that such knowledge is not just specific to mechanical problems, but can also be specific to particular types of problems within the domain of mechanics. For example, formal quantitative laws of mechanics are specific to solving theoretical mechanics problems, whereas knowledge of the kinematic relations between components in a mechanical system is more specific to practical problems such as troubleshooting and design.

On the other hand, the information-processing mechanisms used in mechanical problem solving are more domain general. As in other problem-solving domains, success in solving mechanical problems is due not only to possession of the relevant domain knowledge, but also to the ability to access this knowledge as a problem demands. Whereas this ability is domain general, it may be more critical to mechanical problem solving than to problem solving in other domains because of the variety of different sources and types of mechanical knowledge.

Processes for manipulating spatial information are also central to mechanical problem solving. Different spatial processes are more or less specific to mechanical problem solving. The process of using a spatial representation to reduce search for the relevant information in a problem is applicable to many problem-solving domains such as geometry, games, and computer programming. However, the process of imagining the motions of different components of a mechanical device may be more specific to domains that involve dynamic interacting systems, such as mechanics and electronics. Furthermore, the ability to imagine a mechanical system in motion is dependent on knowledge of the specific kinematic relations between components in that system.

With learning, people acquire new knowledge of mechanical principles; this knowledge becomes integrated with existing mechanical knowledge so that inconsistencies are resolved, and it becomes organized in problem schemata and mental models that include conditions under which different types of knowledge are applicable to solving a problem. As a result, problem solvers learn to consistently access and apply the knowledge relevant to solving different types of mechanical problems.

Finally, the progress that cognitive psychologists have made in understanding mechanical problem solving is evidenced by the success of instructional programs that have applied this understanding to improving the quality of education in the mechanics domain.

ACKNOWLEDGMENTS

I wish to thank Sharon Carver, Erika Ferguson, Richard Mayer, and Catherine Reed for their comments on earlier versions of this chapter.

REFERENCES

Adelson, B. (1984). When novices surpass experts: The difficulty of a task may increase with expertise. *Journal of Experimental Psychology: Learning, Memory and Cognition, 10,* 483–495.

Anzai, Y., & Yokoyama, T. (1984). Internal models in physics problem solving. *Cognition and Instruction, 1*(4), 397–450.

Bennett, C. K. (1969). *Bennett mechanical comprehension test.* New York: The Psychological Corporation.

Bobrow, D. G. (Ed.). (1985). *Qualitative reasoning about physical systems.* Cambridge, MA: MIT Press.

Bureau of Naval Personnel. (1971). *Basic machines and how they work.* New York: Dover.

Brown, J. S., Collins, A., & Duguid, P. (1989). Situated cognition and the culture of learning. *Educational Researcher, 32–42.*

Brown, R. (1973). *A first language: The early stages.* Cambridge, MA: Harvard University Press.

Champagne, A. B., Klopfer, L. E., & Anderson, J. H. (1980). Factors influencing the learning of classical mechanics. *American Journal of Physics, 48*(12), 1074–1079.

Chase, W. G., & Simon, H. A. (1973). Perception in chess. *Cognitive Psychology, 4,* 55–81.

Chi, M. T. H., Feltovich, P. J., & Glaser, R. (1981). Categorization and representation of physics problems. *Cognitive Science, 5,* 121–152.

Chi, M. T. H., Glaser, R., & Rees, E. (1982). Expertise in problem solving. In R. J. Sternberg (Ed.), *Advances in the psychology of human intelligence* (pp. 7–75). Hillsdale, NJ: Lawrence Erlbaum Associates.

Clement, J. (1982). Students' preconceptions in introductory mechanics. *American Journal of Physics, 50*(1), 66–71.

Clement, J. (1983). A conceptual model discussed by Galileo and used intuitively by physics students. In D. Gentner & A. L. Stevens (Eds.), *Mental models* (pp. 325–339). Hillsdale, NJ: Lawrence Erlbaum Associates.

de Groot, A. (1965). *Thought and choice in chess.* The Hague: Mouton.

de Kleer, J., & Brown, J. S. (1983). Assumptions and ambiguities in mechanistic mental models. In D. Gentner & A. L. Stevens (Eds.), *Mental models* (pp. 155–190). Hillsdale, NJ: Lawrence Erlbaum Associates.

de Kleer, J., & Brown, J. S. (1984). A qualitative physics based on confluences. *Artificial Intelligence, 24*, 7–83.

diSessa, A. A. (1982). Unlearning Aristotelian physics: Study of knowledge-based learning. *Cognitive Science, 6*, 37–75.

diSessa, A. A. (1983). Phenomenology and the evolution of intuition. In D. Gentner & A. L. Stevens (Eds.), *Mental models* (pp. 15–34). Hillsdale, NJ: Lawrence Erlbaum Associates.

Egan, D. E., & Schwartz, B. J. (1979). Chunking in recall of symbolic drawings. *Memory and Cognition, 7*(2), 149–158.

Fallside, D. C. (1988). *Understanding machines in motion.* Unpublished doctoral dissertation, Carnegie Mellon University, Pittsburgh, PA.

Ferguson, E. S. (1977). The mind's eye: Nonverbal thought in technology. *Science, 197*, 827–836.

Forbus, K. D. (1984). Qualitative process theory. *Artificial Intelligence, 24*, 85–168.

Forbus, K. D., & Gentner, D. (1984). Learning physical domains: Towards a theoretical framework. In R. S. Michalski, J. G. Carbonell, & T. M. Mitchell (Eds.). *Machine learning: Recent progress.* Los Altos, CA: Morgan Kaufmann Publishers, Inc.

Galton, F. (1907). *Inquiries into the human faculty and its development.* London: Dent.

Gentner, D. (1983). Structure-mapping: A theoretical framework for analogy. *Cognitive Science, 7*, 155–170.

Gentner, D., & Stevens, A. L. (Eds.). (1983). *Mental models.* Hillsdale, NJ: Lawrence Erlbaum Associates.

Ghiselli, E. E. (1955). The measurement of occupational aptitude. *University of California Publications in Psychology, 8*, 101–216.

Hardiman, P. T., Pollatsek, A., & Well, A. D. (1986). Learning to understand the balance beam. *Cognition and Instruction, 3*(1), 63–86.

Hegarty, M. (1988). *Comprehension of diagrams accompanied by text.* Unpublished doctoral dissertation, Carnegie Mellon University, Pittsburgh, PA.

Hegarty, M., & Just, M. A. (1989). Understanding machines from text and diagrams. In H. Mandl & J. Levin (Eds.), *Knowledge acquisition from text and picture* (pp. 171–194). Amsterdam: North Holland.

Hegarty, M., Just, M. A., & Morrison, I. R. (1988). Mental models of mechanical systems: Individual differences in qualitative and quantitative reasoning. *Cognitive Psychology, 20*, 191–236.

Heller, J. I., & Reif, F. (1984). Prescribing effective human problem-solving processes: Problem description in Physics. *Cognition and Instruction, 1*(2), 177–216.

Hinsley, D. A., Hayes, J. R., & Simon, H. A. (1977). In M. A. Just & P. A. Carpenter (Eds.), *Cognitive Processes in Comprehension* (pp. 89–106). Hillsdale, NJ: Lawrence Erlbaum Associates.

Holland, J. H., Holyoak, K. J., Nisbett, R. E., & Thagard, P. R. (1986). *Induction.* Cambridge, MA: MIT Press.

Jeffries, R., Turner, A. T., Polson, P. G., & Atwood, M. E. (1981). Processes involved in designing software. In J. R. Anderson (Ed.), *Cognitive skills and their acquisition* (pp. 255–283). Hillsdale, NJ: Lawrence Erlbaum Associates.

Kaiser, M. K., Jonides, J., & Alexander, J. (1986). Intuitive reasoning about abstract and familiar physics problems. *Memory & Cognition, 14*(4), 308–312.

Kaiser, M. K., McCloskey, M., & Proffitt, D. R. (1986). Development of intuitive theories of motion: Curvilinear motion in the absence of external forces. *Developmental Psychology, 22*(1), 67–71.

Kaiser, M. K., Proffitt, D. R., & McCloskey, M. (1985). The development of beliefs about falling objects. *Perception and Psychophysics, 38*(6), 533–539.

Kieras, D. E., & Bovair, S. (1984). The role of a mental model in learning to operate a device. *Cognitive Science, 8,* 255–273.

Labudde, P., Reif, F., & Quinn, L. (1988). Facilitation of scientific concept learning by interpretation procedures and diagnosis. *International Journal of Science Education, 10*(1), 81–98.

Lancaster, J. S., & Kolodner, J. L. (1987). Problem solving in a natural task as a function of experience. *Proceedings of the Ninth Annual Conference of the Cognitive Science Society.* Seattle, WA. 727–736. Hillsdale, NJ: Lawrence Erlbaum Associates.

Larkin, J. H., & Simon, H. A. (1987). Why a diagram is (sometimes) worth ten thousand words. *Cognitive Science, 11,* 65–99.

Larkin, J., McDermott, J., Simon, D. P., & Simon, H. A. (1980). Expert and novice performance in solving Physics problems. *Science, 208,* 1335–1342.

Mayer, R. E. (1989a). Systematic thinking fostered by illustrations in scientific text. *Journal of Educational Psychology, 81,* 240–246.

Mayer, R. E. (1989b). Models for understanding. *Review of Educational Research 59,* 43–64.

McCloskey, M. (1983a). Intuitive Physics. *Scientific American, 248*(4), 122–130.

McCloskey, M. (1983b). Naive theories of motion. In D. Gentner & A. L. Stevens (Eds.), *Mental models* (pp. 299–324). Hillsdale, NJ: Lawrence Erlbaum Associates.

McCloskey, M., Caramazza, A., & Green, B. (1980). Curvilinear motion in the absence of external forces: Naive beliefs about the motion of objects. *Science, 210,* 1139–1141.

Metz, K. E. (1985). Development of children's understanding in a gears task: A problem space perspective. *Cognitive Science, 9*(4), 431–471.

Mitchell, S. R., & Pellegrino, J. W. (in preparation). *Misconceptions about objects in motion: Variability within and across problems, persons, and time.*

Miyake, N. (1986). Constructive interaction and the iterative process of understanding. *Cognitive Science, 10*(2), 151–178.

Newell, A., & Simon, H. (1972). *Human problem solving.* Englewood Cliffs, NJ: Prentice-Hall.

Nielson, P. E. (1988). *A qualitative approach to rigid body mechanics.* Unpublished doctoral dissertation, University of Illinois at Urbana-Champaign, Urbana, IL.

O'Neill, J. J. (1944). *Prodigal genius: The life of Nikola Tesla.* New York: Ives Washburn.

Reif, F. (1987). Interpretation of scientific or mathematical concepts: Cognitive issues and instructional implications. *Cognitive Science, 11,* 395–416.

Reif, F., & Heller, J. (1982). Knowledge structure and problem solving in physics. *Educational Psychologist, 17*(2), 102–127.

Reiser, B. J., Ranney, M., Lovett, M. C., & Kimberg, D. Y. (1989). Facilitating students' reasoning with causal explanations and visual representations. In D. Biederman, J. Breuker, and J. Sandberg (Eds.), *Proceedings of the Fourth International Conference on Artificial Intelligence and Education* (pp. 228–235). Springfield, VA: IOS.

Rips, L. J. (1986). Mental muddles. In M. Brand & R. M. Harnish (Eds.), *Problems in the representation of knowledge and belief* (pp. 258–286). Tucson, AZ: University of Arizona Press.

Rist, R. S. (1989). Schema creation in programming. *Cognitive Science, 13,* 389–414.

Rogoff, B., & Lave, J. (1984). *Everyday cognition: Its development in social context.* Cambridge, MA: Harvard University Press.

Roschelle, J., & Greeno, J. G. (1987). Mental models in expert physics reasoning. Paper presented at the annual meeting of the Cognitive Science Society, Seattle, WA.

Siegler, R. S. (1978). The origins of scientific reasoning. In R. S. Siegler (Ed.), *Children's thinking: What develops?* (pp. 109–149). Hillsdale, NJ: Lawrence Erlbaum Associates.

Siegler, R. S. (1981). Developmental sequences within and between concepts. *Monographs of the Society for Research in Child Development, 46*(2), 1–149.

Simon, D. P., & Simon, H. A. (1978). Individual differences in solving physics problems. In R. Siegler (Ed.), *Children's thinking: What develops?* (pp. 325–348). Hillsdale, NJ: Lawrence Erlbaum Associates.

Shepard, R. N. (1978). Externalization of mental images and the act of creation. In B. S. Randhava & W. E. Coffman (Eds.), *Visual learning, thinking, and communication* (pp. 133–189). New York: Academic Press.

Smith, I. M. (1964). *Spatial ability: Its educational and social significance*. London: University of London Press.

Stanfill, C. (1983). The decomposition of a large domain: Reasoning about mechanics. *Proceedings of the National Conference on Artificial Intelligence*. American Association of Artificial Intelligence, 387–390.

Sternberg, R. J., & Wagner, R. K. (Eds.). (1986). *Practical intelligence*. Cambridge, MA: Cambridge University Press.

Vernon, P. E., & Parry, J. B. (1949). *Personnel selection in the British forces*. London: University of London Press.

Voss, J., Greene, T. R., Post, T. A., & Penner, B. (1983). Problem solving skill in the social sciences. In G. H. Bower (Ed.), *The Psychology of Learning and Motivation* (vol. 17, pp. 165–213). Orlando, FL: Academic Press.

White, B. Y. (1983). Sources of difficulty in understanding Newtonian dynamics. *Cognitive Science, 7*, 41–65.

White, B. Y. (1984). Designing computer activities to help physics students understand Newton's laws of motion. *Cognition and Instruction, 1*, 69–108.

White, B. Y. (in press). ThinkerTools: Causal models, conceptual change and science education. *Cognition and Instruction*.

White, B. Y., & Frederiksen, J. R. (1986). Qualitative models and intelligent learning environments. Technical Report No. 6277, BBN Laboratories.

Williams, M. D., Hollan, J. D., & Stevens, A. L. (1983). Human reasoning about a simple physical system. In D. Gentner & A. L. Stevens (Eds.), *Mental models* (pp. 131–154). Hillsdale, NJ: Lawrence Erlbaum Associates.

9 Complex Problem Solving in Electronics

Alan Lesgold
Susanne Lajoie
University of Pittsburgh

Electronics expertise has been an object of study within cognitive science for a variety of reasons. It is seen by many as a critical need in our high technology economy. We are often frustrated by failures of consumer electronic devices, and we fear inadequacies of electronics maintenance in the common services on which we depend, such as air travel and the telephone. Further, because many computer science departments originated as subdivisions of electrical engineering departments, many computer scientists have had some training in electronics—they study what they know.

Electronics is also an interesting domain because electronic systems, depending on their nature and complexity, can require a variety of different representation forms. Simple electrical systems, such as a flashlight, have apparently simple descriptions. However, even at the simplest level, the effects of components in a system are in part global. Consider the circuit shown in Fig. 9.1. If the resistance of the resistor is changed, the voltage drop across the light bulb will change. Moreover, the current everywhere in the circuit will be influenced by a resistance change anywhere. Most striking of all, a break anywhere in the circuit causes the current, and hence the voltage drop, anywhere in the circuit to drop to zero.

Because enough of what happens is counterintuitive to people with no formal knowledge of electricity, it is worth studying how principles of electricity are acquired. For this reason, a number of researchers have attempted to characterize the mental models of electrical phenomena that students might have (Caillot, 1987; Gentner & Gentner, 1983) or to specify more useful mental models (e.g., de Kleer, 1984) and how they might be acquired (Caillot, 1987; Gentner & Gentner, 1983; Haertel, 1987). These efforts are important pieces of cognitive

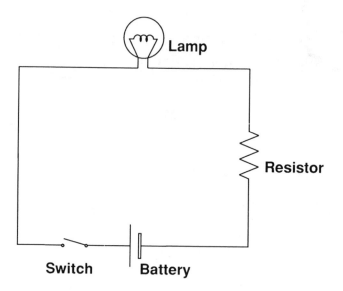

FIG. 9.1. Simple Electrical Circuit.

science, but they differ from the focus of the present chapter. Our peculiar purpose is to describe how expert technicians think as they are diagnosing system failures in electronic equipment.

We cognitive scientists have tended to assume that complete and deep understanding is necessary for success in such jobs as electronics troubleshooting. De Kleer (1984), for example, correctly shows that quite complex knowledge is needed to understand even simple electronic circuits. It does not follow, however, that all of the requisite knowledge is fully developed, verbalizable, and useable in verbal inference. As we show later in the chapter, electronics diagnosis requires rich but possibly intuitive or partial understanding, along with such attributes as confidence and perseverance. The expertise we have observed is grounded in rich experience with particular electronic systems and often is only partly abstracted into "first principles" (cf. Brown & Duguid, 1989, for related ideas).

We make our case based on two kinds of information. First, we have a rich body of experimental data that we and our colleagues have accumulated from task analyses of complex electronics troubleshooting. In addition, we have, between us, had extensive experience with electronics technicians both in our task analysis and tutor development work and in supervising a departmental computer service facility for over a decade. Some of these data are softer than others. Our purpose is not so much to confirm a theoretical position as to begin to develop one that builds on cognitive science but broadens beyond what cognitive scientists have so far done.

STUDIES OF EXPERTISE

We build upon earlier studies of electronics and of expertise in a variety of domains: chess (de Groot, 1966, 1978; Chase & Simon, 1973 a & b), physics (Chi, Feltovitch, & Glaser, 1981; Larkin, McDermott, Simon, & Simon, 1980), programming (cf. Anderson, Boyle, & Reiser, 1985), and real world tasks such as radiology (Lesgold, Rubinson, Feltovitch, Glaser, Klopfer, & Wang, 1988). Although domain specific components of expertise are apparent, there are also some general principles that apply across domains. One such principle is that experts have larger repertoires of domain specific knowledge in their memories than novices, and this knowledge is organized into larger "meaningful" chunks of information about the domain in question. Experts have more memory for information involved in the solution of a problem, and thus better memory retrieval and pattern recognition to specific domains (see Lesgold, 1988).

Contrastive Studies

Many expertise studies have used a methodological framework similar to the contrastive method used to study chess expertise (Chase & Simon, 1973; de Groot, 1966). Based on de Groot's finding that experts could reconstruct a chess board configuration from memory more accurately than novices, Chase and Simon looked at how the reconstruction process took place. They noticed that experts placed more chess pieces on the board at one time, and that they placed the pieces in groups that represented functional units: meaningful chess configurations. To establish that experts had conceptually driven recall rather than generally better perceptual memories, they tested whether experts outperformed novices on memory for random placements of the pieces. The result: experts' memories were superior to novices' only for combinations that were meaningful in terms of the game. Experts' memories had larger "chunks," units that were functional in the domain, available for ready recall.

Egan and Schwartz (1979) developed a set of circuit diagram materials that used a similar methodology to examine electronics expertise. In a series of studies they compared individuals who were skilled in electronics to novices who had no prior instruction in electronics, and found the skilled group differed from the novices on several dimensions: (a) they could reconstruct large circuit diagrams from memory; (b) they recalled circuits in bursts of meaningfully related components, just as chess masters recall board positions in meaningful "chunks"; (c) they had better recall than novices for meaningful circuit diagrams but not for random circuit diagrams; and (d) the size, rather than the number, of chunks that they recalled increased as a function of study time. These findings matched the finding of studies of chess expertise. It seemed, then, that expertise in the electronics domain consisted of better memory recall and conceptual chunking of specific domain knowledge.

Observational Studies

A different (but not inconsistent) viewpoint comes from a long-term study of power plant employees by Rasmussen (1986). Rasmussen studied the diagnostic processes of electronics technicians directly, rather than through laboratory tasks. He observed and interviewed members of the electronics maintenance group of a Danish national electric power laboratory. Although his observational techniques lack the quantified data reports of the earlier laboratory studies, they provide insight into the real job of electronics troubleshooting and hence are of special interest in this review.

Perhaps Rasmussen's most important observation was that experts have several different representations of the systems in which they are searching for faults. First, they have a representation of the function and structure of the system, its anatomy and physiology. Second, this representation also has a topographical extension—they know which components are next to each other physically or via circuit connections.[1] In addition, they are able to move up to a level of principled representation, in which they can represent parts of a system in terms of basic principles of electronics. With these multiple levels of representation, experts can attack fault diagnosis problems in different ways. Part of the time, they simply recognize a fault situation and know immediately what to do. On other occasions, they apply well-learned rule sets to determine the fault from symptoms. They can also trace through circuits topologically, following the circuit path from one component to the next. Finally, if all else fails, they can reason from first principles in an attempt to understand why the device is not functioning as it should.

Having developed this general account of troubleshooting expertise, Rasmussen made a number of specific points (Rasmussen, 1986, p. 27):

• The expert uses "many observations in a sequence of simple decisions." This results in a sequence of judgments that are "informationally uneconomic, but fast."

• The expert technician sees his task as a search for a faulty component, not primarily as an effort to explain why the system is malfunctioning as it is.[2]

---

[1] A circuit connection is not the same thing as physical proximity. Two components may not be connected or related in the functional account of a circuit, but if they are near each other and a drop of solder accidentally connects them, then a circuit failure may occur. Finding these "bridge faults," which involve topographical as well as systematic knowledge, is one of the hardest tasks an expert faces.

[2] In contrast, earlier work (Lesgold, 1988) with radiologists showed that they seem often to impose the higher goal of truly understanding why a symptom is occurring and therefore engage in more explanatory activity. Perhaps this is because deciding to change a person via surgery or medication is a more serious decision than deciding to change a part in a device.

• Fault isolation procedures are organized by means of representations of the system that is being diagnosed. These representations are hierarchical, with systems organized into subsystems, which in turn are organized into units, etc.

• Search is very opportunistic, with switches between recognition, topographical search, symptom-tracing procedures, and functional analysis procedures as these are suggested by the information being gathered.

There are many implications of this view of expertise. For example, task analyses to support training must have more than a limited series of observations of experts at work. What the experts do will depend on the details of the problems they face, and often the switch between recognition, topographical search, and functional analysis will be triggered by factors peculiar to the situation, such as information overload, small knowledge gaps, and accidental observations of potentially useful data. An observer can understand experts' actions only by being aware of the multiple forms of expertise and the experts' ability to move rapidly between them.

Here is an example. Suppose that a technician has isolated the problem in a complex system to a circuit path containing five components in a line, as shown:

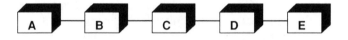

Suppose further that any component can be tested by checking its inputs and outputs. If the inputs are bad, the fault is to the left[3] in the sequence. If the outputs are bad, but the inputs are good, the fault is in the component being tested. Otherwise, the fault is to the right of the component being tested. Suppose further that the fault is equally likely to be in each of the five components. It would seem best to test Component C first, since it is in the middle of the path. If C were good, the fault would lie either in the AB subpath or the DE subpath, so one further test would be required. A first test of C, therefore, has a 20% chance of requiring no more tests and an 80% chance of requiring 1 more test, yielding 0.8 as the expected number of additional tests needed. By similar reasoning, testing A first will yield an expected 1.6 additional tests to be performed. This all seems intuitively sound. Note, however, that testing B or D first is also quite efficient. Suppose B is tested first. Then, if the fault is in B, the work is done. If it is in A, this will be revealed by bad input to B, so the work is done in this case also. If it is in C, D, or E, an average of 1.5 additional tests will be required. So, the expected number of additional tests required after testing B is $0+0+0.60(1.5)$, or 0.9. Even a tiny increase in the probability that the fault is in B will be sufficient to make B the best place to start

---

[3]By convention, the flow is left-to-right.

testing. The implications of Rasmussen's findings, and our own, are that: (a) technicians alter their testing sequences to reflect small probability differences; (b) they do this intuitively and not on the basis of careful probability computations; and (c) they cannot always justify their deviations from strategies that appear to be slightly more optimal.

RESULTS FROM THE SHERLOCK PROJECT[4]

Moving beyond the work of others, much of our acquaintance with electronics troubleshooting expertise comes from a long term research effort we undertook for the U.S. Air Force. This project has had, broadly, three phases: a phase of laboratory-based analysis, a phase of real-world study, and a phase of instructional development. Because the principal product of the third phase is a computer program named *Sherlock*, we refer to the whole research and development effort as "the Sherlock project."

The initial work was Drew Gitomer's (1984) dissertation work on troubleshooting skill. Gitomer, in the spirit of Chase and Simon's chess work (1973) devised laboratory tasks to test components of troubleshooting skill. In the second phase, we followed with work based upon a mixture of laboratory tasks and observations of performance on difficult troubleshooting problems (Lesgold, Lajoie, Eastman, Eggan, Gitomer, Glaser, Greenberg, Logan, Magone, Weiner, Wolf & Yengo; April 1986). The focus was to develop ways of doing cognitive task analyses of complex technical skills that could support the development of training in those skills.

We took the formal results and our extended experience with the cognitive

---

[4]Sherlock was a massive undertaking. It took a lot of work by a lot of people. It was, as a real-world applied activity in a setting with real work that could not be halted, a test not only of ingenuity and hard work but also of courage, patience, tolerance, perseverance, and the love and respect of many players for each other. Joining in the effort at one point or another were Jaya Bajpayee, Jeffrey Bonar, Lloyd Bond, Marilyn Bunzo, James Collins, Keith Curran, Richard Eastman, Gary Eggan, Drew Gitomer, Robert Glaser, Bruce Glymour, Linda Greenberg, Susanne Lajoie, Denise Lensky, Alan Lesgold, Debra Logan, Maria Magone, Tom McGinnis, Valerie Shalin, Cassandra Stanley, Arlene Weiner, Richard Wolf, and Laurie Yengo. Equally important were Sherrie Gott and the many people who worked with her at the Air Force Human Resources Laboratory; Dennis Collins and other Air Force subject matter experts who helped us when we needed it most; and the officers and personnel of the 1st and 33rd Tactical Fighter Wings, at Langley and Eglin Air Force Bases, especially those in the Component Repair Squadrons, who made room in their worlds for Sherlock and his many retainers.

The work was done as part of subcontracts with HumRRO and Universal Energy Systems, who were prime contractors with the Air Force Human Resources Laboratory. Many of the tools and much of the infrastructure that permitted us to conduct this project efficiently were put in place by earlier efforts and the foresight of the Office of Naval Research, where Henry Halff, Susan Chipman, Marshall Farr, and Michael Shafto patiently invested in a future that took a number of years to unfold.

task analyses and went on to develop Sherlock, an intelligent coached practice environment for a specific troubleshooting job. Sherlock is designed for airmen who have just completed technical school training and have started to apprentice in the F-15 manual avionics shops. Influenced by current theoretical accounts and our own academic biases, we began designing Sherlock on the assumption that expert troubleshooting is an act of inference from basic principles and concepts, with substantial automation of recurrent components of the inference process. As it happens, the process of building and testing it taught us a lot about the nature of troubleshooting expertise. In the rest of this chapter, after very brief accounts of the first two phases of the project, we reflect on the lessons we learned in the development phase.

At the time the project began, task analyses for training were heavily behavioral, with intuitive cognitive extensions that were not based on clearly established procedures. We felt it important to develop standard cognitive analysis techniques and spent several years developing some (Gitomer, 1984; Lesgold, Lajoie, Glaser, Bonar, Collins, Curran, Eastman, Gitomer, Greenberg, Logan, Magone, Shalin, Weiner, Wolf & Yengo; May 1986). After completing the cognitive task analyses, we began testing our ideas by actually building intelligent instructional systems based on them and then testing those systems in the field.

Cognitive Task Analysis

Fundamentally, cognitive task analysis is an effort to figure out what knowledge is needed for expert performance of a job, which parts of that knowledge are difficult to acquire, and what facilitates the acquisition. In our task analyses, we started with Air Force information. The Air Force periodically solicits information from supervisors about each job specialty. This information is compiled into Occupational Survey Reports that list specific tasks that the job involves and ranks those tasks according to their frequency, criticality, and difficulty. We chose to focus our attention on tasks that were critical and the most difficult. In the case of the F-15 Manual Avionics Test Station job specialty, the routine work, which is addressed at length during training, is to follow printed algorithms that use the test station to diagnose failures in aircraft navigational system components. The aircraft components—parts of a highly modular system—are relatively simple in most cases (a few, like radar antenna systems, are more complex, but still much simpler than the test station). The hard job is fixing the test station itself.

When the test station fails, problems can sometimes be partially diagnosed by running confidence tests that systematically exercise it, creating an opportunity for any failure to show itself in an easily diagnosed manner. However, these confidence tests take a long time and are necessarily insufficient for diagnosing many faults. As a result, technicians who have not been trained to plan and

TABLE 9.1
Summary of Cognitive Task Analysis

Higher-skill first-term airmen in the test station job:

Are not generally more capable of planning a troubleshooting
strategy outside of their specialty. (SELECTION effect)

Do not show greater basic electricity or electronics knowledge.
(TECH SCHOOL effect)

Do not show greater acccuracy or efficiency in the simplest
cognitive acts, such as comparing a meter reading to the tolerance
given in the Technical Orders (TO). (SELECTION & TECH SCHOOL
effect)

Higher-skilled first-termers do have certain skills that are job
relevant. In addition to making more correct diagnoses, they exhibit:

Better specific methods for troubleshooting the specific equipment
they work with:

Domain-specific strategies.
Schematic tracing skills.
Measurement skills (meters).

More knowledge about the systems they work with:

How components work.
What their function is.
How they relate to system as a whole.

---

execute diagnostic strategies must somehow do so when the station fails. In fact,
they often do not succeed; civilian experts are retained at bases that cannot risk
having test stations down for extended periods. Those technicians who do master
the needed diagnostic skills do so over extended periods of time.

In Gitomer's (1984) work, troubleshooting skill in the test station job had
been found to involve a number of problem-solving abilities. These include the
initial representation of the problem, the further specification of this representation, the availability of a variety of methods, and the efficiency with which these
methods are used. Gitomer found differences between higher and lower competence avionics technicians in: (a) the knowledge available to constrain the search
for a solution to the problem; (b) the refinement of their initial hypotheses; (c) the
types of methods used; and (d) the efficiency with which the methods were used.
We sought to tap these components of troubleshooting in individual airmen.

Most contrastive studies select groups with sharp differences. In one experiment in Egan & Schwartz's (1979) study, the skilled group consisted of Bell

Laboratory electronics technicians who designed electronics equipment for research (range in experience 6–25 years). College students without electronics background served as a novice comparison. In another experiment, the experts were either electrical engineering majors in college or high school students who had one or two courses in electronics, and the novices had no prior electronics instruction.

We wanted to understand not only what specific skills were needed for making complex diagnoses, but also what allows some technicians to acquire these skills on the job while others have difficulty. So, we compared the performances of relatively inexperienced technicians who differed in rated judgments of how well they were learning on the job (Lesgold, Lajoie, et al., Apr. 1986). Our subjects were 17 airmen with less than four years' experience in the job specialty. They were divided on the basis of supervisor ratings and observed performance in troubleshooting verbally-simulated test station failures. A battery of tasks was developed to assess the subjects' relevant job knowledge. The battery included a *manual test station troubleshooting* task, two tasks assessing *basic electronics knowledge,* three tasks assessing *basic operations,* and two tasks assessing *system understanding*.

Manual Test Station Troubleshooting. The manual troubleshooting task was developed as a diagnostic test of troubleshooting skill. The task involved finding faults (the sources of failure) in an electronic device, which was similar to but not exactly like any aircraft avionics device the airmen had ever worked on before. The three problems in the manual troubleshooting task required three different levels of troubleshooting skill. Solving the first problem required only a superficial understanding of the interrelationships between the modules of which the system was composed. Given this understanding, either a few module swaps or a few simple measurements of signals being passed between modules or module swaps would quickly lead to the fault. In contrast, the second problem could not be solved by swapping modules. When a technician localized the problem to the faulty modules and attempted to replace it with a shop standard, he[5] was told that the module could not be swapped because it was physically tied to the unit and that he had to isolate the problem within the module by whatever means he could describe. Thus, finding the fault in this problem meant troubleshooting not only at the module level but also at the component level. The faulty module in the second problem contained only signal routing components such as diodes and relays. It contained no active components or control circuits. In the third and most difficult problem, the module contained both active and passive components. In addition, its circuits were designed to process input signals from both the receiver and transmitter, and to use control and switching data to route those signals through the board. With this added complexity, simple continuity tests

---

[5]We use the masculine pronoun form to simplify exposition. A significant number of technicians in our studies were female.

would not be sufficient to localize and isolate the defective component, and greater skill and understanding of troubleshooting procedures would be required. Thus, the third problem required a more comprehensive approach to solving the problem. Only 3 of 13 airmen who attempted all three problems solved all three.

Declarative Knowledge of Basic Electronics.   Two tasks were developed to evaluate airmen's declarative knowledge of basic electronics, including not only what airmen knew about various electronics concepts and principles but also how such knowledge was organized and how accessible it was. These tasks, built on a set of tasks designed by Gitomer (1984), tested knowledge of basic electronics components and semantic retrieval efficiency. To test knowledge of components, 4 questions were asked for each of 14 basic electronics components. Each question corresponded to one of Weld's (1983) categories of types of knowledge one can have about a concept: physical, functional, operational, and applicability knowledge. A semantic retrieval efficiency task tested the airmen's speed of access to certain important concepts. Using the Posner and Mitchell paradigm (1967), pairs of words or pictures were presented, and the subject had to decide whether the 2 pictures, 2 words, or word and picture were the same.

Basic Operations Tasks.   The basic operations tasks were designed in order to evaluate performance on important low-level components of troubleshooting methods. These relatively simple tasks are used in most troubleshooting situations. We tested the basic operations of reading Technical Orders specifications, interpreting digital multimeter (DMM) readings, understanding waveforms, and understanding relationships between inputs and outputs of logic gates.

Digital multimeter (DMM) comparative judgment task. This task approximates the typical bench testing procedure in which airmen must compare meter readings of voltage or resistance with expected values in their printed documentation. This procedure is performed by airmen hundreds of times a day. This task was designed to assess three abilities: (a) accuracy of judgments; (b) efficiency (speed) in making decisions; and (c) fatigue over numerous trials.

DMM Probe Placement Task. The DMM probe placement task investigated the basic operation of placing the probes of the measurement device in their proper places on a given circuit for a particular measurement.

Logic Gate Computation Task. The purpose of this task was to assess an airman's understanding of the relationship between inputs and outputs for common logic gates. This experiment used the same logic gate types as those used in Gitomer (1984). The question asked for each problem was also the same: given a gate with its output or one of its inputs missing, fill in the blank with either a "high" or a "low."

System Understanding.   There were two system understanding tasks, the radar organization task and the antenna system understanding task.

Radar organization task. The purpose of this task was to examine understanding of a complex system. The task required connecting the names of seven major components of the radar system to show how these components interact.

Antenna system understanding task. This task was based on the findings of Gitomer's (1984) radar antenna task. Gitomer assessed airmen's organization of antenna knowledge by asking them to sort antenna components into meaningful groups. The task we used had two parts, both designed to investigate the same issues in knowledge organization as the sorting task but in a more standardized, directed way.

Part I consisted of 12 questions: 7 baseline questions and 5 questions which predicted skill differences. Each involved choosing which of three antenna components did not belong. In Part II, all 30 components of the antenna system were listed and an airman had to categorize each according to the main category types found by Gitomer (1984). The categories were: RF, electrical, hydraulic, and mechanical.

Results of the Task Analyses

One striking finding was that it was very difficult to obtain skill-related differences on most of the laboratory-type tasks. This result contrasts both with Gitomer's (1984) and with Egan and Schwartz's (1979). Further, skill-group differences in conceptual knowledge tended to be highly related to the specifics of troubleshooting. Only knowledge that is needed to be an effective troubleshooter differentiated high- and low-skill performers. Similarly, metacognitive skills were remarkably uniform across skill groups. What differentiated high-skill troubleshooters was domain-specific knowledge of how to apply general strategies to their work.

Egan and Schwartz (1979) compared true experts to true novices, whereas we were comparing people at the same level of electronics experience but with differential competence, as rated by superiors. This is probably why the differences we found were more limited. Also, certain practices of the Air Force probably attenuate some of the expected differences. First, candidates for the electronics troubleshooting specialties are selected from among the very ablest applicants to the Air Force. The top tier of entrants to the Air Force are an able group indeed and so would be expected to have good metacognitive skills and to quickly learn what is taught in technical school.

Technical schooling in the military is modeled after the world of education to a very large extent. Military and civilian experts decide what knowledge is basic to the career field, and this is taught through lectures, manuals, computer-assisted instruction (CAI) systems, and similar, mostly-didactic approaches. The select group of people we studied would surely do well in such courses. The use of mastery procedures tends to further reduce differences in learning what is taught in technical school.

However, the technical school courses in the period we studied had some specific weaknesses. They tended to start with the most basic concepts and not to reach the level of systems that our subjects actually have to maintain. So, airmen were schooled to do well on our basic concept and basic operations tests, but tended not to understand fully the workings of whole test stations, for example. Technical schooling also has tended to emphasize algorithmic troubleshooting and to ignore heuristic techniques needed for the harder problems. Again, this would have the effect of making everyone look alike on the basic speed and accuracy measures although they might differ greatly in handling really hard problems, as they did.

There is an important lesson in this. Real problem-solving skill is highly adaptive. It requires considerable knowledge, but not necessarily all of the knowledge that seems, from an academic perspective, to be important. In the academic world, we attempt to abstract general knowledge that is powerful enough to generate solutions to many different kinds of problems. This abstractive process is a valid form of extending knowledge and has led to great advances of our civilization. However, it is not the only form of knowledge sufficient for successful job performance. Indeed, it may be the wrong form on which to focus in building an effective work force (cf. Brown & Duguid, 1989).

To some extent we should worry about those whose goal in school is merely to "get the right answer," because many of the activities of schooling have goals that are much broader than the activity itself. However, in practical troubleshooting, getting the right answer (i.e., finding the source of system failure) is the first requirement. Those who are successful will differ from their less successful colleagues at least in their ability to get the right answer. In a sample selected for general academic capability, the ability to acquire and work from basic principles, the primary correlations with job capability that are left to vary are those with the most job-specific knowledge.

Further, not all of the job-critical knowledge need be in the head of the expert, and that which is in the head of the expert may not be stored as an academic might expect. In the real world, colleagues, manuals, overt *aides-memoire,* superficial analogies, automated basic knowledge, and episodically cued recall all supplement principled understanding. One of us functions as a program chairperson without knowing the dean's phone number or the rules for filling out expense vouchers because his secretary knows many of these critical things. Similarly, an electronics technician need not remember information that is easily looked up nor need he understand components that are efficiently tested via mandated algorithms.

Training Study

We set out to build a computer-based system that would promote a grasp of troubleshooting concepts and a facile execution of domain-specific troubleshooting skills. We would emphasize the structure of the device as the basis for a testing strategy that eventually isolates a fault. We would encourage the development of mental models critical to understanding the troubleshooting procedures. We would teach tactics that implement strategy. We would exercise necessary subskills in the context of their use. With these goals, we developed a successful program. Our evaluation of Sherlock at two bases where F-15 avionics equipment was maintained found that a Sherlock group showed significantly better posttest performance than a control group on troubleshooting problems (Lesgold, Lajoie, et al., April, 1988). Independent Air Force tests of Sherlock found it to be a very effective means of teaching fault diagnosis in the test station (Nichols, Pokorny, Jones, Gott, & Alley, in press). In the Air Force analysis, almost all trainees showed improvement, although not all progressed to expert performance. Most also claimed, on questionnaires, greater confidence in their abilities than before.

Sherlock's Curriculum

Strategy.   Strategy in electronics troubleshooting is generally based on one's mental model of the system being diagnosed. When the model is adequate, strategies are often striking in their simplicity; without the right model, strategy can seem impossibly complex or even not worth the bother. In the case of the F-15 manual avionics test station, without an appropriate model of the device, the task of finding a fault is like looking for a needle in a haystack. There are hundreds of printed circuit cards to be tested or replaced. Running the general confidence testing routines can easily take several shifts, making that approach unreasonable, too. In contrast, with the appropriate model, diagnosis can be constrained greatly.

We discuss this model briefly to illustrate the constraints on the problem that come from understanding system function and structure. When the test station is being used, it is being used to conduct tests on aircraft components. When a test of a component points to a specific defect, the technician's documentation specifies a repair that should eliminate the fault. If the repair fails to eliminate the indicated fault, the test station may be malfunctioning. So, the situation in which a possible test station malfunction becomes evident is one in which a single test of an aircraft component is shown to be incorrect. Therefore, the representation a troubleshooter needs in order to build a test station diagnosis strategy is a model of the circuitry that realizes the aberrant test.

At bottom, the circuit involved in any test carried out by the test station consists primarily of a pathway connecting the aircraft unit being tested to a source of patterned electrical energy (the stimulus) and to a measurement device.[6] This configuration can be referred to as the *primary circuit path* or the

---

[6]Specific test steps may lack one of the three components (stimulus, aircraft unit, measurement device). For example, in verifying its own function, the test station routes stimuli directly to measurement devices, eliminating the aircraft component altogether. Also, tests of continuity in an aircraft component may involve no stimulus. More rarely, indicators on a component may be triggered by a stimulus in a test that involves no test station measurement.

signal path. This path is generally sequential. That is, there is a set of components connected one to the next in a sequence. A series of tests can determine which of the components in the sequence is malfunctioning. That component is either faulty or configured incorrectly because it is receiving faulty control inputs (called *data flow*).

The test station is a giant switch that configures the test station into circuit paths that realize particular tests. When a particular test fails, the first part of a sensible diagnosis strategy is to find out which link in the circuit path sequence from stimulus to aircraft device to measurement device has failed. If a test on any component in the main circuit path shows that component's inputs to be good, the components before it in the sequence must be good. If the component's outputs are good, the component in question must be good. If a component has good inputs and bad output, either it is defective or it has received wrong control inputs. For example, a relay card may be working incorrectly either because a relay or diode has failed or because it is receiving incorrect data flow. So, isolating the failure in the primary circuit path to one component really means that the new focus of search is that component plus the circuitry that controls it. These circuit paths, which we call *secondary circuit paths* or *data flow paths,* are often not sequential. However, they are relatively simple. Representing a circuit, then, means representing the primary and secondary circuit paths, the connections between components in those paths, and the specifics of how those components function.

Strategy then becomes very straightforward. Assuming that components are equally likely to fail, the most efficient strategy at each step is to test a circuit path component that splits the suspect region in half. After the component is tested, the fault will be shown to be in it (or the data flow path to it), before it, or after it. This "space-splitting" strategy rules out as large a portion of the circuit path as possible each time a component is tested. Actually, there are a few additional complexities, but the basic strategy is as we have outlined. Since the paths in question tend to involve sequences of at most 5 to 10 components (such as printed circuit boards), there is a handsome payoff to having appropriate representations of what the test station has failed to do properly and of what circuitry could possibly be playing a role. Often, problems that would otherwise be combinatorially impossible end up requiring only 10 to 20 measurements before they can be solved—so long as the representation-constrained strategy is used.

Tactics. What has been left out so far are the tactics, the procedures involved in testing a given component once it has been selected for testing by the overall strategy. For most components, there are relatively standard testing schemes that each technician is taught or works out independently. For example, suppose that the component being tested were a simple electromechanical relay that switches an input to one of two possible outputs if it is energized and to the other if it is not. Suppose further that the relay should have been energized and should have been passing a 5 volt signal from its input to its "closed" output. Then, the tactic for testing the relay would be to check for the 5 volt input. If it is missing, the fault comes before the relay. If it is present, then the next step is to check for the appropriate output. If the output is not present, then either the relay is bad or it is not being energized by its control inputs. So, the final test would be to see if the appropriate activating voltage is present. If so, then the relay is bad and should be replaced. If not, then the path from the solenoid back to the source of the activating voltage needs to be checked.

Just as with strategy, tactics are also heavily dependent on understanding how the components being tested work. Note, however, that what is required is not complete understanding of all of the physics of the system but rather functional, teleological understanding of how the system accomplishes certain purposes. Technicians, even many experts, can have very impoverished understanding of electrical principles so long as their understanding is sufficient to support the kinds of strategy and tactics a particular system requires. For systems that are complex but that carry out simple functions, like the manual avionics test station, the underlying knowledge required to support strategies and tactics is rather limited. For systems in which there are complex feedback processes or in which there are complex transformations of inputs by particular components, more understanding is required.

Further, not all systems have such simple binary decomposition strategies matched to them. For example, a computer network involves many components communicating over a common pathway such as a coaxial cable. Because they share the cable, there is no linear circuit to decompose. In such a case, a totally different strategy may be required. For example, it may be necessary to ask which network "citizens" are capable of generating the faulty patterns that have been observed. Or, it may be necessary to isolate parts of the network to see which parts continue to show the fault. Whatever is done, it will still depend upon a representation of how the system works to achieve particular purposes, and specific tests will rest on some knowledge of how individual components work or what they can do.

The Hidden Curriculum

The development of Sherlock was not entirely driven by the design of the test station. It was intimately tied to real-world expertise and was subject to modification both by our in-house experts (Lesgold, Lajoie, Glaser, et al., May 1986) and by our experience at job sites. In this way, it admitted ad hoc, "cultural," and motivational influences that we have come to believe are essential rather than peripheral to acquiring expertise.

One aspect of expertise is social. A fundamental property of expertise is that it confers responsibility. The electronics expert is expected to fix broken electronics devices. No one is as likely to do so as the expert, but there is no guarantee that the expert knows the right thing to do. Still, he must at least make the decision about whether a repair is possible. Often, he must try to make a repair even if he is pessimistic about his chances of success. Finally, he must carry out his craft in a particular context. That context often will require some tuning of the expert's general knowledge.

Confidence, Persistence, and Motivation.   This brings us to old issues of learning and performance that cognitive science has largely ignored. The fundamental approach of cognitive instructional science, until recently, has been to study expertise by studying the problem spaces for the hard problems of a domain and the steps taken by experts when they work in those spaces. However, there are some other aspects of expertise that are also of great importance. These include understanding how much work it will take to solve hard problems and having the confidence that persisting in the hard work will be fruitful. In the past, we may have ignored these problems because we did not have good ideas about how to address them. Now, we may be entering a period in which the soft issues of confidence and persistence can be fruitfully addressed (for example, Dweck, 1989, discusses inappropriate estimates of task difficulty and confidence levels among high- and low-achieving children). The key is to identify the knowledge that can motivate persistence.

Repeatedly over the past 20 years, we have encountered experiences in which people with low levels of job experience were paralyzed in the face of a task that they were capable of doing. They just did not realize that successful performance was possible. Part of job knowledge is knowing whether a task is doable and how much effort will be required to do it. Even after technicians acquire some facility, they often do not know at the outset of a problem whether their knowledge is likely to be sufficient nor do they know how much work will be required. The relevant expertise is very specific. For example, we have seen many cases of people spending weeks writing software to automate a one-time record keeping task that might only take a day or two to do by hand. This is because they know they can do the programming task but do not know much about manual office procedures. Only when they have written the program does it become clear that it would have been faster to do the job by hand.

Test station diagnosis is strongly of this character. The subgoaling approach that works well does require a considerable amount of specific knowledge. However, many failures can be isolated through repeated application of only a subset of that knowledge. As a trainee acquires expertise, it will often be the case that whether or not he can solve a hard problem depends primarily on whether he attempts to do so and persists in doing the best he can. General instruction to work hard and persevere is never very helpful. Our subjects were very motivated, but they also have a responsibility to call for help if the alternative is extensive down time with no repair afterwards. To be successful, they must have at least partial ability to discern in advance that they are likely to succeed.

Training of persistence.   Sherlock addresses this problem in a straightforward way. All[7] of the activity in Sherlock focuses on solving test station diagnosis problems that are much harder than trainees have ever seen before. We encourage persistence in the diagnostic process by providing advice to the trainee upon request. So, whenever a trainee is unable to proceed, he can ask for help. Providing help, however, might discourage hard thinking. For example, Schofield and Verban (1988) observed students using the Anderson geometry tutor (Anderson et al., 1985) and saw some who do no problem-solving work, but merely press the help button continually.

We solve this problem by building considerable inertia into the advising process. At each point in the course of problem solution, Sherlock will respond to an initial help request (for that point) by providing only a recapitulation of the actions taken by the trainee so far. This recapitulation is structured and summarized, so it has the effect of providing some amount of strategy advice implicitly. However, the overall effect is to be responsive to the trainee, to help him overcome short-term memory capacity limitations, but also to encourage him to think harder. Further requests for help at the same point are answered with incremental amounts of directly useful information. The next hints are bits of conceptual overview that encourage the trainee to continue to think. Each new hint comes a little closer to telling the trainee what to do next. To deal with possible frustrations when the trainee is in too far over his or her head, a student model is used to tune the hinting process. If a trainee asks for help at a point in a problem where the student model predicts that the trainee will have great difficulty, the progression of hints gets explicit and directive much more quickly.

The global experience of trainees with Sherlock is that they have worked hard on every problem and solved it, even though they had no hope of solving such problems prior to the Sherlock experience. Missing domain knowledge is provided as needed through the hinting/advising process. However, the inertia of that process results in some of the needed knowledge being invented or inferred by the airman rather than being provided directly by Sherlock. The trainee gets the most credible indication of what he or she can do by persisting—achieving success in solving problems that he or she initially thought impossible. And it turns out that Sherlock trainees claimed greater confidence in their responses to an Air Force questionnaire (Nichols et al., in press).

It is interesting to look for this aspect of training and resultant expertise in other domains. Medicine and basic military training both exhibit some of the same approach of providing stiff challenges with backup support. After completing medical school, physicians know many basic principles and have fragmentary diagnostic knowledge. Their next experience, the internship, forces them to

---

[7]Actually, each Sherlock problem begins with the mundane everyday task of using the test station to diagnose faults in components from aircraft. To assure that trainees realize that usually the test station is fine and the problem is with the aircraft component, a number of Sherlock problems end with successful repair of the failed aircraft part.

confront a barrage of diagnostic and treatment tasks that go beyond their perceived (sometimes actual) capabilities. As with Sherlock, help is available, but there are social costs to seeking it too quickly. One outcome is that they rapidly gain confidence in their abilities and are also motivated to continue to study hard to fill in the knowledge they still lack. As with Sherlock, inertia in providing help may be inefficient from the viewpoint of telling knowledge to the trainee, but it is important in building domain-specific confidence and persistence. Military basic training also includes a variety of exercises that seem inefficient until the questions of confidence and persistence are taken into account.

In contrast, traditional apprenticeship tended to be much more gradual. Often the apprentice, left to do the dullest tasks, became convinced of his capabilities long before he could exercise them. This made great sense in a slowly changing world where masters wanted to regulate the flow of new competition. However, modern expertise often involves emergent problem-solving jobs, such as repairing new electronic systems. Accordingly, much of the expertise, instead of being slowly crystallized, will necessarily consist of partial knowledge, good weak methods, and, in particular, weak methods involving systematic persistence.

Dialects of Expertise. Our experience in the development phase taught us (as Brown & Duguid, 1989, makes obvious in retrospect) that both skills and strategies are grounded in specific work situations and that tuning of troubleshooting to these varying situations is very important and not possible on the basis of general principles alone. Indeed, even knowledge based in practice is subject to difficult-to-anticipate variations in situations. We cite a very instructive example.

One of our colleagues, Gary Eggan, had worked for the Defense Department in the role of providing expert troubleshooting service and advice in cases where test stations failed in ways that airmen on duty could not diagnose. We relied on his knowledge of the real job, of Air Force doctrine, and of the characteristic errors of Air Force technicians. There came a time when various interested segments of the Air Force sent their own experts to review our work. In a number of cases, senior Air Force experts just like Eggan disagreed strongly with the procedure that he had characterized as the best approach. We went through several phases, first deciding that the other experts were wrong, then wondering if Eggan was as good as we had thought (he was). Finally, we realized that we were seeing dialects of expertise, differences in approach that reflected detailed tuning of performance to subtle environmental differences.

Although system architecture and basic principles are the basis for good troubleshooting strategy, certain data-gathering steps involve small risks that can save great amounts of time. Eggan had gained much of his experience at operational bases with rapid deployment assignments. At these bases, keeping equipment operational at all times is an important mandate. Further, because of their strategic importance, the bases enjoy good logistics and a relatively good budget.

Eggan's critics came from training bases with more of a reserve and support function. These bases had fewer real-time constraints and less luxurious logistic support. The risks that were necessary to solve problems quickly at a forward base were unacceptable at these support bases because parts could not readily be obtained. This mandated a less risky approach and more confirmation of part failure before a replacement was attempted.[8]

In observations of technical jobs done by groups, such as jet engine maintenance, a somewhat different form of dialectal variation can be observed. A group that must work together evolves certain short cuts and anticipatory actions that rest upon their experience working together. Electronics repair is mostly a solitary job. Nonetheless, we can anticipate that real expertise involves some understanding of the social structure in which the troubleshooting occurs. This understanding might include knowledge about the quality of work done by colleagues who may refer hard problems to an expert, for example. Is it worth believing their summaries of what has already been tested, or should their work be replicated? Is their account of the failure likely to be accurate, or should it be challenged? How much can the social structure handle such challenges?

This problem of dialectal variation might seem trivial. Is there something to teach here? Doesn't this sort of thing happen in all jobs? The problem posed by the issue of dialectal variation has two parts. First, without understanding the social structure in which troubleshooting is being done, it is hard to do effective task analyses. Actions of the expert can be difficult to understand if they are grounded partly in deep understanding of the device and partly in the social context of device repair. Second, it is easy to get a limited view of expertise if one sees it expressed only in a particular context. Watching the expert at a training base religiously follow confidence testing algorithms from a book, it might be hard to conclude that the job can also involve complex heuristic reasoning and sophisticated cost-benefit tradeoff analyses.

TROUBLESHOOTING EXAMPLES
FROM EVERYDAY SITUATIONS

So far, we have addressed only a specialized fragment of electronics troubleshooting expertise in the military. Military troubleshooting is characterized by several features that distinguish it from the kind of troubleshooting we all experience when we have a personal computer that fails or when a television set is not working. In everyday business life, replacement is always a competitor for repair. The investment to be made in troubleshooting is limited by the possibility

---

[8]We should emphasize that Eggan shared with his colleagues from the other bases an aversion to diagnosis by part swapping. He did, however, favor techniques that saved much time over the use of full confidence tests as a primary means of data gathering, and these techniques involved minor risks.

of simply replacing the malfunctioning device. With labor becoming increasingly expensive, it is quite common for a very rapid decision to be made that diagnosis is not worthwhile. Cost considerations also constrain the social structure of electronics problem solving in the commercial sector. Ordinarily, the person first sent to provide service at a customer site will be almost a novice. He or she will carry out algorithmic tests of the faulty device and, in most cases, end up making a diagnosis and repair simply by following directions.

The Special Character of Commercial Troubleshooting

The interesting cases, of course, are those in which simple algorithmic activity is insufficient to solve the diagnosis problem. In complex systems, such as large computers, the diagnosis software will usually isolate a fault automatically and indicate the appropriate repair. In smaller systems, some combination of automatic internal diagnosis and a manual will have the same effect. For example, modern automobile control computers are often designed to display a code (via an indicator the mechanic attaches to the electrical system) that is referenced to a shop manual.

However, very often the automatic diagnosis is insufficient. Generally, the diagnosis software is written from a preliminary specification of the device, and sometimes does not perfectly match the final version. Also, if parts of the system needed to run the diagnosis program are faulty, the diagnosis process itself would be interdicted. For example, the disk on which the diagnosis program resides might be damaged, the main power supply for the device may have failed, or the output device whereby the automatic diagnosis would be reported may not be working.

Some faults are not detectable within the context of automatic diagnosis, at least not completely. For example, an intermittent failure of an active bus device, like the bus adapters on large computers, is hard to attribute. If the most common bus activity is disk access, the bus failure may be camouflaged as a disk failure, because the apparent fault would be a failure to transmit information from the disk to the processor. Physical connections can sometimes be inadequate, too. In this case, no device has failed, and strategies asking which component has failed will not work.

Cases like these, in which the algorithmic process fails, usually are not handled by first-level technicians. Ordinarily, the first-level technician will carry out complete algorithmic tests and then call in someone who is more expert. In a large service organization, four or five levels of progressively more expert diagnosticians might be called in, with the last often being a member of the team that designed the device. At each higher level, there is more expertise (generally expressed as more time spent building a mental model of the situation), clearer strategy, and more of an effort to understand the failed system.

Anecdotes

To illustrate the points just made, here are a few examples of real diagnosis episodes from our own experience managing a departmental computer facility. Each helps illustrate the character of commercial electronics diagnosis problems and of the skills they require.

The Map is Not the Territory.   In 1979, our department acquired a VAX "supermini" computer. By the standards of the day, this was a very complex device. Being the first in the design series, it had not yet accumulated much lore or fault experience. Further, it involved dramatic new approaches to computing, approaches most computer people were just beginning to understand. Three of those novel (at least for minicomputers) characteristics were virtual memory, prefetch, and data caching.[9]

A few months after the machine was installed, it suffered a major failure and would not operate for more than a few minutes. The technicians who came to diagnose and repair the computer started by running the diagnostic software. After 10 or 15 minutes, the diagnostic program would recommend the replacement of one of two printed circuit boards. The technicians would make the required changes, but the system would keep failing. The technicians phoned for help,[10] and higher-level service personnel appeared. They, too, were baffled, and a variety of even higher-level people appeared or were consulted by phone. Finally, the senior VAX repair guru was flown in from the main office. He reviewed what had been done so far and almost immediately pulled out the circuit diagrams of the computer.

After comparing the schematic diagrams that show the functional organization

---

[9]**Virtual memory** is a scheme in which not all of a job is in the computer's primary memory at once. The memory addresses contained in computer programs must be mapped onto locations that may be either in the primary memory or on a disk. Memory mapping hardware to do this mediates between the central processor and the primary memory. When the computer requests a datum from virtual memory, the request is translated into the addressing scheme of primary memory if the datum is located there. Otherwise, it is translated into the address for a chunk of disk memory, that chunk is fetched from the disk, and the specific datum is retrieved from the chunk. **Prefetch** is a process in which memory items that will shortly be needed by the central processor are retrieved from memory in advance. For example, while the system is waiting for one datum to be retrieved from the disk by the memory management hardware, it can access the next needed datum, which may be in primary memory already. By having it preloaded into the central processor, some time can be saved. The third mechanism, **caching,** is a mechanism for keeping close at hand data that is likely to be needed again in a few microseconds. Such data, when the central processor wants to store them, are sent out to primary memory but are also copied into an even faster memory cache from which they can be retrieved especially quickly if they are needed again soon.

[10]Informal social constraints, and sometimes company policy, require that before phoning for help the technician must have run the diagnostic software and tried the solutions it recommended (Orr, 1987).

of the computer with the diagrams showing which circuitry was located on which boards, the guru pointed out that the diagnostic software had traced the problem to a particular function. Most of that function was realized in circuitry on a board that was titled by that function (we think it was "memory mapping," but it might have been one of the others). The program had recommended replacing that board. However, in the final design of the computer, it had been found that not all of the circuitry for the function fitted onto one board, so part of it had been moved to another board on which there was extra room. It was the latter board that was the culprit. It was replaced, and the problem was solved.

Consider the nature of the guru's expertise. Novices focus on superficial aspects of problems; experts represent the problem more deeply and operate on their representations (Chi, Glaser, & Rees, 1982). This highest-level expert was representing and diagnosing not only the computer but also the entire process of designing a computer, planning how it will be maintained, creating diagnostic software, and actually doing the maintenance. With such a representation, he could quickly generate the hypothesis that the problem solving representations on which the diagnostic software and its recommendations had been based were incorrect. This domain-specific metacognitive representational and operational capability is the highest level in the electronics repair hierarchy.

But the Book Says. . . . Let's next consider the low end of the expertise scale. Our center had a Diablo printer that was used for typing of form letters. A heavily used, highly mechanical device with many moving parts, it was prone to failure. The person who usually came in to fix it was not very broadly experienced in electronics troubleshooting. However, he was perfectly able to characterize accurately the symptoms the machine was exhibiting and to look up those symptoms in the printed troubleshooting guide he carried on the job. Usually, this resulted in a rapid diagnosis and a quick return of the machine to service. On one occasion, though, this approach failed.

We went through a pattern, day after day, in which the technician would come, exchange a part, test the printer, and then leave. Shortly after he was gone, the printer would fail. On the seventh day of this pattern, one of us stopped in the computer room and asked what was happening. The technician reported that the manual said to replace a particular part when failures of the form we were having occurred, so he had been doing that. Further, he had noticed that each time he removed the suspect part for replacement, it was in fact scorched, suggesting that it had indeed failed.

We then suggested that it was rather unusual to replace a part seven consecutive times and have it fail again each time. He agreed but pointed out that he was doing just what the manual said, and that the parts being replaced were scorched. Further, he suggested that sometimes the service organization would receive a run of bad replacement parts. We suggested that prior to returning the next day when we would surely be calling him again, he should discuss the problem with his supervisor, in hopes of limiting the number of components that were being offered up for sacrifice. With expert assistance, a damaged backplane[11] was discovered, which had been shorting out some of the circuitry and thereby producing the repeated component failures. The backplane was replaced, and life went on.

What can be seen in this incident is a completely algorithmic level of problem-solving performance. The technician had no idea how the device worked and had only the strategy of comparing a superficial description of the failure symptoms with a troubleshooting chart. The possibility that the troubleshooting chart might be incomplete was never considered. Even if it had been, there was no other expertise to fall back on.

Certain kinds of electrical failures are problematic exactly because algorithmic diagnosis approaches are impractical. What usually works can be very valuable, but when it fails, additional heuristics are needed. Sometimes, this is because the failures are in components that are essential even to automated diagnosis. For example, when a primary power supply for a computer fails, that computer will not be able to run diagnostic software. At a more complex level, when a particular memory location fails, the fault can be detected if that location is not used by the diagnosis program. However, if the diagnosis program itself requires integrity of a memory address, then it might not, unless reasonably sophisticated, be able to diagnose failures of that address. Another kind of problem that is difficult for a machine to diagnose is intermittent failure. Sometimes a failure will be manifest only when the computer is carrying out a particular function, or only when the machine is at a particular temperature, or even at random times. In such cases, the system may pass diagnostic tests that it would fail if it had been in the critical state while those tests were being run.

A particularly interesting case is a failure of connections between components. The backplane failure just discussed is of this type. In such a failure, the system has actually become a different system than it used to be, with required connections now absent or with new connections where they do not belong. Such changes violate the fundamental assumptions of ordinary diagnosis and often produce diagnostic impasses. Ordinarily, modern systems are built in a hierarchical modular manner. Diagnosis consists of assessing the adequate function of each high level module. When a high-level module is found to be dysfunctional, then its component modules are examined. Eventually, a specific component is discovered that is not performing as required, and that component is replaced.

From this perspective, then, the hard failures are those in which this hierarchical decomposition will not work. For example, if additional pathways have

---

[11]A backplane interconnects several printed circuit cards. The cards plug into the backplane, which itself is often a printed circuit board on which small cracks can be almost invisible but highly destructive.

been created or usual pathways destroyed, then assumptions about proper device function and decomposition may not be valid. One might find a high-level module that fails but discover that each of its components works fine (because the failure is in connections among the components). Alternatively, components may look bad because their true inputs are not what the technician believes them to be, as when ground connections from highly tuned devices turn out not to be as independent as theorized.

Socially Mediated Diagnosis: War Stories.   Orr (1987) reports interesting examples of a troubleshooting approach often used by technicians of intermediate skill levels.[12] These technicians repair copiers, which are highly evolved systems in which physical connections do not wholly define componential interactions and in which components that look the same may have very different purposes. For example, a common copier design includes three high voltage wires, called corona wires. They are often identical. However, one may make copies darker when voltage is too high and another may have almost the opposite effect.[13]

Because the interconnections among components are complex and involve several different kinds of information (conductive electrical connections, electrical charge relationships, mechanical connections, and even thermal connections), it is not possible to have a simple hierarchical modular model of a device like a copier. Further, because some components can be bent or otherwise physically altered (e.g., a cable gets smashed in a door, resulting in a combination of shorts and open connections), failing systems may require a model that is very different qualitatively from the working system (i.e., more than deletion of a component or a change in gain in an input-output function).

In this tough predicament, copier repair personnel work from a combination of systematic expertise, episodic personal experience, and "war stories." These stories are records of interesting system failures that are retained in the technician culture. When a puzzling failure occurs, technicians discuss it, trying to match its circumstances to one or another story. If a match is made, the story can often be a sufficient guide to enable development and execution of a fault isolation or fault verification strategy.

These community memories serve different functions for novices and for

---

[12]By *intermediate,* we mean that they have the ability to develop a modular representation of the device, build a strategy based on that representation, and execute the strategy with the appropriate tactics. A skilled diagnostician may be rendered "intermediate" by the nature of the fault, as in the present example, or by confronting failures that go beyond his or her knowledge, as when the quality of electrical input from a wall plug is poor, causing a system plugged into that source to fail.

[13]This is because the corona wires are used to "steer" toner particles around. One pushes particles toward the paper while another attracts extra particles from the belt. So, increasing corona wire voltage, which is a possible adjustment, may result in a darker or a lighter print, depending on which wire is adjusted.

experts. Because experts have built up a store of experience with normal failures, they realize that they have heard an account of an unusual incident. They understand why the situation frustrated normal efforts to solve it and appreciate the specific ways in which the situation misled those dealing with it. Further, they will often be able to understand what lesson should be learned from the war story. Is there an inherent weakness in the system that was not previously known? Is there some new use for the system (a new program or the attachment of a new peripheral perhaps) that produces a previously unknown problem? Is the system suffering mechanical difficulties as it ages?

In contrast, war stories can have a negative effect on novice performance. Novices tend in general to be oversensitive to the recency of experiences and undersensitive to their frequency. For this reason, medical interns are warned, "When you hear hoofbeats, think of horses, not of zebras." Just as the medical student suspects he or she may have each new disease learned about, novices tend to invoke war stories too often, trying to match them to situations for which they are irrelevant. A war story can distract a novice from acquiring systematic understanding of device function and systematic troubleshooting procedures.

AN ANALYSIS OF ELECTRONICS TROUBLESHOOTING EXPERTISE

What can we learn from the various sources of information just described? First, it is clear that expertise in complex technical domains is multifaceted. The conceptual knowledge from which effective troubleshooting actions could, in principle, be derived is only one part of this expertise. Specific known methods constitute another part, and certain kinds of social and self-knowledge and experience constitute a third. This division is certainly reminiscent of Sternberg's (1985) triarchic theory of intelligence and helps in organizing the forms of expertise we have noted.

Conceptual Knowledge

The conceptual underpinnings of expertise have been given the most attention by cognitive psychologists and instructional designers. Further, they represent the subset of the expertise that many of us academics have. When one of our personal computers has a hardware problem, we reason about it from first principles. This is very inefficient, but it can work. Because it is inefficient, though, it cannot be the sole basis for truly expert performance. Indeed, in our experience, explicit verbal probing of expert knowledge often reveals gaps in basic concepts. These concepts seem to be present only implicitly and incompletely.

However, conceptual knowledge is surely a primary basis for far transfer. If an expert in fixing the F-15 manual avionics test station is suddenly asked to diagnose and repair other electronic equipment, his ability to go beyond the procedures he uses routinely will rest at least partly in his conceptual knowledge. Without some understanding of the new system and how it relates to the old one, he will have no basis for adapting the procedures he already knows or for developing new ones. Intelligent, adaptive expertise rests on at least a modicum of understanding of the work domain, its artifacts, and how they work. However, such understanding can develop through social discourse mechanisms from situated experience as well as from more academic learning.

Principles

One piece of this understanding is knowledge of principles. In this case of electronics, this includes the fundamental laws of electricity such as Ohm's and Kirchhoff's laws. In order for principles to be useful in problem solving, there must also be methods available for relating them to specific device function and to understanding of analogous or partly analogous systems. Like every form of knowledge in this list, understanding of principles has a procedural as well as a declarative component. This understanding is often not totally articulate. For example, one might know Ohm's law relating current, voltage, and resistance in a circuit. One might also realize that voltage can be thought of as a difference in electrical potential or charge. However, extending this concept to explain why there is a voltage drop across a resistor in an active circuit may require mental gymnastics that are not part of troubleshooting expertise.

Device Models

Perhaps the best studied form of expertise in electronics is representation of the devices that one might be called upon to diagnose. Sometimes this representation is complete. For example, de Kleer's (1984) modeling of a Schmitt trigger captures everything that can be known about such a device. From that knowledge, all aspects of the device's expected behavior can be predicted. Further, given some knowledge of electronics principles, it is also possible to predict how the device would behave if faulted in one way or another. For example, the kind of model envisioned by de Kleer can explain how an amplifier like that shown in Fig. 9.2 works by appealing to Kirchhoff's current and voltage laws and to the defined input-output behavior of the components (transistor, resistor, battery). More properly, the combination of a representation of the circuit connections, knowledge of the component input-output relations, and knowledge of Kirchhoff's current and voltage laws must be tapped by an explanation process that itself represents considerable intelligence.

The problem is that many expert electronics technicians have the ability to diagnose and repair such a circuit, can represent the circuit connections mentally, know the input-output relations in the components and the laws of electricity, but still cannot generate the causal account very clearly. These people would fail

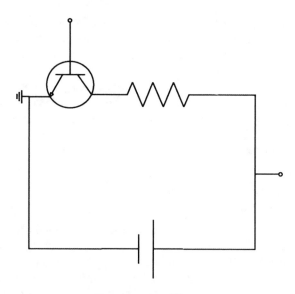

Fig. 9.2. Amplifier.

classroom tests on the apparent prerequisites for the work they do every day. This suggests that we need to understand better how the causal accounts that may not be available explicitly can still be put to use in troubleshooting. Are explicit procedural rules present but not conscious, or is the generative knowledge in some less explicit form perhaps better captured by a connectionist model? We do not have an answer to this question, but we note that it needs to be asked.

There was one related finding in our qualitative task analysis work. This was that the better first-term technicians tended to know more about systems and components at the limits of their job routine. Subsystems that were maintained by other groups or sent to the factory to be repaired were truly outside the knowledge of the less-able technicians but at least partly understood by the more-able. This suggests that expertise may require some amount of explicit learning skill—at least a propensity to go "beyond the information given." We suspect that this tendency to probe the edges of one's current work world is an important part of efficient learning on the job. However, it will be necessary to establish that this capability is a cause of better learning and not an effect of greater prior knowledge (which can "scaffold" broader inquiry).

Methods

Another broad area of expertise is specific procedural knowledge. Experts know methods for doing their work that others do not. In electronics troubleshooting, the methods of greatest importance are those for finding faults in complex systems. Although the distinction can become somewhat arbitrary for certain electronics jobs, it has been useful in our work to distinguish two forms of method knowledge, strategy and tactics. By strategy, we mean the general troubleshooting plans an expert has for deciding which parts of a system to test in what order. By tactics, we mean the specific testing approach taken when testing a particular system part. In medicine, the distinction might be between the general methods for diagnosing diseases and the specific techniques for carrying out lab tests and interpreting their results. Strategy and tactics are discussed in the section on *Sherlock's Curriculum*.

Knowledge Grounded in Work Experience

The sort of metacognitive knowledge that experts have can be seen as grounded in their knowledge of the field. As noted in the discussions of the Sherlock field study, one aspect of expertise is to have confidence that the fault isolation problem can be solved. Experts, simply by virtue of their experience, will know that problems may seem very thorny, but also that they usually give way to continued application of basic strategies. The expert not only knows what to do; he or she also knows that doing it will generally pay off. Novices suffer both from not having as complete a sense of what to do and also from not being as confident that they will succeed. Thus they may give up even when they could have succeeded by just doing the best they could. We note that research in other fields (Dweck, 1989) suggests that low achievers and novices may initially underestimate the difficulty of a task. Experts, in our experience, typically recognize when they face a "hairy" problem. They therefore, presumably, devote more effort to it, and perhaps derive more satisfaction from it when they have succeeded.

Experts know that all problems do not quickly give way to simple strategies. A failure of a system component may turn a system into something other than what it was intended to be. The modified system may exhibit strange characteristics, including mimicking of correct function when function is not in fact correct. Even experts can be stymied. Part of what distinguishes an expert, though, is the realization that almost all fault diagnosis problems can eventually be solved—even if frustrations present themselves along the way.

True expertise also is highly tuned to specific contexts. An expert electronics technician not only is able to diagnose and repair equipment, he also can adapt his operations to local needs. If parts are scarce, he finds ways to minimize part swapping. If time is scarce, he takes relatively prudent shortcuts. If he is teaching a novice, he may behave in an explicitly more systematic way (if he is an expert teacher as well as an expert practitioner). True expertise in this domain, as in others, includes not only conceptually supported strategy and tactics but flexibility and the ability to observe and tune one's activity to specialized situational requirements.

We believe that it is the combination of conceptually undergirded systematic procedural capability with this less visible situationally adaptive flexibility that is responsible for the endless debate over the relative importance of "basic science," procedural practice, and case study methods in teaching real-world expertises. Each has its place. Although it may be incomplete, Anderson's (1983) learning theory helps us understand that three different kinds of training may be required: conceptual or verbal explanation of how things work, practice in carrying out basic procedures, and variation in experiences to permit tuning of procedural knowledge and the development of metaknowledge that can support persistence and confidence. There is less support for insisting that these forms of learning always must occur in strict order from verbal to experiential. Verbally articulate knowledge is a great gift, but it is not always necessary for expert performance.

REFERENCES

Anderson, J. R. (1983). *The architecture of cognition.* Cambridge, MA: Harvard University Press.

Anderson, J. R., Boyle, C. F., & Reiser, B. J. (1985). Intelligent tutoring systems. *Science, 228,* 456–462.

Brown, J. S., & Duguid, P. (1989, May). Innovation in the workplace: A perspective on organizational learning. Paper presented at the Carnegie Mellon Conference on Organizational Learning, Carnegie Mellon University, Pittsburgh. To be published in the conference volume.

Caillot, M. (1987). Modelling the students' errors in the Electre tutor. In J. Self (Ed.), *Intelligent computer-aided instruction.* London: Chapman & Hall.

Chase, W. G., & Simon, H. A. (1973a). Perception in chess. *Cognitive Psychology, 4,* 55–81.

Chase, W. G., & Simon, H. A. (1973b). The mind's eye in chess. In W. G. Chase (Ed.), *Visual information processing.* New York: Academic Press.

Chi, M. T. H., Feltovich, P. J., & Glaser, R. (1981). Categorization and representation of physics problems by experts and novices. *Cognitive Science, 5,* 121–152.

Chi, M. T. H., Glaser, R., & Rees, E. (1982). Expertise in problem solving. In R. Sternberg (Ed.), *Advances in the psychology of human intelligence.* Hillsdale, NJ: Lawrence Erlbaum Associates.

de Groot, A. (1966). Perception and memory versus thought: Some old ideas and recent findings. In B. Kleinmuntz (Ed.), *Problem solving: Research, method, and theory.* New York: Wiley.

de Groot, A. (1978). *Thought and choice in chess.* (2nd ed.). The Hague: Mouton.

de Kleer, J. (1984). How circuits work. *Artificial Intelligence, 24,* 205–280.

Dweck, C. (1989). Motivation. In A. Lesgold & R. Glaser (Eds.), *Foundations for a psychology of education.* Hillsdale, NJ: Lawrence Erlbaum Associates.

Egan, D. E., & Schwartz, B. J. (1979). Chunking in recall of symbolic drawing. *Memory & Cognition, 7,* 149–158.

Gentner, D., & Gentner, D. R. (1983). Flowing waters or teeming crowds: Mental models of electricity. In D. Gentner & A. L. Stevens (Eds.), *Mental models.* Hillsdale, NJ: Lawrence Erlbaum Associates.

Gitomer, D. H. (1984). *A cognitive analysis of a complex troubleshooting task.* Unpublished doctoral dissertation, University of Pittsburgh.

Haertel, H. (1987, September). *A qualitative approach to electricity* (Tech. Rep. IRL87-0001). Palo Alto, CA: Xerox Palo Alto Research Center.

Larkin, J. H., McDermott, J., Simon, D., & Simon, H. A. (1980). Expert & novice performance in solving physics problems. *Science, 208,* 1335–1342.

Lesgold, A. M. (1988). Problem solving. In R. J. Sternberg & E. E. Smith (Eds.), *The psychology of human thought* (pp. 188–213). Cambridge: The Cambridge University Press.

Lesgold, A. M., Lajoie, S., Bajpayee, J., Bunzo, M., Eastman, R., Eggan, G., Greenberg, L. A., Logan, D., McGinnis, T., Weiner, A., & Wolf, R. (1988, April). *A computer coached practice environment for the manual test station shop: Sherlock's influence on job performance* (Technical Report). Pittsburgh, PA: University of Pittsburgh, Learning Research and Development Center.

Lesgold, A. M., Lajoie, S., Eastman, R., Eggan, G., Gitomer, D., Glaser, R., Greenberg, L., Logan, D., Magone, M., Weiner, A., Wolf, R., & Yengo, L. (1986, April). *Cognitive task analysis to enhance technical skills training and assessment* (Technical Report). Pittsburgh, PA: University of Pittsburgh, Learning Research and Development Center.

Lesgold, A. M., Lajoie, S., Glaser, R., Bonar, J., Collins, J., Curran, K., Eastman, R., Gitomer, D., Greenberg, L., Logan, D., Magone, M., Shalin, V., Weiner, A., Wolf, R., & Yengo, L. (1986, May). *Guide to cognitive task analysis* (Technical Report). Pittsburgh, PA: University of Pittsburgh, Learning Research and Development Center.

Lesgold, A., Rubinson, H., Feltovich, P., Glaser, R., Klopfer, D., & Wang, Y. (1988). Expertise in a complex skill: Diagnosing x-ray pictures. In M. T. H. Chi, R. Glaser, & M. Farr (Eds.), *The nature of expertise.* Hillsdale, NJ: Lawrence Erlbaum Associates.

Nichols, P., Pokorny, R., Jones, G., Gott, S. P., & Alley, W. E. (in press). *Evaluation of an avionics troubleshooting tutoring system,* (Special Report). Brooks AFB, TX: Air Force Human Resources Laboratory.

Orr, J. (1987, March). *Talking about machines: Social aspects of expertise* (Tech. Rep.). Palo Alto, CA: Xerox Palo Alto Research Center.

Posner, M. I., & Mitchell, R. F. (1967). Chronometric analysis of classification. *Psychological Review, 74,* 392–409.

Rasmussen, J. (1986). *Information processing and human-machine interaction: An approach to cognitive engineering.* Amsterdam: North Holland.

Schofield, J. W., & Verban, D. (1988). Computer usage in the teaching of mathematics: Issues that need answers. In D. A. Grouws & T. J. Cooney (Eds.), *Perspectives on research on effective mathematics teaching* (pp. 169–193). Hillsdale, NJ: Lawrence Erlbaum Associates.

Sternberg, R. (1985). *Beyond IQ: A triarchic theory of human intelligence.* Cambridge: Cambridge University Press.

Weld, D. S. (1983). *Explaining complex engineered devices* (Tech. Rep. #5489). Cambridge, MA: Bolt, Beranek, & Newman.

10 Computer Interaction: Debugging the Problems

Dana S. Kay
Carnegie Mellon University

Learning how to use a computer is becoming an increasingly important aspect of our society. With this increase in importance has come an increasing interest in understanding the acquisition of computer skills and the best methods for teaching people how to use a computer. Research in this area addresses three primary questions:

1. What is the nature of the knowledge acquired when someone learns to use a computer? That is, what are the knowledge representations and processes that characterize computer skill acquisition?

2. Do the programming skills learned transfer to other problem-solving skills? That is, what are the consequences of learning to program a computer?

3. Does the type of instruction received influence the knowledge acquired and, in turn, the transfer of this knowledge to other domains? That is, what makes instruction good or poor within the domain of computer-skill acquisition?

This chapter discusses in detail each of these questions, drawing on evidence from a decade of research on the learning and teaching of computer interaction. Most of the research presented is part of a program of research addressing at least two of the three questions posed. The research was chosen to illustrate the programmatic nature of research in this area and the tight links that exist between the research questions. In addition, much of the research on computer-skill acquisition addresses learning how to program a computer. However, some of this research pertains to other computer skills such as text editing and the use of software packages.

The three questions proposed map historically onto the evolution of research on computer skills. Initially, this research was performed by computer scientists who were interested in understanding the knowledge possessed by computer science students. They were interested in this issue for the purposes of applying their observations to the design of better computer systems and, in some cases, the design of better instructional materials. To this end, these researchers focused primarily on the nature of computer-skill knowledge representations and the changes in these representations that occur with the acquisition of expertise.

Over time, college students were no longer the only computer users in existence. In particular, children and less experienced adults were learning to use computers. With this change in users, psychologists and educators became interested in research on the acquisition of computer skills. These researchers were especially interested in the transfer of computer knowledge to other problem-solving domains and the use of the computer domain as a complex problem-solving domain that might shed light on instructional design and problem solving in general. The methodologies used were more empirical and led the generation of information-processing models of computer interaction.

What is the Nature of Computer-Skill Knowledge?

Successful performance of a cognitive skill requires the acquisition of the knowledge and procedures relevant to the skill. That is, when people can perform a task, the assumption is that they possess a representation of the domain knowledge and a set of procedures that act upon this knowledge. Research on computer-skill acquisition addresses this issue from two perspectives: analysis of the organization of knowledge for expert and novice computer users and analysis of the learning processes associated with the acquisition of computer knowledge.

User Knowledge Representations.   To better understand man-machine interactions, researchers have investigated the content and organization of user representations of computer knowledge. One method of investigation is the decomposition of user representations into the goals and plans for accomplishing computer tasks. Research has applied this method to text-editing experts and to novice and expert computer programmers.

GOMS.   The GOMS model, proposed by Card, Moran, and Newell (1983), is a comprehensive analysis of expert knowledge representations for text-editing systems. By examining text editing experts using a variety of editors, Card et al. were able to extract four cognitive components that can be used to describe text-editing behavior in an error-free environment. The four components that they proposed are *goals, operators, methods,* and *selection* rules (thus, the GOMS acronym).

In this model, goals define the set of editing tasks to be accomplished (e.g., delete the word "boy"). Operators are the primitive actions that one performs (e.g., type the letter "d"). Methods are procedures for accomplishing goals (e.g., use the line-feed key to locate a line). Selection rules are conditions that direct the use of an appropriate method (e.g., if you are locating a line that is less than four lines from your current location, use the line-feed method.).

Card et al. used the GOMS representation to analyze the sequences of actions necessary to complete a prescribed task and to predict the time necessary to complete the task. They observed manuscript-editing performance for different users and found that they could use the small number of components proposed in the model to predict users' choices of methods to accomplish an editing task. In addition, they were able to derive estimates for the amount of time allotted to each component of the model and then use these estimates to predict how long it would take users to complete a task. Although the GOMS model presents a coherent representation of user knowledge, this characterization was proposed for error-free expert performance, and therefore it cannot easily be used to describe the performance of new users who often make many errors in trying to accomplish a specific task.

Novice/Expert Representations. Adelson (1981) was also interested in the representation of computer knowledge. However, she investigated the representation of programming knowledge for novices as well as experts. In her study, Adelson gave novice and expert programmers a set of individual lines of code that together created a working program. She asked the programmers to judge the similarity of these lines and group them according to these judgments. Novices grouped the code according to syntactic categories. For example, they grouped all the assignment statements together (i.e., the statements that assign a value to a variable). Experts, however, used high-level programming categories to group the code. For example, they saw the statements related to updating a counting variable as similar. Adelson's results showed that novice programmers attend to surface features of the program, the syntax of the language, and experts attend to the deeper features of the program, the semantics of programming.

Ehrlich and Soloway (1982) also analyzed novice and expert computer performance. They proposed that expert programmers encode their knowledge into high-level knowledge structures, called *plans*. These plans, like the methods of the GOMS model, are stereotypic sequences of actions used to accomplish a specific programming goal. For example, they proposed a set of plans for different types of iteration. These plans are called *looping plans*. One type of looping plan is the Running Total Loop Plan. This plan is used to add partial totals and keep a record of the number of numbers used.

Ehrlich and Soloway used their plans to examine the differences in knowledge representations for novice and expert programmers. They gave programmers sample programs that were missing certain statements and asked them to fill in the missing code. The results showed that the experts filled in code that was consistent with the plan represented in the program. Novices were more idiosyncratic in their behavior and more likely to be led astray by surface features of the program. Ehrlich and Soloway argued that these results suggest that programming instruction should focus on programming plans and perhaps teach these plans explicitly. The last section of the chapter discusses a computer system that explicitly uses programming plans to help students debug their code.

Acquisition of Computer Knowledge.   Although the GOMS model and the programming plans analysis are useful for characterizing the content of users' knowledge representations, they do not address the acquisition of these representations. Therefore, other researchers have given attention to describing the learning process that characterizes the transition from novice to expert. Anderson, Farrell, and Sauers (1984) presented one attempt at describing the acquisition of computer programming knowledge. Their account is based upon the mechanisms of Anderson's ACT* theory of cognitive architecture (Anderson, 1983). Using these mechanisms, Anderson et al. simulated the process that underlies learning to program in LISP. In this simulation, programming knowledge is initially encoded as declarative knowledge (a set of facts about computer programming). However, to efficiently solve a programming problem, users need procedural information. Anderson's ACT* theory proposes that, initially, general problem-solving procedures are used to interpret the declarative knowledge and create problem-specific productions or rules. Once the user has solved some programming problems, he or she can structurally map the previous problem productions (e.g., if the goal is to make a list of elements, then use the LIST commands) onto the new problem and use these productions to solve the new problem. Anderson et al. label this mapping process as "structural analogy," in that users are drawing analogies between problems.

With increased exposure to the various types of programming problems, user knowledge is compiled into task-specific procedures. This compilation process entails two subprocesses. In the first subprocess, composition, two related productions (rules) are collapsed into a single rule. That is, productions that follow one another in a problem-solving sequence are combined into one production. The second subprocess of the compilation process is proceduralization. In this step, domain-specific knowledge is incorporated into the productions so that the user no longer has to retrieve this information from memory. Thus, the application of the production or procedure is more efficient.

Once users have learned domain-specific procedures (i.e., they are experienced programmers), they continue to tune their programming procedures. This tuning process entails generalizing across procedures and discriminating among procedures. It is in the context of this tuning process that users can become expert programmers. However, it should be noted that the tuning process may continue beyond the point when a user is considered an expert, in that new programming techniques can always be developed. The ACT* model has been used in the design of LISPITS, an intelligent tutoring system to be described in detail later in the chapter.

Although Anderson et al. describe the processes involved in the acquisition of computer knowledge, they do not directly address the content of the knowledge representations that result from these processes. Kay and Black (1990) used a goal and plan analysis similar to the GOMS representation to trace the changes in the content and organization of knowledge that occur with increased text-editing experience. Their analysis used a methodology similar to Adelson's. They asked naive, novice, and expert computer users to rate the similarity of pairs of text-editing commands. From these ratings, Kay and Black found that, with experience, user representations change from natural language preconceptions to goal/action relationships and then to goal/plan relationships. These results replicated those found by Sebrechts, Black, Galambos, Wagner, Deck, and Wikler (1983), who examined the knowledge representation changes for a command-based word-processing system.

Kay and Black combined their results with the results of a more detailed analysis of text-editing expertise (Robertson & Black, 1983) and proposed a four-phase model of the evolution of knowledge as one proceeds from naive to expert computer user. In this model, phases represent snapshots of the mental structures that exist at varying levels of ability. In this sense, they are similar to the stages that have been presented in developmental psychology. However, the phases in this model are more flexible in that they are not tied to a specific time line. That is, the time that it takes for the evolution of knowledge is, to some extent, the complexity of the domain. In addition, the phases describe local structures, such that different pieces of information can be in different phases for a given individual. However, the phases can be used to classify users by noting the prominent organization of knowledge for the specific user. Fig. 10.1 shows abstract representations of the knowledge organization for each phase.

Phase One.   Phase One of this model describes the knowledge representations that exist before the learning process begins. In this phase, knowledge is organized according to preconceptions about the terminology that will later refer to text-editing commands. That is, the learning process does not begin with a blank slate. It begins with knowledge representations that are based upon prior knowledge associations that may or may not correspond to the associations that will develop as editing experience increases.

The prior knowledge associations exist in a number of forms. They may be metaphorical relationships such as those described in Carroll and Mack (1985) or they may be natural-language associations that result from similarities in the connotations of the terminology. For example, Kay and Black found that people who had never used a computer text editor considered the Center command to be similar to the Balance command because these two words both have an "even something out" connotation. However, in the actual text editor, the Center command was used to center a piece of text, while the Balance command was used to balance left and right parentheses. Thus, we find that people coming to the editing environment for the first time often have the difficult task of overcoming their bias to interpret the editing commands in terms of prior knowledge associations (Fig. 10.1a).

Phase Two.   Phase Two describes the first reorganization of knowledge in the learning process. In this phase, users have had some experience with text editing, but they are still in the early part of the learning process. Because one of the first things that users learn is the goals that the commands accomplish, the new organization of the commands is based upon the relationships between the commands and the relevant goals that they accomplish (Fig. 10.1b). This proposal is based upon results in which novices perceived commands to be similar, if they were used to accomplish the same goal. For example, novices using the Yale text editor perceived the commands Insert, Put, and Replace to be similar because they all add information to the text.

Although Phase Two representations suggest that users have acquired some text-editing knowledge, these representations focus on the result of invoking a command and not the process or procedure that leads to the use of the command.

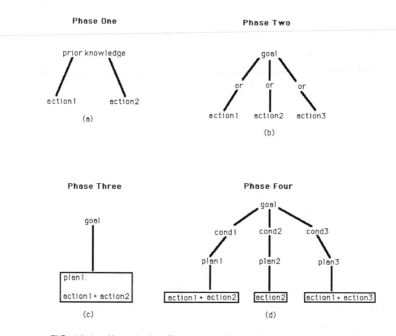

FIG. 10.1.   Knowledge Representations for Four-Phase Model.

Thus, at this level of understanding, users will invoke any of the related commands in attempting to accomplish the goal. To continue with the add information example, novices might use Insert, Put, or Replace to add information to the text without realizing that the source of the information to be added is different for each of the commands. More specifically, the Insert command is used when one wants to "type" the new information. The Put command uses information that has been placed in computer memory as a result of invoking the Delete or Pick commands. The Replace command uses information that has been typed in response to the Search command that looks for a piece of text.

Phase Three.   Having acquired the basic text-editing goals and commands, users begin to note that there are certain commands that are frequently used together in accomplishing a goal. It is this realization that leads to another reorganization of knowledge in which actions that were organized separately in Phase Two are now combined into the plan-based representations of Phase Three (Fig. 10.1c). That is, the goal/action link of Phase Two is divided into two separate links. One type of link is an action/action link, in which the commands are sequenced together into a plan, and the other type of link is a goal/plan link, in which the sequence of commands is linked to the goal that it accomplishes.

Again, Kay and Black extracted this representation from the results of perceived command similarities. However, in this case, the similarities were generated by more experienced users. For these users, commands were perceived as similar when they were used together in a plan. For example, the Replace command that was related to the Insert and Put commands for the novice users was perceived as similar to the Search command for the more experienced users. These two commands are used together in a plan for searching for a piece of text and changing the text. Thus, experienced users have a more complete understanding of the Replace command that not only includes information that this command adds information to the text, but also includes knowledge that the source of this information comes from its use with the Search command.

Phase Four.   The final phase of the model describes the knowledge representations for users who are experts in text editing. The representation proposed for this phase completes the acquisition process (aside from minor forms of tuning that will continually take place) and is similar to the GOMS account of text-editing experts. In this phase, knowledge is reorganized to incorporate (a) compound plans that are composed of the simple plans of Phase Three; and (b) selection conditions for choosing the most appropriate plan for accomplishing a given goal (Fig. 10.1d). As a result of this reorganization, the one-to-one relationship of goal to plan changes to a one-to-several relationship in which a goal can be linked to several plans. It is because of this one-to-several organization that there exist the selection conditions for accessing the correct plan.

The development of compound plans and selection rules was extracted from the results of a study by Robertson and Black (1983). In this study, interkeystroke times were used to investigate the formation and use of plans for a simple experimental text editor. The results of this study showed that with increased experience, the time for pausing between simple plans decreased, suggesting that these plans were combined into complex plans. For example, the time pausing between the cursor movement plan and the change item plan decreased with experience, suggesting a compound move + change plan. There was also a decrease in the time to initiate plans suggesting the formation of rules for selecting a given plan. For example, in the beginning, users would use Delete and Insert to change a word. However, with experience, the same users stopped using the delete/insert plan and began using the overtype plan that is more efficient and appropriate.

By considering the four-phase model in light of the GOMS model, we can propose an ordering for the acquisition of the four GOMS components. The goals and operators (commands) are acquired first, although it is not clear if these components are acquired simultaneously or in an order not captured by the four-phase model. Methods (plans) are the next type of knowledge to be acquired, and finally, the selection rules are acquired. Although this model addresses the changes in knowledge representations as one acquires knowledge, Kay and Black have not as yet defined the processes that underlie these changes. That is, the phases in this model provide subgoals for the acquisition process, but they do not show how to accomplish these goals. However, it is possible to apply many of Anderson's learning mechanisms to explain these changes. For example, the Phase Two to Phase Three transition appears to be a result of the compilation mechanism.

In summary, the nature of the representation of computer knowledge varies with the level of expertise. With minimal exposure to computer interactions, users possess representations that encode simple relationships between computer concepts. These representations can take the form of rules for syntax, goal/action links, and/or declarative facts about the computer domain. With increased experience, these simple relationships become more complex and are encoded into higher level knowledge structures. That is, the computer knowledge is represented as plans, methods, and compiled rules that describe a series of actions for accomplishing a specific goal.

What are the Consequences of Learning to Program a Computer?

In 1980, Seymour Papert published his book, *Mindstorms: Children, Computers, and Powerful Ideas*. This book had a great impact on research in the area of children's acquisition of computer skills. Papert proposed that learning to program a computer would help children learn about their thinking. That is, he believed that once children could program, they would transfer their programming skills to other problem-solving domains and improve their performance in these domains. In addition, he claimed that this learning could take place in a "discovery" learning environment where children were exposed to computer concepts and then given time to work on their own and explore the computer environment. An implication of this proposal is that children would spontaneously acquire the concepts and strategies of computer programming. This implication is addressed more directly in the next section of the chapter. In the past, a similar proposal was made for learning Latin and thus, Papert's proposal sparked a series of investigations of its validity.

Many of the studies investigating Papert's proposals used the LOGO language developed by Papert and his colleagues at MIT. Before discussing these studies, it is useful to give a brief description of the LOGO language. LOGO is a computer-programming language that allows children (and adults) with little programming experience to write programs that generate pictures such as houses and flowers. It also has list-processing capabilities, but most instruction in LOGO is directed at the graphics aspects of the language as these are more inherently interesting to children. The LOGO command names are simple and familiar words, such as Forward (FD), Back (BK), Leftturn (LT), and Rightturn (RT). These commands are used to move the cursor (called the "turtle" for historical reasons) around the screen to draw the graphic output. In addition, LOGO supports more advanced programming concepts such as conditionals (IF/THEN), subprocedures (TO), and iteration and recursion (REPEAT).

Fig. 10.2 presents a simple LOGO program for creating a house. The main part of this program consists of invoking subprocedures that draw a square and a triangle. The individual subprocedures illustrate the use of iteration with the REPEAT command.

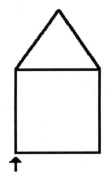

```
TO HOUSE
    SQUARE
    FD 50 RT 30
    TRIANGLE
    LT 30 BK 50
END

TO SQUARE
    REPEAT 4 (FD 50 RT 90)
END

TO TRIANGLE
    REPEAT 3 (FD 50 RT 120)
END
```

FIG. 10.2.   Example LOGO Program.

Early Research on LOGO Led to Mixed Results.   Roy Pea and his colleagues at the Bank Street College of Education performed some of the earliest research addressing Papert's claims. Planning (i.e., organizing the code in the most efficient manner) is a primary programming subskill. Pea and Kurland (1984) proposed that if Papert's claims were correct, then children exposed to LOGO should learn planning and be able to transfer this planning to nonprogramming domains. They used a discovery-learning environment and gave third through sixth grade children about 25–30 hours of LOGO instruction over a 1 year period. This study yielded results that did not support Papert's claims. In the results of two studies, they found that learning LOGO did not improve the effectiveness of planning ability.

Although the Bank Street research did not support Papert's proposal, Clements and Gullo (1984) were able to find some evidence for the transfer of programming knowledge. They compared children learning programming to children who were using the computer for computer-assisted-instruction (CAI). In this study, first grade students were given about 15 hours of instruction over 12 weeks. The results revealed that the children who learned LOGO showed a significant pre-to-post test improvement on measures of reflective and diverse thinking. In addition, they performed better than the CAI students on tasks assessing metacognitive abilities and the ability to give instructions to direct someone through an environment.

These two studies are representative of the contradictory nature of the earlier work investigating the benefits of teaching programming. Given the inconsistency of these results, researchers were not willing to draw conclusions in either direction. An issue of most concern was that this work focused on the number of hours of instruction rather than on the nature of the knowledge that had been acquired. Therefore, researchers proposed that the negative results could be explained by the fact that the students had not acquired the necessary information.

Recent Results Appear More Promising.   Recent research has attempted to remedy this problem by assessing the knowledge that students acquire from the LOGO experience and then using this information to assess the benefits of programming skills for general problem-solving skills. The implication of this new approach is that there are certain subskills that are necessary for proficient programming and successful transfer of this knowledge. There is a trend in the more recent research to focus on these subskills as prerequisites for transfer.

In their study of debugging skill, Carver and Klahr (1986) illustrated one method for assessing student knowledge. They proposed a precise, four-stage model of the subskills necessary for successful debugging of LOGO programs. *Program Evaluation* requires running the program and identifying any discrepancies between the observed and desired output of the program. *Bug Identification* is the generation of a description of the bug that exists. *Bug Location* requires using program cues to find possible locations for the bug. *Bug correction* is the changing of the program so that it no longer generates the identified bug. Before using these stages to assess student performance, Carver and Klahr incorporated them into a computer simulation of the debugging process. The simulation allowed them to test the model on example problems and thereby completely specify the components of debugging.

The fully specified model was used to assess the knowledge that children acquire during a LOGO course. Seven- to nine-year old children were given twelve 2-hour LOGO classes over a 3-week period. Three times during the training students completed a test on their ability to interpret and generate LOGO programs. The results showed that children learned the prerequisites to debugging (e.g., command and program generation), but that they were not able to use these basic skills to interpret a program and identify, locate, and correct the bugs in their code. These results illustrated that students were not acquiring the knowledge necessary to accomplish successful program debugging and therefore, one would not expect them to transfer this information to general problem debugging.

To remedy this situation, Klahr and Carver (1988) designed instruction to explicitly teach the debugging skills described in their model. The details of this instruction are discussed in the next section. In addition to designing instruction, Klahr and Carver assessed the ability of students to transfer what they learned from the explicit LOGO debugging instruction to debugging in nonprogramming tasks. The results of this investigation showed that given explicit debugging instruction, children were able to learn to debug in LOGO and apply the debugging strategies to debugging and correcting instructions for tasks such as arranging furniture in a room and mapping a route from one place to another. These results suggest that once the requisite knowledge is acquired, children can transfer this knowledge to general problem-solving tasks.

Fay and Mayer (1988) provide further support for the necessity of acquiring certain types of knowledge before being able to transfer the knowledge to nonprogramming tasks. In this work, they proposed three components that are necessary for successful use of the navigational commands in the LOGO environment—"syntactic knowledge of LOGO, semantic knowledge of LOGO and semantic knowledge of spatial navigation" (p. 59). Mayer and Fay (1987) describe these components in the context of a model that describes the order of acquisition for the components. Syntactic knowledge consists of the features of the programming language such as commands, punctuation, and the rules for putting these features together in a program. Semantic knowledge consists of the functional relationships associated with LOGO, such as the actions that can be performed with LOGO programs. Navigation knowledge consists of the information associated with maneuvering in a spatial environment. Fay and Mayer proposed that syntactic knowledge is acquired before semantic knowledge and that the navigational knowledge brought to the LOGO environment changes to reflect the acquisition of the syntax and semantics of LOGO. In addition, they proposed that this ordering is important to successful transfer of the LOGO navigational knowledge to other spatial tasks.

In their investigation of this model, Fay and Mayer (1987) focused on the changes in semantic knowledge that occur with exposure to LOGO. They found that children, especially young children, come to the LOGO environment with egocentric misconceptions about spatial relationships and even with initial LOGO experience, these misconceptions continue to exist. They explained this result in light of the inability of children to extract from their ego-centered spatial referents to the spatial referents of the computer cursor (turtle). Therefore, Fay and Mayer proposed that it is not surprising to find that children have trouble transferring spatial knowledge from LOGO to more general spatial tasks.

To support this claim, they assessed the conditions under which children could transfer the knowledge they acquired from the LOGO environment (Mayer & Fay, 1987). Fourth grade students were first given a pretest on their ability to give someone directions from one place to another. Then the children were given LOGO instruction. Using the test booklets from their training, Mayer and Fay categorized the children according to their use of the semantics of spatial relationships. The students were classified as (a) egocentric spatial reasoners (i.e., they could not adopt the referent of the screen); (b) non-egocentric (turtle-centric) reasoners (i.e., they adopted the referent of the screen, or (c) egocentric to non-egocentric reasoners (i.e., during training, they changed in the referent that they used).

The results of this investigation showed that when the children were again tested on the nonprogramming spatial task, performance on the task was related to the egocentric categories. Students who were non-egocentric or changed from egocentric to non-egocentric showed a significant improvement in their ability to give the directions. As mentioned previously, these results support the notion of the importance of acquiring the necessary knowledge before being able to transfer this knowledge to general problem solving. Therefore, researchers interested in transfer must be sure first to assess the knowledge acquired before assessing the knowledge transferred. In addition, both of the studies presented in this section suggest that it is important to define the subskills within the programming environment (i.e., debugging and spatial ability) and then to locate the relevant nonprogramming skills to which these programming concepts might be appropriately transferred.

Transfer Results in Adults.   Most of the recent research on transfer used children as the subject population. This is probably due to the fact that most adults have had some, however minimal, computer programming experience and that most adults have acquired general problem-solving skills. Therefore, the adults would come to the programming environment with not only natural-language preconceptions, but also programming preconceptions. Thus, it would be more difficult to find transfer in the form of problem-solving improvement. Given this situation, programming instruction would have to be designed with the preconceptions in mind and the tests of transfer would have to be more sensitive to changes in performance.

Ehrlich, Soloway, and Abbott (1982) were, however, able to examine transfer in adults for a nonprogramming task considered to be difficult, even for adults. They examined whether learning programming improves the ability to generate equations from algebra word problems. In particular, Ehrlich et al. investigated students' ability to generate equations from word problems such as "There are six times as many students as professors at this university." The correct equation is $S = 6P$, but many students generate the equation, $6S = P$. Poor student performance on this type of problem is proposed to be due to students' lack of understanding of procedurality. That is, students tend to use a static representation for a problem, rather than a more active representation that illustrates a procedural relationship. Ehrlich et al. felt that learning programming, a skill that relies heavily on procedurality, would help students to apply this concept to algebra.

In their study, two groups of students were given a set of algebra problems and asked to generate the appropriate equations. One group of students had just completed an introductory programming course and the other group of subjects had no programming experience. Students who had taken the programming course performed significantly better on the algebra word problems. (This result is not particularly surprising, given that part of learning to program is learning to translate a problem into program code that solves the problem.) These results suggest that, for adults, programming knowledge can produce transfer to non-programming skills, at least for the specific task of translating algebra problems into mathematical equations.

Mayer, Dyck, and Vilberg (1986) also examined transfer with adults. In this study, they examined the transfer of skills from learning programming to general thinking skills that were more abstract versions of the skills assessed by Ehrlich et al. The experimental subjects were computer-naive college students enrolled in a course on the Basic programming language. A control group of computer-naive students who were not taking the Basic course was included for comparison. All subjects were tested on a set of skills, some that directly related to programming and some that represented general intellectual skills. For example, skills related to programming were the ability to translate word problems and the ability to comprehend procedures or directions. The general intellectual skills measured were logical reasoning, visual and verbal ability, and arithmetic ability.

The test was administered at the beginning and at the end of the school semester. The results of this study showed that, for the students who learned Basic, there was a significant change in performance on the thinking skills related to the programming concepts, but that there was no change for general intellectual skills. This study again illustrates that the transfer of programming skills to more general skills will be successful, but only for those tasks that are directly tied to the concepts inherent in programming.

Although the results from the earlier research on transfer from programming skills to general problem-solving skills were somewhat controversial, more recent research addressing this issue tends to support students' ability to use their programming skills in nonprogramming tasks. There are, however, two caveats to this support. The first caveat is that students must be proficient at the skill within the programming environment before attempting to use the skill in general problem solving. Evidence in support of this claim is provided by Carver and Klahr (1986) and Mayer and Fay (1987). The second caveat is that transfer occurs at small grain of analysis. That is, transfer can only be expected if the nonprogramming skill is directly related to a programming skill. We draw this conclusion from the results of Klahr and Carver (1988) and the two studies of transfer in adults, where transfer was limited to specific programming subskills.

What are the Instructional Variables that Influence Learning and Transfer?

Thus far, the discussion has focused on the results of learning to use a computer. That is, we have seen the nature of the representation of knowledge with increased computer experience and the application of this knowledge to nonprogramming skills. Another aspect of cognitive analyses of the acquisition of computer skills is the degree to which the method of instruction influences (a) the knowledge that is acquired and (b) the transfer of this knowledge. In the studies previously discussed, this issue was alluded to, but there exists a set of studies that explicitly manipulated instruction to test what methods of instruction lead to the best computer performance.

This work can be subdivided into two categories. Some of these studies were designed as a response to Papert's (1980) original proposal for the use of a "discovery" method of instruction to teach programming. This method is implemented by giving students a basic introduction to programming and then allowing them to explore the programming environment to "discover" the constraints of the programming environment on their own. The other category of studies is characterized by consideration of information-processing models of the computer user. These studies begin with ideas about the evolution of knowledge with increased computer expertise and/or the goals of learning to use a computer and use these models to design instruction.

"Discovery" Learning—Does it Work?   "Discovery" learning as a method for teaching programming was initiated by Papert (1980), who suggested that children should be given direct, hands-on experience with the computer in a discovery setting. That is, he implied that if children are given the opportunity to explore through the computer environment, they will spontaneously acquire

programming knowledge and then be able to apply this knowledge to other problem-solving tasks. As discussed in the previous section, current research shows that transfer requires that children learn the programming concepts before they can transfer this knowledge. Therefore, a series of studies were designed to investigate whether or not the discovery method of instruction produced the learning necessary for transfer.

Computer learning often takes place in a classroom. Given that these classrooms are located in different schools, one can safely predict that there will be variation in the instruction provided. Marcia Linn and her colleagues in the Autonomous Classroom Computer Environment for Learning (ACCEL) project investigated the characteristics of the classroom environments that lead to the best programming performance. One of the most prominent of these characteristics was the type of instruction given in the classroom.

Linn and Dalbey (1985) studied 17 precollege classrooms where students were learning the Basic programming language. They examined these classrooms in terms of an ideal "chain of cognitive accomplishments" (p. 192) that had been proposed by Linn (1985). The links in this chain are (a) the features of the programming language; (b) the design skill or techniques for combining language features to solve a programming problem; and (c) the problem-solving skills that are general, more abstract versions of the design skills.

Using these accomplishments to assess student performance, Linn and Dalbey categorized the 17 classrooms as *typical* or *exemplary*. Exemplary classrooms were those that explicitly taught the design skills link of the cognitive accomplishments. The typical classrooms allowed students to discover these skills on their own. The results of this study showed that students in the exemplary classrooms performed better in comprehending programs, reformulating a program that wasn't working correctly, and on design skills in general. They found this result for both high- and low-ability students. These results suggest that more explicit instruction on design skills produces more successful performance than pure discovery-based instruction.

Sloane and Linn (1988) performed a partial replication of the Linn and Dalbey study. They examined the instructional characteristics of 14 high school Pascal classes and related these characteristics to programming proficiency. Programming proficiency, in this study, was measured in terms of students' ability to write, understand, and modify programs. The instruction provided in the classroom was measured in terms of explicitness of the teaching, the number of hours/days the teacher lectured to the students, the number of hours/days the teacher worked individually with students, the requirements set before the students had access to a computer (i.e., did the students have to present a handwritten plan before they programmed?), and the quality of the explicit instruction (i.e., explanations provided and illustrations of relationships between concepts).

The results of this analysis showed that the proportion of time teachers worked with individual students and the quality of the explicit instruction were significant predictors of student programming proficiency. Sloane and Linn argued that when teachers worked with students individually or in small groups, they were better able to monitor student knowledge acquisition. That is, they were better able to explain programming concepts and their relationships. Therefore, it is not surprising that the quality of explicit instruction or the teachers' use of explanations was also related to proficiency. The implication of these results is that the more explicit the instruction, the better the outcome in terms of students' acquisition of the requisite concepts for successful programming.

Littlefield, Declos, Lever, Clayton, Bransford, and Franks (1988) performed studies that were more experimentally controlled than the Linn studies. They compared the performance that resulted from discovery learning (or as they called it *unstructured instruction*) to other methods of LOGO instruction. In their first study, Littlefield et al. compared unstructured teaching to a more structured method of instruction. The unstructured lessons consisted of an introduction to new programming concepts and a few examples of the use of these concepts. Students spent the remainder of the instruction time exploring the LOGO environment. The structured instruction contained the same content as the unstructured lessons. However, students were given a set of specific assignments that were designed to encourage the use of the commands that were taught. While the students were doing these assignments, the teacher was available to answer any questions the students might have. The results of this study showed that the structured instruction led to better LOGO performance than the unstructured instruction. Littlefield et al. also found that even though students in the structured condition acquired more LOGO knowledge, they were not able to transfer this knowledge. Therefore, they decided to design instruction that explicitly encouraged transfer.

In their second study, Littlefield et al. designed instructional materials called *mediational instruction*. This instruction stressed how LOGO programming concepts could be applied to general problem-solving concepts. For example, students were shown how the decomposition strategies used in programming could be applied to decomposing other nonprogramming problems. This instruction was compared to the structured method of the first study. Although the results of this study showed no difference in the mastery of LOGO concepts, they did show that the mediational method of instruction led to better transfer to a related nonprogramming task, a map navigation task.

Littlefield et al. noted that their results suggest the importance of the goals of teaching programming. That is, they argue that instruction should be designed according to the desired outcome of the instruction. If the goal of the acquisition of programming concepts is the transfer of these concepts to general problem-solving skills, then the instruction should explicitly point out the relationships between LOGO and problem solving (i.e., mediational instruction). If LOGO is to be learned for its own sake, then one may use structured or mediational types of instruction. Regardless, Littlefield et al. do suggest that acquiring a basic level of programming mastery requires a more structured teaching environment than was implied by Papert's claims.

Carver (1988) reports two pilot studies that also assessed the effectiveness of discovery learning. This research focused on the ability of students to acquire debugging skills on their own. The first study was part of the Carver and Klahr (1986) study discussed previously. In this study, second and third grade students were given 24 hours of LOGO instruction. The instruction was typical of classroom teaching of LOGO except that throughout the instruction, children were given buggy programs and asked to locate the bug and fix it. The results showed that under general instructional conditions, students do not learn how to effectively debug a program. Rather than using the programming cues present in the code to locate a bug, students would serially search through the program until they found the bug. Once they located the bug, however, the students could fix it.

The second pilot study was performed in collaboration with Papert's research group at MIT. In this study, students were given approximately 200 hours of an unstructured LOGO environment. Upon completion of the instruction, Carver administered a debugging test to the top 15 students in the class. The results of this test were consistent with the first pilot study. Even the best programmers had trouble locating the bugs and relied on help from the experimenter. In some cases, students rewrote the buggy procedure rather than fixing the existing code. The results from both of these studies show that when left to their own devices, students do not spontaneously discover the strategies necessary for successful debugging skills.

Papert proposed that children will spontaneously discover programming concepts if given direct, hands-on experience with the programming environment. The studies presented in this section do not provide evidence to support this claim. The results suggest that students must be explicitly taught the programming concepts in order to successfully apply them in the generation, interpretation, and evaluation of computer programs.

Model-based Instruction.   In the first two sections of this chapter, we discussed models of the knowledge acquired while learning to use a computer. One assumption behind the generation of these models is that the model provides a detailed description of the knowledge necessary for successful performance. A natural extension of modeling computer skills is the application of these models to the design of instruction. The goal of this instruction is the acquisition of the knowledge representations in the model and the successful use of this knowledge.

Recall that Klahr and Carver (1988) found that under the right instructional conditions, children could transfer program debugging knowledge to debugging in nonprogramming tasks. This instruction was designed based on their model and simulation of program debugging with the addition of a *problem representation* stage that requires understanding the structure of the program. The primary goal of this instruction was to have students acquire the components of the model and then be able to debug in a fashion similar to that of the computer simulation. This goal was accomplished by presenting students with a 40-minute lesson (given after six to eight hours of LOGO instruction) that described prompts for the students to ask themselves while debugging.

The results of this manipulation showed that students who were given the explicit instruction in debugging heuristics performed better on the debugging tasks than students who had been exposed to LOGO instruction without the debugging lessons. This was evidenced by faster debugging times and more efficient debugging behavior. In addition, as LOGO experience progressed, students were less likely to search serially through the program looking for a bug and more likely to take advantage of the cues present in a well-structured program. These results illustrate the benefits of using a model of cognitive processing to represent the knowledge necessary for successful instruction.

Model-based instruction does not always lead to improved performance. Kay (1987) used the Kay and Black (1990) four-phase model to design instruction for a command-based database system. She compared this type of instruction to other methods of instruction that are currently available with computer software applications. Using an on-line training system, subjects learned how to use the database system. Kay measured performance during training by recording interkeystroke times and errors committed.

The results from these measures indicated that the best performance resulted from task-oriented instruction that organized the computer information according to the tasks that can be accomplished with the software. The worst performance was found for the command-oriented instruction that organized the information according to categories of commands and the instruction designed according to the four-phase model led to intermediate performance. Kay suggested a number of reasons for why the model-based instruction did not lead to the best performance. She proposed that the four-phase model only described the knowledge representations that exist at each level of expertise, but it did not describe the processes that guide the changes in representation. Implicit in this proposal is that the four-phase model describes *what* is learned from the computer, but not *how* it is learned. The research discussed previously suggests that good instruction must address the how as well as the what. These results suggest that in designing model-based instruction, one must be sure to fully specify the model. The Klahr and Carver (1988) study shows one method of accomplishing this goal using a computer simulation of the model.

Intelligent Tutoring Systems (ITS)

One method of model-based instruction that is receiving increasing attention is the design of Intelligent Tutoring Systems (ITS). From an instructional perspective, the benefit of ITS is that it allows for individualized instruction that is not readily available in the classroom setting. Individualized tutoring has been shown to lead to better learning than classroom lecturing (Sloane & Linn, 1988), and because it is not feasible to expect teachers to continually provide this individualized instruction, ITS provides a possible solution to the situation. In addition, ITS provides a forum for research evaluations of different instructional methods. That is, ITS can be used for comparing different instructional variables.

One of the most fully developed tutoring systems is the LISPITS system (Corbett & Anderson, in press) developed by Anderson and his colleagues. This tutor provides instruction for learning the programming language, LISP, and contains information associated with the first 12 chapters of an introductory LISP text (Anderson, Corbett, & Reiser, 1987). The model underlying the tutor is the ACT* model (Anderson, 1983) discussed previously. From this model, Anderson, Boyle, Farrell, and Reiser (1987) derived a set of principles for teaching programming. For example, ACT* assumes that problem solving is goal-driven. Therefore, in teaching programming, LISPITS presents students with the goal structure associated with the problem being solved.

The implementation of the model principles uses a method called *model-tracing*. Model tracing entails comparing a model of observed student performance with an ideal model of successful performance. To do this comparison, the tutor has a set of rules that can be used to generate solutions to the problems presented during learning. These rules are used to (a) model students as they are solving LISP problems, and (b) generate an ideal student model. If there are discrepancies between the two models, the tutor intervenes with feedback on the correct solution step. The goal of model tracing is to help students as they are learning and thus keep them from getting too far off the path for successful learning.

When the tutor was first developed, two investigations were conducted to evaluate its instructional effectiveness. Anderson, Boyle, and Reiser (1985) compared LISPITS instruction to human tutor instruction and to discovery learning. All students used a basic LISP text and solved a series of problems. Although there were no differences between the groups on posttest performance, there were differences in the time to complete the exercises. The students working with LISPITS or the human tutor instruction took approximately half of the time of the students working on their own. These results illustrate that using LISPITS led to more efficient learning.

Anderson and Reiser (1985) investigated the effectiveness of LISPITS as part of the classroom curriculum. The students in this study had some prior programming experience and were taking a LISP course in which they attended lectures and completed a set of out-of-class exercises. Half of the students used LISPITS to solve the exercises and half of the students worked on their own. Students using LISPITS took less time to complete the exercises and performed better on a posttest. These results, again, provide support for the efficiency and effectiveness of the tutor.

More recent LISPITS research uses the tutoring environment as a tool for assessing different instructional characteristics. Corbett and Anderson (in press) conducted two studies that are particularly relevant to the questions posed in this chapter. In one study, they investigated the transfer of experience in code evaluation to code generation. All students in this study solved LISP problems using the tutor. Half of the students were given sample code to evaluate before generating their own code and the other half of the students were not given code evaluation practice. The evaluation exercises consisted of working through the sample code and pressing special keys for noting the order in which the computer would evaluate the function and for noting the result of executing the code. Performance on a posttest revealed that practice in code evaluation helped in later code evaluation, but did not transfer to code generation. This study, like some of the transfer studies presented previously, illustrates that transfer of knowledge may be skill-specific even within the programming language itself.

The second Corbett and Anderson study compared the performances that result from more and less structured tutoring environments. In the structured environment, students had to solve LISP problems in a prescribed order and received immediate feedback if they went off the prescribed path. The less structured environment allowed students to control the order of their coding and the feedback they received. Posttest performance revealed no difference in overall programming performance. However, there was a difference in the time used to complete the exercises. The students in the more structured environment took less time than the students in the less structured environment. These results suggest that if efficiency of learning is an important goal of the instruction, then a more structured environment will allow the accomplishment of this goal.

Reiser, Kimberg, Lovett, and Ranney (in press) are conducting research to improve the benefits of LISPITS. They are developing a LISP tutoring system called GIL. The tutoring system improves upon LISPITS by providing (a) causal explanations for student behavior, and (b) a graphical interface that offloads the constraints of programming syntax onto perceptual representations.

Reiser et al. propose that one of the problems with previous tutoring systems is that they provide feedback based on static domain knowledge, rather than dynamic procedures. Therefore, students must infer the relationship between their actions and the feedback they receive. In GIL, the internal model reasons about student actions and then provides explicit explanations for the student action. Given these explanations, the students can better understand the faults in their reasoning without having to guess why their action is wrong.

Some of the research discussed previously suggests that program syntax had to be acquired before programming semantics because correct syntax is a necessary prerequisite of a working program. However, the research on expert programmers shows that they use high-level structures such as plans to organize their knowledge. The GIL system uses a graphical interface that allows students to focus their attention on the semantics rather than the syntax. That is, the system reduces the memory load for learning to program by delaying the acquisition of syntax during the initial stages of learning.

Initial research on the effectiveness of GIL compared students using the tutor with students learning in a nontutoring environment. The results of this comparison showed that the students using GIL solved the LISP problems significantly faster than students working on their own. In addition, the tutor allowed students to be more flexible in their reasoning. This research illustrates the evolutionary nature of intelligent tutoring systems by showing how the initial LISPITS system has evolved into the GIL system.

Another example of the evolution of tutoring systems is the work of Soloway and his colleagues. As discussed previously, Ehrlich and Soloway (1982) proposed that expert knowledge representations consist of sets of plans for accomplishing specific programming goals. Johnson and Soloway (1983) used this idea in the design of PROUST, a tutoring system that helps on-line debugging of Pascal programs. Students submit a program to PROUST and PROUST uses a catalogue of plans to analyze the program and then output a description of the discrepancies found in the program. The student uses this output to locate and correct the bugs in the program.

Evaluations of PROUST suggest that it improves students' ability to locate and repair bugs in their programs. However, further examination of the model used in PROUST indicates that it is not as flexible as it could be (Sack & Soloway, in press). For example, if PROUST cannot locate the first goal of the problem specification, it stops processing and produces output that is not useful to the student. In response to this situation, Sack (1988) designed a more advanced plan-based tutor, called CHIRON.

CHIRON analyzes a student program by not only checking the implementation of the goals and plans of the problem, but it also checks the flow of control for the program. In addition, it can match parts of a plan and it provides feedback according to the degree of match that it finds. Upon completion of its analysis, as with PROUST, CHIRON outputs a description of the problems found in the program. The student then uses this description to ask CHIRON questions. CHIRON answers these questions by providing possible explanations for the bugs found. CHIRON is still in early stages of its development and, therefore, its effectiveness has not been tested empirically. However, initial subjective evaluations suggest that the additional flexibility in its reasoning leads to more natural instructional interactions than those provided by PROUST.

CONCLUSIONS

I began this chapter with three questions that provide a rough classification scheme for research on the teaching and learning of computer skills. The research presented not only addressed these questions, but also illustrated shifts in the field that have taken place over the past 10 years. In the research on the nature of knowledge representations for computers, we see a shift from the investigation of general domain knowledge representations (e.g., GOMS) to more specific representations of user knowledge (e.g., Kay and Black four-phase model). The transfer research illustrates a shift from focusing on transfer to general problem-solving skills to focusing on transfer to specific programming-based skills (e.g., debugging and spatial ability). Finally, the research on computer instruction has shifted from general "discovery" learning to explicit instruction.

These shifts reflect a deeper understanding of the field of computer interaction. That is, researchers in this field are now more aware of the complexity of the task they are studying and the diversity of behaviors that can be observed. Therefore, when addressing the acquisition, transfer, and teaching of computer skills, they must specify the components of the task and the cognitive processes that relate to each of these components. The most recent research in computer interaction taps into these components and processes and their application to instructional design. However, we have only scratched the surface; future research must continue to investigate these issues while keeping up with the increasing development of new and more complex computer systems.

REFERENCES

Adelson, B. (1981). Problem solving and the development of abstract categories in programming languages. *Memory & Cognition, 9,* 422–433.

Anderson, J. R. (1983). *The architecture of cognition.* Cambridge, MA: Harvard University Press.

Anderson, J. R., Boyle, C. F., Farrell, R., & Reiser, B. J. (1987). Cognitive principles in the design of computer tutors. In P. Morris (Ed.), *Modelling cognition.* New York: Wiley.

Anderson, J. R., Boyle, C. F., & Reiser, B. J. (1985). Intelligent tutoring systems. *Science, 228,* 456–462.

Anderson, J. R., Corbett, A. T., & Reiser, B. J. (1987). *Essential LISP.* Reading, MA: Addison-Wesley.

Anderson, J. R., Farrell, R., & Sauers, R. (1984). Learning to program in LISP. *Cognitive Science, 8,* 87–129.

Card, S. K., Moran, T. P., & Newell, A. (1983). *The psychology of human-computer interaction.* Hillsdale, NJ: Lawrence Erlbaum Associates.

Carroll, J. M., & Mack, R. L. (1985). Metaphor, computing systems and active learning. *International Journal of Man-Machine Studies, 22,* 39–57.

Carver, S. M. (1988). Learning and transfer of debugging skills: Applying task analysis to curriculum design and assessment. In R. E. Mayer (Ed.), *Teaching and learning computer programming: Multiple research perspectives* (pp. 259–298). Hillsdale, NJ: Lawrence Erlbaum Associates.

Carver, S. M., & Klahr, D. (1986). Assessing children's LOGO debugging skills with a formal model. *Journal of Educational Computing Research, 2*(4), 487–525.

Clements, D. H., & Gullo, D. F. (1984). Effects of computer programming on young children's cognition. *Journal of Educational Psychology, 76,* 1051–1058.

Corbett, A. T., & Anderson, J. R. (in press). LISP Intelligent tutoring system: Research in skill acquisition. In J. Larkin, R. Chabay, & C. Scheftic (Eds.), *Computer assisted instruction and intelligent tutoring systems: Establishing communication and collaboration*. Hillsdale, NJ: Lawrence Erlbaum Associates.

Ehrlich, K., & Soloway, E. (1982). *An empirical investigation of the tacit plan knowledge in programming* (Rep. No. 236). New Haven: Yale University Department of Computer Science.

Ehrlich, K., Soloway, E., & Abbott, V. (1982). *Transfer effects from programming to algebra word problems: A preliminary study* (Rep. No. 257). New Haven: Yale University Department of Computer Science.

Fay, A. L., & Mayer, R. E. (1987). Children's naive conceptions and confusions about LOGO graphic commands. *Journal of Educational Psychology, 79*, 254–268.

Fay, A. L., & Mayer, R. E. (1988). Learning LOGO: A cognitive analysis. In R. E. Mayer (Ed.), *Teaching and learning computer programming: Multiple research perspectives* (pp. 55–74). Hillsdale, NJ: Lawrence Erlbaum Associates.

Johnson, W. L., & Soloway, E. (1983). PROUST: Knowledge-based program understanding. In *Proceedings of the Seventh International Conference on Software Engineering*. IEEE, Orlando, Florida.

Kay, D. S. (1987). *Using cognitive models of the users to design computer instruction*. Unpublished doctoral dissertation, Yale University.

Kay, D. S., & Black, J. B. (1990). The evolution of knowledge representations with increasing expertise in using a system. In S. P. Robertson, W. Zachary, & J. B. Black (Eds.), *Cognition, computers, and cooperation*. Norwood, NJ: Ablex Publishing.

Klahr, D., & Carver, S. M. (1988). Cognitive objectives in a LOGO debugging curriculum: Instruction, learning and transfer. *Cognitive Psychology, 20*, 362–404.

Littlefield, J., Declos, V. R., Lever, S., Clayton, K. N., Bransford, J. D., & Franks, J. J. (1988). Learning LOGO: Method of teaching, transfer of general skills, and attitudes toward school and computers. In R. E. Mayer (Ed.), *Teaching and learning computer programming: Multiple research perspectives* (pp. 111–136). Hillsdale, NJ: Lawrence Erlbaum Associates.

Linn, M. C. (1985). The cognitive consequences of programming instruction on classrooms. *Educational Psychologist, 14*, 14–16, 25–29.

Linn, M. C., & Dalbey, J. (1985). Cognitive consequences of programming instruction: Instruction, access, and ability. *Educational Psychologist, 20*, 191–206.

Mayer, R. E., Dyck, J. L., & Vilberg, W. (1986). Learning to program and learning to think: What's the connection? *Communications of the ACM, 29*(7), 605–610.

Mayer, R. E., & Fay, A. L. (1987). A chain of cognitive changes with learning to program in LOGO. *Journal of Educational Psychology, 79*, 269–279.

Papert, S. (1980). *Mindstorms: Children, computers and powerful ideas*. New York: Basic Books.

Pea, R. D., & Kurland, D. M. (1984). *LOGO programming and the development of planning skills* (Rep. No. 16). New York: Bank Street School of Education.

Reiser, B. J., Kimberg, D. Y., Lovett, M. C., & Ranney, M. (in press). Knowledge representation and explanation in GIL, an intelligent tutor for programming. In J. Larkin, R. Chabay, & C. Scheftic (Eds.), *Computer assisted instruction and intelligent tutoring systems: Establishing communication and collaboration*. Hillsdale, NJ: Lawrence Erlbaum Associates.

Robertson, S. P., & Black, J. B. (1983). Planning in text editing behavior. *Proceedings of the CHI '83 Conference on Human Factors in Computing Systems* (pp. 217–221). Boston, MA: Association for Computing Machinery.

Sack, W. (1988). Finding errors by overlooking them. In *Proceedings of International Conference on Intelligent Tutoring Systems*. Montreal, Canada.

Sack, W., & Soloway, E. (in press). From PROUT to CHIRON: ITS design as iterative engineering; Intermediate results are important! In J. Larkin, R. Chabay, & C. Scheftic (Eds.), *Computer assisted instruction and intelligent tutoring systems: Establishing communication and collaboration*. Hillsdale, NJ: Lawrence Erlbaum Associates.

Sebrechts, M. M., Black, J. B., Galambos, J. A., Wagner, R. K., Deck, J. A., & Wikler, E. A. (1983). *The effects of diagrams on learning to use a system* (Rep. No. 2). New Haven: Yale University Learning and Using Systems Program.

Sloane, K. D., & Linn, M. C. (1988). Instructional conditions in Pascal programming classes. In R. E. Mayer (Ed.), *Teaching and learning computer programming: Multiple research perspectives* (pp. 207–236). Hillsdale, NJ: Lawrence Erlbaum Associates.

IV GAMES

11 Skill-Related Differences in Game Playing

Peter A. Frensch
University of Missouri

Robert J. Sternberg
Yale University

SKILL-RELATED DIFFERENCES IN GAME PLAYING

Almost 20 years ago Simon and Chase (1973) suggested that cognitive psychology needed a model organism to study, much like scientists in other areas (e.g., genetics) who are studying model organisms such as Drosophila. Over the past three decades, the Drosophila of cognitive psychology has been a game, namely, the game of chess. Chess, in particular, and games, in general, have been the subject of extensive research not only in cognitive psychology, but also in the related disciplines of artificial intelligence and cognitive science.

Games seem to possess at least four features that make them attractive to researchers. First, most games can be decomposed into sequences of observable moves, allowing the researcher insight into a continuous problem-solving process. Second, most games, at least those that have been selected for study, are complex and nondeterministic in the sense that a current move is not completely determined by previous moves, but rather depends on the player's goals and intentions (Johnson-Laird, 1988). Third, game playing is strictly based on well-defined rules, that is, the number of possible moves at any given time is constrained, which, at least in principle, allows for the construction of the complete problem space that a player might operate in at any given time. Finally, games, particularly those games in which players have to deal with one or more adversaries, possess high external validity, that is, they are in many respects similar to real-life situations (e.g., bargaining for a new car, negotiating in a love relationship, etc.).

In this chapter, we summarize the major empirical findings and theoretical contributions of research on game playing that have evolved over, roughly, the past three decades. The summary focuses primarily on the game of chess, simply because by far most of the research on game playing has been conducted in that area. When available, we extend and contrast the results of the chess research with research on other games, such as bridge, go, gomoku, and poker. As becomes evident, game research has—almost exclusively—adopted a skills-comparison approach, that is, most research has compared players of differing skill levels. Although this approach has yielded a rather thorough understanding of the thought processes of relatively experienced players, it has very much neglected addressing how relatively inexperienced players play the games. In addition, because most of the studies have adopted a strictly static, cross-sectional approach, relatively little is known about the acquisition of game-playing skill, and whether different developmental trajectories might lead to different end results. As a result, the present chapter has much more to say about experienced players' thinking and reasoning processes than about the acquisition of game-playing ability and about inexperienced players' problem solving.

The chapter is divided into three main parts. First, we discuss representational issues of game playing, that is, we are concerned with how game situations are perceived and represented in memory. Second, we discuss search processes in memory, that is, how players search through their memory representations to select a solution to any given game situation. And finally, we briefly discuss whether domain-general or domain-specific abilities underlie skill in game playing.

PROBLEM SOLVING IN GAME PLAYING

In order to understand why game research has so strongly dominated research on problem solving in cognitive psychology in recent years, we need to briefly discuss the major mechanisms that are thought to underlie human problem-solving behavior.

In 1972, Newell and Simon introduced a rather influential general theory of problem solving. They argued that problem solving takes place in an external task environment. Out of the many possible internal mental representations of this external task environment, a problem solver generates his or her own special internal problem representation within which he or she operates. This internal problem space contains three different sets of knowledge: (a) the set of possible knowledge states that the problem can take on; (b) the set of move operators that transform one internal problem state into a different problem state, and (c) the set of restrictions under which the move operators operate. In this general framework, two major components of the *process* of problem solving are identified: (a) the generation of an internal problem representation, and (b) the search through this internal problem representation.

According to Newell and Simon (1972), almost all problem-solving tasks share, at least to some extent, the characteristic that they can be divided into these two separate components, although the two components do not necessarily form a strict temporal sequence. That is, search processes might start already before a complete internal representation of the external problem situation has been formed. Also, an unsuccessful search for a problem solution might lead a problem solver to update or restructure the internal problem representation.

If one agrees with the two-step model of human problem solving, it follows that research on problem-solving behavior should focus on issues of the mental representation of a given external problem situation and on search issues. To the extent that all problem-solving tasks share these characteristics, empirical findings obtained with one task should easily be transferrable and applicable to different tasks. At least partly because in many games the two problem-solving steps are relatively easy to separate experimentally, researchers have turned to games as their favorite experimental tasks. In chess, for instance, the experimental task of recalling briefly viewed chess positions is assumed to target primarily a player's construction of his or her internal representation, whereas the task of choosing a move to a given chess position is assumed to reveal characteristics of the search process.

If this line of reasoning is correct, then the results of experimental research on game playing should hold not only for games, but also for any problem-solving task that is accurately described by Newell and Simon's (1972) theory. That is, the results and findings on game playing reported in this chapter are expected to further our understanding of human problem solving in different task areas. In fact, the experimental methods and theoretical models applied to game research as well as the empirical results obtained in game research have had an enormous impact on our understanding of problem-solving behavior in nongame domains, such as solving physics problems (e.g., Larkin, 1983) and medical diagnosis (e.g., Lesgold, Rubinson, Feltovich, Glaser, Klopfer, & Wang, 1988). It is exactly for this reason that games, and particularly the game of chess, have been called the Drosophilas of cognitive psychology (e.g., Simon & Chase, 1973).

THE LOCUS OF GAME-PLAYING ABILITY

Because most games involve a limited number of legal positions, it is possible, in theory, to generate all possible legal continuations from the beginning to the final move. For adversary games such as chess, this generation of moves can be done by listing all possible legal moves for one player, all possible legal replies for the second player, all counterreplies, etc., until a terminal position is reached. In principle, a player could, after having generated all possible legal continuations, then backtrace his or her way through the "tree" of possibilities and choose the objectively best move to any game situation. In practice, however, it is clear that any *exhaustive* search through all legal move possibilities is doomed to fail from the start. In chess, for instance, there are ten legal moves from the initial position, ten possible replies, roughly ten possible counterreplies, and so on. If one were to generate all possible combinations of moves for only six half-moves (plies), one would arrive at $10^6 = 1$ million different combinations. That is, in order to find the best first move, one would have to evaluate 1 million different configurations that could possibly exist after six plies. If one considers that the average game has about 84 plies and the average position about 38 possible moves, the number of positions that would have to be explored rises to 38^{84}, a very large number indeed. Of course, the number of meaningful game positions is somewhat more constrained, as de Groot (1965) has pointed out. A more realistic estimate of the total number of possible move sequences in a game, based upon de Groot's mean of 32 moves per position and Holding's (1980) count of 78 plies per game, is 32^{78} or about 10^{117}. Clearly, any human chess player's search for a move must reflect a *selective,* rather than exhaustive, search through the vast number of possibilities.

Given the large number of possible game continuations, it is not surprising that many popular accounts of why some humans are better at game playing than others have concentrated on the better players' superior ability to search through the many possible game constellations. One view, for instance, holds that better players, for any line of play, simply are able to look further ahead, that is, to foresee combinations that a less-skilled player cannot foresee. Another view holds that better players might be able to evaluate a larger number of different continuation lines than a less-skilled player. Some of the views have held that the ability to search more effectively and faster is due to a player's general intelligence, whereas others have held that this ability is constrained to a given domain.

Empirical tests of these popular beliefs have a rather long history. In one of the earliest known experimental studies of game playing, eight participants in the Great International Chess Tournament in Moscow served as subjects in a broad series of experimental tests conducted by the Soviet investigators Djakow, Petrowsky, and Rudik (1927). The general purpose of the investigation was to find out which of a rather large number of psychological factors determine chess-playing ability at a high level. Djakow et al. used a wide variety of tests on memory, attention, higher intellectual processes (such as combination power and finding of logical regularities), imagination, will power, and the like. Most of the tests were general in the sense that they were not in any way related to the domain of chess. And most of the tests did not differentiate between the chess masters and a control group of non-chess players.

Djakow et al.'s studies, although later harshly criticized on methodological grounds, might be seen as the earliest experimental indication that skill-related differences in chess playing are not due to domain-general ability, but, rather, are confined to the boundaries of the domain. This particular conclusion has been supported by recent work in artificial intelligence, where researchers are trying to develop nonhuman systems that can mimic intelligent human task performance in a variety of domains (e.g., Feigenbaum, 1989). Most of the early work in artificial intelligence in the late 1950s and early 1960s was based on the assumption that domain-general problem-solving heuristics and domain-general rules of learning were the most important ingredients of an expert system (for a recent review see Sternberg & Frensch, 1989). Early failures to write programs that could compete with human experts (particularly in the area of chess [Berliner, 1978]) have led researchers to acknowledge that domain-independent expert systems do not exist. Rather, different expert systems have to be created for different domains, at least partly because the nature and structure of knowledge differs from one domain to another (Hayes-Roth, Waterman, & Lenat, 1983). In the words of Duda and Shortliffe (1983),

> The early hope that a relatively small number of powerful general mechanisms would be sufficient to generate intelligent behavior gradually waned. When significant problems were addressed, it was often discovered that problem independent, heuristic methods alone were incapable of handling the sheer, combinatorial complexity that was encountered. Similarly, general problem-solving techniques confronted in precisely stated "problems," uncertain "facts," and unreliable "axioms" were found to be inadequate to the task.
>
> When it was asked how people were able to devise solutions to these problems a frequent answer was that people possess knowledge of which the programs were wholly innocent. This knowledge is employed in a variety of ways . . . in clarifying the problem, suggesting the kinds of procedure to use, judging the reliability of facts, and deciding whether a solution is reasonable. (p. 261) (cited after Posner, 1988, p. xxxiii)

Most modern researchers have come to more or less accept this view and have concentrated their efforts on finding skill-related differences within, rather than outside, the domain of game playing.

Modern experimental efforts in this tradition date back at least to de Groot. De Groot's (dissertation) experiments were originally published in Dutch (de Groot, 1946), and only about 20 years later translated into English and thus made accessible to the English-speaking community (de Groot, 1965). In one of his studies, de Groot (1965) showed two groups of chess players (five grandmasters and five experts) a set of unfamiliar positions and asked them to think out loud while choosing a move. The verbal statements were recorded by hand. De Groot's subjects ranged from grandmasters, some of the best players in the world, to club players who would nowadays be rated as Class A to Class C on the USCF rating scale.[1] The results were rather surprising: Although the grand-

---

[1] A player's chess rating depends on performance in organized tournaments, with points won or lost depending on performance and the strength of the competition (for details see Elo, 1978). The United States Chess Federation (USCF) currently recognizes eight different rating classes: senior master (USCF rating of 2400 and over), master (2200–2399), expert (2000–2199), class A (1800–1999), class B (1600–1799), class C (1400–1599), class D (1200–1399), and class E (1000–1199).

masters chose better moves than the less skilled players and did so in less time, the two groups did not differ on any of the quantitative indices of their move-selection processes. That is, both groups considered roughly the same number of potential moves and of initial base moves. Also, they did not differ in how far they were looking ahead to find the best move. Still, four of the five grand-masters ended up choosing the objectively best move whereas none of the experts did so.

It appeared that the major difference between the two groups of players was simply that the grandmasters did not waste any time exploring moves and move constellations that did not lead anywhere, instead concentrating their time and efforts on the exploration of promising moves; whereas the less skilled players wasted much time exploring moves that were not even candidates for the grand-masters' search processes. De Groot (1965) hypothesized that the experts' larger knowledge base guided their better selection of moves. That is, prior experience with similar game constellations led the better players literally to perceive the game situation in a manner that was different from how the less-skilled players "saw" the game situation, and allowed them to limit their search to the most promising continuation moves.

De Groot's (1965) results were largely responsible for steering the interest of fellow researchers away from search-related issues and toward perceptual and knowledge-based issues. The exploration of knowledge-based explanations of game-playing skill has heavily dominated research, and has only recently given way to a more detailed investigation of search processes.

REPRESENTATIONAL ISSUES OF GAME PLAYING

The Impact of Prior Knowledge on Perceptual Processes

That prior knowledge affects the perception of a game situation had been recog-nized as early as 1894 by Alfred Binet. Binet, a pioneer in intelligence testing, had originally assumed that performing a complex task such as chess is primarily an achievement of visual memory. That is, the fundamental task in chess, he believed, is to create a realistic, accurate, visual image of the chessboard and its pieces. Binet studied blindfold chess, a version of chess in which a player plays with his or her back to the game board or is otherwise prevented from viewing the chessboard.

On the basis of expert players' introspective responses to a survey and of a few additional experimental studies, Binet concluded that the ability to play blindfold chess rests on three fundamental capacities: (a) knowledge and experience in the field of chess, (b) imagination, and (c) memory. First, a player's memory for both a specific game situation and a sequence of moves is meaningful in the sense that it is seen as part of a battle that can be described by a few characteristic maneuvers and ideas. It is only because each game can be tied into existing chess knowledge that a master is able to deal with the excessive memory load in blindfold chess. Second, although the reports differed widely regarding the ways in which players internally represent an actual game situation, Binet was able to conclude that most players do not seem to develop and use an accurate internal visual representation of a game situation, although there seem to be a few exceptions to this general statement (e.g., Fine, 1965). Rather, a player "sees" only a rough Gestalt of a game situation, the details of which are continually updated and reconstructed. And finally, because most players reported not seeing the colors and forms of individual pawns on the chessboard, Binet concluded that chess configurations are represented in memory as abstract, rather than as concrete, visual entities. In fact, one of the players (Sittenfeld), on Binet's request, made a drawing representing the abstract nature of his memory representations of a particular game constellation. In this drawing, the particular chess pieces do not appear at all. Rather, the lines of force that go out from them and that schematically represent their dynamic possibilities, together with an indication of which squares are occupied and which are empty, make up the drawing.

Not very long after Binet's (1894) study of blindfold players, Cleveland (1907) conducted a somewhat similar survey, sending questionnaires to 100 sighted, rather than blindfolded, chess players. Like Binet, Cleveland also reported that most of his players commented that their improved ability instantaneously to "see" large portions of the board depended primarily on their ability to extract the meaning of the position, rather than upon the ability to attend to individual chess pieces.

Eye Movement Studies. Somewhat more explicit insights on how the perception of a game situation and the selection of moves is guided by prior knowledge can be gained from studies of eye movements during move selection in chess playing. Tikhomirov and Poznyanskaya (1966), and subsequently, other researchers (e.g., de Groot, 1966; Winikoff, 1967), have recorded the eye movements of human players while the players were searching for the best move in a given game situation. The chess positions used were taken from games that the players had just finished, thus assuring that they were familiar with them. The investigators measured not only where subjects directed their gaze, but also how long they stayed focused on a particular square on the chessboard, and in what sequence the squares were attended to.

The eye-movement data collected by Tikhomirov and Poznyanskaya (1966) and later by de Groot (1966) and Winikoff (1967) show rather consistently that (a) the fixations of subjects move from one square to another square at a maximum rate of about 2–4 fixations per second; (b) chess players fixate only a subset of all possible squares on a chessboard, concentrating primarily on pieces that share significant chess relations ("zone of orientation"); (c) players spend much more time—at least initially—fixating opponent's pieces than their own; and (d) the visual search sequence is nonlinear in the sense that subjects often return their attention to squares that they have attended to before.

Similar findings have been reported when tracings were made of the handling of pieces by blind players. Tikhomirov and Terekhov (1967), for instance, made a series of cyclographic recordings of the hand movements of skilled players who were literally blind and who were thus accustomed to handling both their own and their opponent's pieces while considering a move. They found that the sequences of hand movements seem to share at least some similarities with the eye-movement sequences obtained from humans when they are dealing with the identical chessboard configuration.

Simon and Barenfeld (1969) have described a computer program, called PERCEIVER, that simulates eye movements during roughly the first five seconds a chess player views the board. Like Tikhomirov and Poznyanskaya (1966), Simon and Barenfeld assumed that the sequence of eye fixations is dependent on the meaningful chess relations that the presently fixated square shares with its neighboring pieces. That is, eye fixations are constrained such that they can only move to neighboring squares and cannot skip squares unless the neighboring squares turn out to be empty. When the eyes are fixated on a particular square, PERCEIVER is able to detect neighboring pieces that defend or attack, or that are defended or attacked by the presently fixated square. It can then move its fixation onto one of the neighboring pieces.

Simon and Barenfeld (1969) compared the eye-movement sequence of PERCEIVER over the first 15 simulated fixations, that is, before it began to recycle, with actual eye-movement data from a human subject obtained from Tikhomirov and Poznyanskaya (1966). The trace printed by PERCEIVER seems to show some similarities to the eye-movement data obtained from the human subject. Simon and Barenfeld claimed that both the human player and PER-CEIVER concentrated on the same meaningful and important chess relationships. In fact, the 10 squares that PERCEIVER fixated seem to be squares that are at least next to the human player's zone of orientation. However, only 7 (out of 20 and 15) fixations are common. Holding (1985) has argued that at least part of the reason for the discrepancy between PERCEIVER's and the human subject's eye-movement sequences might be that the human player may be able to notice chess relationships that span more than a few squares and may be able to direct his eye movements toward squares that are not necessarily in the direct neighborhood of the presently focused piece.

The PERCEIVER simulation, the eye-movement recordings, and the hand-movement data all appear to reflect the facts that (a) players do not seem to attend equally to all squares of a chessboard; and (b) their choice of which squares to attend to is affected by meaningful chess relationships among the pieces. It appears that the perception of a chess situation is not just the result of an automatic scanning process that transfers the visually presented information into an accurate and complete visual or more abstract memory representation. Rather, perception is governed, at least to some extent, by top-down processing. In other words, it is affected by information about the meaningfulness of chess configurations. Thus, the perception of a chess pattern is affected by long-term-memory information.

The Memory-Recall Paradigm. The effect of long-term memory on the perception of a game constellation is more obvious in an experimental situation that has come to be known as the memory-recall paradigm (Vicente & de Groot, 1990). The memory-recall situation seems to have been first used by Djakow et al. (1927). It has since been replicated numerous times in different knowledge domains, starting with de Groot (1965). In Djakow et al.'s original study, expert and nonexpert chess players were asked to reconstruct different types of stimulus materials that were experimentally varied so as more or less to resemble a chessboard and its pieces. There appeared to be no difference between the masters' and the control subjects' ability to reconstruct a pattern of pieces presented for about one minute when the board and the pieces did not resemble a chessboard and chess pawns. However, when an 8 × 8 board with moving pieces was used, masters' reconstruction was slightly better than the control subjects'. More importantly, when actual chess positions were used, masters scored "three times as high" as the average obtained in "mass experiments with non-chess players" (Djakow et al., 1927, p. 41).

De Groot's use of the memory-recall paradigm differed from Djakow et al.'s in that (a) the subjects in de Groot's study (a grand master, a master, an expert, and a strong chess player) were shown 16 positions, rather than only 1; and (b) subjects saw the positions for only between 2 and 15 seconds (mean exposure time was 3–4 seconds) in contrast with the full minute that the Russian group allowed their subjects. At the end of each trial, the pieces shown were shuffled and the players were given half-a-minute to organize their memory. After that, they were to indicate which pieces they could recall, the two top players by dictating the pieces they recalled verbally, the two lower players by repositioning the pieces on a chessboard. The results were clear-cut: For 10 positions in which the conditions were nearly homogeneous (about 17 pieces to recall with an exposure time of 3–4 seconds), the two top players recalled 93% of the pieces correctly whereas the expert and the strong player correctly recalled only 72% and 51%, respectively. In addition, the grandmaster was able to recall 4 of the 10 positions perfectly, whereas the master recalled only 2 of the positions perfectly. The two less-skilled players did not recall any of the 10 positions perfectly.

De Groot (1965) interpreted these results as due to the different amounts of experience possessed by the four players. He argued that an experienced player has come to know what to expect in a chess game; that is, what chess configurations are more or less typical and which pieces are more or less likely to occur in certain constellations. Master players can presumably perceive and store relatively large constellations of pieces when these fall into familiar, typical categories. Inexperienced players, in contrast, do not possess this knowledge and are much more likely to view individual pieces as separate entities that are not related to each other.

Note that de Groot's interpretation is vague enough to cover at least two differing accounts of why it is that more experienced chess players are better able to recall briefly presented chess patterns than less experienced players. First, it is possible that, with experience, players generate highly stereotyped, prototypical chess positions that can be used to make educated guesses in the memory-recall situation. In this case, the whole configuration, that is, all pieces on the chessboard, form one or more recognizable and categorizable patterns. Second, an alternative to this proposition could hold that only parts of the configuration of pieces are recognized by experienced players. Because certain part configurations occur again and again in different games, this second alternative would seem to be a more sensitive approach to dealing with the memory-overload problem. A third possibility, finally, could hold that experienced players simply possess a more fine-tuned information-processing machinery than less experienced players, that is, their short-term memory for any kind of information, and not just for chess-piece configurations, is better than the short-term memory of less experienced players.

Enhanced Short-term Memory Capacity.   If the third explanation were correct, of course, then the advantage demonstrated by more-skilled players should hold across a wide variety of domains and should not be true just for chess-related material. For example, Hunt and Love (1972) reported that one of their chess players had a memory span of about 17 digits, clearly far above the normal range of 7 plus or minus 2 (Miller, 1956).

Interestingly, de Groot himself never seems to have believed in this alternative, and he never conducted the simple control experiment, later done by Chase and Simon (1973a), that would have refuted such a possibility. In fact, as Vicente and de Groot (1990) report, he did not even consider it worthwhile to publish the results of just such an experiment performed by one of his students, Lemmens, in 1964. The results of Lemmens' and particularly of Chase and Simon's (1973a) experiments, which we consider later, clearly demonstrate that the advantage of more-skilled over less-skilled players in the memory-recall situation disappears for material that all groups are equally familiar or unfamiliar with and thus cannot be due to a difference in short-term memory capacity.

Prototypicality Studies.   Work by de Groot (1966) himself, and by Jongman (1968) and Goldin (1978a), seems to refute the first possibility. De Groot (1966) looked at various kinds of evidence concerning efficient guessing and concluded that the superior recall exhibited by more experienced players was not due to their general knowledge of the typical chess position. After constructing the stereotyped position "par excellence," that is, the most typical position from a selection of 192 master games that were stopped at the 21st move, de Groot tested master players and less experienced players on memory for a set of positions taken from the 192 master games. As before, stronger players showed superior recall to less experienced players when the positions were only briefly presented. In an additional condition, however, de Groot did not show the positions at all, but had his players guess what the positions they didn't see could have been. If stronger players do, in fact, rely on highly stereotyped positions, then they should have been able to guess better, on average, than the less experienced players—at least on these highly typical master-level games. The masters' guesses at what positions might have been shown, however, were not better than the weaker players', and averaged only a rather disappointing 37% correct. In fact, both groups would have been inferior to a player who simply guessed the stereotypical position all the time, which would have led to a hit rate of 44% correct.

Goldin (1978a), in a series of experiments, more fully explored the effects of typicality on chess memory when she compared memory for typical and atypical chess positions by measuring recall for positions, recognition, and guesswork for more and less experienced players. In her first experiment, eight highly skilled and eight less-skilled players were shown chess diagrams for five seconds and were told to reconstruct the positions on a chessboard. Half of the positions were typical and half were atypical. In addition, half of the typical and atypical positions were taken from games that subjects had studied beforehand, whereas the other half were taken from games that were not studied. The results showed a big difference in recall between positions taken from studied versus nonstudied games (a difference of 26%), and a slight advantage for typical versus nontypical positions (72% correct recalled for typical positions against 62% correctly re-called for the atypical positions). There was, however, no difference between the strong and weak players and, in addition, there was no interaction between skill level and typicality. That is, the 10% recall advantage of typical over atypical positions held for both weak and strong players. Basically the same pattern of results was obtained in a recognition task (Goldin, 1978a).

In her third experiment, Goldin (1978a) used a situation similar to the one used by de Groot (1966) in which he had subjects guess at what positions they might have seen. In contrast to de Groot, however, she gave subjects a set of cue pieces (roughly one third of all pieces to be recalled) to facilitate performance. Again, she found no difference in guessing between strong and weak players, but did find a rather small (5%), though significant, recall advantage of typical over atypical positions. In addition, guessing was better for opening positions than for middlegame and endgame positions.

It appears then that although typicality, or prototypicality, do seem to affect performance in recall and recognition of briefly presented meaningful chess positions, its effects are rather small and cannot explain the recall superiority of strong over weak players demonstrated by de Groot (1965). Thus, although there is evidence favoring a prototypical representation of chess positions in memory, this particular view cannot explain why more experienced players are better at recalling briefly presented chess positions than are less experienced players.

Early Chunking Studies.   A first attempt at investigating the second possible explanation for the superiority of highly skilled over less-skilled chess players in the memory-recall paradigm was made by Jongman (1968), one of de Groot's students at Amsterdam. After comparing hit rates across skill levels in guessing experiments, Jongman looked at the actual guessing sequences obtained from eight master players and eight relatively inexperienced players over 12 trials. His method is probably best understood by analogy to an English language example provided by Holding (1985). Assume you are told to guess a series of successive letters that form a group of words, for instance,

＿＿＿＿＿＿　＿＿＿＿＿,　＿＿　＿＿＿＿＿　＿＿　＿＿＿＿

If this series of letters presents the sentence "ALWAYS CHECK, IT MIGHT BE MATE," then the number of guesses you might need for each letter forms a sequence that might look as follows, "322111 52211, 31 42111 21 1111." Notice that the number of guesses for the first letter of a word is generally much higher than the number of guesses for following letters of the same word. That is, the guessing is constrained by the knowledge of transition probabilities in the English language.

By examining the sequence of guesses for each of his subjects, Jongman (1968) discovered that, although all players start out with roughly the same number of guesses made for a position, the stronger players reduce the uncertainty in the position much more so than the weaker players. That is, by Trial 12, the strong players would have needed fewer guesses to correctly identify the remaining, not-yet-correctly-identified pieces of a position than the weak players. On the basis of this and similar analyses, Jongman concluded that strong chess players literally recognize whole clusters of pieces in a given position. Once they have identified one or a few pieces of a cluster, they can easily reconstruct the remaining pieces by utilizing chess categories in memory. These knowledge categories seem to be organized hierarchically in memory with a broad base of specific groupings that may be accessed directly and with several higher levels of superordinate categories that include more specific subcategories. Jongman's results thus give the first clear indication that subclusters of positions, grouped together in memory, might facilitate processing of meaningful chess positions and might underlie the memory recall advantage of strong over weak players demonstrated by de Groot (1965).

The Chase and Simon Studies.   More recently, the results obtained by de Groot and Jongman were replicated by Chase and Simon (1973a, 1973b), who proposed a somewhat more sophisticated theoretical explanation of the memory recall phenomenon and, more importantly, constructed a whole theory of chess playing based upon the findings obtained in the memory-recall situation. Chase and Simon studied three chess players (a master, a class A player, and a beginner) in a variety of experimental situations. They focused primarily on two chess-related tasks: a memory task, essentially a replication of de Groot's original memory recall studies, and a perception task, in which players were simply asked to copy a configuration of chess pieces that was shown to them on one chessboard to another, empty, chessboard. Players' performances in both tasks were videotaped. Both tasks were set up in the same way. Two chessboards were placed side by side but were separated by a partition. On the left-hand board players were shown a selection of 28 middlegame and endgame positions; the right-hand chessboard was empty. At the beginning of each trial, the partition was removed and players were allowed to view the chessboard on their left for five seconds. In the memory task, the partition was replaced in its original position after the five seconds; in contrast, in the perception task, the view was left open and players could glance back and forth between the two boards.

The positions shown to the three players were either meaningful or randomly generated chess positions. The 20 meaningful positions were either real middlegames or real endgames that were arbitrarily stopped after about the 21st or 41st move, leaving about 24–26 and 12–15 pieces remaining on the board. The eight random positions, four from middle games and four from endgames, were generated by taking actual positions and replacing the pieces randomly on the board. Thus, the meaningful and random positions did not differ in terms of the number of chess pieces that were shown to the players; rather, the only difference was that the meaningful positions could have, and in fact had, arisen during regular games, whereas the random positions could not have been reached in a regular game.

The results in the memory task were clear-cut and essentially replicated de Groot's earlier findings. For the meaningful middlegame positions, the master was able to place about 16 pieces correctly on the first trial, whereas the class A players and the beginner averaged about 8 pieces and 4 pieces, respectively. Furthermore, the master reproduced the board perfectly in three of four trials, whereas the class A player typically required one or two more trials than the master. The beginner, in contrast, needed up to 14 trials to reproduce the entire board configuration. The same qualitative differences between the master, the class A player, and the beginner, although less pronounced, were obtained with the meaningful endgame positions.

When random configurations were recalled, however, the results changed dramatically. There were no differences in the number of pieces that were correctly recalled among the three players. Furthermore, the first-trial performance of all three subjects was even poorer than the first-trial performance of the beginner on meaningful chess configurations.

Chase and Simon (1973a) interpreted these results in the following way, roughly following the conclusions arrived at by Jongman (1968): The superior ability of experienced over less experienced chess players to recall briefly presented meaningful chess patterns cannot be explained by superior storage capacity. That is, masters cannot keep more chess pieces in their short-term memory than less experienced players. Rather, their superiority is based upon a knowledge of a vast number of basic, meaningful chess patterns, called *chunks*, that are stored in long-term memory. Each of these patterns can be quickly identified and can be accessed in long-term memory through a label. When faced with the memory task, expert players match the chess configuration they perceive on the board with their long-term memory chunks. When they find a match, they retrieve the label for the pattern and store this label in short-term memory. At recall time, they can then use the label to access and retrieve the pattern from long-term memory.

This line of reasoning also explains why experience does not aid recall performance for randomly generated chess patterns. In this case, matching long-term-memory chunks simply do not exist. Therefore, the individual chess pieces, rather than labels of chunks, have to be memorized. Consequently, because their short-term memory capacity is not different from less experienced chess players, masters do not perform any better than beginners on random chess patterns.

If this line of reasoning is correct, of course, then it should be possible to identify a master's long-term memory chunks and, furthermore, it should be possible to estimate the number of pieces kept in a chunk. In theory, one might expect that players of varying skill do not differ in how many chunks they can keep in short-term memory, but might differ in how many pieces make up an individual chunk. In subsequent analyses and studies, Chase and Simon (1973a, 1973b) addressed these issues.

By measuring the time between placing subsequent pieces in the copying (perception) task, Chase and Simon (1973a) found that the time taken to place two pieces one after the other rarely exceeded two seconds for pieces that were placed within a glance, that is, without looking back at the left-hand chessboard; whereas it usually took longer than three seconds to place two pieces that were separated by a glance back to the original board. In other words, if one assumes that a glance establishes the boundaries of a chunk, then one might assume that two pieces that are placed one after the other within a limit of two seconds belong to the same chunk while two pieces that exceed an interpiece placement latency of two seconds belong to different chunks. Thus, by adopting the two-second dividing point (arrived at in the perception task), Chase and Simon were able to measure the content, size, and number of chunks processed by their players in both the perceptual task and in the memory task.

The chess pieces placed together in a single chunk in either experimental task might be expected to be related to another in a number of different ways: mutual or one-sided attack or defense, spatial proximity, same color, same type of piece, etc. Many pairs or triplets of pieces might have more than one relationship in common. It appeared that the three players in Chase and Simon's (1973a) study did not differ with respect to the types of interpiece relationships that existed within their chunks. Across all players, Chase and Simon identified four distinct relationships that primarily occurred: (a) castled king-pawn formations; (b) other pawn chains; (c) common back-rank piece positions; and (d) common attack configurations. In fact, the interpiece latencies varied as a linear function of the number of relationships that could be assigned to two pieces: the more relationships they shared, the faster two pieces were placed in succession.

Interestingly, although the four types of relationships showed up roughly to the same extent in the two experimental tasks, the estimates for both size and number of chunks used by the three players varied with the experimental task. In the copying (perceptual) task, the size estimates were not different: 2.0, 2.8, and 2.0 pieces for the master, the class A player, and the beginner, respectively. In the memory task, in contrast, these estimates were 2.5, 2.1, and 1.9 for the three players, respectively. Chunk sizes and chunk-size differences among the players varied as a function of trial. The differences were most pronounced at the first trial (3.8, 2.6, and 2.4 for the master's, the class A player's, and the beginner's recall of the middlegames) and essentially disappeared after five or six trials. For the beginner, the chunk-size estimates were essentially constant across trials, but for the more experienced players the chunk size decreased over trials. Chase and Simon's explanation of this finding was that the more experienced players might simply run off their larger chunks first and that, in addition, because the number of pieces to-be-recalled decreases over trials, the probability to recall larger chunks also decreases.

Counter to the proposed theory, the average number of chunks used by the master turned out to be larger than the number used by the class A player and the beginner (7.7 for the master vs. 5.7 and 5.3 for the class A player and the beginner, respectively), although all players' performances fell comfortably within the normal limit for short-term memory-span size (Miller, 1956). Chase and Simon (1973a) speculated that the larger number of chunks for the master might derive from the way in which chunks are organized in long-term memory. That is, if chunks themselves can be chunked to form a hierarchical pattern (see Jongman, 1968), then one single label kept in short-term memory might, in fact, allow players to retrieve two or more basic-level chunks, thus increasing the observable number of chunks. In fact, later work by Chase and Ericsson (1982) has established that skilled memorizers in various areas of expertise do seem to utilize hierarchical knowledge structures.

Simon and Gilmartin (1973) have described a computer model, called MAPP (*m*emory-*a*ided *p*attern *p*erceiver), that simulates the processes proposed by Chase and Simon (1973a) to be used by subjects to remember and reproduce chess positions they have seen briefly. MAPP combines features of PERCEIVER (described previously) and EPAM (Feigenbaum, 1963), a program that simulates the storage and acquisition of meaningful chess patterns in long-term memory. The actual performance of MAPP is based upon three parts. The first part performs roughly the same function as PERCEIVER, that is, it detects salient pieces on the chessboard. The second part recognizes meaningful chess patterns, that is, groups of pieces around the salient pieces, and stores labels for these patterns in short-term memory. The third part uses the labels stored in short-term memory to access and decode the meaningful patterns stored in long-term memory.

The performance of MAPP was tested by growing two different EPAM networks, one containing 447 and the second containing 572 different chess patterns. These memory sizes were large enough to recall about 39% or 43% of the pieces, respectively, from the set of middlegame positions used by Chase and Simon (1973a). The behavior of the program seemed to compare favorably with the behavior of the human chess players observed by Chase and Simon. For example, MAPP reconstructed 50–60% of the pieces that the master had recalled, but only 30% of the pieces that the master had missed. Furthermore, 16 of the 22 chunks recognized by MAPP were either identical with those used by the master or overlapped with them.

Simon and Gilmartin (1973) estimated that in order to achieve master-level performance in the memory recall task, the program would need to store between 10,000 and 100,000 patterns in long-term memory, and suggested that at least 10 years of concentration on the game are needed by a human player to acquire such a large number of meaningful patterns.

Evidence from Other Games

The theoretical formulations put forth by Chase and Simon (1973a, 1973b) and Simon and Gilmartin (1973) to explain skill differences in the memory-recall situation have until recently been widely accepted in the literature of chess psychology and have had an enormous impact on both the topics that fellow researchers interested in game playing have chosen to investigate and on the theoretical explanations that were acceptable. The general finding that "knowledge is power" has led researchers to generalize the Chase and Simon (1973a) findings and theoretical explanations to games other than chess, such as go, gomoku, and bridge, probably preventing at the same time alternative explanations from flourishing.

Go and Gomoku. The game of go is a boardgame like chess, but is played by adding, rather than moving, successive identical pieces or "stones" to intersections on the lines of a 19 × 19 grid so as to surround opposing stones and territory. Gomoku is a much simpler game in which the object is to complete an unbroken line of stones in any one direction.

Gomoku seems to have been studied first by Rayner (1958a, 1958b), who focused, however, primarily on the acquisition of strategies, rather than on memory issues. Eisenstadt and Kareev (1975) studied the effects of go and gomoku skill on players' memory for patterns of stones that could have derived from either go or gomoku. They trained subjects to play both games and, in one experiment, asked subjects to recall a go and a gomoku position. In fact, subjects were shown the exact same pattern for the go and the gomoku recall, except that the pattern that was shown second was a rotated version of the one that was shown first. In addition, the color of the stones had been reversed. Interestingly, instructing players that the patterns had arisen from one game or the other had a big effect on the reconstruction of pieces. Believing that a position had arisen from go led to a different level of accuracy, and a different pattern of errors than believing the position to have been derived from gomoku. Eisenstadt and Kareev's (1975) model of subjects' performance during memory recall is somewhat different from the one proposed by Chase and Simon (1973b) and more similar to the prototype explanations discussed earlier. Memory for meaningful go or gomoku patterns, according to Eisenstadt and Kareev, appears to be achieved by a top-down strategy, with a winning pattern acting as prototype to which the tested, to-be-recalled patterns are matched.

Reitman (1976) performed a series of studies of go that was directly modeled after Chase and Simon's (1973a) perception and memory tasks. Like Chase and Simon, she asked a beginner and a professional-level go master to recall and copy briefly presented (for five seconds) meaningful and meaningless go positions. In addition, she obtained the master's penciled delineations of the chunks he remembered six months after the experiments had been completed.

In line with the Chase and Simon findings, the go master was far better at recalling the briefly presented meaningful go patterns (66% correct vs. 39% correct on the first trial), but was not able to recall meaningless patterns any better than the go beginner (30% correct vs. 25% correct). In addition, the master and the beginner needed, on the average, 4.25 and 3.75 trials respectively to reproduce the random patterns. On meaningful patterns, in contrast, the beginner took 3.4 trials, the master nearly a full trial fewer (2.5).

Of more interest are Reitman's findings on the content of chunks. Like Chase and Simon (1973a), she constructed a cutoff interpiece time from subjects' between-glance and within-glance interpiece times in the copying task. However, a detailed comparison of the contents of the chunks as defined by glances in the copying task and of the chunks inferred on the basis of the cutoff interpiece time in the memory task showed that they were not identical. In fact, trying out a range of ten different interpiece times still failed to identify memory chunks in the two tasks that matched in content.

In explaining these difficulties, Reitman (1976) argued that the technique of identifying chunks on the basis of between-glance and within-glance interpiece latencies rests on several assumptions, particularly, the ideas that the chunks form a linear, rather than hierarchically, structured set, and that all elements of a chunk are recalled before any element of a different chunk is recalled. In fact, the penciled delineations of chunks as seen by the master player six months after the experiment seemed to indicate that his chunks were neither linear, nor hierarchically organized. Rather, they were often serially overlapping. That is, because the final elements of one chunk are often the first elements of a different chunk, a player's chunking might be somewhat arbitrary and unstable. This finding casts considerable doubt on the reliability of the cutoff interpiece latency technique, and demonstrates at the very least that chunk structures might differ across different domains of knowledge.

Bridge.   Engle and Bukstel (1978) compared four bridge players of varying degrees of skill on the by-now-familiar recall and copying of briefly presented meaningful and random bridge hands. Meaningful bridge hands were structured by sorting them into suit and number order. In addition, they unexpectedly asked their subjects to recall which bridge hands they played in an earlier tournament simulation. Not surprisingly, all of their tasks showed a bridge expert and a life master to have superior memory and perception for meaningful bridge hands, but not for random hands. Skill seemed to determine also which bridge cards the players attended to, with the lower-rated players attaching more prominence to the presence of honor cards than to the number sequences within a hand.

Charness (1979) studied a sample of 20 bridge players, ranging in skill from novice to life master. Level of skill affected performance on a series of bridge-related tasks: planning the play of a contract, rapid bidding, incidental learning of bridge hands, and memory for briefly presented meaningful bridge hands. Again, the only task on which more-skilled and less-skilled bridge players did not differ was the recall of briefly presented randomly sorted bridge hands.

The results on unexpected recall where players were asked to recall hands evaluated earlier for planning the play revealed that the more-skilled players had encoded the hands more efficiently despite having spent less time on encoding. It appeared that all players performed better on hands that they had evaluated correctly, and that the better players used the value of bridge contracts as a cue to recalling the cards seen.

Frensch and Sternberg (1989) reported the results of a series of three experiments that demonstrate that the meaningful patterns formed in long-term memory by highly skilled and less-skilled bridge players follow different organizing principles. Frensch and Sternberg hypothesized that less-skilled players would organize their patterns primarily on the basis of perceptual features, and more experienced players would form more abstract, strategy-based patterns (e.g., Chi, Feltovich, & Glaser, 1981; Larkin, 1983).

In their first experiment, bridge players of varying levels of skill were asked to play 12 simulated bridge games on a computer. Half of the games were played under normal conditions. In the other half, players were introduced to slightly different versions of bridge. Version 1 introduced new nonsense names for honor-cards and suits; Version 2 rearranged the order of honor-cards and suits; and Version 3, the lead-rule change, modified the rule determining who began each play. Instead of the player who won the last trick, which is the common rule in bridge, the player with the lowest card in the last trick led into the next trick. If, in fact, players at different levels of skill base their long-term memory patterns on different features, then the two groups of players should have been differentially affected by the rule changes. That is, Versions 1 and 2 were considered perceptual modifications that should affect less-skilled players most, while Version 3 was expected to exert its effect on a deeper, more abstract and strategic level and, therefore, to affect highly skilled players most.

The most important results of the study were that: (a) highly skilled players were more affected by the strategic rule change than by the two perceptual changes whereas less-skilled players were most affected by the two perceptual changes; and (b) the highly skilled players were, even in the modified games, on average still the faster and better players. Interestingly, the difference between surface and abstract changes for expert bridge players appeared to be most pronounced in a reaction-time variable, namely, the speed of choosing a play; whereas for nonexpert players, the difference between these two types of rule modifications seemed to manifest itself most clearly in a quality measure, namely, the number of games won. Apparently, experts used the additional time they needed when dealing with the abstract change to employ new and effective game strategies, perhaps reflecting a difficulty in adapting their existing knowledge base.

In their second experiment, Frensch and Sternberg (1989) had the same 34 bridge players generate opening bids to given bridge hands as quickly as possible. As Charness (1979) pointed out, even novice bridge players are able to generate a reasonable opening bid. Furthermore, the choice of opening bids is based primarily on the distribution of honor-cards and on the number of total cards per suit in a given hand. Although there are a large number of different bidding systems to determine a bid, these systems are based upon the same, primarily perceptual, properties of hands and, generally, do not arrive at different opening bids. Thus, more and less experienced bridge players were not expected to differ in their classification of hands into bid categories, which is exactly what Frensch and Sternberg found. In addition, both groups' generating of opening bids was, as expected, much more affected by the perceptual changes than by the strategic, more abstract modification.

Frensch and Sternberg's (1989) last experiment tried to locate the locus of difficulty for the two perceptual changes. That is, it might be argued that the perceptual modifications affected all subjects primarily at the level of encoding and only to a minor degree at a conceptual level. Or alternatively, it might be argued that experts were most affected at a perceptual level whereas nonexperts were most affected at a conceptual level or vice versa. The study used a somewhat modified version of the memory-recall paradigm.

In this study, players of differing skill levels were shown slides of bridge hands (13 cards displayed in a fanned position), presented in the natural way. Slides were visible for only five seconds. After slide-offset, players were asked to write down as many of the cards as they could remember. They had the option of watching the same slide as often as they wanted to until they had written down all 13 cards of the seen hand. Half of the bridge hands shown were structured in the same way players usually structure their hands; for the other half, features of the visual display were changed so as to correspond to the name-change and rank-order-change conditions used in the previous experiments. In the name-change condition, the letters on honor-cards were changed to new ones. In the rank-order condition, the familiar rank orders of suits and high cards were changed; consequently hand displays mirrored the new rank orders.

The results of this study demonstrate that the two types of display changes did not differ in their effects on subjects' encoding abilities. Furthermore, experts and nonexperts were not differentially affected by the two types of changes of the visual display, indicating that the effects of the perceptual rule modifications obtained in the previous studies might, for both expertise groups, be partly due to the disruption of normally occurring encoding processes. The findings did not support the argument that the perceptual changes affected experts primarily at a perceptual level and nonexperts primarily at a conceptual level of information processing or vice versa.

Problems for the Chunking Model

The work on non-chess games generally confirms that highly skilled players are better than less-skilled players at recalling briefly displayed meaningful information, but are no better at recalling nonmeaningful information. The non-chess research also suggests, however, the need for several modifications to the chunking theory as proposed by Chase and Simon. The work on go performed by Reitman (1976), for instance, casts considerable doubt on the use of pauses to define chunk boundaries and suggests that the organization of chunks in long-term memory might be more complex than the chunking theory implies. Additional evidence against the plausibility of Chase and Simon's account has been raised by studies that have tried to decrease subjects' reliance on short-term memory in the memory recall task.

Charness (1976), for instance, compared class A and class C players' performance in the memory-recall situation when interfering tasks were inserted between the presentation of the to-be-recalled material and the actual recall. He reported that interfering non-chess tasks such as repeating random digits, computing running sums of random digits, copying abstract symbols on paper, and carrying out mental rotations, had as little effect on subjects' ability to recall the briefly presented material as had interfering chess-related tasks such as solving chess problems and naming the pieces on a second chessboard. Over all tasks, interference decreased memory recall only by about 6% to 8%. Similar results have been reported by Frey and Adesman (1976), who showed that neither counting backward nor remembering additional chess positions had a profound effect on recall of briefly presented meaningful information.

In addition, a series of studies by Lane and Robertson (1979) points to the impact of the degree of processing on the recall of briefly presented information when short-term memory participation is excluded. Lane and Robertson examined the effects of a semantically oriented task (find the best move) and a purely formal task (counting pieces) on intentional and incidental learning in the classic memory-recall paradigm in which a group of low-skill chess players viewed chess positions for 20 seconds and were then given a 10 minute interfering test of spatial ability. The experimenters found that for incidental, but not for intentional learning, the semantically oriented task led to better recall than the formally oriented task. Similar, even more pronounced results were reported for a group of highly skilled players.

Taken together, these studies seem to suggest that performance in the memory recall task might not be mediated by short-term memory. That is, the findings that interfering tasks do not affect recall performance seem to suggest that the information to-be-recalled might be stored directly in long-term memory. Furthermore, the Lane and Robertson (1979) studies (see also Goldin, 1978b, 1979) seem to suggest that the recognition of familiar chess configurations is not simply a mechanical matching process, as suggested by Chase and Simon, but can be consciously manipulated.

Recent Developments

Lane and Robertson (1979) argued that an important component of chess skill is the ability to integrate large configurations of pieces into coherent schemata. Like the memory prototypes discussed above, these schemata enhance recall by preserving the meaning of a chess position. Similarly, Chase and Ericsson (1981, 1982) have proposed a new theoretical explanation of the memory recall phenomenon that takes the criticisms formulated above into account. *Skilled memory theory* has evolved from Chase and Ericsson's studies of expert mnemonists and is based primarily on detailed analyses of individuals who were able to increase their digit spans far beyond the seven plus-or-minus-two limit (Miller, 1956). Essentially, the theory proposes that experts have developed not only content skill, but also skill in long-term memory encoding and retrieval that basically enhances their short-term memory capacities. Chase and Ericsson (1982) characterize experts' efficient use of long-term memory in terms of three principles: (a) the meaningful encoding principle; (b) the retrieval structure principle; and (c) the speed-up principle.

Similar to Chase and Simon's (1973a) account, the meaningful encoding principle states that highly skilled individuals explore both the content and the structure of prior knowledge to encode meaningful information. In contrast to Chase and Simon's theory, however, the retrieval structure principle assumes that experts develop memory mechanisms called retrieval structures to facilitate the retrieval of information stored in long-term memory. Retrieval structures are used to encode meaningful information together with retrieval cues that can later be regenerated to retrieve the stored information without a lengthy search (Tulving & Thomson, 1973). The third principle, the speed-up principle, states that both long-term memory encoding and retrieval processes speed up with practice such as to approach the speed and accuracy of short-term memory encoding and retrieval.

Skilled memory theory has so far not been tested extensively in domains other than digit span, for which it was originally proposed. Ericsson and Oliver (1984; Ericsson & Staszewski, 1989) have, however, reported some experiments on blindfold chess playing that were performed with a single highly skilled chess player. These experiments seem to suggest that the player's retrieval structure preserved a representation of the chessboard that allowed him to explore the board as if it were perceptually available. For example, the player was able accurately to identify the contents of randomly probed squares (over 95% correct) almost as fast when he had never actually seen the position as when he was allowed to view the position on a chessboard. Ericsson and Oliver (1984) suggest that the retrieval structure used by the player contains retrieval cues that point to the individual squares on a chessboard.

Skilled memory theory might be viewed as an extension of Chase and Simon's (1973a) original chunking theory. Both theories assume that stored domain knowledge is used to encode meaningful new knowledge and that therefore the experts' advantage in the memory-recall situation is limited to meaningful domain information. Unlike chunking theory, skilled memory theory claims that meaningful new information is stored directly in long-term memory and that experts have at their disposal mechanisms for indexing the new knowledge such that it can be rapidly, reliably, and efficiently retrieved at a later point in time. In addition, skilled memory theory assumes that long-term memory storage and retrieval operations speed up with practice.

The Impact of Prior Knowledge on Move Selection

So far, we have presented only that part of Chase and Simon's (1973a, 1973b) chunking theory that is directly concerned with subjects' performance in the memory-recall situation. Somewhat less formally stated and quite certainly less well investigated is that part of the theory that is concerned with the selection of moves. It develops from and is directly based upon the chunking model that we have reviewed so far and that suggests that a large pattern repertoire is available to the skilled player. The basic idea is that these patterns act as move generators. That is, each of the patterns stored in long-term memory is assumed to be associated with an internal label, which in turn is said to be associated with information about plausible moves. The two kinds of information are linked in a production system, in which the necessary conditions are satisfied by the stored and perceived patterns and the corresponding actions consist of attending to plausible moves.

Also associated with the internal label is a set of instructions allowing the player to regenerate the pattern as an internal image ("a concrete internal representation") in the mind's eye. When the skilled player perceives a meaningful chess position, he constructs an internal image and executes the plausible move associated with the perceived pattern. The result of the move, that is, the new internal image, is then passed back through the pattern-recognition system, which generates new plausible moves that can be executed in the mind's eye, and so on. To ease the memory load imposed by the internal image of the position, Chase and Simon (1973b) assumed that a player is able to form a composite picture by blending the external and internal piece configurations, allowing him to remember the possible lines of play he has generated and searched through so far. That is, only the labels for patterns encountered during search need to be kept in short-term memory; the real actual position is always available for inspection on the chessboard.

Charness's (1989) model of planning in the domain of bridge playing is similar in many respects to Chase and Simon's theory. Charness assumes that specific card distributions are associated with play strategies for the more experienced bridge players. In contrast, the novice player's search for the next move and for a general game plan is, in any given situation, guided by domain-general problem-solving rules. With increasing experience, the domain-general rules become refined and associated with certain card distributions (see Hayes-Roth, Klahr, & Mostow, 1981, for a description of a set of possible mechanisms that achieve such a knowledge refinement in the game of hearts). Like Chase and Simon (1973b), Charness likens the association between memory for card distributions and specific game strategies to a production system, in which the condition side represents the encoded card patterns, and the action side indicates the intended sequence of play.

As Holding (1985) points out, there appears to be no clear evidence in favor of the Chase and Simon (1973b) theory as it is outlined herein. There is, however, some evidence that at least is very difficult to reconcile with the theory. First, as we pointed out earlier already when we discussed the early introspection-based work by Binet (1894) and Cleveland (1907), it is by no means clear that chess players construct concrete visual images of the chessboard and its pieces.

Milojkovic (1982) has recently reported an experimental study concerning the use of imagery in chess playing. In his experiment, he showed a group of chess novices and a single master simple chess positions (involving only three pieces) on a tachistoscope. The positions presented varied in the orientation of the board as well as in the distances among the pieces. All positions were shown for only three seconds after which they were replaced by a colored card, indicating subjects which move to imagine. Subjects were instructed to make the required move in their head and press a button when they were ready to continue. The results showed that, for the novice players, the response times, presumably reflecting the time taken to amend the image of the position, varied as a linear function of the distances among the pieces. The master, however, did not show an effect of piece spacing. This experiment, thus, seems to indicate that the representation of chessboard configurations varies with level of skill. The comparison seems to suggest that perhaps the master's representation of the position was more abstract, less visual, and therefore less affected by the physical details of the layouts than the perhaps more visual form of representation used by the novices.

The apparent use of visual imagery in chess was also demonstrated in an experiment, described by Church and Church (1983), in which a class A player was shown a series of positions, each involving a single white piece (queen, rook, or bishop) and a black king. The task was simply to decide whether or not the king was in check. Overall, it took the player longer to decide on a check when the check was diagonal, rather than parallel. In both cases, however, the decision time varied as a linear function of the distance between the pieces.

Both the Milojkovic (1982) experiment and the study described by Church and Church (1983) seem to indicate that some chess players, possibly the less-skilled ones, construct visual internal representations of the chessboard while others don't. Of course, the evidence in favor of this conclusion is based upon reaction times that vary with the physical layout of the actual positions. As Anderson (1978) has argued quite convincingly, no experiment can ever decide whether imagery or some other form of representation underlies any cognitive process. It is possibly partly for this reason that this particular aspect of the internal mental representation of chess positions has not been subjected to a more vigorous empirical examination.

More serious objections against the theory stated by Chase and Simon (1973b) concern the proposed associations between stored patterns and plausible moves. First, the chunks described by Chase and Simon (1973a, 1973b) seem much too small to determine meaningful moves in a complex chess position (Holding, 1985). And second, the theory does not seem to be able to account for findings that demonstrate skill differences in choose-a-move tasks for unfamiliar chess patterns (Holding & Reynolds, 1982; Saariluoma, 1985).

Holding and Reynolds (1982) asked chess players of differing skill first to reconstruct a set of randomly constructed chess configurations consisting of 24 pieces. The random positions were shown for eight seconds and were followed by the players' attempt to reconstruct the position. Next, the reconstructions were corrected by the experimenters and players were asked to choose the best continuation move to the random positions. According to Chase and Simon's theory, there should have been (a) no skill-related differences in recall performance for the random patterns, and (b) no skill-related differences in the choose-a-move task because the random patterns should not have been stored in long-term memory and thus should not have been associated with plausible moves.

The experimenters found in fact that prediction (a) was correct, but (b) was wrong. That is, even in the absence of skill-related recall performance there were still skill-related differences in the quality of the moves chosen for the random positions. In fact, the correlation between the quality of the moves chosen and skill rating was about 0.75, while the correlation between level of skill and recall performance was not significant. The study thus demonstrates that game playing as exemplified in the choose-a-move task cannot simply be a function of the associations between remembered meaningful patterns and plausible moves, but has to be at least partially dependent on additional processing.

Similar results have been obtained by Saariluoma (1985). In three different experiments, he tested players of varying skill levels for how fast they could identify whether or not a king was in check, how fast they could count the number of minor pieces (bishops and knights) on the board, and how well they could recall briefly presented positions. Positions were either meaningful or randomly generated. For all tasks involving meaningful chess positions, level of skill correlated with the speed or the quality of task performance. More importantly, the skill-related differences were identical for random chess positions with the exception of recall performance. That is, highly skilled players were faster in detecting whether the king was in check and in counting the number of minor pieces on the board, regardless of whether the chess positions were meaningful or randomly arranged.

Again, it may be concluded that skill differences in chess cannot be solely due to differing numbers of meaningful chess positions that are stored in long-term memory and are associated with plausible moves.

THE SEARCH PROCESS

It seems rather strange that the important issue of search could have been relatively neglected in game research for so long. After all, novice game players are capable of choosing moves in a game, admittedly rather slowly and error prone, but they can do so nevertheless. In the absence of experience with the game, how could they possibly achieve their performance other than by means of search processes? Also, even more experienced players will certainly face game situations that are new to them, that they have not been in before. Again, in the absence of stored patterns for these particular situations, how could they possibly come up with a decent move other than by means of heuristic search?

The relative absence of research on search processes until very recently can probably partly be explained by researchers' emphasis on understanding skill-related differences, rather than performance processes that are common to players at all skill levels. Even so, de Groot's (1965) basic contention that highly skilled and less-skilled players do not differ in the quantitative characteristics of their search processes does by no means imply that the players were performing qualitatively identical processes. That the overall depth of search, for instance, appeared to be comparable for grandmasters and experts (de Groot, 1965) does not at all imply that both groups use identical search strategies; after all, the moves selected by the grandmasters are different from the ones selected by the experts.

Strategies and Plans

It seems intuitively obvious that the process of searching for a move should, at least for highly skilled players, be guided by general strategies or plans. In fact, Murray Campbell, one of the designers of "Deep Thought," arguably the most powerful chess computer of our times, has recently argued that what differentiates the best available computer programs from skilled human chess players is primarily the ability to plan ahead (Leithauser, 1990). Unfortunately, there is very little information on how human game players use strategies and plans in their search process, although it appears clear from an inspection of verbal protocols that players do, indeed, use general plans (Holding, 1985).

One piece of evidence comes from Rayner's (1958a, 1958b) early studies on how young adults and children learn to play pegity, a game also known as gomoku. The objective of pegity, or gomoku, is to form a uninterrupted line of five pegs on a board. Rayner (1958a), studying a group of subjects as they acquired skill in playing gomoku over a 5-week period, was able to describe the types of patterns that players gradually learn to look for, and the associated strategies for each pattern. Although some of the players never progressed beyond forming single-line patterns, most eventually learned to use crossed-line strategies which both maximize the chances of preventing defensive moves by the opponent and increase the likelihood of forming lines of five pegs. Interestingly, the switch from single-line to crossed-line strategies was accompanied by an increase in the time taken to make the move, indicating perhaps that the different strategies had differential effects on search processes.

Tikhomirov and Terekhov (1967) present some further evidence that suggests that the use of general strategies and plans affect search processes in chess playing. Recording the hand movements of blind players during move choices, Tikhomirov and Terekhov discovered that the hand movements tended to involve fewer squares on the board, thus decreasing the effective search size, when a sequence of moves appeared highly predictable. More interestingly, search size seemed to be affected by whether an opponent move was thought to be consistent or inconsistent with the opponent's plans and intentions. That is, when an opponent move was subjectively judged as consistent with the opponent's plans, then search size—the number of squares visited by the blind player's fingers—was smaller than when the move was judged as inconsistent with the opponent's plans. This was true regardless of whether the opponent's move was objectively consistent or inconsistent with his or her plans, although the difference in search size was more pronounced for objectively discrepant moves.

Findler (1978) reports some findings that indicate the usefulness of strategies in the game of five-card draw poker. In draw poker, five cards are dealt initially, followed by a first betting round, which, in turn, is followed by the possibility to discard up to five cards that are replaced by new cards. A player is allowed to see only his or her own cards, and can, therefore, only use his or her knowledge of objective probabilities of card configurations to restrict the search space to within operable limits. Findler developed a number of computer programs that play poker on the basis of fixed static strategies and/or adaptive learning processes. It appears that the most successful programs use not only objective criteria, such as the objective probabilities of certain card configurations to limit the search space, but also more subjective criteria, such as the desirability of staying in the game and the opponents' playing styles as they become apparent over a sequence of games. Findler reports that human players are usually unable to tell whether they are playing against a computer program or against human players when the game is played over computer terminals, indicating perhaps that human players restrict their search in similar ways.

Quantitative Characteristics of the Search Process

Although only very little is known about how players use plans, strategies, and goals to guide their selective search, there is some research—mostly based upon the analysis of verbal protocol data in choose-a-move tasks—that is concerned with the quantitative and qualitative aspects of the search process.

Search through the space of possibilities is generally assumed to take the form of a search through a search tree (Charness, 1981a, 1981b; Newell & Simon, 1965; Wagner & Scurrah, 1971). Following a procedure developed by Newell and Simon (1965), the actual search process in chess, for instance, can be divided into a number of episodes, with each episode defined as beginning with a base move and continuing with an evaluation of its consequences. Episodes are continued to a certain depth, which may be expressed in plies. The last node in an episode is called a terminal node; alternatives to any move after the base move are called branches. Base moves may be unique or repeated; alternatives may be implied, rather than actually mentioned.

Based on such or a comparable analysis of protocol data, it is possible to derive quantitative estimates of the search process, such as the total number of moves considered by a player, the maximum and average search depth, and the number of different base moves mentioned. It is also possible to some extent to describe the qualitative aspects of the search process, that is, whether and when a player returns to the same base move, when he selects to switch to a different base move, and so forth.

De Groot Revisited

As we described in the opening paragraphs of this chapter, the first quantitative descriptions of the search process were obtained by de Groot (1965) who analyzed the verbal protocols of his subjects obtained while they were choosing a move to a given chess position. De Groot is often quoted as having shown that the quantitative indices of the search process, such as the maximum search depth, are not different for players of differing skill levels. As Holding (1985) points out, however, de Groot's analysis was based on only a small sample of players who, in addition, were all excellent players. Furthermore, the results were based on the verbal protocols obtained for a single position with possibly some idiosyncratic features. In fact, later research on the very same position has shown that strong players can push their maximum search depth far beyond the 5.3 plies reported by de Groot for his grandmasters.

Newell and Simon (1965), for instance, report a depth of 9 plies for one of their players and Wagner and Scurrah (1971) a depth of 15 plies. In fact, the player described by Wagner and Scurrah achieved a *mean* depth of 6.8 plies for an endgame position, which is larger than the *maximum* search depth reported by de Groot for his grandmasters.

In addition, even though de Groot's two skill groups did not significantly differ on most of the quantitative indices, all of the measures obtained were in favor of the better players. The grandmasters achieved a maximum search depth of 6.8 plies to the experts' 6.6 plies; they considered an average of 35 moves to the experts' 30.8 moves; and they searched faster, taking 9.6 minutes against the experts' 12.8 minutes to decide on a move.

More recent research by Charness (1981b) and by Holding and Reynolds (1982) has cast considerable doubt on the assumption that level of skill does not affect the quantitative aspects of the search process. Charness (1981b), for instance, comparing 34 players of differing skill, found systematic, skill-related differences in the depth, breadth, and speed of the search process. For example, the average maximum depth of search appeared to change by about 1.4 plies for each standard deviation in skill rating. That is, in Charness' sample, the maximum search depth varied from about 3.6 plies for his lowest-rated player to about 9.0 plies for his highest-rated player. Essentially similar results have been obtained by Holding and Reynolds (1982) for random test positions.

A similar, though less pronounced increase with skill rating was also obtained for the mean depth of search (varying from about 2.3 plies to about 4.1 plies in the sample). Skill level also affected the total number of moves explored and the total time taken to choose a move for a given situation. On the basis of these results, it appears that an increase in skill level leads to a deeper and broader exploration of the search tree.

Qualitative Characteristics of the Search Process

Perhaps one of the most interesting qualitative characteristics of the search process that emerged from de Groot's (1965) analysis of verbal protocols was what he termed the concept of "progressive deepening." This concept refers to players' reinvestigation of moves that have been explored already. De Groot argues that the progressive deepening of the search, which in fact includes progressive broadening as well, is not the result of a player simply having forgotten that he or she explored some of the moves already, but serves the goal of systematically extending and exploring the tree search in manageable portions.

Newell and Simon (1965) formulated some rules that supposedly govern the search process and explain when a player uses progressive deepening—continuing a line of search; or progressive broadening—considering alternative moves. The three most important of Newell and Simon's six rules are: (a) the analysis of any base move is independent of the analysis of other base moves; (b) the first episode of a base move involves normal moves, whereas later moves involve increasingly unusual moves; and (c) if the evaluation of an episode is favorable, then analysis of the base move is continued; if it is unfavorable, then a different base move is chosen.

Work by Scurrah and Wagner (1970; Wagner & Scurrah, 1971) seems to indicate that the first two rules are essentially correct while the third rule—the win-stay/lose-shift principle (Holding 1985, 1989)—seems to be doubtful. In Scurrah and Wagner's (1970) analysis of a single player, it appeared that the player often failed to shift to a new base move after coming up with a negative evaluation.

Reynolds's (1981) reexamination of de Groot's (1965) verbal protocols seems to indicate that the use of the win-stay/lose-shift principle, which he calls "homing" heuristic, varies with the skill level of a player. That is, it appears that de Groot's grandmasters and masters seemed to have complied with the homing heuristic more frequently than the experts and class players. Even the highly skilled players, however, tended to diverge from the heuristic a great deal of the time.

The Evaluation of Chess Positions

A player's compliance with the win-stay/lose-shift principle is, of course, closely tied to his or her ability to judge a given as well as anticipated positions accurately. In general, the whole search process is meaningful only if a player is able to accurately judge alternative possible continuations of the play. Interestingly, very little is known about how players evaluate current and anticipated positions.

Holding (1979) and subsequently Charness (1981a) have demonstrated that the quality of a chess player's evaluation of a given position seems to vary with the player's level of skill. Holding asked 50 players to evaluate five middle game and five endgame positions, all taken from world-class games, on a numerical scale. The rating was to be expressed in terms of the advantage of the winning over the losing side and could vary from 10 to 20. Holding's results clearly indicate that the quality of the evaluation, that is, whether the actual outcome of the game was correctly predicted or not, increases with increasing playing strength. In addition, the advantage of the better players was more apparent in the endgame than in the middlegame positions. There was also some evidence indicating that players frequently base their evaluations not on the static features of the situation, but on anticipated future game constellations. That is, players do not seem to evaluate a poorly positioned pawn negatively if the position can easily be modified to a better one on the next move.

Work by Charness (1981a) has confirmed the basic contention that highly skilled chess players more accurately evaluate given positions than less skilled players. In Charness's study, the players received evaluation tests as an interpolated task between move choice and later recall of chess positions. In these evaluation tests, players had simply to decide, as quickly as possible, which side would win or whether there would be a draw. The times needed to come up with an evaluation were divided into those that were smaller than 10 seconds— presumably reflecting static evaluation; and those that were larger than 10 seconds—presumably reflecting dynamic, search-based evaluations. Although the players' average response time was not correlated with skill level, the proportion of correct evaluations for the static evaluation increased significantly with increasing playing strength.

Although the findings on the general quality of the evaluational judgments of players are important, they do not address the more interesting question of what features of a given or anticipated game situation a player bases his or her evaluation upon. Horowitz and Mott-Smith (1973), for instance, provide a normative system of "point count chess," in which points are awarded and deducted for positional features of a chess position. Features that deserve to be awarded could be, for instance: center control, more space, file control, advanced pawn, pawn majority, etc. Weaknesses that require deductions might be, for example: doubled or isolated pawns, holes, king in center, and so on. In Horowitz and Mott-Smith's system, point-counts are calculated separately for the two sides and are then compared. The point-count system shares many similarities with recent, advanced evaluation functions that are used in chess-playing computer programs, such as the complex function used by the CHESS 4.5 program (Slate & Atkin, 1983).

In an attempt to find out upon which features human players base their evaluations, Holding (1979) compared the evaluations obtained from his human players with evaluations obtained from three chess-playing computer programs. The first program used a relatively simple evaluation function, basically a count of the relative mobility of the white and black pieces. In the second, somewhat more sophisticated and complicated program, evaluation depended on "square control," "a measure of the relative chess values of the pieces occupying and attacking each of the squares on the board" (Holding, 1989a, p. 105), and the third program (CHESS 4.5) exemplified the best currently available complex, knowledge-based evaluation function.

Correlations between the players' and the programs' evaluation scores differed depending on the players' skill levels. For relatively low-skilled players, all of the correlations were significantly different from zero (0.68, 0.63, and 0.80 for the comparisons with the mobility, square control, and CHESS 4.5 evaluation functions, respectively). For highly skilled players, in contrast, only the comparisons with the square-controlled-based and the CHESS 4.5 based evaluation functions were significant (0.44, 0.58, and 0.91 for the comparisons with the mobility, square control, and CHESS 4.5 evaluation functions, respectively).

The data seem to suggest that (a) players of differing skill levels do, in fact, base their evaluations on different features of the game situation; and (b) that evaluations increase in complexity with increasing skill level. Interestingly, the high correlations of both skill groups with the complex evaluation function employed by CHESS 4.5 might imply, as Holding (1989a) argues, that both humans and computers operate in a very similar manner, perhaps basing their evaluations on roughly the same set of features.

Looking Ahead

Real games are unlike experimental situations in that players must be able to evaluate not only the current, visually present chess position, but also future, anticipated ones. In fact, the success of any search process can be said to depend substantially on the ability to evaluate unseen, anticipated chess positions which, in turn, depends on players' ability to accurately predict and imagine the unseen positions. In contrast to chess-playing programs that have no difficulty performing evaluations of predicted positions, human players might become overloaded by the process and increasingly less accurate in their evaluations of increasingly distant future positions.

Holding and Pfau (1985) have recently addressed this problem. In their experiment, Holding and Pfau had chess players of differing skill levels first make preliminary evaluations of middle game positions that were taken from actual games. Then, the experimenters dictated three pairs of moves and told the subjects to imagine the new chess positions. After each pair of moves was dictated, the players were asked to reconsider and revise their earlier evaluation. After all three pairs had been dictated, the pieces were moved to their terminal positions by the experimenters and subjects were asked to give an evaluation of the final, now visually present position.

An analysis of the differences between the final evaluations and the three previous evaluations of the unseen positions indicated that for both a group of highly skilled and a group of low-skilled chess players, the initially given evaluations differed considerably from the ones given last. However, these discrepancies were continuously reduced the closer the players got to the final position. In addition, the highly skilled players' difference scores were substantially smaller than the less-skilled players' scores, indicating that the better players can see ahead more clearly than the less-skilled players.

In a recent experiment, Holding (1989b) demonstrated that these differences between players of differing skill levels increase considerably when players are asked to evaluate unseen trees of play, rather than simple lines of play. In this study, the evaluations of players of differing strengths were compared with evaluations provided by a senior master and, again, with the final evaluations. It appeared that the difference scores of the highly skilled players descended virtually as before the closer the position evaluated was to the final position. For the less-skilled players, however, this trend was now essentially flat, showing no improvement with decreasing distance to the final position.

In addition, Holding (1989b) argued that the highly skilled players might be more consistent than less-skilled players in how they utilize search trees. That is, having evaluated a potential end node as the best possible position, good players seem to be able to trace their way back through the maze of possibilities and choose the next move that will actually lead to the predicted best move; whereas poorer players seem to make many mistakes when they work their way back through the search tree.

THE LOCUS OF GAME-PLAYING ABILITY: DOMAIN-GENERALITY VERSUS DOMAIN-SPECIFICITY

It appears then that, contrary to de Groot's (1965) original contention, skill in game playing might in fact depend a good deal on the ability efficiently and yet accurately to search through a complex tree of possible future game constellations. As we have noted before, interest in research on the quantitative and qualitative aspects of the search process has only recently been rekindled and might be expected to provide a good deal of important information on game playing in the foreseeable future.

Somewhat unfortunately, it appears that the two major bodies of research on game playing, the one concentrating on memory effects, and the other on search issues, respectively, are largely independent of each other and have only rarely been tied together (but see Holding, 1985). Although it appears relatively uncontested that memory for prior game situations must to some extent affect search, it is less clear how exactly this interaction works. Aside from Chase and Simon's (1973b) early, by now at least partially disconfirmed, account, there have been no other "grand theories" of game playing.

An additional issue that we have not yet considered concerns the debate we briefly alluded to in our introduction, namely, the debate between those who argue that the ability to play games depends primarily on domain-general problem-solving abilities versus those who argue that game playing is primarily determined by domain-specific skill. This controversy is really related to two different issues. First, there is the problem of whether humans rely more on domain-general problem-solving abilities or on domain-specific domain knowledge when they play a game. And second, there is the issue of what drives the knowledge-acquisition process in game playing; that is, the problem of whether the rate and quality of improvement in game playing is based on domain-general ability and/or on domain-specific skill.

The answer to the first problem should be relatively clear given the empirical evidence we have reviewed in this chapter, and is generally also supported by related work on artificial, nonhuman machines that play games (e.g., Berliner, 1978). It appears that beginners in any game seem to be relying primarily on domain-general problem-solving abilities, whereas experienced players utilize an extensive body of domain-relevant knowledge. One might expect, therefore, that measures of general intelligence, which supposedly reflect domain-general abilities more than domain-specific knowledge, be related to novices', but not experts' game-playing ability.

Surprisingly, there appears to be very little data linking general intelligence to game-playing ability. Consistent with the prediction formulated previously are Djakow et al.'s (1927) early findings that seem to suggest that skill in highly skilled chess players does not depend on general problem-solving ability. Using a battery of early psychometric tests that included measures of the speed of evaluating arithmetic calculations, the discernment of logical patterns, a test of concentration and various indices from the Rorschach, they found that chess masters appeared to have more willpower than nonchess players. None of the other tests, however, differentiated between the two groups. Cleveland (1907), on the basis of a survey of 100 players, had earlier arrived at the same conclusion.

On the other hand, summaries of biographical data obtained by de Groot (1965) and Elo (1978) seem to indicate that expert chess players do not represent a random sample from the general population. Elo's (1978) more comprehensive sample of 180 highly skilled players indicated that 63% of the players had obtained at least some education at the university level, as had 38% of their parents. Also, 40% of the players reported as their profession chess journalism, a profession that seems to require at least some verbal ability which, in turn, has been shown to be one of the better indicators of general intelligence (Sternberg, 1985). In addition, 96% of the players reported proficiency in at least two different languages, with 25% reporting proficiency in five or more languages, again indicating that the sample was very unlikely to be randomly derived from the general population.

It appears then that there may be, in fact, some relationship between general intelligence and game-playing ability. We might speculate that the level of general ability affects primarily the *acquisition* of domain-specific skill and knowledge. That is, a player of relatively higher general ability may be faster and better than a less intelligent player at acquiring domain-related knowledge. If this were true, then the relationship between general intelligence and game-playing skill might show up in the correlation between general measures of IQ and measures of speed and rate of acquisition, but not necessarily in a correlation between general IQ and measures of achieved level of excellence. If we assume that the acquisition of game skill follows a power function (e.g., Newell & Rosenbloom, 1981), then we might expect the relationship between general intelligence and achieved level of game skill to be obscured by a restricted-range effect at the upper end of the ability continuum (e.g., Ceci & Liker, 1986).

Charness (1989) has recently reported the results of a longitudinal study of game-playing ability that are roughly consistent with this view. The author had a single chess player, who had originally participated in a series of two experiments (Charness, 1981a, 1981b) perform the same experiments again about nine years later. At both times, the subject, who was 16 years of age at the time of original testing, was asked to think out loud while choosing the best move for four different positions, to evaluate 20 endgame positions as rapidly and accurately as possible, to reproduce the four choose-a-move positions (incidental recall), and to recognize the four choose-a-move positions from a set of 30 different game constellations.

It appeared that the player's transition from an about average-performance player to one of the top-ranked (7th) players in Canada was accompanied primarily by an increase in the ability to choose the correct move for the positions presented, and to do so in less time. Interestingly, most of the quantitative measures of the player's search processes (total number of moves considered, maximum and average search depth, etc.) did not seem to change by much, although he tended to search fewer base moves, and the total number of moves searched also seemed to have declined. Charness (1989) argued that the most dramatic change occurred in the player's chunk size, which increased from about 1.8 pieces per chunk in 1978 to about 2.7 pieces per chunk in 1987. These findings are roughly consistent with Chase and Simon's (1973b) account of skill acquisition in chess.

More importantly, the player's rise to a master level could not have been predicted on the basis of any of the domain-specific measures that were taken at the original time of testing. That is, the player differed from the total sample in only 2 out of 18 chess-related measures that were computed in 1978, namely, the quality of the move selected in the choose-a-move task, and the time taken for the endgame evaluations (where he was slower than average). Given that simply by chance, as Charness (1989) noted, 1 of the 18 tests could have produced one significant difference, the results seem to indicate that the player's domain-specific ability at the earlier testing time did not provide any indication that he would be any different from the rest of the sample nine years later. Although this finding does not demonstrate that the player's domain-general ability, if measured in 1978, would have been a significant predictor, it leaves the door open for such an explanation. (In fact, the player was, at the time of the second testing, a graduate student in mathematics at a major Canadian university.)

On the other hand, however, Radojcic (1971) describes a domain-specific, chess-related task (a knight's tour of the board), said to have originated with L. Cherny, that seems to predict to some extent subsequent chess-playing ability. In fact, Radojcic reports that all of the four boys who turned in the fastest times when tested on this task together with a large sample of chess-playing Czech school children, are now prominent, master-level chessplayers.

Thus, although there is still the possibility that domain-general ability might affect the acquisition of domain-specific knowledge, the issue is debatable, and cannot be decided without further empirical research. In addition, there appear to be a variety of noncognitive factors, such as motivation (e.g., Deci & Ryan, 1985; Ericsson, Krampe, & Tesch-Römer, 1989; Pritchard, Campbell, & Campbell, 1977), personality (Bloom, 1985), and instruction, that might affect the acquisition of game-playing skill, thus vastly complicating the deceptively simple picture drawn so far.

GAMES AS THE DROSOPHILAS
OF COGNITIVE PSYCHOLOGY

In summary, it appears that experienced game players differ from less experienced players in that they have acquired vast amounts of game-related information, and have stored this information in long-term memory in a way that allows efficient and rapid access. Stored knowledge eases the perceptual processes required in game playing and, to some extent, also eases move selection.

In addition, experienced players seem to have acquired the ability to search efficiently and rapidly through their internal representations of the current and anticipated game situations, and appear to be more accurate and more consistent than less experienced players in evaluating potential game continuations. It is an empirical question at this point whether the acquisition of game-playing skill is affected by a player's general intelligence.

Games, particularly the game of chess, are easily the most thoroughly investigated and best understood complex problem-solving tasks in cognitive psychology. The experimental methods and theoretical models applied to game research have had an enormous impact on the methods and theories applied to tasks outside the games domain (e.g., physics, computer programming, medical diagnosis). It is in this regard that games have been the Drosophilas of cognitive psychology. On the other hand, however, it has been increasingly noticed in recent years that different games require different human abilities for successful performance. Whereas chess, for instance, seems to be an excellent task for studying search processes, bridge, for instance, seems more suitable for examining pattern-driven planning processes (Charness, 1989).

Thus, now that research on game playing has progressed to the point where important insights into global aspects have been gained that seem to apply to many complex problems, more specific questions and problems can be addressed and studied that might be unique to some tasks but not to others. In the foreseeable future we might expect, therefore, the Drosophila-like status of games to decrease markedly. Not necessarily because games will cease to attract researchers' interests, but because the findings obtained in game research will be less likely to be applicable to different tasks and to different knowledge domains.

REFERENCES

Anderson, J. R. (1978). Arguments concerning representation for mental imagery. *Psychological Review, 85*, 249–277.

Berliner, H. (1978). A chronology of computer chess and its literature. *Artificial Intelligence, 10*, 201–214.

Binet, A. (1894). *The Psychology of great calculators and chess players.* Paris: Hachette.

Bloom, B. S. (Ed.). (1985). *Developing talent in young people.* New York: Ballentine.

Ceci, S. J., & Liker, J. K. (1986). A day at the races: A study of IQ, expertise, and cognitive complexity. *Journal of Experimental Psychology: General, 115*, 255–266.

Charness, N. (1976). Memory for chess positions: Resistance to interference. *Journal of Experimental Psychology: Human Learning and Memory, 2*, 641–653.

Charness, N. (1979). Components of skill in bridge. *Canadian Journal of Psychology, 33*, 1–16.

Charness, N. (1981a). Aging and skilled problem-solving. *Journal of Experimental Psychology: General, 110*, 21–38.

Charness, N. (1981b). Search in chess: Age and skill differences. *Journal of Experimental Psychology: Human Perception and Performance, 2*, 467–476.

Charness, N. (1989). Expertise in chess and bridge. In D. Klahr & K. Kotovsky (Eds.), *Complex information processing. The impact of Herbert A. Simon* (pp. 183–208). Hillsdale, NJ: Lawrence Erlbaum Associates.

Chase, W. G., & Ericsson, K. A. (1981). Skilled memory. In J. R. Anderson (Ed.), *Cognitive skills and their acquisition* (pp. 141–190). Hillsdale, NJ: Lawrence Erlbaum Associates.

Chase, W. G., & Ericsson, K. A. (1982). Skill and working memory. In G. H. Bower (Ed.), *The psychology of learning and motivation* (Vol. 16, pp. 1–58). New York: Academic Press.

Chase, W. G., & Simon, H. A. (1973a). Perception in chess. *Cognitive Psychology, 4*, 55–81.

Chase, W. G., & Simon, H. A. (1973b). The mind's eye in chess. In W. G. Chase (Ed.), *Visual information processing* (pp. 215–281). New York: Academic Press.

Chi, M. T. H., Feltovich, P. J., & Glaser, R. (1981). Categorization and representation of physics problems by experts and novices. *Cognitive Science, 5,* 121–152.

Church, R. M., & Church, K. W. (1983). Plans, goals, and search strategies for the selection of a move in chess. In P. W. Frey (Ed.), *Chess skill in man and machine* (pp. 131–156) (2nd ed.). New York: Springer Verlag.

Cleveland, A. A. (1907). The psychology of chess and learning to play it. *American Journal of Psychology, 18,* 269–308.

de Groot, A. D. (1946). *Thought and choice in chess.* Amsterdam: Noord Hollandsche.

de Groot, A. D. (1965). *Thought and choice in chess.* The Hague: Mouton.

de Groot, A. D. (1966). Perception and memory versus thought: Some old ideas and recent findings. In B. Kleinmuntz (Ed.), *Problem solving: Research, method and theory* (pp. 19–50). New York: Wiley.

Deci, E. L., & Ryan, R. M. (1985). *Intrinsic motivation and self-determination in human behavior.* New York: Plenum.

Djakow, I. N., Petrowsky, N. W., & Rudik, P. A. (1927). *The psychology of chess.* Berlin: de Gruyter.

Duda, R. O., & Shortliffe, E. H. (1983). Expert systems research. *Science, 220,* 261–268.

Eisenstadt, M., & Kareev, Y. (1975). Aspects of human problem solving: The use of internal representations. In D. A. Norman & D. E. Rumelhart (Eds.), *Explorations in cognition* (pp. 308–346). San Francisco: Freeman.

Elo, A. (1978). *The rating of chessplayers, past and present.* New York: Arco.

Engle, R. W., & Bukstel, L. (1978). Memory processes among bridge players of differing expertise. *American Journal of Psychology, 91,* 673–689.

Ericsson, K. A., Krampe, R. T., & Tesch-Römer, C. (1989, November). *Prudent practice makes perfect: An examination of the daily lives of elite violinists.* Paper presented at the Annual Psychonomic Society Meeting, Atlanta, GA.

Ericsson, K. A., & Oliver, W. (1984, November). *Skilled memory in blindfolded chess.* Paper presented at the Annual Psychonomic Society Meeting, San Antonio, TX.

Ericsson, K. A., & Staszewski, J. J. (1989). Skilled memory and expertise: Mechanisms of exceptional performance. In D. Klahr & K. Kotovsky (Eds.), *Complex information processing. The impact of Herbert A. Simon* (pp. 235–267). Hillsdale, NJ: Lawrence Erlbaum Associates.

Feigenbaum, E. A. (1963). The simulation of verbal learning behavior. In E. A. Feigenbaum & J. Feldman (Eds.), *Computers and thought* (pp. 297–309). New York: McGraw-Hill.

Feigenbaum, E. A. (1989). What hath Simon wrought? In D. Klahr & K. Kotovsky (Eds.), *Complex information processing. The impact of Herbert A. Simon* (pp. 165–182). Hillsdale, NJ: Lawrence Erlbaum Associates.

Findler, N. (1978). Computer poker. *Scientific American, 239,* 112–119.

Fine, R. (1965). The psychology of blindfold chess: An introspective account. *Acta Psychologica, 24,* 352–370.

Frensch, P. A., & Sternberg, R. J. (1989). Expertise and intelligent thinking: When is it worse to know better? In R. J. Sternberg (Ed.), *Advances in the psychology of human intelligence* (Vol. 5, pp. 157–188). Hillsdale, NJ: Lawrence Erlbaum Associates.

Frey, P. W., & Adesman, P. (1976). Recall memory for visually presented chess positions. *Memory & Cognition, 4,* 541–547.

Goldin, S. E. (1978a). Memory for the ordinary: Typicality effects in chess memory. *Journal of Experimental Psychology: Human Learning and Memory, 4,* 605–611.

Goldin, S. E. (1978b). Effects of orienting tasks on recognition of chess positions. *American Journal of Psychology, 91,* 659–671.

Goldin, S. E. (1979). Recognition memory for chess positions: Some preliminary research. *American Journal of Psychology, 92,* 19–31.

Hayes-Roth, F., Klahr, P., & Mostow, D. J. (1981). Advice taking and knowledge refinement: An iterative view of skill acquisition. In J. R. Anderson (Ed.), *Cognitive skills and their acquisition* (pp. 231–254). Hillsdale, NJ: Lawrence Erlbaum Associates.

Hayes-Roth, F., Waterman, D. A., & Lenat, D. B. (1983). An overview of expert systems. In F. Hayes-Roth, D. A. Waterman, & D. B. Lenat (Eds.), *Building expert systems* (pp. 3–29). Reading, MA: Addison-Wesley.

Holding, D. H. (1979). The evaluation of chess positions. *Simulation and Games, 10,* 207–221.

Holding, D. H. (1980). Captures and checks in chess: Statistics for programming and research. *Simulation and Games, 11,* 197–204.

Holding, D. H. (1985). *The psychology of chess skill.* Hillsdale, NJ: Lawrence Erlbaum Associates.

Holding, D. H. (1989a). Adversary problem solving by humans. In K. J. Gilhooly (Ed.), *Human and machine problem solving* (pp. 83–122). New York: Plenum.

Holding, D. H. (1989b). Evaluation factors in human tree search. *American Journal of Psychology, 102,* 103–108.

Holding, D. H., & Pfau, H. D. (1985). Thinking ahead in chess. *American Journal of Psychology, 98,* 271–282.

Holding, D. H., & Reynolds, R. I. (1982). Recall or evaluation of chess positions as determinants of chess skill. *Memory & Cognition, 10,* 237–242.

Horowitz, I. A., & Mott-Smith, G. (1973). *Point count chess.* London: Allen & Unwin.

Hunt, E., & Love, T. (1972). How good can memory be? In A. W. Melton & E. Martin (Eds.), *Coding processes in human memory.* Washington, DC: Winston.

Johnson-Laird, P. N. (1988). A taxonomy of thinking. In R. J. Sternberg & E. E. Smith (Eds.), *The psychology of human thought* (pp. 429–457). Cambridge, MA: Cambridge University Press.

Jongman, R. W. (1968). *The eye of the master.* Amsterdam: Van Gorcum.

Lane, D. M., & Robertson, L. (1979). The generality of the levels of processing hypothesis: An application to memory for chess positions. *Memory & Cognition, 7,* 253–256.

Larkin, J. H. (1983). The role of problem representation in physics. In D. Gentner & A. L. Stevens (Eds.), *Mental models* (pp. 75–100). Hillsdale, NJ: Lawrence Erlbaum Associates.

Lesgold, A., Rubinson, H., Feltovich, P., Glaser, R., Klopfer, D., & Wang, Y. (1988). Expertise in a complex skill: Diagnosing x-ray pictures. In M. T. H. Chi, R. Glaser, & M. J. Farr (Eds.), *The nature of expertise* (pp. 311–342). Hillsdale, NJ: Lawrence Erlbaum Associates.

Miller, G. A. (1956). The magical number seven, plus or minus two. *Psychological Review, 63,* 81–97.

Milojkovic, J. D. (1982). Chess imagery in novice and master. *Journal of Mental Imagery, 6,* 125–144.

Leithauser, B. (1990, January, 14). KASPAROV Beats Deep Thought. The New York Times Magazine.

Newell, A., & Rosenbloom, P. S. (1981). Mechanisms of skill acquisition and the law of practice. In J. R. Anderson (Ed.), *Cognitive skills and their acquisition* (pp. 1–56). Hillsdale, NJ: Lawrence Erlbaum Associates.

Newell, A., & Simon, H. A. (1965). An example of human chess play in the light of chess-playing programs. In N. Weiner & J. P. Schade (Eds.), *Progress in biocybernetics* (pp. 19–75). Amsterdam: Elsevier.

Newell, A., & Simon, H. A. (1972). *Human problem solving.* Englewood Cliffs, NJ: Prentice-Hall.

Posner, M. I. (1988). Introduction: What is it to be an expert? In M. T. H. Chi, R. Glaser, & M. J. Farr (Eds.), *The nature of expertise* (pp. xxix–xxviii). Hillsdale, NJ: Lawrence Erlbaum Associates.

Pritchard, R. D., Campbell, K. M., & Campbell, D. J. (1977). Effects of extrinsic financial rewards on intrinsic motivation. *Journal of Applied Psychology, 62,* 9–15.

Radojcic, M. (1971). What is your chess IQ? *Chess Life & Review, 26,* 709–710.

Rayner, E. H. (1958a). A study of evaluative problem solving: I. Observations on adults. *Quarterly Journal of Experimental Psychology, 10,* 155–165.

Rayner, E. H. (1958b). A study of evaluative problem solving: II. Developmental observations. *Quarterly Journal of Experimental Psychology, 10,* 193–206.

Reitman, J. (1976). Skilled perception in GO: Deducing memory structures from interresponse times. *Cognitive Psychology, 8,* 336–356.

Reynolds, R. I. (1981). Search heuristics of chessplayers of different calibers. *American Journal of Psychology, 95,* 383–392.

Saariluoma, P. (1985). Chess players' intake of task-relevant cues. *Memory & Cognition, 13,* 385–391.

Scurrah, M., & Wagner, D. A. (1970). Cognitive model of problem solving in chess. *Science, 169,* 209–211.

Simon, H. A., & Barenfeld, M. (1969). Information-processing analysis of perceptual processes in problem solving. *Psychological Review, 76,* 473–483.

Simon, H. A. & Chase, W. G. (1973). Skill in chess. *American Scientist, 61,* 394–403.

Simon, H. A., & Gilmartin, K. (1973). A simulation of memory for chess positions. *Cognitive Psychology, 5,* 29–46.

Slate, D. J., & Atkin, L. R. (1983). Chess 4.5—The Northwestern University chess program. In P. W. Frey (Ed.), *Chess skill in man and machine* (2nd ed., pp. 82–118). New York: Springer Verlag.

Sternberg, R. J. (1985). *Beyond IQ: A triarchic theory of human intelligence.* Cambridge, MA: Cambridge University Press.

Sternberg, R. J., & Frensch, P. A. (1990). Intelligence and cognition. In M. Eysenck (Ed.), *Cognitive psychology: An international review* (Vol. 1, pp. 57–103). Chichester, England: Wiley.

Tikhomirov, O. K., & Poznyanskaya, E. D. (1966). An investigation of visual search as a means of analyzing heuristics. *Soviet Psychology, 5,* 3–15.

Tikhomirov, O. K., & Terekhov, V. A. (1967). Evristiki cheloveka [Human heuristics]. *Voprosy Psikhologii, 13,* 26–41.

Tulving, E., & Thomson, D. M. (1973). Encoding specificity and retrieval processes in episodic memory. *Psychological Review, 80,* 352–373.

Vicente, K. J., & de Groot, A. D. (1990). The memory-recall paradigm: Straightening out the historical record. *American Psychologist, 45,* 285–287.

Wagner, D. A., & Scurrah, M. J. (1971). Some characteristics of human problem-solving in chess. *Cognitive Psychology, 2,* 454–478.

Winikoff, A. W. (1967). *Eye movements as an aid to protocol analysis of problem-solving behavior.* Unpublished doctoral dissertation, Carnegie-Mellon University, Pittsburgh, PA.

V CONCLUSIONS

12

Some Comments on the Study of Complexity

Earl Hunt
University of Washington

This chapter is intended to be a commentary on the study of complex problem solving, with special reference to the earlier chapters in this volume. Every such commentary carries with it a constraint; the commentator ought to mention all the other authors. This poses a problem if the commentator feels obliged to follow the Thumperian principle, a technique of rhetoric formulated by Thumper, the rabbit in Walt Disney's movie *Bambi*. Thumper advised: "If you can't say something nice, don't say nothing at all." My problem is to mention everyone and still obey the Thumperian principle.

Fortunately, there is precedent. Psychologists, more influenced by rat than rabbit, have not always heeded Thumper's advice. Besides, in this case the Thumperian constraint is not terribly restrictive. Most of the papers in this volume are rather good, and I am not under any obligation to agree with everything that the authors said. Here is what I shall attempt.

First, I make some remarks about the procedures that are appropriate for the scientific study of complex problem solving. Second, I try to extract a theme from the different empirical findings. The theme is considered in terms of cognitive science's current model of the mind.

The stress on "scientific" study is important. Some investigations of human thought are properly termed *scientific investigations*. Other, equally respectable investigations are *humanistic* or *engineering investigations*. All three traditions are illustrated by various papers in this volume. The distinction is not meant to be pejorative. However, since the term *scientific* has come to have excess value among academic psychologists, the distinction between traditions needs some explanation.

Scientific, engineering, and humanistic investigations of thought produce results that are useful for different purposes. In general, scientific knowledge permits objective generalization. A "good scientific explanation" ought to be stated so unambiguously that a robot could use it. Furthermore, the generality of a scientific explanation is important; science is supposed to present unified explanations of a variety of different phenomena.

Engineering explanations are supposed to provide instructions that are useful for solving a particular problem. In educational psychology, for instance, useful prescriptions for teacher-student interaction (e.g., Minstrell & Simpson, 1990) are engineering explanations. Engineering explanations are often derived from scientific principles, but there is no necessary reason that this be so, even in the physical sciences.[1] Engineering explanations are valid if they work and if it is clear when they should be used.

Scientific and engineering explanations both have to satisfy objective criteria. Humanistic explanations are judged more subjectively. A humanist's audience must feel that something has been revealed, but different members of the audience can disagree over precisely what has been revealed. How many different interpretations are there of *Hamlet?*

These philosophical remarks may seem very far from the psychological study of complex problem solving. They are not. Thought can be studied from scientific, engineering, and humanistic perspectives. Each has a contribution to make. However, these contributions are different, so the procedures appropriate for producing one type of knowledge are not always appropriate for producing another. In evaluating a specific study of complex problem solving one has to consider the type of knowledge that the study produced. I shall concentrate on the production of scientific knowledge.

SCIENCE AND THE SYSTEMS APPROACH
TO COMPLEXITY

Scientific analysis takes place in two steps: the observation of empirical laws and the elucidation of general principles from which these laws can be derived. The emphasis throughout is on laws, that is, on regularities in the behavior being observed. A second emphasis is on simplicity; the principles used to derive a law

---

[1]The assertion that engineering does not necessarily depend on science may sound surprising. In our society, engineering is certainly associated with the physical sciences. But consider the following examples. Six or seven hundred years ago the best engineers in the world were the Chinese government officials charged with the construction of public works, and their contemporaries, the cathedral builders of medieval Europe. Neither the Chinese nor the Europeans had anything approaching the correct model of physical mechanics. To bring the point closer to home, in modern applied psychology there have been two broad approaches to teaching the retarded. One stems from radical behaviorism, and the other is based on an avowedly cognitive theory of presenting mental challenges to the child. Butterfield (1990) has pointed out that although the theoretical orientation of these groups could hardly be more different, they recommend almost identical educational practices.

are supposed to be simpler than the law itself. To put the statement in statistical terms, a scientist shouldn't draw conclusions from an observation without degrees of freedom. Sometimes we forget, but we ought to be embarrassed when we do.[2]

Scientists develop laws by studying systems. In mathematics, a system is a set of interdependent variables, such as a set of linear equations. In empirical observation we distinguish between open and closed systems. A closed system is one whose state is determined only by those variables that are explicitly represented within the system. An open system is one whose state is subject to perturbations from variables outside the system itself, and hence outside of the range of observation.

Suppose an observer is presented with an empirical system. How is it to be understood? A scientific explanation will be stated in terms of the operation of a closed system that approximates the real, open one. This means that a scientific explanation (a) must be based on regularities, and (b) will only be approximately true. However, the degree of approximation is really of little interest to the scientist, so long as regularities can be explained.

The behavior of a scientist is in marked contrast to the behavior of an engineer, who is very concerned with controlling certain key variables, in an admittedly open system. The engineer needs a statement of relationships in a system that is "closed enough" so that those variables that have practical importance can be kept within bounds by setting the values of other variables that the engineer can control.

Hegarty (this volume) offers an interesting example. She distinguishes between an ideal system of pulleys capable of lifting an object weighing 100 lbs with a 50 lb force and an actual system of pulleys that would let a farmboy lift a 100 lb bale of hay with a 50 lb pull. In the ideal system the weight would be lifted by any pulley arrangement with a mechanical advantage of 2. The farmboy, who has to deal with sticky ropes and rusty pulleys, ought to use a system with a mechanical advantage of 3.

Let's turn this example around. Suppose that we did not know about Newtonian mechanics. How would we discover "the laws" that apply to pulley systems? The answer to this question depends upon the type of laws that we want to discover. If we are interested in engineering laws, we want to observe how people lift real bales of hay, with real pulleys. We would, presumably, develop engineering knowledge of how to build such systems.[3] However, if we wanted to

---

[2]During a symposium on intelligence at the 1990 American Psychological Society meetings, one speaker (S. Ceci) illustrated his point by contrasting learning curves in two groups, each containing a single sample point (n = 1 per group). Remarks from the audience suggested skepticism. The skepticism was appropriate, since Ceci was presenting in a scientific forum, and asking his audience to draw a scientific conclusion based on a statistical contrast without any degrees of freedom. Ceci's approach would have been acceptable by humanistic standards.

[3]This is what the Chinese and medieval builders did. Pulley systems were used extensively well before Newton's time.

develop scientific knowledge of the laws of force, we would have to deal with abstractions of our knowledge of factual pulley systems.

I doubt that these abstractions could ever be developed by studying the complicated pulley systems that were used to build cathedrals and castles in the Middle Ages. We would want to study very simple (and, in practice, useless) systems consisting of "close to ideal" arrangements of light pulleys and strings, where friction could be disregarded. These systems would not be of much use to a medieval construction contractor, who might look on our work with scorn. The medieval master would, correctly, realize that his apprentices needed to practice with real pulleys. That's because the medieval master was trying to transmit engineering knowledge, not scientific knowledge.

The arguments for and against studying closed systems apply to psychology just as they apply to physics and engineering. If we are going to develop scientific knowledge, we are most likely to succeed if we study closed systems. Engineering knowledge can only be acquired and verified by studying important but more open, realistic systems. Because verification is important, we want to study enough of these systems so that we can be sure where the principles apply. Finally, humanistic insight may be obtained by careful analysis of single cases. The cases should be chosen because they are likely to yield important insights, whether or not they are important in themselves.

Although psychology loudly asserts that it is a science, many psychological investigations are more properly thought of as quests for engineering knowledge. This remark, which is not a criticism, certainly applies to many contemporary studies of complex problem solving. Consider Lesgold and Lajoie's (this volume) analysis of their experience with SHERLOCK. In their paper they point out that electronics repairmen express a great deal of their knowledge in the form of "war stories" about previous experiences. They use analogies based on the war stories to guide problem solving in difficult situations.

Lesgold and Lajoie's paper is in itself a "war story," addressed to cognitive scientists. They are telling us how to build a tutorial system that provides technical instruction. In doing so they invite us to draw analogies between the development of SHERLOCK and any tutorial development problems that we may face in the future. Lesgold and Lajoie do make occasional references to abstract scientific theories such as ACT* (Anderson, 1983) but no real use is made of theory in any formal way.

Historically, psychologists acting as scientists have tried to mimic the physicist's approach to studying complexity, by studying simple systems and then extrapolating the results to the complex systems. This approach has a mixed record. A great deal of time has been devoted to studies of such things as paired associates learning and maze-running behavior of the rat, without learning much of use to education. On the other hand, there are examples of success, especially in the field of perception. We can use performance in tests of vernier acuity to predict the visual performance of myopics outside of the laboratory.

There are several reasons why psychologists have not made great practical advances by studying simple systems. Probably the most important reason is that we have not spent enough time developing theories of complex systems that could be used to guide us in developing appropriate and manageable models. A closely related point is that we have not spent enough time considering what properties of a complex system might be due to the action of simpler subsystems within it and what properties of the entire system might be due to the interactions between component systems. Both these topics are dealt with in some detail in the next section. For the present, it is enough to note that, unlike physicists studying pulley systems, we don't have enough of a theory of system construction to be able to isolate the vital components of complex problem solving for study, if you will, *in vitro* rather than *in vivo*.

In recent years some psychologists appear to have concluded that we are inherently unable to extrapolate from simple to complex situations. They argue, therefore, that we should study complex, ecologically valid behavior directly. See Funke (this volume) and Neisser (1978) for arguments to this effect. Those who advocate studying complex systems directly also appear to want to draw scientific rather than engineering conclusions from the research. Other psychologists have questioned the practicality of this approach. The skeptics maintain that complex, ecologically valid systems are so open that regularities cannot be observed, and hence scientific conclusions often cannot be drawn (Banaji & Crowder, 1989).

The important dimension here is the one between open and closed systems, not between simple and complex systems. Some things are inherently complex, and a scientist seeking to understand them simply has to accept that complexity. Probably the best example in psychology is the study of the visual system. The visual system is a very complex neurophysiological and neuroanatomical system. We are quite sure that whatever the mechanisms of vision are, they are all located in an identifiable region of the brain, stretching from the eye to the visual cortex. The system is closed, but complicated.

Put another way, to the extent that behavior in a complex problem-solving system depends upon the interaction between system components, there is no way to understand the complex system, scientifically, without studying it directly. On the other hand, to the extent that the systems we study are open we simply cannot find scientific laws, let alone develop scientific theories.

THE STUDY OF COMPLEX
PROBLEM SOLVING SYSTEMS

Suppose that we are satisfied that we are studying a relatively closed problem-solving system. To go further we have to find a way of analyzing the system so that we ourselves can understand it. This is not a trivial limitation. Suppose I handed you a complete neurophysiological explanation of the neurological events inspired when a dance lover watches a ballet. The explanation would be of no use whatsoever, because you could not understand mental action at that level of detail.

Simon (1969, 1981) has argued that many apparently complex systems can be broken down into relatively simple, manageable subsystems. The complexity of the system arises because of the interaction between the simpler, analyzable subsystems. Simon used as an example the path of an ant across a beach. Braitenberg (1984) has extended Simon's idea by showing how very simple autonomous vehicles can interact with their environment to display what looks to an observer like purposeful behavior. The philosopher Fodor (1983) has argued that mental behavior can similarly be analyzed as the product of interactions between understandable, modular systems.

There is no guarantee that a given complicated system can be broken down into independent, interacting modules. However, some can, so it seems reasonable that as a first step someone interested in complex behavior ought to try to break down the system under study into its modules.

Stanovich and Cunningham's (this volume) treatment of reading illustrates how successful this method can be. They argue that reading can be broken down into two systems: a lexical system that translates from visual stimuli to linguistic arguments, and a more general language system that analyzes the products of the lexical system. Furthermore, they show that the two systems operate in fundamentally different ways. The lexical system is driven by environmental stimuli, in a "bottom-up" fashion, and the language system is more directed "top down," by expectations generated from goals and from the results of earlier analyses.

Sokol and McCloskey (this volume) provide a somewhat similar systems analysis of mental calculation. They break mental calculation down into two subsystems, a subsystem that retrieves mathematical facts and a subsystem that executes algorithms based on those facts. Hegarty's paper on mechanical problem solving parallels the logic of Sokol and McCloskey's paper, although the content is very different. Hegarty breaks comprehension of mechanical systems into two parts: A process of retrieval of knowledge about mechanics and a more general purpose visual-spatial mechanism that can simulate movement of parts "in the mind's eye" in order to reason about how a particular device will behave.

There is a marked contrast between the approach taken in the three papers just cited and the holistic approach taken by Funke (this volume) and by Voss, Wolfe, Lawrence, and Engle (this volume). Voss et al. provide insightful, careful accounts of debates about crucial events in modern history: the US intervention in Korea in the 1950s and the Cuban Missile Crisis in the 1960s. Voss et al.'s analysis left me with a subjective feeling that I had a better understanding of events that exerted a major influence on my own life. I found their contrast between the style of meetings conducted by presidents Kennedy and Truman to be especially revealing. The general principle that I drew from Voss et al.'s study was that there is one way to run a meeting if you have decided, in advance, your general course of action but you want your plan checked and approved (Truman), and another if you honestly are not sure what to do and want to explore your alternatives (Kennedy).

The pronoun "I" appeared in the last paragraph more than is usual in scientific communications. This was intentional. I gave *my* reactions to Voss et al.'s paper. Other people might draw other conclusions, and they could be equally valid. The paper invites a variety of future intellectual inquiries, but it does not dictate its conclusions in the sense that a tightly organized scientific paper does. Voss et al. did not even enunciate the variables they were studying, let alone try to demonstrate that the system was closed.

That is the way things are in humanistic studies. Voss et al.'s paper is fine scholarship, but it does not provide scientific knowledge. It is a humanistic evaluation with suggestions for engineering knowledge.

A scientific analysis of a complex system is more than an assertion that modules exist; there has to be some way of verifying that they do. Plato is supposed to have said "carve nature at its joints," which captures the idea nicely. But how do you know where the joints are?

The predominant approach of cognitive psychologists has been to do a logical analysis of the functions required to do a complex task, and then to assume that the functions are executed by independent modules. This is the approach taken by Stanovich and Cunningham, by Sokol and McCloskey, and by Hegarty. It has also figured prominently in the literature, for example, in Sternberg's (1977) analysis of intelligence tests and in Coltheart's (1985) analysis of the neuropsychological basis of reading. However, just doing the analysis isn't enough.

Analyses by function alone often reduce to necessary truths. These are statements that have to be true, on logical grounds alone. Of course, mathematical calculation depends upon retrieving facts about arithmetic and executing the algorithms associated with operators. Of course, reading requires conversion of visual symbols to lexical entries. Therefore, a functional analysis has to be verified by some test that shows that the functions are being conducted by separate modules. This test has to be an empirical truth, that is, it must involve evaluation of a statement whose truth cannot be determined without empirical observations.

One way to do this is to show that the presumed modular functions have biological reality. In order to establish a biological fact you have to manipulate biological variables. This is what Sokol and McCloskey have done for calculation, and what Coltheart (1985) did for reading. Whereas neuropsychological observations can be a dramatic way to show that one's ideas are right, they can never be the only way. There are the obvious practical reasons; we cannot count on people being injured in just the right way to allow us to test a scientific hypothesis.

There is also an important theoretical reason for not relying solely on biology to verify theories of system modularity. As Stanovich and Cunningham point out, modularity of functioning can be produced by learning. Therefore, behavioral evidence will often be used to verify a hypothetical systems analysis. The statement that the prelexical system must execute purely visual processes and must access the lexicon is a necessary truth. The observation that dyslexia is not associated with visual defects is an empirical verification of the separateness of the visual and lexical access components.

My remarks thus far could be read as an argument for laboratory science on isolated modules, and against the study of complex problem solving per se. If that were the case, what is the point of the volume? That is not quite the case. Just knowing what the modules of the system are doesn't tell us anything, unless we know how the modules are put together to solve complex problems. There are two issues: How does the control system work and what limits its overall functioning?

One of the strongest arguments for studying complex problem solving directly is that this is the only way that we can understand how control systems work. To illustrate my point, I again turn to Sokol and McCloskey's analysis of disabled mental calculators. Their performance is particularly illuminating if we contrast it to the performance of superior mental calculators (Hunter, 1968).

Sokol and McCloskey's study verifies the existence of separate modules for arithmetical fact retrieval and algorithm execution. Studies of "lightning calculators" show how superior performance can be achieved. The time and potential for errors in mental calculation is essentially linear in the number of operations required (Hitch, 1976). Lightning calculators achieve their eminence in two ways. One is to shift the burden from the error-prone calculation system to the more efficient memory system. Some calculators memorize substantial portions of the three digit multiplication table. The other is to use an algorithm for multiplication that is closer to the standard algorithm for vector multiplication than the algorithm that is taught in U.S. schools. In most cases, fewer intermediate results have to be kept in memory when a person uses the vector multiplication algorithm than when a person uses the U.S. school algorithm.

Many studies of complex problem solving produce results like these. The research produces a description of the problem-solving strategies used to solve a particular class of problems. Such results are useful by humanistic and engineering standards. Accepting an account of strategies as scientific evidence is a bit more problematical. I demonstrate this by considering Amsel, Langer, and Loutzenhiser's paper (this volume) contrasting causal reasoning by lawyers and by psychologists.

Amsel et al. found that lawyers prefer to offer deterministic causal reasons for an event, whereas psychologists are more likely to accept probabilistic explanations. Consider a case that is right on the borderline: explaining why Martina Navratilova won the 1990 Wimbledon tennis tournament. A psychologist could, rightly, point out that from 1970 through 1989 Ms. Navratilova won a very high percentage of her matches. Therefore, on statistical grounds alone, she was one of the most likely players to produce the string of six straight wins required to win the tournament. A lawyer could counter that Ms. Navratilova won the tournament because she had prepared herself with exceptional concentration, and that she had an awesome forehand.

What Amsel et al. do is to show that psychologists are most likely to accept the statistical argument, whereas lawyers are more likely to accept the mechanistic argument. This is a finding about strategies. Because a strategy is, in Pylyshyn's (1984) terms, cognitively penetrable, it can be described to another person, and that other person can use the strategy. Those of my readers who would, on their own, prefer the statistical explanation can understand the mechanistic one, and vice versa. This a humanistic criterion. In this case, though, "humanistic" refers to the thinking of Amsel et al.'s participants. Amsel et al., themselves, were working within the statistical confines of a closed system. They were searching for regularities using some of the traditional criteria of science.

Amsel et al.'s conclusion is also useful engineering knowledge. It could be used to teach psychologists how to play lawyer, and vice versa. A somewhat more useful engineering example is found in Hegarty's work. She showed that people often make errors in pulley problems because they count the number of pulleys in a system without considering their arrangement. A teacher who knows this fact is in a better position to explain how pulley problems should be solved than is a teacher who doesn't know what the students are thinking.[4]

Descriptions of strategies are less clearly acceptable as scientific explanations. The reason is straightforward. Strategy descriptions are descriptions that apply to a particular situation. Scientific descriptions are supposed to apply to a wide range of situations. Most studies of strategies in complex problem solving only approach this. More importantly, it is not clear how the abstractions that are developed can be applied beyond the situations used to make the original abstractions.

Consider studies of how people play formal games, such as chess and bridge. Probably more attempts have been made to abstract general principles from behavior in this area than in any other area of complex problem solving. In reviewing the literature, Frensch and Sternberg (this volume) repeat the argument that game playing is a useful thing to study because it serves as the Drosophila of cognitive science.

Does game playing serve this purpose? I doubt it. Geneticists have a theory that explains how one generalizes from inheritance in the fruit fly to inheritance in human beings. Cognitive psychology does not have a theory to explain how

---

[4]Minstrell and Simpson (1990) have shown that paying attention to the students' beliefs can improve instruction in elementary physics dramatically.

we move from game behaviors to behaviors in other situations. Indeed, there is a good deal of reason to question the generalization. Most of the games studied are games in which the player either has full information or explicitly probabilistic information about the state of the world. Wagner (this volume) points out that this is precisely the sort of information a manager does not have. Yet managers solve problems. So how can we generalize from the board game to the board room?

The present focus on describing performance in complex problem solving may be misplaced . . . especially if the goal of the investigation is to produce scientific knowledge. Recall Simon's (1969, 1981) point that complex cognitive behavior is produced by the interaction between the problem solver and the environmental system. Without a theory of both, I do not see how we are going to go beyond abstracted descriptions. This gets us a little way toward understanding complex problem solving, but only a little way. (I consider how far in the next section.)

If the goal is to make generalizations, it seems to me that the study of learning would be a more fruitful area of study. Instead of trying to find out what behaviors are common over a large set of complex problem-solving behaviors, why not examine how people learn to adjust their own behavior to a complex environment? There are theories of cognitive learning (Anderson, 1983; Newell, 1990; Singley & Anderson, 1989). Although these are at present stated rather vaguely, they are a start. Even if these theories do not stand up over time, studies of how we acquire complex problem-solving skills may be more generalizable than descriptions of the limited number of problem-solving situations that we can study.

Unfortunately, studying complex learning takes a long time. It can literally take years to acquire a problem-solving skill. Ergo, it takes years to observe the acquisition process. Do psychologists (and granting agencies) have long enough attention spans to perform this sort of research? I am not sure that we do.

Given all these caveats, we have learned something from studies of complex problem solving. The next section considers what it is.

THEMES ABSTRACTED FROM THE STUDIES

If any one theme runs through all of these studies, it is the dominance of the concrete. The expert trouble shooters studied by Lesgold and Lajoie utilized their prior experiences to solve new and difficult cases. Frensch and Sternberg remind us that game players recall piece configurations they have seen before. Computer programmers learn and use fairly specific tricks, such as the plan for programming an iterated loop (Kay, this volume).

Being concrete is a useful problem-solving strategy, because it ties an action to some perceivable element in the environment. Unfortunately, the concrete can lead us into trouble. The students Hegarty observed counting pulleys were using a strategy that is easy to execute, but they were not calculating the mechanical advantage of the pulley system.

The dominance of the concrete extends to goals. In all but a few cases, problem solving is done with some goal in mind. The goal, therefore, is the very first cue that a person has and, it seems, we learn to execute problem-solving methods that are associated with that goal. This is shown in two very different papers. Amsel et al. demonstrate that lawyers learn to look for causes that can be associated with the legal goal of assigning blame, whereas psychologists learn to look for causes that can be stated as specific cases of a general rule. At a more exalted level, Voss et al. observe that Presidents Kennedy and Truman, and their advisors, only considered policy alternatives that were consistent with certain broad principles, such as resisting aggression.

There seems to always be a good side and a bad side to any problem-solving method. If you have a goal, it is good to have some general way of achieving it. On the other hand, associating problem-solving methods with goals limits transfer. Kay (this volume) points out that the study of computer programming does not translate into an improvement in general problem-solving skills. This is true in spite of the fact that programming forces people to make their problem-solving strategies explicit. Why not? Because people learn programming with one goal in mind: to program computers. It is not immediately obvious that the principles of programming can be applied to a variety of other activities with other goals.[5]

The dominance of the concrete has an important implication for psychological theory. The assertion that people follow some abstract problem-solving principle simply is not true. Decision theory provides the clearest case. Wagner's managers did not enumerate and evaluate opportunities; they poked at a problem until the solution revealed itself. We see some of the same behavior in Voss et al.'s discussion of high level decision making. The policy makers framed the issue this way and that, until a clear-cut solution appeared. There was little explicit weighing of options, and certainly no calculation of subjective expected utility!

Beach (1990) has presented a more detailed theoretical exposition of decision making that fits quite well with many of the reports in this book. Beach sees decision making (and problem solving more generally) as the unfolding of successive mental representations. According to Beach, problem solvers usually rely more on developing a believable mental scenario than on analyzing alternatives.[6] Beach was concerned with decision making, but his remarks could equally well apply to many forms of problem solving. Hegarty remarks that

---

[5]Singley and Anderson (1989) present interesting examples of how transfer is controlled by common goals within the domain of computer programming.

[6]Beach does acknowledge that there are times when we actually sit down and use analytic tools. In fact, Beach himself has been involved in the developmental of decision aids to facilitate formal analysis.

when people solve mechanics problems they try to envisage how the machine will run. In other words, they produce a concrete scenario rather than a general analysis.

The picture that emerges is one of a problem solver who has memorized a huge number of tricks of the trade, rather than one who has developed a single powerful strategy for reasoning. Local optimality acquired at the expense of global consistency. This bothers people (particularly academics) who like to think of themselves as Homo sapiens. Shouldn't we value pure reasoning?

We should. Pure reasoning is an extremely valuable cultural tool for understanding the world, which is what science is all about. At the individual level, though, it seems that pure reasoning is not a very good way for getting about in the world. Kay makes the point that when students are trained using the discovery learning technique they learn what to do, but not always why it works. Lesgold and Lajoie's electronics troubleshooters—and certainly Voss et al.'s decision makers—also seem to operate in discovery mode. They operate by learning what to do in local situations rather than learning abstract principles.

Let us return to Simon's point, that complex behavior is the result of an interaction between modular systems. The dominance of concrete reasoning may well be an example of what Simon was talking about. Imagine a device that has a very large long-term memory, reasonably good pattern recognition mechanisms, and a decidedly error-prone working memory. Such a device should ought to emphasize concrete, memorizable solutions to local problems. It certainly ought not to rely on applying general principles that, inevitably, lead to long chains of reasoning, and thereby tax the device's error-prone working memory. Since that imaginary device is us, humans emphasize local, concrete reasoning.

SOME CONCLUDING COMMENTS

If the analysis just given is correct, we may want to change the way in which we study complex problem solving.

There needs to be more emphasis on isolating and verifying the components used in complex problem solving. The characteristics of these components can then be studied, in isolation, using a variety of standard laboratory techniques. Note, though, that I am not advocating a return to the days of paired-associates learning. Components should be studied in isolation if and only if those components can be verified as part of the process of problem solving itself.

The direct study of complex problem solving will always be useful, but I think more for gains in engineering than in scientific knowledge. Research on complex problem solving reveals the local knowledge and strategies that are used in those problems. The data on transfer suggest that you learn about how people deal with the problem you are studying, and not about how people deal with complex problems in general. Because general knowledge isn't being gained, one has to apply the usual criterion for engineering knowledge: Will what I learn be useful? The argument for studying ecologically important problems, such as electronic troubleshooting, mechanics, or national policy making, is clear. There seems to be less of an argument for studying highly artificial situations. Game playing is not the Drosophila of cognitive science. Funke's goal of studying complexity per se is even more questionable.

This is a disturbing conclusion, because it essentially says that we cannot have a science of complex problem solving, simply because all complex problems have local solutions. I think that this is the case. However, I do think that we can develop a scientific understanding of how people learn to deal with complexity. The reason is that the principles of learning may be general, whereas the result of learning is specific to the situation in which the learning takes place. Expert-novice contrasts are a start, but only a start. We need to look at the process of moving from novice to expert. This will require some long, slow, studies.

REFERENCES

Anderson, J. R. (1983). *The architecture of cognition.* Cambridge, MA: Harvard University Press.

Banaji, M. R., & Crowder, R. G. (1989). The bankruptcy of everyday memory. *American Psychologist, 44,* 1185–1193.

Beach, L. R. (1990). *Image theory: Decision making in personal and organizational contexts.* New York: Wiley.

Braitenberg, V. (1984). *Vehicles.* Cambridge, MA: MIT Press.

Butterfield, E. C. (1990). *Similarities among behavioral, cognitive, and instructional design systems for deciding what to teach.* Paper presented at the Second Meeting of the International Association for Cognitive Education, University of Mons-Hainaut, Mons, Belgium.

Coltheart, M. (1985). Cognitive neuropsychology of reading. In M. I. Posner, & O. S. M. Marin (Eds.), *Attention and performance XI* (pp. 3–37). Hillsdale, NJ: Lawrence Erlbaum Associates.

Fodor, J. A. (1983). *The modularity of the mind.* Cambridge, MA: MIT Press.

Hitch, G. (1976). The role of short term working memory in mental arithmetic. *Cognitive Psychology, 10,* 302–323.

Hunter, I. M. L. (1968). Mental calculation. In P. C. Wason & P. N. Johnson-Laird (Eds.), *Thinking and reasoning.* Baltimore: Penguin.

Minstrell, J., & Simpson, V. C. (1990, April). *A teaching system for diagnosing student conceptions and prescribing relevant instruction.* Paper presented at the American Educational Research Association Meetings, Boston, MA.

Neisser, U. (1978). Memory: What are the important questions? In M. M. Gruneberg, P. E. Morris, & R. N. Skyes (Eds.), *Practical aspects of memory* (pp. 3–24). London: Academic Press.

Newell, A. (1990). *Unified theories of cognition.* Cambridge, MA: Harvard University Press.

Pylyshyn, Z. W. (1984). *Computation and cognition: Toward a foundation for cognitive science.* Cambridge, MA: MIT Press.

Simon, H. A. (1969). *The sciences of the artificial* (1st ed.). Cambridge, MA: MIT Press.

Simon, H. A. (1981). *The sciences of the artificial* (2nd ed.). Cambridge, MA: MIT Press.

Singley, M. K., & Anderson, J. R. (1989). *The transfer of cognitive skill.* Cambridge, MA: Harvard University Press.

Sternberg, R. J. (1977). *Intelligence, information processing, and analogical reasoning: The componential analysis of human abilities.* Hillsdale, NJ: Lawrence Erlbaum Associates.

Author Index

Subject Index